A SHAMEFUL ACT

ALSO BY TANER AKÇAM

From Empire to Republic:
Turkish Nationalism and the Armenian Genocide

Praise for

A Shameful Act

"Magnificently researched . . . No scholar has mined and synthesized the Ottoman Empire's internal documents and memoirs with Akçam's assiduous skill. Like Raul Hilberg's *The Destruction of the European Jews*, *A Shameful Act* is destined to become a touchstone for other studies."

—Carlin Romano, *The Philadelphia Inquirer*

"Richly sourced . . . An important work of record, comprehensively chronicling the destruction of the Armenians, its causes, unfolding and consequences."

—Adam LeBor, *The Nation*

"Timely and well-researched . . . Helps to explain why the conditions in which these events might be freely discussed in Turkey have never quite fallen into place."

—*The Economist*

"A clear, well-researched work . . . As Turkey now petitions to join the European Union, and ethnic cleansing and collective punishment continue to threaten entire populations around the globe, this groundbreaking and lucid account by a prominent Turkish scholar speaks forcefully to all."

—*Publishers Weekly* (starred review)

"Akçam is unsparing in his evidence. . . . Of profound importance to history—and certain to stir up nests of hornets."

—*Kirkus Reviews* (starred review)

"One of a handful of scholars who are challenging their homeland's insistent declarations that the organized slaughter of Armenians did not occur, Akçam is the first Turkish specialist to use the word 'genocide' publicly in this context. His work . . . is breaking new ground."

—Belinda Cooper, *The New York Times*

"Some important Turkish scholarship has attempted an honest admission of the Armenian genocide and a critique of the official rationalizations for it. Taner Akçam is the only Turkish historian to have talked of genocide."

—Christopher Hitchens, *The Atlantic Monthly*

"What makes Akçam's work stand out—apart from the fact that the author is a Turk—is that his is the first serious scholarly attempt to understand the genocide from the perspective of the perpetrator, rather than the victim."

—Levon Sevunts, *The Gazette* (Montreal)

"Akçam's work is the state of the art in this field."

—Erik Jan Zürcher, author of *Turkey: A Modern History*

A SHAMEFUL ACT

THE ARMENIAN GENOCIDE AND THE QUESTION OF TURKISH RESPONSIBILITY

Taner Akçam

A Holt Paperback
Metropolitan Books/
Henry Holt and Company • New York

Holt Paperbacks
Henry Holt and Company, LLC
Publishers since 1866
175 Fifth Avenue
New York, New York 10010
WWW.HENRYHOLT.COM

A Holt Paperback® and ® are registered trademarks of
Henry Holt and Company, LLC.

Library of Congress Cataloging-in-Publication Data
Akçam, Taner, 1953–
    A shameful act: the Armenian genocide and the question of Turkish responsibility /
by Taner Akçam ; translated by Paul Bessemer.—1st American ed.
    p. cm.
Includes index.
ISBN-13: 978-0-8050-8665-2
ISBN-10: 0-8050-8665-X
1. Armenian massacres, 1915–1923. 2. Genocide. 3. War crimes. I. Title.

DS195.5.A418   2006
956.6'21154—DC22   2005058401

Henry Holt books are available for special promotions and premiums.
For details contact: Director, Special Markets.

Originally published in hardcover in 2006 by Metropolitan Books

First Holt Paperbacks Edition 2007

Designed by Meryl Sussman Levavi
Map by Mapping Specialists based on a map by Ara Sarafian, Gomidas Institute, 2005.

Printed in the United States of America

P1

I would like to dedicate this book to the memory of Haji Halil, a devout Muslim Turk, who saved the members of an Armenian family from deportation and death by keeping them safely hidden for over half a year, risking his own life. His courageous act continues to point the way toward a different relationship between Turks and Armenians.

CONTENTS

A SHAMEFUL ACT

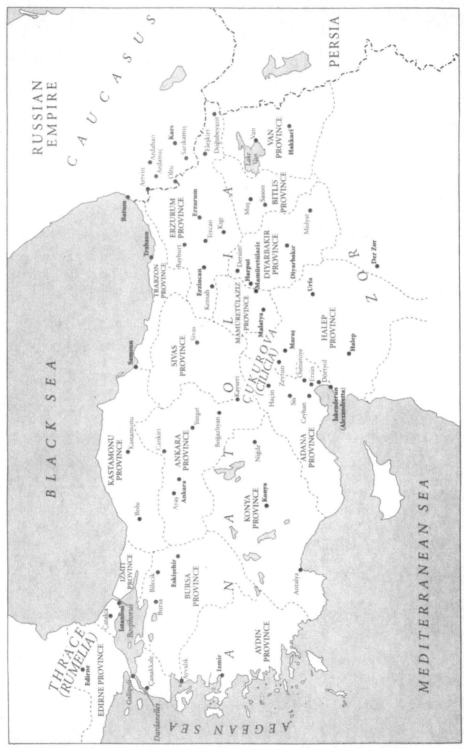

Based on a map of the Armenian Genocide by Ara Sarafian, Gomidas Institute, 2005.

PREFACE

ANY ACCOUNT OF THE DECLINE AND FALL OF THE OTTOMAN EMPIRE IS necessarily also a history of the creation of many new nation-states within its imperial borders. Inevitably, the desire of ethnic-national groups that had coexisted for centuries to break off into their own exclusive states led to expulsion or worse for the other ethnic groups living in the same territory. Great suffering followed, suffering that formed a crucial component of each new nation's collective memory. Of course, this is not unique to the Ottoman Empire: Communities, whether national, religious, or cultural, tend to memorialize not the wrongs they have inflicted but those they have endured. Bulgaria, Serbia, Greece, Iraq, Syria—indeed, all the entities established on Ottoman soil—remember their histories as a series of expulsions and massacres inflicted on them by "others." This is the basis of the historiography of nation-state building in the late nineteenth and early twentieth centuries in the Middle East. Turkish national historiography is no different, memorializing massacres of Muslims by Armenian, Greek, Bulgarian, and other ethnic-national groups while making no mention of suffering inflicted by Muslims on non-Muslim groups, such as the massacre of Christians, let alone the Armenian genocide.

This book breaks with that tradition. It is a call to the people of Turkey to consider the suffering inflicted in their name on those "others." The reason for this call is not only the scale of the Armenian genocide, which was in no way comparable to the individual acts of revenge carried out against Muslims. It is also because all studies of large-scale atrocities teach us one core principle: To prevent the recurrence of such events, people must first consider their own responsibility, discuss it, debate it, and recognize it. In the absence of such honest consideration, there remains the high probability of such acts being repeated, since every group is inherently capable of violence; when the right conditions arise this potential may easily become reality, and on the slightest of pretexts. There are no exceptions. Each and every society needs to take a self-critical approach, one that should be firmly institutionalized as a community's moral tradition regardless of what others might have done to them. It is this that prevents renewed eruptions of violence.

When on 24 May 1915 the news reached Europe that Ottoman Armenians were being killed, England, France, and Russia issued a joint declaration: "In view of these crimes of Turkey against humanity and civilization, the Allied governments announce publicly to the Sublime Porte that they will hold personally responsible [for] these crimes all members of the Ottoman government and those of their agents who are implicated in such massacres."[1] After the Allies' victory in World War I—and the death of some one million Armenians (the numbers vary widely depending on the source)—the Great Powers were expected to make good on their promise. However, it soon became clear during the 1919 Paris Peace Conference that the arrest and prosecution of individual members of the wartime Ottoman government would be no easy task since many of those involved in the genocide remained in power. It also quickly emerged that the Allies had divergent political interests in the region, which directly caused serious differences over the prosecution of war criminals. Finally, and most important, there were inadequate institutions and legislation within international law to deal with the problem of "crimes against humanity."

While the Allied Powers had the right to prosecute war criminals and specifically the perpetrators of the Armenian massacres—as granted in the 1920 Treaty of Sèvres, signed with the Ottoman Government—this prerogative was never fully exercised.[2] There were three separate attempts, however, to try and punish the guilty. The first was the series of extraordinary courts-martial set up by the Ottoman Government itself, prior to the Treaty of Sèvres, in the hope of obtaining more favorable results for Turkey at the Paris Peace Conference. These courts, which began their pretrial interrogations in November 1918, started hearing cases in February the following year and continued until 1922. They were ultimately disbanded because of pressure by the Turkish nationalist movement and because the trials were no longer seen as offering any advantage to the new nationalist government, especially after the Treaty of Sèvres was concluded and partition of the empire had begun.

The second attempt was initiated by the Allied Powers at the Paris Peace Conference itself, with the goal of creating a legal corpus for the trial of crimes against humanity and their subsequent prosecution in an international court. Allied conflicts of interest, however, as well as the fact that international law at the time applied only to crimes committed by one state against the citizens of another doomed these efforts as well. Armenians, as Ottoman subjects, were excluded from this category and no international convention existed to cover crimes perpetrated by a state against its own people.

One final attempt to try those responsible came from Great Britain, which, wary of the Ottoman courts in Istanbul, moved to take suspects into British custody and ship them to colonial Malta. As the Turkish extraordinary courts-martial began to lose domestic support, the British continued to work to try the suspects under British law. In the absence, however, of sufficient evidence in the American and British archives against specific individuals—as opposed to the Ottoman archives, which contained ample evidence—their efforts proved fruitless. Thus, despite their many deficiencies, it was the Ottoman military trials in Istanbul—the indictments, telegrams, eyewitness accounts, and other testimony produced during the trials themselves and the investigations and interrogations leading up to them—that proved to be the most successful in documenting and establishing responsibility for the genocide.

*　*　*

The question of Turkish responsibility invariably prompts great controversy, but in all the debate there is only one clear question to be answered: Is there evidence of intent and central planning on the part of the Ottoman authorities for the total or partial destruction of the Armenian people? The official Turkish position is that the death of hundreds of thousands of Armenians (Turkish estimates range from 300,000 to 600,000) was a tragic but unintended by-product of the war. This argument rests on the claim that the Ottoman sources contain no evidence showing a deliberate policy of systematic killing. In this book, which makes the most extensive use to date of Ottoman materials, I will argue otherwise.

As noted, the evidence produced during the extraordinary courts-martial conducted in Istanbul is of unparalleled value to any effort to assess Turkish responsibility for the Armenian genocide. Of the approximately sixty-three military tribunals, beginning in February 1919,[3] three major trials—of the wartime cabinet ministers, the central committee members of the Committee of Union and Progress (the CUP, the party in power during the war), and the regional party secretaries—dealt at length with the question of political responsibility. A clear attempt was made to prove that the Armenian massacres had been a centrally planned operation, an unequivocal case of genocide. Along with the other Istanbul trials, which focused on concrete instances of atrocities in different areas, these court proceedings yielded important information about how the massacres were carried out and about the division of labor among various paramilitary and irregular organizations. Leaving aside documents published by Aram Andonian (which academic researchers have tended to avoid due to accusations of inaccuracy or forgery),[4] the investigations leading to the trials also produced crucial records concerning the genocide's planning and implementation. It is noteworthy that much of this material was provided by Ottoman army commanders and other high-ranking officers and bureaucrats who knew what was happening, some of whom refused to participate in the crimes. The commander of the Third Army, Vehip Paşa, and Aleppo provincial governor Celal Bey are two such examples.

Until recently, these documents did not attract the attention they deserve from scholars, for several reasons. First, to this day we do not know the whereabouts of the complete official court records. Some copies are filed in the archives of the Armenian patriarchate in Jerusa-lem, but they are handwritten copies, not originals. Second, the extant materials on the trials are scattered and incomplete. These comprise the proceedings, including indictments and verdicts for twelve of the sixty-three trials, that were published as supplements to the Ottoman government's official gazette, *Takvîm-i Vekâyi;* the daily newspapers of the period, which provided extensive coverage of the events sur-rounding the trials; and finally, various other Ottoman archival mate-rials. The dispersal of these sources in a number of different locations is an obstacle to the compilation of a full record, while the archives are not easily accessible for scholars. Third, all these sources are in the Ottoman language—Turkish written in Arabic script, with a strong influence from Persian and Arabic—and require special skill to read. Finally, even those Ottoman documents that are accessible have been dismissed by Turkish scholars, along with the trials themselves, as "victor's justice," imposed by the Allies as part of their effort to dis-credit the Ottomans and carve up the empire.

While there is ample reason to believe that these long-neglected archives were "pruned" after the 1918 armistice—many of the rele-vant documents were destroyed or, according to the Istanbul public defender in the military trials, "confiscated"—the immensity of the crime and the extensive nature of the records meant that these docu-ments could only be partially purged. In the course of implementing the state-wide genocidal policies, hundreds if not thousands of pages of correspondence were exchanged at various government levels. While we are missing a significant portion of these papers, what remains in the Ottoman archives and in court records is sufficient to show that the CUP Central Committee, and the Special Organization it set up to carry out its plan, did deliberately attempt to destroy the Armenian population.

To give just one example of the kind of evidence that belies the official Turkish state version, in 1995 the Directorate-General of the State Archives published a large collection of documentation, *The Armenians, [as they appear] in Ottoman Documents, 1915–1920,* that was carefully selected to prove the accepted thesis. The volume included a telegram, dated 12 July (29 Haziran) 1915, from Talât Paşa, the minister of the interior, to the governor general in the province of Diyarbakır, commenting on recent deportations in the region. The telegram clearly shows genocidal intent. Acknowledging that more than two thousand Christians had been killed in Diyarbakır, Talât Paşa warned the governor that "Since it is categorically forbidden for other Christians to be included under the disciplinary and political measures adopted in regard to the Armenians, an immediate stop should be put to this sort of occurrence, which will have a bad effect on public opinion, and will indiscriminately place the lives of Christians in extraordinary danger."[5] Thus the policies deliberately enacted against the Armenians were explicitly to exclude other Christian groups.[6]

The evidence in the Ottoman archives is augmented by the documents found in Germany and Austria, which give ample confirmation that we are looking at a centrally planned operation of annihilation. These records are particularly significant because Germany and Austria were military and political allies of the Ottoman Empire. Their troops fought at the same military fronts, and their consular officials enjoyed freedom of movement within the country and uncensored communication with their foreign ministries back home. Beyond their activities in the provinces, the various consulates maintained regular contact with the centers of Turkish political and military decision-making and had firsthand knowledge of events. Initially, German and Austrian officials wanted to believe that the Armenian deportations were limited only to the war zones. They consequently adopted positions in line with and even supportive of this view.[7] But as the deportations began to exceed the consuls' original assessments, their position became more complicated and their disapproval more explicit. Their reports included eyewitness accounts of the horrors in the provinces, as well as telling comments from the capital, such as the following from Talât Paşa: "What we are dealing with here . . . is the annihilation of the Armenians."[8]

After its defeat in the war Germany was at pains to disprove allegations of war crimes and complicity in the Armenian genocide, trying all the while to ensure a more favorable outcome at the Paris Peace Conference. To shape opinion, Germany published collections of archival documents on its foreign policy before and during the war, *Die Grosse Politik der Europaischen Kabinette, 1871–1914.*[9] Johannes Lepsius, who was entrusted with this publication, also produced an additional collection of archival documents dealing with the Armenian question from 1914–18. Because the goal here was to prove the Germans blameless in the Armenian genocide, Lepsius either avoided publishing a number of reports of an incriminating nature or he published them in censored or abridged form.[10] Later research revealed that most of the distorted documents contained information about Germany condoning the deportations or about its participation in suppressing the Armenian uprisings that erupted in response. Likewise, expressions of Turkish opposition to the deportations and massacres were partially removed from the reports, in order to create a more negative image of the Turks. All mention of Armenians being armed and fighting with the Russians was removed to enhance their innocence, as were some descriptions of the horrors and Armenian suffering, to make the whole situation less shocking for the reader.[11] We now know, however, that German involvement was not limited to simple awareness of the events and remaining silent. Instead, some German officers even signed some of the deportation orders.[12] Today researchers have an almost complete set of original German documents, and after the Ottoman archival materials these comprise the most important evidence showing the genocidal intent of the Ottoman authorities.

Another important source of information is the documents found in the U.S. archives.[13] As the United States did not enter the war until 1917, American consular officials were able before that date to travel freely around the empire. They witnessed some of the events and received hundreds of reports from survivors as well as from foreign observers, such as missionaries, working in the affected areas. These sources are supplemented by recollections and memoirs written by survivors of the massacres and foreign observers as well as further Turkish-language documents, such as the memoirs of central figures in the CUP,[14] parliamentary minutes after 1908, reports of parliamentary commissions, official army and government bulletins, and the daily press.

Taken in their entirety, these sources leave us in no doubt that the scale of the operations would have been impossible without planning at the political center. More specifically, the sources lead us to conclude that there is a very strong likelihood that a decision was made by the CUP's Central Committee during a series of meetings at the end of March 1915 to remove Armenians from their homes to be killed. The CUP, also known as Unionists or Young Turks, took this decision ultimately because they saw it as the only means to guarantee the territorial integrity of the empire and the elimination of the related and long-standing Armenian question once and for all. In Talât Paşa's letter of 26 May 1915 to the head of parliament, the grand vizier, he alludes to this CUP-originated plan of genocide, now government policy: "necessary preparations have been discussed and taken for the complete and fundamental elimination of this concern, which occupies an important place in the exalted state's list of vital issues."[15] But we can conclude from the documents and our knowledge of the workings of the cabinet at this time that the decision was essentially made by the party's central committee and not by the Ottoman cabinet—an important distinction, since pockets of resistance against the CUP remained within the state apparatus.

Beyond arguing that it was the CUP's intention to destroy a people, one of the basic claims of this book is that the Armenian genocide was not an isolated aberration. Indeed, it can only be understood within a broader historical context, which is the process of the demise of the Ottoman Empire and the response of the political leadership to that demise. Following their shocking defeat in the Balkan War, 1912–13, the Ottomans lost more than 60 percent of their European territory. A deep belief developed that it was impossible to live side-by-side with the empire's remaining Christian population, or even worse, that Ottoman Christians posed a threat to the empire's very survival. Thus the ruling Ottoman-Turkish authorities formed a policy which aimed at homogenizing the population of Anatolia, the territorial heart of the empire. This policy had two main components: the first was to disperse and relocate non-Turkish Muslims, such as Kurds and Arabs, among the Turkish majority with the purpose of their assimilation. The second component involved expelling non-Muslim, non-Turkish people from Anatolia, which resulted in the removal of two million people in all, essentially the region's entire Christian population. While Armenians as well as Assyrians were targeted by special measures aimed at their annihilation, Greeks were also expelled. In total, almost one-third of the Anatolian population was either relocated or killed. What is crucial is that this ethnic cleansing and homogenization paved the way for today's Republic of Turkey.

This view is unacceptable in Turkey. Indeed, because of the long-standing Turkish policy of denial, the very term "genocide" has become contested—sacred to Armenians, taboo to Turks. Both sides attach supreme importance to the question of whether or not "genocide" should be used. I have used the term in line with the United Nations definition adopted in 1948. Accordingly, genocide includes the partial or complete destruction of an ethnic, national, racial, or religious group, whether in periods of peace or war. The definition covers various means of destruction, be it killing members of a particular group, exposing them to grave physical or emotional harm, inflicting such physical damage that ends the group's continued existence, preventing the group's members from giving birth, or forcibly removing their children and merging them with other communities. Under the terms of the UN definition, and in light of all the documentary evidence, we cannot but call the acts against the Armenians genocide.

The important thing, however, is not the term, but rather the moral position that recognizes the crime and condemns it. However we define it, whatever word we use, we must acknowledge that this history involved the deliberate destruction of a people. In 1915 Çerkez Hasan was an Ottoman officer commissioned to "resettle" Armenians in what are now the Syrian and Iraqi deserts. When he realized that the real aim of the deportations was not resettlement but annihilation he resigned. "You may argue whether or not the word 'killing' is synonymous with 'deportation,'" he said. "Use it any way you want; it doesn't change what actually happened in any real sense. . . . There is only one terrible way to understand what happened, and of which the whole world is aware."[16] The failure of the official Turkish state approach is its insistence that this immense crime was a justifiable act of state necessity, which therefore allows the country to avoid taking any moral stance on it.

In line with the argument of necessity, the state claims that the destruction of the Armenians was not the deliberate policy of either the government or the party but a series of isolated events that occurred, without intention and in the course of harsh wartime conditions, during a "normal" deportation. It remains, however, extremely difficult to explain how 300,000–600,000 people (the numbers variously cited in official Turkish sources) died within a year—1915—as a result of disease, random attacks, and general wartime conditions while raising no alarm among the central authorities.

The denials are problematic for other reasons, even without the accumulation of documentary evidence. The official reason given for the deportations was that the Armenians posed a danger to the military at a time of war and needed to be distanced from the theater of fighting. Yet Armenians were deported from areas well behind the front lines which were in no way connected to the war. More significantly, they were in fact sent *into* war zones, "placed close behind the Ottoman Sixth Army in Der Zor, or behind the Fourth Army in Hauran."[17] Additionally, no plans were made to ensure the well-being or even basic survival of the deportees, either on their journey or when they arrived at their places of resettlement. Moreover, assistance offered by Germany, America, and international aid organizations was all refused. Research for this book uncovered many new documents that clearly show the Ottoman authorities' genocidal intent. These documents, some of which appear here for the first time, relate to such issues as the use of confiscated Armenian property to finance the war and the reallocation of assets to create a Muslim bourgeoisie which would replace the Armenian middle class that had been wiped out.

In light of the decisive weight of evidence, why, we must ask, has Turkey insisted on repeating its scarcely credible denial? Perhaps the government fears that if Turkey were to acknowledge the genocide and its responsibility there would be serious repercussions in terms of compensation for territory and property. Setting aside the issue of territorial claims, which have no validity in international law, the issue of financial compensation is real.

Another reason, the moral factor, is related to the connection between the Armenian genocide and the founding of the Turkish state in 1922. The Turkish Nationalist Movement, the driving force behind the establishment of the Turkish Republic, was led by members of the CUP, the same party that was responsible for the genocide. Many of the CUP members who later became central figures in the Turkish government admitted openly that the republic could only have been established by eliminating the Armenians and removing their demand for self-determination in Anatolia. As in every other nation-state, the Turks glorified their founding fathers as heroes. The first parliament passed decrees proclaiming as national heroes CUP members who had been tried for crimes against the Armenians. In 1926 parliament passed a law awarding land and pensions to families of former CUP members, including two who had been executed as a result of the Istanbul trials and those who had been assassinated by Armenian revenge killers. There has been no fundamental change in this position from the founders of the republic to Turkey's current ruling elite, and the continuity has made it very difficult to conduct an open discussion on the beginnings of the republic. More profoundly, declaring some of Turkey's founders war criminals would call into question the state's very identity.

Finally, there is the psychological factor compounding the difficulty of an honest historical reckoning in Turkey. In general, Turkish society is disinclined to consider its past. In the prevailing culture, not only the Armenian genocide but much of Turkey's recent history is consigned to silence, the Kurdish question and the role of the military being but two examples. The Alphabet Reform of 1928, which changed Turkish script from Arabic to Latin letters, served to compound the problem. With the stroke of a pen, the Turkish people lost their connection to written history. Turkey is a society that cannot read its own newspapers, letters, and diaries if they were written before 1928. It has no access to anything that happened prior to that date. As a result, modern Turkey is totally dependent on history as the state has defined and written it. Of course, the state has a stake in how history is represented, certainly when that history touches on its very legitimacy. In this light, it becomes clear why Turkish society has consigned the Armenian genocide to oblivion.

This avoidance of history is also due to the trauma of the Ottoman ruling elite during the late nineteenth and early twentieth centuries. The final hundred years of the empire were darkened by the specter of collapse and disintegration. Between 1878 and 1918, the empire lost 85 percent of its territory and 75 percent of its population. The fear of obliteration was a constant presence throughout the empire's long demise. Reminders of this period—and of the Turkish Republic's filial relationship to the empire's history of decline—are to be avoided at all cost. The Armenians constitute a symbol of this most traumatic era. If the Turks conceive of themselves as a phoenix rising from the Ottoman ashes, the Armenians are the unwelcome traces of those ashes.

But there has always been another narrative of the past, an oral tradition at odds with official state historiography. This is especially true in eastern Anatolia where the events occurred, and among the Kurdish and Alawite minorities. The two narratives have coexisted, side by side, for as long as Turkish society—fatalistic and reticent—avoided challenging the state version of history. But with the rise of the democratic movement in Turkey, fuelled by the country's bid to enter the European Union, the contradiction between state and society has been forced into the open, and one by one the taboos are being confronted and torn down.[18]

Just as there are two narratives, there are two historiographical approaches. On the one hand, there is the story of an empire dismembered by Europe's Great Powers, a drawn-out process of collapse and disintegration. This history served to create a powerful sense of battling the West to survive and it has produced strong anti-Western sentiment in Turkey, especially among the ruling elite, which persists until today. On the other hand, there is the story of persecution, massacre, and annihilation of different religious and ethnic groups, the Armenians in particular.

In line with these two histories, basic works on the Ottoman Empire all conform to one of two mutually exclusive approaches: Most Ottomanists and Turkish historians tend to write the empire's history as one of partition and demise. The entire process is cast as a struggle between the Great Powers and a weakening Ottoman state, with barely a reference to the massacres and genocide of the late nineteenth and early twentieth centuries. Then there is the history of this period as written by the victims, which excludes mention of the empire's partition. The intervention of the Great Powers is always presented as an act of good, done in the name of human rights. One of my central arguments in this book is that these two mutually exclusive versions must be reconciled and viewed together: Their strong interrelationship is inextricably part of the same history.

For Turkey to become a truly democratic member of the society of nations, it has to confront this "dark chapter" of its history, this "shameful act," as Mustafa Kemal Ataturk, founder of the republic, called the Armenian genocide.[19] Only full integration of Turkey's past can set the country on the path to democracy.

This book is dedicated to Haji Halil, whose story I first heard from Greg Sarkissian, president of the Zoryan Institute, when he delivered a paper at a conference in Armenia in 1995. Eight members of his mother's family were kept safely hidden for some six months in Haji Halil's home under very dangerous circumstances: Any Turk protecting an Armenian was threatened with being hanged in front of his house, which would then be burned. I was deeply moved by the story, by the humanity that triumphed over evil and by the fact that an Armenian could find it in his heart to praise a Turk, in a public forum, for that humanity. The memory of Haji Halil reminds us that both people, Turks and Armenians, have a different history on which they can build a future.

AUTHOR'S NOTE

THE TERMS "TURKS," "ARMENIANS," "GREEKS," AND "KURDS" ALL appear here frequently. I have often used them in much the same way they were used at the time, both by those involved and by contemporary writers. But the generalized use of these terms, which involves oversimplification and is the product of a certain nationalistic approach, is in fact the very cause of the problems explored in this book, as well as being incorrect. Those who acted collectively in history were not the entirety of "Turks" or "Armenians," but certain organizations or groups that shared a common interest and claimed to be acting in the name of the nation or religion to which they belonged. In some cases, this meant the government; in others, a political party; in still others, the representatives of a clearly defined class or subclass. It is even questionable whether the broad mass of Muslims in Anatolia at the time understood themselves as Turks, or Kurds, rather than as Muslims. In all cases, however, these actors never comprised the entire national or religious group that they claimed to represent.

Where possible, I have tried to steer clear of such descriptions, which nevertheless figure repeatedly in the relevant publications.

Instead, I have selected more precise terms for the people involved in any particular action. The terms "Turks" and "Armenians," which are widely used in historiography and conversation, are not historical categories, but rather ahistorical constructions. They are used to express only that one group is not Armenian and the other not Turk. This not only misrepresents history but exacerbates public perceptions and prejudices today.

It also seems to me necessary to point out that this history focuses on the decisions and actions taken by part of the Ottoman political establishment that resulted in the Armenian genocide, as well as the causes and consequences of those decisions. I feel obliged to warn readers against the error of assuming that they will find here a comprehensive history covering all aspects of the genocide.

PART I

THE ARMENIAN QUESTION PRIOR TO THE DECISION FOR GENOCIDE

CHAPTER 1

THE OTTOMAN STATE AND ITS
NON-MUSLIM POPULATIONS

MANY BOOKS AND MUCH OF THE WRITING CONCERNING THE ARME-
nian question claim that the Armenians under Ottoman rule lived in
a state of peace and tranquility until the nineteenth century. "Despite
their second-class status, most Armenians lived in relative peace so
long as the Ottoman Empire was strong and expanding."[1] This assessment only makes sense in the context of the greater conflicts taking
place during the nineteenth century and so cannot be considered
objective. It is true that compared to the violence of the twentieth
century, this period might be seen as relatively peaceful. However, due
to its theocratic character[2] and its dependence on the sultan's unlim-
ited authority, the Ottoman state was a despotic regime, and the communities under its control were not citizens but subjects of the sultan.
These communities, which to a large measure lived with minimal
legal safeguards, were vulnerable to the oppression—both legal and
illegal—of the central and local authorities, especially under the pretext of tax collection.

In addition to the general subjugation of all its subjects, the
Ottoman state specifically oppressed and discriminated against non-
Muslims. Indeed, in the course of Ottoman rule, long-standing

assumptions of Muslim superiority evolved into the legal and cultural attitudes that created the background for genocide. This is not to say that the Ottoman Empire rested only on violence,[3] but that without a grasp of the particular circumstances of the Muslim–non-Muslim relationship, we cannot understand the process that led to a decision for a "final solution" to the Armenian question. While the genocide was not a direct or inherent result of the cultural and legal conflicts at work, the decision for genocide could not have been reached without the prior existence of a special set of conditions. The Muslim-Christian clashes of the nineteenth and twentieth centuries and the Armenian genocide must be considered against this background. Accordingly, the view that relative peace prevailed prior to the emergence of nineteenth-century nationalism, is not only incorrect but also misleading.

The Ottoman Empire comprised many different religious and national groups. Apart from Islam, the state religion, various rights were recognized for other monotheistic religions, also known as "peoples of the book." These lived for centuries with a certain degree of religious communal autonomy. This principle of social organization formed the foundation of the Ottoman state, which, based on the principle of heterogeneity and difference rather than homogeneity and sameness, functioned in an opposite way to modern nation-states. Consequently, historians have endlessly debated the question of how to characterize such a state. Turkish historian İlber Ortaylı likens the Ottoman state to a third Roman empire, functioning within the framework of Mediterranean customs and traditions: "Within this empire, it was possible to be accepted into the life of the state and society and to join the administration by adopting its ethnically based multi-state ideology, and adapting to its conditions."[4]

Other historians argue that since Islam formed the state's ideological foundation—a fundamental premodern characteristic—the Ottoman Empire should be seen as an Islamic state. Not limited to governing only questions of faith and worship, Islam also prescribes rules for every aspect of legal, social, and political organization involved in running a state. In this sense, the Ottoman state could, along very general lines be considered Islamic. But there always remained an area of *örfî*, or "customary" law, operating alongside

Islamic Shari'a law. According to Inalcık, "Custom (*örf*), in its specific meaning, is the authority to impose laws in areas which fall outside the scope of the Shari'a, and based solely on the will of the sovereign."[5] There is no clear determination regarding the areas in which Shari'a and *örfî* were applied, or where the boundary between the two lay. This is the subject of an ongoing and partisan historical debate.

We do know that in principle, "public law, . . . especially . . . concerning administration, finance and organization, along with certain penal laws, was generally directly administered through the orders and imperial edicts, known as *fermans*, of the Sultan himself. . . . Nevertheless, areas of civil law concerned with personal law . . . especially marriage and inheritance, remained both in content and form subject to the rulings of the Shari'a."[6] But frequently the sultans overlooked this distinction, sometimes narrowing the scope of Islamic law by issuing decisions contrary to the Shari'a.[7]

Neither field of Ottoman law, Islamic or customary, was codified in a single corpus. Some Shari'a rulings were collected in volumes that appear to be fundamental books of law, but it was never clear that one binding system covered the entire empire.[8] A similar problem existed in customary law. No single comprehensive body of legislation was ever issued. Laws were only promulgated in response to the specific needs of each region. The administration frequently left existing legal frameworks intact, making partial changes over time that eventually accumulated into a varied set of special laws that differed in each locale.

Legal statutes for the empire's non-Muslim communities were basically determined according to Islamic law. But there were exceptions to this general framework. Sometimes, in addition to imperial edicts, laws evolved out of special letters of privilege or diplomatic understandings with foreign governments. Thus four sources of law governed non-Muslim subjects in addition to the Shari'a: Church law to the extent that it was recognized by Islamic law; the Capitulations—a series of terms granted to foreign countries by the Ottoman state, especially after the conquest of Constantinople in 1453; various peace treaties; and changes enacted by a set of reforms legislated in 1839 in response to the influence of European modernity.[9]

To understand which of these sources were dominant, it is necessary to divide the six centuries of Ottoman history, from 1299 to 1922, into two periods. The first encompasses the time from the founding of the state until the reforms of 1839. The second begins in 1839 and ends with the collapse of the Ottoman Empire. The first of these two periods itself warrants subdivision into two eras, from the founding of the state through the reign of Süleyman the Magnificent in 1566; and from 1566 to 1839. During the first period, the principles of Islamic law were dominant. But beginning in 1535, the series of Capitulations and changes in the legal statutes concerning non-Muslims went beyond the limits of Islamic law, forming exceptions to it.

The legal status of non-Muslims in Islamic law is based on various passages in the Koran in addition to agreements the Prophet Muhammad made during his life with non-Muslim communities and religious opinions attributed to the Caliph Umar. Accordingly, the first and fundamental division is between Muslims and non-Muslims, who are further divided between "peoples of the book" (monotheists possessing a revealed scripture) and others (idolaters, atheists). These groups are also politically divided, into those fighting against Muslims and those who have entered into a pact with Muslims. This last category, the "people of the treaty," is then subdivided into subgroups: the most important of these for our concerns being the "people of the debt," or those who accept the protection of the Islamic state in exchange for a poll tax.

An important principle determining the political status of any specific non-Muslim is the nature of the country in which he lives. Islamic law divides the nations along general lines into two main groups: Islamic and non-Islamic. The non-Islamic countries are comprised of those that are at war with Muslims, the "abode of war," and those that have made peace with Muslims, or the "abode of reconciliation." What concerns us here specifically is the legal status of *dhimmî*—people living under the protection of the Islamic state, or under Muslim sovereignty.[10]

According to Islamic civil law, Muslims in an Islamic nation enjoy the full rights and duties of "citizenship," while the *dhimmî's* rights are limited to protection from violence and depredation. The *dhimmî* are to be endured. Their presence is not contested so long as they accept the authority and superiority of Muslims and the Islamic order. The meaning of *"dhimma,"* a notion in Islamic jurisprudence, reflects the Islamic "obligation" to protect the *dhimmî*; the word also connotes "right," "agreement," or "mercy." According to the understanding reached by the *dhimmî* and the Islamic state, their lives and property are inviolate, and their freedom of religion and worship are guaranteed. In exchange, the *dhimmî* are obliged to display subservience and loyalty to the Muslim order and to pay a tax known as the *jizya*'.[11] The relationship is not one of equals, but one of tolerance and forbearance.

The twenty-ninth verse of the Koran's Ninth Sura forms the foundation of the *dhimmî*'s legal status. "Fight against such of those who have been given the Scripture as believe not in Allah nor the Last Day, and forbid not that which Allah hath forbidden by His messenger, and follow not the Religion of Truth, until they pay the tribute readily, being brought low." Throughout the history of Islam, this verse has served as the basis for the debasement of the *dhimmî*, and has governed their relationship to the state.[12] Given that the Islamic statutes relating to believers do not apply to *dhimmî*, their lives were thus administered differently. Within clearly delineated limits, these communities were allowed to· order their own social and religious lives and apply their own laws to questions of marriage and inheritance, which fell under civil law. Only in regard to penal law were they subject to Islamic regulations.[13]

Under Ottoman rule the *dhimmî* were organized according to religion or sect, and these groups were known as *millets*. The autonomy of each *millet* was recognized through a sultanic letter of permission. Each *millet* administered the great majority of its own affairs, "not only the clerical, ritual, and charitable affairs of their flocks, but also education and the regulation of matters of personal status like marriage, divorce, guardianship, and inheritance."[14] A high-ranking member of the clergy from each religious group was chosen by his community as its leader, to act as a state official, responsible to the sultan. Apart from penal matters—and even here exceptions were made—the *millet* leaders had the authority to adjudicate between congregants and collect taxes.

Far from a body of institutions or an empire-wide administrative system, the *millets*, their leaders, and their governance amounted to a series of ad hoc arrangements made over many years. Initially, these arrangements were restricted to distinct regions. However, in the nineteenth century they were regularized and institutionalized as the "*millet* system."[15]

Inevitably, the *millet* authorities sometimes transgressed general Islamic principles.[16] Despite their autonomy, the *dhimmî* were not considered the equals of Muslims and their inequality was manifest in a series of political and legal limitations. For example, *dhimmî* men were barred from marrying Muslim women. Testimony by *dhimmî* against Muslims was not accepted in court.[17] In penal law, a Muslim who killed a *dhimmî* was generally not executed, although there are examples of Muslims sentenced to death for killing a *dhimmî* with premeditation.[18]

Apart from such legal inequalities, the *dhimmî* were also subject to humiliating practices. They were forbidden from conducting their religious observance in a way that would disturb Muslims. The ringing of church bells and construction of churches or synagogues were forbidden.[19] Permission from the state was required to repair existing churches. Additionally, *dhimmî* were prohibited from riding horses and bearing arms and were obliged to step aside for approaching Muslims when traveling on foot. The color of the *dhimmî's* clothing and shoes and the quality of the fabrics had to be distinct from that of Muslims. We know from various imperial edicts, such as this example from the sixteenth century, that at one time non-Muslims were prohibited from wearing collared caftans, valuable materials (silk, in particular), fine muslin, furs and turbans.[20] Other edicts dictated the colors to be worn. Armenian shoes and headgear, for example, were to be red, while the Greeks wore black and Jews turquoise. Their homes too were painted different colors. They were forbidden to wear clogs and had to attach small bells to the coverings worn in the bathhouses.

The *dhimmî's* debasement included a prohibition on building their houses higher than those of Muslims, as a reflection of their inferiority. Their windows were not to look over Muslim quarters. Jews and Christians were discouraged from living within a town or city's Muslim quarters, although there was no specific prohibition. Breaching these restrictions was punished by fine or imprisonment, or even, during the harsher reigns, with death.

In sum, the pluralist Islamic model rested on both humiliation and toleration. It was expected that non-Muslims would willingly accept this status; acting otherwise was violation of the *dhimma* agreement. The non-Muslims' demands for equality in the nineteenth century were indeed seen as a violation of the agreement, and the Muslim communities of the Ottoman Empire had no intention of acquiescing. This cultural-legal framework, forming as it did the basis for the separation of Muslims and non-Muslims, would prove decisive in the clashes between Armenians and Muslims at the end of the nineteenth century.

The second important institution that determined the status of non-Muslims in Ottoman society was the body of agreements reached between the empire and foreign powers, known as the Capitulations and treaties. After the Ottoman conquest of Constantinople in 1453, these agreements—a series of legal and commercial privileges—formalized existing Arabic and Byzantine commercial arrangements, originally in place to encourage foreign trade and shipping. At first, these privileges affected only foreigners in their dealings with the Ottoman authorities, but as the empire expanded to include ever more diverse and far-flung populations, and then as its power waned, the European governments exerted pressure to extend these protections to subjects—mostly Christian—living under the sultan's rule.

According to the agreements, the protected subjects could not be tried in Ottoman courts; the laws of taxation were differently applied; their homes were immune from searches by the authorities and they received a number of significant advantages in commerce.

The first such agreement was concluded with the king of France in 1535. Additional agreements were signed with France in 1604, 1673 and 1740. Initially, the privileges affected those subjects of France and its allies. In the agreement signed in 1673 between Sultan Mehmet IV and King Louis XIV, France became protector of all Catholics in their dealings with the Ottomans, including those living in the empire. This role was expanded in 1740, when other non-Muslims began to enjoy the privileges accorded to French subjects.[21] The Austrian Empire also negotiated privileges in its treaties of 1699, 1718 and 1791. The Austrians claimed that these also extended to Ottoman Catholics and intervened accordingly in domestic Ottoman affairs. Later, British and German subjects enjoyed similar rights.

On the basis of such agreements, the Great Powers interfered frequently in the internal affairs of the Ottoman state. Not surprisingly the Ottomans considered these acts violations of their sovereignty. Most controversial in this regard was the Küchük-Kainarji Treaty of 1774 with Russia, which claimed that the agreement involved protective rights over the Ottoman Orthodox Christians. However, the other European powers uncharacteristically shared the Ottoman position that this was a violation of Ottoman sovereignty. On 28 December 1854, they issued a memorandum to Russia condemning its misinterpretation and requiring Russia to renounce the "erroneous interpretation" of the Küchük-Kainarji Treaty.[22] Significantly, none of these countries were likely to forego their own claims regarding Ottoman subjects.

The foreign consuls habitually assisted all Ottoman Christians in taking advantage of the privileges secured for their own subjects, and this assistance was not limited to handing out letters of consular protection. They also issued or sold passports to Ottoman religious minorities, since simply being registered with a local consulate was often enough to receive foreign citizenship. Those who availed themselves of this were then largely immune from Ottoman justice and taxation, and also received advantageous customs rates when engaging in commerce. Indeed, these activities of the European powers expanded so extensively over the nineteenth century that in many parts of the empire the consuls tended "to conduct themselves like little lords."[23] Their power was often great enough to ensure the dismissal of local officials who failed to cooperate with them. "If a provincial governor or lieutenant governor did not accommodate the local consul, in short, if he was unwilling to abrogate his duties and rights in the service of the consul's interests," the official could be removed from his position "simply through an official letter of complaint from the consul to the dragoman, or interpreter, of his country's embassy."[24]

Given the opportunity, non-Muslims inevitably chose the protection of a foreign power, both to escape Ottoman state oppression and to take advantage of the attendant benefits. In Istanbul alone an estimated fifty thousand Ottoman subjects opted to become subjects of a foreign power. In his memoirs, Edmund Hornby, the British Consular Court judge in Istanbul from 1856–65, claimed that the number of "so-called British protected subjects" under Ottoman rule in 1856 was "little short of a million."[25] Although a law of Ottoman Citizenship was issued in 1869 to curtail the protection system, it failed to stem it completely.

From the late eighteenth century on, wars between the Ottomans and different European powers resulted in peace treaties that brought significant privileges to Ottoman Christian subjects which, in turn, paved the way for the eventual independence of these non-Muslim communities. The Christian minorities, infected with the spirit of progress and freedom blowing in from Europe, began to revolt against political and economic oppression and demand equality, followed by autonomy, and eventually territory. The Ottomans generally met these demands with violent suppression and terror, whereupon foreign powers would intervene, even to the point of war. After defeat, the Ottomans were then forced to accept the insurgents' demands and agree to reforms granting autonomy. But these were usually reforms only on paper, and new revolts would ensue, followed by new foreign interventions, beginning the cycle all over again. This process would continue until the rebellious community achieved independence.

The Serbian revolt of 1804 is widely viewed as the beginning of this development. This uprising and ongoing conflict over the fulfillment of promises made in various treaties, including the 1814–15 Congress of Vienna, culminated in the 1829 Treaty of Edirne, in which Christian communities were for the first time accorded the right to participate in local Ottoman administrations. Similarly, the 1861 decree reorganizing administrative ordinances for the province of Lebanon was drafted under Western pressure following massacres against Christians in 1860.[26] While the decree was limited to Lebanon, it served as a reference point and precedent for communities in other regions.[27] Additionally, the treaties of Paris (1856) and Berlin (1878) belong among the various agreements that paved the way for important changes in the legal status of non-Muslims.

Among the fundamental problems that plagued the Ottoman state during the nineteenth century was the question of placing non-Muslims on an equal level with Muslims and ending their oppression and humiliation. The non-Muslim communities were involved in a tireless struggle for basic rights and freedoms, and the Great Powers repeatedly used this as a pretext for interfering in domestic Ottoman affairs. Considered the "Sick Man of Europe" since the 1830s, the state was on the verge of collapse; the Great Powers were conveniently able to present their ambitions to partition the empire as "humanitarian interventions."

In addition to the pressure of the foreign powers, Ottoman rulers were influenced by the changing political climate of Europe after the French Revolution to take steps in the direction of equality for all their subjects. The *millet* system might have been progressive compared with medieval Europe but held up against the principle of equality introduced by the French Revolution it was revealed as utterly backward. Recognizing this, the Ottoman rulers began the Tanzimat (or "reorganization") reform period of 1839 to 1876 with the aim of forestalling the danger of the state's collapse and binding the Christian population more closely to the state. As Ortaylı wrote,

> The Tanzimat period and its reforms were aimed at stemming the territorial losses that had begun with the eruption of Balkan nationalism. It was the product of those who believed that the empire could be saved through a new type of patriotism, through Ottomanism.[28]

The ruling elite understood that Muslim-Christian equality was the sole means to preserve Ottoman unity.[29] When Greece attained independence in 1829 it became clear the state's Islamic principles would only alienate its remaining Christian population. Although it was not the preferred route, the empire's survival depended on the creation of a new political and cultural identity. The main problem revolved around how to go about forging such an identity. With this aim, the state unveiled its Imperial Rescript of 1839, a document that was reluctantly accepted by Ottoman rulers who felt they had no choice but to introduce Western institutions. When it was introduced to the empire it appeared to be a reaction to crises.[30] The "Western institutions" that emerged were in fact neither the result of a cultural awakening nor the enthusiasm of intellectuals. Political scientist Taner Timur noted that "These were the concessions Ottoman statesmen were forced to make—usually without believing in them . . ."[31] There was consequently great resistance among state functionaries and Ottoman-Muslim subjects. Roderic Davison discusses this lack of enthusiasm in his general assessment of the reform period, claiming that, on the issue of equality, "such statements made for public and foreign consumption were often not followed by action, and were sometimes hypocritical."[32] Yet these utterances were not always insincere. The difficulty was, Davison claims, that the leaders were often in advance of popular opinion and could only proceed with caution.[33]

The Imperial Rescript promised that steps would be taken to ensure that the physical security, property, honor, and well-being of the empire's Christian and Muslim populations would be protected without consideration of religion. Taxation and military service were to be reconfigured justly. All subjects were declared equal before the law. However, the text failed to list the promised rights in detail. Critics therefore claimed that the decree "was written first of all in defense" and merely published "to deceive the foreigners. . . . [These promises] were simply a sort of document produced under the pressure of external and internal events, and which, once such events had passed, would more or less be shelved."[34] Any doubt about the reluctance to implement the reforms is quickly put to rest by the fact that legal changes needed to implement the principle of equality were completed only in the 1880s, almost half a century after the edict's promulgation. Its delayed implementation notwithstanding, the edict's most radical aspect—an intention to achieve Muslim-Christian equality—has been characterized as a "great revolution."[35] Indeed, this equality "represented the most radical breach with ancient Islamic tradition," as historian Bernard Lewis noted, "and was therefore most shocking to Muslim principles and good taste."[36] For this reason, the edict frequently met with hostility. This hostility, together with the state's poor planning to implement such equality, rendered all relevant efforts impotent.

The second great step toward Muslim-Christian equality was taken with the Reform Edict of 1856, a "program prepared by the foreign powers which the Sublime Porte was obligated to adopt."[37] With the 1856 decree, the principle of universal equality—announced with the 1839 Tanzimat reform edict but not yet made into a fundamental legal principle—formed the basis of a system of law. The edict's intention was to remove the obstacles created by the *millet* system and establish a principle of citizenship valid for all peoples of the Ottoman Empire. In addition to the principle of equality before the courts, the decree confirmed that equality would also be achieved in matters of taxation, military service and acceptance of Christians into civil and military schools and government office.[38] It also announced the continued protection and preservation of the autonomous organizational structure of the various religious communities, but in a move to secularize these institutions allowed for lay or non-religious representatives to sit on administrative bodies.

This was a major blow to the non-Muslim religious leadership. Prior to the reform, religious leaders had wielded near-absolute power over their congregants. Consequently, the move met with tremendous opposition at first, particularly within the Greek Orthodox Church. But in 1862–63, despite this reaction, the sultan asked each community to restructure its organization and prepare new regulations, or charters. These charters, prepared by the communities' leaders, were very significant. The Armenian Constitution, approved on 29 March 1863, served as a model for the subsequent Ottoman Constitution of 1876.[39]

Even prior to the reorganization of the *millet* system, a series of changes to the administrative and judicial branches eventually altered the situation of the Christian population. Local administrative councils had been formed as a result of the 1839 Tanzimat Edict, and non-Muslim communities were represented in these councils by their religious leaders. The councils were recognized as the most liberal outcome of the Imperial Rescript ". . . through their emphasis on legal equality among all the empire's subjects, regardless of religious or racial difference, not only in principle but in practice as well."[40] In reality, though, the councils were less than a breakthrough because even "in the areas in which the Christians formed the majority, the Muslim members still held a majority over the Christians."[41]

Although new reforms were enacted in 1849 and 1852 with the aim of encouraging greater Christian participation in these councils, they also proved less than successful. A Provincial Reform Law promulgated in 1864 was based on the French model. Administrative councils were formed at the provincial, sub-provincial and district level, and it became obligatory for representatives of the various non-Muslim *millets* to serve on these councils beside their Muslim compatriots. The system, which was originally implemented as a pilot program in a limited number of provinces, was extended throughout the empire with additional reforms in 1867 and 1871. As for penal law, a new criminal code was prepared and adopted in 1840. It was further developed with revisions in 1850–54 and 1857 and took its final form from the French model in 1877. This was an effort to simultaneously adopt "modern" (i.e., Western) legal principles and ease out Islamic penal laws. Through a series of similar reforms in the judicial system, secular courts were established.[42]

A process that began in 1840 with the establishment of commercial courts, on which sat both Christian and Muslim judges, continued in 1865, with the first courts to be established fully outside of Shari'a law. Then in 1869, they were granted authority over all other courts. But the elimination of the Islamic justice system led to chaos. The selection of Christian judges and the testimony of Christian witnesses were neglected. The rights that these reforms granted to Christians were forcibly withdrawn. Almost immediately after the implementation of the judicial reforms, enacted largely due to foreign pressure, a "witch hunt" against "infidels" was implemented as official government policy.[43]

Thus basic rights and liberties for all the state's religious communities presented a fundamental challenge to the framers of the 1876 Ottoman Constitution. In this document the term "Ottoman" was used for the first time to refer to all imperial subjects, Muslim and non-Muslim. Furthermore, equality before the law was made into a constitutional principle, which was repeated in the document's eighth, ninth and seventeenth Articles.[44] The new Constitution proclaimed universal equality, and established the separation of judicial decisions and their execution, as well as the rules of criminal trials and public prosecutorship, all put into effect in the 1880s.

Despite all these efforts at reform, there remained great attachment to the millet system, which resulted in Article 11 of the Constitution guaranteeing collective religious privileges while at the same time confirming the equality of all subjects as Ottoman citizens. What resulted was the emergence of two separate legal systems, one based on universal equality and individual rights and the other based on group rights and the principle of inequality; this made the Constitution's realization nearly impossible.[45] This dual legal framework, which became known as the "Tanzimat duality," would continue to plague the Ottomans until the very end of the empire.

While the reforms were expected to bring about closer relations between Muslims and non-Muslims, in fact the very opposite occurred. The conceptual basis for such transformation simply didn't exist, either among the ruling elite or within the general society. According to leading Tanzimat reformer Mustafa Reşit Paşa, the full equality promised in the Imperial Rescript would erase the differences between the groups,[46] and thereby end the 600-year dominance of Ottoman Muslims. This was unacceptable to the general Muslim population. Mustafa Reşit Paşa maintained that without proper preparation, Muslims would resist the reforms, even possibly respond with violence. Just as he feared, Muslims created disturbances and these led to massacres.[47] The concessions that Muslims were being asked to make in regard to the principle of fundamental inequality were, as Bernard Lewis states, "no less great an effort of renunciation than is required of those Westerners who are now called upon to forego the satisfactions of racial superiority."[48] Therefore, "[a]mong the Turkish population an initial reaction which was favorable to the promises of security of life and property, of tax reform and of conscription reform, was followed by an opposite reaction directed primarily against the doctrine of equality. The sacred law of Islam, they said, was being subverted."[49]

While the Muslim population was generally unhappy with the rights granted to non-Muslims, the clergy and lay leadership did their part to incite the masses.[50] A massive propaganda campaign was launched, pointing to the erosion of religion and the decline of the state, which was due to the influence of Christian customs.[51] This attack on Christian equality reached its apex with the 1856 Reform Edict. The reformist statesman and chronicler to the sultan, Cevdet Paşa, described the day of its proclamation as one "of mourning and sorrow" for "the people of Islam."[52]

The most difficult aspect for Muslims was to lose their sense of superiority toward the "infidel." "We have lost our sacred right that our forefathers won with their blood. [The perception that] the nation used to ruling has lost this right is not merely held by the ignorant masses, but by our statesmen as well."[53] The Muslims had begun to lose their dominant status. Furthermore, non-Muslims refused to forego the various privileges traditionally accorded them in exchange for their lower status, even while demanding universal equality. In other words, in some regards it was not in their interest to override Islamic law. As one British diplomat put it, "The idea of equal rights for all Ottoman subjects bothered the other communities within the empire . . . because it indirectly threatened their old established privileges."[54] Reportedly, when the 1856 Reform Edict was returned to its red satin pouch after its ceremonial reading at the Sublime Porte, the sultan's court, the Greek Metropolitan of İzmit uttered "İnşallah— God grant that it not be taken out of its bag again."[55]

Thus, "although the Ottoman Christians may have wanted equality in theory, they preferred in practice to pay a tax and so gain exemption from five years of military service and possible death, and to devote their time to trade or agriculture."[56]

In some ways, Christians were better off than the average Turkish peasant, given their exemption from military service, and often the support of a foreign consulate, which excluded them from Ottoman courts, protected their homes from being searched by the authorities and freed them from Ottoman taxes.[57] "The maligned Turkish peasant, at the other end of the social scale, was generally no better off than the ordinary non-Muslim and as much oppressed by maladministration. . . . He was as much in need of reformed government as the Christian, but [h]e had neither treaty, foreign power, nor patriarch to protect him, and his lot was generally unknown to Europe."[58] The consular reports from various regions of the empire at various times bear witness to this fact.[59] If we add to this the fact that Christians were more easily able to secure control of land and trade in the absence of Muslims,[60] who were forced to serve in the army, and were seen as taking advantage of foreign protection, it becomes easier to understand why plans to create equality fostered the growth of hostility and resentment within Ottoman society.[61] These sentiments were expressed openly in the daily press:

[Turks] are being killed on Crete, slaughtered on Samos, massacred in Rumelia, cut into pieces in the Yemen, mown down in the Hauran, throttled in Basra. But it's not the Greeks, Armenians, Bulgarians, Vlachs, Jews, Arabs or Albanians who are sent there, is it? Let them sit in their houses . . . devoting themselves only to their own affairs. Let them grow rich, marry, and have children. We wouldn't want to anger them, to trouble their elevated souls or wear out their delicate constitutions. Otherwise, how could we coax their love of Ottomanism? We simply must make them happy, so that they will be polite and kind and remain Ottoman.[62]

To the empire's Turkish-Muslim population, the Christians were not only defeatists who wanted to carve up the empire, but more important, they were a force that sought themselves to occupy a position of power and superiority. Clearly, Muslims would not willingly abandon their eroding position of superiority. As Norbert Elias explains:

> If they perceive that the means of power of their potential rivals and enemies has grown greater than their own, that their values are being threatened and that their superiority had disappeared . . . they become as dangerous as wild animals. A series of developments in the conditions of two peoples living together, in the past as in the present, is an extremely normal and common situation which compels them toward the use of violence. It is one of the conditions under which such wars appear.[63]

This well describes the experience of Muslims, who lived through a long process of declining superiority vis-à-vis the Christian population. Losing power over "the Bulgarian dairymen, Serbian pig farmers, and Greek tavern owners, over whom [they] had lorded for 500 years,"[64] was such a blow to their honor that the Turks declared openly that they would never surrender power peacefully, and that much blood would flow before they would surrender it at all. Young Ottoman leader Ziya Paşa, who complained that implementing the principle of equality had vaulted the Christians far beyond the Muslims, predicted that Muslims would find the situation unbearable. "Although the nation of Islam has up to now endured" this development, the events were now reaching "intolerable levels, unacceptable to the honor and will of Muslims . . . a day will come when this will be impossible to bear, and things will get out of control."[65] Ali Suavi, also of the Young Ottomans, went even further, warning that Muslims "would not only refuse to accept the superiority of a subject nation, they would never tolerate being ruled by them. They will be ready to risk everything and shed blood [in order to prevent] that."[66]

Accordingly, throughout the nineteenth century, Muslim assaults and revolts against Christians occurred because of anger at their own loss of power. Incidents in Lebanon in 1844, in Mecca in 1855 and in Jeddah and Syria in 1858 are but a few examples. The cause of the Serbian uprising of 1856–61 was the inability of the Muslim population to accept its loss of dominance. According to the Convention of Akkerman in 1826 and the Treaty of Edirne in 1829 Turkish peasants had to sell their lands and abandon Serbia. But many Turkish peasants refused to comply. What's more, "they were unable to digest the fact of suddenly emerging from the situation of being Lords of Serbia and entering into one in which they were sometimes equal, and at others subject to the [Serbs]. . . . On the other side, it was slowly entering the Serbs' consciousness through the concessions that they had won that they were slowly becoming a nation. . . . The transformation taking place in the Turkish and Serbian psychologies was the reason for the violent clashes and bloody struggles between them."[67] One of the main causes of the massacre of Armenians in certain regions was, again, the perceived Muslim loss of power in relation to their Armenian neighbors. "The Muslims in the province of Van resisted the Armenians, whom they had ruled for centuries, and were utterly incapable of accepting . . . them as leaders or rulers."[68] The same writer argued that the attacks against Armenians were, therefore, to be seen as "rational." Bernard Lewis portrays the result thus: "From the late eighteenth century through the nineteenth century, expulsion, outbreaks of mob violence, and even massacres became increasingly frequent."[69]

The hatred that the Muslim population felt toward the Christians only increased with the Russian, English, French, and later German interference in Ottoman internal affairs. The loss of superior status had shaken the Muslims' confidence, which resulted in the loss of their tolerance. Massacres against Armenians, which by the late nineteenth century had become almost routine, can best be understood against this background.

Sultan Abdul Hamid II and the Armenian Question, 1876–1908

Although the Armenian question only became an issue of international importance with the Berlin Conference following the Russo-Ottoman War of 1877–78, the problem already existed. Long before the conference, the Armenians had been seeking an end to oppression and injustice. The Armenian Communal Council, which assumed its duties in 1862, collected peasants' complaints from Anatolia, where most Armenians lived, and petitioned the government on their behalf. "These grievances were assembled by the council in 1870 . . . processed during 1870 and 1871, and a report was produced and debated before being submitted to the government."[70] The complaints included looting and murder in Armenian towns by Kurds and Circassians, improprieties during tax collection, criminal behavior by government officials, and the continued refusal to accept Christians as witnesses in trials.[71] Overall, the report, submitted to the Ottoman government on 4 March 1872, summarized twenty years of grievances, including 73 offenses during tax collection, 154 cases of abuse of power by government officials, and 249 cases of kidnapping, robbery, and illegally preventing religious functionaries from performing their duties.[72] In response, the government set up a commission composed equally of Muslims and non-Muslims. "It was decided that those responsible for the conditions mentioned in the report were to be punished, recommendations were to be made for the future, and the actions advised were to be reviewed."[73]

The revolt in Bosnia-Herzegovina in 1875 and the Bulgarian and Serbian uprisings that quickly followed were turning points in the Armenian question. Leaders in Europe, incensed by the bloody suppression of these revolts, went into action, arguing that the 1856 Paris Treaty that gave them the right to protect the empire's Christian population also implied the right to intervene.[74] A first meeting in Istanbul in December 1876 ended in failure. To block the interference of the Great Powers, the Ottoman government hurriedly declared a constitutional monarchy. The Great Powers, upset by these diplomatic maneuvers, left Istanbul and came together in London which ultimately resulted in the London Protocol of 1877. The ninth Article of the protocol granted the foreign signatories the authority to undertake joint action if they were disappointed with proposed Ottoman reforms.[75] After the protocol was signed they returned to hold talks in Istanbul, but the Ottoman government refused to sign the agreement, rejecting it as a violation of its honor and sovereignty. The sultan was prepared to risk war with Russia rather than to accept the conditions of the agreement.

During these negotiations, the Armenian patriarchate submitted his people's demands to the British and the Ottoman rulers. These included conscription of Armenian recruits rather than paying the price of military exemption; payment of taxes directly to the government rather than taxing farmers; appointing independent inspectors in the provinces; abandoning Shari'a courts; increasing the number of secular courts; disarming belligerent Kurds and Circassians; and granting Armenians the right to bear arms. The report also protested against "forced land seizure, profaning churches and places of worship, and in particular the forced conversion of women and children, arson, protection extortion, rape, and murder. These are some of the things Armenians frequently encounter."[76]

Following the Russo-Ottoman War the Armenians looked toward victorious Russia. The Armenian officers successfully serving in the Russian Army, enlisted from the large Russian-Armenian population, had played a significant role in this shift.[77] The Armenian patriarch in Istanbul decided to send a memorandum to the exilarchate in Etchmiadzin in Russian Armenia, considered the spiritual center of the Armenian Church, to be passed on to the czar. The memorandum demanded the following: that the large part of eastern Anatolia occupied by Russia and considered historic Armenian land, should not be returned to the Turks and that the standard rights recognized for Bulgarians be applied to Armenians as well. Furthermore, if these lands should be returned, then the Ottoman government must be pressured to enact reform and Russian soldiers remain in the area until such reform is realized. Additional demands called for acceptance of Armenians into government service and the military and allowing a significant role in the provincial and municipal leadership. The memorandum finally demanded settlement of the nomadic Kurdish and Circassian tribes.[78]

A decision was made to submit similar requests to the czar and the British prime minister, as well as to dispatch a delegation to the Russian commander in Edirne. Doubtless, the Ottoman rulers must have been aware of these actions. Once Russian Armenians undertook similar initiatives, instructions were sent to the Russian ambassador to the Porte, Count Nicholas Ignatiev, asking that the Armenian question be raised during the forthcoming Ottoman-Russian peace talks. As the Russian patriarchate had requested, an arrangement similar to the Lebanese autonomy was agreed upon although never ultimately established.

At the beginning of the peace talks, held at San Stefano, the possibility arose that there would be no article in the final treaty concerning the Armenian question. The Armenian patriarch, "taking upon himself all responsibility, went to the Russian army in San Stefano."[79] As a result, the sixteenth article was added, which turned the Armenian question into one of the central issues of international diplomacy. This article states:

> As the evacuation of the Russian troops of the territory which they occupy in Armenia, and which is to be restored to Turkey, might give rise to conflicts and complications detrimental to the maintenance of good relations between the two countries, the Sublime Porte engaged to carry into effect, without further delay, the improvements and reforms demanded by local requirements in the provinces inhabited by Armenians, and to guarantee their security from Kurds and Circassians.[80]

According to this agreement, Russian units were to remain until reforms had been carried out in the Armenian areas. Russia thus became a permanent supervisor and guarantor. But Great Britain could not accept Russia's attainment of so much "sovereignty" over the Ottoman Empire, and immediately sent a naval force into the Bosphorus. London contracted a separate, secret agreement with the Ottoman government, which in any case was unhappy with Russia's new role. Then, announcing that they would not recognize the Treaty of San Stefano as binding, British leaders called for a new peace conference in which all of the Great Powers would participate.

The Congress of Berlin convened on 13 June 1878, and concluded one month later, on 13 July. England and Russia had previously reached an understanding on the fundamental issues in a protocol signed by both states on 30 May. The Armenian organizations, led by the church, sent delegations and submitted reports on the Armenian situation. Their greatest fear was that their achievements at San Stefano would be lost. In a letter the Armenian delegates stressed that they did not desire independence from Turkey but only an Armenian governor and a measure of autonomy in those areas where Armenians formed a majority.[81] They also proposed detailed plans to support such a structure.

The sixty-first article of the Berlin Treaty brought the Armenian question fully into the European field of vision:

> The Sublime Porte undertakes to carry out, without further delay, the improvements and reforms demanded by local requirements in the provinces inhabited by the Armenians, and to guarantee their security against the Circassians and Kurds. It will periodically make known the steps taken to this effect to the Powers, who will superintend their application.[82]

This was an advance from the Armenian point of view, but the failure to achieve autonomy, as well as the clear indication of the withdrawal of Russian soldiers, were seen as losses in relation to the San Stefano Treaty.

In 1879, shortly after the Berlin Treaty was signed, Great Britain reminded the Ottomans of their promises. When Sultan Abdul Hamid II showed no interest, the British sent another note to the Porte.[83] This message produced no result, and so "an English flotilla arrived at Beşik Bay in an attempt to apply pressure. It was also assumed that the English warships would put pressure on the Dardanelles."[84] At this point, the Porte decided to take up the issue of reform in the provinces and dispatched to the region "commissioners possessing broad authority to study the principles of reforms."[85] The Armenian patriarchate prepared further detailed reports about the necessary reforms.

On 13 June 1880, the signatories to the Berlin Treaty delivered a new note to the Porte regarding Armenian reform. On 5 July the Ottoman government forwarded its response, a memorandum listing the regional commissioners' activities and complaining about exaggeration. Additionally, the government took pains to prove that Armenians did not form a majority in the eastern provinces but admitted that up to that point, no concrete reform initiatives had been taken. Further European entreaties to the Porte on this matter were made in 1883 and 1886, but the Ottomans ultimately proved successful in their attempt to drag the matter out and do as little as possible.

Beyond this state resistance to reform, the Kurdish situation complicated the problem. The Ottomans argued that they wanted to include the Kurds in any comprehensive reform plan. However, the Great Powers failed to support this position because they believed the Kurds to be "primitive" and suspected the plan was an Ottoman tactic designed to forestall Armenian change.[86]

Ultimately, all such efforts were doomed, because, as Turkish historian Enver Ziya Karal has pointed out, stern measures against the Circassian and Kurdish tribesmen who constituted the Armenians' central complaint were almost impossible. Without forced settlement, these tribesmen remained nomadic. More important, Muslims had united in response to massacres in the Balkans and ongoing assaults of the Great Powers.

> Actions taken since 1875 by both the Balkan Christians and Christian states of Europe to the detriment of Turkish and Muslim populations had produced a sense of solidarity among the Muslims. A good number of high Ottoman statesmen, Adbul Hamid II first among them, advocated a foreign policy intended to preserve the power of the state by tapping into this solidarity, a policy which over time began to be known as Pan-Islamism.[87]

The empire of Abdul Hamid II came to see the remaining Christian communities as a lost cause and directed its efforts toward binding its Muslim subjects more closely to the throne.

Using the pretext of increased activity by Armenian revolutionary organizations, the Ottoman government established irregular Kurdish cavalry forces, the Hamidiye Regiments.[88] In the middle of November 1890, the Istanbul dailies published the sultan's imperial decree concerning their establishment. They were formed of Kurds from regions bordering the Russian Caucasus who had remained obedient to the Porte.[89] Although the official histories depict these units as having been established to redress a shortfall in military manpower and provide security on the Russian border, a good number of Turkish sources claim that their real target was the Armenians.[90] Hungarian Orientalist Armenius Vambery recounts that the sultan told him of the units' true purpose: "I tell you, I will soon settle those Armenians. I will give them a box on the ears which will make them smart and relinquish their revolutionary ambitions."[91]

In 1894, a revolt broke out in the Cilician village of Sasun (near Muş) because the Armenian villagers were being forced to pay taxes to the Kurdish tribes over and above those paid to the government. They were being crushed by the burden of dual taxation. Refusing to pay, the villagers lodged a formal complaint with Istanbul and the courts ruled in their favor, but "the governor-general of the province, an ignorant and stubborn person, incited the local Muslims against the Armenians."[92] The Armenian peasant revolt was suppressed and looting and murder continued. Then, as a result of the propaganda of the Armenian revolutionary organization, Hunchak, the villagers finally rebelled. When the news of an "Armenian revolt" was relayed to the palace, military units were dispatched to the village. Turkish sources relate that these units behaved savagely toward the Armenian villagers, and a good number were slaughtered."[93]

After this bloody suppression, Great Britain, Russia and France prepared a memorandum based on the principles laid out by the Armenian patriarchate and outlining a reform plan to include the six east Anatolian provinces of Erzurum, Bitlis, Van, Sivas, Diyarbakır and Harput. The Ottoman government sent a committee of inquiry to the region on 27 November 1894. But the committee's explicit task was "to investigate the looting and murders which Armenian gangs had committed,"[94] causing Great Britain to issue a strong protest, demanding the dismissal of the governors-general in the "Armenian provinces."[95] Abdul Hamid II appealed to the Germans, but without the desired result, the Ottomans were finally forced to establish a reform commission with Britain, France and Russia. The foreign members of the commission strongly condemned the Porte, but France and Russia hinted to the Ottomans that they would not be overly insistent on the question of reform. Russia had little interest in its western border, caught up as it was in a conflict with Japan in the Far East which would culminate in war in 1904.

As a result of this joint initiative, a far-reaching reform package was submitted on 11 May 1895 to the Ottoman government. This plan remained a point of reference for years to come. Initially, Abdul Hamid II rejected the package, believing that its proposals violated the sovereignty of the sultan. On receiving the reform scheme, the sultan is said to have remarked, "This business will end in blood."[96] As the pressure upon him increased, he compromised and suggested a reform package just for the Armenians. He promised to make changes in the fields of administration, justice and taxation, appoint Christians to government positions and include them in the police and gendarmerie.

With discussions dragging on while incidents in the region continued, the Armenians, under the Hunchak leadership, demonstrated in Istanbul at the end of September 1895. A massacre of the capital's Armenian population was organized on the pretext that violence had erupted during the protest.[97] The Great Powers then forced the sultan to accept the original reform package on 20 October 1895. The new program also called for supervision of the Kurdish tribes, and a prohibition on the members of the Hamidiye Regiments from wearing their uniforms or carrying their weapons when not on active duty. But like previous reform attempts, these changes never actually occurred.[98]

Meanwhile, the Anatolia region was again engulfed by the flames of revolt. Organized massacres of Armenians were carried out in Zeytun, Trabzon, Erzurum, Bitlis, Van, Harput, Diyarbakır, Sivas and Çukurova.[99] Although there is no direct evidence that the sultan ordered the massacres, the timing is suspect, with the events occurring just after the reform decree was issued.[100] On August 26, 1896, when the Armenian Revolutionary Federation, the Dashnaks, raided the Ottoman Bank in Istanbul, hoping to draw attention to their cause, a large-scale massacre of Armenians followed. Various figures have been given for the total number of dead resulting from the different incidents between 1894 and 1896. Kaiser Wilhelm II claimed, on the basis of reports he had received, that by 20 December 1895 some eighty thousand Armenians had been killed.[101] The figures given in French and English reports are two hundred thousand and one hundred thousand, respectively.[102] Johannes Lepsius, the German pastor and Armenian advocate, puts the total figure at eighty-eight thousand,[103] while the Armenian patriarchate argued that the real number was in the area of three hundred thousand.[104]

Once again, the Great Powers applied pressure. New promises of reform were made, and new programs were drawn up.[105] But Sultan Abdul Hamid II again succeeded in weathering the storm of protest. The reforms were watered down and a good portion lost and forgotten in the course of subsequent events. Disputes among the Great Powers played an important role. Despite the language of humanitarian intervention, the European states were each pursuing their own economic and political interests. During the 1890s, they made it clear to the Ottoman rulers that they would not undertake any action solely for the sake of the Armenians. Due to Europe's hypocritical policy, the Armenian problem continued to go unresolved.[106]

In sum, the various foreign interventions and agreements had a negative effect, produced no lasting reforms, and played a significant part in both the killings of 1894–96 and the Armenian genocide of 1915.[107] Thus, after 1880, the Armenians experienced oppression and massacre rather than progress, and after the 1894–96 massacres the Armenian question was removed from the international agenda until the revolution of 1908.

The massacres directed at Christian minorities throughout the nineteenth century were mostly either in response to provincial revolts calling for social change, or they were the result of reactions to national independence and separatist movements. In a great many cases, the clashes were quickly transformed into interreligious or intercommunal clashes between Muslims and Christians.

The Armenian massacres that occurred after the 1890s began to take on a very different character from earlier ones. In this period, the Ottoman state was laboring to achieve a sort of national unity on the basis of Pan-Islamist ideology, in an attempt to stem the process of decline and collapse. The social exclusion of a national-religious group preponderantly on religious grounds (and the Armenians in particular) began as conscious state policy during this period. The Armenians were made into scapegoats.

For instance, at one point, after claiming that the Armenians were extremely wealthy, constituted a full third of the members of the Ottoman bureaucracy, paid very few taxes and didn't do military service, Abdul Hamid II said that "the Armenians are a degenerate community. . . . Always servile. . . ."[108] He also claimed that their advantageous position derived from their economic power, and began exerting pressure on merchants, stockbrokers, and the rest of the Armenian bourgeoisie.[109]

The belief began to take firm root that the empire was faced, in the words of Abdul Hamid II, "with the endless persecutions and hostilities of the Christian world."[110] Enemies wanting to carve up the empire surrounded the Ottomans on nearly every border. This challenge was seen as a constant source of erosion. Abdul Hamid II said:

> By taking away Greece and Rumania, Europe has cut off the feet of the Turkish state. The loss of Bulgaria, Serbia and Egypt has deprived us of our hands, and now by means of this Armenian agitation, they want to get at our most vital places and tear out our very guts. This would be the beginning of totally annihilating us, and we must fight against it with all the strength we possess.[111]

In this light, any reform would be interpreted as tantamount to the collapse of the empire. With this in mind, the sultan told the German ambassador to the Porte: "I swear that . . . I would rather die than accept reforms that would produce self-government [for the Armenians]."[112] The German liberal Friedrich Nauman described the Ottoman mental state thus: "The Turkish killing of the Armenians is not simply persecution of the Christians. On the contrary, it is part of the life-and-death struggle of an old and great empire not willing to die without exerting one last, bloody effort to save itself."[113] In such an environment, it was easy to spread the idea that the Armenians were simply an internal extension of external enemies. More and more, the Armenian question came to be seen as a question of the empire's very survival. Solidarity among the empire's Muslims, no matter what, was the psychological product of decline and disintegration coupled with the belief of being surrounded by hostile forces desiring the state's elimination. Thus Pan-Islamism was transformed into state ideology.[114]

For this reason the attacks, mainly against the Armenians, had the nature of pogroms. The state unleashed its attacks on the slightest provocation, calculating that this would bind Muslims more closely to the empire. The Austrian ambassador to the Porte reported that Muslims were being armed and set into action against Christians, calling this policy a "Muslim Crusade."[115] From reports of the various diplomatic missions in Istanbul and eyewitness accounts,[116] it is clear that the massacres of 1894–96 were centrally planned. The British and French ambassadors to the Porte reported information that the slaughter was directed from the palace itself.[117] The German and Austrian embassies gave similar accounts.[118] In the Great Powers' memorandum to the Ottoman government in 1896, it is mentioned that the attacks began simultaneously in many different areas and that a portion of the perpetrators had the same weapons and wore the same clothing. The memorandum also reported that state officials directed the attackers to their targets.[119] French ambassador Paul Cambon recounted that Ottoman foreign minister Tevfik Paşa admitted that state functionaries had participated in the massacres.[120]

Summarizing the general lines of Abdul Hamid II's Islam-based policies, one author wrote:

> He gathered around him experts from a number of diverse Muslim communities; he reduced the number of Christians at the higher level and increased the number of Muslims. . . . By arming Muslim groups he recognized their right to defend themselves against Christians, who had been armed by Europe, and he gave the impression that the state was on their side. No longer were Muslims penalized simply because Europe demanded it; and if they were, the penalties [were such that] they could have been called rewards.[121]

The goal was for Muslims to look upon attacks against Christians as the fulfillment of a religious duty.

European consular reports and testimonies of travelers from various regions of the empire confirm this situation. The dragoman at the British Embassy, whose Turkish was superb and who based his reports on the views he heard from local Muslims, said of the 1894–96 massacres:

> [The perpetrators] are guided by the prescriptions of the Shari'a. The law prescribes that if the "rayah," or cattle, Christians try, through their recourse to foreign powers, to overstep the privileges allowed them by their Mussulman masters and free themselves from their oppression, their lives and property are forfeited, and they are at the mercy of the Mussulmans. To the Turkish mind, the Armenians tried to overstep those limits by appealing to the foreign powers, especially England. They therefore consider it their religious duty and a righteous thing to destroy . . . the Armenians. . . .[122]

Witnesses to massacres in Urfa reported that before killing the Armenians, whose hands and feet were bound, the Muslims recited passages from the Koran and prayed.[123] It is no coincidence that the massacres generally occurred after Friday prayers. The slaughter, which commenced in response to a specific signal given when the prayers ended on Friday, would continue until a second signal was given to stop.[124]

The belief that Muslims were carrying out a religious duty by killing Armenians might not have been a motive at the decision-making level, but was an important factor for those participating in the genocide of 1915 and influenced the aftermath. Yusuf Kemal Tengirşenk, a member of the investigative commission formed by the Ottoman parliament after the Adana massacres of 1909, and later the second foreign minister of the Turkish Republic, listed the reasons—on the basis of the British consular report—that Muslims participated in the slaughter: "I am of the opinion that the great majority truly believed that their government, their lives, and their religion were under threat." Another reason he cited was the "thirst for plunder."[125] Voices began to be heard during Abdul Hamid II's reign calling for a resolution of the Armenian problem through wholesale killing. Armenius Vambery recounted that İzzet Paşa, the architect of Abdul Hamid II's Armenian policies, thought the way to eliminate the problem was to eliminate the Armenians.[126]

With the establishment of the Hamidiye Regiments, we can see that the "reward" mechanism for dealing harshly with Armenians began to gain a more systematic character. The expenses for these units were covered by revenue accrued through the oppression, theft and murder they carried out. Members of these units were exempt from taxes and their tribes were often given land by the state. These rewards and their institutionalization would play a crucial role as an exacerbating factor in the mass slaughter to come.

CHAPTER 2

THE UNION AND PROGRESS ERA

PRIOR TO 1915, THE MASSACRES DIRECTED AT ARMENIANS WERE "local" in nature, even if they were the product of central Ottoman policies. Their purpose, beyond binding the Muslim population to the sultan, was to cow the Armenians into submission. The events of 1915–17 differed in their purpose, which was, as Talât Paşa wrote in a 1915 memorandum, to achieve "a complete and fundamental elimination of this concern."[1] If indeed a decision for such a radical act was taken, when and how did that happen? And what were the factors permitting the making of such a decision?

Turkish nationalist ideas gradually came to predominate within the Union and Progress party, the governing party during the war years, and played an important role in the Armenian genocide. To explain the factors that pushed the nationalists· toward annihilating the Armenians, some general information about the movement's character is necessary. Rather than discuss all of the aspects of Turkish nationalism,[2] I will instead shed light on the intellectual framework and background of the idea of eliminating the Armenians and show how a concrete plan gradually evolved.

One clarification is necessary. It would be a mistake to conclude from the following analysis that genocide was inevitable. Even immediately prior to the genocide decision, there were always other options available to the Ottoman leadership. It is easy to fall into the trap of inevitability when describing historical events. The context and circumstances need not have necessarily resulted in genocide.

Among the empire's Muslim-Turks a belief in the "ruling nation" or *Millet-i Hakime* prevailed, according to which they were superior to its other peoples and nations, and therefore possessed the inherent right to rule over them, a concept due in part to the influence of Islamic ideas. The Ottoman-Turkish ruling elite identified with Islam and saw themselves as superior to other religious groups.

It has been generally accepted that Islam has played a particularly negative role in the development of Turkish national consciousness. As Bernard Lewis stated, "Among the different peoples who embraced Islam, none went farther in sinking their separate identity in the Islamic community than the Turks."[3]

The Young Ottoman movement that formed in the mid-nineteenth century and its successor, the Young Turks—another form of referring to the Union and Progress organization—accepted Turkish domination of the Ottoman Empire as a situation so natural and obvious as not to merit discussion. Its representatives frequently asserted that Turks would recognize the rights of other communities and nations only on the condition that they accept Turkish domination. Throughout the ideological changes among the ruling elite during the modern period, Ottomanism, Pan-Islamism and Turkism, Muslim superiority remained a constant idea, even during a time when a cosmopolitan attitude, such as Ottomanism, was dominant. During the period of Tanzimat reform, statesman Ali Paşa, "having observed the conflicting interests and aspirations of the various nationalities in the Empire, commented on the particular role of the Turks as the unifying element. . . ."[4]

Turkism emerged after the Tanzimat period in the 1880s as a movement to simplify the Ottoman Turkish language. There was still no "political" Turkish nationalism;[5] the early pioneers of "Turkist" ideas in language and literature saw themselves more as Ottomanists or as Islamists. Writer Ahmet Rasim, referring to the debates of that era, said that the term "the Ottoman nation" was equated with

"Turk."[6] Yusuf Akçura, widely considered the father of the idea of Turkish nationalism, argued that the early pioneers of Turkist thought in language and literature (Şinasi, Namık Kemal, Ahmed Vefik, Mustafa Celâleddin and Süleyman Paşa) were not "Turkists" politically speaking, but that they advocated a "policy of Ottoman Nationalism" or "the Unity of Islam."[7]

For all their differences, these divergent currents—Ottomanism, Islamism, Turkism, and Westernism—shared one core premise: the nationalism of a dominant ethnic group, which was understood to mean the Turks.[8] The Union and Progress movement continued this tradition and gave a new coloration. Namik Kemal, a leader of the Young Ottoman movement, laid the ground for this process, which inspired and preceded the Young Turks and the CUP, when he claimed that "We can compromise with the Christians only when they accept our position of dominance."[9] Kemal based his supremacist ideas on openly racial grounds: "The Turks, who, on account of their great numbers and abilities, possess excellent and meritorious qualities, such as 'breadth of intelligence,' 'cool-headedness,' 'tolerance and repose,' occupy the preeminent position in the Ottoman collective."[10]

A similar idea was expressed by Ali Suavi, another Young Ottoman leader, who advanced the thesis "that the Turkish race [is] older and superior . . . on account of its military, civilizing, and political roles."[11] Şinasi, considered one of the first Ottoman secularist intellectuals, also defended the principle of the "ruling nation." In fact, he began to publish Tercüman-ı Ahval, a nationalist newspaper, because he believed that the idea was insufficiently disseminated.[12]

Although the Union and Progress movement did not, in its early years, have a systematic ideology beyond its embrace of modernity and its wish to limit the sultan's power, the idea of "Ottomanism" predominated.[13] Ahmet Rıza, an important figure in the movement, understood Ottomanism to mean Turkish rule. To him, success would mean Turkish dominance. Rıza's Ottomanism was one in which the Turk could be "proud of being a Turk."[14] The Union and Progress movement's publications repeatedly emphasized the need for a "primary element" or dominant group, even in multinational societies. In the 20 May 1903 edition of the Unionist Şura-yı Ümmet, Britain was criticized for not "supporting the Turks, who are the ruling nation, but rather [treating them as] a component part. . . ."[15]

Hüseyin Cahit Yalçin, whose newspaper *Tanin* was considered the official Unionist organ, defended the idea of Turkish sovereignty, writing, "Say what you want, but the ruling nation in this country is and will be the Turks."[16] Cahit continued to defend this thesis, on the assumption that the Christian communities had no aim other than to destroy the country. According to him, "The country was only a 'homeland' for the Turks. . . . In that case, it was essential that the right to steer and decide the fate of the country and make the essential decisions be in Turkish hands."[17]

The enormous reaction to the 1904 article "Three Types of Policy" by Yusuf Akçura, founder of Turkish political nationalism, provides another example of the widespread belief in a "ruling nation" among the Ottoman elite. Akçura, claiming that Ottomanism could not possibly resolve the empire's problems, publicly called for a shift of government policy to Turkish nationalism. The prevailing understanding among his readers was that Islam, Ottomanism, and Turkism were indivisible, one and the same. Among the responses the article received, a frequent argument was that for Turks "it is impossible to separate Turk from Muslim, Muslim from Turk, or either Muslim or Turk from Ottoman, or to divide what is one into three."[18] Mizancı Murat, a Young Turk leader, called his newspaper *The Turk* and frequently wrote that he was both a Muslim and an Ottoman. One reader claimed that this was a contradiction. Murat responded: "Let's not err in praying in the name of Turkishness, Ottomanism, or Islam, which our friend has mistakenly taken as distinct from one another."[19]

Thus even before Turkish nationalism was fully formed as a political ideology, the Turks viewed themselves as the ruling nation in the Ottoman state and defended the need to bring the minority communities to heel.[20] This understanding of "ruling nation" would play a crucial role as a political and cultural foundation for the Armenian genocide.

At the same time, the multinational character of the Ottoman state placed the ruling Turkish community in a dilemma. Because the main aim as the dominant group was to preserve the existing status of the multinational state, the Turks were never able to embrace openly their own national identity. Integrationist ideologies that would gather other national groups under its wing were always presented as the "official state ideology." Thus prior to the defeat in the Balkan War in 1913, the ruling group could never openly claim to be Turkish nationalists, opting instead to hide behind the ideology of Ottomanism. In his memoirs, Halil Menteşe, president of the Ottoman Chamber of Deputies and later foreign minister, relates that because the Turks had to unite the different ethnic and religious elements within the empire, they could not say "We are the Turks" within the Ottoman Parliament.[21] The Union and Progress movement's Central Committee, responding to calls from provincial members to recognize its Turkish character, responded that everyone in the empire should call themselves "Ottoman."[22] Provincial members wished to separate themselves from the Christian communities, which is what led them to demand recognition as "Turks."

There are several other reasons for the late development of Turkish nationalism, the most significant being that the term "Turk" was used among Ottomans as a pejorative. In an article from an 1875 edition of the newspaper *Basiret* there is mention of "youth who are not ashamed of being Turks."[23] As a means of preserving the crumbling empire, Turkish nationalism would have seemed the least attractive of the leaders' options, because of the exclusion not only of Christians but non-Turkish Muslims. Ottoman leaders persisted in hoping to establish unity around the rallying point of Islam. After all other options had been exhausted, they were compelled to choose Turkism, an undesired but necessary option.

An additional obstacle to the acknowledgment of Turkism was the empire's weak position in relation to the European states. In the letters they wrote to Turks and other Muslim subjects, Union and Progress leaders openly expressed this trepidation, as well as their objections to embracing Pan-Islamism: "We oppose as unsound any overt or public effort on behalf of the idea of Islamic unity. . . . At present our enemies are far more powerful than we are. In such a weakened state, it would be inappropriate to make Europe suspicious of us."[24] Yet despite the prevailing Pan-Ottoman and Pan-Islamic atmosphere, there was already a current within these trends that stressed the importance of the Turkish element. Descriptions such as "the refinement particular to the Turks" and the "national dignity among the Turks" found in various journals and special reports confirm this.[25] But those who made such claims were simultaneously

writing articles in which they stated that Pan-Ottomanism was identical to Turkish nationalism.[26]

Dr. Mehmed Nazım (as he is always referred to) and Bahaettin
Şakir, Unionist leaders who played central roles in the Armenian
genocide, were strong representatives of the Turkist stream. In their
correspondence, the two openly grappled with both Turkish nationalist and Pan-Islamist ideas. In a joint letter of 2 June 1906 to the
committee's Kızanlık branch in Bulgaria, they speak of "our committee [being] purely Turkish," and state that the organization "would
never submit to the ideas of the enemies of Islam and Turkishness."[27]
The acceptance of non-Muslims into the committee was possible only
on the condition that they worked within the Union and Progress
program "for the triumph of Ottomanism."[28]

In short, Ottomanism was necessary to preserve the state.
"Although the classical political ideal of Ottomanism appeared to
make little sense in the face of numerous challenges, the political
cadres who wanted to prevent the dissolution of a multi-ethnic construct were unable to replace it with another value. This remained the
central problem that the committee found itself unable to solve."[29]
Thus it was only at the outset of the twentieth century that Turkish
Muslims began to think seriously about their national identity.

Hungarian Orientalist Vambery wrote in 1898 that he had "never
met a single Turk in Istanbul who seriously concerned himself with
either the question of Turkish nationalism or Turkish languages.[30] In
1896, Ziya Gökalp, the leading ideologue of the CUP, began to display
an interest in ancient Turkish history after reading the writings of historian Leon Cahun on the Turks. During this period—and even into
the early 1900s—Ottoman schools taught nothing concerning the
history of the Turks. Even as late as 1911, "of the assigned textbooks in
Turkish middle schools dealing with modern history, two thirds of
the pages were devoted to the history of France, while the remainder
dealt with the other states of Europe; almost nothing at all was mentioned of Turkey or of the Turks."[31] Until the 1908 revolution (which
brought about the proclamation of a second constitutional monarchy), Islamic seminaries barred the study of the Turkish language. To
the extent that the seminaries taught history, it was Ottoman-Islamic
history, beginning with the life of the Prophet Muhammad.

One important result of the delay was the influence of racist and social Darwinist ideology.[32] The first Turkish nationalist thinkers admired the works of Arthur de Gobineau, a nineteenth-century French racial theorist.[33] His influence was felt in the journal *Genç Kalemler,* the Unionist intellectual publication that began in Salonica in 1911.[34] The German concept of nation, which emphasized race, blood and culture, became dominant. In Ziya Gökalp's opinion the German approach "happened to more closely match the condition of 'Turkishness,' which was struggling to constitute its own historical and national identity."[35] Gökalp laid the foundations for an expansionist version of Turkish nationalism. He argued that the political borders of the homeland of the Turks "would extend as far as their language and culture stretched."[36]

The Union and Progress movement continued to blur the Turkish nationalism in its program until the Balkan Wars, but then, given the loss of much territory and the non-Muslim population of the Balkans, it felt free to pursue a Turkist policy openly.[37]

The attitude of the Union and Progress movement toward the empire's Christian communities was not based on clear ideological preference, but primarily on political exigencies. It had inherited a state-based philosophy that had lasted more than six hundred years and left a deep mark, in which the ruling elite recognized no principle other than the preservation of the centuries-old state and the need to continue its existence at any price. Thus, for Ottoman leaders, ideologies could be discarded and exchanged like clothing when the situation called for it.

Renowned Turkish social scientist Tarık Zafer Tunaya has claimed that the question "How can this state be saved?" was the Union and Progress movement's core concern. Their "aim and greatest concern, the beginning and end of their thoughts were with rescuing the state."[38] Therefore, the Unionists were not overly concerned with philosophical ideas. They "did not mind which particular element of the [Pan-Islamic or Pan-Turkic] ideology was emphasized" because they knew that in the end leadership would always remain in the hands of the Turks.[39] If it became necessary to jettison one ideology and adopt another, they had no compunction in doing so.

Celal Bayar, a well-known Unionist who later became the third president of the Republic of Turkey, noted that "there were some [members] who remained faithful to the Ottomanist policies of the

Tanzimat, others who were inclined toward Islamic or Pan-Islamic, Turkist, or nationalist policy as well. There were also groups of opportunists. These were far more evident among the men of state and high-ranking officials."[40] This pragmatism made it possible to unite members with diverse opinions under the umbrella of the movement's political party, the CUP. The reason Ziya Gökalp became a leading party ideologue was because of his attempt to find a middle way among these divergent ideas. His "Islamic-Turkish-Western" synthesis became the official Unionist slogan, produced and repeated according to occasion and need.[41]

Above all, the movement was driven by its fear of partition. The Ottomans passed what İlber Ortaylı has termed "the Empire's longest century"[42] in fear of a partition that could come at any time. The "Eastern Question," one of the main problems engaging European diplomacy throughout the nineteenth century, was simply the question of how to divide the carcass of the ailing Ottoman Empire among the various imperialist powers. The primary reason that the "Sick Man of Europe" was able to survive was the failure of the Great Powers to agree among themselves as to the proper allotment of the spoils. Both Ottoman leaders and their political opponents well knew that the future of the empire lay not in Ottoman hands but in those of various foreign powers. It was widely believed that the "sick man's" days were numbered and that even the empire's ruling circles were simply waiting for a verdict on their future.[43] As one deputy put it, "A disaster continued to roil. Crete is gone, Trablusgarp (Libyan Tripoli) is going, Turkey is going, the Islamic world is going. . . ."[44] "This week I looked at a map. Most of it (Ottoman territories) is gone; little remains. This too will go very shortly."[45] When British and Russian diplomats met in Reval in June 1908 the Ottomans were certain that the final decision about their destiny was at hand. Since the empire had remained only by virtue of the inability of Russia and Britain to reach an agreement, the negotiations could only mean that the last obstacle to partition was now being removed.[46] Ottoman fears were confirmed when the two powers agreed on a solution of the Macedonian problem.

The CUP felt compelled to act and its military wing launched the

July 1908 revolution to force a constitutional monarchy. The Unionists believed that through the revolution they could halt the empire's dissolution and cure the patient. Unionist leader Enver Paşa declared liberty before the government mansion in the Macedonian town of Köprülü on 23 July 1908, shouting. "We have cured the sick man!"[47] But the joyous mood of the first days of the revolution proved to be short-lived, and an air of panic returned. The empire continued to slip away. The Austro-Hungarian Empire, taking advantage of the situation, moved troops into Bosnia-Herzegovina, announcing its annexation. Bulgaria proclaimed its independence shortly thereafter and Crete followed by declaring its union with Greece. Several years later Italy's occupation of Trablusgarp (Libya) followed, and the 1912 Balkan War. When one of the Arab deputies in parliament protested that "there was a retreat from Rumelia; Bosnia-Herzegovina was abandoned; Eastern Rumelia too had to be evacuated. Mighty Egypt has met with military occupation. . . . Gentlemen, the province of Trablusgarp is slipping away from this state. . . . The Arab nation is weeping bitter tears," another deputy leapt from his seat and shouted out in reply: "Not just them, all Ottomans—all Muslims, even—are weeping tears of bitterness!"[48] The Islamic feeling of superiority, European intervention, and the imbalance in social status between Muslims and non-Muslims all worsened with the rise of Balkan nationalism.

Thus Turkish national identity developed amid pronounced and continuous anxiety over the Turks' future and their very existence. As a result, the Unionists sought explanations for the empire's decline. The answer appeared to lie in the struggle of the Christian minorities for equal rights and reform.

The CUP opposed Christian demands of autonomy and equality, fearing separatism. "It had been opposed to reform from the outset, either for local autonomy or [reforms] for a specific Ottoman community . . . and, the self-government that could result from this."[49] In an article on the Macedonian question in the Union and Progress newspaper Meşveret, dated 15 Subat (1 March) 1899, Ahmet Rıza clearly expressed the attitude of the CUP by criticizing the revolutionary committees operating in the region, and their demands for autonomy: "We cannot reach a compromise with them on a matter of principle. We will not accept self-government, which means some sort of partition of the Ottoman State."[50] In another Unionist newspaper, *Osmanlı*, a number of articles appeared arguing for the indispensability of one 'shared culture that could unite all Ottoman subjects, and warning that, if each religious community adopted its own culture, it would lead to the breakup of the state. These articles also called for the creation of a shared language for the purpose of uniting the various elements, claiming that this language would have to be Turkish.[51]

Although within the organization Ahmet Rıza was considered something of a "cosmopolitan" and "Christianophile" in his ideas, and his writings along these lines alienated him from members of the organization for a time,[52] he also claimed that "autonomy is treason; it means separatism. . . . Our Christian compatriots shall be Ottomanized citizens."[53] Various committee publications admitted that the Christian minorities suffered injustice. Scorn was nevertheless heaped upon the Christians for their various struggles for autonomy and reform. One of the main critiques of the revolutionary movements was that they "intentionally created incidents so as to be grounds for foreign countries to meddle in the internal affairs of the Ottomans." In *Meşveret*, Ahmet Rıza wrote that "the Armenian and Macedonian Revolutionary Committees have always admitted that the revolts are only staged in order to draw the attention of Europe and win their intervention."[54]

Assessing the period years later, Hüseyin Cahit Yalçın, who in his newspaper, *Tanin*, was often the spokesman for the CUP, summed up the Unionist leaders' approach to the subject thus: "For the State . . . [and] the Constitutional Regime, the greatest danger came from the non-Turkish elements within Ottoman society." Therefore, "the history of the Constitutional period is the history of the Turks, who perceived the danger, and struggled not to drown in the flood of peoples."[55]

It was both the CUP's hostility to and mistrust of the Christian minorities and its predominant political culture of violence that pushed the group to perpetrate the Armenian genocide. The Unionists had a propensity to use violence and nondemocratic means—not only against non-Muslims but against every force that opposed them.

The movement's perception of itself and of its mission was a critical element of this style of leadership.

Faith in science—especially in the natural sciences—held a central place in the Young Turks' philosophy. Through their modernist and science-based philosophy, the Unionists saw themselves on a historical mission entrusted to them by a force outside their own society, that is, by "science." It was a bewitching concept, one that explained the superiority of the West and Ottoman backwardness. In attempting to solve social problems, the first Unionist response was always to refer to the natural sciences for assistance. This enthusiasm for science was so all-encompassing that even the various Young Turk journals devoted a significant amount of space to such things as chemistry lessons. The young Turks described themselves as "societal" physicians: Just as medical doctors cured their patients by means of medicine, they would cure society's ills through the proper application of science.[56] They were convinced that, because of this special role, they represented a special group, separate from the rest of society. Its illegal status, outlawed for its opposition to the sultan's broad power, only heightened the CUP's sense of separateness. "Being a Unionist [was] almost a type of God-given privilege."[57] Thus, to oppose this messianic force, to struggle to keep it from power, was tantamount to opposing Divine will, and to political treason.

The logic of this sentiment is openly expressed in the CUP's founding statutes. Every member swore

> upon his religion, conscience and honor, and upon the glorious name of the sultan not to disclose the Committee's secrets or the names of any members . . . and to work within the statutes of the Ottoman State and until the end of his days for the right of sovereignty to remain with the House of Osman, to be passed down to its glorious descendants . . . and to fully execute all the decisions of the Committee and be willing to die if he were, by chance, shown to have committed treason. . . . [58]

The penalty for those who fell afoul of the party or left was death. According to the first paragraph of the "Section on Procedures for Trials and Punishment," a person, whether a member of the Committee or not, [shall be punished] in the event that he [is responsible for] a situation or action that would place either the physical homeland or the Committee in danger, or that would hinder or frustrate the Committee's actions, or would cause partial or total injury and damage to the Committee.[59]

Crimes committed against the committee were divided into three separate categories. The first two comprise mild disciplinary transgressions; the third category, "Criminal Offenses," is defined as follows:

Article 10. The Commission of Crimes; First, the revealing or reporting to the government of either Committee secrets or the names of one or more of its members, either out of malicious intent or out of groundless fear or cowardice; second, the carrying out of treacherous actions which either place the Committee organization in danger or obstruct and foil its aims; . . . fourth, the attempt by one or more non-members of the Committee, who, regardless of their aim and intent, to obstruct the sacred patriotic aspirations of the Committee through either secret or overt surveillance, with the intent of uncovering the organization and members of the Committee. . . .[60]

The organization saw its task as the elimination of anyone, regardless of who they were, who seemed an obstacle to its sacred calling.

It was with this in mind that the committee established its secret organization of *fedâiin,* a group of brave, self-sacrificing, obedient young men, who would undertake "special operations"—usually the murder of political opponents—on orders. Membership was entirely voluntary, but once one entered, there was no going back. Members were obliged to carry out every duty assigned and those who failed to do so were punished, usually within twenty-four hours. Furthermore, independent actions were strictly forbidden. The only orders to be carried out were those from the Central Committee. The particulars are found in the forty-eighth through fifty-fifth Articles, in the section of the Organization Statutes titled "*Fedaî* Branches."[61] On the basis of this document, there is a fair probability that various Unionist murders that occurred after 1908 were directly ordered by the Central Committee.

The organization also tended to see everyone outside of the committee as a traitor or potential danger to be eliminated. The CUP was greatly influenced by the various Balkan revolutionary organizations, and admired and imitated their nationalist and terrorist tendencies. "Upon seeing up close that they were brutal and ruthless even toward their coreligionists, and that they engaged in the most low and inhumane behaviors," the Unionists thought this "a very effective form of nationalism" and it is clear that the chauvinism and prevalent political culture within the CUP "influenced the decisions and behavior of the Unionists in events such as the Armenian deportations."[62] Indeed, the same people who became prominent in the organization's first struggles with armed militias and formed the first *fedaî* groups, later founded the notorious Special Organization that played a direct role in implementing the Armenian genocide.

From the outset, the CUP and the Armenian revolutionary organizations maintained contact, though the nature of their relationship changed over time and according to circumstances.[63] Despite this relationship, the Unionists approached other groups with the assumption of subservience. Even when understandings were reached with the Armenian organizations, or joint decisions made, the façade of unity concealed the assumption that accounts would some day be settled with the Armenians. Soviet Armenian researcher Y. A. Petrosyan was not far off when he described the collaborative agreements between the Unionists and the Armenian Dashnak organization in 1907 as "an understanding reached on the basis on hatred and enmity."[64]

The first period of Unionist relations with Armenian groups lasted through the middle of the 1890s. In the CUP's fledgling era, a series of meetings were held to work out a shared approach to Abdul Hamid II's oppressive regime. These contacts ultimately proved fruitless, partly because of the highly conservative views of the Unionist leaders on the preservation of institutions such as the sultanate and caliphate. They also opposed the Armenians' national and democratic demands. Turkish historian Yusuf Hikmet Bayur described these relations as "the desire to actually get along, mixed with political fatigue and mistrust."[65] It is possible that the Unionists saw the Armenian revolutionary committees as perpetual rivals, against whom they were constantly comparing themselves. It was, in part, resentment at the activities of the Armenian organizations that prompted the existence of the CUP.

In September 1895, the Hunchak demonstration held in Istanbul to deliver demands for reform to the sultan brought the CUP into action. The CUP called for a halt to "Armenian impudence," hanging flyers in Istanbul that read: "Muslims and our most beloved Turkish compatriots! The Armenians have become so bold as to assault the Sublime Porte, which is our country's greatest place and which is respected and recognized by all Europeans. They have shaken the very foundations of our capital. We are greatly distressed at these impudent actions by our Armenian compatriots. . . ."[66] This was the first organized public action by the CUP.

At first, relations with the Armenian organizations abroad were more orderly and organized. The first known contact was in meetings held by early CUP leader Mizancı Murat in London.[67] Even though they failed to produce any tangible results, upon Murat's recommendation, interorganizational contacts were established in Erzurum (in today's eastern Turkey). Some of the people involved were arrested when their documents were obtained by the authorities and the first joint demonstrations against Abdul Hamid II were organized in response.[68] Ahmet Rıza held a second series of meetings in London in 1896,[69] but these encounters failed to produce any plan for joint action. The main issue between the two sides was the Armenians' demand for the reforms promised in the 1878 Treaty of Berlin and for the assistance of foreign countries, if necessary, to achieve these goals.

Mutual attempts to achieve certain agreements continued until the first Congress of Ottoman Opposition Parties in Paris in 1902. Armenian and Unionist appeals and declarations[70] found in the various Unionist journals, calling for cooperation between Muslims and Armenians, all testify to these efforts.[71] Additionally, one of the central issues in the CUP's French-language journal *Mechveret* was the reforms in the Armenian provinces, and the journal published frequent reports to the effect that a way to unite their causes was continually being sought and that meetings were held for this purpose.[72] But the "mistrust of these groups [the Armenian Revolutionary Committees]" by the Unionist leaders[73] essentially eliminated the possibility of any active collaboration. Additionally, it was at about this time that Ahmet Rıza was expelled from the committee for an article calling the Greek population "justified" in undertaking a revolt in Crete. But various examples of mutual solidarity, such as joint participation in various international congresses, joint meetings with representatives of foreign countries and joint military operations between local groups on the ground continued.[74]

The proposals for collaborative efforts came largely from the Armenian organizations rather than from the Unionists[75] who leveled much harsh criticism at Armenian demands for autonomy. Nevertheless, consideration was given to the idea of continued dialogue. A piece written in response to the massacres of 1896, for instance, claimed that "We [the Unionists] are disposed to identify, to the great shame of our government, that the massacres were a crime perpetrated on an official level."[76] Şerif Mardin, a Turkish sociologist, has stated, however, that this *Mechveret* article met with a fierce response from the Union and Progress cadres, and that this was a manifestation of the essentially racist approach to the subject found within such circles. Despite the criticism of the crimes directed against the Armenians, the main target of their barbs, Mardin claims, were the Armenian organizations. According to this same *Mechveret* piece, for instance: "The Armenian committees planned the bombing of the Ottoman Bank in 1896 in order to attain Europe's unilateral intervention, and they sacrificed Turkish-Armenian relations for the sake of achieving this goal."[77] Another article, from August 1897, claimed that "those who have unfurled the flag of separatism have declared Turkey their enemy."[78]

Indeed, the main critique of the Armenian organizations was their demand for autonomy. The CUP criticized the Armenians for acting on their own, saying it was a mistaken approach, and that "it was necessary to act in unison with the Young Turks as had been agreed."[79] Unionists argued that "the Armenians demand equality, justice, liberty and public order. It is one's right and duty to desire such things, and we stand by them. . . . But the Armenians do not stop there, they also want self-rule in an area they call Armenia. To demand this does not mean to bring about a revolution, it means making war against us."[80] This, for the CUP, was the most sensitive

point. In their eyes, the Armenian demands meant loss of the homeland and territories.

At the Union and Progress Committee's Paris congress in 1902,
the differences between the two groups became clearer. The Young
Turk movement itself was divided: On one side were the centralists
who rejected the Armenian demands and foreign intervention. On
the other side was Ottoman prince Sabahettin, who headed the faction that looked most favorably on the Armenians' demands, and
who later would found the moderate Committee for Decentralization
and Personal Initiative. Thus, the basis for a political division that
would profoundly affect Ottoman political life after 1908 was laid at
this time. Prince Sabahettin, who opposed the excessive centralization
of state functions, managed to win a majority at the 1902 congress by
virtue of the support of the Armenian and Greek delegates.[81] The
Armenians at the congress called for reforms as required in the sixty-
first article of the 1878 Berlin Treaty and the memorandum of 11 May
1895, and they demanded the intervention of a foreign power. Ahmet
Rıza, Dr. Nâzim, Bahaettin Şakir and their faction of the CUP reacted
sharply to the idea of foreign intervention. "From this viewpoint, the
problem [revolved around] the [issue] of Turkishness and the
demands of the minority."[82]

In the wake of the congress, the criticisms of the Armenian revolutionary committees sharpened. In the journal Şurayi Ümmet, published by Bahaettin Şakir, Ahmet Rıza and the centralist faction after
the congress, the Turkish nationalists' perceptions of the Armenians
and their methods were heard for the first time. The Armenian committees were attacking the Muslim population to provoke the Muslims to attack, whereupon the Armenians would demand European
intervention.

On this point, at least, the Unionist leaders and Sultan Abdul
Hamid II were of one mind. According to the sultan, "the apparent aim
of the Armenians is to incite the Turks, and then, after enough force has
been used to suppress them, to cry of oppression and elicit the sympa-
thies of Europe, especially of England."[83] Şurayı Ümmet claimed that,

> Because the Armenian and Macedonian revolutionary committees
> know that the only way to get the attention of world opinion and to
> cause their intervention, is to [provoke the] massacre [of] Chris-

tians in our country they have never refrained from provoking the anger and fury of the Muslims, which pave the way for [such massacres].[84]

Contemporaneous Turkish sources are full of such interpretations concerning the Armenian tactics. For example, Dr. Cyrus Hamlin, the founder and first director of Robert College, reported in an American newspaper dated 23 December 1893, about such tactics, which he had heard about from an Armenian revolutionary:

> The *Hunchak* armed gangs will look for the opportunity to kill Turks and Kurds, to raze villages, and then flee into the mountains. The Muslims, who become beside themselves with rage over this, will then rise up and attack the defenseless Armenians, killing them with great ferocity, so that Russia will then advance and occupy the country in the name of humanity and Christian civilization. The English Ambassador, Sir P. Currie, wrote in one report that "the primary goal of the [Armenian] Revolutionaries was to provoke civil unrest and, by bringing inhumane reactions upon themselves, to open the way for [other] states to intervene in the name of humanity."[85]

This is the approach that contemporary Turkish histories of the period favor. For example:

> All of the Christian communities played the game of causing bloody slaughter and inciting the Muslim population to respond with even bloodier actions, and then they embarked upon a campaign of "Let's rescue the poor oppressed Christians!" in European public opinion.[86]

And other examples: "[This was] the traditional way of separating from the Ottoman state. . . ." All Christian minorities acted in this way: "armed actions, undertaking revolts, and, when either the government or the Muslim population itself reacted against this, to raise the cry of 'massacre' . . . [and] to impel the great powers to action. . . ."[87]

In 1906, Bahaettin Şakir, Dr. Nazım and Ahmet Rıza held discussions with the Hunchaks about undertaking a joint struggle against the sultan. The Hunchak leaders declared that they wanted to see the Reform Program of 11 May 1895 carried out and the Armenian-populated region of Cilicia to be included within the areas subject to the program. Sabuh Külian, a Hunchak leader, described the effect this had on his Turkish counterparts:

> The Young Turks became grieved, struck dumb with surprise. Our arguments had brought them to a moral crisis. Even the color of their faces changed. . . . The addition of Cilicia to Armenia would split the empire in two. We said that self-rule would preserve the unity of these parts of the empire, that it didn't mean total separation or independence. Dr. Nazim, in replying to our demands, said that this division was merely a precedent for independence, if not today, then in 5–10 years.[88]

In a letter to Bulgaria sent in 1906 by Bahaettin Şakir in the name of the party, the general attitude toward such demands is clearly reflected:

> You are well aware that we cannot in any way countenance the loss of even the smallest portion of our homeland. . . . Anyone who would attempt to divide the country piece by piece or people by people is our opponent and our enemy.[89]

And again, in another letter from 1906 addressed to the Muslims of the Caucasus:

> Do you not see that the Armenians are not working to ease the burden of human sorrow or for the progress of industry, but to produce the tools of destruction that will kill their Muslim neighbors easily and in large numbers. . . . Beginning with the assumption that you are Muslims, each and every one of you should not only consider the atrocities committed by the revolutionary Armenians, who are the enemies of your religion, against the Muslims of the

Caucasus, but against your coreligionists within the Ottoman state and against the Islamic Sultanate.[90]

The directive given to the Muslims of the Caucasus was not only to spread propaganda against the Armenian revolutionaries; it was also suggested that they take over their wealth: "It is necessary to weaken the Armenians, who are, above all, one of the obstacles to freeing ourselves from Russia's stranglehold; with this in mind, we must also destroy their wealth, which is their greatest strength."[91]

At the Second Unionist Congress in Paris, in 1907, the CUP and the Armenian Dashnak Revolutionary Federation established a joint front and decided to participate together in the armed struggle against the sultan. But the manner in which the decisions made at the congress were reported to the CUP Central Committee in Salonica[92] is significant because it shows the Unionists' attitude to these alliances:

> The Armenians, who have spilled unnecessary blood and are con-
> tinually calling for foreign intervention, which would be detrimen-
> tal for the independent life of the nation, [have been] drawn into
> this circle of unity. . . . [By virtue of this] the deleterious actions of
> [Armenian groups] who spill blood unnecessarily and call for for-
> eign intervention [have been] frustrated.[93]

From this language, which prevails throughout the letter, we can understand that "there were quite significant currents within the Salonican center who opposed the understandings concluded with the Greeks and Armenians."[94] Arguments were put forward to per-suade the Central Committee to acquiesce to such agreements. In one internal document feelings on the issue were clearly expressed: "After we topple the [Ottoman] government and reconvene the Chamber of Deputies (i.e., parliamentary rule) . . . , we will no longer have to fear either a handful of Armenians . . . or the government[s] of Europe."[95] In the same document:

> Let us topple the current government, let us convene the national
> assembly; after this it will be easy to explain things to those who
> revel in the thought of self-rule, because the authoritarian regime

that has paralyzed our material and spiritual will/shall have been
eliminated. . . .

Bayur, who cites this document, asserts that "its meaning is
clear. . . . Regardless of the basis on which the understandings with
the other organizations were reached, they have no importance."[96]
After gaining power, it would be easy to settle accounts with these
groups.

Thus despite the various attempts at achieving unity prior to
1908, the Unionists approached the Dashnak organization with great
suspicion and perceived that Armenian action was designed "to
divide the homeland." The Unionists repeatedly declared that they
would not remain silent in the face of such provocations and the
Armenian organizations, which constantly pleaded for foreign assistance, were accused of "stabbing the Ottomans in the back" and of
treason.[97] Clearly, the Unionists never had any intention of granting
liberty, including even regional autonomy.[98] Instead of considering
democratic solutions such as policies that would foster an Ottoman
identity and citizenship, the Unionists preferred to "enter the field of
battle with a shield of constitutionalism," to save the state at all costs.
Its position of constitutionalism was a tool to achieve this goal.[99]

In a report dated 20 February 1894, French ambassador Paul Cambon
describes a high-ranking Turkish official telling him that "the Armenian question does not exist, but we shall create it." Indeed, if we
closely examine the ambassador's account, we see that in regard to the
Armenian problem, "As if it were not enough to provoke Armenian
discontent, the Turks were glad to amplify it by the manner in which
they handled it."[100] This was a powerful hint of what was to come.
Despite the "united front" produced at the second congress organized
by the Unionists and Dashnaks in 1907 and the spirit of brotherhood
and friendship that arose after the declaration of the constitutional
government in 1908,[101] the same attitude to minorities predominated
among the Unionist leaders. But once the CUP took power in 1913,
both sides came out in open opposition to each other.

In July 1908, in response to the revolt, the sultan called for parliament to be reconvened. This was the start of the second constitutional
regime, the first constitutional regime having been suspended in

1878. The way to political power was open for the Committee of Union and Progress.[102] Nevertheless, it was not until January 1913 that the Unionists were able—or wished—to take sole control of the empire. The question of why they did not assume full political control until then remains a significant topic of debate among scholars. In part, this delay occurred because of the sultan's popularity and the essentially conservative program of the CUP, which never aimed fully to remove the caliphate or the sultan. "The majority within the Young Turk movement was a conservative group of people, a group that had no desire for societal transformation."[103] The CUP had always advocated the continuation of the sultanic institution, calling for the reinstatement of the 1876 Ottoman Constitution, Therefore, between 1908 and 1913, the Unionists ruled in something of a "supervisory" role).[104]

After the sultan's proclamation elections were held for a new parliament convened on 17 December 1908. The CUP ran in an alliance with the Armenian Dashnaks, and received a majority in the new Chamber of Deputies (the lower house of the Ottoman parliament), and they intervened in the functioning of every government formed during this period, preferring to direct from outside by "monitoring" the affairs. Significantly, no serious attempts were made to force reforms. Historian Yusuf Hikmet Bayur, grandson of one of the important grand viziers of this period, Kâmil Paşa, published some of the CUP's memos to the Sublime Porte, which he found among his grandfather's papers. Not a single word about reforms is found in any of the notes, despite being full of other Unionist demands. The CUP basically only interfered in government affairs to prevent specific key appointments.[105]

It is thus clear that the Unionists were never attempting "to resolve the country's political problems through a revolutionary struggle, but by seeking a consensus with the feudal-authoritarian powers, appealing to the Sultan's [sense of] 'justice' and 'good intentions.'"[106] Even in its most radical period, in 1907, the CUP wanted to insert an article into its common declaration with the Dashnak organization saying that "the statutes of the Sultanate and Caliphate would be adopted" because "there could be no Turkish power without them."[107] For the Young Turks, the key to saving the state was in training a "moral" and "good" elite. What they desired, then, was "a just ruler," and what they expected from the sultan was simply that he would carry out his duty of "being just."[108] "All of the Young Turks looked upon Sultan Abdul Hamid II as a father who had failed to fulfill his paternal duties."[109] The issue, then, was one of replacing the "wicked" administrators who had allowed the corruption within the country, and to bring to power "science-conscious" cadres like themselves.[110]

The 1908 declaration of the second constitutional regime was greeted with great joy. The prevailing hope and expectation was that the despotic regime had come to an end, liberty had arrived and long-awaited reforms would finally be enacted. After the July revolution, the Armenian revolutionary committees announced that they would make every effort to protect the constitutional regime.[111] The various Armenian, Bulgarian, Greek and Turkish militias and revolutionary committees, who had until that point struggled against the regime from their mountain hideouts, now returned to the cities and were met with celebrations. Interreligious ceremonies were held for the fallen in the struggle against Abdul Hamid II, and many speeches expressed the hope that "Turks and Armenians would work together like brothers for the good of their country."[112]

But such optimism did not continue for long. Instead of reforms, what came about was the "counterrevolution" of 1909 and a subsequent massacre in Adana. On 31 March (13 April, according to the Western calendar), some military units in Istanbul revolted against the new government. The Islamic seminary students, or *softas*, a religious component grouped around the conservative religious newspaper *Volkan*, provided the ideological leadership for the revolt. Because the demand for the return of Islamic religious law, or Shari'a, was so prevalent at this time, a good many historians have depicted the events of 1909 as reactionary or counterrevolutionary. But this assessment is far from universally held. The rebels themselves quickly went on a hunt for Unionists, but they did not oppose the constitutional government.

The events are closer to an unplanned military coup attempt, lacking a program or any hope of success, organized by the political opposition, directed against the CUP, and supported by some of the Christian communities in Istanbul, the Greeks among them.[113] The counterrevolution lasted for ten days, supported by regimental (*ala-lyi*) officers, who had risen within the ranks, were often illiterate, and resisted modernization and change. One of their demands was to purge those officers who were the product of military academies (*mektepli*), many of whom were killed by the rebel forces, along with one government minister and a deputy of parliament, mistaken for a prominent Unionist journalist. The power vacuum created by the action was finally ended when the rebel forces were crushed by the Action Army, which had hastily regrouped in Salonica, the bastion of Unionist power, and from there marched on Istanbul. Dashnak actively participated in the Action Army. The court-martial that was established in the wake of the debacle handed down numerous death sentences, and the bodies of those executed were prominently displayed at central points throughout the capital.[114]

The massacre in Adana began in the wake of the developments in Istanbul, the result of both national and local factors. As the news reached Adana on March 31 that a counterrevolution had occurred in Istanbul, rumors circulated that the CUP had been forced out of power. Local Muslims, who had opposed the modernizing mission of the 1908 revolution, began to attack Armenians as the catalyst of the new ideas and as agitators for independence. Adana's Armenians had indeed visibly supported the aims of the revolution. There was also an important economic factor. Local Armenians "were the richest and most prosperous class in the region. In Adana . . . the Armenians had attained a high standard of living. In every field, they were ahead of Turks." Armenian wealth and prosperity in the region meant a reversal of their social status in relation to Muslims, who were envious and resentful. It was no coincidence that the violence in Adana targeted not only Armenians but also their new technology—tractors and other kinds of mechanized equipment. An estimated fifteen to twenty thousand Armenians were killed during the course of the massacres. The Ottoman parliament, only able to reconvene in May, sent a commission of inquiry to the region to investigate the events, while the CUP distanced itself from the killings. In both the courts-martial and the local trials that were held over the next eighteen months (10 June 1909 to 13 December 1910) some 124 Muslims were executed after being convicted of involvement in the events in Adana. Seven Armenians were executed, largely with the aim of appeasing the local Muslim population.[115]

Even if the CUP had no direct connection to the events in Adana, there are a number of accounts that claim local Unionist leaders were involved. In a speech to the French parliament on 17 May 1909, Foreign Minister Stephan Pichon recounted that the Ottoman units sent from Damascus and Beirut to restore order had also participated in the massacres.[116] In letter written 20 May 1909 by a Turkish soldier to his family that came into the possession of the German consul, a soldier wrote: "We killed thirty thousand of the infidel dogs, whose blood flowed through the streets of Adana."[117]

The director of Tarsus American College had been told by Turkish officers that they had received orders "to kill the Armenians."[118] According to some sources, Dr. Nâzım said after the events at Adana: "The Ottoman Empire must be Turkish alone. The existence of foreign citizenship is a tool for European intervention. The empire must be Turkified by force of arms."[119] This nationalist position would gain the upper hand in the CUP in the near future.[120]

In response to the counterrevolution and the Armenian massacres in Adana, the CUP and Dashnak concluded an agreement in September 1909 whereby they promised to "work together for progress, the Constitution, and unity." Both parties declared that rumors of Armenian efforts toward independence were false. The Unionists took care to have an Armenian minister present in the governments formed after 6 August 1909, which could also be interpreted as an attempt to demonstrate the CUP's distance from the Adana events. Further, the CUP and Dashnak established joint committees that met regularly to review such issues as the confiscation of Armenian land and mistreatment by local authorities. In the 1912 elections, an agreement was reached to run jointly. Nor was this cooperation limited to activities within the Ottoman Empire. The CUP supported the Armenian revolutionary movement against the czar in Russia and from 1910 on, for example, allowed the revolutionaries to organize against Russia within the empire. Armenians in the capital and Anatolia held fund-raisers to collect money for legal assistance to Armenians imprisoned in Russia. This extra-territorial cooperation lasted until 1914. In general, throughout this period, Unionist-Dashnak relations vacillated between understanding and antagonism.[121]

After 1908, the main goal of the Union and Progress movement was the creation of a modern, centralized state. For this reason, a collision with the old imperial structure and institutions was unavoidable. One of the most fundamental principles underlying the creation of such a state is citizenship. The general principle of the equality of all citizens and their responsibility to the state would have to be implemented. No institution or organization could take precedence over the state as mediator or representative for a specific group, or assume any state functions. But the Ottoman *millet* system ran fundamentally contrary to this notion. Ottoman society was still divided into a number of religious communities, with each group granted special rights. The institution of citizenship in the full sense was thus never established. A number of the functions of the state (tax collection, judicial functions, and so forth) continued to be carried out by the religious communities. The state was comprised not of individuals but of representatives of these communities as well as of tribal groups, and in some senses, it performed an administrative function mediating between these groups.

Out of this compartmentalized society the CPU wanted to create a modern state in which all of its citizens would be bound by a shared identity and on the basis of universal equality. Even the simplest responsibilities necessary for the proper working of a modern state, such as taxation and military service, failed to function as they should. Among the first planned reforms was centralizing control over the regions that were not providing conscripts or paying taxes. In a declaration published on 27 July 1910, the following issues were addressed: "Securing troops and money form the foundation of a nation's sovereignty, of national security and state administration. Those who fail to pay taxes or serve in the military have done nothing for the homeland. . . ."[122]

But the fundamental question remained: What would this shared emotional tie, this cultural identity be, and how could it be created? The question was extraordinarily simple. In the words of Yusuf Akçura:

The history, customs, religion, relationships, hopes and dreams, manner of thinking, occupational patterns and levels of civilization of the peoples who were Ottoman subjects were so different from one another that it was strange even to imagine them uniting in some compatible way. What sort of point of contact could a Christian

Serb, who farmed on the plains of Kosovo, have with a Muslim Arab who lived as a Bedouin in the deserts of Najd? . . . I ask: Is it possible to find a single Muslim who would make even the smallest concession from his clearly defined religious identity for the sake of a union? . . . Within the broad expanses of the Ottoman realm, there are two civilizations, two ways of looking at life and the world, two very different philosophies colliding. Is their coexistence at all possible?[123]

In order to resolve the issue of shared cultural identity, as the process of centralization demanded, the Unionists chose a well-worn path. They opted to unite the principle of universal citizenship, according to which everyone was to be treated equally, with a cultural identity to be formed around the values of the dominant national group. For this purpose, they enacted forced-assimilation policies. When such policies became unworkable, they began to add a dimension of violence.

One can track this development in the CUP's party programs, in political reports and in laws that were passed. At the party congress of 1909, "after it was recalled that the Ottomans were obliged to view their advantages as shared, it was announced that 'legal means' would be employed against those who desired to create schisms and strife by promoting racial or confessional differences or through other means."[124]

In line with this goal, the Law of Associations was promulgated on 16 August 1909. It became "unlawful to form an institution that is contrary to public morals, . . . and violates the political integrity of the state or changes the present form of government, or sows political divisions between the various Ottoman peoples (Article 3). It is forbidden to form political organizations on the basis of nationality or race or bearing the name thereof (Article 4)." Thereby it became forbidden to establish political associations or other entities that bore the name of a country.[125] This prohibition "was followed immediately by the closure of the Greek, Bulgarian, and other minority clubs and societies in Rumelia [the European Ottoman territories]."[126] With some minor amendments, the relevant articles of this law were added to the Constitution on 21 August 1909. On 14 September a temporary

law was issued to establish a special military unit with the aim of disarming Armenian, Greek and Bulgarian militias.

The forced assimilation program manifested itself most concretely in the area of education. The CUP's 1908 program already
included sections dealing with this issue: Government schools shall
be opened that will include [members of] all the communities. The
Turkish language will be the mandatory language of instruction for
primary education. Primary education will be free in government
schools."[127] When citizens graduated from state high schools, their
possibilities of getting a position in the state bureaucracy would be
improved. However, this Law of Public Education was drafted, but
never passed.[128] In 1910 a portion of the draft was prepared as the Law
of Primary Education, which foresaw the creation of a single, centralized educational system, but it too failed to be adopted by the chamber. Only in 1913 was it implemented, and then as a temporary law.
All attempts at bringing the minority schools under central control
and supervision were met with great resistance, and "this situation
continued so until the year 1330 (1914). Then, after the repression of
the minorities with the outbreak of World War I . . . these schools
were disciplined with the imposition of a new set of regulations."[129]

In this period other laws were issued that were aimed at holding
the multinational Ottoman society together. Since the Tanzimat era,
the conscription of non-Muslims into the Ottoman army had been a
lingering problem.[130] In June 1909, the Law on the Conscription of
Non-Muslim Communities passed through parliament.[131] Until this
time the Christian communities had vehemently opposed the idea of
being conscripted into military service. Because of this resistance, in
1909 it was decided that educated conscripts would be taken into the
army as "reserve officers" or exemptions could be purchased from the
state.[132] As in the case of education reforms, the full implementation
of the plan was not complete until 1914.[133]

These policies, implemented under the rubric of an "Ottomanism" that aimed at achieving a "union of peoples" (İtthad-ı anasır) were
an effort to homogenize society culturally around an Islamic-Turkish
identity and were understood as such by the empire's various component groups. It was not only Christians who resisted central control
and supervision. The various non-Turkish Muslim communities of

the empire were subjected to similar policies, as they too were forced to learn Turkish.[134] In the field of education, in particular, the Arab and Albanian communities came out in firm opposition to the attempt to make them learn and use Turkish in primary schools.[135] As a result, resistance became inevitable. The Albanian revolt of 1910 was an important turning point in this regard. The government's education policies were one of the primary causes of the revolt.[136] It was a clear sign that the "union of peoples" policies were not working. This revolt "convinced the Turks that it would be impossible to reconcile different national interests and attain a unified empire."[137]

All of these efforts at centralization were seen and experienced as reductions of freedoms. Indeed, after the counterrevolution of 31 March/13 April, Unionists used it as an excuse and the government declared martial law on 25 April 1909. Martial law continued until 15 July 1912, and was then reintroduced a few months later, remaining in effect until the end of the empire. After 1909, a number of legal prohibitions were issued. With the promulgation of the Law Regarding Vagrants and Suspicious Persons on 14 May 1909, individual freedoms were largely restricted. The Law on Public Gatherings, passed on 17 June 1909, made it illegal to hold meetings and demonstrations. The Laws on Press and Publishing Institutions, which were promulgated on 31 July 1909, seriously restricted press freedoms. In addition to the legal limitations on the press, killing anti-Unionist journalists was another relatively common strategy in this period. The editor of *Serbestî*, Hasan Fehmi Bey, was killed by unknown assailants on 6 April 1909; Ahmet Samimî Bey, the editor of *Sada-yı Millet*, was assassinated on 9 June of the following year, while *Şehran* editor Zeki Bey was slain on 10 July 1911.[138]

Today Turkish scholars wryly refer to the 1908 revolution as the "Declaration of the Lack of Liberty" because of the excessive repression and prohibitive legislation.[139] The CUP steered an oppressive regime under the influence of a handful of people,[140] who were reviving "a period of repression and evil," in the words of Prince Sabahettin, a main opposition figure, to further their "base political ambitions under the guise of reform."[141]

The Union and Progress leaders were greatly disillusioned in the summer of 1910. They came to see the bankruptcy of the program that was intended to bring all of the disparate peoples of the empire together. This period had taught them that the time had long since passed for "the 'Ottomanist' dream of the free, equal and peaceful association of peoples in ... a multi-national, multi-denominational empire," and it had therefore "ended forever."[142] Because of "the deepening antipathy between the different nations and between Islam and Christianity, no possibility remained of creating an Ottoman unity that would unite the empire's nations and reconcile them."[143]

On 27 July 1910, the second anniversary of the revolution, the CUP underwent some soul-searching and declared Ottomanism bankrupt. In its "Declaration to the Nation," the CUP

> confessed that its measures to bring about the union of the different communities had failed, owing to the excessive zeal it had shown in the first two years of constitutional rule. It now recognized the opposition of the ethnic communities to Ottomanism, and would therefore leave them alone. The Committee would continue to pursue the cause of unity in a different way, namely, by concentrating all its energy on the material and educational development of the Empire, hoping thereby to unite all the elements through a community of interests.[144]

It has been reported that Talât Bey (later Paşa), who, together with Finance Minister Cavit Bey was touring Macedonia in an effort to repair the committee's failures and to shore up low morale, spoke at a meeting of the committee's "secret conclave" in Salonica. He made some interesting remarks on the reasons that the policy of Ottomanism was destined to fail and on new directions that the committee would take. The acting British consul in Monastir (Bitolj) reported the speech:

> You are aware that by the terms of the Constitution, equality of Mussulman and Ghiaur [infidel] was affirmed by you. One and all know and feel that this is an unrealizable ideal. The Sheriat, our whole past history and the sentiments of hundreds of thousands of Mussulmans and even the sentiments of the Ghiaurs themselves, who stubbornly resist every attempt to ottomanize them, present an impenetrable barrier to the establishment of real equality. We

have made unsuccessful attempts to convert the Ghiaur into a loyal Osmanli and all such efforts must inevitably fail, as long as the small independent States in the Balkan Peninsula remain in a position to propagate ideas of separatism among the inhabitants of Macedonia. There can therefore be no question of equality, until we have succeeded in our task of ottomanizing the Empire—a long and laborious task, in which I venture to predict that we shall, at length, succeed after we have at last put an end to the agitation and propaganda of the Balkan States.[145]

Several days later the English ambassador to the Porte, Gerald Lowther, made the following comments on this report: "To them 'Ottoman' evidently means 'Turk' and their present policy of 'Ottomanization' is one of pounding the non-Turkish elements in a Turkish mortar. . . ."[146]

The French consul in Salonica reported on the meeting in a more detailed fashion. According to his account, among the Unionists there were those who thought that it would be impossible for the different communities to live together and others who argued that "military force alone" would solve the problem. Furthermore, the debates on the Macedonian question and the Bulgarians of Edirne were so detailed that the Unionists even came to the point of voting for the options of either "deportation" or "massacre." Forced transfer of the Christian population of the region to inner·Anatolia and settling Muslims in their place was proposed, and if that did not solve the matter, it was suggested, the Christians could be killed. He also reported that the Union and Progress leaders were inclined to resort to violence in the event that "the peaceful efforts to achieve the unity of Turkey meet with failure." The Austrian, French and British reports on the 1910 Salonica gathering all agree.[147]

These accounts indicate that with increasing frequency CUP members supported the idea, in the words of Yusuf Hikmet Bayur, "of solving [problems] through the army."[148] In an interview he gave to a newspaper at the end of 1909, Dr. Nâzım said that Muslim emigrants coming from Bulgaria and Bosnia—and even the Jews—would be resettled in Rumelia.[149] In other words, the idea of achieving Ottoman unity through the settlement of Muslims in regions with a Christian majority and solving the population problem through

forced population transfer was not new. Solving issues through violence "slowly began to form and take root."[150] Nevertheless, even as
late as at the 1909 party congress, the Istanbul delegation, which
advocated Turkish nationalism as its foundation, was not allowed to
address the assembly.[151] But by 1910, within a short time, the skir-
mish between the "Ottomanist" and "Turkist" factions in the party
had become acute and the Turkist wing was becoming more vocal.

At the 1911 congress, the CUP undertook a general reassessment
of the situation. Past and future policies were reeevaluated. The questions remained, How should the state understand "Ottomanism" and
how could it achieve a "Union of Peoples"? A report read at the congress stated that the committee was decisively opposed to "those who
understood Ottomanism to mean a [federated] state formed from an
amalgamation of forces and communities possessing political rights";
it also opposed those who argued that Ottomanism "was composed
only of individuals, and that, in order for Ottoman unity to be complete, it would be necessary for the various groups and communities
in which these individuals were found to merge into the greater
Ottoman whole."[152]

In the report, Ottomanism was described in a manner that left no
room for misunderstanding: the unification of all of the component
peoples of the empire around the pillars of Islam, Turkishness and the
caliphate. The report emphasizes that Ottomanism is defined in the
Constitution as aiming to preserve the homeland, national unity, its
language, Islam and its political and legal institutions, such as the
caliphate, the Sheikh ul-Islam (the highest religious authority in the
empire), Islamic jurisprudence and customs.[153] Ottomanism was
defined as the supremacy of Islam, and as such, it was the fundamental goal of the CUP. "In our opinion, it is the aim of the Committee of
Union and Progress to establish a united and progressive Ottomanism. . . . The Committee of Union and Progress considers Islam to be
the basis of Ottomanism and attributes its existence to this spiritual
force."[154]

At the same congress, it was stated that the CUP had previously
attempted to organize minority groups as social and cultural entities
(according to characteristics such as language, confession, and literature), but that it had failed: to "preserv[e] the language and national
identity of the various peoples and . . . strengthen . . . historical ties

that would bind them to one another . . ." within a united Ottoman social fabric.[155]

Many researchers consider this congress the moment when the transition from Ottomanism to Turkism was complete.[156] Some first-hand observers also reported that the issue of organizing systematic Pan-Islamist activity in the Caucasus and Central Asia were discussed in detail as well. The Austrian consul in Salonica reported that there were eight CUP committees active in the Caucasus, and seventy-two in Iran, China and India. He further reported that it had been decided that more resources should be set aside for propaganda work.[157] From other sources, we learn that a large number of agents were sent to the Caucasus and Central Asia after this date. The British consuls in these places regularly sent detailed reports regarding the agents sent to Central Asia and their activities.[158] Some scholars argue that the decision to suppress all ideas opposed to Turkism, and even the decision for the Armenian genocide, were made at this congress. However, there is no information to confirm this thesis.[159]

There are many reasons why the Unionists' "unity of peoples" policy met with failure, which we have addressed here. In addition, party leaders, while outwardly espousing Ottomanism, were at the same time propagating the dominance of Turkish nationalism. Ziya Gökalp, a member of the CUP's Central Committee since 1910, is a good example of this kind of contradiction. He favored Ottomanism, continuing to publish articles supporting it as late as 1911,[160] but at the same time, he directed the newspaper *Genç Kalemler* (Young Pens), which openly advocated Turkism. Finding mere cultural nationalism insufficient,[161] Gökalp published his poem "Turan" (the geographical area in which all Turks live) and worked to imbue the Turkish nationalist idea with political content.[162] Gökalp once claimed that it was he himself "who supplied the theoretical basis for the Turkist movement. . . ."[163]

In an article, "The Things That are Happening to Turkishness," Gökalp made a surprising and sincere admission concerning the failure of the CUP's Ottomanism: Neither the Tanzimat reformists nor the CUP leadership were sincere in their promise to give national and cultural rights to the various ethnic and religious groups.

The Tanzimatists desired to pull a veil of disguise over the face of Turkishness. . . . None of the [minority] peoples believed this lie. . . . When, after the declaration of the Second Constitutional Regime . . . [the CUP perpetuated] the "deception" the Tanzimatists began, the minorities began to complain loudly, crying, "You want to turn us into Turks!" And indeed, the Ottomanization policies were nothing other than a covert beginning of the Turkification process.[164]

This was an open confession that Ottomanism was only a cover for Turkification and this was the reason for its failure. According to Gökalp, what needed to be done was to stop hiding behind the mask of Ottomanism and to promote Turkish nationalism explicitly. In this way the idea of a "union of peoples," which had been advanced as a way to keep the different religious and national groups together, slowly but surely began to disintegrate. Turkish nationalist ideas gradually came to predominate.

Another reason for the failure of Ottomanism was the CUP's undemocratic approach. "More than any Western notions, [it was] the military character of the regime they created" that determined [its] behavior.[165] The party advocated fierce struggle, sometimes using fundamentally nondemocratic methods, not just against non-Muslims, but against all who opposed it. This pattern emerged during the 1908 elections. The CUP worked tirelessly to ensure that the country went into the elections as a one-party system. With the claim that it represented all Turks, it entered into an understanding with the Armenians and Greeks and accused the other parties, who objected, of "betraying Turkishness." Certain people associated with Prince Sabahettin's opposition party were arrested as they tried to organize a campaign in Anatolia. Some were even subjected to death threats.[166] "The CUP claim[ed] that it [alone] represented the Turks and desired that everything be done under its supervision."[167]

Another cause of the CUP's failure was the policies of the Great Powers, who aimed to partition the empire. As Bernard Lewis has stated, "It is difficult to judge how sincere the Young Turks may have been in their promises and declarations of freedom and equality; it is, however, undeniable that the immediate response of Europe and of the Balkan Christians to the heart-lifting events of July 1908 was what, in Turkish eyes, could only be described as aggression and betrayal."[168]

As a rule, rather than support the various efforts of the reformers within the empire, the Great Powers preferred to extend their sphere of influence whenever an opportunity arose. There are countless examples of this. The Great Powers both chastised the Ottoman government for failing to carry out reforms and then created obstacles to these same efforts. This was a common topic of discussion among Unionists before 1909. In 1894, Ahmet Rıza rightfully asked the Great Powers, who had badgered Sultan Abdul Hamid II mercilessly for reforms in the Armenian provinces and exerted pressure to tie a solution to a timetable, why they had not employed the same pressure and effort to reinstate the 1876 Ottoman Constitution.[169] Another example was England's hostile attitude toward the second constitutional regime. The British were afraid that a reformed Turkey would exert a very strong influence in European diplomacy, and this would have an effect on the world's Muslims that would be detrimental to England. Therefore, they adopted the strategy of "giving the appearance of supporting reforms" while simultaneously "being prepared to act in unison with Russia at every opportunity."[170] Sir Edward Grey, the British foreign minister, wrote to his ambassador at the Porte:

> If Turkey indeed establishes a Constitutional administration and is strengthened by reviving it, it will advance further, to the point that none of us can foresee the outcome of such a situation. . . . Until now, wherever we have had Muslim subjects, we have been able to tell them that there was a merciless authoritarian rule in the countries ruled by the heads of their religion. In any case, our authoritarian rule is compassionate. . . . But if a parliamentary life now commences in Turkey and things are put in order, the demand for constitutional rule will grow in Egypt and our ability to act against this will diminish greatly.[171]

In the eyes of the Great Powers, Ottoman land was simply an object for exploitation. In 1913 Austria even sent representatives to Anatolia with the aim of "determining whether or not these areas were worth occupying."[172] Since 1883, the German government had continuously been preparing detailed plans for German colonies that would likely be established in Anatolia and Rumelia.[173]

Despite these intentions, the Great Powers presented their interventions in Ottoman affairs as humanitarian. This produced within Unionist circles a tendency to equate slogans like "Human Rights" and "Democracy" with imperialism and colonialism, creating resistance to the ideas and sometimes outright hostility. The Turkish press often asserted that "the claims by Europe, which acts as a spokesman for human rights, of humanity and civilization are simply impossible to believe. . . . Europe's humanitarianism and justice are nothing but hypocrisy."[174] They saw beyond the façade of Western humanism the desire to partition the empire.

Such a view was expressed openly in *Genç Kalemler*, which advocated Turkish nationalism. In an article called "Homeland! Only the Homeland," the author, "rejecting the idea of internationalism and the illusion of 'humanity,'" claimed that he would prove just how terrible and destructive these concepts were for the homeland." Further, he argued that the Europeans' actual goal . . . was "to swallow us." He demanded that the Ottomans use "the idea of nation, the love of the homeland" to struggle against the Europeans who "were crushing the peoples of the East, who trampled the humanity of the East underfoot, and who engaged in civilized brigandage which was anything but compassionate and merciful, and which desired to imprison and curse all who were not like themselves."[175]

In the end, it was the empire's Christian communities that suffered the greatest damage from the CUP's failure to create a "unity of peoples."

CHAPTER 3

TURKISH NATIONALISM

FROM 1908 TO 1913 TURKISH NATIONALISM WAS PURSUED MORE openly in the Unionist movement. However, it was not declared the ideological basis for Union policy until 1913, after the defeat in the Balkans.[1] The ideological roots of Turkish nationalism can be described as the following: 1) the scientific field of Turkology, which developed in Europe (and was then transported to Turkey by Ottoman students in Europe and political refugees); 2) Turkish nationalist currents developing in Russia; 3) Turkish historians and linguists; and 4) the nationalist ideological movements that developed in the Ottoman state.[2] Politically, the origins were the Ottoman reaction to Balkan nationalism; the Tatar rebellions against Russian Pan-Slavism and the influence of European nationalism on Turkish and Tatar intellectuals. All of these factors, ideological and political, encouraged the growth of Turkish nationalism.[3]

Like all Eastern European nationalist movements, Turkish nationalism initially developed largely within language and literature studies.[4] Turkish nationalism took on a more political character after 1904. Yusuf Akçura's article, "Three Types of Policy," is considered a turning point in the transformation of Turkish nationalism into a political movement. From 1906, the Committee of Union and Progress began to perceive itself as a "Turkish" organization, even while its leaders labored to conceal this and avoided admitting it on an official level.

In the period following the 1908 revolution, a number of lengthy debates arose around the fundamental question of how the empire could be saved. Various ideological currents came to the fore, whether Turkish nationalist, Ottomanist, Westernist, Islamist or some combination of these, and each one had its own answer to the question.[5] In the course of these debates, Turkish nationalism gradually took on a more political character. Three groups were influential in this transformation. The first was the Turkish cultural nationalists, who had begun to develop their theories in the last part of the nineteenth century. The second was the participants in the *Young Pens (Genç Kalemler)* journal in Salonica after 1908. The third group was made up of Turks from the Russian Empire who had begun to trickle into the Ottoman Empire after the constitutional revolution. These three streams found common ground in the Turkish Hearth association.

As we have seen, because of the policy encouraging a union of the various peoples of the empire, efforts towards Turkish nationalism could not be encouraged.[6] Its advocates' propaganda was not well received.[7] However, because the Committee of Union and Progress gradually came around to viewing Turkish nationalism as a compulsory belief system, not a doctrinal preference, it failed to perceive it as a complete break with all of the other doctrines then circulating, such as Pan-Islamism or Ottomanism.[8] Even when the CUP became Turkish nationalist, the committee wanted to continue seeing it as a type of Ottomanism.

Only after its disappointment with Ottomanism did the Young Turk leadership turn more definitely to Pan-Turkism, although they did not discard Ottomanism entirely and continued the policy of Turkification. Rather, Ottomanism and Pan-Islamism were downgraded and applied only intermittently, whenever the occasion demanded. In practice, the attitudes of rank-and-file members of the Committee of Union and Progress towards Islam—and Pan-Islamism—varied considerably. However, the top leadership was pragmatic in its approach.[9]

For this reason, switching from one ideology to another through a political decision was perfectly natural behavior for the Unionist leaders.

Ottomanism continued to be the keynote of internal politics; Turkish nationalism the keynote of relations with the Tatars of Russia . . . ; Pan-Islamism, that of relations with the Arabs and other non-Turkish Muslims within the Empire and of the Moslem peoples of North Africa and elsewhere outside of it.[10]

All was secondary to the goal of maintaining the empire.[11] Ziya Gökalp's series of articles "Turkification, Islamification, Modernization," which he published in the journal *Türk Yurdu* (Turkish Homeland) beginning 20 March 1913, laid the necessary theoretical foundation for this pragmatic approach. According to Gökalp, not only had Turkishness never been a contradiction to Ottomanism, on the contrary, it had always been its strongest supporter. He saw no contradiction between Turkishness and Islam. "Turkism is simultaneously Islamism."[12] In this way, Gökalp smoothed over the ideological differences between Ottomanism, Turkism, Islamism and Westernism. One of the most significant signs that the Turkish nationalism of the CUP was the result of political calculation, and could be dispensed with at any time, was the lack of political influence of Turkist ideologues within the Unionist movement. Astonishingly, the theoreticians of Turkish nationalism, like Akçura, never played an important role in the inner circles of the party.[13]

The CUP's pragmatism was evident in 1913, when Turkism was the dominant ideology. The party nonetheless decided to "pursue an Islamist course" as a concession to the Arab provinces.[14] Accommodation was made with the Arab population in education, language and administration.[15] However, this opportunistic approach was harshly criticized by traditional Islamists.[16]

A new stage of Turkish nationalism began with the tremendous shock of the defeat in the Balkan Wars.[17] It was seen by the Ottoman world as "Allah's divine punishment for a society that did not know how to pull itself together."[18] To rise above this calamity was only possible by wholeheartedly grasping the idea of Turkish nationalism. "The Turks, who could not have said 'I exist' before the Balkan Wars, now could say these words and even craft a plan for nationalization."[19]

At the time, the Unionists were struggling and failing to consolidate control over the government. In late 1912, they were compelled to go into the opposition. In this weakened state, the CUP began to call openly for Turkish nationalism, especially after the Italian invasion of Libya in 1911. After the defeats in the Balkans, they used the Ottoman surrender at Edirne as a pretext for a grab for renewed power through a military coup on 23 January 1913.[20] Many sources claim that the first Balkan War in 1912 had broken out as a result of the Balkan countries' attack on the Ottoman state and their plans and aspirations to acquire more land. But this is only partially correct. In Istanbul, the Unionists had been pushing for war in the newly independent Balkan states. Unionist leaders had tried to outdo each other in their bellicose rhetoric.[21] In the beginning of 1912, the war drums started to beat. Great demonstrations were organized, both by the Unionists and other parties. University students were herded out into the streets and speeches were given reminding the Turks that they were "the heroic descendants of [their] glorious grandfathers, who had caused the entire earth to tremble through their military heroism"; poems were recited, claiming that the Turks were "the Ottomans, who have struck fear [into the hearts of] all the world / . . . if angered they shall set the world suddenly ablaze." Calls for war were published in the newspapers: "To say 'Ottoman' is to say soldier. Long live the army, long live war!" The land that had been lost would absolutely have to be retaken: "The natural border of the Ottoman state is the Danube. We shall [re-]take our natural border. Forward, Ottomans—to the Danube!"[22] The CUP encouraged this war furor.[23] Talât Bey was one of the leading organizers of meetings that were held in Istanbul. Protestors demanded war in the Balkans, shouting "Attack Filibe [Philipopolis]; attack Sofia!"[24] The minister of war, Nâzim Paşa, claimed, "After war is declared, not a week shall pass before the Ottoman flag shall be seen [flying] over Filibe and Sofia."[25] The war broke out in October, and after a devastating campaign, the shocked Ottomans had lost "mighty Rumelia"—the birthplace of almost the entire CUP leadership and now only a nostalgic memory.

To understand the total collapse brought on by the Balkan Wars, it is necessary to grasp what these territorial losses meant for this generation. The continuous military defeats that the Ottoman Empire had experienced throughout the nineteenth century, and the Balkan loss in particular laid the foundation for a deep desire for revenge.

The story of war in the period of the empire's decline during the nineteenth century is not simply one of the massacre of rebellious Christian communities. A full history of these events would also include the slaughter and dispossession of the Muslim populations in the Christian areas.[26] After the 1840s, there were a significant number of Muslims, who, to save themselves from oppression and massacre within the Christian regions, "left behind their murdered grand-parents, children, and relatives and their property and belongings, in an attempt to reach the ever-shrinking borders of the Ottoman Empire."[27] Between the years 1855–66 alone, the number of Muslims migrating to Anatolia and Rumelia in the wake of the Crimean War was around one million.[28] Hundreds of thousands more fled the rebellions in Serbia and Crete, only to be followed by thousands fleeing the 1877–78 Russo-Ottoman War. These were followed by the further massacre of Muslim inhabitants of the Balkans.

Thus, a persistent yearning grew among Ottoman Muslims to regain lost territories, and "not to leave unavenged the blood of Muslims who had been murdered." Beginning in Abdul Hamid II's reign, this spirit of revanchism came to dominate the empire's military academies. The mood at these schools is recorded in the memoirs of cadets who attended during this period. One example of such memoirs:

> War would certainly break out one day and in that war, these young officers would take their revenge for the war of 1878, which ended in defeat. They would then demand a new accounting for the 1897 Greco-Ottoman War, which despite the Ottoman victory ultimately resulted in a setback [for the empire].[29]

The Balkan defeat only served to reinforce this sentiment. Societies established by and for the refugees flooding into Istanbul at the end of the war saw as their central task taking revenge for lost land and for fellow Muslims who had been slain. In a journal published by one of these societies, we read: "Let this be a warning. . . . O Muslims, don't get comfortable! Do not let your blood cool before taking revenge."[30] British historian Arnold Toynbee, who had the opportu-

But the greatest advance for Turkish nationalism came when the CUP itself decided to become directly involved. The *Türk Ocağı*, or Turkish Hearth Society, established in March 1912, began its activities in earnest in July at the Ottoman military medical school, where the CUP had begun some three decades earlier.[49] The CUP succeeded in amassing impressive support. The figures and publications advocating the society's establishment were all Unionist-affiliated. Ahmet Ferid Bey, who "appropriated" the movement from students, was a Unionist deputy from Kütahya. *Türk Ocağı*'s elected committee held its first meeting at the CUP's Central Committee, a meeting at which both Talât and Ziya Gökalp were present. In addition, Talât, Cemal and Enver Paşas, as well as the *Tanin* editor-in-chief all provided financial assistance.[50] Later, *Türk Yurdu Cemiyeti* and *Türk Ocağı* merged, and *Türk Yurdu* became the mouthpiece of both. Ziya Gökalp was the leading ideologue of the organization. After the Balkan Wars, *Türk Ocağı* even assumed the role of ideological standard-bearer for the CUP.[51]

A whole series of other Turkish nationalist organizations sprang up in the period following the Balkan Wars. *Türk Gücü*—Turkish Strength—was among the most aggressive, claiming its goal to be the "rescue of the Turkish race from collapse," and it used extremely racist, virulent language to express its view.[52] The society's slogan was "Turkish strength is sufficient for all things."[53] As for the society's aims, it intended, along with the other Turkist organizations, to enforce the Turanic idea. It would:

> cover the entire world with its raging torrents, . . . leave no neck unbowed, no sword unbroken, no fortress not struck. . . . The custodian of Turkish strength, the watchman of the Turkish hearth, the defender of the Turkish homeland—they shall be the vanguard of Turan. The iron fist of the Turk shall take hold of the world again, and the world shall again tremble before it.[54]

After the Balkan defeat, the CUP took the leading role by establishing the "Society for National Defense," whose aim was national unity and social mobilization to cure the nation's ills.[55] A number of guild associations were set up and smaller guilds in particular were reorganized along nationalist lines. This effort extended even to the

nity to tour Anatolia at this time and observe the situation firsthand, wrote: "The arrival of the Rumelian refugees from the end of 1912 onward produced an unexampled tension of feeling in Anatolia and a desire for revenge."[31]

This last point is crucial for the subsequent Armenian genocide, because it was precisely those people who, having only recently been saved from massacre themselves, would now take a central and direct role in cleansing Anatolia of "non-Turkish" elements. The dimensions of this migration and its results become easier to understand when we recall that between 1878–1904 some 850,000 refugees were settled in predominantly Armenian areas alone.[32]

The Balkan War, the humiliating defeat, and the loss of territories had a radical effect on the CUP as well, as the party completely reformulated its policy. "Turkish nationalism became an official current from the spring of 1913."[33] At the 1913 party congress, the Unionists decided:

> Just as it shall struggle to end the . . . economic concessions and exceptions that prevent an independent national economic policy and involve foreigners, the Union and Progress Party [also] considers as the most sacred of objectives the employment of means to eliminate all of the Capitulations.[34]

Unionists were beginning to conceive of the implementation of a nationalization program—one in which there would be a prominent economic aspect. Ziya Gökalp took up the questions and problems of national emergence and expounded upon the ideological, political and economic foundations necessary for a Turkish state.[35] The most significant dimension of his theoretical writings was a sharp critique of the measures carried out following the Tanzimat reforms. In Gökalp's view, the greatest mistake of the reformers and their successors was their desire to establish the principle of equality by elevating the non-Muslim population to the status of citizens:

> The Tanzimat [reforms] strove to broaden the understanding of "Ottoman" to Muslim and non-Muslim alike in order to satisfy Christian elements that had supposedly expressed dissatisfaction through their desire for [their own separate] nationality. . . . But

it could [never] have worked as the Tanzimat [reformers] had hoped. . . . The Christian peoples did not consider the right to be Ottomans as a gift or a favor.[36]

According to Gökalp, what was needed was a return "to the former meaning of 'Ottomanism'" and an end to "the illusion of Muslim-Christian equality."[37] This statement was found in a secret memorandum sent by the CUP to its cadres on educational matters. The open embrace of Turkish nationalism was the next, necessary step.

In Gökalp's opinion, coexistence, whether willing or unwilling, was no longer to be attempted and Turkishness was to be the basis for policy. In a 1911 article for the journal *Yeni Hayat (New Life)*, Gökalp wrote that the "Turks are the 'supermen' imagined by the German philosopher Nietzsche. . . . New life will be born from Turkishness. . . ."[38] He believed that the Turks needed to embrace their Turkishness. In his article "The Three Currents" in *Türk Yurdu*, Gökalp dealt at length with the negative effects of the opinion: "I'm not a Turk, I'm an Ottoman."[39] One cannot create a shared homeland for different cultural, ethnic, religious and national groups. For Gökalp, the problem was painfully clear: "A state that is not based on a shared consciousness" cannot survive. This shared consciousness was "the national idea." Thus Muslims had to use "the weapon of nationalism."[40]

Gökalp's national economic model also developed under the influence of German nationalism, according to which the state was likened to a living organism that, by definition, had to be an organic whole. The nation should be considered a "social totality." The stages necessary to achieve this were "cultural unity," "economic unity" and "political unity." Economic unity could only be established together with national consciousness.[41] The theory of a national economy emphasized "the formation of Muslim-Turkish guilds," and stressed the need to focus on the ethnic dimension. A national economy could be realized through ethnic uniformity: "The modern state emerged from the division of labor which developed in a single ethnic community."[42]

This theoretical framework is crucial for an understanding of the Armenian genocide because it provided ideological grounds and therefore legitimacy. Gökalp gave "the nation" an important mystical component. In his work, "he transferred to the nation the divine qualities he had found in society, replacing the belief in God with the belief in the nation: and so nationalism became a religion."[43] The national is deified, thus expanding Durkheim's idea that "society can do as it pleases." So, if a nation perceives itself in danger, it feels no moral responsibility in its response to that danger. The Unionist "scientific approach" gained a "sacred" character through Gökalp's theories.

Evidence exists that Gökalp compiled special studies of the empire's minorities, including the Armenians. These were done as part of a wider plan to amass detailed knowledge of the ethnic-religious structure of Anatolia. A special department, the Office for the Settlement of Tribes and Immigrants, established within the Interior Ministry in 1913, dealt especially with questions of population dispersal and resettlement. The office commissioned various scholars to conduct field studies within Anatolia and even invited German specialists on ethnicity to contribute reports.[44] The office's publishing branch translated foreign-language books on legal and political aspects of ethnicity, migration, and resettlement into Ottoman Turkish. Ziya Gökalp coordinated one of the Anatolian studies, specifically about the Armenians. While we have little solid information about the report's content, one of Gökalp's students, Enver Behnan Şapolyo, noted a connection between his teacher's investigation into the "Armenian Question" and the "Armenian deportations."[45]

More concrete expressions of Turkish nationalism were making themselves felt as well. The first organization devoted to the cause was the *Türk Derneği*, or Turkish Society, founded on 7 January 1909.[46] But the society sparked little interest, and was eventually forced to close its doors when its founders left Istanbul. It was primarily a scientific and literary, rather than political organization, which included Muslim and non-Muslim Turks and Europeans on its executive committee, such as Orientalist professors Goldlevski and Martin Hartmann.[47] This first failed effort was followed in 1911 by the *Türk Yurdu Cemiyeti*, or Turkish homeland society, established on 18 August.[48] This society also published a journal of the same name, *Türk Yurdu*. Cultural goals were at the forefront of this second attempt. Ziya Gökalp himself became a member of *Türk Yurdu Cemiyeti* in 1912.

porters guild. Significantly, "Christians were to be . . . excluded from these institutions."[56] Another important CUP institution was the *İstiklal-i Milli Cemiyeti*, or National Independence Society, which was founded on 3 July 1913 and fostered the establishment of a large number of new companies. The aim was to create a bourgeoisie comprised solely of Turks and to replace Christians with Muslims in traditional economic roles. CUP member and minister of supplies, Kara Kemal,[57] was in charge of the creation of this new bourgeois class. The Turkish language became mandatory for all commercial correspondence within the empire. This was enshrined in a 1916 law "concerning the use of Turkish in the correspondence and business transactions of public works, institutions, and concessionary companies."[58]

Organizations formed through Unionist assistance often made immense profits through various illegal means, such as corruption and black marketeering. The committee defended this on the grounds that the ultimate goal of creating a Muslim-Turkish bourgeoisie was sacred. In a 1917 parliamentary speech defending the government's budget, Unionist finance minister Mehmet Cavit Bey said, "Even if we suppose that the support and assistance was unlawful, as some have claimed, the benefits have, as a result, been obtained. The economic advantage could, in my view, negate this illegality."[59]

The use of force, such as the requisition and seizure of Christian property, was one of the more important features of the economic policy implemented in the spring of 1914. After the outbreak of war the government established the Committee to Prevent Hoarding[60] to curb speculation. But the committee primarily targeted non-Muslims and greatly helped smooth the way for Muslim-Turkish merchants by eliminating competition.[61]

One of the main subjects of the postwar interrogations of Unionists members was the relationship between the CUP's economic organizations and the suppression of opposition party members and Armenian deportations. During the trials in Istanbul, Unionists were frequently asked about their economic policies. One important aspect was the use of the economic organizations established by the Unionists to fund the special organizations formed to carry out the genocide.[62] In fact, an entire session of the main trial against the Unionist leaders (Third session, 6 May 1919) was devoted entirely to this subject.[63]

As Turkish nationalism evolved, its primary goal—to rid the empire of its non-Muslim populations—became clear. A notion that took hold among the Unionist leaders was that for "Turkey to survive in possession of its territories," it would have to be "free of foreign peoples,"[64] as Talât Paşa claimed.

> These different *blocs* in the Turkish Empire . . . always conspired against Turkey; because of the hostility of these native peoples, Turkey has lost province after province—Greece, Serbia, Rumania, Bulgaria, Bosnia, Herzegovina, Egypt, and Tripoli. In this way, the Turkish Empire has dwindled almost to nothing.[65]

Prominent Unionist Halil Menteşe claimed in his memoirs that it was "Talât [Paşa who] proposed that the country be cleansed of its treacherous elements."[66] According to Kuşçubaşı Eşref, who played a central role in the "cleansing" operations, non-Muslims were "internal tumors" that needed "to be cleaned"; such an act was "a national cause."[67]

The leaders of the CUP, after acquiring complete political control, began to devote themselves fully to the problem of ridding Anatolia of its "cancerous" concentrations of non-Turks. For this purpose it was necessary to devise a comprehensive plan that would be not only ideological in nature, but also social, political, and economic. The first step was to rescue those "Turks in the Ottoman state who were living with no consciousness," who never spoke up, out of deference to the "union of peoples" policy. It was necessary "to throw back the perfidious curtain [of Ottomanism] that had shielded Turkish eyes" since the Tanzimat, and "ignite the idea of Turkishness."[68] The next step was to extend the empire to include reliable elements, to construct a whole new political entity together with the Muslim-Turkic peoples of the Caucasus and Central Asia. The question—Where is the Turkish nation's homeland?—would have to be answered anew. Ultimately, Ziya Gökalp had already provided the answer in 1911.[69] The new homeland was "Turan," an idealized entity that "would gather all Turks together and reject foreigners." Turan "is the entirety of all the countries in which Turks live, in which Turkish is spoken."[70] The borders of Turan would extend as far as the languages and political culture of the Turks.[71] Turkish nationalism was thus perceived as an expansionist idea which had political, cultural and ideological components known as Pan-Turanism or Pan-Turkism.[72] However, Pan-Turkism had not completely severed its ties to Islamic ideology and so the term was often employed interchangeably with Pan-Islamism. In any case, the CUP had a grander objective: "the streams of Turkish nationalism are directed at uniting the Islam[-ic world], and those Turks who remain outside of Turkey."[73] By 1914, Gökalp had crystalized these ideas in a phrase: "The enemy's country shall be laid waste; Turkey shall grow into Turan with haste." Enver Paşa was the idea's most ardent proponent. "The objective took such immense shape in the minister of war's imagination until finally, [he envisioned] himself as the ruler of a resurrected Ottoman empire, one which, after uniting the Turks and Muslims of Asia and winning back the countries we had lost in Europe, would stretch from the Adriatic Sea to the waters of India."[74]

The Unionists developed a plan with the aim of extending the empire through Central Asia to make up for lost territory in Europe. Enver Paşa in particular believed that the collapse of Russia would clear the path for a powerful Turkish Empire to replace the weak and heterogeneous Ottomans and gather all the Turkish "race under its mantle."[75] Shortly thereafter, these ideas would be declared as a specific Ottoman war aim.

To realize this Pan-Turanist vision, the CUP founded the Special Organization. Unfortunately, because a great many relevant documents were destroyed, we do not possess definite and detailed information as to exactly when or how it was established. Kuşçubaşı Eşref, a central figure, claimed that it was set up between 1911 and 1913.[76] There are a number of different records concerning its origins. Unionist party secretary Cemil, writing under the nom de plume A. Mil, stated that discussions on the matter began after the Balkan defeat, and that the Special Organization was actually established in July 1914. Historian Tevfik Bıyıkoğlu reports that the organization was established "through a secret order by Minister of War Enver Paşa in August 1914." Some argue that it was actually founded in 1911. Unionist Fuat Balkan, on the other hand, claims that the Special Organization was established during the 1913 Balkan defeat. In his memoirs, Cemal Paşa mentions Special Organization activity taking place during the Balkan Wars. But Tevfik Bıyıkoğlu, on the basis of a 1953 conversation with Fuat Balkan, claims that in this period "the Special Organization had neither name, nor separate existence."[77]

The journalist and historian Cemal Kutay has claimed, on the basis of Kuşçubaşı Eşref's memoirs, that the Special Organization was established as an official entity by imperial decree.[78] But there is no information from any member of the government regarding such a decree. The Unionist grand vizier Said Halim Paşa, during interrogation by the parliamentary commission of inquiry after the war, claimed that he was unaware of such an organization, and said that it was not a matter to concern the Porte or the government, because there [was] no government decision or initiative in this regard." Both the finance and justice ministers gave similar statements to the commission.[79] The defendants at the main trial of the Unionist leaders in the Istanbul extraordinary court-martial also pleaded ignorance when asked about an imperial decree.[80] However, they did claim that the Special Organization had operated as a unit within the Ministry of War.[81] In his memoirs, Talât Paşa writes that the Special Organization was a state office. During the postwar Istanbul trials, the public prosecutor attempted to prove that the Special Organization had been established following a CUP Central Committee decision. This, in turn, would prove that the Armenian deportations and killings had been a CUP initiative. Thus the Special Organization received special attention. The indictment claimed that the CUP had set up "a committee named 'the Special Organization' to prepare the ground for the murderous work of the criminal gangs released from prison. . . . "[82]

The extant information leads us to conclude that in 1911 a group associated with Enver Paşa began to call itself the "Special Organization." This group was initially founded to organize a guerrilla war in Libya against Italy at the end of 1911.[83] It is probable that the organization was formally established in 1913 under the leadership of Enver Paşa and played an important role in the Balkan Wars in the summer of 1913. It was reconstructed in January 1914, when Enver Paşa was the minister of war.[84] From a good number of memoirs and recollections, we know that some significant differences arose between Talât and Enver as to its control. They eventually agreed that the organization should be attached to the CUP Central Committee, which decided that "the War Ministry would have to demarcate its program and course of action."[85]

During the trials after the war, the judge concluded, on the basis of a document from the War Ministry, that the Special Organization was first formed at CUP party headquarters and later moved to the Ministry of War.[86] After the reorganization, the "official" Special Organization was comprised of representatives from the CUP Central Committee, the Interior Ministry and the War Ministry. The organization's first chairman was Süleyman Askeri, and his assistant was Atıf Kamçıl. In time, Askeri would be replaced by Halil Paşa and a certain Cevat Bey. In his testimony before the extraordinary court-martial, Cevat would claim that the needs and requirements of the Special Organization were met by the War Ministry, and he coordinated the correspondence between these two bodies.[87] Additionally, the director-general of security, Aziz Bey, was the representative for the Interior Ministry, while Dr. Nâzım and Bahaettin Şakir were the members from the CUP Central Committee and coordinated the overall activities of the Special Organization in Istanbul.[88] In time, government security chief Cevat Bey assumed "the task of ratifying and implementing the [committee's] unanimous decisions."[89] During the trials, Atıf also testified that the Special Organization was actually comprised of at least four separate bureaus, saying that "there was the Rumelia desk, the Caucasus desk, the Africa and the Tripoli desk," but claimed not to remember the exact number.[90]

Rıza, a member of the Special Organization, provided other important information. During the trial's Fifth session on 12 May, Rıza testified that not one but two kinds of Special Organization existed. One was subject to the authority of the War Ministry, and the other to the CUP. Individual Special Organization units were formed under party control, independently in Anatolia on the orders of either local administrators or party secretaries. He also explained that these secondary Special Organization units were set up especially for the deportation of Armenians.

> A second Special Organization was . . . created . . . to carry out these deportation operations due to insufficient gendarme forces. . . .
> These forces and the ones deployed by the [first] Special Organization are two completely different matters.

When asked for the identity of the leader of this second organization, Rıza replied that he himself was only "local."[91] Other witnesses confirmed the statement that a second kind of Special Organization was established to implement the deportations. The governor of Erzerum gave similar testimony and revealed that Bahaettin Şakir was the leader of the second Special Organization.[92] Governor of Kastamonu Resat Paşa gave the same testimony, adding that he personally had received written orders from Bahaettin Şakir as the leader of the Special Organization.[93]

During the Armenian genocide, there was a great deal of collaboration between the Special Organization and the Central Committee as well as the local organizations of the CUP. In the 1919 trial of Unionist leaders, many documents and several defendants testified to the fact that the Special Organization worked hand in hand with the CUP, even as it was officially tied to the War Ministry.

According to one of its founders, the aim of the Special Organization was concrete and twofold: "The first was Pan-Islamism that would gather all Muslims under its banner; the second was [a] Pan-Turkism that would place the entire Turkish race under one political unit."[94] To achieve this Turkish-Islamic unity, the organization operated domestically and abroad. In the "foreign" struggle, agents were sent to countries colonized by the West—especially by Britain—and to Central Asia to foment revolution:

> It was widely agreed that we would send our [more] capable people. Everywhere they went they would work with doggedness and determination, like Jesuit priests. We were going to incite India, Baluchistan, Iran, Afghanistan and all the Muslim peoples of Africa. The world of Islam would come under the command of the Caliph. Revolutions would follow one after the other. Britain and France would find themselves in a disastrous situation, where they would be routed out of crucial regions.[95]

The domestic objective was every bit as important. After its reconstitution in 1914, in particular, the organization became "the foremost institution for both internal and external security for the Ottoman state."[96] According to Cemal Kutay,

During these years the Special Organization perform[ed] services which the visible government forces . . . would not necessarily be able to do, not only through covert intelligence gathering, but also through measures implemented outside the Ottoman state, as well as in areas which were still within its borders but whose connection and loyalty to the central government were always suspect, and in which non-Turkish races and nations formed a minority.[97]

Actions directed at the "enemy within" had begun even before World War I. The expulsion of the Aegean Greek population through terror and expropriation of property was done as part of the plan to homogenize Anatolia. With the outbreak of war, this plan was expanded, and the Special Organization was now given the task of directly organizing the Armenian genocide.

The Armenian question had become a burning issue once again in the wake of the Balkan Wars. After the loss of the Balkan territories, the Ottomans were utterly weakened, and every faction involved knew that it was now the Armenians' turn to press their advantage. Various foreign countries, the Ottomans, and the Armenian revolutionary organizations entered into a sort of competition to seize the initiative. The Unionist leaders knew full well that the debate on the issue of reforms for the Armenian-populated provinces affected the political future of the last territories remaining under Ottoman control.

Anatolia had become the focus of nationalist interest. The newspaper *Tanin*, the mouthpiece of the CUP, pessimistically predicted, "It is impossible to save Anatolia from the destiny awaiting Rumelia."[98] Even though the Dashnaks were part of the CUP's coalition, all efforts toward Armenian reforms were fruitless. On 16 July 1911, the Armenian patriarchate had delivered a list of grievances, which included incidents of looting and killing, and demanded certain improvements. "Since the beginning of [1911], as many as fifty people have been killed in the Eastern provinces, and there have been a great number of attacks and wrongful seizure [of property]."[99] In its response to this petition the government promised to implement certain changes in the areas of minority education, language, and military service, as well as legal reforms, such as the recognition of Christian witnesses before the courts. But resistance to these changes, especially on the part of Kurds and local notables, was so strong that nothing was achieved. Kurdish deputies in the Ottoman parliament blocked every reform attempt and relations between Kurds and Armenians deteriorated. In 1912 the Armenians presented another list of grievances, among them pillaging, rape, and killing in the eastern provinces. The patriarch threatened to resign and close the patriarchate if Armenians in the provinces were not protected.[100]

After the Balkan Wars, the Armenians repeated their demands for reform. On 31 March 1913, the Armenian patriarch appealed to the grand vizier, delivering a letter stating that "the situation of the Armenians has deteriorated even further, to the point that we fear for their wholesale elimination."[101] He announced that he was calling on the Ottoman state's sense of responsibility as a last resort. When the request went unanswered, the General Council of the Armenian patriarchate resigned on 4 May 1913, claiming that this was the only possible option, "because it had not, until now, seen a single result from initiatives and requests concerning the situation in the provinces, which had been sent numerous times to the Porte."[102] In a meeting with the grand vizier on 12 May 1913, these complaints were summed up:

> The Armenians are being killed, wounded and forcibly converted to Islam, and those who are responsible pay no penalties. The Armenians have had their weapons confiscated, while the Muslims still have theirs. The refugees from Rumelia are being settled in Eastern Anatolia. . . .[103]

There was also a noticeable increase in Armenian activities in foreign capitals, appealing for the governments to supervise the Armenian reforms. The Russian Armenians in particular were especially active, sending a variety of demands to the czar's government to occupy the part of Armenia still under Ottoman rule.[104] Although he rejected this demand, Russian foreign minister Sazanov promised that he would assist in the matter of the reforms.[105]

An important reason for this flurry of activity was that Russia's interest in the Far East had largely waned. It now set its sights on the Bosphorus and Anatolia, and in 1912 Russia's Armenian policy underwent a significant transformation. Having implemented a pol-

icy of extreme repression against the Armenians under its own control, Russia now became an enthusiastic advocate and an important
center for political activity for Turkish Armenians.[106] The Russian-
Armenian Catholicos, the highest religious authority in Russian
Armenia, requested that the czar take the Turkish Armenians under
his protection.

Russia's policy was to prevent other powers, especially Germany,
from controlling areas of the crumbling Ottoman Empire and to
widen its own area of sovereignty. The Russians incited Kurds and
Armenians in the region and armed both parties to facilitate future
military intervention.[107] As a result of this incitement and the Kurds'
fear that reforms would hand over the region to Armenians, they
revolted in Bitlis and the surrounding region. This revolt was forcibly
suppressed, and fourteen Kurdish leaders were executed.[108]

In addition, the Russians supported sending a delegation of
Russian-Armenians, headed by Bogos Nubar, to Europe. They
arranged the transfer of letters of complaint, sent by the Armenian
patriarch to the Russian consulates in the eastern provinces, then on
to the Porte. And they organized petitions by Armenians demanding
Russian citizenship. Additionally, in December 1912, Foreign Minister Sazanov, through the Russian ambassador in Istanbul, drew the
attention of Britain and France to the plight of the Armenians, giving
the impression that Russian occupation of the region was inevitable.
Britain and France were warned that they needed to insist on the
reforms listed in the Treaty of Berlin. The Ottoman government's
plans to resettle Muslim refugees from the First Balkan War in eastern
Anatolia triggered these diplomatic moves because the policy would
have reduced Russian influence in the region.[109] Thus, the Armenian
question returned to the top of the European agenda.

As a result of this increased involvement, reports began reaching
Istanbul that the Great Powers were engaged in negotiations over the
partition of Anatolia. The CUP knew that preventive measures were
needed to avoid a repeat of disaster in its eastern provinces. For this
reason, some reforms were implemented that were aimed at forestalling Russian and European interference. There was an attempt to
strengthen local administration through the Law on the General
Administration of the Provinces, dated 26 March 1913.[110] Ultimately,
this was nothing more than remaking a law that, according to the

Constitution, should have been enforced anyway. A draft had been prepared after 1908 but its passage blocked in parliament. Now, as pressure from the foreign powers began to mount, this law was, with several amendments, taken out again and passed, seen as the lesser of two evils.[111]

The Reform Commission was also created within the Interior Ministry. Plans were made to divide the Armenian provinces into two parts, to be administered by commissions composed of Ottoman Christians, Muslims and foreigners.[112] This was part of a larger plan according to which the empire was to be divided into regions, each containing three or four provinces. The intention was to begin the reorganization immediately with the Armenian provinces. On 24 April 1913, the Ottoman government made an official appeal to Great Britain, requesting assistance for the implementation of these reforms.[113] The Ottomans wanted Britain to send officers and administrators to this region to prevent a problem in eastern Anatolia such as the ethnic clashes and revolutionary turmoil that had occurred in Rumelia. The fact that it was the British who had admonished the Porte about the Armenian reforms emboldened the Ottomans to ask them for assistance. But after a period of evasiveness, the British turned down the request so as not to disturb their relations with Russia. In this way, the issue was transformed into a shared problem for Russia and the other European states, and on St. Petersburg's initiative, it was decided that reform for the Armenian provinces should be examined at a series of meetings to be held in Istanbul. In June of the same year, a commission composed of British, French and Russian representatives met and announced a draft resolution on the reforms.

Subsequently, there was a great deal of negotiation and maneuvering. Britain, France and Germany entered into the process in mediating roles, but the struggle over which country would have relative advantage, and how to divide Anatolia were more important than the reforms themselves. For them, the Armenian reforms were "the step toward partition."[114] During the discussions on reform, the French chargé d'affaires in St. Petersburg suggested that the best way to solve the Armenian problem was to do what was done in Rumelia, that is, to establish small states based on nationalities—such as Armenian or Syrian.[115] The German ambassador at Istanbul, Hans von Wangenheim, claimed on 30 June 1914 that "this matter means the beginning of the partition."[116] André Mandelstam, the Russian representative at the discussions who prepared Russia's first reform proposal, described the initiative as "the first step toward rescuing Armenia from Turkish oppression."[117] Meanwhile, the Austrian ambassador to the Porte, Count Pallavicini, reported that the Russians told him that, with the realization of the reforms, "the dividing up of the Asian part of Turkey was already a done deal."[118]

Germany was absolutely opposed to any initiative that would result in eastern Anatolia coming under Russian hegemony. Finally, Germany and Russia reached an understanding, known as the Yeniköy Accord, on 8 February 1914. Accordingly, the eastern provinces would be divided into two and a foreign inspector, possessing complete authority, would be appointed for each group. The inspectors were to be appointed in April 1914, but with the outbreak of the First World War, the reform package was quickly shelved.

The Unionist leaders knew that

> for the Turks, the Armenian movement was the deadliest of all threats. From the conquered lands of the Serbs, Bulgars, Albanians and Greeks, they could, however reluctantly, withdraw, abandoning distant provinces and bringing the Imperial frontier nearer home. But the Armenians, stretching across Turkey-in-Asia from the Caucasian frontier to the Mediterranean coast, lay in the very heart of the Turkish homeland—and to renounce these lands would have meant not the truncation, but the dissolution of the Turkish state.[119]

The Armenian reforms appeared as "the final blow to strike the Ottoman Empire . . . [and] the time chosen was seen as so propitious as to give the blow sufficient force to topple the Empire."[120]

The Great Powers did not approach the issue with the goal of reforms, but with the aim of discovering "whether what would be left of Turkey would be able to survive alone, or if it was destined to collapse."[121] The prevailing assessment, in the wake of the Balkan Wars, was that "Asian Turkey did not have the strength to defend itself with its own forces."[122] The Great Powers participated in the talks to prevent the negative effects of "premature" partition—i.e., Russian domination—and to make sure that when the likely partition did finally occur, they would be able to make off with a reasonable share of the pie.

Ultimately, fear of this plan was a critical factor in the decision to turn to genocide because the partition would have created an independent Armenian state in Anatolia, destroying the empire. In fact, after the Ottoman defeat in World War I, the Treaty of Sèvres, signed in August 1920, would have established an Armenian state in these very provinces had there been any Armenians left. After the war, many former Unionist leaders said openly that the Armenian genocide made the establishment of a Turkish national state possible. In the words of former Unionist press doyen Hüseyin Cahit Yalçın, "Those who devised and carried out the deportation of the Armenians thereby rescued Turkey."[123] Similar sentiments were uttered by the former Unionist parliamentary leader, Halil Menteşe, who wrote that "had we not cleansed our eastern provinces of the Armenian revolutionaries who were collaborating with the Russians, there would have been no possibility of bringing our national state into existence."[124]

In June 1913 Grand Vizier Mahmut Şevket Paşa, who was close to the Unionists, was assassinated by the emerging opposition within the military that rejected the CUP's modernization process. This event gave the Unionists the chance they needed to seize power and eliminate the opposition, once and for all.[125] Enver Paşa's appointment as minister of war in January 1914 was a major step toward realizing the creation of a homogenized Turkish state. To that end he began reorganizing not only the Special Organization but also the army.[126] According to Kuşçubaşı Eşref, in a meeting at the Ministry of War on 23 February 1914[127] Enver said that the only way out of the dismal position in which Turkey had found itself was to achieve a unity of the Turkish and Islamic worlds. The non-Muslims had proven that they did not support the continued existence of the state and that its salvation would necessitate stern measures against them. The Special Organization would, in this regard, carry out "services which government and public forces could never hope to perform." In Kuşçubaşı's words, "The first task was to separate the loyal from the traitors."[128] That meant eliminating the danger posed by the empire's Christian communities.[129]

Kuşçubaşı provided important details about the plans to realize this goal. At the beginning of 1914, Ottoman leaders concluded that they faced two important problems: "1) an enormous opposition, which exploited all liberties; 2) separatist, non-Turkish elements who threatened the integrity and unity of the empire through overt and covert means." The first problem ". . . was a political issue which could be solved. But the second was a more difficult, even deadly ailment, the cure for which demanded steely measures."[130]

Secret meetings at the Ministry of War focused mainly on liquidating concentrations of non-Turkish populations that had accumulated at strategic points, and which were susceptible to negative foreign influences.[131]

Kuşçubaşı says in his memoirs that these meetings were held throughout May, June and August 1914. Also participating were some of the CUP's "reliable . . . valuable, self-sacrificing, patriotic elements" in Anatolia, "having been summoned individually to Istanbul." Significantly, "certain members of the Cabinet did not even know" about the meetings.[132]

Detailed plans were prepared for the Turkification of Anatolia by the elimination of its Christian population. The same measures were implemented in the Aegean region in the spring of 1914.

> The [Committee of] Union and Progress made a clear decision. The source of the trouble in western Anatolia would be removed, the Greeks would be cleared out by means of political and economic measures. Before anything else, it would be necessary to weaken and break the economically powerful Greeks.[133]

According to Unionist leaders, the most immediate threat in Anatolia lay in the Aegean region. It was decided to concentrate activities around Izmir, as the center of subversive activities. "The measures themselves can be divided into three main categories: 1) general measures taken on a governmental level; 2) special measures enacted by the army; and 3) measures to be taken by the Union and Progress Party."[134]

Kuşçubaşı went to the region and submitted a report about his findings, stating in it that foreign influences in İzmir would make it very difficult to carry out Turkification. He predicted that any local initiative would bring the Ottoman government under suspicion by foreign powers. "In this regard, any nationalization action is conditioned upon their implementation by serious, resolute, strong-willed and honorable patriots."[135]

The war had not yet begun and there was still hesitancy to act, due to the fear of provoking foreign intervention. The Unionist government organized terror campaigns, raids and robberies, but all through the Special Organization so as to mask any direct government connection. Halil Menteşe said that so that "the provincial governors and other officials would not appear to be intervening, the Committee's organizations would administer the affair. . . . "[136] It was possible to make it seem as if there were no government decisions involved, but high-ranking officials were required to monitor the process.

> The "cleansing" operation in the Aegean basin was implemented militarily by Chief of Staff Cafer Tayyar Bey of the 4th Army, which was under the command of Pertev [Demirhan] Paşa, and by the governor of the Izmir Province, . . . Rahmi Bey as the local administrative director and, on behalf of the Party of Union and Progress, by Responsible Secretary Mahmut Celâl Bey (subsequently Republican President Celâl Bayar). The state's forces would act according to orders given by the Ministry of War and the Supreme Military Command to implement this plan.[137]

> The greatest part of the work fell to Kuşçubaşı Eşref.

> The Greeks were harassed through a variety of means and compelled to emigrate as a result of the pressures that were brought to bear. Armed gangs under the command of Kuşçubaşı Eşref . . . conducted raids on Greek villages. . . . Greek youths . . . [were] gathered together in . . . "labor battalions," in which they were forced to work building roads in forestry and in construction.[138]

Despite all the precautionary measures taken, the events provoked a strong reaction in Europe. As a result of foreign pressure—especially from France—the Unionists were forced to halt the Greek emigration, and even to commission a committee of inquiry, headed by Talât Paşa, including members from each foreign embassy.[139]

Regarding the "cleansing" of the Aegean region of its Christians, historian Arnold Toynbee reported that the Turkish reprisals against the West Anatolian Greeks became general in the spring of 1914. Entire Greek communities were driven from their homes by terrorism, their houses and land and often their moveable property were seized, and individuals were killed in the process.[140]

Unaware of Kuşçubaşı's memoirs, Toynbee nevertheless claimed that

the procedure bore evidence of being systematic. The terror attacked one district after another, and was carried on by "chetté" bands, enrolled from the Rumeli refugees as well as from the local population and nominally attached as reinforcements to the regular Ottoman gendarmerie.[141]

The forced migration of Greeks from the Aegean region resumed during the First World War. This second wave, however, was based more on military needs although these too "were carried out with great brutality."[142] From Ayvalık, for example, the entire population between the ages of twelve and eighty was forcibly relocated to inner Anatolia. What is significant is that this second wave of forced migration was organized by the German general Otto Liman von Sanders. In a report he submitted to the Ottoman government, Liman von Sanders wrote that "he would be unable to take the responsibility for the security of the army" so long as such resettlement had not taken place. He further reported that he wanted to begin the deportations immediately upon arriving in Ayvalık, posing the rhetorical question, "Couldn't they throw these infidels into the sea?"[143] On 23 November 1918, a few days after the armistice, at a meeting of the Ottoman Chamber of Deputies, questions were raised about whether action had been taken against General Liman von Sanders.[144]

American ambassador Henry Morgenthau drew attention to the similarity between the methods used to drive the Greeks out of the Aegean and those used during the Armenian genocide:

The Turks adopted almost identically the same procedure against the Greeks as that which they had adopted against the Armenians.

They began by incorporating the Greeks into the Ottoman army and then transforming them into labor battalions, using them to build roads in the Caucasus and other scenes of action. These Greek soldiers, just like the Armenians, died by thousands from cold, hunger, and other privations. . . . The Turks attempted to force the Greek subjects to become Mohammadans; Greek girls . . . were stolen and taken to Turkish harems and Greek boys were kidnapped and placed in Moslem households. . . . Everywhere, the Greeks were gathered in groups and, under the so-called protection of Turkish gendarmes, they were transported, the larger part on foot, into the interior.[145]

Morgenthau claims that although there is no certainty about the number of people deported, estimates run between 200,000 and 1 million.[146] The Greek premier Eleutherios Venizelos announced at the Paris Peace Conference that 300,000 Greeks had been killed, and another 450,000 had fled to Greece, while the Turkish historian Doğan Avcıoğlu claims that "there is no existing information that would testify to large-scale massacre of the Greeks having been carried out."[147]

Celal Bayar, who became Turkey's third president, directed the economic aspects of the plan. He redistributed confiscated Greek properties to Muslims. He estimated the number of Greeks deported at around 130,000.[148] Halil Menteşe puts the number of Greeks deported from the İzmir region at 200,000.[149] Kuşçubaşı Eşref claims that during the first months of the war alone the number of "Greek-Armenians . . . deported totaled 1,350,000."[150] In a June 1918 report sent by the British Intelligence Services to the French Ministry of War, the figures for killed and deported are close to those given by Kuşçubaşı:

The number of persons dispatched from Thrace and Anatolia exceeds 1.5 million; half of this number were either killed or died due to distressed conditions. Turkish government officials and military officers declare without hesitation that the Christians are no longer allowed to live in Turkey and that the Greeks will be forcibly converted to Islam. The value of those Greek properties seized by the Turks is around 5 billion French Francs.[151]

In discussions in the Ottoman Chamber of Deputies in 1918, the figures given for the number of Greeks evicted from Thrace were between 300,000 and half a million.[152] Heated debate on the ethnic cleansing raged in the Ottoman parliament on several occasions. During its eleventh session (4 November 1918), Aydın deputy Emanuel Emanuelidi Efendi demanded an explanation "concerning the activities of the former government," saying that while expelling the Greeks, "the property of some 250,000 . . . was confiscated," and that "550,000 more . . . were killed in the coastal regions of the Black Sea, Çanakkale, Marmara and the Aegean Islands and other areas, and their property was seized and looted."[153]

On 11 December, other requests for clarification were submitted by Tekfurdağı deputy Dimistoklis Efkalidis Efendi and Çatalca deputy Tokinidis Efendi on the question of the forced emigrations from Ayvalık, Edirne, and Çatalca. According to their figures, some 300,000 Greeks in the Edirne and Çatalca areas had their houses and possessions seized and were deported to Greece. Additionally, "armed gangs carried out massacres in this region." The deputies announced that the total number of those who had perished was 500,000.[154]

As the discussions continued, it emerged that the leaders of the massacres had been rewarded. "Just as the governor of Edirne Province, Hacı Adil Bey, was subsequently made president of the Chamber of Deputies, the governor of Tekfurdağı, Zekeriya Bey, was elevated to the governorship of Edirne."[155] Deputy Efkalidis Efendi claimed that the massacres had been a part of the CUP's Turkification policies systematically implemented since the end of the Balkan Wars.[156]

The CUP had acted, he claimed, with the goal of reducing non-Muslim wealth by looting, and thereby enriching the Muslim population.[157] Efkalidis Efendi explained how what he called "the policy of destruction and annihilation" had been carried out. The world was made to think that the Greeks were under the influence of Greek prime minister Venizelos's propaganda and had voluntarily moved to Greece. They were forced to sign documents to this effect.[158] Efkalidis Efendi related that Talât Paşa showed him cables with statements such as "We are unhappy in Turkey. . . . We want to go to Greece. . . . Why won't you let us go?" Although a parliamentary deputy, Efkalidis himself had his property looted, and when he demanded that it be returned he was told to appeal to a regional commission and seek redress there.[159]

In the parliamentary session on 12 December, Armenian deputy Nalbantyan Efendi drew the chamber's attention to the parallels between this "cleansing" operation and the Armenian genocide, and reminded the assembly that "Turks may well be opposed to the oppression and actions repeatedly carried out, but the injustices were done in their name." He too claimed that the acts were the result of systematic policies in place since 1913, and were done to "achieve Turkish domination." The issue was thus the collective responsibility of all Turks.[160]

Dimistoklis Efkalidis Efendi's speeches were repeatedly interrupted by Turkish deputies shouting, "That's how it was done in Bulgaria and Greece!" The Turks had also faced oppression, they claimed. Some Turkish deputies said, "We learned about deportation from our neighbors. We didn't do it ourselves."[161] The Greek deputies were accused of acting as "defense counsel for the Greek Government."[162] The Turks in parliament were referring to expulsions, often on a religious basis, that had occured in the Balkan states against the Muslim population. There is abundant information in the consular reports regarding the mutual "ethnic cleansing" policies in the Balkans.[163] As a result of the "massacres and forced expulsions," hundreds of thousands of Muslims were compelled to migrate or flee to Anatolia. Historian Arnold Toynbee gives the figure of 413,992 Muslims expelled during the course of the Balkan Wars.[164] Almost the same number is given in Turkish sources.[165]

PART 2

THE DECISION FOR GENOCIDE AND
SUBSEQUENT DEVELOPMENTS

CHAPTER 4

WHAT LED TO THE DECISION FOR GENOCIDE?

THE 1914 GREEK DEPORTATIONS AND MASSACRES WERE A PRECURSOR of what was to come. Unionist leaders were encouraged by their success at forcing the migration of the Greek population. According to Henry Morgenthau, "Bedri Bey, the Prefect of Police at Constantinople, himself told one of my secretaries that the Turks had expelled the Greeks so successfully that they had decided to apply the same method toward all the other races in the empire."[1] The question remains, however, as to why the measures against the Armenians took a genocidal form compared to Greek massacres and expulsions.

It is widely acknowledged that war creates a favorable climate for genocide. At the time of the Greek expulsions the war had not yet begun and the Ottoman government, which did not want to damage or sever its relations with the European powers, behaved extremely cautiously. It was forced to be conservative in the implementation of its policies against the Greeks and also distanced itself from them. When the Greek patriarch complained, the authorities depicted the events as the actions "of certain compatriots, as a result of personal anger."[2]

With the outbreak of war all foreign pressure was lifted. Under such conditions, plans for the Turkification of Anatolia could proceed apace and without any major hindrances. Historian Ahmet Refik, who served long years as an Ottoman army officer, wrote in 1919 that the annihilation of the Armenians had become one of the national objectives of the Unionists. They planned, by means of the annihilation policy, to avoid carrying out reforms in the six eastern provinces, and to solve the Armenian "problem" at its root.[3]

The prevailing opinion in Turkey today is that the Ottoman government did not voluntarily enter the war but was forced to enter it on Germany's side, unable to resist the pressure of the Great Powers. This is not correct. The evidence shows that the Unionists devoted a great deal of effort toward entering the war. After the defeat, an interrogatory committee was established by the Ottoman government to investigate the actions of the wartime cabinet, among them the Ottoman entrance into the war. Some members of that cabinet confirmed, in the testimony they gave to the Fifth Department of the Ottoman parliament and in the trials of the former Unionist leaders in the Istanbul extraordinary court-martial in 1919, that efforts were made to join the war. The CUP made a conscious decision to join the war as a way to solve its pressing problems.

By entering the war, the Ottomans expected to benefit in three ways.[4] It would mean an end to the international agreements that had brought the empire to the point of collapse, including the hated Capitulations and the reform agreement for the Armenian provinces. The war would also serve Pan-Turanist and Pan-Islamic objectives, and provide an opportunity to regain lost territories, especially in the Balkans, and seek revenge in the Christian communities.[5]

Grand Vizier Said Halim Paşa, in a remorseful remark after the war had begun, said, "Come, let us abandon the conquest of Turan and Egypt, our hopes for Tripoli, Tunisia and Algeria. . . ."[6] This well-intentioned call came way too late, since the Unionists had seen an opportunity to stem the collapse of the crumbling empire and expand to establish a new union with more reliable fellow Turks. Ottoman public opinion agreed that "the war was an immense opportunity for Turkdom and for Islam. . . ."[7]

As early as 1910, the Unionists had begun organizing Muslim and Turkish communities in regions outside the empire. In the wake of the Balkan Wars these efforts acquired the character of government policy. British consuls reported on agents sent to Central Asia and their activities in detail: "Even at that time, Enver imagined a union of all Turkic peoples from Edirne to the Chinese oases along the Silk Trade Road. He allegedly was unconcerned about Greece and Serbia having achieved their independence, so long as a substitute empire, with its capital in Samarkand, the historic Turkic center, could be set up."[8] As soon as the Balkan Wars were over, Enver Paşa established concrete ties with the Turks of Central Asia. This region became one of the most important fields of activity for the Special Organization.

The Ottoman aim in the war was, in part, to rescue Muslims from Russian rule, which fully complemented the Germans' overall war strategy. A note written by Kaiser Wilhelm II on a cable from his ambassador in St. Petersburg expressed this lucidly: "Our consuls in Turkey and India, our people must incite the entire Islamic world to a savage revolt against this . . . cursed, perfidious, conscience-less nation [Russia]. . . ."[9]

The German General Staff was put in command of the Turkish armies, under Defense Minister Enver Paşa, at the outbreak of war. The objective was to reach the Muslims of north Africa and India, and to unite with the Turks of Central Asia. On 11 November 1914, the day the Ottoman Empire officially entered the war, the CUP made the following declaration in a memorandum sent to all of its branches: "The ideal of our nation and our people leads us toward the destruction of our Muscovite enemy, in order to obtain thereby a natural frontier for our Empire, which should include and unite all branches of our race."[10] Enver, who departed Istanbul on 6 December 1914 to lead the military campaign to take Kars, said that "he was going to India, via Afghanistan."[11] Ali Fuat Erden, a staff officer of Colonel von Frankenberg, the head of the General Staff of the Ottoman Second Army, later recalled:

> In the great room in which the army general staff was present I found its head (von Frankenberg) along with officers from the Turkish General Staff leaning over an atlas, engaged in determining the details of the borders that the Ottoman State would acquire as a result of the general war. . . . This border would pass through the Caucasus in the north, through the Volga river region, and fully include Egypt. The present discussion concerned the Crimea and Turkistan.[12]

The Armenians formed a major territorial obstacle to the realization of this goal. "The strong-handed exile of the Armenians may be
partly seen as motivated by the wish to eliminate a barrier between
Turkey and several Turkic groups in Russia living near the frontiers."[13]
In October 1918, Enver Paşa ordered his brother Nuri, commander of
the Ottoman forces in Baku, to "cleanse" Azerbaijan of Russians and
Armenians, with the aim of attaining "territorial continuity" between
Turks.[14] Interior Minister Mustafa Reşit Paşa declared from the podium
of the Ottoman Chamber of Deputies after the defeat in 1918 that the
country had entered the war out of a desire for an illusory goal.[15]

After the war, despite their defeat, the Ottomans still believed in
uniting the Turks of Central Asia and that the Armenians were an
obstacle and should be eliminated, policies that were clearly stated at
an Istanbul meeting held by the Turkish Hearth Association on 18
February 1920.[16] The newly established government in Ankara continued this same policy after 1919. Foreign Minister Ahmet Muhtar
said on 8 November 1920 that the Entente nations had given Armenia
the task of "cutting our lines of communication with the East. . . . It is
of the utmost necessity that Armenia, which is situated in the middle
of a large Islamic region, be politically and materially eliminated."[17]

The "desire not to forget" lost territories, and feelings of revenge
were among the most important reasons for the Ottomans' entry into
World War I. In the words of historian M. Cemil Bilsel:

> I suppose that, among all of the reasons for the Ottoman Empire's
> entry into the World War, there were two factors that were most
> influential. One of these was psychological, mental . . . it derived
> largely from the Balkan disaster. . . . On the day that war broke out,
> every Turk whose heart burned with the bitterness of the Balkan
> disaster and the fire of revenge sensed that the opportunity had
> come to redeem his sullied honor . . . and every Turk knew he had
> been brought to this point by the policies Europe had for the last
> two centuries followed against his country, and longed to settle
> accounts.[18]

Taking back land that had been lost as a result of Europe's "crusade" was a question of honor. In a letter to his wife from 8 May 1913,
Enver Paşa summed up this feeling:

Everywhere there are signs of the wretchedness brought by the most recent Crusade. If I could tell you of the savagery the enemy has inflicted, . . . a stone's throw from Istanbul, you would understand the things that enter the heads of poor Muslims far away. But our anger is strengthening: revenge, revenge, revenge; there is no other word.[19]

The powerful effect of territorial losses is evident in Halil Menteşe's opening address to parliament in 1914:

Other nations do not forget parts of their homeland that they have lost through war; they keep the [memory] alive for coming generations. The reasons for the disaster live on with them. . . . From this exalted seat, I call on my nation: Let it not forget! Do not forget beloved Salonica, the cradle of the flame of Liberty and Constitutional Government, not to forget green Monastir (Bitolj), Kosovo, İşkodra (Scutari), Yanya (Jannina) and all of beautiful Rumelia.

The chamber responded with cries of "We shall not forget!"[20]

Among Unionist leaders, the goal of retrieving lost territory became an idée fixe. Hüsamettin Ertürk recalled a speech by Enver Paşa:

How could a person forget the plains, the meadows, watered with the blood of our forefathers; abandon those places where Turkish raiders had hidden their steeds for a full four hundred years, with our mosques, our tombs, our dervish retreats, our bridges and our castles, to leave them to our slaves, to be driven out of Rumelia to Anatolia: this was beyond a person's endurance. I am prepared to gladly sacrifice the remaining years of my life to take revenge on the Bulgarians, the Greeks and the Montenegrans.[21]

Ertürk goes on to say that Enver became increasingly excited when speaking about the subject, that his face would become red and overheated, that his eyes flashed like lightning.

This yearning for vengeance is also found in Unionist correspondence. Hilmi, the CUP inspector for Erzurum and Van provinces, writes in a 1914 letter to a Kurdish agha that "we Unionists are proud to rescue the mosques, madrasas and Muslims of Edirne. If we succeed in this election, we shall, God willing, not give up hope of returning to Rumelia. We are about to begin, God willing, to settle accounts with those Greek dogs."[22] Poems about the lost territories appeared in the press, with lines like "Alas, alas" and "Thou art not satisfied" and titles like "Rancor": "Oh, my father, who rests peacefully in his grave and who earned a name / now the name of his children is Joyous Revenge."[23]

In particular, it was the pain of the Balkan defeat that could not be forgotten. Again, M. Cemil Bilsel:

> The people of the Balkans turned Rumelia into a slaughterhouse of Turks. . . . The Turks have not forgotten this bitterness. By retelling the story to students at school, to children at home, to soldiers in the barracks, Turks have awoken a national spirit, a national grudge. They have infected people with a spirit that longs one day to settle accounts for the humiliation and oppression suffered by Turkdom. In maps Rumelia now appears in [mourning] black. The entire army is urged to avenge its besmirched honor. Soldiers went to training every day singing the song "In 1328 [1912] Turkish honor was sullied, alas. Alas, alas, alas, revenge!" Soldiers returning to their villages would sow more seeds by singing this song.[24]

Even children were imbued with a desire for revenge.

> It was that desperately feverish year in which the Balkan War came to an end. We children were immersed in the bitterness of a defeat which we could accept no more than the adults, who had learned to bow their heads with their gaze averted. Every song spoke of strange vengeance marches.[25]

With the outbreak of war, "the day had come when we would have our revenge on unjust and oppressive Europe."[26] At its session on 21 December 1914, the Ottoman Chamber of Deputies decided to send an encouraging message to the army:

> That day of revenge, which has been awaited for centuries by the nation's young and old, by its martyrs and by its living, has finally arrived. You find yourself facing the Muscovites and their allies, the British and the French, the greatest enemies of the Ottoman Empire

and of Islam. . . . Take revenge for the homes they have set ablaze, for the wounds they have inflicted, for the martyrs they have trampled underfoot.[27]

Even before the Ottomans officially entered the war, Special Organization units were organizing campaigns in Russia. In August and September 1914, declarations were prepared for distribution to the people of the region:

If we have not yet taken advantage of the disaster befallen Russia, when shall we? . . . Oh, people of faith, our dawn is breaking. . . . From the graves of our martyrs, wrapped in their bloody shrouds, we shall hear them shouting "revenge, revenge, revenge."[28]

With the outbreak of the war, Unionist journalist Hüseyin Cahit Yalçın wrote an article, "The Awaited Day," in which he stated that the war "had come like a stroke of good fortune upon the Turkish people, who had been sure of their own decline."[29] "The day had finally come," Cahit asserted, when ". . . the Turks would make an historical accounting with those . . . whom they had been previously unable to do so." The Turks would extract "revenge, the horrors of which had not yet been recorded in history."[30] Ziya Gökalp composed bloodthirsty poems: "Run, take the standard and let it be planted once again in Plevna / Night and day, let the waters of the Danube run red with blood. . . ."[31] And the one who would realize these dreams, the one who would bear the good news that "The Turks have been saved!" was Enver Paşa.[32] In his memoirs, Galip Kemal Söylemezoğlu, a diplomat under both the Ottoman Empire and the Turkish Republic, claimed:

A number of crimes were perpetrated during the war. . . . These crimes occurred for a number of reasons. . . . I only remember that 350,000 Muslims were murdered during the Balkan War. . . . It must not be forgotten that the world war was a struggle for our state's very existence, and that those who committed the atrocities were partially subject to feelings of revenge.[33]

It was this kind of feeling that was used to justify the killing of Armenians.

* * *

The other important factor in the Ottoman entry into the war was the desire to eliminate its responsibilities under the Capitulations and other international agreements. Cemal Paşa summed up this desire:

> Our sole aim was, by virtue of this war, to rid ourselves of the lot of them, however many international decisions there were. Each one represented a blow to our . . . independence. . . . And, just as it was our dearly held goal to lift the Capitulations and the Mt. Lebanon concessions, we also desired to destroy the signed understanding concerning the reforms in Eastern Anatolia. . . .[34]

These reforms, affecting the Armenian provinces, were the most threatening of all, seen as they were as the path to partition. On 1 August 1913, German ambassador Wangenheim sent a cable stating that "Russia desires an autonomous Armenia . . . [but] autonomy is to be thought of as one step on the path that [ultimately] leads to Istanbul."[35] In a letter written to British prime minister David Lloyd George after the war, Halil Menteşe confirmed this view:

> [Russia] . . . succeeded in acquiring England's collaboration for imposing the draft of the Armenian reform plan. Had this policy been implemented, Eastern Anatolia would have been snatched away from Turkey. If Russia had not met with German resistance, Turkey would have been partitioned in 1912.[36]

This was a recurring theme throughout 1914 to 1916, particularly invoked to explain the Ottoman government's decision to enter the war. In a 1916 party congress, Grand Vizier Said Halim Paşa expressed concern that the level of interference by the Entente Powers and the danger of the partition had become critical.[37] Thus the connection between Russian pressure to implement the Armenian reform plan and Turkey's entry into the war on the side of the Germans was not coincidental. In the words of historian Kurt Ziemke,

> The danger posed to the unity of the Turkish Empire by the Armenian reforms was correctly assessed in Istanbul. The entry into the World War coincided with the abrogation of the reform agreement.

The desire to free themselves of this fetter played an important role in determining the Turks' decision to join the war on the side of the Germans.[38]

Immediately before the war, the Ottomans had tried to rid themselves of the various reform plans. The Dutch inspector-general appointed to oversee the reform plan in September was delayed in beginning his duties "due to the critical situation in which the world then found itself" and was sent back to his country.[39] A second inspector-general, from Norway, met with similar obstacles. Ultimately, his position was terminated and at the beginning of February 1915, he was given six months' salary as compensation.[40]

Abrogation of the Armenian reform agreement was one of the first orders of business of the Ottoman entry into the war. Signed in Yeniköy on 8 February 1914, it was declared invalid on 16 December 1914,[41] abrogated together with other treaties and agreements that had bound the Ottoman state to Europe. Thus the Ottoman government had rid itself of all international legal commitments and removed the legal basis for foreign intervention in its internal affairs.

Prior to the war, when the Armenian reform plan had been high on the international diplomatic agenda, Unionists had repeatedly asked the Armenian revolutionary organizations to cease their appeals to foreign powers. They demanded that the reform issue remain a domestic matter. Their demands were rejected by the Armenian organizations, which was perceived by the Unionists as advantage taken of Turkish weakness. According to Halil Menteşe,

> Along with Interior Minister Talât Bey, I was involved in numerous discussions at this time with the leaders of the Dashnaksoutiun [Armenian Revolutionary Federation] to bring the Armenians back from their dangerous path. . . . We said to them: "This measure is a Russian trap; let neither yourself or ourselves fall into it. . . . Come, leave it, let us implement these reforms through collaboration." But it was impossible to convince these dream-chasers.[42]

The Unionists leaders never forgave the Armenians. This perceived treachery and the looming reform package seriously worsened the position of Ottoman Armenians. There are countless reports of

Unionists who perceived the Armenian attitude as enormous "ingratitude." On 12 May 1915, when the Armenian deputy Vartkes came to see Talât Paşa, he was told, "When we were weak . . . you kicked us and demanded the Armenian reforms." And Talât said he would do the same in return. Vartkes then asked Talât, "Then will you continue the work of Abdul Hamid?," referring to the massacres of 1894–96. Talât's answer was short. "Yes."[43] After the war, when he was detained in Malta, Halil Menteşe wrote to British foreign secretary Lord Curzon:

> The Armenians imitated the Balkan countries, but they did not bear in mind the geographic differences. God had settled two or three million Armenians in the midst of thirty million Turks and Kurds. . . . This being the case, they entered into a war against nature. They attempted, through destructive methods, to achieve the rule of the minority over the majority. And they suffered the consequences of their failure.[44]

. Joseph Pomiankowski, military attaché in the Austrian Embassy in Istanbul between 1909 and 1919, made an incisive observation:

> A great number of Turkish intellectuals have sincerely expressed the sentiment that the reason for the Ottoman Empire's loss in recent years—and more generally, over the last two centuries—of [many of] its provinces in Europe and Asia lies first and foremost in the excessively humanistic behavior of the previous sultans. What should have been done was either the forcible conversion to Islam of the population in the provinces . . . or their utter and total extirpation.[45]

According to Pomiankowski, the Young Turk government used the war as an opportunity to undo the mistakes of previous sultans.

Many foreign observers made similar observations. Ambassador Morgenthau, who had the opportunity to meet frequently with the Young Turk leaders, related the following:

> The conditions of the war gave to the Turkish Government its longed-for opportunity to lay hold of the Armenians. . . . They criticized their ancestors for neglecting to destroy or convert the Chris-

tian races to Mohammedanism at the time when they first subjugated them. . . . They thought the time opportune to make good the oversight of their ancestors in the 15th century.[46]

Lewis Heck, American high commissioner in Istanbul, concurred. "The Young Turk Government has exploited the opportunity provided to them by the wartime conditions in order to attempt to eliminate the Armenian population of Asia Minor, and to thereby finally relieve themselves of the 'Armenian problem.'"[47]

Dozens of eyewitness accounts, which confirm this view, are found in the reports of the German consulates in Turkey. The German vice-consul in Erzurum, Max Erwin von Scheubner-Richter, writes in a report dated 28 July 1915 that the Unionists

frankly admit that the ultimate objective of the actions against the Armenians is complete annihilation. The utterance "After the war, not a single Armenian shall remain in Turkey" belongs, word for word, to one of the prominent [Unionist] individuals.[48]

The German consul in Aleppo, Walter Rössler, who personally witnessed the expulsions and massacres, wrote in a report dated 27 July 1915, that the only possible explanation for the events was that the Unionists' aim was undoubtedly to exploit the possibilities afforded by the war to solve the Armenian problem in decisive fashion, by leaving as few as possible alive.[49] In June 1915, Talât Paşa said to the German consular functionary, Dr. Mordtmann, that it was "clear that the deportation of the Armenians was not merely being carried out with an eye toward military considerations." Wangenheim's assessment was that "the Porte wished to use the World War in order to fundamentally get rid of the internal enemies—local Christians—without being disturbed by the diplomatic intervention of foreign countries."[50]

After Wangenheim's death, the new German ambassador, Count Wolff-Metternich, tried to intervene on behalf of the Armenians. Talât Paşa sent a request to Berlin to recall him. In his memo, Talât claimed that the war had given the Turks a great opportunity to solve the Armenian problem, and added that "the work that is to be done must be done *now;* after the war it will be too late."[51]

Pallavicini, the Austrian ambassador to the Porte, recounts that Halil Menteşe "openly stated and admitted that his fellow ministers [Talât, Enver, and others] aimed to solve the Armenian problem through their own methods during the war, and to present the Great Powers with a *fait accompli*."[52] The opportunity to eliminate the Armenians under the cover of wartime was viewed by Unionist leaders as something that would bring great political relief. In the words of German Turkophile Ernst Jäckh: "Talât clearly saw the annihilation of the Armenian people as easing the political situation."[53]

Indeed, the Ottoman entry into the war and the subsequent Armenian genocide succeeded in foiling plans for the partition of Anatolia since few Armenians remained in the eastern provinces.[54] As a result of the Armenian genocide, the conditions necessary for a Turkish state in Anatolia had been created. Halil Menteşe: "Had we not cleansed our Eastern Provinces of Armenian revolutionaries collaborating with the Russians, there would have been no possibility of establishing our national state."[55]

A postwar commission of inquiry that heard the testimony of CUP ministers clearly established that Unionist leaders had gone to lengths to enter the war on the side of the Germans. Systematic preparations were made. Unionist finance minister Mehmet Cavid Bey, who had been opposed to the war, noted:

> Everything possible was done at the time to act in a way that would violate our neutrality toward the Entente countries. . . . German soldiers and officers continued to arrive in Istanbul, in civilian dress, by way of Rumania and Bulgaria.[56]

These preparations were not limited to the importation of a few German troops or warships. Incursions by armed gangs had been organized to goad the Russians into the war as part of the German General Staff's plan to "incite Muslim fanaticism" in India and Egypt, against the British, and in the Caucasus.[57] Austrian Ambassador Pallavicini confirmed that in July 1914 plans were devised with Enver Paşa for revolt against the Russians in the Caucasus and in Azerbaijan.[58] On 6 August, Enver had reported to Berlin that "revolts were about to begin in the Caucasus and in Azerbaijan," and that "transport of weapons and supplies were needed to strengthen revolts in Egypt, Libya, Tunis, Iran, Afghanistan and India." Two weeks later he demanded that "the transport of German weapons be speeded up."[59]

Çürüksulu Mahmud Paşa, former Ottoman public works minister, gave the following account of the activities consciously intended to provoke a war with Russia:

> Recourse was made to a number of means that were contrary to neutrality. . . . And a great many preparations and incitements were planned and carried out—particularly on the borders of Syria and Anatolia—that shows that [they] were in favor of the war.[60]

He also revealed that the Special Organization coordinated attacks and massacres inside Russia by provoking Kurdish villagers. And according to him, Enver and Talât hoped that Russia would declare war.[61]

Indeed, during the Istanbul extraordinary court-martial established after the war, defendants also testified that the Special Organization's gangs had been sent on assault missions inside Russia with the goal of provoking war. When the judge attempted to establish the veracity of reports that "these units adopted certain plans even before the war to unite with the Islamic peoples residing there," defendant Atıf, a leader in the Special Organization, replied that "these reports are correct."[62] On 14 April 1919, at the eleventh session of the trial, concerning deportations and massacres in the Trabzon region, defendant Yusuf Rıza Bey testified that he had gone into Russia with a group to carry out military actions. The judge then asked whether war had been declared at the time, to which Rıza replied in the negative, adding that he was already inside Russia when war was declared.[63] The attacks against Russia were frequent enough that at the beginning of October, "a real war had indeed begun on the Ottoman border."[64] In a cable sent at the beginning of December, German ambassador Wangenheim put the number of people in revolt in the Caucasus at fifty thousand.[65]

According to the memoirs of party secretary Arif Cemil, attacks on Russia had already begun by the end of August. By the beginning of September, "coded telegrams sent to the [Special Organization] Erzurum headquarters from various local branches reported that the skills and abilities of the armed gangs were being tested and sent into Russia. . . ."[66] Cemil stated that "the entire front was already under the clear command of Yusuf Rıza Bey."[67] Cavid Bey characterized the mood within Unionist circles before the war: ". . . being opposed to the war was interpreted as a crime and as betrayal of the homeland."[68]

But the historic opportunity to resurrect the great empire was eventually revealed as illusory. Fear of total collapse replaced dreams of former glory. At the time of the forced deportation of the Greeks, Ottoman leaders continued to believe in their state (and with it, their rule); they were operating under the conviction that they could emerge from their desperate situation. But by the time of the decision for the Armenian genocide they had lost all such illusions, being in the grip of the profound realization that all they had worked for was coming to an end. If past deportations had been a matter of Turkification they were now, according to the well-known intellectual Doğan Avcıoğlu, tied to the issue of "continuing or not to exist as a state."[69] This change had a direct effect on the ultimate decision to annihilate the Armenians.

Until the nineteenth century, the Ottomans had traditionally disdained the West, to the point where "learning a foreign (i.e., European) language was something of a humiliation."[70] Even the Ottomans' numerous defeats in the seventeenth and especially eighteenth centuries failed to change this attitude. But then, over time, the Ottomans' sense of elevation turned painfully into inferiority. But memory of the "great and glorious past" was too recent to erase, making the Empire's "humiliation" and "debasement" that much harder to accept. The Ottomans were crushed under the weight of the empire's former glory.

One consequence was increased longing for the "golden age," and the desire to recapture it was transformed into a "sacred" goal. The Pan-Turanist ideal was a product of this longing. A second response to being the West's "whipping boy" was a loss of security and sense of worth, accompanied by strong feelings of humiliation and a desire for revenge.[71] In the words of Bernard Lewis,

> military defeat and political humiliation had indeed shaken the tor-
> pid and complacent trust of the Turks in their own invincible and
> immutable superiority, but the ancient contempt for the barbarian

infidel, where it yielded, often gave place to rancour rather than emulation.[72]

The war was, simply, "the last chance for the CUP and for the empire."[73] By playing it right, the Turks could reverse their ill-fortune and put a stop to their empire's decline.

But the series of military defeats experienced in the first months of the war ended all dreams of renewed glory, bringing, instead, a certain moral collapse. The disaster at Sarıkamış in January 1915, where between 60,000 and 90,000 Turkish soldiers died, mostly from the cold, represented a turning point that "brought the Unionists . . . face to face with great disillusionment. . . . The defeat extinguished their Turanist and Islamist dreams."[74] Like the Nazis in World War II, the Ottomans felt that "the defeat was due to a treacherous deception, to a conspiracy of murderous criminals, to our fighting units being stabbed in the back by the traitors among us."[75] In numerous Turkish writings, it was the Armenians who filled this traitorous role, which was continuously explained through leaflets and reports distributed by a Ministry of War department. According to Ahmet Refik, a young officer attached to the military and later a historian,

> In Istanbul, the propaganda work necessary to justify an enormous crime was fully prepared: the Armenians had united with the enemy, revolution was about to break out in Istanbul, they were going to kill the Unionist leaders, they were going to force open the [Bosphorus and Dardanelles] Straits.[76]

Anti-Armenian agitation was coordinated by the War Ministry's "Second Department," the Department of Intelligence. Numerous articles on the subject appeared in the ministry's weekly *Harb Mecmuası*, published by Colonel Seyfi [later Düzgören].[77] After the 1918 armistice, the daily *Sabah* reported that, as the officer responsible for the political department in Ottoman military headquarters, in collaboration with the Special Organization and in close coordination with Unionist Bahaettin Şakir, he had been among those who had devised the plan for the murder of the Armenians.[78]

The defeat at Sarıkamış was followed by others, and the enemy forces were pressing on with their campaign at Gallipoli. The end of the empire seemed at hand. Almost everyone believed that the capture of Istanbul was only a question of time. At the main trial of Unionist leaders after the war, Cevat testified that "it wasn't known what sort of condition Istanbul would be in eight hours hence."[79] The battle of Gallipoli lasted for 259 days and was a complete "inferno,"[80] a "ritual of fire and death."[81] Every one of those days was a back-and-forth struggle between death and resurrection. The fall of Istanbul and the loss of Anatolia, the last refuge of the Turks, seemed imminent. This drama, enacted over and over in the past two hundred years, was being staged yet again, but this time it was far worse, and with even worse results. With this defeat, the last territory left to the Turks would be handed over to the Armenians and this would be more devastating than the losses at Rumelia or Macedonia. Anatolia itself would be lost.[82]

As a British functionary had perceptively commented:

> If the Great Powers . . . attempt to force [the Ottomans] to accept autonomy for Armenia, those who are today found in power in Istanbul shall not bow their heads and submit, but shall set all of the provinces ablaze. If the Russian draft [for reforms] is accepted, it shall open the way to massacres in the entire country.[83]

It was not a coincidence that the Armenian genocide took place soon after the Sarıkamış disaster and was contemporaneous with the empire's struggle at Gallipoli. As a rule, the acceleration of the process of a country's decline and partition helps to strengthen a sense of desperation and "fighting with one's back to the wall." As the situation becomes increasingly hopeless, those who have failed to prevent the collapse become more hostile and aggressive. When the crisis deepens, they resort to increasingly barbaric means, and come to believe "that only an absolute lack of mercy would allow one to avoid this loss of power and honor."[84] A nation that feels itself on the verge of destruction will not hesitate to destroy another group it holds responsible for its situation.

A prediction made by German ambassador Wangenheim is worth mentioning. With the outbreak of the war in August 1914, Henry Morgenthau warned him that the Turks would massacre the Armenians in Anatolia, to which Wangenheim replied, "So long as England does not attack Çanakkale or some other Turkish port there is nothing to fear. Otherwise, nothing can be guaranteed."[85] However, this is precisely what happened.

In addition to the broad Unionist plans for Turkification, a detailed military plan had also been prepared on how to proceed in case of a military defeat. Şeref Çavuşoğlu, a young officer who participated in secret meetings in Istanbul, writes in his memoirs:

> The Central Committee had, after examining every possibility, decided that in the event of our defeat, weapons would not be put down and, withdrawing to Anatolia, the Turks would continue their struggle by degrees, and a plan had even been prepared.[86]

The plan generated much discussion and correspondence between various military commanders over such issues as where to place the army's headquarters.[87] And this documentation provides some important clues as to the immediate background to the Armenian genocide. The Turkification of Anatolia was not the only objective; Unionists had also planned for a drawn-out war of resistance in Anatolia. Another account relates that in November 1918, Ahmet Şükrü Bey, a prominent Unionist serving as minister of education, said: "The government has previously thought about this angle and already taken measures. Weapons, ammunition and organization: all is ready for the struggle in the mountains as well as armed militias. We will hold out for 50 years!"[88] Memoirs of the period do not provide any information about when the plans for this resistance were drawn up. However, from the account given by Kuşçubaşı Eşref, we can assume that they were at least initially considered in a series of meetings between May and August 1914.

Was this plan implemented? We know that it became increasingly probable after the defeat at Sarıkamış, and in March 1915, during the attack on the Dardanelles, when "for the first time the plan appeared necessary and . . . those who had been entrusted with duties [now] went into action."[89] Instructions were sent to officers regarding establishing local defense organizations in various regions and stockpiling weapons. Çavuşoğlu had been enlisted in preparing for long-term resistance. His specific task was to organize resistance movements in the Bursa and Bilecik regions. The plan called for transferring the central government from Istanbul to inner Anatolia, to Eskişehir or Konya, along with a portion of the Treasury and archives.[90] Foreign embassies were informed that the necessary preparations were being made for their transfer.[91] At the Istanbul court-martial after the war, Cevat Bey testified that preparations were being made to move the entire government.[92]

Çavuşoğlu provided the names of officers entrusted with implementing the plan in Anatolia, and they were well-known members of the Special Organization, which organized the Armenian genocide. But there is no document that shows a clear connection between the long-term resistance plan in Anatolia and the Armenian genocide. But it is certain that the decisions to enact the two events were made during the same period and their simultaneous start is significant. Thus, the strong possibility exists that these leaders thought a war of resistance in Anatolia would be easier with the elimination of the Armenian population, or at least a reduction of its numbers. In this light, the decision to carry out a forced migration of the Armenians from western and central Anatolia becomes more comprehensible.

From a number of the memoirs of the period, we can see that a mood of complete panic reigned in Istanbul during the Gallipoli campaign. Meetings were held on the topic of the resistance, with participants asking how the Turks would be able to defend themselves against the Armenians, who would revolt the moment the enemy entered Istanbul. Talât Paşa (then Bey) was a participant in these meetings, where there were discussions about who would remain in Istanbul and who would depart for Anatolia, and about what form the resistance would take.[93]

When defeat seemed inevitable, the Armenian presence in Anatolia posed the greatest obstacle to plans for resistance, which for the Unionists ultimately led to the idea of mass deportations. Journalist Ahmet Emin Yalman claims that "for certain influential Turkish politicians, [deportations] meant the extermination of the Armenian minority in Turkey with the idea of bringing about racial homogeneity in Asia Minor."[94]

The Unionist leaders knew the implications of their actions, and they were prepared to be condemned. Yalman wrote:

Dr. Bahaettin Şakir, a member of the CUP Central Committee and a leader of the Special Organization, thought thus: "It was clearly understood that the continued existence of the Armenians living around [and along] the border with Russia represented a great threat to the country's future. It was necessary for the nation's well-being to do whatever was possible to remove this danger. To take such a route would perhaps mean to act contrary to the laws of nations and of humanity. I am ready to pay the price for this with my own life. Whether I achieve the goal or not, there will be many who will castigate me. This I know, but there will also be those who in the distant future will understand that I sacrificed myself in the name of serving my country."[95]

Bahaettin Şakir's letters contain similar explanations. These are included among the documents published by Aram Andonian. For instance, in a letter of 25 March 1915 to Cemal Bey, the Unionists' special representative in Adana, he writes:

the Committee is ever ready to rescue the homeland from the blemish of this accursed nation [i.e., the Armenians]. It has been decided to wash our hands of the responsibility for this stain that has been smeared across Ottoman history.[96]

Even with hindsight, members of the postwar Turkish nationalist parliament praised those responsible for the genocide:

You are aware that the deportation matter was an event that has caused uproar in the world and all of us to be thought of as murderers. We knew even before it was carried out that the Christian world would not stand for it and they would direct their wrath and fury at us. But why should we call ourselves murderers? Why have we taken on this vast and difficult matter? These things were done to secure the future of our homeland, which we know is greater and holier than even our own lives.[97]

The official date given for the beginning of the Armenian genocide is 24 April 1915, but it is largely symbolic. On that date, some 235 leading members of the Armenian community in Istanbul were arrested on the pretext of an Armenian revolt in Van.[98] This was followed by the arrest of 600 more people. On 24 May, the Ottoman government announced that all together, some 2,345 people had been arrested in Istanbul.[99] In many of the empire's provinces, the arrests had begun as early as 19 April.[100] Johannes Lepsius reports that "three days before the arrests of the Armenian intellectuals in Istanbul, Armenian notables had begun to be arrested in many cities. These arrests continued in systematic fashion over the course of three weeks, from April 21 to May 19."[101] There were some who died from torture while in custody.[102] A large portion of those arrested were executed in public places to intimidate the Armenians. Between May and August 1915, the Armenian population of the eastern provinces was deported and murdered en masse. This was followed by deportations from western Anatolia and Thrace. By the beginning of 1917, the Armenian problem had been thoroughly "resolved."

Anti-Armenian measures had already begun with the declaration of general mobilization on August 2. At the same meeting at which the mobilization was confirmed, the CUP Central Committee issued orders regarding the formation of Special Organization units in eastern Anatolia.

> On the evening of the day in which the general mobilization was announced (August 2) an important meeting was convened at the CUP's Central Committee, at which a comprehensive decision was taken to be implemented in the very near future. This decision aimed at the creation of a "Special Organization" that would facilitate our army's actions on enemy soil, whether we entered the world war or not. On the outbreak of the war, the irregular groups, which were to be armed through the Special Organization, would carry out raids against enemy territory.[103]

During the postwar trials of former Unionist leaders, the defendants testified that the decision to reform the Special Organization was made at this August 2 meeting.[104] These units would be active primarily in eastern Anatolia, where they would operate with the intention of contributing to "Islamic unity and Turkish nationalism, which related to uniting Turks outside of Turkey."[105] As we know, this plan involved provoking revolts in Egypt, the Caucasus, Iran and India against the English and the Russians.[106] Domestically, as a cable sent by Hilmi, the Unionist inspector for Erzurum, to Bahaettin Şakir testifies: "there are individuals inside the country to be eliminated. We are pursuing this perspective."[107] The "individuals" were the Armenians.

An executive commission for the reorganized Special Organization, with representatives from the Ministry of the Interior, the Ministry of War and the CUP Central Committee, was established within the Ministry of War. During the postwar trials, Atıf Bey testified that "the Ministry [of War] granted the authority, and we corresponded with the provisions department, with the [Committee for] National Defense, the Committee of Union and Progress and all of the ministries and national institutions."[108] Coordination between the various government ministries, the CUP Central Committee and various provincial branches was delegated to this commission. Ministry of the Interior code was even used in this commission's correspondence between Istanbul and the party and Special Organization functionaries in the provinces. At the trial, the judge asked why an institution connected to the Ministry of War would use the code of the Interior Ministry for its correspondence, but he did not receive a satisfactory explanation.[109]

The main task of this executive commission was to build Special Organization units for operations in Russia and Iran. We can find extremely detailed information regarding its intensive coordination efforts in documents and testimony from the Istanbul trials. Numerous telegrams and letters were read during the trial pertaining to correspondence between local governmental leaders and local party branches on the one hand, and the CUP Central Committee in Istanbul and the Special Organization on the other.[110]

Bahaettin Şakir was entrusted with the task of the practical organization of the armed gangs in the region. He was also sent to the northern Caucasus, while "Ömer Naci Bey and Ruşeni Bey traveled to Iran . . . [and] Rauf Bey and Ubeydullah Efendi to Afghanistan."[111] Additionally, the CUP's responsible secretaries traveled to the region, but this was kept under the strictest secrecy.[112]

At the Istanbul trial, Atıf claimed:

We sent individuals into Russia who were patriotic and knowledge-
able about local conditions. By means of these people we created an
organization that targeted the innocent Muslim population of the
area . . . and that would ensure assistance to us in the event that our
army advanced to those regions.[113]

As we have seen, not only did this activity begin before the outbreak of war, but it was intended to draw the empire into war. On 19
August 1914, Enver Paşa reported to Berlin that "the transformation
of the Islamic world into one of revolution, as His Majesty has
desired, had been in preparation for some time and had now been put
into action."[114] The Austrian consul in Trabzon wrote in a report
dated 2 September 1914 that one hundred fighters had entered Russia
to start a rebellion.[115] From other accounts, we know that this figure
was in fact much higher.

Erzurum was chosen as the central staging area for all activities.
Accordingly, a separate Central Committee for the Special Organization was formed in Erzurum. There is in the evidence of the fifth session of the Istanbul trial, a telegram sent by Süleyman Askeri to
Bahaettin Şakir, appointing Riza Bey a member of the Central Committee of Erzurum. From another cable introduced at the same session, we understand that Şakir was the person responsible for this
Central Committee.[116] In his memoirs, General Ali İhsan Sabis
recounts that Enver had mentioned Bahaettin Şakir as "the Chief of
the Special Organization, Central Committee member Bahaettin
Şakir Bey."[117] Şakir's duty "was to investigate Russian military actions
in the Caucasus, to create an organization among the Islamic peoples
[there] and to exploit this [organization] in time of war."[118]

Due to the importance and the secrecy of these policies, it was
necessary to appoint trustworthy officials in the regions. Cemal Azmi
Bey, who became known by the moniker Sopalı Mutasarrıf (the
cudgel-wielding lieutenant governor) and who would later play a very
important part in the Armenian genocide, was appointed governor-
general of Trabzon, which had been selected as a second base of operations.[119] Tahsin Bey, who was a loyal party member, was appointed
governor at Erzurum.[120] Mahmut Kâmil Paşa, who was later a central
figure in the genocide, was appointed commander of the Third
Army.[121] Army Commander Ali İhsan Sabis claimed that Bahaettin

Şakir continually intervened in the army's internal affairs, even to the point of having officers with whom he was dissatisfied replaced.[122] In addition to Bahaettin Şakir's delegation to Erzurum, Central Committee member Kara Kemal also came to Trabzon with a second group, which included a number of German functionaries. These Germans would later be active inside Russia, particularly in liaison work with the Georgians.

The secret nature of these activities necessitated organization outside government and party channels. In August, Bahaettin Şakir and Kara Kemal established the Revolutionary Committee of the Caucasus:

"... the discussions continued for several days ... a detailed plan of action was devised and a statement of regulations written up. .... It was then distributed to the Special Organization branches and relevant individuals.[123]

According to the plan, the Eastern Front was to be divided (for the moment) into two administrative divisions, Trabzon and Erzurum. Later, Van and its environs would also be made into a separate administrative front under the direction of Ömer Naci. Due to the distance between these two regions, both were authorized to communicate separately with Istanbul. As part of the evidence introduced at the trial, there are several telegrams making it clear that Talât Paşa was responsible for coordination between the two regions. In one cable, for instance, Talât wrote to Bahaettin Şakir: "In any case, you have no more business there. ... Move on to Trabzon immediately, to take up a very important task; Yakup Cemil Bey, who will be departing from here, will bring you the necessary explanations and instructions."[124]

The irregular armed militias came under the umbrella of the Third Army, while their orders came through local administrative functionaries. In a cable sent to the office of the lieutenant governor of Erzıncan and officials of the provincial districts of Bayburt, Tercan and Kığı, for instance, it was stated that "at the suggestion of the Third Army Commander, an Islamic militia unit was formed under the leadership of Dr. Bahaettin Şakir Bey."[125] Either army officers or party branch secretaries were appointed to head these gangs.

The gangs' activity was coordinated under the direct control of Bahaettin Şakir. In September 1914, the Third Army compiled a list of secret instructions for the militias. These were distributed to the gang leaders only and local agents in charge of "creating these militia organizations."[126] Some German officers also assumed the task of organizing the gangs. For example, the gangs active in the Kars-Artvin region were under the direction of the German colonel Stange.[127]

The decision to include these armed gangs as part of the Third Army was made in Istanbul. At trial, Cevat Bey recounted that the irregular "volunteer" units sent to the region "carried out their duties within the framework of the army command." When the judge asked whether or not the Special Organization detachments were completely subject to the orders of the military commanders, Cevat replied: "Without a doubt. . . . They were included within the army cadres."[128] In fact, irregular militia units were not restricted to the Third Army. From general military correspondence sent to all army units, dated 17 Kasım 1330 (30 November 1914), we understand that militias were created in each of the armies.[129]

The formation of the Special Organization units began in the second half of August 1914. Three main sources of manpower were drawn upon for the task: Kurdish tribes, jailed convicts, and recent emigrants from the Caucasus and Rumelia. Hilmi, Unionist party inspector for the Erzurum region, was entrusted with putting these gangs together in his region. In a letter to a Kurdish tribal chieftain, he wrote:

> The time has nearly come for the matter we discussed in Erzincan. . . . I will require 50 young men from you. . . . I will prepare all manner of leisure and comfort for them here. . . . Pay no heed to the age of the men . . . , merely make sure the individuals . . . are steadfast and sufficiently resolute that they would gladly die for their country and nation. You are to depart upon receiving the first notice from us. . . . . Only ready yourself and inform Bahaettin Şakir Bey that you have done so. For now, I kiss you with the greatest respect. My brother Bahaettin Bey sends his personal greetings.[130]

Regarding the second source of manpower, the prisoners, Erzurum party secretay Hilmi wrote to Istanbul in August calling for the release of "people held in the Trabzon prison . . . to form them into irregular units under the command of [regular] officers, and especially, to promote prisoners who have a reputation leading outlaw gangs."[131] In the reply from Istanbul, "it was reported that permission would be granted to release the prisoners if it appeared necessary."[132] Talât Paşa continued that "the people imprisoned who are needed for the irregular units will be released and a list will be prepared and sent in regard to these."[133] In reality, releases had begun even before the order arrived from Istanbul. The Erzurum Central Committee made a decision to this effect at the beginning of September[134] and former justice minister İbrahim Bey testified that the prisoners' release had begun long before the law was passed. Subsequently, the Justice Ministry issued a special amnesty[135] not only for the eastern provinces, but throughout Anatolia. From a document of the trial's sixth session, we understand that a memo to this effect had been sent to the various regions on 15 September 1914.[136] This temporary law, after passing through parliament, became permanent in 1916.[137]

The third source for the gangs, immigrants, came from Anatolia and the Caucasus. In the main trial, telegrams from Musa, Unionist inspector for Balıkesir and the CUP district branch office in Bursa, testify to the fact that the CUP Central Committee had sent a "secret order" to provincial party branches on 15 October 1914 regarding the inclusion of immigrants in the armed gangs.[138] In a cable sent by the Unionist responsible secretary for Samsun, Rüştü, on 29 October 1914, we read that "it is respectfully requested that a 55-man unit of armed irregulars, the fifth such group, under the command of Artvinli Tufan Ağa, be dispatched by motorized transport."[139] A communication between the Special Organization and Mithat Şükrü, dated 13 November, also shows that orders had been sent earlier to all regions.[140]

This picture is further confirmed in some memoirs of the period. Falih Rıfkı Atay, for instance, while calling these gangs "an army of murderers," claims that it was mentioned to him that "the Central Committee had created armed gangs of civilians, and that people we knew were commanding them, and that I should go and see Dr. Nazım."[141]

Throughout the Unionist leaders' trial, the defendants gave testimony indicating that their duties were generally coordinated and organized by the Special Organization headquarters and the CUP Central Committee in Istanbul. It was the local party secretaries who were accountable for the creation of the local armed gangs.[142]

The gangs were either brought to Istanbul and trained and outfitted there, or they were moved between the provinces. The Austrian consul at Trabzon reported on 8 November 1914 that such gangs were being trained on the coastal road and in various other locations.[143] The defendant Cevat testified that there was a special office in the War Ministry concerned with equipping and training those who came to Istanbul. A letter written in the name of the Ministry of War by İsmet İnönü, who later became the second president of the Republic of Turkey, shows that all of the regional volunteer units in Macedonia, Thrace and elsewhere answered directly to the army through the War Ministry in Istanbul.[144] The claim that these gangs were actually trained in Istanbul for the purpose of carrying out the Armenian genocide is mentioned in other sources. Ahmet Refik, for example, claims that "these gangs were composed of murderers and thieves who had been released from incarceration. They received a week's worth of instruction in the courtyard of the War Ministry and were then sent to the Caucasus border through the agency of the Special Organization. During the Armenian atrocities [it was] these gangs who perpetrated the greatest crimes."[145]

By the beginning of November 1914, the work of emptying the prisons had progressed. In Trabzon, for instance, a unit of some 700 to 800 had been formed.[146] The Austrian consul in Trabzon also confirms that the irregular units formed in Rize contained convicts, and were under the leadership of German officers. According to his report, a 169-man unit created from convicts in Trabzon had been sent into the Caucasus. This group was to be followed by a 1000-man-strong Hamidiye unit made up of Kurds.[147] As for the total number of gangs and members, different estimates exist. Phillip Stoddard, who held a series of discussions with Kuşçubaşı Eşref, puts the number of people involved at about thirty thousand.[148]

In August 1914, there was a Dashnak congress in Erzurum to which, standard sources concur, the CUP sent a special delegation. The CUP offered to grant autonomy to the Dashnaks in exchange for fomenting a rebellion inside Russia. However, the Dashnaks rejected this proposal, apparently deciding to avoid intrigues and perform their duty as Ottoman citizens.[149] Historians tend to place great importance both on the fact that the Unionists would send a special delegation to the congress, and that the Armenians rejected the proposal. Turkish sources see this as a turning point in Unionist-Armenian relations, going so far as to say that the Dashnaks actually decided to embark upon a secret revolt against their Ottoman overlords.[150] Thus, the subsequent deportation order was unavoidable.[151]

However, this version is incorrect. As the evidence from the post-war Unionist trial shows, the CUP went to Erzurum not to participate in the congress but to form irregular units of the Special Organization. The congress appears to have been simply a means to disguise the true purpose for traveling to Erzurum. We also learn that the Unionist participants intended to liquidate the Dashnak members attending the congress. In one document we read: "The necessary preparations have been made for those individuals . . . who have left Erzurum. . . . Instructions for those things that are essential for our organization's freedom of action should be given."[152] The author of this document confirmed that Bahaettin Şakir had wanted "those people [mentioned in the telegram] apprehended on the way and liquidated." But the Armenians "succeeded in escaping from the gangs by covering their tracks."[153]

Bahaettin Şakir, who met with the Armenians at the congress, reported the results to Istanbul. In reply, party secretary Mithat cabled him that "it has been understood from your communication of 15 August 1330 (28 August 1914) and from the accounts of certain people with whom you spoke that the Armenians are not inclined to joint action with us," and he issued a directive that "it is therefore necessary to conceal from them the path we have adopted."[154]

After the gangs were formed in August, military operations began in Russia and against the Armenians. In September, along the Ottoman-Caucasus border in particular, the militias began to stage attacks on individual Armenian villages as well as on Armenian intellectuals, politicians and religious leaders. According to Johannes Lepsius, "The armed gangs saw their main task as raiding and looting Armenian villages. If the young men escaped their grasp, they would rape the women and force them to hand over all their money and whatever other objects of value they possessed."[155] In a report sent to Talât Paşa in September, Bahaettin Şakir openly wrote of the looting, saying, "I am supervising our organization. . . . I am very hopeful. We have probed; we have broken the Russian forces everywhere. Up to now as many as one thousand sheep and four hundred cattle have been seized as booty."[156]

Turkish army officers who were active in the area gave detailed information about the raiding, pillaging and looting of Armenian villages by these gangs. Şerif Köprülü, for instance, recounts:

> Upon the orders of Hasan İzzet Paşa, the most distinguished officers and most courageous individuals in the units of the 9th Army Corps in Erzurum were given to the armed gangs formed by Bahaettin Şakir. Later, I saw how these gangs didn't go in ahead of us, but instead followed behind us and engaged in looting villages.[157]

The same information is found in German consular reports.[158] The gangs displayed an extreme lack of discipline, attacking and looting Muslim villages as well as Christian ones. "In the places they went, they . . . behaved cruelly and intimidated the local population. The gangs made sure that they were well taken care of. They did whatever they felt like."[159] It was this behavior that would later strain the relations between the Special Organization and the army.

German colonel Louis Mosel, who served with the Special Organization units in the Caucasus during this period, reported lootings carried out by these gangs, which he described as "criminal." At this time, the gangs and their leaders "saw their main task as self-enrichment through theft, and undertook evil operations to increase the misery of the local population."[160] The gangs operating in the Van area were no different. One German officer in the area noted, "It was impossible to keep . . . them [the gang members] from looting and pillaging."[161] Colonel Mosel, in a second report sent nineteen days later, told his superiors that "the Young Turk committee, . . . should be distanced from such affairs." In response, Ambassador Wangenheim decided to undertake an initiative to end such actions in this region by the Young Turk committee.[162]

Once war broke out, in the very first months of hostilities massacres were carried out under the cover of the fighting, in the Artvin, Ardahan and Ardanuç areas, all of which were under the direction of the Special Organization. Ahmet Refik quotes a German journalist who witnessed some of these events: "You should see . . . just how cruel their actions were! Curse them. . . ! They have no regard for Muslims, for Christians, for anything."[163] Johannes Lepsius gives detailed figures for the number of people killed in the massacres in the area. "The villages in the areas of Ardanuç and Oltu . . . were pillaged. 1,276 Armenians were killed. . . . The number of Armenians killed in the Artvin and Ardanuç region is estimated at seven thousand."[164] The leaders of the Special Organization units involved in the massacres include many who would later play significant roles in the later Turkish War of Independence, such as Deli Halit Paşa, Yenibahçeli Nail and Topal Osman.

Similar massacres took place in the Van region, considered a third operational front for the Special Organization.[165] American and German missionaries living in Van reported that in the winter of 1914–15 all of the fifty-two Armenian villages in the Doğubeyazit and Eleşkirt areas were raided, pillaged and destroyed by the irregular Kurdish Hamidiye regiments.[166]

In the initial months of operation, the gangs had some important military successes against Russia, taking back Ardahan, and advancing to the outskirts of Batum, areas lost in 1878. But they soon suffered a series of military defeats in the Caucasus. These were due, at least in part, to the role played by volunteer Armenian units assisting the Russian forces. After their own success in battle, the Russian troops and their Armenian allies began to conduct operations against Muslim villages that greatly resembled the Special Organization's attacks on the Armenian villages. German officers serving in the Erzurum region reported Muslim villages being razed and looted as well as forced expulsions.[167] Similar developments seem to have taken place in the Van region as well, where the First and Second Armenian volunteer units saw success against the Turkish irregulars and attacked and looted Muslim villages.

An important motive for the subsequent massacres of the Armenians in the Caucasus and the area of Lake Van was taking revenge for these defeats. According to historian V. N. Dadrian, the attacks directed at the defenseless Armenian population in the border region were exceptionally brutal because of the string of military failures inflicted on the Special Organization units by the Russians and their Armenian volunteers.[168] Even Turkish sources report that local Armenians were killed in the clashes around Van. When the Turks took Van Province back from the Russians, they killed the city's entire Armenian population.[169] The actions of the Armenian volunteers with the regular Russian army units would have an important effect on the Unionists' decision to carry out the genocide. Memoir accounts claim that Bahaettin Şakir, in particular, was very moved by these events. In Ardahan he himself was saved from death at the last moment.[170]

Early attacks on Armenian villages occurred not only on the Caucasus frontier but also in Anatolia, where they were carried out under the pretext of collecting taxes, requisitioning supplies and rounding up military deserters. Lepsius writes that

the situation in the province of Sivas before the general deportation was the same as in Trabzon and Erzurum. The armed gangs looted the villages. The gendarmes raided houses on the pretext of searching for weapons and then looted them, violating the women and torturing to attain money. Those who complained were arrested.[171]

Foreign observers in the region registered similar reports.

Toward the end of October [1914], when the Turkish war began, the Turkish officials started to take everything they needed for the war from Armenians. Their goods, their money, all was confiscated. . . . Only a tenth perhaps was really for the war, the rest was pure robbery.[172]

These accounts are confirmed by several cables used as evidence at the postwar Istanbul trials. For instance, at the 8 February 1919 session of the Yozgat trial, the presiding judge read a telegram that reported pillaging and looting by the gendarmes in the Yozgat area. It stated that "one of the unfortunate situations is the prevalence of horrible looting and pillaging in the Armenian villages by replacement gendarmes, Circassian cavalry units, and the [local] Muslim population . . ." and added that it was not known how far "this looting, which has continued in these places," would spread.[173]

Another telegram reported that the gendarmes "were causing distress to the [local] population" and that the Armenians were being arrested and robbed on the pretext that they were outlaws.[174] Some

Turkish officers' memoirs mention that even before the war had started, there were units that took part in actions such as "looting villages and violating women," and that there were among the soldiers and officers "groups who had no compunction against taking everything without paying."[175]

These activities increased, and by early October, the Dashnaks began making entreaties to Talât Paşa in Istanbul. "At this, Talât sent an order by cable stating the need for better treatment of the Armenians—and especially the Dashnaks."[176] Similar developments occurred in Trabzon and the surrounding countryside. The military commander of Trabzon, who was made uneasy by the armed gangs, ordered those in the area to be disbanded.[177] In a cable sent to the province, Talât announced that the criminal acts against Armenians should cease.[178] But these cables must have been simply formalities, since reports of violence continued to stream in.

Immediately after the general Ottoman mobilization began, Armenians were declared a suspect national group. On 6 September 1914, the government sent a coded memorandum to all the provinces in which there was a large Armenian population, ordering that prominent members of Armenian political parties and intellectuals be monitored.[179] That same month, the Third Army declared that in light of Russian announcements of Armenian assistance in the Caucasus, Armenian soldiers in Ottoman military units were considered a suspect group. In a subsequent published memorandum, all Armenian soldiers were ordered disarmed. The situation was reported to Istanbul in a coded cipher on 24 September 1914. After describing the activities of the Russians, the telegram said that

> to counter this, special [directives] have been ordered among the troops. . . . Those non-Muslims who have crossed the border without a passport in their possession shall be arrested. Those who attempt to smuggle weapons and ammunition across the border shall be immediately executed. The Armenians shall, to the extent possible, be separated into non-combatants. And, in the event of any action against us, it shall immediately and forcefully be suppressed and those who would presume to such deeds shall be liquidated.[180]

The document also relates that Russians had transported ammunition across the Ottoman border and created stockpiles within the empire.

Armenian men between ages twenty and forty-five had been conscripted into the military with the general mobilization, while those between fifteen and twenty and forty-five and sixty were enlisted in labor battalions or as porters for the army.[181] Hans Humann, a close friend of Enver Paşa's who worked in the German Embassy, reported that the labor battalions, comprised of Greeks and Armenians, were formed after October 1914.[182] The Venezuelan-born officer Rafael de Nogales, who served voluntarily in the Ottoman army during the war, says in his memoirs that the labor battalions were formed as a response to the high rate of desertion among the Armenians in the Ottoman army.[183]

On 29 December 1914, Ambassador Wangenheim reported information he had received from the Armenian patriarchate regarding the eastern provinces:

> men able to bear arms between the ages of 20 and 45 were taken into the army, the others are being used for transporting goods and similar tasks, thus the [Armenian] villages have been left defenseless before the excesses and attacks of military deserters.[184]

Austrian military attaché Pomiankowski reported the existence of 120 such Christian "transport" battalions in April 1915.[185] Several foreigners serving in the region also provided ample information on how the Armenians were being used for transporting heavy burdens. American ambassador Morgenthau, for instance, wrote that the Armenians,

> instead of serving their country as artillerymen and cavalrymen . . . had been transformed into road labourers and pack animals. Army supplies of all kinds were loaded on their backs, and, stumbling under the burdens and driven by the whips and bayonets of the Turks, they were forced to drag their weary bodies into the mountains of the Caucasus.[186]

We read in another source the following regarding the Armenians around Muş:

It was necessary to have food, etc., carried to the front, on the Caucasian frontier. For this purpose the government sent out about 300 old Armenian men, many cripples among them, and boys not more than twelve years old, to carry the goods—a three-week journey from Moush to the Russian frontier. As every individual Armenian was robbed of everything he ever had, these poor people soon died of hunger and cold on the way. They had no clothes at all, for even these were stolen on the way. If out of these 300 Armenians thirty or forty returned, it was a marvel; the rest were either beaten to death or died from the causes stated above.[187]

Such events were not limited to the region of Muş. The Armenians in the Sivas region were also enlisted into the labor battalions as porters, and some lost their lives as a result of deprivation, exposure, or beatings and torture. Those who fled had their houses razed.[188] Of the Armenians employed as porters in the province of Bitlis, "half died on the roads, and at most one in four managed to return."[189] According to the numerous reports from many other provinces that began to accumulate in Istanbul in February and March 1915, the situation was not much different anywhere.

The defeat at Sarıkamış was a turning point in the treatment of the Armenians, especially those in the army and labor battalions, who were no longer just mistreated but frequently murdered. In many regions, propaganda claimed that the Armenians had stabbed the Turks in the back. Enver Paşa himself attempted to attribute the defeat to Armenian treachery, and referred to Armenians as a "threat." According to Hüseyin Cahit Yalçın, editor of the Unionist *Tanin,* Enver claimed that the threat could be eliminated by "removing the Armenians from the places where they lived and sending them to other places."[190] At the same time, immediately after the defeat, Enver conveyed his thanks to the Armenian patriarchate for the sacrifice and heroism of the Armenian soldiers in the war. In a letter sent on 26 February, Enver requested that the patriarch convey his "pleasure and thanks to the Armenian Nation, which was known to represent an example of complete loyalty to the Ottoman Government."[191] German consular reports corroborate this account. One from November 1914, for instance, states that, since the official declaration of war, Turkish officers had frequently recounted the self-sacrifice shown at the various fronts by the Armenians, who had organized campaigns to raise funds for war.[192]

Nonetheless, the first measure taken after the Sarıkamış disaster was the order sent to army units on 25 February 1915, instructing them to disarm all Armenian soldiers. Signed by Enver Paşa, the order noted that "Armenian individuals are absolutely not to be employed in armed service, either in the mobile armies or in the mobile and permanently deployed gendarmerie [units], nor in service in the retinue or offices of the army headquarters."[193] These measures had already partially begun in the Third Army.[194] Now, however, they were broadened to include the entire armed forces. Reports followed, claiming that the annihilation of Armenians serving in the army had begun. German missionary Jakob Künzler, who worked with the medical personnel at the Urfa missionary hospital, recounts that the Armenians taken into the labor battalions were killed in March 1915, and that, "mostly knives were used, because the ammunition was needed for the foreign enemy."[195] Something similar was related by Ambassador Morgenthau:

> In almost all cases, the procedure was the same. Here and there squads of 50 or 100 men would be taken, bound together in groups of four, and then marched out to a secluded spot a short distance from the village. Suddenly the sound of rifle shots would fill the air, and the Turkish soldiers who had acted as the escort would sullenly return to camp. Those sent to bury the bodies would find them almost invariably stark naked, for, as usual, the Turks had stolen all their clothes. In cases that came to my attention, the murderers had added a refinement to their victims' sufferings by compelling them to dig their graves before being shot.[196]

Other eyewitness accounts by foreigners serving in the area corroborate the fact that the murder of the labor battalions began only after the defeat at Sarıkamış.[197]

The liquidation of the labor battalions accelerated when the deportation orders were issued, in May 1915, and continued into 1916. Dr. Ernst Kwiatkowski, the Austrian consul for Trabzon, reported being told by a Turkish officer that in the first days of July 1915, some 132 Armenian soldiers had been killed in the village of

Hamzaköy.[198] Jakob Künzler writes that another thousand Armenian soldiers were murdered in Urfa in August.[199] The German consular reports provide a great deal of information on the subject. Walter Rössler, the consul in Aleppo, reported that a German officer had told of seeing bodies all of young men from the labor battalions, all with their throats slit.[200] Between Diyarbakır and Urfa, likewise, in a report dated 3 September 1915, the consul described the killing of hundreds of Armenians who had been forced to work in road construction in his region.[201] Indeed Armenian soldiers engaged in road construction in the area under the control of Third Army commander Vehip Paşa and those sent to the Fourth Army were killed after being dispatched from Sivas. Vehip Paşa immediately ordered an inquiry and established a court-martial, at which he ruled Sergeant Nuri Efendi responsible for a particular incident and sentenced him to death.[202] Ambassador Morgenthau, basing his claims on American consular reports, reported that some two thousand Armenians who had worked in the labor battalions were killed during their transfer from Harput to Diyarbakır, and stated that there were other, similar reports like this for other such events in other regions.[203]

The Armenian deportations began in February 1915 as a local war measure in Cilicia. One cable reported that "not a single Armenian should be left in the Erzin region," and that "the Armenians of Dörtyol should be sent off to Osmaniye, Adana and Ceyhan."[204] British espionage activity in these areas was the given reason. Of those deported to Adana, four were publicly executed. Young men were taken to work on the roads but news soon arrived that these workers "had been murdered by their armed Muslim colleagues."[205]

This was followed in March by an operation aimed at the population of Zeytun, a town in Cilicia, who were deported to inner Anatolia in early April and then soon redirected to Der Zor in the Iraqi desert.[206] The "official" Turkish account presents Zeytun as the first place to attempt a rebellion against Ottoman authority. However, the governor-general of Aleppo at the time, Celal Bey, claims that the district lieutenant governor was responsible for the incident and it could hardly be considered a revolt. According to Celal Bey, the new lieutenant governor attributed political motives to the presence of a few military deserters in Zeytun and then rounded up some forty or fifty

Armenians. Celal released some of the detainees to pacify the region but Istanbul removed Zeytun from his authority, declaring that "the Provinc[ial government] [no longer had] the right to intervene in [the affairs of] Zeytun."[207] According to Celal, the subsequent violent suppression at Zeytun and the deportation of the elderly, women and children from the region was absolutely unnecessary. Celal's account is corroborated by the reports of the local German consul.[208] Thus, the Turkish account is quite different from the one related by the various consuls and eyewitnesses.[209] After the Zeytun and Dörtyol incidents, in April, the entire Çukurova region (the areas around Adana and Maraş) began to be systematically emptied. The destinations for resettlement were, again, inner Anatolia and Der Zor.[210]

Ultimately, the decision to deport the Armenians from these regions was strongly influenced by information that the British were making preparations to land at Iskenderun (Alexandretta). According to Malkon, one of the arrested Zeytuni Armenians, they had been told "that the English would land at Iskenderun." The British had asked the Armenians to "revolt to make things more difficult for the government, and support the British by hindering [the government's] efforts to mobilize."[211] A report sent on 13 March 1915 by Büge, the German consul in Adana, agreed with this assessment. He claimed that British ships could easily approach the coast and land troops to forge a connection with Armenians working under their orders.[212]

The German consuls, who went to the area to investigate the events for themselves, reported that, in addition to the deep sympathy for Britain and France found among the people of the region, the British had managed to win over a number of Armenian collaborators. While the level of organization was tentative, the British were indeed seeking ties to help with a possible landing.[213] A number of sources also reported that, due to Russian pressure, England was making serious preparations to open a southern front in Iskenderun, the attack on the Dardanelles in March 1915. It is highly probable that the Unionists, who feared Armenian assistance to the British during a possible landing, decided to evacuate the area as a precautionary measure. The same German consular report also claimed that the measures taken in Dörtyol were only taken after an English naval squadron appeared off the coast, and that all the young men had been removed from Dörtyol and its surroundings with the aim of "preventing the possibility" of a British landing and collaboration with the Armenians there.[214] According to British accounts, they planned not only on close cooporation with local Armenians but also with Armenians abroad. An Armenian delegation offered the British a volunteer force of around twenty thousand people.

> Monsieur Varandian delegate of Armenian Committee and speaking in its name requested me to ask you if his Majesty's Government would be disposed to utilise service of 20,000 Armenian volunteers to operate a descent upon the coast of Cicia [sic] in region of Alexandretta. Half of the troops are ready in America rest Balkans. Several committees exist for sending troops to destination chosen by His Majesty Government: Cyprus is suggested as base.[215]

Another report of the war office shows that "the arming of these Armenians was part of a scheme for the occupation of Alexandretta."[216] But the British gave up this plan.

Some official Ottoman correspondence from the following months shows clearly that the decision to deport Armenians from the region was tied to instructions from Istanbul, both oral and written. A letter to the Ministry of the Interior from the general command on 26 May 1915 stated that "It was orally decided that the Armenians be sent from the eastern Anatolian provinces, from Zeytun and from such areas which are densely populated by Armenians, to the south of the province of Diyarbakır, to the valley of the Euphrates, to the vicinity of Urfa and Süleymaniye."[217]

To conclude, the measures against the Armenians began even before war broke out. Four types of methods were used: 1) the oppression of villages on the pretext of tax collection, forced conscriptions, confiscation of property, and the pursuit of deserters, which began with the general mobilization in August; 2) assaults and massacres in the border villages, perpetrated by the Special Organization units, which began in September and increased during the winter; 3) disarming the Armenian population; and 4) strategic deportations in certain "problem" regions at the very beginning of the war.

It is worth considering the disarming of the Armenian population in greater detail. Some of the Armenian revolutionary organizations were indeed armed. German officer Mosel, who served in the eastern provinces, reported in March 1915 that the Armenian revolutionary organizations were "arming themselves."[218] Aleppo consul Rössler also reported that the Dashnaks in Maraş and the surrounding region were smuggling in weapons. The Erzurum consul, Scheubner-Richter, while reporting on 15 May 1915 on the incidents in Van, stated "that in many places, weapons were stockpiled with the goal of defending against a possible massacre, and later, for an insurrection."[219]

However, it was quite normal to carry firearms given the general lack of security. A British consul in Mersin stated that, "According to the Constitution, everyone may bear arms. . . . Thousands of revolvers have been purchased."[220] Furthermore, the CUP itself had distributed a good portion of the weapons during the 31 March 1909 uprising, when the Armenians formed volunteer units to suppress the revolt with the Unionists: some "160 mausers and 200 martinis along with enough ammunition for distribution among several hundred volunteers."[221]

After the 1909 revolt and the Adana massacre, when the CUP and the Dashnaks agreed to defend the Ottoman Constitution jointly, "weapons were distributed by the Young Turks to the Armenian villages that they believed would fight against reaction."[222] These weapons were now seized through force and torture.[223] But weapons were not taken from Muslims, however. On the contrary, some Muslim civilian populations were now armed. The Austrian consul in Trabzon, for instance, reported in November 1914 that "the Greek and Armenian populations were extremely worried due to the arming of the Muslims."[224] Similar consular reports came from the eastern provinces.[225]

It appears that, when all these various measures against the Armenians seemed insufficient to solve the problems facing the Ottomans, together with the defeats of the winter of 1914–15 which heightened the prospect of total collapse, the decision for genocide was taken, to provide "a complete and fundamental elimination" of the Armenian problem.

CHAPTER 5

THE DECISION AND ITS AFTERMATH

AFTER AUGUST 1914, MANY PEOPLE FELT THAT THE ANNIHILATION OF the Armenians was imminent. In memoirs from the time, the authors claim they had heard that the decision regarding the Armenians had already been made, during the winter of 1914. Whether or not these reports are accurate is not critical. The importance is that these memoirs show the atmosphere in which people were living.

At the beginning of March 1915, the Istanbul Dashnak organization, which received frequent reports from the provinces, wrote in its newspaper that "the government's intention is in the direction of moving the Armenians from their areas of settlement." The entire Armenian nation was "living with the dread of a general massacre." Armenians were told that they were the reason for Turkish defeat in the war and that they would be destroyed. Journalists reported that the "fear of a general massacre hovers."[1] On several occasions, Armenians appealed to the German consul for protection from coming atrocities, as in the case of the Special Organization's attacks on Armenian villages near the Russian border.[2] German reports from the region had anticipated that Bahaettin Şakir, the head of the Special Organization, was preparing for just such an assault. But they also noted that the governor-general of Erzurum had prevented him from carrying them out.[3] Rumors of an imminent massacre reached foreigners throughout the empire. Jakob Künzler, the Swiss-German missionary and doctor, reported hearing from Unionists that "it [was] impossible to work with the Armenians. This war will give Turkey the chance to either get rid of them or kick them out."[4] Johannes Lepsius reported that Armenians in Erzurum had been warned by their Turkish colleagues of an impending massacre.[5]

Alma Johansson, a Swiss nurse, claimed that such thoughts were expressed openly in Muş as early as November 1914:

> Already by November we had known that there would be a massacre. The mutessarif of Moush, who was a very intimate friend of Enver Paşa, declared quite openly that they would massacre the Armenians at the first opportune moment and exterminate the whole race. . . . Toward the beginning of April, in the presence of a Major Lange and several other high officials, including the American and German Consuls, Ekran Bey openly declared the government's intention of exterminating the Armenian race. All these details plainly show that the massacre was deliberately planned.[6]

A Danish nurse by the name of Marcher reported that Erzincanlı Sabit, the governor of Harput, told Max Scheubner-Richter, the German vice consul in Erzurum: "The Armenians in Turkey must and were going to be killed. They had grown, he said, in wealth and numbers until they had become a menace to the ruling Turkish race; extermination was the only remedy."[7] Scheubner-Richter himself reported that a senior official told him "there will be no Armenians left in Turkey after the war."[8]

There are many sources reporting that Turks warned Armenians of the Unionists' intentions. Even though these reports largely came from opponents of the CUP, the significant number of independent sources corroborate each other.[9]

The Special Organization units had sustained successive defeats on the Eastern Front, and this, along with subsequent rout of the Ottoman army at Sarıkamış, pushed the Unionist leaders to conduct a serious reappraisal of the situation. Their objectives had not been achieved, the CUP's Pan-Turanist dreams had been destroyed, and

Armenian volunteers were believed to have played a major role in these losses. The defeats also served to highlight the intensified conflict "between some [army] command centres and the Special Organization." There had even been reports of direct clashes between the army and Special Organization units. One reason for this conflict was that some officers had never been informed about the existence of the Special Organization units.[10] The army, believing that public order in the region was breaking down, increased its security staff.[11] Stange, a German officer stationed in the region, wrote that the armed gangs' operations and their lack of discipline were the cause of continuous friction with the army.[12]

Furthermore, in the wake of military defeat, many of the Special Organization members either fled or took to general looting and disruptive behavior, even creating problems for Muslim villages.[13] In some areas, gangs began executing Muslim villagers whom they deemed suspicious, without interrogation or trial and at times even conducting mass executions by firing squad.[14] The army took the view that the gangs had to be either disbanded or incorporated fully in regular army units. Those in the Special Organization closest to the party, and therefore Talât, vehemently opposed this.

The history of tension within the CUP between Enver and Talât, the heads of the military and civilian wings of the party, respectively, carried over into an ongoing feud between the Special Organization and the army. At the end of February or beginning of March, before returning to Istanbul, Bahaettin Şakir convened a meeting in Erzurum, where it was decided that the leadership in Istanbul had to remove the Special Organization entirely from the supervision of the army.[15] From now on the party, rather than the government, would take the initiative in implementing military policy.[16]

In early March, Bahaettin Şakir headed to Istanbul,[17] leaving Hilmi in Erzurum as his deputy. Almost every day, Hilmi sent cables to Bahaettin Şakir in Istanbul, warning that "unless an order is issued to free the Special Organization from the army, [you can] forget about coming back to the Caucasus Front." In addition to the question of the army command, fundamental changes in the Special Organization's activities were also under discussion. "The Armenians' anti-Turkish attitude and the help they gave the Russian army convinced [Bahaettin Şakir] that dealing with the enemy within was as necessary as the enemy without."[18] Having assembled evidence of Armenian gang activity in the region, Şakir now tried to persuade his friends in Istanbul that it was time to get rid of this threat.[19]

It is very likely that the key decisions concerning the massacre were made within the CUP in Istanbul during March 1915. "In these discussions a decision was made that Bahaettin Şakir Bey would resign from his duties pertaining to the country's foreign enemies and concentrate solely on its internal enemies." Şakir was put in charge of dealing with "the Armenians inside. . . . These discussions concluded with the formulation of the Deportation Law. When Bahaettin Şakir Bey returned to the Caucasian front a short time later the new arrangements had been completely determined."[20]

This information is confirmed by Ottoman documents. In a telegram sent by Talât to the local authorities in Erzurum on April 5, 1915, he notes that "Bahaettin Şakir will come soon" and that he was bringing money with him.[21]

We have other evidence that the decision was made at the end of March, during the critical days of the Gallipoli campaign, and that it was discussed with the Germans. While the battle for Gallipoli was raging, Enver remarked to Hüseyin Cahit that the solution to the Armenian threat was to "remove them. . . . and send them somewhere else." In his memoirs, Halil Menteşe wrote that the government sent him to Berlin on 18 March to ensure German assistance in holding on to the Balkan road, a German supply corridor. As soon as he reached Berlin, Menteşe began holding meetings. At around this time, he received a telegram from Talât telling him, "Wait! We have some important tasks for you." Menteşe proposed that the task be entrusted to Cavit Bey, who was also in Berlin at the time. "No," came the answer. "This is not something Cavit Bey can do. Wait there." When Menteşe returned to Istanbul in May, Talât met him at the railway station. "Tell me, dear Halil," he reportedly said. "What did you discuss in Berlin regarding the deportation of Armenians?"[22]

From Cavit Bey's journal we know that he learned that Menteşe was coming to Berlin on 28 February 1915. Menteşe duly arrived on 6 March, not March 18. After several trips elsewhere, Cavit returned to Berlin on 22 March, and met with Menteşe on the following day. This meeting is entered in Cavit's diary on 30 March. At the meeting Menteşe told him about the cable from Istanbul with the orders to remain.[23] Thus, the telegram from Istanbul must have been sent before March 23. Halil himself claimed that the instructions he received, or was about to receive, were to discuss the deportation of Armenians with the Germans. What we may extract from all this is that the decision was made toward the end of March, and that it was probably discussed with the Germans. Cavit Bey's diary indicates that he had no knowledge of these discussions. The timing of the decision is especially significant because it was taken ahead of the Armenian uprising in Van in late April 1915, even though the uprising is usually presented as the reason for the decision.

In a report, Paul Rohrbach, a friend of Talât Paşa, quoted a speech given by a Russian deputy in the Duma. The deputy, Miljukow, mentioned a meeting between Enver and Wangenheim, the German ambassador to the Porte, quoting from Wangenheim's own report. The passage he quotes is identical to Enver's comments to Hüseyin Cahit. Enver reportedly told the ambassador that the interests of state necessitated the deportation of the Armenians, and he asked the Germans not to stand in the Ottomans' way, and even to help. According to the Russian deputy's allegations, Wangenheim reported the conversation to Berlin as a "ready plan."[24]

We have many indications that the decision for genocide was made by the CUP Central Committee deliberately and after long consideration. The postwar indictment of Unionist leaders provides some valuable information. "The massacre and eradication of Armenians," it states, "was the result of a decision made by the Central Committee of the Committee of Union and Progress." These decisions were made after "wide-ranging and in-depth discussions." The indictment records Dr. Nâzim's statement that the Armenian question "had been decided by the Central Committee after long and in-depth discussions," and that "this initative would settle the Eastern Question."[25]

The governor-general of Aleppo, Celal, said in his memoirs that he heard this from a deputy from Konya. The deputy told Celal that if "he were to oppose their point of view on this matter, they would get rid of him."[26] Further, İhsan Bey, head of the Special Bureau of the Interior Ministry, gave testimony in Istanbul that when he was prefect of Kilis, Deputy Director of the Office for the Resettlement of Tribes and Refugees Abdul'ahad Nuri Bey, coming to Aleppo from Istanbul, told him that the intention behind deportation was extermination. "I was in contact with Talât Bey," said Nuri, "and personally received the annihilation order." He tried to convince İhsan Bey by arguing that "it [was] for the safety of the country."[27]

Vehip Paşa, who was appointed commander of the Third Army in February 1916, said in his written testimony of December 1918:

> These atrocities, committed according to a clear program and with absolute intent, were carried out at the orders and supervision of first, members of the Union and Progress Central Committee, and second, by leading members of government who, by casting aside law and conscience, served as tools for the designs of the Committee.[28]

Vehip added that government officials, despite being fully aware of these crimes, did nothing to stop them and even encouraged them.[29] The verdict in one of the postwar trials in Istanbul mentions the decision to massacre as having been made by the Central Committee and conveyed to the provinces by special couriers.[30]

Foreign observers confirmed this account. Stange, a German officer who worked with the Special Organization's armed gangs on the Caucasian front, wrote that the government had a "fear of Armenians that was out of all proportion to the powerless condition in which they lived." He added that had the decision to deport the Armenians been made by the army, one would have expected steps to be taken to protect the deportees' lives and possessions. "Hundreds and thousands were murdered," Stange wrote, "the authorities helped themselves to anything left behind, houses, shops, goods . . . the Armenian church had assests worth about 150,000 lira . . . the evictions were carried out in inhumane conditions and families and women were driven away with no protection. . . . One feels justified surmising that military considerations were of secondary importance, and that the main aim was to take advantage of this excellent opportunity to implement a long-held plan to weaken, if not destroy, the Armenian people, while there would be no protest from the outside world. The military imperatives and the various rebellions only provided welcome pretexts."

Stange also observed that "the Young Turks in Constantinople" had decided on the expulsions and destruction, "organized and implemented it with the help of the army and voluntary militias. Members of the committee were stationed locally," among them Bahaettin Şakir in Erzurum, who coordinated the plan.[31]

The most important document to reveal the real intent behind the decision to deport the Armenians—that it was not simply related to wartime security—is a statement sent to the grand vizier from the Ministry of the Interior on 26 May 1915. The document states that the deportations need to take place so that the Armenian question is "brought to an end in a comprehensive and absolute way (*esâslı bir suretde hal ve faslı ile külliyen izâlesi*)." The document has been cited in various publications but the complete text has not been reproduced, except for an extensive summary,[32] since it was first published in its entirety in the newspaper *Ati* after the Armistice.[33]

The text explains the reasoning behind the deportations from a historical perspective: "[A] reform entirely related to internal Ottoman affairs became an international issue, whereby some regions of the Empire, coming under the influence of foreigners, demanded certain privileges and special administrative organizational regulations. . . . It became bitterly clear that this reform and reorganization, done under duress and due to foreign influence, caused the fragmentation of the Ottoman nation. . . . After consultation with local officials and the military commanders the state, of necessity, began . . . an action believed to be completely within the interest of the state, in keeping with the proper rules and procedures. . . ."[34]

Most significantly, the document goes on: "preparations and presentations have been proposed and considered for a final end, in a comprehensive and absolute way, to this issue, which constitutes an important matter among the vital issues for the state."[35] Talât Paşa made similar remarks to American ambassador Henry Morgenthau. In his memoirs, Morgenthau recorded a meeting of 9 July 1915 with Talât: "Talât said that they had discussed the matter very thoroughly and arrived at a decision to which they would adhere. When I said they would be condemned by the world, he said they would know how to defend themselves; in other words, he does not give a damn."[36]

Morgenthau recorded an additional conversation on the subject with Talât, attributed to 3 August 1915:

Talât . . . told me that the Union and Progress Committee had carefully considered the matter in all its details and that the policy
which was being pursued was that which they had officially
adopted. He said that I must not get the idea that the deportations
had been decided upon hastily; in reality, they were the result of
prolonged and careful deliberation.[37]

Based on his conversations with various Turkish officials during
his service, Scheubner-Richter reported that the elimination of the
Armenians was planned well in advance. People had told him that
"the empire must be rebuilt on a Muslim and Pan-Turkist foundation. . . . Non-Muslim communities have to Islamicized by force or,
failing that, eliminated." One such source told him that war was the
most suitable condition in which to put the plan to action.[38] Mahmut
Kâmil Paşa, the commander of the Third Army at the time, was
among those who told him there would be no Armenian question
after the war.[39]

The most incriminating evidence confirming that the intention
behind the deportation was genocide comes from Mordtmann, the
German consul general in Istanbul. In his report of 30 June 1915, he
writes that leading Unionist and Istanbul director of police İsmail
Canpolat, pointing to a map of Anatolia, said that the deportation of
Armenians would extend to the whole of Anatolia. "This cannot be
explained by military exigencies," Mordtmann wrote, recalling that
Talât had told him "a few weeks" earlier: "'What we are talking
about . . . is the elimination of Armenians.'"[40]

Many members of the government were unaware of the genocidal
decision that we believe was made by the party in late March and carried out under the veil of the government's deportation decree at the
end of May. In later operations too, the government was excluded as a
matter of principle. In convincing statements made after the war by
Grand Vizier Said Halim Paşa and İbrahim Bey, the minister of justice, they claimed that, "This business was not carried out through
any orders from the government." Said Halim Paşa said, "As with
everything else, I learned of this disaster after it was over. . . . Not a
single word was said about it in the cabinet."[41] İbrahim Bey said much
the same thing.[42]

As Eşref Kuşçubaşı put it, the government was never informed of the meetings and plans related to the deportations and massacres.[43] Only two or three members of the government were involved, and so there are no records in the minutes of cabinet meetings. Kuşçubaşı illustrates the extent of government ignorance: when the wartime grand vizier Said Halim Paşa was assassinated in Rome in 1921, purportedly in connection with the Armenian massacres, Kuşçubaşı said that he, "as an insider of these events," knew that the grand vizier had nothing to do with the genocide. He had been killed for nothing.[44]

From the Ottoman assembly's postwar investigations carried out by the Fifth Department, we learn that many topics actually discussed in cabinet meetings were excluded from the minutes. Çürüksulu Mahmud Paşa, minister of public works, confirmed this several times during his questioning, and added that in many meetings, minutes were not taken at all: "This was not part of the record because no records were taken."[45] If we can believe Ahmet Şükrü, the minister of education, even "the decision to mobilize the army was taken orally."[46]

In his memoirs, Talât Paşa notes that a law of 11 February 1915, which allowed parliament to go on early recess on March 1, was connected to the desire to solve the Armenian question without parliamentary involvement.

> The Special Organization was aware that some non-Turkish members of both the Chamber of Deputies and the Chamber of Notables would leak vital information and decisions to the patriarchy and the embassies. As long as the assemblies were in session, it would be impossible to prevent such individuals, who supposedly represented the nation, from such action.[47]

Parliament gave the cabinet the authority to issue temporary laws and then went into recess at the beginning of March. This eased the Unionists' situation greatly. It is significant that all official decisions related to the deportations were indeed issued as temporary laws.[48]

In light of the party's decisions, the Special Organization was reorganized. The most important change was that the organization and its irregular units were finally fully detached from the army and brought under the control of Bahaettin Şakir. The end to its relationship with the army had begun in early February. The Ministry of War sent a circular to the various armies on 3 February 1915, ordering a halt to the formation of armed gangs.[49] Cevat testified that "by April, we had no more dealings [between the army and the Special Organization]."[50] According to defendant Atıf, the Special Organization office within the ministry was dissolved at the end of April.[51]

It was the reorganized Special Organization units—under direct control of the party—that carried out the genocidal campaign. Ahmet Refik testified that the perpetrators of the massacres at Pozantı, some thirty to forty kilometers from Adana, were "reorganized by gangs sent to the Caucasus."[52] Carl Schimme, a German officer sent to Trabzon by Scheubner-Richter, said that during his journey, he saw dead bodies on the roads and the gangs just waiting to carry out further massacres.[53] Scheubner-Richter reported on 18 June that in the Kemah-Erzincan area, twelve hours away from the Third Army headquarters, the gangs eliminated some twenty thousand to twenty five thousand people between 10–14 June.[54]

The German Major von Mikusch reported how members of a Special Organization gang composed of convicts told him with great pleasure of the massacres they had committed with their commanders. The major saw bodies tied to each other drifting down the Euphrates.[55] Wedel-Jarlsberg, a Norwegian nurse, saw members of the gangs on horseback patrolling the area between Erzincan and Sivas and many corpses of murdered Armenians.[56] German consular reports contain a wealth of information to the effect that units of the Special Organization were directly involved in the massacre.[57]

The 1919 trials of the CUP leaders, and regional trials in Yozgat and Trabzon further document the direct involvement of Special Organization units. In the Yozgat trial, for example, Halil Recai and Sahabettin, both army officers, testified that the "slaughter" was carried out by the armed gangs and that they themselves had received orders not to interfere. In the trial's final summary:

With the assistance of collaborating gendarmes, the units guarding the columns [of deportees], comprised of habitual criminals and degenerates, drove the defenseless Armenians out of towns, ostensibly for deportation. When they had been [sufficiently] distanced from the towns, they were set upon by gangs of bandits . . . who, after looting what they had in their possession, had them killed. . . .[58]

As a rule, the Special Organization units carried out the massacres outside of towns. The judges in the Trabzon trial wrote that "it has been proven in all [the war crimes] trials, and we are all convinced, that the murder and looting did not take place inside the town of Trabzon, but were entirely carried out outside in an organized way."[59] One of the most striking features of the Trabzon trial was that a large number of Muslims appeared as state witnesses, including military and civilian officials such as Colonel Muhtar, chief of staff of the forces in Trabzon and Lazistan; Lieutenant Ahmet; Colonel Arif, Giresun's military commander; Nâzım, former governor-general of Van; Tahsin, former governor-general of Erzurum; judicial inspector Kenan; Trabzon's recruitment bureau chief Necmettin; retired colonel Vasfi, also chief of staff in Trabzon; and Trabzon military commander Avni Paşa. They all confirmed the involvement of the Special Organization in the deportations and killings.[60] Colonel Vasfi testified that he had been sent to investigate reports of executions in the Erzurum region, organized by Bahaettin Şakir, but Third Army commander Mahmud Kamil had hindered him from his work.[61] This information was repeated in almost all of the major trials. In the trials of the party secretaries, Turkish and Armenian witnesses testified to the killing of Armenians sent from Istanbul to Çankırı by the Special Organization unit under the control of Party Secretary Cemal Oğuz.[62]

The relevant Armenian survivors' memoirs recount hundreds of similar versions of these events.[63]

From the telegrams that were sent, it is clear that the first wave of deportations from Zeytun and Dörtyol were strategically motivated. On March 2 Talât Paşa wrote to Adana: "It is confirmed that the Armenians should be transferred to the indicated region as communicated in the Feb. 13th telegram. As the situation has been evaluated by the state, the probability of rebellion and protest indicates the need to take action. The increasing possibility of Armenian uprisings requires that every effective means of suppression needs to be applied."[64] The turn from strategic to genocidal deportations occurred during the Van uprising, to which we shall return.

When reports of this uprising reached Istanbul the deportations already underway were redirected to the deserts of Syria. The earliest document to indicate a change in the policy regarding the deportation is a telegram dated 24 April 1915 to Cemal Paşa, Fourth Army com-mander. The telegram declares that "the Armenians expelled from the Zeytun and Maraş areas" should no longer "be sent to the area of Konya," in Anatolia, and that those to be "expelled from Iskenderun, Dörtyol, Adana, Haçin and Sis, should be transferred to the South-east, to the Zor and Urfa regions." Another telegram from 26 April 1915, sent to Adana, Halep and Maraş, repeated the same informa-tion. Yet another coded communication, sent to the Maraş governor's office on 3 May 1915, ordered the "complete expulsion" of the Arme-nians of Zeytun.[65]

At around the same time (24 April 1915) arrests were made in Istanbul and the prisoners were to be sent to Ayaş, a city in central Anatolia. A telegram sent to the region requested that it prepare "the military warehouse in Ayaş for the arrival of the Armenian detainees to be sent there." A second order sent on the same date states that "180 Armenian . . . leaders" would arrive on train #64, and of these, "67 of the individuals would be secured in the military warehouse" while the others would be sent to Çankırı.[66]

Then on 6 May orders were sent to the governor's office of Maraş for "the complete expulsion of [the Armenians] from Zeytun." In later telegrams, Talât Paşa began to inquire as to the numbers of Armenians deported. One telegram sent to Adana on 12 May asks "How many Armenians have been expelled from Haçin and Dörtyol and where have they been sent to?"[67]

Telegrams were also sent to the other eastern provinces. On 9 May, the Ministry of the Interior sent an encrypted message to the Van and Bitlis provincial governors, communicating the decision to deport the Armenians of the Van area, noting that it was his direct and personal responsibility. The cable ordered that the deportation was to extend to the south of Erzurum, Muş and the Sason area and stated that a similar cable had been sent to Erzurum. Another encrypted telegram, sent from the ministry to Erzurum on 18 May 1915, ordered that Armenians already deported from the Erzurum area be sent to the southern districts of Musul and Urfa and to the provincial district of Der Zor. These documents tell us that deporta-tions from that area began in late April or early May. From German consular reports, we know that deportations from villages around Erzurum had already begun in April, and that by "May 15 all the villages . . . had been emptied."[68] From a memoir by Başkatipzade Ragıp Bey, an Ottoman bureaucrat, we learn that he arrived in Erzurum on 14 April 1915 and left on 26 April, and that "the helpless deported Armenian girls and women broke our hearts with their miserable, wretched, humiliating conditions."[69]

German documents from May 1915 record the change of destination, as well as a change in the scope of the deportations. Wide-ranging explusions began in May and June 1915. On 6 May Ambassador Wangenheim noted that "the clearing out of Armenians from their areas of large-scale settlement continues." Walter Rössler, the German consul to Aleppo, reported on 10 May that in the wake of the Zeytun and Dörtyol deportations, expulsions had been extended to Maraş. "The measures taken seem aimed at eliminating all Armenians in the region," he added. Other consular reports recount a similar story: hundreds of thousands of Armenians driven from their homes in convoys and killed, either on the road or after having arrived at their assigned destinations.[70]

The killings themselves have been extensively described in a wide array of documents and published sources, all of which prove the almost identical pattern of massacres. We will return to the genocide itself in greater depth.

The genocide was implemented through a dual mechanism. First, an official deportation order was sent to the provincial regions by the Interior Ministry. Specifically, the Department of Public Security and Dispatches within the ministry was responsible for overseeing all the practical matters involved in the deportations. The orders were sent to the government's local representatives (governors and prefects) in the provinces, who were expected to carry them out. Then there were separate, unofficial orders for the annihilation of the deportees, issued by the CUP Central Committee and conveyed to the provinces through party channels.

When the local governors received deportation orders from the Interior Ministry they would forward them to the security forces in their area, usually to the gendarmerie, the body responsible for keeping provincial order (and part of the Interior Ministry). At the same time, the CUP would send the liquidation orders to the local governors. The messenger, usually a party secretary but on occasion

Bahaettin Şakir himself, would travel from province to province transmitting a written document or conveying the order verbally. In cases where local governors resisted, they were removed from office.

Following receipt of the deportation order, the gendarmerie would summon the Armenians to a central point and then accompany them on their route. When the convoy reached the provincial borders, the gendarmerie was supposed to deliver the deportees to the gendarmerie of the next province, however this was often the point where the Special Organization took over—set in motion by the secret liquidation order—and deportation became elimination. The Special Organization units, in cooperation with the gendarmerie, would join the convoys of deportees and set about their murder.

In some regions there were strict orders to prohibit military involvement. In the postwar Trabzon and Yozgat trials army officers confirmed that they had been instructed to stand aside and act only if the civil authorities asked for help. However, in some regions massacres were carried out directly by the military. In one official deportation order, the army was granted the authority to make decisions. The division of labor and the question of responsibility was a source of tension between the civil and military authorities throughout the deportations.

Reşit Akif Paşa, a cabinet minister in the first postwar Ottoman government, relayed this crucial information. In an important speech to parliament on 21 November, 1918, he described the process of the Armenian genocide:

> During my few days of service in this government I've learned of a few secrets and have come across something interesting. The deportation order was issued through official channels by the minister of the interior and sent to the provinces. Following this order the [CUP] Central Committee circulated its own ominous order to all parties to allow the gangs to carry out their wretched task. Thus the gangs were in the field, ready for their atrocious slaughter.[71]

Some newspapers published Reşit Akif Paşa's speech in full, citing its "extreme significance" and "particular import."[72] Unfortunately, however, he did not give dates for these secret documents.

Vehip Paşa's testimony confirms Reşit Akif Paşa's discovery. He testified that the deportation orders were circulated through the provincial governors' offices, whereas the massacre was organized by Bahaettin Şakir. As the head of the Ottoman Third Army Vehip Paşa launched an investigation into the reported February 1916 massacres of Armenians, arresting the gendarme officers and their assistants, whom he thought responsible for the liquidation of convoys leaving Erzurum and Trabzon, even interrogating them himself. They told him they "had received orders from Memduh Bey, . . . Lieutenant Governor of Erzincan, and that the people who had actually taken part in the unfortunate events had received orders from Bahaettin Şakir Bey."[73]

The postwar trials paid special attention to the roles played by Bahaettin Şakir and the regional party secretaries in organizing the killings. Turkish historian Cemal Kutay said of the party secretaries: "The fact of the matter is that the final decision on all important questions was theirs." Scholar Tarik Zafer Tunaya describes them as "the bearers of Unionism," adding that they were chosen from the most reliable elements of the party apparatus.[74] They had great influence over many government officials, from simple civil servants all the way to governors. The responsible secretaries, to borrow an expression from the supplementary indictment of the main trial, functioned as a "special cadre" inside the party and they formed a secret arm within government.[75]

The secretaries were put in charge of forming the gangs in the provinces. A letter sent from the Special Organization to the CUP Central Committee on 13 September 1914 demanded that "the Responsible Secretaries should secretly and within one week summon all the individuals willing to cooperate." Other similar telegrams were read at the main trial. One such cable came from one Rüştü, the party secretary for Samsun, who announced that he had managed to form the gangs requested for his region. Other defendants claimed that contact with the responsible secretaries was not made directly through the Special Organization, but rather via Mithat Şükrü, the CUP party secretary.[76] Due to their principal role in the massacres, the secretaries were tried separately, and the verdicts stated that they were "accessories in the . . . crimes of the [Union and Progress] Party."[77]

The responsible secretaries were given broad powers over Special

Organization units sent to their regions. They were the ones who carried the extermination orders to the relevant governors, as was documented in the Yozgat and other trials. Governors who refused to obey the secretaries' orders were, at the latters' behest, removed from their posts. Mazhar Bey, the governor-general of Ankara Province, Reşit Paşa, the governor-general of Kastamonu and Cemal Bey, the lieutenant governor of the provincial district of Yozgat, were all sacked upon responsible secretaries' requests.[78]

Mazhar Bey, who was removed from the governorship of Ankara, described in his testimony how he was removed from his position:

> When I received orders from the Ministry of the Interior regarding the deportation of Armenians I pretended not to understand. As you know, other provinces were done with the deportations before I had ever started. Then one day Atıf Bey came to me and orally conveyed the interior minister's orders that the Armenians were to be murdered during the deportation. "No, Atıf Bey," I said, "I am a governor, not a bandit, I cannot do this, I will leave this post and you can come and do it."[79]

The story of Reşit Paşa, the governor of Kastamonu, is the same. The trial record of the responsible secretaries mentions how Reşit said, "I will not stain my hands with blood." He was subsequently fired at the request of Hasan Fehmi, the responsible secretary for Kastamonu.[80]

There are various documents that show that the liquidation order from the Central Committee was delivered to the provinces by special couriers. Ahmet Esat was the director of the Second Branch of the Security Office of the Ministry of the Interior. After the armistice, he tried to sell the British what he claimed to be the minutes of a meeting in which the Armenian massacre was decided. He gave the British four documents, two of which were in his own handwriting.[81] According to Esat's information, the orders were delivered to the governors of the provinces by special couriers, usually the party secretaries, with instructions to read and return them to be destroyed.[82]

Evidence submitted at the Istanbul trials confirmed that the orders were indeed sent in this manner. The presiding judge at the main trial asked each of the defendants: "Responsible emissaries were sent to places such as Ankara, Kastamonu, Erzincan, Yozgat, Trabzon,

Sivas, where they gave the governors and lieutenant governors certain secret orders: Are you aware of this?"[83] The former lieutenant governor of Yozgat, Cemal, said that he had received an unofficial order from Necati, the responsible secretary for Ankara, calling for the murder of the Armenians. Necati, Cemal claimed, had said the order was issued at the behest of the CUP Central Committee and that he also possessed a written version, although he did not allow Cemal to read it.[84] Cemal gave the investigative commission written testimony on 12 December 1918 that echoed the experience of Mazhar Bey.[85] Cemal made many incriminating statements against the defendants in the Yozgat trial, statements which they could not refute satisfactorily.[86]

Prefect of Bayburt Nusret, who was condemned in the postwar trials, testified that he had received orders from Istanbul to leave not a single Armenian alive, and anyone standing in the way of this order should be executed.[87] The Venezuelan Rafael de Nogales, who served as an officer in the Ottoman army, witnessed the massacres at Diyarbakır. When he subsequently spoke about them with the province's governor-general, Dr. Mehmet Reşit Şahingiray, the latter told him that the killings had been ordered, and that the responsibility belonged with those who had given the orders. He hinted unambiguously that he had received a telegram from Talât Paşa to that effect.[88]

The various telegrams presented at the trials show that Şakir was, in practice, in charge of directing the Armenian massacres. As we know, he was chief of the Special Organization. One trial verdict concludes that

> The defendant CUP Central Committee member Dr. Bahaettin Şakir Bey, left Istanbul for the Trabzon and Erzurum provinces and other regions as the "head of the Special Organization." He assumed leadership of the armed gangs (çete), which had been set up and formed by a procession of criminals released from prison. . . . He sent them into action by delivering secret orders and instructions, some verbal, others encoded, to certain people and officials, . . . [to carry out] the atrocities and evil massacre of the population and the plunder of their possessions, which were committed at different times and places during the deportation of the Armenians . . . the Special Organizations had been formed for the purpose of destroying and annihilating the Armenians.[89]

Bahaettin Şakir, who was not an elected official, "toured the eastern provinces, met with governors, lieutenant governors and others, and, acting at the level of government official, informed them of the decisions made by the Central Committee of the CUP.[90] Tahsin Bey, the governor-general of Erzurum, testified that Bahaettin Şakir Bey, a man with no state position, nonetheless "had two different ciphers for communication, one with the Ministry of the Interior and one with the Sublime Porte."[91]

One telegram sent by Şakir Bey to the Mamüretülaziz party secretary asks: "Are the Armenians being dispatched from there being liquidated? Are these troublesome people you say you've expelled and dispersed being exterminated or just deported? Answer explicitly."[92] Also at the trials, Sabir Sami Bey, the former lieutenant governor of Antalya, said that he had received a coded telegram from Şakir inquiring about his plan of action: "Now that the Armenians have been dispatched to Zor, so that not a single one of them remains in the areas around Erzurum, Van, Bitlis, Diyarbakır, Sivas and Trabzon, what is being done in Antalya?"[93] Additionally, German consular reports from the region confirm Şakir's role and that the killing operation was organized in Erzurum.[94]

Telegrams ordering the annihilation were supposed to be destroyed. In one indictment, it was shown that Ali Suat, lieutenant governor of the provincial district of Der Zor, was ordered to destroy telegrams after reading them.[95] The prefect of Boğazlıyan, Kemal, testified in the preliminary investigation that he had received telegrams with orders to destroy them after reading.[96] At the 24 March session of one trial, Kemal was asked again about these orders, and he retracted his statement, saying that he had been "very tired while being interrogated." The prosecutor disagreed: "I was a member of the Criminal Investigation Commission and I therefore know this not to be true. He took three or four hours to think about it before writing his statement."[97]

Some of the governors refused to accept the Central Committee's instructions that deportation was to be understood as annihilation. In several cases, uncooperative officials were actually murdered. Hüseyin Nesimi, the prefect of Lice, refused to obey the verbal order and asked for a written copy. He was fired, called to Diyarbakır, and murdered on the way.[98] Abidin Nesimi, the prefect's son, wrote that the liquidation of government officials was ordered by Mehmet

Reşit,[99] the governor of Diyarbakır, among others. The murdered include "Ferit, the governor-general of Basra, Bedri Nuri, the lieutenant governor of Müntefak, . . . Sabit, the deputy prefect of Beşiri, İsmail Mestan, a journalist." The reason for these murders was clear: "The administrative cadre that opposed the massacre had to be liquidated. . . ."[100] The prefect of Midyat too was murdered on Reşit's orders. "The Prefect of Midyat defied orders to kill Christians in his area; before long he was murdered by order of the governor-general of Diyarbakır."[101] Kenan Bey, an inspector at the Ministry of Justice, said at the 11 May 1919 session of the Trabzon trial that he had gone to Samsun to investigate; while there, he "saw the deportation as it took place" and "the prefect of Bafra was murdered."[102]

Another example of a governor who did not obey the secretaries' orders was Tahsin Bey. In an 11 December interview with the Armenian newspaper *Zhamanak,* Tahsin Bey claimed he had "interceded with headquarters many times in order to stop the deportation of Armenians."[103] One of these attempts was a coded telegram he sent to Istanbul on 24 May 1915, in which he said that both the deportation decision and the justification for it were wrong. Tahsin Bey argued that the Armenians to be deported from Erzurum were in fact "far from the front" and that the "spying and disruption" of which the Armenian population was accused "did not happen."[104]

The German vice-consul to Erzurum reported Tahsin saying to him, "I am against" the deportation decision, adding, "I have to obey, but I will try to soften it."[105] He carried out the orders but excluded from deportation women, children and the sick. Yet Mahmud Paşa, the commander of the Third Army, sent all the remaining Armenians away. The German vice-consul to Erzurum said of Tahsin: "He did what he could, but he had no power."[106] Celal, the governor-general of the province of Aleppo, defied the deportation order outright. In his reports, Consul Rössler said that Celal was popular in the district because he had succeeded in establishing peace and order.[107] But he was ultimately removed for his insubordination. Rahmi Evranos Bey, the governor-general of Izmir, and Nabi Bey, the lieutenant governor of Malatya, were among those who initially defied the deportation order. Their efforts too ultimately came to naught.[108]

There is sufficient evidence to conclude that the deportation was to be understood as annihilation. A. Nuri, who was stationed in

Aleppo, reported that Talât Paşa said: "The intention of the deportations is annihilation."[109] The Yozgat trial featured a large number of telegrams on this particular point; twelve were read at the ninth session alone on 22 February 1919. Statements in these telegrams repeatedly say that deportation meant elimination and massacre. For example, a telegram sent by the Boğazlıyan recruitment bureau chief Mustafa to Halil Recai, acting commander of the Fifth Army Corps, informed him that "the Armenian vermin gathered tonight from the townships and villages have been led to the predetermined places."[110] Halil Recai replied the same day, inquiring what "being led to the predetermined places" meant.[111] The gendarme officer replied, also on the same day, "They said the Armenians were killed because they were vermin."[112] Halil Recai, who testified at the trial, claimed that a telegram from Colonel Sahabettin in Kayseri stated that "deportation" meant "massacre." A telegram sent from Hulusi, the gendarme officer at Boğazlıyan, used similar language, stating "deportation means annihilation."[113] Finally, it should be added that the party secretaries were also active in inciting the local Muslim populations against the Armenians, looting Armenian property and enriching themselves. The defendants were questioned about this in the trial of the party secretaries; and the verdict of that trial mentions many instances of the secretaries encouraging the people to engage in mass demonstrations, appropriating Armenian houses and property and organizing looting raids.[114]

The documents leave no doubt that Talât Paşa was the overall coordinator of the deportations and massacres. Mordtmann, the German chief consul in Istanbul, described him as "the [guiding spirit behind] the Armenian persecution."[115] Of the many telegrams Talât sent to the provinces, some were recovered and listed in the main trial indictment. In general, they refer to such issues as how to clear the corpses from roadsides and punishing people who refused to obey orders. In one coded cable sent on 21 July 1915 to the governors-general and lieutenant governors of Diyarbakır, Mamüretülaziz, Urfa and Der Zor, Talât Paşa writes that "the dead on the roads should be buried, not thrown in lakes, wells or rivers, and their belongings are to be burned." A "coded order from the governor-general of Mamüretülaziz Province to the lieutenant governor of the Malatya provincial district" notes that "contrary to emphatic reports, we have news that many bodies have been left by the roadside," and adds that "the Interior Ministry has ordered severe punishment for any officials negligent in this regard."[116] The German consul to Jerusalem sent a telegram to the embassy in Istanbul on 9 September, in which he reports Cemal Paşa's claim to only carry out the plans while "—Talât Bey decides the dimensions of the expulsions."[117]

Many telegrams sent by Talât are used in Turkish sources to prove that the Ottoman government did not intend to annihilate the Armenians, but merely deport them. In these telegrams he talks about orderly deportation and humane treatment of the deportees. Most of these were sent by Talât to appease the German ambassador in Istanbul. When the German and Austrian ambassadors received word of slaughter in the provinces, they interceded with the Turkish government. The German government's notes of 4 July and 9 August are but two examples of these efforts. This intervention prompted Talât to send repeated cables to the provinces, referring to humane treatment, but despite all promises to rectify the situation, nothing changed. Word continued to arrive claiming that the slaughter was continuing unabated. "Further reports from the imperial consuls . . . confirm that the well-known telegraphic instructions from the Sublime Porte to improve the state of the deported Armenians have on the whole not fulfilled their purpose."[118] The consuls kept up their pressure, while Talât Paşa kept reassuring the Germans that no massacres were taking place and that he "would do whatever he could [about the situation]."

For this reason Talât is mentioned in the consular reports as a liar. The German ambassador described Talât as "ruthless" and "two-faced."[119] Austrian ambassador Pallavicini called him a person "playing a double game."[120] German consular reports afford a striking example of this duplicity. The Germans pleaded with the Turkish government to at least exclude Protestants from the deportations. They obtained a promise and a corresponding order was sent to the provinces. But the German consul to Adana had this to say:

> The Sublime Porte's explanation to the Chancellor's Embassy on August 31 is a great deception. The Porte has sent an inspector, Ali Münif Bey, to cancel this order . . . and the deportations continue without regard to faith.[121]

Talât sent telegrams to the provinces merely to silence the foreign ambassadors and then immediately followed them up with a second cable cancelling the first; sometimes he sent envoys to the provinces as well.

Even some of Talât's close associates described him as a liar. His closest friend, Hüseyin Cahit, said that Talât "regularly lied in government and political affairs."[122] Falih Rıfkı Atay, Talât's private secretary, described him as a man for whom "lying and injustice did not count as immorality." Atay said that sending an order only to cancel it shortly afterward by coded cable was business as usual for Talât.[123] From the memoirs of both Ambassador Morgenthau and Halil Menteşe, we learn that Talât, a former telegraph operator, had a line installed at his house and conducted his communications from there.[124] The ambassador once paid a sudden visit to Talât's house and over the course of several hours, his "involuntary host paus[ed] now and then in his telegraphing to entertain me with the latest political gossip."[125]

But Talât was not alone in his duplicity. The practice of cancelling orders with a secret, follow-up communication was widespread among Ottoman administrators. Hans von Seeckt, who served as chief of staff for the Ottoman armies, said that as a rule, one had to pay attention to official orders, secret instructions, and the intimations and clues that indicated which were valid and which were not.[126] Captain Selahattin, a Turkish officer who knew Enver, said in his memoirs that Enver too used this method.[127]

Neville Henderson, the British Embassy chargé d'affaires during the armistice period, sent Talât's telegrams calling for humane treatment for the deported Armenians on to London. Largely unaware of the Ottoman practice of multiple orders, Henderson's comments about Talât's telegrams are strikingly prescient:

> These lines are worthy of being read and kept in mind as a living example of Turkish administration and mentality. Whether they were cancelled by secret orders or had been sent in the certain knowledge that they would be useless in the face of natural brutality and indifference is a matter for academic conjecture.[128]

The Army's Role in the Genocide

An important question is whether regular army units took part in the killings. It seems that a central decision determined that regular army units would not participate. At the seventh session of the Yozgat trial (11 February 1919) Halil Recai said that he had received orders from Enver Paşa, the minister of war, that the army was not to interfere in the deportations. He said the same thing at the trial's fourteenth session (26 March 1920).[129] These instructions contain the same information as the documents given by Ahmet Esat to the British:

> The manner in which the deportation of Armenians is to be carried out and the responsibility therefore rest with the civilian authorities. The civilian authorities are not to be hindered or interfered with in this respect, and are to be afforded help only when they ask for it.[130]

In the sixteenth session of the Trabzon trial (5 May 1919) Avni Paşa, the commander of the local garrison, claimed that he had received orders from the Ministry of War not to interfere with affairs of the provincial governor, and added that the massacres had occurred outside the city limits, carried out by the armed gangs.[131] Aram Andonian published two similar documents from Talât Paşa, in which he persuaded the Ministry of War to order local garrison commanders and military branches not to interfere with the expulsions. A circular to this effect was sent to the provincial military authorities.[132] This clearly shows that the Interior Ministry's gendarme units were to play a part in the killing operations, while regular army units were not. Indeed, many gendarme units took part in the slaughter alongside the Special Organization. Arnold Toynbee points out this difference in the level of involvement between the military units and the gendarmes, and notes that "the behaviour of the gendarmerie . . . was utterly atrocious. . . . A very large proportion of the total misery inflicted was the gendarmerie's work."[133]

Nonetheless, despite the orders to the army not to interfere, some units—of the Third Army, in particular—did get involved. Shortly after the Van uprising, in areas such as Bitlis and Muş, residents were slaughtered by local army units.[134] In this connection, the role of

Mahmut Kâmil Paşa, as Third Army commander, is crucial. A telegram issued by General Kâmil stated:

A Muslim who protects an Armenian will be executed in front of his house and the house burned. If he is a civil servant, he will be dismissed and sent before the Court-Martial; members of the military who consider it appropriate to protect [such persons] will come before the Court-Martial for military insubordination and be tried.[135]

As already mentioned, the Turkish officer Vasfi testified about General Mahmut Kâmil's role at the fourth session of the Trabzon trial (3 April 1919). He had received orders from General Ali Paşa, his commander, to go to Erzurum to investigate reports of massacres, but was blocked by Kâmil, who basically told him that the matter was none of his business.[136] Necmettin, head of the recruitment office, and Ethem, another officer, provided information on Kâmil Paşa's involvement in massacres at the fifth (5 April 1919) and fifteenth sessions (30 April 1919) respectively.[137] According to a newspaper report of 20 May 1919, Süleyman Faik Paşa, deputy commander of the Second Army Corps in the Harput region and former lieutenant governor of Harput, was still in possession of the document containing Mahmut Kâmil Paşa's order to eliminate all Armenians.[138] Corroborating evidence is provided in a report by German officer Stange, who also mentioned Kâmil Paşa's role in the deportation process. The massacres in the region, Stange reported, were coordinated by Hilmi Bey, the Unionist "inspector," Bahaettin Şakir Bey, and Seyfullah Bey, deputy for Erzurum (the three of them working on behalf of the party), as well as by Hulusi Bey, the police chief, and Mahmut Kâmil Paşa.[139]

The army's involvement in the deportations and killing included the intelligence branch of the General Staff, run by Colonel Seyfi. According to documents collected for the trials by the postwar investigation committee he was also in charge of the Special Organization's financial affairs.[140] Colonel Seyfi's branch was responsible for planning the massacres and drawing the maps for the Armenian deportation. Secret documents seized by the police in December 1918 and later given to the commission investigating the deportations, confirm that Colonel Seyfi, in coordination with Bahaettin Şakir, sketched out the plans.[141]

The British archives provide further information, included in the minutes of secret meetings that Ahmet Esat gave the British authorities after the war. Colonel Seyfi is listed among those present, alongside Talât, Dr. Nâzim, and Bahaettin Şakir. Esat said that this meeting saw the emergence of the first crude plans for the massacres. Seyfi was there as someone who enjoyed the full confidence of Enver Paşa. "This gave him considerable power," say British documents.[142]

Other documents also show that some army commanders played a direct role in the massacre, by eliminating the civilian Armenian population within the military zones, and murdering Armenian soldiers within the army units.[143] Halil Kut Paşa, Enver's uncle, and Ali İhsan Sabis, one of the Unionists later exiled to Malta by the British, are two cases in point. The soldiers in Halil Paşa's units carried out "a veritable massacre."[144] An American, Willam A. Shedd, who worked in the American Presbyterian mission in the city of Urmia, recorded that Halil Paşa had the Armenian soldiers serving in the units under his command liquidated.[145] Not stopping at that, Halil himself said he was "working to destroy the Armenian nation to the last person."[146] Scheubner-Richter, the German consul in Erzurum, who served in Halil Paşa' s army, relates that he received orders to attack and "punish" some Armenian villages. Protesting that this was an "internal Turkish affair," the consul refused to carry out the orders and transferred them to a Turkish officer. Scheubner-Richter said of Halil Paşa: "[His] campaign in northern Iran resulted in the liquidation of the Armenian and Syriac Christian units under his command and in the expulsion of the Armenian, Syriac and Iranian populations. It also created great fear among the Turks."[147]

As for Ali İhsan Sabis, he not only worked to organize the deportations, but also proudly told German officers that he himself had killed Armenians. According to one consular report:

Ali İhsan, Commander of the Sixth Army in Mosul, who studied in Germany and spoke perfect German, said on countless occasions in the presence of Germans that he would not leave a single Armenian alive in his command zone. He took pride in telling German officers that he killed Armenians with his own hands.[148]

The Genocide

It is of course impossible to tell the entire story of the forced deportations and the murderous campaign that accompanied them. But a
general overview is necessary.

Some regional variations notwithstanding, the expulsions and
massacres proceeded in the same way everywhere and are well documented in American, British and German archival materials, missionary reports, and survivors' accounts. The very persistence of the
pattern indicates central planning. In some provinces the Armenians
were given two weeks' notice; in others, merely two hours. As a general rule, however, the deportations began before the announced date.
In some areas the deportees were allowed to prepare and take some
belongings: in others they were forbidden from carrying or selling
anything. The Third Army, in control of the eastern provinces, issued
a warning that Muslims caught helping Armenians would be killed in
front of their homes and the homes then burned. Similarly, deportees
who took valuables with them only hastened their deaths. Some officers gave the Armenians something to eat; others let them starve to
death by the roadside. As noted, convoys were accompanied by gendarmerie units to the provincial border and then handed over to the
gendarmerie of the next province. Killings were coordinated among
the gendarmerie, the Special Organization and also Kurdish tribes.

In urban areas, either a town crier conveyed the deportation
order or representative Armenians were summoned to city hall to
hear the information. In some cases notices were put on walls; in
others, the gendarmerie surrounded a neighborhood and emptied
the houses with almost no notice. Usually the male population (generally the elderly, who had not been conscripted) were arrested at
night, taken outside the city limits and killed. If they were among the
convoys of deportees, the men were separated from the women and
children before being sent away, shot or butchered soon after their
convoys set out.[149] Leslie A. Davis, the American consul to Harput,
quoting an Armenian who had somehow survived, states that eight
hundred or so Armenians who were held in the prison of Harput
were taken to the outskirts of town in groups of fourteen and either
shot or bayoneted to death, in this case by the gendarmes.[150]

In some areas the Armenians were forcibly converted to Islam, those who did so being spared. The German consul to Samsun reported that the Ottoman government was sending fanatical Muslims to Armenian houses, forcing them to convert under threat of deportation, and claiming that, by that time, "all the Armenian villages in and around Samsun had been Islamicized."[151] Similar reports arrived from the Erzurum, Trabzon, and Adana regions. In some cases, Armenian churches were turned into mosques.[152] A German report of 12 December 1915 said that at the beginning of that month a government directive ordered that Armenians converted by force sign papers stating they had done so voluntarily.[153]

The policy of forced Islamicization was abandoned, however, when it turned out that most Armenians were willing to convert to escape death. A telegram from Talât Paşa sent on 1 July 1915 announced: "Some Armenians are converting to Islam collectively or individually to be able to stay in their areas of residence," and ordered that "they must be transferred despite their conversion." Similar telegrams were sent later.[154] An eyewitness who came upon a convoy of deportees an hour away from Erzincan reported that the women implored his party, "Save us! We will become Muslims! . . . We will become Germans! We will become anything you want, just save us! They are taking us to the Kemah Pass to cut our throats."[155] Armenians who survived the massacres and managed to reach Syria and Lebanon were again faced with pressure to convert to Islam. Consular reports from the beginning of 1916 offer information on the process.[156] As the Austrian ambassador put it on 6 January 1916, at first the CUP pursued a policy of intense Islamicization, but when the number of converts began to swell, that policy was abandoned. After the expulsion of the deportees, efforts were resumed to force them to convert.[157]

All the Armenians who belonged to the Gregorian Church—the vast majority—were deported. Catholic and Protestant Armenians were deported as well, although with some interruptions, due to German pressure.[158] Although Germany's efforts to soften the Turkish government's position were dismissed as "interference in domestic affairs,"[159] the German and American ambassadors continued to focus on saving Catholic and Protestant Armenians from the expulsions.

Their intercessions persisted during the summer of 1915, and at last Talât Paşa allegedly yielded to their entreaties and ordered the deportation of Catholic and Protestant Armenians halted.

The earliest existing relevant telegram is from 4 August 1915, after most of the deportations from the eastern provinces were complete. It specified that "the deportation of the remaining Catholic Armenians is to stop." A similar telegram, dated 15 August 1915, contained instructions that "Armenians of the Protestant denomination who have not yet been deported are to remain."[160] From these telegrams, we may surmise that Catholic and Protestant Armenians were being deported at least up until the dates mentioned.

It was soon discovered, however, that these decisions were part of Talât's double dealings aimed at mollifying foreign ambassadors. Consular reports from the provinces claim that these deportations continued, despite orders to the contrary.[161] A second set of contradictory orders had been sent, delivered through a variety of channels, such as Ali Münif's mission to Adana. Bekir Sami Bey, the governor-general of Aleppo, told Rössler that the special treatment afforded to Catholic Armenians had been cancelled and all Armenians were now being deported without exception.[162] J. B. Jackson, the American consul to Aleppo, reported a message received on 17 August allowing "Protestant Armenians to stay where they are." But the following day, a second cable arrived, also ordering "the deportation of all Armenians without discrimination."[163]

On 21 August, Dr. Mordtmann was summoned to the Ottoman Interior Ministry and informed that special treatment for Catholics and Protestants had been repealed in Ankara and Adana.[164] On 31 August, Talât visited the German ambassador and told him that the orders cancelling the special treatment had in turn been cancelled themselves—in short, Catholic and Protestant Armenians would be allowed to remain where they were.[165] On 2 September Talât presented the embassy with three telegrams, translated into German, ordering an end to the deportation of Catholics and Protestants. Yet reports continued to arrive from the provinces that Armenians of these two religions were being deported and murdered along with the others.[166] Some reports said that these orders were "nothing but a hoax," others even gave figures for the number of murdered Catholic and Protestant Armenians.[167] Ottoman documents not only corroborate these claims but also show how the dual mechanism worked. According to the documents, Talat would send a second telegram in which he annulled his prior order. So, for example, after ordering a halt to the deportations of the remaining Protestants in a specific region, he sent a second order the same day canceling his previous telegram and instructing that the deportation of all Armenians should continue.[168] On 18 September 1915 cables sent from Kayseri, Eskişehir, Diyarbakır and Niğde report that all the Armenians had been deported from these provinces and that none remained.[169] In a last-ditch attempt, Ambassador Hohenlohe-Langenburg pleaded with Talât to at least allow the Protestant and Catholic Armenians deported to Aleppo to remain there. But Talât was obdurate—he insisted that these Armenians be moved again, from Aleppo to the Syrian and Iraqi deserts.[170]

The situation remained unchanged in 1916. The German Embassy kept protesting and kept receiving the same promises. Meanwhile, reports kept coming from the provinces that Protestants and Catholics continued to be deported.[171] According to a report dated 3 March 1916, all fifteen of the Armenian Catholic congregations in Anatolia, apart from those in Bursa and Istanbul, had been dissolved.[172] The German ambassador forwarded these reports to the Turkish government, only to be told by various ministers—the foreign minister, in particular—that they knew nothing about these allegations. Count Wolff-Metternich, who replaced Hohenlohe-Langenburg in the autumn of 1915, summed up these developments and admitted the failure of German policy in his report dated 18 September 1916:

> The Sublime Porte's easing of the Armenian deportations is again to be reversed. . . . Turkey is set on fulfilling, in its own way, a policy that will solve the Armenian question by destroying the Armenian people. Neither our intercession, nor the protests of the American ambassador, nor even the threat of enemy force . . . have succeeded in turning Turkey from this path, and nor will they succeed at a later date.[173]

These intercessions and appeals nevertheless did succeed in saving a small number of Armenian Catholics and Protestants from deportation in some provinces, such as Ankara, Urfa and Aleppo.[174]

A report dated 14 July 1917 said that "the killings have stopped, but the destruction has not." The survivors were mostly women and children and they were living in buildings under German control.[175] On 16 December 1917, the Armenian Catholic archbishop reported that only 23 percent of the prewar Catholic population of Anatolia remained alive.[176]

One letter, sent by the General Staff to the grand vizier's office, from 26 May 1915, shows that the relocations were based on a demographic principle that limited Armenians to 5 to 10 percent of the population in any given region. Scholars have long dismissed this demographic consideration as an attempt to disguise the real reasons for the deportations. Now, however, newly discovered documents from the Ottoman archives indicate that this was not in fact a strategy of diversion, but rather a calculated policy applied not only to Armenians, but Arabs, Kurds, Albanians, Bosnians and others. For example, a telegram sent from the Interior Ministry to different provinces in May 1916 demanded that the Kurds be separated from their religious leaders and sheiks and that they be settled in Anatolia in numbers not exceeding 5 percent of the indigenous population.[177] Another telegram sent by Talât Paşa to Ankara dated 1 October 1915, notes that Albanians and Bosnians would be dispersed among the Turkish population without exceeding 10 percent of the native population.[178]

The same was true for Armenians. Some telegrams say that in regions where Armenians constituted less than 5 or 10 percent of the population, no relocation was necessary.[179] In each region, the government kept continual track of population percentages, constantly checking the numbers of expelled groups and relocated groups in any particular place. In regions to which Armenians were deported, they were not to exceed 10 percent of the population. A telegram sent to the Syrian and Iraqi provinces, clearly states that the Armenian population there should never exceed 10 percent.[180] In the Der Zor region, the Armenian population exceeded 10 percent, and the Interior Ministry sent telegrams to the governors of Adana, Erzurum, Bitlis, and Aleppo drawing their attention to the fact.[181] This explains the 1916 massacres in those areas and why Der Zor was the center. This also shows that the deportations were hardly simply a matter of relocation. The issue was Armenian population density.

As for the attitude of the Muslim population, we have an ambivalent picture. Evidence exists showing that in some regions the Muslims participated in the genocide while they actively resisted it in others.[182] A significant part of the male Muslim population was serving in the army. Many, no doubt, experienced the same feeling of emptiness described by Officer Çerkez Hasan: "When I returned from the war I found that Avadis Ağa the blacksmith's shop, Nikogos the cook's place and many other neighbors had been pillaged. They had been sent to Arabia and other places."[183] In some areas Muslims protected Armenians, hid them and tried to stop the deportations. In others, they began looting Armenian homes even before the occupants had left, attacking the convoys and massacring the deportees. Scheubner-Richter, who followed the events closely, suggested that while the strategy of extermination suited the Unionists, the Turkish people would never approve of solving the Armenian question this way.[184] The consul to Trabzon, Heinrich Bergfeld, concurred that the campaign did not have the support of the people. "One has to give the Turkish people their due. The majority of Turks do not think it right to deport women and children."[185] In his report of 5 August, Scheubner-Richter repeated this view. "A broad section of the Turkish people," he wrote, "those blessed with common sense and reason . . . do not support the annihilation policy," and he reported that many local figures condemned the crimes and distanced themselves from them, denouncing them as a Unionist policy. "Despite the commandments in the Quran," one man said, "thousands of innocent women and children are being killed. It is not people in a state of rage who are doing this, but the government, the Committee."[186] In another report, Scheubner-Richter named people who had saved Armenian lives such as Mustafa Ağa, the mayor of Malatya.[187]

In the main indictment in the trials of the leaders, we read that the people of Kastamonu complained to their governor-general about how "Armenians from the neighboring provinces were being bundled off to the hills with their children and families, as if to a slaughterhouse, and were killed there." Objecting to such things taking place in their region, they insisted that "the government cannot take part in such sacrilege."[188] The subsequent trial sessions more clearly revealed the opposition of broad sections of society to the campaign against the Armenians. In the Trabzon and Yozgat trials, the majority of witnesses were Turkish and Muslim, and they presented damning evidence against the defendants. At the Yozgat trial, for example, the mufti's written statement was among the most incriminating documents against Kemal, the prefect of Boğazlıyan, and was critical in the court's decision to execute him.[189] Julius Neumann, the Austrian consul in Izmir, reported that the Turks in Akşehir had protested the measurements taken against the Armenians.[190] In some areas, such as Dersim and Mardin, the Kurds, singly and in groups, followed the convoys and saved as many people as they could.[191] Although it is impossible to give precise numbers, Kurdish villagers are estimated to have rescued between twenty thousand and thirty thousand Armenians.[192] However, this was not a completely altruistic endeavor. Armenians paid the Kurds out of the little money they had left, and the rescue became a lucrative activity.[193] But there were also massacres in the Dersim area. In his testimony as a witness before the Mamüretülaziz trial, Tahsin, the governor-general of Erzurum, said that the majority of the convoys "were intercepted around Dersim."[194] The prosecution claimed that Bahaettin Şakir had arranged for "members of the Special Organization to incite the Kurds and local villagers to kill the Armenians and loot their property . . . after they had departed from the towns and villages."[195]

There are also examples that confirm that the civilian population in some provinces took part in the massacres with the intention of looting.[196] One report sent by the Austrian consul in Aleppo said that "overall, the Turkish population approves of the actions taken against the Armenians."[197] In some instances, there were even volunteers "to kill Armenians." Walter Rössler, German consul in Aleppo, names such people in several of his dispatches.[198] Ironically, in other cases, the gendarmes tried to protect the convoys from local attacks, even engaging in armed scuffles with Kurdish tribesmen.[199] But the very same gendarmes later slaughtered the Armenians, as the same eyewitnesses testified.[200] In some places the Kurds attacked Armenian villages and massacred the population even before the deportations.[201] Mikusch, a German officer in the region, said he counted two hundred corpses in one such village. Other eyewitnesses said the attackers killed both women and men and stole clothes from the dead and dying.[202] Looting was not the only motive for murder; in many cases young girls and women were kidnapped or bought from the gendarmes, either on the way to or at their final destination.[203]

In some areas the Armenians had their hands bound behind their backs before being taken away. The judge in the Yozgat trial pointedly asked one defendant, Tevfik: "Did you tie deportees' hands?" and the straightforward answer was yes.[204] After the armistice, there was coverage in the Istanbul press about the governor-general of the province of Izmir, Rahmi Evranos, and how "he besieged the Armenian neighborhood of Izmir with a military force; had two thousand Armenians handcuffed like criminals, paraded them through the markets and streets on the way to the prison and then deported them."[205]

In the Black Sea region, the Armenians were loaded onto boats and then thrown overboard—confirmed by eyewitnesses at the Trabzon trial. At the trial's fourth session (3 April 1919), "one woman's confirmed testimony" said that "Cemal Azmi Bey ordered the gendarmes to collect Armenian men and take them by boat to Kumkale. On the way they were all killed—some shot, others thrown into the sea. . . . Niyazi Efendi was in charge of the boats.[206] "Around Değirmendere," said the same indictment, ". . . the women and children were loaded onto boats, taken to the sea and thrown off to drown."[207] Mehmet Emin Bey, a deputy from Trabzon, said at a session in the Chamber of Deputies, that he witnessed Armenians being taken by boats and thrown overboard: "Your humble servant saw this. There was a prefect in the Ordu District. He loaded the Armenians onto boats ostensibly to send them to Samsun and then had them thrown overboard."[208]

Norwegian nurse Wedel-Jarlsberg, serving in Erzincan, made notes of a gendarme's description of the events: "They're mowing them all down." The gendarme told her that there were specific execution sites along the roads; but on the way, whenever the convoys passed a populated area, they were also attacked and pillaged. Those too sick or exhausted to march were killed where they fell. The gendarme said he had accompanied a convoy of three thousand people; in his reports he claimed: They're all gone; finished![209]

The deportations from the eastern provinces were carried out between May and July, followed by deportations from western and central Anatolia and Thrace. The first stop in these expulsions was Aleppo. Those who survived the journey were crowded into concentration camps until they could be sent on to their final destination. The appalling sanitary and humanitarian conditions turned these into death camps; survival was nothing short of miraculous, but meant being sent on to southern Syria and eastern Mesopotamia—that is, to the Arabian deserts and certain death. Reports from Der Zor, one desert destination, said that the deportees were denied food, medical attention, or shelter. People were simply left to die. In some cases, the living were forced to eat the dead.[210] These deportations continued until late 1916.

Immediately after Armenians were removed from their homes, Muslim settlers were brought in to occupy the empty towns and villages. In some regions, resettlement of Muslims began even before the general deportation order. A report sent on 2 April 1915 said that two thousand immigrants had been settled in Armenian villages in the regions of Malazgirt and Bulanık. Cevdet, the governor-general of Van, was also reported preparing to settle Muslims in and around Muş.[211] Migrants from Macedonia were settled in evacuated Armenian villages in the Zeytun area by the beginning of May.[212] Muslim refugees coming from the war zone in Erzurum were resettled by mid-May.[213] Reporting on this, the German consul to Erzurum said, "Creating places for these immigrants could well be the reason behind the deportations."[214]

The documents indicate that the time between deportation and resettlement was no more than one week in some regions. There was therefore a great deal of preparation beforehand. One telegram from 18 May 1915, appointing an official to oversee Muslim settlement, made reference to a previous telegram dated 16 May 1915 about the Armenians' expulsion. Another telegram sent to Erzurum on 18 May 1915 inquired about the number of immigrants in the province and the resources needed to feed and settle them.[215]

The resettlement continued systematically throughout the summer of 1915. Telegrams sent to Elazığ and Van on 27 June ordered the resettlement of immigrants. The information in Istanbul was not sufficient to fully compile a "settlement policy." So cables were sent to twelve provinces and provincial districts on 12 July ordering a full accounting of Armenians deported and their property vacated so as to facilitate resettlement.[216] This evidence refutes the Unionists' repeated claims that the deportations were a temporary war measure—in fact, they knew that the deportees would never return. When combined with the fact that in some areas all Christians and sometimes even non-Turkish Muslims were deported, the settlement policy strengthens the argument that the Unionists were following a well-formulated demographic policy aimed at Turkifying and homogenizing the whole region.

The total number of people killed as a result of the deportations is not certain. The prewar Armenian population within Ottoman territory was 2.1 million, according to the Armenian Church, although Turkish sources put the number at 1.3 million. Only a fraction remained in Anatolia after the war. Estimating the number of survivors is no easier, since the figures are conflicting. All the available estimates are based on a political agenda. Some sources put the number of survivors at 600,000, of whom 150,000 to 200,000 lived through the deportations. The number of women and children given to Turkish and Kurdish families or kidnapped is impossible to estimate. Some sources put this number at 200,000, but, like all the other figures, this is no more than conjecture. The estimates of those killed swing between 600,000 and 1.5 million.[217]

There is, however, one official number. On 14 March 1919, the Istanbul government announced after its investigation that the number of Armenian victims during the war was 800,000. This was the result of the commission established by Interior Minister Mustafa Arif Değmer in December 1918. The announcement was made on 18 March 1919 by Interior Minister Cemal Bey.[218] The ensuing reaction of scandalized deputies and others forced Cemal to modify his statement; the 800,000 figure, he clarified, was the number of all Armenians deported, not just those killed. He confessed not to know how many had survived.[219] Nonetheless the figure of 800,000 people killed gained some currency. Mustafa Kemal and Grand Vizier Damat Ferit Paşa both mentioned it on various occasions. In 1928, the General Staff of the Turkish Army published a book on the issue of World War I losses, and the figure of 800,000 Armenian dead was repeated. Turkish historian Y. H. Bayur has stated that this figure must be considered accurate.[220]

Deportation or Elimination? The Treatment of the Deportees

In November 1918, at the CUP's final congress, where the party disbanded, Talât Paşa laid the groundwork for the "official Turkish version" of the deportation and killings:

> . . . there were many such incidents during the deportations. But in
> none of them did the Sublime Porte act according to some pre-
> determined decision. In many places long-harbored hostilities
> erupted and led to abuse that we never intended. Many officials dis-
> played excessive injustice and violence. In places, countless inno-
> cent people were killed. This much I admit.[221]

This is the position of the Turkish government ever since: The Armenians were victims of wartime conditions, disease, and isolated acts of
violence. There was no state intention to kill them as a people. There
are, however, a few significant but often overlooked discrepancies.
The first is between the reason given for the deportations and the
places to which the Armenians were sent. Officially, the Armenians,
who constituted a danger to the army, were distanced from the war
zone. In fact, they were deported from areas far removed from the war
zone directly into the theater of operations, from inner Anatolia to the
front where the Fourth and Sixth Armies were fighting the British.[222]
Furthermore, at no point during the deportation—not at the start,
nor on the road, nor at the final destinations—were any preparations
made for the mass movement of people. This alone was enough to
demonstrate that the campaign's aim was deliberate extermination.

Proposals made to protect the convoys were rejected. Scheubner-
Richter reports that Tahsin Bey, governor-general of Erzurum, said
that he had petitioned Third Army commander Mahmut Kâmil Paşa
to guard the roads and delay deportations until they were secured, but
this request was turned down.[223] As mentioned earlier, Tahsin Bey
had already proposed, in a coded telegram, that the expulsions be
postponed for security reasons.

> Sending 60,000 people from the borders of the Caucasus to Mosul
> and Baghdad cannot be done with orders alone. Who will protect
> these people and safeguard their money and property? If the army

can protect them then it should assume that responsibility. Your humble servant has not taken any efforts [toward the ordered deportations], nor will I be able to [given the present state of affairs]. Therefore, I appeal in the name of the safety of the nation for the operation to be postponed until such point when this danger is given [serious] consideration.[224]

The deportees were denied any help offered, "in money, food or any other form." This we know from many consular dispatches.[225] German ambassadors and consuls were prevented from providing assistance. On 9 December 1915 Ambassador Wolff-Metternich was informed that his proposal to help the deportees had been rejected, "in order not to raise the Armenians' hopes of help from abroad."[226] Several months later, the embassy made another attempt, and on 28 April 1916, it received the same reply.[227] On 12 August 1916 the Germans learned that a similar offer made by the Americans had also been rejected.[228]

Further evidence that the aim was extermination, not deportation, comes from Ottoman government officials. Celal, governor-general of Aleppo, believed that moving Armenians out of the war zone was a war necessity. He asked the Ministry of the Interior "to make provisions for housing those Armenians to be deported." The request was rejected.[229] Later transferred to Konya, Celal, divested of his illusions, tried to prevent the deportations, but failed. He later recalled:

In Konya, I was like a man standing by a river without any means of rescue. But instead of water, the river flowed with blood and thousands of innocent children, blameless old men, helpless women and strong young people all on their way to destruction. Those I could seize with my hands I saved; the others, I assume, floated downstream, never to return.[230]

In Syria, Cemal Paşa turned down all offers of help, citing firm orders from Istanbul. Hardegg Loytved, the German consul to Damascus, declared his willingness, and the American government's, to extend such humanitarian aid as soup kitchens and sanitary centers to the deportees. "When I informed Cemal Paşa of our intention," wrote

Loytved, "he told me that he was doing his best to lessen Armenian losses, but he had received firm orders from Istanbul to prevent the Germans and the Americans from providing assistance.[231] Consular dispatches claimed that Cemal Paşa had indeed tried, despite his orders, to ease the situation for the Armenian deportees. He had even agreed to accept money from the Germans unofficially and distribute it secretly among the refugees.[232] Hüseyin Kâzım Kadri, who coordinated Cemal Paşa's efforts, told the German consul to Damascus that

> his orders are ignored; in fact, government offices do exactly the opposite. . . . The government has not the slightest desire to help Armenians; he is afraid it may even be planning to exterminate them all. This barbaric policy will be a source of shame for Turkey.[233]

Hüseyin Kâzim resigned from his post in protest and later wrote in his memoirs that "200,000 people were sacrificed to the government's evil designs in Lebanon alone."[234]

The clearest illustration that the deportations were intended as extermination came from Çerkez Hasan Bey, Hüseyin Kâzım's successor. Local government officials welcomed him to his new post hoping that he would finish the job of "'cleansing' those Armenians."[235] At first Hasan Bey thought this was just a local policy, and so he sought confirmation from Cemal Paşa, who had told him to organize a humane deportation. But this humane deportation was considered "traitorous" and the Ministry of the Interior removed him from his position. Cemal Paşa was warned not to interfere with civilian authorities.

> The civilian authorities are solely responsible for the resettlement of the Armenian deportees. Army commanders are not to interfere in this matter. Therefore, deporting an Armenian from one district to another can only be done with the permission and order of the Interior Ministry.[236]

The Ottoman authorities' genocidal intent is further demonstrated in Talât Paşa's cable to the local authorities in Diyarbakır, dated 12 July

1915. Talât said he had been informed that Armenians and other Christians were being murdered, that "700 Armenians and other Christians were taken by night to the outskirts of the city and slaughtered like sheep," and that the total number killed in that province had reached two thousand. His response was to issue the order, quoted earlier, that "the disciplinary and political measures taken against Armenians should absolutely not be extended to other Christians. Any measures threatening the lives of local [non-Armenian] Christians are to end immediately and should be reported."[237] In other words, he had no concern about the killing of Armenians.[238]

The Ottoman authorities' genocidal intent becomes clear if we look at the issue of Armenian property. In support of the position that there was no intent to annihilate the Armenians, official reports quote at length the provisional laws, regulations, and orders issued in the context of the deportations, claiming that Armenian property under the control of the state and the owners compensated.

The first set of regulations concerning confiscated property and plans for relocation were published on 30 May 1915. The deported Armenians were to be provided for, en route and at their final destination, through an existing government fund for refugees. In the deportees' new location the government would provide land, housing, agricultural equipment, seed grain and other necessary supplies. The deportees were to be compensated for property and valuables left behind. Abandoned property was to be registered and distributed to incoming refugees. The remaining "olive, berry, and orange groves, gardens, storefronts, inns, factories, depositories and similar immovable property [would] be sold by way of auction or its rental equivalent paid."

This cabinet decision[239] was expanded by the Interior Ministry department for the Settlement of Tribes and Immigrants, and its implementation began on 31 May 1915 with the details published in a manual of fifteen sections. An addendum to the manual included language describing how the Armenians would be able to take their movable property and livestock with them and how they would be settled into new villages. It explains that they would be prohibited from abandoning these villages and that their newly assigned lots of land would be registered to them.[240] In accordance with this law, the state would form joint commissions of the ministries of interior and finance to implement the plan.

A second manual, consisting of thirty-four separate sections, published on 10 June,[241] contained a detailed guide to the registration, administration and transfer of Armenian property to the new Muslim settlers. However, other than the statement that "money obtained from the sale or lease of such properties . . . will be paid to the rightful owners . . . ," there are no explanations of how the property should be returned to the Armenians.

More regulations appeared at later dates. The most important was issued on 26 September 1915.[242] This law made several modifications to the May thirtieth law, amounting to the "liquidation of all property" owned by Armenians.[243] This law was the result of pressure from German business interests, which had lost significant investments in Armenian concerns. The law, according to historian H. Kaiser, was intended to compensate for German commercial losses in particular and to protect the interests of foreign companies. There is no mention of compensation to Armenians for their losses. However, "the law mentioned that Armenian properties would be distributed free of charge to Muslim settlers."[244]

A temporary measure, the law was announced three days before the opening of parliament and was immediately put into effect. Retroactively, Ahmet Rıza, the president of the Chamber of Notables, the upper house, argued that the law should not be put into practice until it had been approved by the Chamber of Deputies, but he was effectively ignored. Ahmet Rıza told his fellow notables, "By the time this law comes up for debate in this chamber, no possessions or property will be left. . . . What will be left for us to discuss?" To him, this law was "an oppressive measure. Seize me, throw me out of my village, then sell all my property; this is never lawful." According to Ahmet Rıza, "the law's intention was to complete the looting as soon as possible . . . by the time the law is rejected, it will all be over." As was often the case, while the Constitution demanded that temporary laws be approved by the Chamber of Deputies, this law never even came up for discussion in the assembly.[245]

There were two fundamental principles underlying this law. First, the Armenians would never be coming back, and the property left behind would, according to certain criteria set by the government, be distributed to the settlers who replaced them. Second, the Armenians were to be compensated for those properties left behind.

Yet despite the dozens of documents outlining the use of Armenian property, there is not a single piece of evidence showing that any compensation was actually paid to any deportee. This absence provides a strong argument for the genocidal intent of the Ottoman government. There is also no evidence that any parcel of land was given to the deportees at their final destination, nor any goods. Had the intention been, as stated, to resettle the Armenians elsewhere, proof of this would exist in the archival documentation. Hundreds of Ottoman documents have been made available, but not a single one to confirm the official Turkish position of compensation for Armenian losses. Further proof of the complete lack of any effort to pay compensation is provided by the various postwar decrees allowing deported Armenians to return to their homes. The first decree was issued on 18 October 1918. Then a cabinet decision on 4 November cancelled the September 1915 law allowing for confiscation of Armenian property, thus opening the way for the deportees to reclaim their assets. The Interior Ministry also sent detailed instructions to the local provincial authorities on how to organize the restitution of Armenian property. A great many other regulations followed, but what is notable is that not one of them refers to any compensation already paid.[246]

On the contrary, we have examples of documents that clearly illustrate the systematic ways in which the money and property were put to other uses. We can see from the documents that there were five chief concerns governing the distribution of the resources.

1. TO EXTEND THE MUSLIM BOURGEOISIE

Much of the Armenian property left behind was given to Muslim individuals or companies for the purpose of creating a Muslim bourgeois class, often without demand for any payment or on very favorable terms, including installment plans. Examples are found in the archives of the Cipher Office of the Ministry of the Interior.

a) A telegram sent by the Ministry of Interior's Office of Tribal and Refugee Settlement (IAMM) to Adana (Dörtyol) and also from the Directorate of General Security, known as the *Emniyet Umum Müdürlüğü* (EUM), to the Diyarbakır provincial governor's office states that "[i]t may be fitting that the properties owned by Armenians prior to the deportation be sold and transferred to the Muslim population at a reasonable rate."[247]

b) Telegrams sent by the IAMM to the regional governments in Erzurum, Adana, and Edirne, as well as to local government offices in Urfa, İzmit, Kayseri, Marash, and others, and to the presidents of the Commisions for Liquidation in Tekfurdağ, Adana, Aleppo, and Gemlik state that to increase the number of Muslim businesses, Armenian property should be transferred by using shares to be acquired by business owners and farmers. To further this end, all offices should take any action necessary to develop trade among Muslims.[248]

c) A telegram sent by the IAMM to the president of the Commission for Liquidation in Trabzon states that "to transfer the establishments connected to craft and trade to Muslims, the abandoned stocks of stores should be sold to honorable, young people on installment plans."[249]

d) A telegram sent by the IAMM in the Interior Ministry to the president of the Commission for Liquidation in Istanbul outlines how Armenian establishments connected to craft and trade should be transferred to Muslims, and to whom they should be transferred.[250]

e) A supplemental telegram sent by the IAMM in the Interior Ministry to the provincial governments of Edirne, Adana, Ankara and others, as well as to the governors' offices of Kayseri, Canik and elsewhere and to the offices of the presidents of the Commissions for Liquidation in Adana, Aleppo, İzmit and elsewhere, gives instructions regarding renting Armenian factories and stores to Muslim companies at a low cost to prevent their lying vacant and unused.[251]

2. TO PROVIDE FOR THE NEEDS OF NEW IMMIGRANTS

Property was also distributed to Muslims who settled in the areas formerly inhabited by Armenians. This resettlement goal was openly declared by the cabinet in the regulations decreed on 30 May 1915 and 10 June. Several communications sent to various regional offices provide examples of this program.

a) A telegram sent by the IAMM to the regional governments in Ankara, Adana, Aleppo, Hüdavendigar, and elsewhere, as well as to the governors' offices in İzmit, Urfa, Canik and other places, discusses assigning empty houses to incoming immigrants.[252]

b) A telegram sent by the IAMM to the president of the Trabzon Commission for Liquidation gives instruction to use the stock left behind in warehouses and stores to provide clothing for the new Muslim refugees.[253]

c) A telegram sent by the IAMM to local government offices in Ankara, Adana, Aleppo, and elsewhere, as well as to the governors' offices in İzmit, Eskişehir, Urfa, and other places, orders that refugees from the war zone in need and without support be settled in abandoned property and given provisions, and be placed in available jobs.[254]

3. TO MEET THE NEEDS OF THE MILITARY

One of the most important uses made of Armenian property was to help the armed forces. This was done by commandeering buildings, which were then used for military operations, and through the sale of commodities produced by Armenians. The policy of using abandoned property for military purposes was not, however, confined to that owned by Armenians; abandoned Greek property met with the same fate. Examples or relevant communications follow:

a) A telegram from the IAMM sent in response to a communication from the governors' office in Urfa refers to the milling and processing of abandoned Armenian crops and their consignment to the military.[255]

b) A telegram sent by the secretariat of the Ministry of War to the governor's office in Kütahya asks for information about the type, quantity, and value of property and goods to be redirected to the military.[256]

c) A telegram sent by the AMMU to the governor's office in Kala-ı Sultaniyeye (Çanakkale) refers to the value of grapes from abandoned vineyards prior to their delivery to the military.[257]

4. TO COVER THE EXPENSE OF THE DEPORTATIONS

Records in our possession show that income received from the sale of Armenian properties was used to compensate the state for expenses associated with deporting their owners.[258]

a) A telegram sent by the IAMM to the president of the Commission for the Administration of Abandoned Property in Aleppo concerned the use of part of the income received from the sale of livestock for deporting and providing for Armenians.[259]
b) A telegram sent by the IAMM to the director of immigrants, Şükrü Bey, in Aleppo, ordered that income derived from abandoned property in Aleppo, along with money to be sent from Eskişehir, be used to cover the expense of deporting the Armenians and their upkeep.[260]
c) A telegram sent by the IAMM to the office of the deputy governor of Aleppo orders that the income derived from abandoned property be consigned to the treasury to cover the cost of the deportations.[261]

Some documents discuss the fact that the state's expenses in connection with the deportations were not covered and explicitly indicate that Armenian property would be used for that purpose, and that the costs would thus be compensated. "Since the maintenance of the Armenians deported from Zeytun cannot be met by the state alone, they must provide their own sustenance. Please communicate regarding the amount spent on their maintenance thus far and how many *kuruş* [Ottoman currency] are required for continued residency."[262]

5. TO COVER OTHER STATE NEEDS

In some circumstances, Armenian-owned buildings were used as prisons or for other state requirements. What follows are several examples of exchanges about the need for prison facilities.

a) A telegram sent from the Office of Prisons to the regional and governors' offices in Edirne, Adana, Ankara, İçel, Niğde, and elsewhere inquires about the availability of abandoned buildings large enough to be converted to prisons and their state of repair.[263]

b) A telegram from the General Health Office (*Sıhhıye Müdiriyeti Umumiyesi*) to local offices in Erzurum, Bitlis, and Sivas provinces and elsewhere seeks to reserve buildings and medical equipment left behind by non-Muslims for use in these regions.[264]

These documents reveal why the government frequently sent representatives to the provinces to investigate local pillaging of Armenian property, which was wanted by the Ottoman authorities for their own ends. There was thus no tolerance for private looting; the goal was high-level looting. When the German consulate called the 26 September 1915 law "legalized pillaging," it was not far from the truth.[265] Even as the genocide was occurring, ex-Unionist Ahmet Rıza, speaking before the parliament, decried the pillaging that resulted from this law.[266]

After what he witnessed in the region, Çerkez Hasan summed up the whole abomination: "Stop talking about deportation and murder and instead say that this was a decision to kill the Armenian nation and that will be an end to the arguments."[267]

The Documentation

Of the official documentation of the massacres, many important papers were destroyed. In the main indictment of the postwar trial, we read:

From close inspection of the remaining documents of the Special Organization we understand that most of that body's documents, and all the Central Committee's documents, have been destroyed. Interior Ministry records and eyewitness testimony prove that the files of then-Director-General of Security Aziz Bey were taken from that office before Talât Bey's resignation, and these, containing

important information and correspondence, were not returned
after his resignation.[268]

Mithat Şükrü and Ziya Gökalp, defendants in the trial of the Unionist
leaders, claimed that Dr. Nâzım took all the Central Committee's documents. When asked what became of these papers after the party
was dissolved, Mithat Şükrü explained, "What I understand is that
Dr. Nâzım Bey took them, or so the staff said." Ziya Gökalp was asked
whether Dr. Nâzım had seized the important documents. "Dr. Nâzım
asked for documents on the Committee's history, saying, 'I brought
them from Europe and I shall keep them safe. . . .' But I later learned
that the documents weren't separated from any others. He took them
[all] away in boxes."[269]

In the same trials, postal minister Hüseyin Haşim admitted to
ordering all military telegrams burned, on the instructions of the War
Ministry.[270] On 24 January 1919, the British armed forces intercepted
a telegram from the Turkish interior minister to the provincial governor of Ayintab about burning the originals of telegrams.[271] Furthermore, it was reported that before his flight from the country Talât
Paşa took "a suitcase full of papers to his friend's seaside mansion in
Arnavutköy and had the papers burned in the furnace. . . ."[272]

In a British report on Ahmet Esat's documents, he is quoted as
saying: "Shortly before the Armistice, government staff raided the
archives department by night and destroyed the greater part of the
documents."[273] In a trial in 1926, Kör Ali İhsan Bey, a member of
the CUP Central Committee, said he had burned all the documents in
his possession.[274] This destruction continued after the Unionists
withdrew from government. In fact, they chose their replacements
specifically for this purpose. On 14 October 1918 Ahmet İzzet Paşa
formed the first postwar Ottoman cabinet, with himself as both
grand vizier and minister of war. He ordered an end to the operations
of the Special Organization (referred to euphemistically as the "Office
of Eastern Affairs") and the destruction of its archives.[275]

From the documents that do exist, we know that the official government deportation decision was made on 27 May 1915 and published in *Takvîm-i Vekâyı*, the official government gazette, on 1 June
1915[276] as the "temporary law on military measures against opponents of government policy in time of war." Before this temporary

law, other documents confirm the deportation decision, such as two memoranda from the General Staff to the Interior Ministry dated 2 and 26 May; and an inquiry from the Interior Ministry to the cabinet dated 26 May 1915 regarding the need for a temporary law. Again on 30 May, the cabinet passed a regulation regarding the rules of deportation that was subsequently published.[277] These official documents give no real sense of the course of events. As we have seen, the expulsions had begun long before the date on which the decrees came into force (1 June). And these decisions may well have been issued merely to serve as official cover to assuage the unease of foreign countries.

The 26 May memo from the General Staff to the Interior Ministry noted that the first decision and orders concerning deportation were given orally.[278] İbrahim Bey, the minister of justice, confirmed that the expulsion orders were issued long before the government's official decree. In his statement before the postwar commission of inquiry, he stated that "during the war the commanders of the armed forces were given certain powers. These were necessary for operations to secure the army's rear. The armed forces carried out these operations and the deportation law was issued later."[279] As we have seen, there are a number of documents, different orders of the Interior Ministry to local governors for deportation of local populations dated from late April and early May that show the expulsion had already started at the beginning of May.[280]

The deportation law issued by the Ottoman government must have owed something to the Allies' declaration of 24 May 1915, when the governments of Britain, France and Russia jointly issued a note stating "In light of the crimes against humanity and civilisation committed by Turkey, the allied powers warn the Sublime Porte that members of the Ottoman government involved in the mass murder will be held personally responsible for these crimes."[281] The Interior Ministry's efforts to give the expulsions a semblance of legality began two days after this note was issued. Talât Paşa demanded a decree from the government to give official cover to his actions.[282]

As Toynbee correctly pointed out: "Glancing back . . . , we can discern the Central Government's general plan. . . . It was a deliberate, systematic attempt to eradicate the Armenian population throughout the Ottoman Empire, and it has certainly met with a very large measure of success."[283] Thus, Talât Paşa could tell the acting

German ambassador, Prince Hohenlohe-Langenburg, on 31 August 1915, that "*la question Armenienne n'existe plus.*"[284]

The Role of Armenian Unrest

The true scale of the Armenian uprising, which was used by the Ottoman authorities as a pretext for the deportations, is still a subject of debate. One reason is the Turkish policy of denial, which has hampered academic debate. As a result, most scholars have ignored addressing the question of the Armenian organizations' activities, which has suggested a causal link between the activities and the genocide. This link must be rejected. The only way to do this is to begin an open debate about the Armenian uprising. Here we will only make several observations.[285]

Official Turkish history argues that the deportations were prompted by Armenians having volunteered to fight with Russia, forming armed gangs inside the country, and staging uprisings. Thus, according to this theory, the Dashnak promise that "the Armenians [would] remain loyal to the Ottoman government and do their military duty" was a sham. Their real purpose was to organize an Armenian uprising in coordination with the Russians.[286] However, there is a clear distinction between the "Armenian" units in the Russian army and the so-called "Armenian uprisings" in eastern Anatolia. On the first issue, it must be noted that the presence of Ottoman Armenians and Armenians from Europe and America in Russian ranks made a far greater impression on the Unionists' imagination than their real military significance. The first volunteer units were formed by Russian Armenians; Ottoman Armenians participated during the war.[287] The total number of the Armenian volunteers was four thousand, in groups of one thousand.[288] The presence of some prominent Armenians in these units was used by the Ottomans as damning evidence.[289]

After the outbreak of war, the Ottoman Dashnaks sent a delegation to Tiflis in an attempt to dissuade people there from fighting the Ottoman Empire, arguing that it would be used as a pretext for persecuting Armenians. But they were unable to stop the march of events. On 17 February 1915, Ambassador Wangenheim reported that he had asked the Armenian patriarch to intervene and warn the Russian

Armenians. But the patriarch declined; "even if we intervened," he said, "it would be claimed that we did so under pressure and we would achieve nothing."[290] Armenian historian Leo (Arakel Babakhanian), claims that, in any case, the Armenians in Tiflis did not take the Turkish Armenians' pleas seriously because the Dashnaks in Istanbul were secretly encouraging the volunteer movement in the Caucasus.[291]

Russian soldiers, guided by Armenians, raided Muslim villages in the Caucasus, Van and Bitlis. Louis Mosel, a German officer, reported that in the Caucasus, "a large part of the population is fleeing death at the hands of Russians and their Armenian collaborators."[292] In Turkish sources as well, we have similar examples[293] of such incidents in the Caucasus and at Van, which prompted feelings of revenge among the Muslims.[294] The first Armenian volunteer unit, commanded by Antranik Toros Ozanian, and the second unit, commanded by a former member of the Ottoman parliament, achieved some military successes in the Van area, and also looted Muslims' houses in the surrounding villages.[295] Yet Muslim villages were not the sole target of these raids; the gangs also attacked Armenian villages that did not willingly provide them support.[296]

Attacks on Muslim villages had become common even before the Van uprising.[297] A German journalist in the region reported to his consulate that the gangs killed two hundred Muslim families in Van including women and children.[298] Yet the operations against Muslims in Van began in earnest only around mid-May, after the Russian occupation of the city. "On May 18, Armenian units entered Van and began a cleansing operation around the lake."[299]

There were, of course, Ottoman Armenians who joined their coreligionists from Russia in the volunteer units. "Armenian privates in [Ottoman] units deserted at the beginning of the battle and joined the enemy."[300] German consuls reported that during the Caucasian campaign, Armenian soldiers in the Ottoman army "turned their guns on the Turks."[301] Militias were formed in Ottoman Armenia in the autumn of 1914 despite the Dashnak Congress's Erzurum decision and pledge of loyalty. Aziz Samih relates, for example, that some two thousand Armenians took to the mountains around Erciş.[302] A similar situation existed in the Zeytun area, where deportations had begun in March 1915. German consular reports say that some Armenians in the region refused to join the army and hid in the mountains as a form of passive resistance, but that the Armenian people on the whole were uneasy about the militias formed in their name. Some of these gang members were captured and tortured to death by the Ottoman Army.[303] The situation was the same at Dörtyol, where the first deportations took place. "Almost all" of the Armenians preferred to either flee or stay in their homes rather than serve in the Ottoman army.[304]

Hovhannes Kachaznuni, the first president of independent Armenia and several times the leader of the Dashnak Party, said that despite the Dashnak congress's decision to support the Ottoman regime, inevitably some Armenians would refuse. "It could not have happened otherwise. For a quarter of a century, Armenian society has nurtured a certain and inescapable psychology. This psychological state had to come to the fore and of course it did."[305] The operations of Armenian gangs behind the front lines are mentioned in Turkish as well as non-Turkish sources.[306] Kurdish nationalist Nuri Dersimi gives details of Armenian volunteers' raids and massacres in Kurdish villages at the beginning of the war.[307] Some Armenian memoirs also mention the volunteer Armenian gangs.[308]

Due to war conditions, a certain level of chaos prevailed on the Caucasus front, especially after the defeat at Sarıkamış. Soldiers " . . . would throw down their weapons and flee at the first encounter with the enemy; the army was no longer an organized force."[309] With each successive military defeat, the number of Ottoman deserters rose sharply—and not just among the Armenians. The German consul to Adana reported on 18 March that after the outbreak of war, almost everybody in town, regardless of ethnicity or religion, was a deserter; and that these deserters committed acts of banditry, which were therefore widespread.[310] Pursued by the gendarmes, the deserters (Turkish, Kurdish and Armenian) attacked whichever village happened to be on their route. Describing the Turkish deserters, a Turkish officer claimed: "They had even run off with the officers' personal belongings and the regimental coffers."[311]

Fed up with being pillaged by the army, villagers began to defend themselves by uniting with the bandits and firing at army units. Aziz Samih reports that the villagers of Erzurum Aşkale, Kara Kilise, and the Tercan Plain carried out many such attacks.[312] In some places (Erzurum, Dersim), local Kurds and Alevis joined the Armenian gangs shooting at soldiers. "The people of Dersim . . . became outlaws themselves."[313]

Some of the attacks attributed to Armenian volunteers were in fact carried out by the irregular Kurdish cavalry Hamidiye regiments; later they blamed the attacks on the Armenians, increasing the tension between the two communities and provoking the Kurds to attack in reprisal.[314]

Some consular reports claimed that the CUP provoked the Armenians to rebel.[315] We also have reports of Turkish army units photographing their own weapons and then using the photographs for propaganda, claiming the weapons had been found in Armenian houses and churches. Rafael de Nogales witnessed one such incident and said that the purpose was to lay the groundwork in public opinion.[316] The American consul to Harput reported on 24 July 1915 that "people were tortured to confess that [they had] guns and pistols when in reality there was nothing. . . . It is understood that all this had been planned months ago."[317]

Some events cited in Turkish sources to justify the deportation—uprisings and weapons seizures—were simply fabrications. Erzurum is one example. When German chief consul in Istanbul Mordtmann appealed to Talât Paşa at the end of May to exclude the women and children of Erzurum from deportation, or at least afford them better treatment, the interior minister said that an uprising was in the works and that the place was full of weapons and bombs.[318] This information was forwarded to Scheubner-Richter in Erzurum, who discussed it with the provincial governor, Tahsin Bey. "The governor confirmed that there are no bombs and weapons in and around Erzurum," the consul reported.[319] Preparations for an uprising were, in Tahsin Bey's words, "improbable." Talât must have known this, for he had received a coded cable from Tahsin on 24 May—five days before his interview with the German ambassador on 29 May—refuting claims that an uprising was planned.

Yozgat is another example. At the Yozgat trial, some defendants who had claimed an uprising had taken place later admitted that this was not true. At the second session, Kemal Bey, the district prefect, said that an uprising had taken place in Boğazlıyan. The trial judge responded by reading a telegram sent by a witness named Şahabettin from Yozgat to the Fifth Army in Ankara: "There is no evidence of a rebellion in the district of Boğazlıyan."[320] This claim of an uprising was repeated many times during the Yozgat trials. At the eighth session (20 February 1920), Şahabettin testified that he had sent two hundred officers to stop a rebellion that he later admitted was only five or six deserters.[321] Moreover, public order "was being violated by the gendarmes," his telegram noted, and "looting is still going on."[322] At the trial's eleventh session (March 5), Cemal, lieutenant governor of Yozgat, said that when he investigated this "uprising," he found that the incident consisted of a few Armenian deserters hiding out in their houses in some villages.[323]

The same is true for all the Armenian "uprisings" in Anatolia cited in Turkish sources to defend the deportations. In fact, most of the resistance, such as in Şebinkarahisar on 3 July 1915[324] and in Urfa in October 1915, came in response to the deportations. The Urfa uprising in October was started by Armenians deported from Van and Diyarbakır, since Urfa was a stop on the deportation route. Some Armenians of Urfa also had been deported and killed. In May, eighteen families were deported and in June, fifty people were arrested, ruthlessly tortured, and then sent off to Diyarbakır to be killed on the road. In August and September, survivors of massacres elsewhere began to arrive in Urfa. In mid-August, massacres began in Urfa itself, and between 15 and 19 August, four hundred people were taken to the outskirts of town and murdered. The Armenians in Urfa preferred to resist rather than be driven away and killed.[325] Celal, the governor of Aleppo who was sacked for defying the deportation order, said of these events, "Each human has the right to live. A trampled worm will squirm and wriggle. The Armenians will defend themselves."[326]

The Van uprising deserves to be examined separately, for regardless of the fact that it took place after the secret deportation and extermination decisions were made, it served as the main reason used by the government (and later Turkish historians) to justify the deportations. What really happened has yet to be researched thoroughly. However, there are enough accounts from the region that we can make some general assessments. Ömer Naci, who arrived in Van to organize Special Organization units in August 1914, reported that he "found the Armenians here far more docile than in Erzurum."[327] Rafael de Nogales said that the local leaders of the CUP blamed Armenian volunteers for the Russian defeats during the winter of

1914–15, and sought revenge against the local Armenians. This pushed the Armenians in Van to rebel[328] since, before the uprising, the Unionists had made no secret of their intention to eliminate the Armenian population. Cevdet Paşa, the governor of Van, is reported to have held a meeting in February 1915 at which he said, "We have cleansed the Armenians and Syriac [Christian]s from Azerbaijan, and we will do the same in Van."[329] Hüsnü Bey, the head of the court-martial in Van, was aware of the preparations; he warned the Armenians and later remained by their side when the plan was put to action.[330]

Tahsin wrote that "there was not and could not have been an uprising in Van. Through our constant pressure [of the local population] we have created a mess from which we can no longer escape, and we have put the army in a difficult position in the East."[331] A similar assessment was offered by Celal, the governor-general of Aleppo. Rössler, the German consul there, reported that the governor said, "Muslims are razing Armenian villages to the ground near the Russian borders." And "the Turkish government . . . sees all Armenians as guilty, as the enemy."[332]

İbrahim Arvas, a Van deputy in the Ottoman parliament, was in the city at the time, and he reported that the CUP was secretly provoking people to attack Armenians.[333] A consular report dated 2 April 1915 claims that Armenian villages in the Van area had been attacked and looted and a massacre had taken place in and around Saray.[334] Joseph Pomiankowski, the military attaché at the Austrian Embassy in Istanbul, described the Van uprising as "a desperate effort by Armenians, who witnessed the beginning of the murders and understood that their turn would come."[335] L. Spörri, a Swiss national who oversaw the German missionary efforts in Van, reported that Armenians in the area kept receiving news of massacres.[336] After the war, American missionary Stanley E. Kerr collected the memoirs of people who witnessed the events in Van. He claims that more than fifty-five thousand Armenians had been killed (including beyond the border) before the uprising had even started.[337]

The Dashnak organization was very powerful in Van. In a report submitted to the Socialist International in Copenhagen in 1910, the Dashnaks claimed that armed young men in the region had gathered under its banner.[338] German consular reports say that Armenians in the region were arming themselves, probably for protection from massacre initially, but later on in preparation for an uprising.[339] Even sources that describe the event as a "forced rebellion" admit that the Dashnak organization held certain parts of the city under its control and bargained with government officials.[340] Some Armenian historians claim that the provocation of the Dashnaks played an important part in the events.[341] For a government to lose control over some areas under its sovereignty and to be forced into "bargaining" with nongovernmental organizations also sheds light on another aspect of the affair.

It can be argued that military necessity drove the evacuation in certain regions. Based on the information we have, this is indeed possible in the case of Van. The German embassy also repeatedly informed the Turkish government that it was willing to support the deportation if it was for military purposes and for the protection of the local civilians.[342] The critical point is that people were not just deported from militarily sensitive areas, but from the entire empire. This nullifies the argument of military necessity. The governor-general of Erzurum, Tahsin Bey, who readily admitted that the disturbances in the area were the result of Unionist policies, still agreed with the deportation from the border region; but he objected to it being extended to areas of no military importance and to its being justified by such fictions as "bombs found" and "uprisings."

An overall assessment of all these accounts of rebellion leads to the conclusion that, in fact, the deported Armenians for the most part obeyed the deportation orders without much resistance. An eyewitness who survived the massacres claims that a convoy of ten thousand only required twenty gendarmes to guard it.[343] The American consul to Harput noted that "the most striking observation on the situation is the Armenians' helplessness and their lack of any power to resist." In some cases, only two or three gendarmes would massacre a whole village.[344] Consular reports confirm that when the deportation campaign began in Zeytun in February and March, the Armenians showed no resistance and followed orders.[345]

The striking part of all these arguments is that they are used to justify the death of eight hundred thousand people. No actions by gangs or individuals can justify the death of eight hundred thousand people. Nonetheless most Turkish work on the subject sticks to the official story. One can find legitimization of the crime in statements like the following:

> The Ottoman Empire was caught between two great threats that surrounded Turkey and endangered its very existence. In the west, there was the British and French campaign in Gallipoli and the naval blockade; in the east and southeast, there was the Russian encirclement. A state in such a dire condition is faced with an Armenian rebellion along its internal communication lines. . . . Surrounded by enemies on all sides . . . what is a state to do with [its] minority communities? What state would put itself at the mercy of this network of treachery and crime and its [active] communities?[346]

Herein lies the problem in Turkey today. From this perspective, it becomes acceptable, when deemed necessary, for one ethno-religious group to carry out mass murder against another. The attempt to justify and rationalize the death of a whole nation, including women, children, the old, and the infirm, must itself be considered a crime against humanity.[347]

Leaving aside the allegations of uprisings, the issue of Armenian volunteers serving with the Russians is very important,[348] for its impact on the Unionist leaders. Behaettin Şakir almost lost his life at the Caucasian front and the experience colored his actions for the rest of the war. It became very easy for the Unionists to blame the Armenians for the end of the Pan-Turanist dream. The volunteers were then successfully used as a pretext for implementing a project planned long in advance. Even events entirely unrelated to war and the military defeat were held up as evidence of "Armenian treason."[349]

It bears repeating that the implementation of the Armenian reform plan was at stake. Had Russia occupied the eastern provinces, the Muslim population would have been removed, so the thinking went, and the territories forever lost. This threat seems to have given the Unionists the psychological strength to make their final decision. Had there been no Armenian campaign, the Unionists would likely have made a similar decision for fear that a Russian victory might lead to the implementation of the reform plan. The problem for the

Unionists was not the Armenian gangs or an Armenian rebellion, but the fact that Armenians lived in the eastern provinces at all. As we have seen, the Treaty of Yeniköy with Russia on 8 February 1914 was considered the beginning of the loss of Anatolia for the Ottomans. Numerous statements by foreign diplomats deemed the reform plan "a step towards partition."[350] Pallavicini, the Austrian ambassador at Istanbul, reported the Russians saying they felt no need to conceal the fact that, with the implementation of reforms, "the partition of Turkey in Asia will be as good as done."[351]

Official Ottoman correspondence clearly shows that the authorities also understood this, and that the purpose of the deportations was to prevent the emergence of an Armenian state. A general circular from the Ministry of the Interior, sent by telegram to all the Ottoman provinces on 29 August, stated that "the government's aim in deporting the Armenians . . . is to prevent them from pursuing any nationalist action to promote an Armenian government."[352]

PART 3

THE INVESTIGATIONS AND PROSECUTION
OF THE WAR CRIMES AND GENOCIDE

CHAPTER 6

THE QUESTION OF PUNISHING THE "TURKS"

WHEN IT BECAME CLEAR THAT THE WAR WAS IRREVOCABLY LOST, Talât Paşa's cabinet resigned. His successor, Ahmet İzzet Paşa, formed a new cabinet on October 14 and immediately set about its first task: discussing the conditions for the armistice with the British. The armistice agreement was signed at Mondros on 30 October 1918. One copy of the agreement was passed to the Germans on November 7, and this terminated the alliance between Germany and the Ottoman Empire. The most important articles of the armistice agreement were:

> Article 7. The Allies will retain the right to occupy any and every strategic point if a situation arises that would threaten security. . . .
> Article 24. In the event of disturbances in the Six [Eastern] Provinces, the Entente countries reserve the right to any or all parts of the aforementioned provinces.[1]

Somehow, the agreement was presented to the Turkish people as a victory. Minister of the Navy Rauf Orbay Bey, who signed the agreement, claimed:

The independence of our state, the rights of our sultanate have been preserved in their entirety. This is not an armistice concluded between victor and vanquished; rather it is more a situation in which two equal powers, both desiring to end a state of war, cease hostilities.

Based on a confidential letter received from Admiral Somerset Arthur Gough-Calthorpe, commander of the Royal Navy in the Mediterranean, Rauf Bey claimed that no enemy soldiers would be entering Istanbul or Adana, and there would be no occupation of Ottoman territory. But in the days after his speech, Allied soldiers did enter Istanbul, and the occupation of Ottoman territory followed quickly.[2] First, two English officers made an appearance in Istanbul on 7 November 1918. The next day, four French officers arrived, and on 10 November three generals—two English, one French. Finally, on 13 November the city's occupation was declared. A flotilla consisting of 67 British warships, 22 French, 10 Italian and one Greek anchored before Istanbul's Dolmabahçe Palace.[3] On 8 February 1919, in an official ceremony to inaugurate the occupation, French general Franchet d'Espérey entered Beyoğlu in the heart of Istanbul on a white horse, in the footsteps of Sultan Mehmet II, Mehmet the Conqueror, who had entered the walled city of Constantinople 466 years earlier.

In addition to the usual expectations for punishing a defeated nation, there appeared to be unusually good justification for punishing the Ottomans. When the 1920 Treaty of Sèvres—the Allies' peace treaty with Turkey—was criticized for being too harsh, British prime minister Lloyd George responded: "This is justified by the Turks' entering the war on Germany's side, which prolonged the conflict by two years and cost Britain huge losses in men and materiel."[4] But there were three further reasons why the Turks were thought to merit harsh punishment.

The first involved the desire to partition Anatolia. By the eve of World War I, the Great Powers had concluded various agreements among themselves that resolved how they intended to carve up Ottoman territory. While these plans appeared at first glance to be limited to the economic sphere, their ultimate goal was the political division of Anatolia, thereby disemboweling the Ottoman state.

The French ambassador to Berlin, in charge of the talks between the Great Powers, wrote on 25 September 1913 that the discussions taking place would settle "collectively and finally [the] future shares and present spheres of influence in Asia Minor." The ultimate outcome was a series of bilateral agreements among France, Germany, Britain and Italy, which divided Anatolia into zones of economic influence. On 16 March 1914 the French ambassador noted that "the aim of this bargaining was not merely . . . to divide up Asia Minor in an economic sense, but also to partition it politically. In March 1914, the German ambassador to London, Prince Lichnowsky, signed the Baghdad Treaty with Britain. "In reality the aim of this agreement," he wrote, "is to divide Anatolia into zones of influence. But in order to appear respectful of the Sultan's rights, utmost care must be taken never to use this expression."[5] These plans were interrupted by the war and by Germany's defection, so a new series of secret agreements and treaties followed to determine the share of the wartime Allies. These agreements, some of which provided for new independent states in the region, were as follows:[6]

1) Treaty of Istanbul (March–April 1915): After long discussions and much haggling, Russia succeeded in securing, in separate arrangements, France's and Britain's acceptance of its claim over the Straits of the Bosphorus and the Dardanelles.

2) Treaty of London (26 April 1915): This agreement recognized Italy's right to occupy Antalya in the event of the partition of Anatolia.

3) The Hussein-McMahon Correspondence (July 1915–March 1916): The outcome of correspondence between Sir Henry McMahon, the British high commissioner in Egypt, and Arab leaders was a British promise to support, outfit and arm an Arab revolt against the Ottomans in the area between Iran and the Mediterranean. In return, the Arab leaders would recognize Great Britain's claims in Mersin, Alexandria, and large parts of Syria.

4) The Sykes-Picot Accord (May 9–16, 1916): Signed by Britain and France and later approved by Russia, it confirmated the Treaty of Istanbul. The accord also provided for international administration of Palestine, French occupation in the coastal areas of Syria, British rule in lower Mesopotamia and an Arab state in between, as well as an overall confederation of these states. This accord had great influence on the postwar peace agreement and its implementation.

5) The Saint Jean de Maurienne Treaty (1 April 1917): This treaty was devised as a way to include the newest member of the wartime alliance, Italy, in the Sykes-Picot Accord. It granted Italy the right to occupy additional areas in Anatolia in the event of a breakup of the Ottoman Empire, pending Russian approval. The October Revolution removed Russia both from the war and from the series of agreements, which in turn led to a dispute between Italy and the Allies about the treaty's legal validity. On 30 October 1918, Lord Balfour announced to the strong protest of the Italians that the 1917 treaty was void. This issue dogged the peace talks in Paris and later led the Italian government to support the Turkish struggle for independence.

6) The Balfour Declaration (2 November 1917): The British government promised the World Zionist Organization a national homeland for the Jews in Palestine.

7) The Hogarth Message (January 1918): The Bolshevik government in Russia published the Sykes-Picot and Istanbul agreements, forcing the British government to confirm that it was bound by the promises made to the Arabs in these accords. The publication of these secret accords put the British government in a very difficult position. In a speech on 5 January 1918 Lloyd George was also forced to reaffirm that Britain was "not fighting to deprive Turkey of its capital or of rich and famous lands such as Thrace and Asia Minor where the majority of people are from the Turkish race."[7] This statement, made at a time when it was not yet clear how the war would end, was interpreted as a retreat from the secret accords. British foreign secretary Lord Curzon was to announce later that the statement had been made "to pull the Turks out of war" and was no longer valid.[8] Once the Allied victory was clear, France and Britain jointly reiterated the goals of the secret accords.

8) The Fourteen Points (8 January 1918): These were proposed by U.S. president Wilson as the basic points for peace. The twelfth point directly concerned the Ottomans:

> The Turkish portions of the present Ottoman Empire should be assured a secure sovereignty, but the other nationalities which are

now under Turkish rule should be assured an undoubted security
of life and an absolutely unmolested opportunity of autonomous
development, and the Dardanelles should be permanently opened
as a free passage to the ships and commerce of all nations under
international guarantees.[9]

9) *The Four Principles* (11 February 1918): These were intended to
enforce and redefine the right of self-determination proclaimed by
Wilson. The Sèvres peace treaty reiterated that the position of the
people living in each area would be taken as the basis for determination, and that their interests should not be violated by any past or
future conflict.

10) *Declaration to the Seven* (June 1918): In this declaration,
Great Britain reassured seven Arab leaders that it would guarantee
full independence for the Arabs.

Yet, despite (and perhaps to some extent because of) the various
agreements, in the end the Great Powers were unable to come to
terms on how to divide Ottoman territory. There were many reasons
for this, not least of which were the absence of a single, comprehensive agreement signed by all parties, the contradictory promises made
in various treaties and accords (as in the case of Palestine) and the
sudden withdrawal of Russia from the equation. The Turks' success in
founding their national state after the war was to a large extent due to
the Great Powers' failure to agree on the partition of the Middle East.

The second compelling reason for punishing the Turks was to exploit
the opportunity of throwing them out of Europe, which had perhaps
been in the back of Europe's mind since the Ottoman conquest of
Constantinople. By the end of the eighteenth century, this idea had
become one of the most potent cultural-political weapons used by
the Great Powers to mobilize the Ottoman Empire's Christian communities in their nationalist struggles. They went so far as to draw up
concrete political plans to this end. Tsarist Russia, for example, had
always seen itself as the third Rome, the heir to the Byzantine Empire,
and as such evolved a mission of delivering Constantinople. This mission acquired more weight after 1774 with the preparation of a "master

plan for the Eastern system," which proposed the destruction of the Ottoman Empire and the establishment of a "Greek State" in its place.[10] Forcing the Turks out of European territory was one of the main demands of Christian communities fighting for independence, and European support for these movements, whether by governments or organizations, was mobilized by this motif.

During World War I the idea of liberating the Christian nations from the barbaric Turks was stated openly, even by the British. Lloyd George rejoiced when Turkey entered the war on Germany's side, since this offered an opportunity for a necessary final settlement with the Turks. "I am very pleased," he said on 10 November 1914, "that the Turks are finally being called to account for the crimes they committed against humanity."[11] In Lloyd George's mind, the Turks were "a human cancer, a creeping agony in the flesh of the lands which they misgoverned." Lloyd George warned his detractors that a Turkish victory might well mean "the torch of war, pillage, outrage and murder" moving from Asia to Europe, and must therefore be prevented.[12] Ridding Europe of the Turks, therefore, was "far from being a simple issue" and one that had "plagued European political life for nearly 500 years." War and the Turks' defeat offered the chance to settle this question "once and for all." Europe ought to use this opportunity, "which she has been awaiting for nearly 500 years and which shall not come again."[13]

Wilson expressed similar views at the Paris Peace Conference. "I have studied the question of the Turks in Europe and every year confirmed my opinion that they ought to be cleared out."[14] This was the shared position of the other countries represented at the Paris Peace Conference. When Damat Ferid Paşa went before the Council of Ten—the most powerful body of the states' representatives—on 17 June 1919 to present the Ottoman position on the peace terms and to object to the West's anti-Turkish cultural bias,[15] the reply he received made the cultural aspect of the punishment very clear.

> History tells us of many Turkish successes and many Turkish defeats. . . . Yet in all these changes there is no case to be found, either in Europe or Asia or Africa, in which the establishment of Turkish rule in any country has not been followed by a diminution of material prosperity and a fall in the level of culture; nor is there any case

to be found in which the withdrawal of Turkish rule has not been followed by a growth in material prosperity and a rise in the level of culture. Neither among the Christians nor among the Moslems . . . has the Turk done other than destroy whatever he has conquered."[16]

Neither the Great Powers' desire to partition Anatolia, nor the impetus to expel Turkey from Europe could be openly cited as justification for punishment. So the claim of Turkish crimes committed against the Empire's own people, the Armenian genocide in particular, was given as the primary reason. In fact, the call had been made throughout the nineteenth century to throw the Turks out of Europe on the grounds of human rights; the argument was that a nation that rode roughshod over human rights had no place in civilized Europe. The allegations of the Armenian massacre went to the heart of the human rights question and gave Europe strong justification for its position. As Balfour put it, "The massacres in Syria and Armenia are far more terrible than any that history has recorded in those hapless countries."[17]

News of the Armenian atrocities provoked a strong reaction from the public in the West, in Britain in particular, which had a powerful humanitarian movement. The first reaction came from Sazanov, the Russian foreign minister, who visited London and Paris in April 1915 and argued for a letter of protest to be sent to Istanbul. He wanted members of the Turkish government held personally responsible for the crimes. What ultimately pushed the Allies to support such a letter was not simply revulsion and outrage at the deportations. Sazanov argued, for example, that the intervention would prompt the Turks to ease or even halt their anti-Armenian campaign, something that would no doubt boost the morale of Armenian soldiers in the Russian ranks. To Russia this effort signified a means to advance its claims over the Straits.

Arnold Toynbee claimed that the tsarist government had yet other, more sinister calculations behind the strong position it adopted: the Armenian massacres would deflect attention from the atrocities perpetrated by its own soldiers against the Jews in Poland during their retreat before the Germans on the Eastern Front.[18] "The French ambassador to Russia described this brutality toward Jews, claiming that more than eight hundred thousand were violently expelled from war zones in Poland and Lithuania."[19]

France immediately backed Sazanov's proposal, while Great Britain continued to dither. Under pressure from public opinion, however, and fearful of losing its historical role as chief protector of the Christians of the Ottoman Empire, the British government issued a joint memo with France and Russia on 24 May 1915. The first draft, proposed by Russia, contained the phrase "crimes against Christianity and civilization," but France and Britain feared this would offend their own colonial Muslim populations and succeeded in changing the phrase to "crimes against humanity."[20] This paved the way for the concept to assume its place after the war as one of the most important categories in international law.

American ambassador to the Porte Henry Morgenthau delivered the letter to Grand Vizier Said Halim Paşa on 3 June. But it produced no effect whatsoever, seen merely as foreign meddling. The grand vizier declared that the deportation measures the Turkish government deemed fit concerning its Armenian population was of no concern to the other powers, and that it was fully within its sovereign rights to do so. The Sublime Porte, after consultation with the German ambassador Wangenheim, issued a forceful statement of its own. "Far from having condoned or organized mass murders, the Porte declared, it had merely exercised its sovereign right of self-defense against a revolutionary movement, and the responsibility for everything that had happened in the Armenian districts had to be borne exclusively by the Entente Powers themselves, because they had organized and directed the revolutionary movements in the first place."[21]

The British government continued to issue warnings throughout the war, even declaring the punishment of the Turks for their crimes as one of the Allies' central war objectives. In reply to a 1916 memo from President Wilson on how to end the war, the Entente countries replied on 18 December 1916 that one of the main aims was "the liberation of nations living under the bloody injustice of the Turks."[22] The French foreign minister used similar words on 10 January 1917, citing as one of the "supreme goals of the war":

The liberation of the peoples who now lie beneath the murderous tyranny of the Turks, and the expulsion from Europe of the Ottoman Empire, which has proved so radically alien to Western civilization.[23]

This view would later be reiterated at the Lausanne Peace Conference in 1922–23 when Lord Curzon claimed the "protection of Christian minorities, and if possible their liberation" as one of the Allies' war aims.[24]

After the war the Allied Powers tied the terms of the peace treaty to the Ottoman government's attitude toward punishing the perpetrators of the massacres. Commanders of the Allied forces who came to Istanbul to monitor the conditions of the armistice wasted no time in impressing upon the government the need for urgency and firm, decisive action in this respect. General Franchet d'Espèrey, for example, the French commander who oversaw the official commencement of Istanbul's occupation by Allied troops, symbolically entering atop his white horse as had previous conquerers, said to the incumbent grand vizier, Tevfik Paşa, who stood before the white horse, "If your government does not take severe measures the judgment passed on you shall be dire." When Tevfik Paşa reported this to Ali Fuad, Sultan Vahdettin's chief secretary, he asked uncomprehendingly, "Sir, what do they want done?" To which Tevfik Paşa replied, "They want us to do what Fuat Paşa did in Damascus"—referring to the execution of Muslims responsible for a Christian massacre in 1858.[25]

The British were adamant that the Turks be punished. In a note to the Turkish Foreign Ministry on 18 January 1919, Admiral Calthorpe, now the British high commissioner in Istanbul, wrote that "His Majesty's Government is resolved to have proper punishment inflicted on those responsible for Armenian massacres."[26] Ten days later he sent a telegram to London reporting that

it was pointed out to Government that when massacres became known in England, British statesmen had promised the civilized world that persons connected would be held personally responsible and that it was [the] firm intention of H. M. Government to fulfill promise.[27]

British occupation officials went to pains to treat the Turks coldly to emphasize the point. In Admiral Calthorpe's words, "If I used strong language in my note it is only out of my desire to be a faithful translator of the feelings of the British Government and people." And,

"Our first duty, regardless of our interest, is to embrace the Christian subjects. . . . The vile treatment to which they have been subjected must not be forgotten."[28] During the first months of the occupation, the sultan's attempts to establish some sort of relationship with the high commissioner or the British Command Headquarters were rebuffed.[29] Said Molla, founder of the Turkish-British Friendship Society, asked one British official, "Why is the British High Commissioner behaving in such a conspicuously cold manner towards Turkey?" The answer came, "So as not to leave any doubt in a single Turkish mind that Turkey's punishment will be heavy indeed."[30]

When General Milne, commander of the British forces in Caucasia, said that "the Turks must be taught a harsh lesson," he expressed a sentiment shared by all the Allies.[31] Lloyd George stated at one point that "when the peace conditions are announced the Turks will see what heavy punishment will be meted on them for their madness, their blindness, their crimes. . . . The punishment will be such that it will satisfy even their greatest enemies."[32] Lord Curzon described Turkey as "a culprit waiting to hear the sentence."[33] After the armistice was signed in October 1918, Western public opinion demanded "the liberation of peoples long living a life of captivity under arbitrary, murderous rule." The massacre of "Armenian and Greek populations" headed up a long list of what were seen as "the atrocities and crimes of the Turks."[34] But what did punishing Turks for the Armenian massacre actually mean in practice?

As early as 20 December 1917, Lloyd George mentioned one aspect of this punishment: "What would become of Mesopotamia should be left to the Paris Congress. Yet there is something that should not be allowed to happen again. The Turks' bloody dictatorship will not be restored."[35] Positions on this point would become clearer after the war. Just as there was no one single reason for punishing the Turks, there was no single form of punishment. Admiral Webb, deputy high commissioner in Istanbul, wrote in 1919 to the Paris Peace Conference:

> Punishing those responsible for the Armenian atrocities means punishing all Turks. That is why I propose that the punishment, on the national level, should be the dismemberment of the last Turkish

Empire, and, on the individual level, putting on trial the senior officials on my list so as to make an example out of them.[36]

Turkish Attitudes Toward Punishing the Unionist War Criminals

In the immediate postwar period in Turkey, especially after 1919, two
competing centers of government evolved. Ankara was the center of the
Nationalist Movement (founded mostly by former CUP members),
while Istanbul was controlled by the sultan and largely by former opponents of the wartime CUP. The emerging Turkish Independence Movement, centered in Ankara, organized around two main concerns: to
prevent the partition of Anatolia and to liberate the sultan from the
"custody" of the occupation forces. These two centers were in a constant state of negotiation, at times agreeing and at others in bitter conflict depending on the composition of the Istanbul government.

Initially, both political centers favored trying war criminals, hoping to secure a more favorable outcome for Turkey at the peace talks.
But they both categorically rejected any punishment that involved dismemberment of the empire. When during the Paris conference the
Allies insisted on treating the punishment for war crimes and the partition of Anatolia as one and the same issue, the initial goodwill shown
by the Turks quickly evaporated. Both the Ankara and Istanbul centers
now began to see the desire to partition Anatolia as the real motivation
lurking behind the Allies' demands for trying war criminals, and they
hardened their stand against such prosecution. In the beginning, however, there were some differences between their positions.

Even postwar grand vizier Damat Ferid Paşa, the most ardent
Turkish advocate of prosecution, said that the real culprits were "those
three missing people: Talât, Enver and Cemal, who had fled to Germany
in October 1918. There are also a handful of secondary accomplices."
But that was where he drew the line. Ferid Paşa rejected the notion that
an entire nation could be held responsible for the deeds of "a couple of
thugs," and asserted that "the innocent Turkish nation [was] free of the
stain of injustice."[37] In his view, "the whole blame rested squarely on the
few leaders of the CUP, who, through their alliance with Germany and
their control of the army, had terrorized the rest of Turkey into

submission. Not only had Christians been persecuted, but three million Muslims had felt the terror of the CUP as well."[38] In the 17 June memorandum presented to the Council of Ten, the grand vizier announced that he opposed the partitioning of Turkey as retribution for what had happened. "The Ottoman Government will not accept the dismemberment of the empire or its division under various mandates."[39] The Allied Powers reacted to Ferid Paşa's statements with amazement. "Wilson commented that he had 'never seen anything more stupid,' while Lloyd George called the memorandum 'good jokes.'"[40]

On 25 June 1919, the Council of Ten gave its formal reply, stating clearly that the Turks as a people would not be able to evade responsibility and announcing that culpability for the massacres fell on the whole Turkish people, They "are guilty of murdering Armenians without any justification. Therefore the Turkish people must bear the whole responsibility."[41] The council stated that "a nation must be judged by the Government which rules it."[42]

The rival Turkish political centers disagreed about whether the Unionists' taking the country to war constituted a crime. While the successive postwar governments in Istanbul weighed the idea that the CUP had led the country to war to satisfy its own adventurism, the Nationalist Movement in Ankara rejected it out of hand. The Nationalist Movement held that the war had not been a matter of choice but was instead forced on the nation. At its congress in Sivas on 4–11 September 1919 the Nationalist Movement elected a Representative Council headed by Mustafa Kemal (Atatürk). In response to the Istanbul government's efforts to sabotage the congress, the nationalists organized a campaign of disturbances of the communication lines between Anatolia and Istanbul, which became known as the "telegram war" against Damat Ferid Paşa. The disturbances ultimately forced Damat Ferid Paşa to resign at the end of that month.[43] The new cabinet, headed by Ali Rıza Paşa and appointed on 2 October 1919, sent a telegram to Mustafa Kemal putting forward a series of conditions for holding talks on a general parliamentary election. Istanbul demanded that the Representative Council declare: 1) It had no connection whatsoever with the Unionists; 2) the Ottoman state's involvement in World War I had not been justified, and the names of those responsible would be made public and legal proceedings initiated against them; and 3) none of those guilty of crimes during the war would escape legal sanction. These conditions were considered essential to "prevent misunderstanding at home and abroad."[44]

Mustafa Kemal wrote a lengthy reply to these demands. Ankara would not acknowledge any inherent guilt for entering the war, let alone accept punishment. "Staying out of the World War would have been desirable, of course, but there was no material possibility of doing so." Kemal listed several factors that made war inevitable for the Turks and it was therefore unfair to "see [the Ottomans'] entry to the war as a crime. . . ." What needed to be done, then, was obvious: "To tell the truth openly, and acknowledge that defeat is accompanied by inescapable consequences but not to interpret the actions of this great nation that fought so heroically as a crime . . . therefore these accusations must be rejected along with the demand that the nations be punished."[45]

Notwithstanding the differences in position, Mustafa Kemal accepted that the Unionists included a small faction that had led the country to ruin by its mismanagement and exploitation," and argued that they could be held responsible for their crimes.[46] The two parties met in Amasya between 20 and 22 October 1919 and agreed that "the government shall not be drawn into the controversy over whether or not our involvement in the war was justified. Nevertheless, it is necessary for the country's safety that opinions approving this involvement be suppressed for now."[47] If nothing more, the Istanbul regime had at least persuaded its counterpart in Ankara not to speak its mind openly on the subject.

As a result of this agreement, general elections were held in autumn 1919. The Ankara faction would be represented as a bloc in the Ottoman Chamber of Deputies when it reconvened in Istanbul the following January. Mustafa Kemal drew up a draft bill for this bloc to present that demanded "legal proceedings against cabinets that bear responsibility for the war and placed themselves above the law through their attacks on the Constitution,"[48] thereby indicating that any punishment for past actions should be restricted to former cabinet members themselves.

Leaving aside their differences over the details, Ankara and Istanbul were fundamentally in agreement about punishing those guilty of the massacres. The Ankara government conveyed to Istanbul in its September 1919 correspondence that it was important to "make it understood that the reign of law has begun, with impartiality and proper justice." Furthermore, "concrete punishment was more useful in terms of showing friends and foes than simply writing declarations that only cause controversy."[49] However, public relations were not the primary motive, but rather the right allocation of responsibility.

The question of trials was discussed during the meetings held between the Ankara and Istanbul centers in Amasya on 20–22 October 1919. Both sides agreed that blame should be restricted to the leaders of the CUP. The talks produced five protocols, three of which were signed and made public while the other two were unsigned and kept secret. The first protocol, dated 21 October 1919, read in part:

> Article 1: A resurgence of Unionism and its ideas, or even traces of the [Committee of] Union and Progress, would be politically harmful. . . .
> Article 4: The lawful punishment of those who committed crimes during the deportations is an imperative of justice and of policy.[50]

The third protocol[51] dealt with elections. The parties agreed that Unionists suspected of any involvement in the massacres would be barred from standing for office and that Ankara reserved the right to intervene in the election process.

> Since such a presence is unacceptable, all means shall be applied to prevent people connected to the misdeeds of Unionism or sullied by the deportations and killings or other misdeeds contrary to the true interests of the nation from appearing in the Chamber of Deputies to be convened.[52]

The first protocol consisted, in Mustafa Kemal's words, "almost entirely of items proposed by [the Istanbul government] and which we saw no harm in accepting."[53] The secret protocols are significant in that they show Ankara's different attitude. The Ankara faction sought to halt the war crimes investigations by the British against some military commanders; return Turkish prisoners exiled to Malta by the British; and prosecute Armenians accused of crimes.[54]

The public protocols were drawn up with the Allied governments in mind since the Paris Peace Talks were underway. These openly mention that the Allies had opposed the Unionist government, that taking no action would produce "a negative result at the conference," and that taking a decision in favor of prosecution was necessary to prevent "hostile opposition and intervention."[55]

These initial positions on the prosecution of those involved in war crimes changed when it appeared that punishment would involve the partition of Anatolia. The Turks wanted individual retribution, as in Germany and Bulgaria. "Our old allies, such as Germany and Bulgaria, were defeated along with us and to the same extent, but their existence and right to life has not been placed in peril."[56] Since partition was considered a "death sentence"[57] for Turkey, protecting those being prosecuted for war crimes eventually became an important part of nationalist policy.

Allied Efforts to Prosecute Ottoman War Criminals

The 1918 armistice agreement marked the first concrete step toward prosecuting the perpetrators of the massacres and other subsequent war crimes. Efforts in this respect took place at three different levels. The first was the Paris Peace Conference, where proposals were submitted for an international court to try the suspects. This attempt, which took the form of certain articles in the Treaties of Versailles and Sèvres, ultimately came to nothing. The second occurred through the measures taken by several postwar Ottoman governments. These efforts were at least partially successful. The third level was a series of initiatives of the British Occupational Forces in Istanbul. The initial result of all these efforts, in Paris and in Istanbul, was multiple arrests of people associated with the wartime regime and their exile to Malta, but the British did not in the end achieve their desired results.

With the Allies' declaration of 24 May 1915, the concept of "crimes against humanity" was used for the first time. Further, the principle of holding perpetrators of such crimes personally responsible regardless of rank and authority also emerged for the first time. The declaration gave crimes against humanity a concrete definition as a discrete legal category and made clear that anyone suspected of such a crime would face criminal prosecution regardless of position. This precedent came to form the legal framework and foundation of the 1946 Nuremberg Trials. It was also mentioned in the Preamble of the United Nations' Convention on the Prevention and Punishment of the Crime of genocide, which was adopted on 9 December 1948, and thereby become an international legal norm. On 29 July 1950, the United Nations accepted the "Nuremberg Principles" as one of the foundations of international law. Other such decisions would follow.[58]

It was through this process that the notion of "crimes against humanity," now an integral part of international law, made it possible to try those accused of genocide in places such as Yugoslavia and Rwanda. Of course, international tribunals are not the only legal venues in which cases of crimes against humanity can be heard; they tend to function poorly in practice, being susceptible to pressures from powerful states and the prejudices of the nation-states involved. Thus many countries, having learned the lesson of past experience, prefer to incorporate crimes against humanity into their national jurisprudence. Such countries include Germany, Israel, France, Canada, Australia, the United Kingdom and the United States of America.[59]

The State of International Law Before 1919

In 1625, Hugo Grotius published his monumental book *De Iure Belli ac Pacis*, which collected the historic precedents on the subject of war crimes and laid the foundation for the modern law of nations. The first theoretical exposition of the subject was Rousseau's 1762 *Contrat Social*. "War produces a legal relation," he wrote, "only between two sovereign nations participating in it and does not cover the civilian population."[60] The law of nations, which began to take shape in nineteenth-century Europe, was built on this principle. This was an attempt to construct and implement laws to limit the effects of wars, which were becoming ever more deadly and destructive. Rules attempting to limit unnecessary violence in time of war came about with the rise of national armies. The 1856 Treaty of Paris ending the Crimean War spelled out rules on maritime law as well as the legal treatment of piracy. The first international convention on the treatment of those wounded in combat was signed in Geneva in 1864.

During the American Civil War, for example, Union troops were subject to rules of conflict. But it was the congresses and international conventions held in The Hague in 1899 and 1907 that served as a turning point.

Concepts such as "principles of humanity" and "public conscience and the law of humanity" were first used in these conferences. The Hague Convention of 1907, for instance, binds the signatories to serve "the interests of humanity and the demands of civilization" and remain true to the principles of a law of nations based on "settled traditions of the civilian population, the laws of humanity and public conscience," even in the absence of clear rules and laws of war.[61] Thirteen governments signed the convention.

The document certainly had its shortcomings. One of these was that the basic principles declared referred solely to moral values. None of these principles were defined in any technical legal way. Moreover, the penalties for violations were not clear. Further, the convention's provisions only concerned the actions of one national army or state against another—no provision was made for an army's actions against its own people. The eighth paragraph of the preamble to the convention declared: "The inhabitants and the belligerents remain under the protection and the governance of the principles of the law of nations, as they result from the usages established among civilized peoples, from the laws of humanity, and the dictates of the public conscience."[62]

Extending restrictions on states' behavior to cover not only other countries' citizens, but also each state's own was one of the major legal questions of the Paris Peace Conference. The accusations against the Ottoman government concerned its own citizens, a situation not addressed by any international agreement.

However, the Hague Convention did provide a loophole for colonialist aspirations:

The only exception to the general principle of the binding force of the rules of warfare is in the case of reprisals, which constitute retaliation against a belligerent for illegitimate acts of warfare by the members of his armed forces or of his own nationals.[63]

This transforms the right of reprisal into a legal principle which was particularly useful for the Great Powers, who did not want to relinquish sovereignty over their colonies. Combined with certain other articles, the reprisal clause gave the occupying power the right to "punish" acts of resistance on the part of the local inhabitants.[64]

Additionally, the concept of personal responsibility for transgressions had not yet evolved at the time of the Hague convention. It had, of course, long been established that soldiers and officers were responsible for their acts and should be prosecuted by any state that captured them. But military and political officials who had not played a direct role in the military operations were not yet included in this notion of responsibility. Before the First World War, in many places military officers who had not taken part directly in operations became liable one way or another under the jurisprudence and military law of their own countries. But the question of prosecuting the political authorities—the people who ran the country—had not yet been considered. Calls during the war to hold the Ottoman political elite and the German kaiser personally responsible for the Armenian massacres and to prosecute them on those grounds heralded a turning point. From that point on, personal responsibility and prosecution—even of those in the political sphere—became one of the most important principles of international law.

The Ottoman government had become a member of the "family of Europe," when it signed the 1856 Paris Treaty and accepted the burdens and obligations of international law. The seventh article of the treaty stated these responsibilities explicitly: The Sublime Porte [is] admitted to participate in the advantages of the Public Law and System of Europe."[65] In years to come, more such treaties were signed by the Ottoman state, even the Hague Convention of 1907.

The Ottoman government had also signed two binding international treaties which directly addressed the Armenian question, the first being the Berlin Treaty of 1878, which demanded a series of reforms and was guaranteed by other signatory countries. The second pertinent agreement was the Treaty of Yeniköy, signed with Russia on 8 February 1914, in which the Ottoman Empire promised to implement broad administrative reforms for Armenians. As we have discussed, Ottoman administrators had no intention of fulfilling the terms of either agreement, particularly the Yeniköy Treaty, since the reform plan carried an implicit threat of dividing Anatolia. Thus the Ottomans saw the Armenian reforms as a thinly veiled attempt to take those territories. Earlier territorial losses had mainly involved withdrawal from distant border areas and, however undesirable, had not been a matter of choice. But the Armenian reforms were "the deadliest of all threats. . . . To renounce these lands would have meant not the truncation, but the dissolution of the Turkish state."[66] So with the coming of war these obligations were revoked one by one. One of the early actions taken by the Ottoman Empire after its entry into the war was the cancellation of the Yeniköy Treaty, followed by withdrawal from other related agreements which called for international intervention in the event that the Armenian reforms were not implemented. Later, on 5 September 1916, the Ottoman cabinet withdrew from the 1856 Paris Treaty, the London Declaration of 1871 and the Berlin Treaty of 1878. "These three international treaties," according to Halil Menteşe, who delivered the announcement, "imposed political restrictions on the Ottoman state, and the Sublime Porte wanted to be free of them."[67] These decisions freed the Ottoman government from all obligations under international law and removed the legal foundations for other countries' political intervention. It is significant that the decision came soon after the first phase of the Armenian deportation.

At the Paris Peace Conference the question of punishing the Turks followed the individual political calculations of each of the Great Powers.

Britain: The Liberal-Conservative coalition that won the elections of 1918 favored an extremely hard-line policy in keeping with public expectations in Britain. But this inclination was directed more at Germany and Austria than Turkey. The question of how to deal with the Ottomans barely featured in the elections. The main concern behind British policy toward the Ottomans was to prevent Bolshevik activity in their zone of occupation. For this reason no final decision had been made regarding disarming and decommissioning the Ottoman army or over the fate of the Unionist leaders, despite the detailed conditions set down in the armistice agreement. This indecision was to play a major part in the Allies' inability to reach a successful conclusion at the final peace talks.

British policy at the Paris Peace Conference was governed by three considerations. The first was the intention to spread British sovereignty as far as possible, with the aim of securing the road to India. The second was the desire to minimize all points of friction with France. The third was the conviction that the long-term British policy of supporting the Ottoman state and the Istanbul government would not achieve these goals.[68] Britain's insistence on keeping the Allied Aegean Fleet under its command, its exclusion of France from signing the armistice agreement and its arrival in Istanbul as the first army of occupation were all results of these policies. As a direct consequence of Britain's third consideration in particular, the government decided in December 1918 to try to keep Palestine under British control, strengthen the Greek presence in the essential regions on the road to India, and establish an Armenian state as a barrier against Russian expansion. Placing the Armenian state under an American mandate was Britain's great dream.

On the future of Istanbul the British failed to agree even among themselves. Both the War Office and the India Office strongly opposed seizing control of Istanbul from the Turks, since the resulting Turkish upheaval would make peace impossible and would also offend Indian Muslims. For its part, the Foreign Office favored ending Turkish rule in Istanbul, and attempted to advance its position through an anti-Muslim campaign in the press and parliament. When it became more or less clear, with Wilson's arrival in Paris, that the Americans would not accept a mandate in Armenia, the various British government offices held a meeting on 30 January 1919 to formulate overall policy. Among other decisions, the compromise that emerged on the question of Istanbul involved placing the city under international administration and removing the Turks from control. While the British government remained resolved to punish the Turks for the Armenian genocide, this resolve was balanced by all the other political considerations.

France: France saw itself as the natural guardian of the Ottoman Christians and considered itself entrusted with an important mission. It had territorial claims over Lebanon, Syria and Cilicia, and was uneasy about increased British control in the area. Far more important for France, though, was the European peace—that is, bringing Germany to its knees and establishing favorable border arrangements between the two countries. Therefore, it was willing to be more conciliatory in regard to British demands in the Middle East for the sake of securing a more advantageous arrangement for itself within Europe.

Italy: As part of its wartime agreements, Italy had obtained the right to occupy large parts of western Anatolia, but postwar exigencies resulted in some of these areas being given to Greece instead. Italy's primary goal was simply to obtain the land it had secured in the prior agreements. When Greece was authorized by the Paris Peace Conference on 30 March 1919 to land in Izmir, the Italians quickly switched their support to the Turks, first in their own zone of occupation and then throughout Anatolia.

United States: Throughout the First World War, the United States never declared war on Turkey, mainly out of concern for the fate of American missionaries and the country's assets in the region. Moreover, the United States generally believed that Turkey was an instrument in the hands of Germany. In the fall of 1917, as part of a general study, a committee of American experts examined the question of a peace treaty with Turkey. According to the recommendations of this inquiry, dated 22 December 1917:

> It is necessary to free the subject races of the Turkish Empire from oppression and misrule. This implies at the very least autonomy for Armenia and the protection of Palestine, Syria, Mesopotamia and Arabia by the civilized nations. It is necessary also to establish free intercourse through and across the straits. Turkey proper must be justly treated and freed from economic and political bondage.[69]

These ideas would later reappear as the twelfth point of Wilson's Fourteen Points.[70]

The concrete meaning of these principles was formulated on 31 July 1918: "Turkey shall remain a separate country under a Turkish government. This could be the existing government or some other government."[71] A report by Robert Lansing, the American secretary of state, was presented to the peace delegation on 21 September 1918 and dwelt on the idea of putting Syria and Armenia under protection for a short period of time before they would be allowed their own governments. American policy was to place German and Turkish colonies under the control of the proposed League of Nations and thence to distribute them as mandates to the Great Powers. But the

Americans rejected a British proposal for putting Turkey under an American mandate. The stumbling block, for the U.S., was the incompatibility of the imperialist secret agreements signed by the Allies and the Wilsonian principles of self-determination. The Americans had no intention of recognizing the prior agreements.

Wilson's principles also constituted the Turks' great hope, since the twelfth of the Fourteen Points unambiguously recognized Turkish sovereignty in the areas where Turks constituted a majority. Yet at the beginning of the Peace Conference, it seemed that the Allies were agreed on placing Istanbul under international protection, while simply contesting how that should be done. The delay that resulted from this disagreement allowed the Turks enough breathing space to reorganize. At a meeting on 20 March 1919 to discuss Turkey's future, Wilson announced his belief that "the Sick Man on the Straits"—meaning the Ottoman Empire—would die. "Only one thing must be said to Turkey," Wilson said, referring to the reach of the empire. "If peace is to be achieved: that she will have nothing."[72] On 14 May the president proposed putting northern Anatolia under French control and setting up an independent Turkish state centered on Konya, a city in Anatolia. As the discussion dragged on and the pressure mounted to find a quick solution, Wilson proposed yet another arrangement on 25 June 1919. He "believed that putting Turkey under a mandate would be a mistake, but favored evicting the sultan and his government from Istanbul."[73]

No plan to partition Turkey ever came to fruition, partly because France and Italy had each chosen to pursue their own ends. As each of the Allied Powers tended to its own imperial benefits, and because the differences between them were too great to reconcile, the determination to prosecute those responsible for perpetrating the Armenian genocide subsided. The ultimate concern of the Great Powers was their own interests, not the prosecution of war criminals.

Even before the peace talks began, the question of how to try war criminals was the subject of intense debate between the British and the French. Both countries were bound by their proclamations made during the war regarding Ottoman crimes against humanity and Ottoman government responsibility. More important, promises had been made to try Kaiser Wilhelm II before an international tribunal.

Throughout the war the drive to "Hang the kaiser!" had been a prominent idea, to the point that it became one of the main issues in the British elections of 1918. Thus, the idea of setting up international tribunals had been broached even during the war.

France was the first country to take concrete steps in this direction. A draft proposal was presented by the French government as soon as the guns fell silent. The basic idea was to get the Germans to accept formal responsibility as the side that intentionally started the war, thereby laying the legal foundation for their subsequent punishment.[74] The issue was brought up in discussions between the French and British prime ministers on 2–3 January 1918. Britain had been making its own, similar preparations, and in the end it was decided to put the kaiser on trial before a tribunal to be set up by the Allies. Any legal difficulties that might arise would be solved by making modifications to the structure of the tribunal, which the Allies were free to form in any manner they liked, provided it adhered to the general tenets of justice.

Before the first session of the Peace Conference on 18 January 1919, France distributed an expert report on the possibility of holding Wilhelm II criminally responsible. Britain had drawn up a similar report—the content and conclusions of both were the same. The French report concluded that the kaiser could not be put on trial because the proposed charges of starting a "war of aggression" and violating Belgian sovereignty were not defined as crimes under international law. The actions were not punishable because of German sovereignty and the kaiser's political immunity. Nonetheless, such gross injustice could hardly go unpunished. Wilhelm could only be tried before a future international tribunal on the basis of a future, not current, law of nations. A new law was in the process of taking shape.[75] The Allies' adoption of Wilson's fourteenth point regarding an association of nations is the first indication of the acceptance of this new law of nations.

At first Wilson was not especially keen on the idea of trying war criminals and the German emperor before an international court. In January 1919 a conference of the five great powers (the United States, Britain, France, Italy and Japan) recommended setting up the Commission on the Responsibility of the Authors of the War and the Enforcement of Penalties—the Commission of the Fifteen—to determine the rules applicable to the prosecution of war crimes and their perpetrators.

The commission, set up on January 25, divided its activities among three subcommittees, which between them looked into five separate questions: Who had instigated the war; who had violated the laws of war and how; what were the criteria according to which responsibility would be determined for those who had committed crimes; and how were the accused to be tried.

Apart from the question of trying the kaiser, punishing the Turks for the massacres was one of the most important issues on the commission's agenda. The commission unanimously concluded that the war had been started by the Germans in a planned and premeditated fashion. Turkey and Bulgaria were considered responsible for helping Germany start the war.[76] The conclusion read: "The war was conducted by the Central Empires and their allies, Turkey and Bulgaria, in a barbaric or illegitimate manner that violates established laws, the traditions of war and the principles of humanity."[77]

A significant part of the report dealt with clarifying "the law and justice of war" and actions that violated "the law of humanity." Relevant actions, described as "primitive barbarism," implemented by a "terrorist system," included all the campaigns of the Ottoman government against Greeks and Armenians during the war. The commission classified these crimes according to two categories. The first involved crimes committed by one state against the armed forces of another state or its subjects while under occupation—war crimes in the classical sense of the term. The second was for crimes committed by Germany and Turkey against their own citizens on their own sovereign territory. The main crime under this category was the Turkish massacres of Armenians and Greeks. For the first time a distinction had been made between "war crimes" and "crimes against humanity." Although the distinction had not yet been formulated in legal terms, future legal definitions would depend upon it.

The commission then faced the difficult question of under which law and in what manner the crimes should be prosecuted. The Hague Convention of 1907, which was the basis of the whole process, said nothing about prosecution. Nor did it refer in any way to the crimes governments commit against their own citizens. The commission therefore had grave doubts, having established that at least two hundred thousand Armenians were killed, about going forward with criminal charges. This point was the subject of some debate among the members of the commission, who, in the end, recognized the need for a new body of law. While there was no international law yet in existence regarding a state's treatment of its own citizens, the campaigns waged during the war were clearly against "human and moral law." The 1907 Hague Convention had decreed that in cases where no law of war is clearly applicable, action should be taken based on "the established customs among civilized peoples, the laws of humanity and the demands of public conscience."

Thus it was decided to try the leaders of the Committee of Union and Progress on the basis of the humanitarian principles of the Hague Convention. Hence, "any person within enemy countries accused of crimes against humanity or against the laws and customs of war shall be criminally prosecuted, regardless of [their] position or rank, including heads of state."[78]

There was no disagreement among commission members as to the suspects or their moral responsibility or the classification of their crimes. The only dispute was over whether to try the defendants before an international court or a special court set up by the Allies, and about the jurisdiction such a court might possess. Lansing, the American delegate on the commission, argued for trial under the laws of the countries concerned, not under international law, since he had strong reservations regarding the notion of a "law of humanity," when the criminal code for such a law did not actually exist. Criminal punishment could only be meted out on the basis of written law, Lansing argued, whereas the "law of humanity" was in fact only an ethical principle that varied among different countries and communities. One could even make the case that war itself was a violation of such a principle. Furthermore, it was not possible to carry out a criminal investigation solely on the basis of an ethical principle. Trying suspects on that basis was legally indefensible. Lansing's specific objection was to the proposal to try Ottoman Turks for crimes against fellow Armenian citizens under this law of humanity. Although his objection did not feature prominently in the commission's report, it was to prove definitive in later agreements. Excluded from agreements signed with Germany and other countries, crimes "against humanity" and against the "law of humanity" appeared only, as we shall see, in Article 230 of the Sèvres Treaty with Turkey.

Another important problem was whether individuals could be held responsible for crimes committed in the name of their countries.

Some among the Allies wanted to hold the kaiser responsible in the German case, and the Unionist leaders personally responsible for the massacre of Armenians in the case of the Ottomans. But this was not possible, since the law of nations then in force in 1914 did not offer any procedure for the criminal prosecution for campaigns carried out by states. What was needed was a legal framework to put these campaigns, which were clearly in breach of the law of nations, into the realm of criminal prosecution. However, this way was blocked by the fact that all jurisprudence forbade the retroactive application of new laws. The Americans made it clear they had no qualms about incriminating future acts and trying those who committed them under the law of nations. Despite the American argument, the commission as a whole accepted that the principles of the 1907 Convention left the door open for prosecution. The discussions came to an end, however, with an American veto on the commission's decision.

The commission presented its report on 29 March and the issue then passed on to the highest authority, the Council of Ten. As the dispute continued here, the whole peace conference was soon threatening to unravel. Finally, the Americans dropped their objections, and on 9 April 1919, members of the conference accepted a proposal drawn up by President Wilson himself.[79] On America's insistence, the defendants were to be tried not for "crimes against humanity," but for "crimes against the law of war." Furthermore, the emphasis shifted from the international court to military tribunals to be set up in large part by the Allies. Wilson himself acknowledged that the points as passed were very weak and rendered any international prosecution impossible.[80]

Clauses on this subject were inserted in the treaties signed with the countries concerned. In these clauses the Allies reserved the right to bring suspected war criminals to trial before an international court. Among the conditions for peace was the surrender of any and all war criminals and relevant documents to the victors. Articles 227 to 230 in the Versailles Treaty with Germany (signed 28 June 1919), and Articles 226 to 230 of the Sèvres Treaty with the Ottoman Empire deal with the prosecution of war criminals.

The most relevant articles of the Sèvres Treaty are as follows:

Article 228: The Turkish Government undertakes to furnish all documents and information of every kind, the production of which may be considered necessary to ensure the full knowledge of the incriminating acts, the prosecution of offenders and the just appreciation of responsibility.

Article 230: The Turkish Government undertakes to hand over to the Allied Powers the persons whose surrender may be required by the latter as being responsible for the massacres committed during the continuance of the state of war on territory which formed part of the Turkish Empire on August 1, 1914. The Allied Powers reserve for themselves the right to designate the tribunal which shall try the persons so accused, and the Turkish Government undertakes to recognize such tribunal. In the event of the League of Nations having created in sufficient time a tribunal competent to deal with the said massacres, the Allied Powers reserve to themselves the right to bring the accused persons mentioned above before such tribunal, and the Turkish Government undertakes equally to recognize such tribunal.[81]

It was widely agreed that the Sèvres Treaty was stillborn, due to conflicts of interest among the Allies and the Turkish War of Independence, to which we shall return.

British Initiatives to Punish the Turks

The Paris Peace Conference was not the only assembly to debate the issue of prosecuting suspects accused of mass murder. Britain, having realized that the conference would not deliver results in this area, decided to go its own way. It is generally agreed that Britain's interference on behalf of "Armenians and Greeks held under duress" was against its interests, that it nonetheless pursued that policy vigorously and that it consequently repeatedly rebuffed friendly Turkish advances.[82] Britain's sensitivity, however, reached beyond the Allied memo of 1915 and its promises, going back to the Abdul Hamid II period.

A sense of guilt and obligation toward the Armenians was one of the most important reasons for British action on their behalf. After Russia's victory in 1878 over the Ottomans, with the Treaty of San Stefano, the Armenian provinces had been put under Russian rule until the completion of reforms. Britain annulled this agreement, returning the area to Ottoman control, leading to the massacres of the Armenians in 1894–95 and again in 1915–17. Thus, the British felt responsible. In an eloquent recounting of forty years of Armenian travails, Lloyd George expressly laid responsibility for Armenian misfortune at his country's door. "Had it not been for our sinister intervention," he wrote,

> the great majority of the Armenians would have been placed, by the Treaty of San Stefano in 1878, under the protection of the Russian flag.
>
> The Treaty of San Stefano provided that Russian troops should remain in occupation of the Armenian provinces until satisfactory reforms were carried out. By the Treaty of Berlin (1878)—which was entirely due to our minatory pressure and which was acclaimed by us a great British triumph which brought "Peace with honour"—that article was superseded. Armenia was sacrificed on the triumphal altar we had erected. The Russians were forced to withdraw. The wretched Armenians were once more placed under the heel of their old masters, subject to a pledge to "introduce ameliorations and reforms into the provinces inhabited by Armenians." We all know how these pledges were broken for forty years, in spite of repeated protests from the country that was primarily responsible for restoring Armenia to Turkish rule. The actions of the British Government led inevitably to the terrible massacres of 1895–1897, 1909, and worst of all to the holocausts of 1915. By these atrocities, almost unparalleled in the black record of Turkish misrule, the Armenian population was reduced in numbers by well over a million. Having regard to the part we had taken in making these outrages possible, we were morally bound to take the first opportunity that came our way to redress the wrong we had perpetrated, and in so far as it was in our power, to make it impossible to repeat the horrors for which history will always hold us culpable.
>
> When therefore in the Great War, the Turks forced us into this quarrel, and deliberately challenged the British Empire to a life and death struggle, we realized that at last an opportunity had been given us to rectify the cruel wrong for which we were responsible.[83]

After a debate in the House of Commons on 18 November 1918, the country's responsibility for the state of the Armenians was accepted: "This country is indebted to Armenia. For we, above all, obstructed Armenia's liberation from the Turks' tyranny by the Russians. Had we not done this, all this terrible suffering since would not have happened."[84]

Another reason for Britain's particular sensitivity regarding the massacres was the strong Armenian solidarity movement in the country. The roots of this movement went back to the second half of the nineteenth century, a period during which Ottoman persecution of Christian minorities had increased. Thus news of the Armenian massacres were received with outrage, and, feeding on anti-Muslim feeling, led to a powerful bloc of support for the Armenians, especially in parliament and in the press.[85] An article published in both the *Guardian* and the *Times* toward the end of 1916 expressed these feelings:

> One thing remains to be said of Armenia: the whole people of this country was massacred and cleansed in the worst atrocity the world has seen since the birth of Jesus Christ. That country should never again and under no conditions be left in the hands of Turkey.[86]

The sense of guilt over the murder of Armenians and the pressure of popular solidarity pushed Britain to take a principled position on the prosecution of the perpetrators, even when this attitude clashed with its colonial interests.

So when Admiral Calthorpe was appointed first high commissioner to Turkey on 6 November 1918, Lord Balfour wrote to the Ministry of War urging it to issue orders for the .

> rejection of all offers of hospitality from the Turks and the restriction of encounters between the Allied occupation forces and the Turks to the minimum necessary for the preservation of the strict formal nature of these occasions and until peace is signed.[87]

Balfour wanted to ensure that no behavior on the part of the British might do anything to raise the Turks' hopes.

A personal letter from Lord Balfour to Admiral Calthorpe, sent on 9 November 1919 to clarify these instructions, said that the British-occupied territories in Syria, Iraq, and Arabia would not be returned to Ottoman sovereignty or administration, that this was an unalterable part of British policy and that no action must be taken that might mislead the Turks in advance of the upcoming peace conference. Lord Balfour reminded the admiral of the widespread feeling among the Turks that the armistice agreement had given them favorable conditions and that they should instead be made to comprehend their utter defeat:[88] The British therefore wasted no opportunity to remind the Turks of their determination to bring to justice those accused of the massacres of Armenians.

In the first months after the armistice in 1918, the British began to arrest Ottoman officials suspected of war crimes and crimes against humanity. The British authorities' attention first focused on field commanders, stemming from their belief that these were more important than fugitive Unionist leaders and those civilians with direct responsibility for the wartime atrocities. In one set of instructions from the Foreign Office (sent on 5 February 1919) to the British high commissioner in Istanbul on who would be arrested and according to which criteria, the first four points dealt directly with Turkish officers and their treatment of British prisoners of war both during the fighting and following the Armistice. The Ottoman government had already come under pressure in November and December 1918 to fire these officers. On 3 January 1919, the British Ministry of War had sent a lengthy coded telegram to its commanders in Istanbul, Baghdad and Cairo instructing them to consider the Turkish army's stocks of food as Armenian property and to arrest any Turkish officers with these provisions in their possession. Another cable, sent on 15 January 1919, named nine Turkish commanders and demanded their arrest.[89]

Also in January the British began actively to seek out those responsible for the Armenian massacres. The High Commissioner's Office wrote to London that "behavior towards the Armenians is, as always, extremely aggressive," and proposed that he himself be invested with the power to arrest and hand over to the Allied military authorities any member of the Istanbul government against whom evidence existed.[90] Yet the same letter warned that "capturing all those who must be punished is a great task," and drew attention to the impossibility of achieving such a goal. What mattered was to "frighten" the Turks, "show respect to the Armenians," "facilitate the implementation of the armistice" and make the Turks "understand very well that they have been defeated."[91]

The first officer arrested by British forces in Istanbul was Colonel Ali Rıfat Bey from the Army of the Caucasus. He was arrested in January and sent to Batum in the Caucasus for trial by Britain's military tribunal. Other arrests followed. The first officer to be exiled to Malta was Ali İhsan Sabis Paşa, the commander of the Sixth Army. On 7 January the British high commissioner met the Ottoman foreign minister and demanded the punishment of Turkish "war criminals." "Good intentions are not enough, we want results," he added.[92] Turkish promises to try the perpetrators had so far only resulted in preliminary interrogations.

Thus the British authorities intervened with the Ottoman government to arrest suspects. Admiral Calthorpe met with the Turkish foreign minister on 7 January, 1919, stating that the British government was determined to mete out to those responsible for the Armenian massacres the punishment they deserve.[93] Ten days later, he reported the reaction to his letter:

> The sultan indicated that he is ready to punish anyone we want, but said he feared that disturbances would be inevitable if action were to be taken on a wide scale, in which case he might be deposed or even killed. . . . He wanted to know whether he can count on Allied protection for his person were he to implement severe measures.[94]

On 23 January 1919, the British foreign minister, minister of war, and the first lord of the admiralty met in London to decide on policy toward Turkish war criminals. The meeting laid out the crimes and how to go about prosecuting them, ultimately establishing seven different categories. On 5 February these decisions, with some changes, were sent to Istanbul as instructions. The high commissioner was ordered to give instructions to the Turkish government to make arrests based on these categories and to surrender the individuals to the nearest British or Allied forces.[95] This program was to form the basis of British activity.[96] The February 5 letter also reports that "courts have been set up in the British zones of occupation [the Caucasus, Syria and Iraq] to try any Turk who offended against the laws and customs of war."[97]

The essential question that remained, however, was whether these trials could be held under British jurisdiction. Britain found it "unacceptable" for war crimes suspects in the parts of Turkey outside Allied occupation "to be tried and punished by Turkish authorities." Thus those suspects were also to be surrendered to Britain and "sent to the detention camp in Malta where they will be tried and punished in accord with the decisions to be taken by the Allies."[98] The French argued that these trials should take place outside of the Allied occupation, but the British carried on with their activities regardless. In line with the decisions of 23 January 1919, the minister of war wrote to commanders in the region ordering them to establish military courts and to begin the trials of the Turkish suspects.[99] This caused an uproar among Turkish officers, who even talked to the government about a "mutiny." For a military officer, the idea of being tried before a foreign court was deemed particularly "dishonorable."

> If a foreign government can haphazardly arrest our division commanders, and if our government has no right or word in their defense, then where are we heading? If these arrests and punishments are necessary, then let our government do it. Under what law in the world, under what logic, can the commander of an Ottoman division be tried before a British military court?[100]

The French objected to all these British efforts. The British occupation of Istanbul was not yet official, thus Ottoman sovereignty and Ottoman jurisdiction still held sway. General Franchet d'Espèrey, the commander of the French occupation force, wrote to Admiral Calthorpe on 11 February 1919 saying that he agreed on the issue of punishing war criminals, but that "finding suspects in the non-occupied zones of the Ottoman Empire, prosecuting and punishing them is up to the Turkish authorities—naturally, under the control and supervision of the Allied military authorities."[101] The French government in Paris agreed with the commander, arguing that this type of court-martial would only increase sympathy for the Turkish officers.[102]

Then D'Espèrey, backed by his government, acting without telling the British, presented Grand Vizier Tevfik Paşa with a list of twelve suspects he wanted arrested, including former Grand Vizier Said Halim Paşa.[103] Tevfik Paşa basically shelved the request and none of the suspects were arrested.[104] Meanwhile, the British demanded the surrender of twenty-three people suspected of mistreating British prisoners of war. This demand was rejected by the Ottoman government as "a direct contravention of the rights of sovereignty." The Ottomans sent a note of protest on 16 February 1919. They argued that trying Ottoman officers before foreign military courts was against established laws.[105] After the French and Ottoman reactions, British authorities decided to take no further steps for the moment, waiting "until it is clear whether or not the French are convinced."[106] So the British limited their activities, for the time being, to presenting lists of suspects to the Ottoman authorities.[107]

The Ottoman foreign ministry next proposed that the British hand over the evidence and documents in their possession and that the suspects be tried before Ottoman courts. On March 5, responding to the installation of a new grand vizier, Damat Ferid Paşa, and overriding French objections and Ottoman protests, the British simply submitted another list of suspects with the directive to surrender them to British authorities, along with a reminder of the sultan's words: "I am ready to arrest anyone you want." This time, the new Ottoman government arrested twenty-two members of the CUP on 9 March, but refused to hand them over to the British. The British high commissioner therefore wrote to London:

> By overly insisting on their being handed over to us I am afraid that this trotting horse will fall tired and stop dead in its tracks. If I do that I will have put the new cabinet in an impossible position without any hope of a better, more honest cabinet. Here is what I propose: Let us for the time being . . . content ourselves with seeing that the arrested are held in a safe place.[108]

And so the British had to satisfy themselves with having suspects in Turkish custody.

Fearful of foreign intervention, and with an eye to the ongoing peace conference, the Ottoman government took the initiative and by 1919 had established military courts and begun trials. But that did not settle the issue for the Allies. The British had no confidence in either the ability or good intentions of the Ottoman authorities. As discussions on how to prosecute war crimes suspects continued in Paris, the Ottoman government made some attempts to satisfy international doubts.

Toward the end of February 1919, Tevfik Paşa's cabinet appealed to the Danish, Swiss, Swedish, Dutch and Spanish governments, asking for opinions on how the Armenian issue might be resolved. The cabinet proposed:

> the election of an impartial body from the delegations of Spain, Switzerland, Denmark, Holland and Sweden to investigate the bloody events that took place in our eastern provinces and to determine what share of the responsibility fell to Muslim suspects and what share to the Armenian committees.[109]

A note submitted to the Danish Embassy in Istanbul read:

> The Ottoman government has begun legal proceedings against the individuals responsible for the deportation of Ottoman citizens, both Muslim and non-Muslim, during the war. . . . Commissions of Inquiry have been set up in Istanbul and the provinces to identify the suspects. In order to cast the light of sublime justice and impartiality on this undertaking the Ottoman government has decided to include foreign members, chosen from the judiciaries of the neutral countries, in the Commissions of Inquiry.[110]

Denmark was asked to appoint two judges, bringing the total number of neutral participants invited to sit on the commissions to ten. The British, however, blocked this move, saying that the final decision would be made at the Paris Peace Conference. In the meantime, Britain sought to clarify who could be tried before military courts and who could be deported to Malta to be tried before an international court. On 2 April the Foreign Office sent Lord Balfour at the peace conference a clear decision: Turkish war crimes suspects could not be tried before British military courts; an international court would be required. The peace conference was asked to come to a quick decision on the establishment of an international tribunal and on the suspects' exile to Malta.[111]

But the peace conference itself was in no hurry, and the British remained firmly against the trials being conducted solely under

Ottoman law: "Since such suspects cannot be tried before military courts in the full meaning of the word, it remains nevertheless not desirable to leave their punishment to Turkish officials."[112] Additionally, the question of the jurisdiction of British courts in the occupied zones was still to be determined. At various meetings in late May, many British jurists insisted that the British Military Courts in the occupied zones were within their rights to carry out the trial and punishment of Turkish offenders in accordance with the "Common Law of War." The "Common Law of War," it was argued, subsumed the violations of the customs and laws of war.[113]

An important development came with the appointment of Grand Vizier Damat Ferid Paşa. On 19 May the Ottoman Foreign Ministry sent another note of protest against British practice of military courts but received no reply. On 12 June Ferid Paşa sent a message to the high commissioner, suggesting the establishment of a mixed British-Ottoman military court in Istanbul. Not impressed, the British dismissed the idea out of hand.[114]

In an effort to break the deadlock, the British Foreign Office asked the crown prosecutor to review the legal obstacles that stood in the way of trying and punishing people involved in one of the seven categories of crimes established earlier. The prosecutor would also determine which, if any, of these crimes could be tried before a military tribunal and which before an international court.[115] The crown prosecutor responded on 7 August 1919 by detailing the various options and their legal consequences, arguing that British military courts in the occupied zones did have the right to hear these cases, "provided they are approved by the British government." Such crimes, the legal experts argued, came under the jurisdiction not of national law, but of the law and customs of war.[116] Regarding crimes committed outside the occupation zone, British military courts were allowed to try these only with permission of the Ottoman government.[117]

The crown prosecutor recommended "proceeding according to the conditions" still to be determined in Paris when it came to prosecuting suspects of the Armenian massacres. But there was no legal barrier against detaining the suspects until their cases were heard; for this was an act of state whose validity could not be challenged in a court of law. The British legal experts, believing in the Turkish government's reluctance to try the suspects, finally concluded, "It is 'practical and desirable' to provide rules to override Turkish punitive procedures."[118] The Ministry of War duly sent a note on 17 December 1919 to the British consulates in Istanbul, Cairo and Baghdad informing them that military courts in the occupation zone had the authority to try current crimes committed in their zones. A letter sent to the military court in Batum, for example, said the court had jurisdiction to hear cases for "1. Insufficient application of armistice conditions; 2. Obstructing the fulfillment of these conditions; and 3. Insulting British commanders and officers,"[119] provided the crimes were committed in that zone of occupation. Other suspects—mostly those involved with the massacre of Christians—were "to be sent to Malta pending trial before an international court."[120] The Malta exiles would in time become a bone of contention between the political center in Ankara, which was steadily growing in size and power, and the British.

CHAPTER 7

OTTOMAN GOVERNMENT INITIATIVES

ALTHOUGH THE TALÂT PAŞA CABINET RESIGNED ON 8 OCTOBER 1918, the Unionists were still determined to direct the country's affairs, and to do so by choosing their successors. According to Halil Menteşe, "Talât Paşa . . . wanted to leave the government to a committee whose patriotism he could count on."[1] But the Unionists' main concern was that they would be brought to account for the Armenian deportations. Later, Mithat Şükrü and Dr. Nâzım both testified that the Armenian question was decisive in the Unionists' decision to flee.[2] (Mithat Şükrü himself decided to remain in Istanbul, however, since he had at that time no proven connection to the Armenian deportations.[3])

The Unionists' efforts to remain in charge resulted in extensive negotiations over the composition of the next cabinet.[4] Talât Paşa's direct intervention led to army general Ahmet İzzet Paşa, Talât Paşa's candidate, forming the new cabinet.[5]

Having signed the armistice agreement, İzzet Paşa's government knew that the country's final destiny would be determined by the Allies at the Paris Peace Conference, which opened in January 1919. It was clear that to secure the most favorable terms at the conference, the incumbent Ottomans would have to act to distance themselves from those responsible for the Armenian massacres and other war crimes. However, İzzet Paşa's cabinet had received a vote of confidence, on 19 October 1918, on the basis of a program that avoided all criticism of the CUP's wartime policies and actions. The "deportation affair" was described as something "compelled by the exigencies of the war." Still, despite this neutral description, mention had been made of the "great torment" suffered by the "children of the homeland," i.e., the minorities. Plans were announced to return their property and possessions, or provide compensation if this was not possible. In addition, the cabinet supported changes to the electoral laws to allow for the minorities' equal participation in government. With regard to foreign policy, the government affirmed the Wilsonian principle of "the right of every nation to determine its own destiny," but also that the state would be "safe from the imperialist ambitions of foreigners."[6] The Arab provinces were to achieve autonomy with strong ties to the Caliphate and Sultanate.[7]

As for the CUP, Ahmet İzzet Paşa resisted sanctions or punitive measures against them, and even in his memoirs years later, he wrote of the Unionists only in the most positive terms.[8] He said that he "desired no enmity or hostility be shown to the Unionists, or that they be treated harshly. . . ."[9]

Not only did he block investigation of the Unionists, he also destroyed incriminating documents that could lead to such an inquiry. In his new office he took charge of the Ministry of War, changed the name of the Special Organization to the Office of Eastern Affairs, put a stop to its activities, and ordered its archives destroyed.[10]

The government was concerned about how to protect Unionist leaders from acts of vengeance by Armenians or Greeks. Rauf Orbay Bey, chief aide to the grand vizier, noted that: "[Enver] Paşa's protection is the duty of the government. I am personally obliged." Regarding the pressure the occupation powers applied to the government to arrest members of the former regime, Rauf Bey stated "that the İzzet Paşa government would never acquiesce to these demands of the Entente powers."[11] He added, "it never occurred [to the government] to initiate steps against the Unionists."[12] On the contrary, the government even assisted Unionist leaders and others to flee the country.

The grand vizier himself ensured that people being sought for their involvement in the Armenian genocide were able to leave Istanbul. Yenibahçeli Şükrü, a member of the Special Organization, claims in his memoirs that Deputy Hilmi's escape from Ardahan, and Ebulhindili Cafer's and Yenibahçeli Nail's flight from Istanbul, were due to Ahmet İzzet Paşa's direct intervention.[13] From various German diplomatic reports, we also know that the government gave permission for CUP government members to escape the country on 1 November 1918:

> Talât Paşa, Enver Paşa and the others in power want to leave the country. On the one hand, the grand vizier desires to help them, but on the other he is afraid he will be attacked for this in the future. He asks whether we are willing to guarantee that we will hand these people over on request of the [Turkish] government.[14]

The news of the Unionist leaders' flight was explosive. Many had expected the arrest of those responsible for the war. When it emerged that this would not happen, much of the public response was decidedly hostile. The article "Where Do You Think You Are Going?" that appeared in an Istanbul newspaper asks,

> Where have the pashas gone, running from place to place with cudgels in their hands, scimitars in their belts, blood in their eyes? . . . Political opponents? Bring them down. Writers? Beat them. Turks? Send them to their deaths. Greeks? Take their money. Armenians? Chop off their heads. Arabs? String 'em up. . . . Bandits? We'll be with you shortly. Hooligans? Show them right in. . . . And now where have you gone, scampering from one bolt hole to the next like sly little weasels? Have you had your fill of slaughter? That's what we've been denied asking you.[15]

Under mounting pressure from within and without, the government was forced to step down on 8 November 1918. The new government, formed by Tevfik Paşa on November 11, took a more distant approach to the Unionists, influenced by the general mood.[16] The government grasped that its own interests would be served by trying the wartime leadership. The calculation was simple: All crimes committed during the war could be seen as the work of a few prominent Unionists sparing the Turkish nation any and all responsibility. Good relations with the Allies would follow, and a more positive result for the Ottomans at the Paris Peace Conference.

⋇   ⋇   ⋇

The occupying powers were not alone in demanding trials for those guilty of war crimes and massacres. The political opposition and Ottoman press had grown louder and more assertive and were also demanding that the Unionist leaders be tried for war crimes and the Armenian massacres. The press, in particular, seemed determined to "utterly dismantle and neutralize the Unionists in this country."[17] Writers asked the grand vizier, "The people responsible for the war, what business do they have in your cabinet?"[18] All they wanted, they claimed, was "that the perpetrators be punished, the secret organizations be dissolved to the point of elimination forever. Is there any Ottoman who does not expect these things?"[19] Clearly, the winds were shifting against the Unionists, something they likely sensed before they fled.

But before their escape, Talât Paşa and others left a letter for Ahmet İzzet Paşa that stated:

> I see that the country will remain under foreign control and influence for a while. Nonetheless, I was of a mind to stay and stand trial before the nation. But all of my friends insisted that I leave for the sake of the future. . . .
>
> I would like to give an accounting before the nation, to endure with courage the punishment given in judgment. I promise the Illustrious Person [of the Sultan]: The day when my country is free of foreign control I shall obey your first command (i.e., to return home).[20]

Similar sentiments were expressed by Cemal Paşa:

> There is nothing in the world that could make me turn from the law . . . With a clear conscience, I am prepared to answer for each and every one of my political and administrative orders and actions, and to do so before the court of public opinion. . . .[21]

However, the way to avoid immediate investigation was to flee.

The press, in particular, began to provide detailed information about the genocide. The crimes done to the Armenians were reported with fierce condemnation. In *Minber,* a daily endorsed by Mustafa

Kemal and published by his close friend Fethi Okyar, the destruction of the Armenians was deemed sheer madness, described as "the greatest and most unpardonable act in history."[22] The press also took up the issue of the indequate investigations.[23] The names of suspects who participated in the massacres and the looting and were being sought by the authorities were published in the press, with the observation that these people "were living freely and comfortably in Istanbul." The press demanded that these people "be brought in and interrogated immediately, so that unlike certain rich types [Enver, Talât and Cemal] they won't be able to sneak off to some place or another."[24] Pressure increased for an honest, straightforward investigation, and the press tried to help the relevant judicial bodies and offices. Articles calling for the execution of those responsible for the genocide appeared more frequently:

> The gallows are not good enough for these individuals. Their heads need to be ripped from their bodies, laid on the chopping block, chopped for days, then hung from the obelisk in front of Topkapı Palace! . . . No lesser punishment than death is right for these people.[25]

The main opposition party, Liberty and Concord (*Hürriyet ve İtilaf*), crushed by the CUP during the war, now began to make its voice heard, most loudly on the issue of war crimes trials. The party was reconstituted on 10 January 1919, and the imperial prince Damat Ferid Paşa was made chairman.[26] One of the party's founding principles was the need to try those guilty of the massacres. Both the sultan and the public were asked to support this demand and it was publicized and discussed at frequent events. The party's platform demanded "that documents related to the war be published and the guilty be punished."[27]

Additionally, a concerned group of individuals drew up a petition calling for the sultan to outlaw the CUP, which had reorganized under a new name, and arrest those members who remained at large, "as if being invited to escape." This was the necessary condition, the petition claimed, to reestablish the country on a stable footing and alter the decisions forthcoming from the Paris Peace Conference.[28] When former Diyarbakır governor-general Dr. Reşit Bey escaped from prison on January 25, the opposition's protest seemed all the more justified, and many other groups were mobilized into action. The Liberty and Concord Party gathered an enormous crowd that marched to the grand vizier to protest the escape.

Debate Within the Ottoman Parliament

The press was not alone in its discussion of the responsibility for the war and the massacres. The subject was repeatedly taken up by deputies in the Ottoman parliament, if not in the government. As noted, there was no debate on the issues in October, as the Unionists remained in power. Indeed at the opening of the parliamentary session on 10 October 1918, speaker Halil Menteşe gave a lengthy defense of the decision to enter the war. But with the establishment of İzzet Paşa's government, deputies who had been silent now began to speak up, even though the cabinet had explicitly distanced itself from criticism of the wartime CUP.[29] In the debate over the new government's program, some called for punishing those who for four years had crushed thousands of innocent people through their oppressive policies. Domestic peace and security could only be achieved "by rescuing the nation from tyranny and oppression and punishing the oppressors, who have been swimming in wasteful extravagance and wallowing in pleasure while sucking the nation's life's blood."[30]

Trabzon deputy Mehmet Emin Bey scolded the new government, saying,

> Your humble servant sees one thing lacking in the cabinet's program, and it is . . . that it will investigate those responsible for the atrocities, murder and persecution that occurred during the World War, and pursue their legal prosecution.[31]

He noted that the guilty parties were still driving around in their cars, in public, and that the situation was unbearable.[32] Mehmet Emin Bey, himself a Unionist, claimed that the entire Turkish nation was being burdened with guilt for these crimes. He proposed that trying the real culprits would prevent the blot from staining all the Turks.[33] His speech seemed like a confession:

> We have kept quiet about these events until now. . . . "Let's not say a word while the war is going on," we said. . . . We shuddered when we silenced discussion about this in the chamber. . . . The law must punish those who pursued the crimes, for personal profit or gain. . . . The government must tell us that it will carry out these prosecutions. This nation is innocent. But its innocence must be visible to the judgment of history while others must receive their due punishment.[34]

Mehmet Emin Bey warned that he would not support the new government if it did not vow to pursue the necessary prosecutions.

The only serious initiative taken by the government on the subject was its proposal for urgent consultation on the temporary laws regarding deportation and the sale of Armenian properties, which were both still in effect. The subject was taken up in the parliament's 24 October session. Foreign Minister Fethi Okyar Bey explained that the government's intention was to rescind the laws. The proposal was sent to a sub-commission and at the 18 December session the temporary laws were declared illegal.[35]

Harsh debate over the genocide began in the chamber's eleventh session on 4 November. Through a variety of motions, proposals, speeches, and questions, war crimes, genocide, and other abuses were brought to the chamber's attention. A proposal submitted by Aydın deputy Emanuelidi Efendi called for new elections to be held for the president of the chamber, or the speaker, claiming that the present chamber would never address the crimes of the former government, especially since some of these crimes were directly related to Halil Menteşe, who had maintained his position as president of the chamber.[36] He should, Deputy Emanuelidi Efendi argued, be forced to step down from his post and new elections be held. The proposal was ultimately rejected.

Another deputy from Aydın, Veli Bey, suggested that the Ottoman parliament be closed. He argued that the events of the previous four years had changed the nature of the parliament and impaired its moral standing, declaring that the chamber itself was responsible for what had happened. To the public, he asserted, the chamber had lost its dignity and worth and no longer had the power to represent the nation. If the assembly truly wanted "to stand before the nation, before history and before the law with a clear conscience, it should dissolve itself."[37] Fethi Okyar Bey, acting interior minister, thought this proposal too emotional and that what parliament needed to do was to get down to work.

The same assembly, on 4 November, considered a ten-point proposal put forward by Fuat Bey, the deputy for Divaniye, to try former government members in the High Court of Justice. It was this proposal, ultimately accepted, that paved the way for the first commission of inquiry on the genocide. Fuat Bey's concerns were echoed by Hudeidah deputy Muharrem Hıfzı Bey and his colleagues, who proposed trying in absentia the Unionist leaders who had fled, as well as confiscating their property.[38] This was referred to the relevant government department.

At the same parliamentary session, Deputy Emanuelidi Efendi, together with two Greek deputies, brought a second motion, one which dealt with the Armenian genocide. In an eight-point proposal, the deputies called for the punishment of Talât Paşa and his colleagues and that the Unionist persecution of "the Armenian nation" as well as the "noble Arab people" should not go unpunished.

According to this motion:

- One million people, including women and children, people who had committed no crime other than being part of the Armenian nation, were cut down and killed.
- Some 250,000 members of the Greek community, which has for at least the last forty centuries been the true agent of civilization in this country, were expelled from the Ottoman Empire and had their property confiscated.
- After the war, some 550,000 more Greeks were murdered at sea and on land, and their property was seized.
- Since non-Muslim communities within the Ottoman empire were barred from conducting trade, and commerce was left to the thievery of the authorities, the entire nation has been cheated.
- Deputies Zohrab Efendi and Vartkes Efendi were assassinated.
- The abuses inflicted on the noble Arab nation are the main cause for the current disaster.

- Some 250,000 people serving in the Labor Battalions, formed as a result of the general mobilization, perished from hunger and deprivation.
- The country entered the war without reason and a portion of its territory was abandoned to the Bulgarians in order to attain this dubious honor [referring to the Ottoman exchange of territory to gain Bulgarian entrance into the war].[39]

The government was then asked what knowledge it had of these various charges and what steps it would now take in response.

Emanuelidi Efendi said that the motion had not been raised "out of a desire for revenge." The aim was not to reopen wounds but rather to:

> understand what sort of serious ideas the new government has to guarantee that there is no repetition, but an end to, abuses which we know about, as does the entire world—including our recent allies who encouraged us [in these]—that they were carried out against several of our communities.[40]

Emanuelidi Efendi added that the responsible parties could not only have been three or four people but "a mighty stream that carried out this business." Thus, future events could not be prevented by punishing only a few. What was important was whether the new government had significantly different policies from its predecessor. Emanuelidi Efendi then called for a program, or for a series of measures, to ensure that such horrors would never occur again.

Responding for the government, Minister Fethi Okyar Bey claimed that any mention of the sufferings of the Greek, Armenian, and Arab peoples must also include the Turks, who were, he said, "perhaps more abused and mistreated than anyone." He promised to improve the position of non-Muslims and said the government was committed to "return those who had been expelled [and to] compensate, to the greatest extent possible, those who had suffered material losses." He added that it was the government's duty to make sure that such things should not be repeated, and that anyone involved in these actions should be punished. To see proper and thorough redress, anyone with a complaint had to lodge it with the appropriate departments:

There won't be results by just writing letters to the newspapers, or making speeches here. Let anyone who has a complaint make it directly; we are prepared to carry all necessary investigations and to follow them up.[41]

The minister's words were met with shouts of "Bravo!"

In his answer to Fethi Bey's speech, Emanuelidi Efendi asserted that those responsible for the genocide were not only isolated individuals but an entire political movement, and suggested that whoever supported this movement—even the entire nation—bore political responsibility, prompting harsh responses from some Turkish deputies, who called out: "This is an indictment of the whole Turkish community. . . . We cannot accept it!"[42]

Overall, the government's conciliatory reply to the demand for clarification elicited a strong reaction from the Turkish deputies. "The speaker is making a number of accusations to which the government has responded with forebearance," several deputies argued. "They say that one million people were brutally killed—and without cause—by the Turks, a blot on our nation for all time."[43]

A second request for the government's response on the Armenian genocide was submitted by the Armenian deputy for Kozan, Matyos Nalbantyan Efendi, and his colleagues. They asked that

the government explain its position on the laws and regulations enacted during the war, and on the crimes, the deportations, the lootings, and the killings that were done as a result of those laws.

The Government was asked to quickly debate the abrogation of the Temporary Decree of [27 May 1915] and of 26 September 1915 concerning the abandoned property and possessions of the deportees.[44]

As we know, the Unionists' method of governance relied on temporary decrees unratified by parliament. Fethi Bey reported that measures were being taken to abrogate these decrees and ensure the return of Armenians' property, "But the actual implementation is not as simple as we had imagined." For those Armenians who wanted to return, they needed "a dwelling and a hot bowl of soup"; however, a large number of deportees did not wish to return, the government claimed. Thus the goal was to find shelter for the few returning deportees.[45] Fethi Bey reiterated his promise to hold an inquiry into all injustices: "Let them appeal to us and we shall verify their claims. . . . We do not wish that the officials responsible should escape the law in any way."[46]

Later, this proposal was joined to the memorandum asking that the government abrogate the relevant wartime decrees, and thus the debate over the specific laws in question began. The Armenian deputy from Aleppo, Artin Boşgezenyan Efendi, spoke about the deportation law:

> The matter is not finished simply by ending the law. . . . The law is a knife, an ax, responsible for so many crimes. Let us not attempt to correct these crimes just by blunting the knife. . . . A great deal of innocent blood has been spilled as a result. . . . It is impossible to determine the number of burned or destroyed homes. This three-line law is a fearful thing. We must overturn it in both form and substance. . . . But along with cancelling it, we must also move to the punishment, without exception, of those who destroyed the country on the basis of this law; those who used and exploited the law by conspiring to murder must be punished. The matter is not ended just by putting away the weapons.[47]

Boşgezenyan Efendi's speech was followed by shouts of "We are with you!"

Meanwhile, some Turkish deputies disputed the figures given for Greeks and Armenians who had been killed. Trabzon deputy Mehmet Emin Bey claimed that the numbers were exaggerated and condemned the matter as an injustice being done to the Ottomans:

> It is not right to wipe out one injustice with another. . . . Yes . . . I say that our government slaughtered a great number of Armenian women and children. And their property was looted. But the number is not one million, as claimed. It is around 500–600,000. And furthermore, it is not right to say that these people "were killed because they were Armenians."[48]

When Boşgezenyan Efendi then asked for a reason why the Armenians had been killed, Mehmet Emin Bey answered that "there were revolts here and there" and gave an example from the Black Sea region, where Russian military units had assisted irregular Greek armed units. Therefore there had been some solid reasons for the deportations, he claimed, adding that army commanders had killed a great number of Turks as well, and many Arabs had been executed and deported for no reason. The discussion became extremely heated. A government minister intervened, saying, "Let's not dig into it." This stormy 4 November session finally came to an end with cries of "May Allah curse the oppressors!" and "Amen, amen!"

A vote was then taken, as a result of which the temporary decrees issued on 27 May 1915 and 29 September 1915, concerning the Armenian deportations and the sale of the deportees' property, were annulled. (These laws would make a reappearance on 14 September 1922,[49] enacted by the nationalist assembly, even though they had been deemed contrary to the Constitution.)

The lengthy 4 November session also resulted in a commission established to "form a committee of inquiry to examine the documents upon which entry into the World War was based." Fuat Bey's proposal to try members of the previous government in the High Court of Justice was considered insufficient because it only targeted top officials, excluding individuals in the lower levels of government service. "Certain abuses had been perpetrated, not only in the government ministries, but also in the Commissions of Provisioning and for the Prevention of Hoarding. . . ."[50] Thus, in addition to cabinet members, it would now be possible to try anyone involved in such abuses.[51]

The parliamentary debates over the Armenian genocide continued after the fall of Ahmet İzzet Paşa's government and during the formation of the Tevfik Paşa government that succeeded it. In its program, presented on 18 November, the government stated that first among its aims was "a peace agreement in line with the honor and dignity of the Ottoman State and Nation." Additionally, the government considered its most fundamental task to be

> to attain sincere commitment and mutual friendship among all the classes and segments of the population, without regard for racial or religious difference, and to enact all religious and legal statues

through the speedy elimination of the illegal actions that have continued for several years.[52]

Following this presentation, many of the Turkish deputies gave
emotional speeches. The Entente Powers' occupation of Istanbul was
called contrary to the armistice agreement. Better to "die with honor"
than sign a peace treaty on the basis of the present conditions, one
deputy argued, adding that the Muslims were victims of great injustice, and that there would be some future reckoning.

Boşgezenyan Efendi stated that the only way to secure a favorable
outcome at the Paris Peace Conference—something which the government claimed as one of its objectives—was to undertake certain
actions in regard to the Armenian genocide. "Let us not come to that
table with our hands empty," he said:

> Let us come with certain commendations that might act as our
> advocate, that might preserve our rights. I say to you openly: Gen-
> tlemen, you are well aware that in the eyes of the civilized world and
> the world of politics, the Turkish nation today stands accused. . . .
> Today there is an enormous crime which stands as the most sor-
> rowful and bloody page of Ottoman history. This immense crime,
> which has shaken both heaven and earth, is known as the massacre
> of the Armenians, as the Armenian calamity. For this reason the
> Turkish nation is accused, but the real perpetrator is not the
> Turkish nation but the former Turkish government and adminis-
> tration. . . . The nation is one thing, the government is another. . . .
> I say that this great crime, of which an entire nation stands accused,
> was carried out by the former regime, or, more correctly, by the
> hooligan regime. . . . It is not right . . . to accuse an entire nation
> for the crimes of a handful of murderers and madmen.

To avoid collective punishment, the guilty parties

> must be arrested with all due haste, and punished through trials
> and the justice system, to prove that we are not strangers to the con-
> cepts of justice and righteousness. These people are roaming
> around with impunity.[53]

Boşgezenyan Efendi added that Interior Minister Fethi Bey's stance of awaiting the complaints of the innocent was not sufficiently active, because the fact was that no one was left to file a complaint. Instead, he argued that

> the government must issue forceful directives to its officials and to public prosecutors, and it must pursue those responsible for these crimes and bring them to trial.

Boşgezenyan Efendi stood firm against denunciations from some Turkish deputies. The outcome he wished, he said,

> is that those officials and civilians who are convicted be punished, that the widows and orphans scattered here and there in captivity be provided for by the government, have their property and possessions returned, and be compensated for the injuries they suffered.[54]

Several Turkish deputies tried to justify the deportations as a result of wartime conditions and the armed gangs that had collaborated with Russian military units. If a crime had been done, they claimed, "the sole reason for it" was the Armenians. İlyas Sami Efendi, a deputy for Muş, claimed that the issue was not "a crime," but "a battle." Among other things, he criticized the Armenians for having fought with the Russians, and for having taken part in the massacre of Muslims in the Van area. The accusations were "a calumny against the Turks."[55] Later, Sami Efendi was arrested for his participation in the Armenian genocide, at first standing trial in the Istanbul extraordinary court-martial, then, on 29 August 1920, being exiled to Malta by the British, as he was considered among those primarily responsible for the massacre of Armenians.[56]

The Armenian deputies reacted harshly. Nalbantyan Efendi reminded the chamber that a large number of the deportees appeared to have been women and children, and that the regions from which they were deported were not war zones. He added that, even after making excuses for a few individual instances, these "reasons" could not begin to explain the annihilation of an entire people:

> If one armed gang appears here, or there, or if it undertakes certain
> actions, or if the residents of an area participate in these actions,
> and if they take part in a number of illegal acts, does this situation
> really warrant that everyone in any place in the whole country, even
> its remotest reaches, that all Armenians—even down to the handful
> who lived in Edirne, İzmit and on the coast, for instance—be
> expelled and killed? That their honor and dignity be violated? That
> their land and property be confiscated and looted?[57]

The sharp exchange over the Armenian genocide continued
throughout discussion of other proposals, including an inquiry
regarding General Liman von Sanders, a German. The deportation of
the Greek population of the Ayvalık region had been carried out on
von Sanders's orders, and a great many people had died as a result.[58] A
new request for clarification protested that the government continued to resettle people on Armenian land and property, and asked
what the regime planned to do about this.[59] Another dealt primarily
with "the deportation of the Greeks of the Province of Edirne and the
Sanjak of Çatalca." Heated argument broke out once again in the
chamber, turning into an open debate on the issue, and the Armenian
deportations as well, lasting for two full parliamentary sessions and
marked by mutual recriminations.

The Armenian and Greek deputies did not limit their accusations to
the Committee of Union and Progress, instead speaking of Turkish collective responsibility overall. The Turkish deputies, who immediately
moved to counterattack, then delivered speeches in defense of both
Turks and Turkishness. Mehmet Emin Bey, the deputy from Mosul, said:

> Although we have not refrained from cursing the oppressors and
> expressing sympathy for the oppressed . . . there are those who
> desire to attribute this calamity to Turkdom as a whole. . . . I reject
> this in the name of the high moral character of my nation.[60]

Emin Bey's speech reflects a certain mental state then prominent
among Turks. He emphasized the tolerance of the Turkish people and
deemed the nation "strong as a bull, innocent as a lamb . . . and merciful." The Turks were the nation that had truly suffered throughout

history. They "had given blood from their weakened veins, wept until the founts of their sorrow ran dry, shed tears of death and lamentation . . . pursued from dungeon to dungeon, exile to exile." It was they "who bore, like the red brand of the accused, the stain of oppressors' crimes and transgressions . . . they who received no expression of comfort . . . bereft of the mercy and protection of humanity." The frequent applause and expressions of support from the chamber indicated that the speech reflected the feelings of a broad sector of the Turkish population.

In reply the Greek deputy, Yorgi Yuvanidis Efendi, listed the massacres. He then asked the assembly, "Now, let's suppose that Nikolai does something bad: Does this give one the right to drive five or six hundred Apostolic Christians into the mountains, loot their property, and slaughter them?" The issue, he said, "was not deportation, it was annihilation."[61]

Even as he was speaking, Yuvanidis Efendi was interrupted by Turkish deputies shouting, "Go ahead and say what the Greeks did! Why don't you talk about their crimes? Go and talk about the Muslim children who were dismembered."[62] A ferocious back and forth followed. Mehmet Faik Bey, a Muslim deputy for Edirne, stated that "We learned how to do these deportations from our neighbors. We didn't invent it," at which point the chamber erupted with harsh shouts of recrimination on both sides.[63]

Deputy Emanuelidi Efendi changed the tenor of the debate by reminding the chamber that all of the deputies during the war had applauded subjecting the Greeks to expulsion. Listing the politicians by name, he recounted how a consciously anti-Christian policy had developed, and gave examples of the theories that had been advocated as justifications, such as Pan-Islamism and the Turkification of Anatolia.

When Mehmet Emin Bey then spoke, he provided some important information regarding the Armenian genocide: "There was an official in the district of Ordu. He loaded the Armenians on a caïque with the pretext of transporting them to Samsun and then threw them into the sea." Emin Bey said that he had the official removed from his post, but he was not able to remove the governor-general of Trabzon, who had Armenians killed in the same way.[64]

Deputy Dimistokli Efkalidis Efendi sharply attacked the Turkish deputies' equation of "We were wronged, you were wronged" and the notion that some sort of balance could be reached in this way, as well as their desire "to be thus reconciled." The Turks had no doubt suffered because of the war, Efkalidis Efendi said, and he supported the prosecution of any Greek who had massacred Turks or looted Turkish homes. "If for some reason our Muslim fellow citizens had been wronged by a Greek, I would press for the law to be applied doubly. I would even approve of that Greek being sent to the firing squad, and then hung."[65]

The Armenian deputy Nalbantyan Efendi then stated that as a member of the Armenian nation, his words should nonetheless not be understood as "an insult or calumny directed at Turkdom born of the Armenian nation's sorrow or revenge." With the president of the chamber continually interrupting him, Nalbantyan Efendi claimed "that Armenians had been slashed to pieces like a leek," that things had been done "that far overshadowed the barbarity of Nero," that the Armenians "had been exterminated," that inner Anatolia "had been turned into a graveyard," that his family had been deported and that he himself had only been saved from execution at the last moment because he was a parliamentary deputy. Recounting what he had seen on the roads, he stated that "these are not stories from the Arabian Nights, they are present conditions." These things, he claimed, "were done in a systematic way."[66] The most significant element of Nalbantyan Efendi's speech was in connection with collective responsibility. Those responsible for the crimes, done "to eliminate an entire nation," were the political echelon, acting in the name of their nation.

> For a long time, in this country . . . sovereignty has meant the sovereignty of the Turks. The true Turks may well be opposed to the persecutions that were repeated again and again. . . . It is spoken of three to five people who did this. . . . Three to five people could not have done this. . . . Those who did these things shouted: "We do this for Turkish sovereignty!" and "Our strength is Turkish bayonets!" . . . Those who did these things are individuals who belong to the Turkish nation.

Nalbantyan Efendi then claimed that the Turks as a nation would not escape responsibility:

Both world opinion and the victims will demand an accounting and compensation, and the Turks will have to provide it. The Turks, who claim that their hands are clean, must give an accounting, they must punish those who deserve punishment . . . without regard for the station or the numbers involved, they must return the rights to those who lost them. Only afterward will they be able to stand true before humanity and the world. Otherwise, how will we ever be able to bring a complaint against any other people?

He concluded by denouncing the Turks' demand to place their own victims with others: "The Turks who suffered injustice," he stated, "did so as the ruling nation."[67] There was only one way to solve the problem:

Redemption is possible, but we must find every person who committed these crimes and we must punish them, and we must return and restore those rights that were trampled and abused. And after this we will go before the civilized world as a delegation and declare that we are going to do this, even if it means punishing one hundred thousand . . . this is the soundest and most righteous path.[68]

In response, Muş deputy İlyas Sami Efendi deployed the logic that we still hear even today. Sami Efendi claimed that in the Ottoman Empire non-Muslims "had been protected like favored children for eight centuries," and that they must consider the reason this happened to the Armenians. Parliament must not be afraid of asking the question "why?"

Nalbantyan Efendi interjected, "No action could ever cause this to be necessary," to which Sami Efendi snapped, "Don't interrupt me when I'm speaking," asserting that, although some 80 percent of the Armenians were innocent, it was still they themselves who were to blame for the decision to deport them. According to him, the deportations were the Turks' revenge against those who had been conspiring to kill them.[69]

At the end of this fiery two-day debate, a government official declared that further discussion would serve no purpose other than to be divisive. Attacks on the government had no validity unless proof was provided. In its absence, the government continued to deny culpability.[70]

The Armenian genocide was taken up for the last time on 21 December 1918, when under pressure from the Allied Powers, the sultan dissolved the assembly. The final debate, initiated by Karesi deputy Hüseyin Kadri Bey and his colleagues, questioned the government's resistance to acting against those responsible for the massacres. In his reply, given on behalf of the government, Foreign Minister Mustafa Reşit Paşa first mentioned the destruction that the Unionist government had allowed to happen by pushing the country into the war, and then the impossibility of righting all these problems in such a short period of time. He also commented on some of the disastrous results of the genocide and their correction:

> The government has begun to fulfill the needs of justice by moving toward prosecutions and legal investigations of the criminals who sullied the reputation of this country before world opinion. . . . Despite the lack of available means of transportation from the time we came to power until today, through the government's instructions some 2,525 Muslims, 19,695 Greeks and 23,420 Armenians from among the refugees and those deported and exiled have been resettled in their . . . homes.[71]

In sum, until the Chamber of Deputies was closed, the most fundamental issues were the debates over the Greek and Armenian deportations and the punishment of the guilty parties. But apart from Deputy Fuat Bey's ten-point proposal, which resulted in investigations by the Ottoman parliament's Fifth Department, no concrete results were achieved. The president of the chamber, Halil Menteşe, and his assistant, Unionist propagandist journalist Hüseyin Cahit Yalçın, in particular, worked with the regime to prevent discussion of the matter. Their tactics included refusing to read proposals and motions coming from Armenian and Greek deputies, omitting them from the chamber's agenda, not giving these deputies the floor, and continually interrupting them while they were speaking.

Fuat Bey's ten-point proposal of 4 November 1918 was ultimately forwarded to one of the parliamentary commissions, the Fifth Department, with the aim of beginning investigations. The proposal, which demanded that the Said Halim Paşa and Talât Paşa cabinets be brought before the High Court of Justice, called for people who had served in those governments to be questioned, and, if necessary, tried on the grounds that they had entered the war without cause and at an inopportune time, that they had made false declarations before parliament, that they had rejected peace proposals, enriched themselves at the expense of the people and imposed unnecessary political and military censorship.

Points five and ten of the petition dealt with the question of the Armenian deportations, charging the guilty with

> (5) transforming the country into a landscape of disaster through the enactment of temporary laws, orders, and decrees that were entirely opposed to the spirit and explicit direction of legal and human principles, and of our Constitution in particular; ...
> (10) active involvement in these disasters, which they brought about through their support of gangs that violated the right to life, property, and honor so as to create a state of chaos in the country.[72]

Fuat Bey's request was based on the Thirty-first Article of the Ottoman Constitution, which provided detailed instructions on the proper procedure for taking a member of the Ottoman parliament or cabinet to the High Court of Justice. The procedure called first for presidential consideration, then debate in the Chamber of Deputies if the president deemed it necessary, and possibly consideration by a relevant commission, which would recommend the matter to the Chamber of Deputies for a vote. To ratify the decision for a trial, a two-thirds majority vote was necessary. If this majority was achieved, the petition would then be submitted to the grand vizier, who would deliver it to the High Court via sultanic decree.[73] The proper procedure to be followed by the court was laid out in Articles 92–95. According to these, two separate offices would be constituted: an Office of Indictment and a Court of Judgment, together composed of thirty members. These would be drawn from the High Court of Justice, the Chamber of Notables (the upper house of parliament), the Council of State and the Appeals Court. Decisions in both offices required a two-thirds majority vote.[74]

The Fifth Department's inquiries began on November 9, 1918, with the questioning of the former grand vizier, Said Halim Paşa. They concluded more than a month later, on 14 December. Despite the month of inquiries, since parliament was dissolved in December no concluding decision was ever released.[75] However, the inquiries helped shed light on the manner in which the wartime government ran its affairs, especially on the two pressing questions of Turkey's entry into the war and the killing of Armenians. It became clear that the decision to enter the war had been made without the knowledge of all the members of the cabinet. For example, during the deposition of former public works minister Çürüksulu Mahmud Paşa, the minister claimed:

> The cabinet was not aware of the discussions and correspondence being carried on with the [foreign] ambassadors; thus, we also learned of the situation through newspaper editorials reports, and certain accounts that I was told.[76]

But we also know, from the testimony of Grand Vizier Said Halim Paşa, given to the Fifth Department, that those questioned did not always answer truthfully. When asked about his knowledge of and involvement in the decision to enter the war, Said Halim feigned ignorance, saying that he had known nothing about it, that he had only learned of the decision later. This was patently untrue, as German sources confirmed his involvement in the decision-making process.[77]

Again and again, cabinet ministers claimed that the deportations had been carried out without their knowing the details, on the orders of the Ministry of War. Again, Said Halim Paşa's testimony is a typical example. In response to questions about the treatment of Armenians during the deportations he replied,

> ...the inhumane actions were within the normal [course of events]. When a country is at war and its army is attacked by its own subjects and the dispatch of its troops disrupted, it is not right to object [to such measures]. Therefore, a law was enacted to secure the army's rear during the fighting.... It was a necessity. That being the case, I would only like to say that whatever the nature of the law itself, the question of its implementation is another matter entirely.

The Fifth Department's committee chairman then asked, "Did the law explicitly mention that women and children should be removed from their homes and executed?" In his response, Said Halim Paşa chose to deny any personal responsibility for the events, replying instead:

> The Minister of War and the army commanders said that the areas where Armenians lived posed a danger for the army, and proposed moving them elsewhere. But "Move them" does not mean "Kill them".... The implementation was a disaster. Now, if you were to write a law, and the official implemented it in a disastrous way, are you to blame because you were the one who created the law?

The chairman of the Fifth Department's investigation then asked, "But didn't you hear about some of the disasters during the implementation?" Said Halim Paşa claimed not to remember much, replying, "As with everything else, I heard about these disasters after they had already happened." According to Said Halim Paşa, "In the end, it was the Ministry of War that informed us of the reasons behind all this and provided reports. That's where you need to ask, because I am unable to say anything that would convince you [otherwise]." He defended the government, saying that during the events a commission of inquiry had been established but thwarted in its task by Talât Paşa.

> The commissions of inquiry . . . returned, having carried out their task. But the Interior Ministry did not wish to report on the results of these investigations. Despite all manner of insistence and badgering, [the ministry] steadfastly insisted on keeping the truth hidden. As long as Talât Paşa was at the Interior Ministry he saw to it that the investigations would remain fruitless.[78]

After the armistice, the Interior Ministry supplied clarifying information about these commissions, which were never intended to examine the actions of officials during the deportations, but only the economic crime of misappropriating Armenian property. All together, there were three commissions of inquiry although none had any authority, and some did not even visit the regions they had been ordered to investigate. Just as Said Halim Paşa claimed, their reports were disregarded.[79]

During questioning, Said Halim Paşa gave very general replies to inquiries about the executions carried out by Cemal Paşa in Syria: "Regarding the Armenian, Iraqi and Syrian problems, no correspondence, not even a line, was sent to the Sublime Porte." He also claimed that he had only heard about the murder of Zöhravi (Zohrab Efendi), an Armenian deputy in the Ottoman parliament, some time after the event, and that all of his inquiries went unanswered. On the formation of the Special Organization units, his position was the same: "This question does not concern the Sublime Porte or the government, because . . . the government never made any decision or took any initiative in this regard." Asked whether he was aware of the organization, Said Halim Paşa replied in the affirmative, but "only after everything was finished."[80] He claimed he had heard about the dreadful actions of the Special Organization, and had "repeatedly and insistently [told] Enver Paşa that the organization was an evil thing, and demanded that an end be put to it immediately." But all of his attempts in this direction were either ignored or left unanswered. Despite any doubts about Said Halim Paşa's testimony, we can be sure that the CUP largely bypassed the government.

Similarly, former justice minister İbrahim Bey claimed that "the extraordinary actions during the implementation of the Law of Deportation were reported only after the fact" and that the government was ignorant.[81] In his deposition he made the significant claim that the deportations had begun before the actual decision was taken:

> During wartime conditions, the military commanders possessed a certain degree of authority regarding decisions to secure the army's rear; the Law of Deportation was decreed only afterward.[82]

Although İbrahim Bey claimed that the deportation decision had been taken for military purposes, he was reminded that "a great number of people were deported [from] places that were not in the theater of war. And many others were executed in places outside the military sectors." In reply, he gave the standard response, claiming "we were not aware."[83] The minister's assertion that he had no knowledge of the executions during the period of the deportations is highly significant, because any such orders would have had to be issued by the wartime military court, the cabinet, and approved by the sultan himself.[84]

Thus, the cabinet should have been aware of the order for murder. But what appears to be true is that no legal procedures were observed in relation to the executions.

İbrahim Bey testified similarly with regard to the Special Organization. As minister of justice, he only learned of the release of convicts from prison after the fact, and the relevant law was also issued later so as to give the whole matter a veneer of legality.

> A provincial district attorney, I cannot remember from which province, reported that the convicts had been released by the provincial administration to send them to the front, and upon hearing this, I went to the appropriate ministry and made a scandal demanding that they be sent back, saying that "a convict who has not been pardoned by imperial decree cannot be released." The military sector also insisted that it was not right to use this power so carelessly, which was happening with significant frequency. We issued a law concerning their [the prisoners] dispatch and this was ratified by your lofty council as well.[85]

Since parliament was dissolved in December 1918, the Fifth Department transferred the minutes of its sessions to the chief prosecutor of the extraordinary court-martial that was established later, on the order of Ferid Paşa.[86] One of the reasons for the sultan's decision to dissolve parliament was the perceived impossibility of prosecuting cabinet members through the courts. The heavily Unionist character of the Chamber of Deputies would have prevented this.

In the upper house of the Ottoman parliament, or Chamber of Notables, the first debate on the issue of the Armenian deportations was held as a result of the opening speech given by chamber president Ahmet Rıza, a former Unionist who had broken with the party. In it, Ahmet Rıza hinted that the sultan, who directly appointed all the notable deputies, felt as troubled by the massacres as he himself did.

> The Mercy of His Imperial Majesty would not leave the orphans and widows of those Armenians who were brutally killed, of those Arabs who were hanged or deported, to be crushed under the

weight of their poverty and despair. There will no longer be any weeping or moaning.[87]

In response, some members took Ahmet Rıza to task. Field Marshall Osman Paşa said:

For justice and equality to be done in place of the Mercy of His Imperial Majesty, your most humble servant [believes] it would be appropriate . . . to consider all of the citizens who experienced this oppressive treatment; let us not forget the orphans and widows of those poor Turks and Kurds who were cruelly killed by Armenians and Arabs.[88]

Ahmet Rıza's reply is significant. He noted that the Armenians had been killed as a result of a premeditated state plan, and pointed out that there was thus an important difference between theirs and other deaths.[89]

Replying to the sultan's speech that had opened parliament, in which he referred to the chamber's "difficult task" in confronting the recent past, the notables included the term "deportation" in the text of their response. This was criticized by Damat Ferid Paşa:

I am surprised at the word "deportation." These people were forcibly expelled. "Deportation" gives the sense that they were relocated or settled. Were they resettled? No. . . . They were driven into the mountains after their homes were taken away. Only God knows what became of them. For this reason, the word "deportation" is not appropriate here. The term "expelled" would better describe the true situation.[90]

He added that

the number of our Armenian fellow citizens who succumbed to disaster in the recent past is 800,000, the number of Greek citizens 550,000; if we add the two million Muslims wrongfully mistreated, one can speak of three million people who perished as a result of hunger, poverty, oppression and bad government.

He told the chamber that it would be almost impossible to document the properties seized from people who had been killed, and that it was of the highest importance to form a commission to investigate these matters. His proposal to set up such a commission was rejected by the chamber on the grounds that this was a matter for the government itself to deal with.[91]

At the 4 November 1918 session of the chamber Vice-President Çürüksulu Mahmud Paşa submitted a proposal demanding that all the secret agreements and related documents that brought the Ottomans into the war be made public. He also proposed that separate military and political commissions of inquiry be established to investigate the issue and punish those responsible.[92] After some debate, the Chamber of Notables set up the Special Council to advise the government on establishing a commission to examine the previous government's actions. The government did indeed establish a number of commissions of inquiry at this time, among them, the Fifth Department's investigations.

Said Halim Paşa, now a notable deputy, proposed that a high court be constituted to examine the documents relating to his grand vizierate and the war. However, the Chamber of Notables was not empowered to establish such a high court and so his suggestion was referred to the Special Council. At the same session, Ferid Paşa claimed that the parties responsible "were three missing people . . . Talât, Enver and Cemal. . . . [Though] in truth, there are also a number of secondary accomplices." In his view, Ferid Paşa stated, these people were traitors.[93]

Another important debate followed a proposal submitted by Ahmet Rıza on 21 November. In it he said:

> A great many crimes were inflicted on the Ottomans as a whole: political injustice and atrocities, massacres, looting, and violations of . . . property; these atrocities, which are without parallel in Ottoman history, particularly affected our Arab, Armenian, and Greek citizens.[94]

Even if a high court was established to investigate the events that took place during the deportations, it would be insufficient, limited only to former government members and would also take a great deal of time. For the state to demonstrate its responsiveness, the government needed to act immediately, rather than wait for the parliamentary commissions to conclude their work. Rıza Bey called for a criminal investigation by the public prosecutor:

> I demand that the Imperial Government establish a trial venue in the name of the public and with the . . . Public Prosecutor's Office, to ensure that the individuals' rights are protected and that the murderers are identified as soon as possible and delivered to the hands of justice.[95]

Ahmet Rıza explained why he called for individual trials to be held for people responsible for aiding and abetting the crimes: "My wish," he said, "is that the conscience of humanity be satisfied."[96]

This debate prompted discussion of the important question of who was actually responsible and who had given the orders. Ahmet Rıza claimed that, ultimately, it was the government: "I do not recognize the CUP or any other element as the perpetrators. . . . I only recognize the executive power. . . . The executive government is responsible for the war and for the crimes." İbrahim Bey asserted that the responsible party was not the government as a whole, but only certain individuals within it. But many members of the chamber disagreed; Damat Ferid Paşa, for example, cited the wartime government's own book, published during the war, justifying the measures against the Armenians:

> It has been said that a mistaken impression should not be given regarding the former government. Yet leading members of that government have published a long book and even submitted it to both chambers. In the book the main reasons for the atrocities and persecution are presented. It says "If we evicted one million Armenians from their homes and villages, if the birds and beasts feasted on their bones on the roads to Baghdad; [it is] because they would have cut our army's lines, attacked our army from the rear, and presented a danger to the state." These reasons are fictitious and ridiculous. . . . Neither humanity, nor civilization, nor the Islamic world can accept them.[97]

He went on: "There are only one or two wretches responsible for the disasters. . . . The degenerates who carried them out are nothing but Bolsheviks," and thus, the Turkish nation cannot be held responsible. Ferid Paşa then called on the Western powers, who had acted to try to save the Russian nation from Bolshevism, saying, "Truth and justice demand that they must say 'Let us save the Turkish nation, which has lived with honor, dignity, nobility and decency for 600 years.'"[98]

Damat Ferid Paşa put forward another proposal in the chamber, on 2 December, calling for an immediate inquiry into the Armenian genocide. He claimed that the present parliament did not represent the nation, and that many of the deputies were members of the CUP. As such, parliament was unable to investigate the genocide since it had supported the war and the things done during the war, and had shared power with the government of the time. "No matter what you call the individuals within a party, it is unacceptable that they act as both judge and accused." What was needed, he said, were new elections. The constitution of the High Court should be decided by a new parliament.

However, Ferid Paşa went on, a court-martial should begin its work immediately, without waiting for new elections. The British Occupational Government had moved toward swift trials and the government should do likewise. He claimed that if the nation wished to cleanse and purify itself, it had to try its own criminals. Therefore, the Ottoman government needed to take immediate action against the former ministers and others. This was the only way to put a stop to certain people using the slow-moving parliamentary investigations to buy time.[99] The demands outlined by Ferid Paşa amounted to a cabinet program that he began to implement when he eventually came to power, appointed by the sultan, soon thereafter.

In this discussion, all of the chamber's members agreed that those responsible for the Armenian genocide should be brought to trial at once. However, they differed on the question of the parliamentary investigations. Çürüksulu Mahmut Paşa, for instance, supported the parliamentary inquiries because he held the government responsible for the crimes, arguing that they were "decided on and organized by active members of the cabinet in power at the time." He added that the "armed gangs" had been attached, through various means and in varying degrees, to the Special Organization. All these circumstances, he concluded, properly placed the responsibility with the wartime regime. "For this reason," he claimed, the High Court had to, of necessity, reach a speedy decision.[100]

In the end, these various debates in the Chamber of Notables came to nothing. The chamber had no real power and the dissolution of parliament also played a role.

The question of dissolving the Ottoman parliament had appeared on the agenda at its first postwar session, on 10 October 1918. The parliament was hampered by its relationship to the past government and was therefore unable to act decisively.[101] But it remained possible to resolve a number of important issues, such as delivering the former regime to the High Court of Justice and discussing amnesty laws. However, articles began appearing in the press arguing that parliament should have been dissolved when İzzet Paşa's cabinet stepped down because the majority of deputies were Unionists.[102] But the new sultan, Vahdettin, was opposed to the idea of dissolving parliament because he feared this might be interpreted as acceding to the permanent occupation of areas of the empire. He also feared that annulling parliament would be understood as de facto recognition of the occupation. However, the Unionist majority in the Chamber of Deputies worked hard to obstruct both the opposition's and the government's activities.[103] Finally, both the sultan and Tevfik Paşa concluded that it was necessary to close parliament to take appropriate measures against the Unionists. The Allied Powers, who "held the CUP responsible for the Greek and Armenian 'deportation' operations," continued to apply pressure, leaning heavily on the sultan "to disperse the Chamber of Deputies, which had given a vote of confidence to a group of murderers."[104] The sultan realized that it would be impossible to pass a motion to prosecute Unionists because of their strong majority and active opposition to any such measures.

Thus he issued a decree on 18 December dissolving parliament and announced that he was acting on the demand of the British Occupational Forces. "Only God and I know what I have endured, night and day, . . . at the hands of the foreigners; they have pressured us into dispersing the Chamber of Deputies. They have not merely insinuated their opinions—they have announced them loudly."[105] Although the Ottoman Constitution required that new elections be held no later than three months after the old parliament was dismissed, this provision was not observed. In fact, new elections would become one of the most significant demands of the Nationalist Movement in Ankara. The government, appointed by the sultan, continued to function but elections were only held in the fall of 1919, and the new parliament began its work on 12 January 1920.

Measures Taken by the Postwar Governments

In all the parliamentary debates in both chambers, deputies expressed their concern with the question of returning the deported Armenians from exile and restoring their property and possessions. The short-lived cabinet of Ahmet İzzet Paşa, which had characterized the wartime treatment of Armenians as "the internal deportation and relocation from one region to another,"[106] decreed that the deportees were free to return to their homes, and claimed to have issued communiqués to this effect to the provinces.[107] Meanwhile, in the Chamber of Notables, Fethi Bey informed the members that the government had decided "that the deportees should gradually return to their homes" and that it "had begun to take action to this end."[108] With regard to locating and repatriating the women and children who had somehow been separated from their families, the cabinet took only a very limited number of steps. As for prosecuting those responsible for the genocide, not a single action was taken.

As we have seen, the fate of Armenian property during the deportations was ostensibly governed by laws and regulations. According to the regulations, Armenians were allowed to leave with their possessions but this was not in fact what happened; in most cases, Armenians had to leave their belongings behind. Legally, their property should have been placed under state supervision, but in reality there was wholesale pillaging. The Armenians were either compelled to sell their possessions at a negligible price, or the Unionists simply closed their eyes to the looting, hoping thereby to earn Muslim support. In many regions, Muslims saw the deportations as an opportunity to take over Armenians' possessions at a minimal price.[109]

The looting and dispossession was carried out in so public a fashion that numerous reports reached the foreign embassies in Istanbul. The German, Austrian and U.S. consular reports vividly illustrate the treatment of Armenian property. In an account from 13 August 1915, the American consul in Trabzon stated:

There is no attempt at classification and the idea of keeping the property in "bales under the protection of the government to be returned to the owners on their return" is simply ridiculous. The goods are piled without any attempt at labeling or systematic storage. A crowd of Turkish women and children follow the police about like a lot of vultures and seize anything they can lay their hands on and when the more valuable things are carried out of a house by the police they rush in and take the balance. I see this performance every day with my own eyes.[110]

The Austrian consul of Bursa also described the systematic looting of Armenian possessions and property. The Armenians were ordered to go to the local registrar's office to register their property, after which they were obliged to sell it. They were also forced to sign documents stating that the sale had been voluntary and that the money they had received was due compensation. In fact, the price paid was whatever amount was grabbed from a sack full of money and generally far below the true value of the items. In any case, the money was reclaimed by a functionary waiting at the exit and then returned to the sack, to be used again to "purchase" the next person's possessions.[111]

This was clearly not simply "run-of-the-mill" looting, then, but a conscious effort to "create a new class" of Muslims. In 1917, the Austrian ambassador quoted some sections of an annual report sent by Mustafa Abdülhalik Renda, the governor-general of Aleppo, to the Ministry of Trade:

It is with great pleasure that I report that we have succeeded in completely transforming the conditions here and in the provincial district of Maraş, in accordance with the government's aims. My province has been cleansed of Christian elements. Two years ago, eighty percent of the merchants and business owners were Christian; today ninety-five percent are Muslim and five percent Christian.

The report then supplied a precise and detailed list of all of the businesses transferred into the hands of reliable Muslims.[112]

Turkish author Halide Edip has drawn attention to the decisive role played by economic considerations in the Armenian genocide: "Besides [the] political argument . . . there was a strong economic one, supported morally by the Germans. This was to end the Armenians' economic supremacy, thereby clearing the markets for Turks and Germans."[113] One foreign consular report notes that "not only have members of the Committee [of Union and Progress] and Jews become rich by purchasing properties left behind by the Armenians at ridiculously low prices but state institutions [are also] taking material advantage from the mass deportation of the Armenians."[114] As a result, "with the Armenian properties acquired for a song, a group of nouveau riche have now sprung up, while those who had been wealthy before were able to increase their assets."[115] A new class of the wealthy was formed in Anatolia, essentially a continuation of the Unionist policy of homogenizing the area.

After the war, on 18 October 1918, İzzet Paşa's government decided:

> to allow all of the people—first and foremost, of course, the Armenians—who had been moved from one place and dispatched to other regions as a result of the wartime situation and military decisions to this effect, to return to their homes, and to ensure that their journey is safe.[116]

Two days later, other decisions allowed those who had been forcibly converted to return to their former religion if they so desired, and orphaned children to be reunited with relatives.[117] On 22 October 1918, the Ministry of the Interior sent a coded telegram to the provinces informing them of the decision permitting Armenians and Greeks to return to their homes, with the expectation of receiving some provisions.[118] Another coded telegram was sent the next day saying that officials remiss in this regard would be punished.[119] Various government offices then exchanged correspondence about facilitating the Armenians' return and ensuring their needs were met. Another letter, written on 1 November, from the Interior Ministry to the Foreign Ministry, reports that the number of Armenians and Greeks who had returned from other provinces was approximately 10,600.[120]

The government took another step through the Chamber of

Deputies when it cancelled the wartime deportation and confiscation laws. With this decision, both the deportations and the sale of Armenian property were retrospectively declared illegal. For its part, Tevfik Paşa's government made several very determined efforts to locate displaced Armenian women and children and reunite them with relatives, as well as return property to Armenian refugees. [121]

By 21 December, Foreign Minister Mustafa Reşit Paşa told parliament that "despite the lack of necessary transportation from the time we came to power up to now, . . . some 2,552 Muslims, 19,695 Greeks and 23,420 Armenians have, upon the government's instructions, been returned to their places of residence and resettled in their homes."[122]

On this issue, Great Britain continually applied pressure. In an interview published in the Armenian-language newspaper *Azadamart* on 11 December, a British official said, "You may be assured that we shall earnestly demand that an immediate end be put to the torments [suffered by] the Armenians."[123] This pressure produced the important result that on 24 February 1919 a commission was established to oversee all questions of restoration and repatriation, and was dispatched to various places in Anatolia for this purpose. The government also decided to include both the occupation forces and the Armenian patriarchate in the commission, and that the expenses incurred would be met by the Finance Ministry.[124]

But the British were not satisfied with these efforts, and so they directly commissioned the Armenian-Greek Section, established and housed in the high commissioner's office, to monitor the situation. Primarily, this department was entrusted with preparing lists of people involved in the genocide, and there is little information about its activities on behalf of returnees and kidnapped women and children. In a report sent on 29 July 1920, the British high commissioner, Admiral de Robeck, gave the following information:

> During the last year and a half, the Armenian-Greek Section of the High Commission . . . has been instrumental in rescuing from Moslem hands thousands of [Christian] women and children who have been forcibly Islamised and in obtaining the restitution of their property to thousands of returned deportees. Its activities have of late been greatly restricted by the spread of the National Movement.[125]

In his memoirs of the period, Sir Robert Graves, who directed this section, had the following to say:

> In A.G.S., as it was called for short, I found Heathcote Smith and others doing their best to rescue Armenian and Greek women and children who had been forcibly converted to Islam from the Turkish houses and institutions into which they had been taken, and also to obtain the restitution of their rights to owners of Christian properties which had been arbitrarily confiscated. There were also half a dozen Relief Officers with knowledge of the country and the languages, who were employed in reporting on the condition of the native Christians who had remained in the interior, and in ministering to their needs as far as they were able.[126]

But despite its efforts, the section had little success in either resettlement or the return of confiscated property. In truth, the conditions were prohibitive, because "in accordance with the List of Directives on Abandoned Properties the property belonging to the minorities had passed into the possession of Muslims (recent immigrants, officials, etc.), some as temporary dwellings, some having been appropriated for public use, and some actively seized."[127] Additionally, most of the original owners had been killed.

There was also increasing resistance to this policy from local Muslims, especially those who had been settled in the vacated homes. According to the news reports, these Muslims formed an organization called the Immigrant Society, which claimed there were "approximately 150,000" homeless Muslims because of the returning homeowners.[128] The numbers of those returning were similar.

In a report dated 18 October 1918, British high commissioner Admiral Calthorpe noted the Muslim resistance to the Armenians attempting to return and that it was Turkish officials and their offices that were proving an obstacle.[129] A twelve-point note was delivered to the Ministry of War on 11 February 1919 regarding the increase of this type of resistance, and the difficulties being created by Turkish officials such as Sixth Army commander Ali İhsan Sabis Paşa regarding the implementation of the conditions of the armistice.[130]

Another example of British attempts to remind the Ottoman government about its responsibilities to the Armenians came on 4

March 1919, when acting British high commissioner Admiral Webb stated that

the Armenians and the Greeks . . . are resolved and insistent on the matter of full compensation for their losses . . . and that the matter concerned the confiscation of lands, domiciles, orphans and women, young men and children who had been forcibly converted [to Islam] and in many cases, possessions that had been sold.[131]

It is difficult to believe that the Ottoman leaders actually desired to correct the situation, since each successive government made resolutions on the matter, but little was actually accomplished.[132]

The occupation forces were continually critical of the fact that those who were returning were not being given enough support and aid. In response to this, the Ministry of the Interior sent a statement, dated 20 March 1919, to the Ministry of Foreign Affairs (a copy was also sent to the Allied forces), in which the number of those returning (including the Greeks) was now given as 232,679.[133] There is no differentiation between Greek and Armenian in this calculation. The important point is that the memo says that there were insufficient funds to feed and maintain this group and that the British were asked to do some fund-raising for this purpose. A similar statement was given to the press by the Ministry of the Interior around the same date (11 March 1919),[134] in which it was reported that a total of 230,000 people—118,352 Greeks and 101,747 Armenians—had been settled. Damat Ferìd Paşa sent a report dated 7 June 1919 to the British high commissioner that put the number of returning Greeks and Armenians at 276,015. The purpose of the statement was to obtain free transportation for the returning population, and for this reason the number may have been exaggerated.

This problem was not easily solved and continued to be an issue. On 8 January 1920, the government issued a decision "decree[ing] the return of property, which according to a decree from 8 November 1918 was registered in the treasuries of the Ministries of Finance and the central office that oversaw foundations within the Ottoman empire, the Pious Foundations, in accordance with the temporary law of 26 September 1915 and the regulations of 8 November 1915."[135]

The greatest challenge was identifying the seized properties and possessions, because no comprehensive list existed. During the geno-cide, the continual stream of requests from the German Embassy that, at the very least, Armenians belonging to the Catholic Church be allowed to return to their homes was refused by Talât Paşa on the grounds that "this is impossible, because they will not be able to find their property."[136]

The return of Armenian women and children kidnapped by Turks or Kurds was another ongoing problem. Despite the govern-ment's intentions, there were great difficulties, and major mistakes were made. It was difficult to find the Christian women and children in Turkish homes. Families had been torn apart intentionally. Chil-dren had been taken away, forced to convert to Islam and often placed in orphanages. Some had been sent to surrounding villages and the girls forcibly married to Muslims. Many relevant memos were sent to the provinces during the genocide period,[137] which itself also shows the genocidal intent of the deportations. For example, a telegram from the Interior Ministry sent to various provinces and districts ordered that people with no living relatives or protection should be dispersed among the villages and towns in which there were no for-eign or Armenian populations; young girls and widows were to be married, and the children placed in orphanages.[138]

One example is the Sivas region. In the investigation of the provin-cial governor of Sivas, Muammer Bey, the Commission for the Investi-gation of Criminal Improprieties reported that all remaining local Armenian boys had been circumcised.[139] One telegram clearly shows that Armenian families were split up. While the men were deported, the women and children were separated and dispersed in villages and towns where there were no foreigners or other Armenians.[140] The CUP had also seen to the deportation of children placed in orphanages who refused to convert to Islam. Such actions were met with continuous protest, especially in the orphanages run by German missionary groups.[141] In the face of these protests, orders were sent from Istanbul with the directive that the children in these orphanages were not to be touched "for now."[142]

Admiral Webb, who wrote three detailed memos on the missing Armenian women and children, reported on 27 February 1919 that "a great number of the women have become attached to those persons with whom they have now lived for four years; if they were to leave they do not even know . . . to whence they would be returning, or who of their relatives are still alive." Similar difficulties affected the children. To all these practical obstacles a number of political and administrative difficulties were added. Admiral Calthorpe said in a report of 13 January 1919 that "despite the official assurances which report the good intentions of the Turkish officials, they are pursuing an actively obstructionist policy which they mask with words."[143]

Thus, on 1 March 1919 Webb proposed: "I am of the opinion that, under present-day conditions, it would not be appropriate to attempt direct activity in order to rescue them (i.e., the Armenian women and children). . . . Experience has shown that the question is fraught with danger and that, instead of being helpful, hasty action may even be detrimental."[144] Indeed, we know from many of the recollections of the period that errors were made; when officials simply relied on guesswork, Turkish children were taken from their homes, sometimes by force, which Turkish sources frequently cited as an important demonstration that Armenian claims were groundless. Celal Bayar, for instance, wrote in his memoirs that "it was dangerous for Turkish children who had dark eyes and a swarthy complexion to go out into the street."[145] The government was ultimately forced to announce that there was no way for it to intervene on this issue.[146] During debates held in the final Ottoman Chamber of Deputies assembled in January 1920, several motions for clarification were submitted.[147] During the later Lausanne Peace Conference the French representative on the Sub-Commission on Minorities admitted that certain errors had been made in implementation, but they were minor and had been corrected.[148] The occupation of Izmir by the Greeks on 16 May 1919—a result of the Paris Peace Conference—and the widespread abuse that followed essentially brought all efforts on restitution and family reunification to an end. In his report of 11 November 1919, Admiral de Robeck states that "all the satisfactory activities by the officers of the High Commissioner's Office to return the deportees' property to them have suddenly been blocked."[149] British officials in the provinces, grappling with the return of looted or confiscated property and missing women and children, cited the need to put at least a temporary stop to their activities. In one report, "Sergeant Derring, from Samsun on 1 October 1919, requests of the High Commissioner that the matter of returning property be shelved."[150]

The reasons that these efforts bore little fruit are clear. A new class of "notables" had been created through their acquisition of Armenian property, having become wealthy as a result of the genocide and the attendant looting. To return the looted property was unthinkable for them. After a tour through the Black Sea region, one British representative wrote on 29 October 1919, "it is as if the Armenian community has completely disappeared. The Greek and Armenian properties were not returned; there are many who are making a living out of selling these properties."[151] Such people would come to support the Turkish National Movement so as not to have to give back the property now in their possession. As Turkish historian Doğan Avcıoğlu wrote, it is no coincidence that wherever the Nationalist Movement flourished, a halt was put to "operations to return Greek and Armenian property and punishing those guilty of the injuries to the Greeks and Armenians." On 1 October 1919, Admiral Webb expressed this clearly, informing Lord Curzon that "those guilty of the deportations have become a symbol of Turkish patriotism."[152] Similarly, the measures taken by the different Ottoman governments in Istanbul were blocked by the rise of the Nationalist Movement.

In response to increasing criticism of Turkey within the League of Nations, especially claims that thousands of Armenian and Greek women and children were still being secretly held in "harems," in 1922 the Ottoman Interior Ministry published a report providing information on the measures taken since the armistice. Despite strenuous denials of negligence, the report also admitted that efforts to return surviving deportees were largely unsuccessful. According to the report, the Ottoman government had allocated more than one million lira and devoted hundreds of officials to "return the Greeks and Armenians." Moreover, sixty-two different delegations had been established,

> formed of British police, Ottoman officials and one person from each of the other countries involved, appointed by the British High Commissioner . . . and sent to every corner of the country . . . with the authority to return those who had been deported and to restore their property.

These delegations "invited every Christian woman who had married a Muslim with consent" and asked them what they wished to do. For this reason, "it wasn't [a question of] hundreds of thousands of Armenian or Greek women and children [being held] in harems or orphanages—there weren't even two children being held."[153] The failure of this policy was not limited to efforts in Istanbul but throughout the country.[154]

The question was prominent at the Lausanne peace talks as well, especially during the December 1922 talks on minorities. The Turkey delegation was uncompromising in its opposition to any article in the peace agreement regarding the search for lost women and children or the return of confiscated property. When the British made such a proposal "in order to attain the return of those persons, regardless of their race or religion, who have been lost or separated from their families since the date August 1, 1914,"[155] the Turkish delegation reacted strongly. Delegate Rıza Nur approached the subject as a problem "that remains in the past" and declared that "he would absolutely refuse to accept" such an article.[156]

Ultimately, the question was papered over in the 1923 Treaty of Lausanne, with an article inserted into the signed protocol concerning the general amnesty. The only concession that Turkey made was not to "object to actions, carried out between the dates 20 October 1918 and 20 November 1922 under the protection of the Entente Powers, to reunite families separated since the war and to restore properties to their lawful owners."[157] Nevertheless, on 14 September 1922, the nationalists in power attempted to restore the 1915 decree regarding the confiscation of Armenian property, nullified earlier by the Chamber of Deputies as a violation of the Constitution.[158]

Despite the various debates in parliament about the Armenian genocide and the discussions over returning the deportees, direct investigation of the killings by the government proceeded at a decidedly plodding pace. In an article published in the British *Daily Mail* on 24 November 1918, Sultan Vehdettin complained to the reporter that the continued delays were the fault of İzzet Paşa's cabinet:

> It was with great distress that I learned of the actions carried out against the Armenians by certain political committees within

Turkey. . . . As soon as this news reached the Sultanate, I ordered
the start of immediate investigations into those responsible and the
severest possible punishment. Various causes have prevented this
order from being properly carried out, but today this problem is
being investigated in detail.[159]

Indeed, the first steps toward a real government response were
taken by Tevfik Paşa's cabinet, appointed after İzzet Paşa's resignation.
On 20 November, the government prohibited Unionist leaders who
had fled abroad from transferring their property to third parties and
soon after ordered the confiscation of leading Unionists' possessions
and properties, targeting Talât, Enver, Cemal, and İsmail Hakkı Paşa,
Dr. Nâzım and Bahâettin Şâkir.[160] Days later, on 26 November, the
government decreed a special court-martial for Enver and Cemal
Paşa within the Defense Ministry, to try them in absentia.[161] On 12
December, the special court-martial declared that Enver and Cemal
Paşa had to surrender to the authorities with ten days; if they failed to
do so, they would be deprived of their civil rights, as well as their
property and possessions.[162] While this trial was limited in scope—it
did not address questions relating to the Armenian deportations and
killings—it was nonetheless the very first court-martial to investigate
the wartime military leadership, and it was an important starting
point for the trials that followed. The government subsequently
decreed (on 30 December 1918) the confiscation of the National
Development Bank's assets and those of a number of other Unionist-
created companies—National Manufacture, National Imports, and
National Textiles—in connection with alleged improprieties.[163]

More important were the cabinet's efforts to launch a thorough
investigation into wartime crimes through a commission of inquiry.
The Commission to Investigate Criminal Acts (*Tedkik-i Seyyiyat*) was
announced on 24 November. News coverage revealed that the commission had been unveiled in the assembly by the interior minister,
that the "former governor of Bitlis, Ohrili Mazhar Bey," had been
appointed to preside over it, and that its members were comprised of
state and judicial appointees.[164] The publication *Sabah* dubbed it a
"commission of investigation into a catastrophe."[165] The commission
was endowed with broad authority and the right to exert it over all
state functionaries, regardless of rank or position. It was allowed to

subpoena, search people and premises, confiscate property, place suspects under surveillance, and carry out arrests. To exercise this authority, police and military assistance was required.

In its next decision, made in early December, the cabinet appointed additional commissions, manned jointly by ten appointees of the Justice and Interior Ministries, to travel to various relevant regions as extensions of the Investigation of Criminal Acts.[166] "These bodies were charged with . . . listening to the complaints of the locals, investigating them, and when necessary forwarding the complaints to the local prosecutor's offices for criminal proceedings." These traveling commissions were given full authority to detain and punish at their discretion.[167]

Mazhar Bey, commission president, joined the first group to investigate the provinces. While the precise legal relationship between the Investigation of Criminal Acts and the traveling commissions was somewhat unclear, there was an unambiguous decision to allow each individual commission to act independently. However, if an individual under investigation changed his location, the commissions would share information and jurisdiction. All the commissions were directly tied to the Justice Ministry[168] and all were acting in the service of the military tribunals, or courts-martial, which were soon to be set up.[169]

Once the commissions had identified the people to be prosecuted, those individuals were sent to the military tribunal in Istanbul. Over the course of two months, the commissions would find, in the twenty-eight different provinces under investigation, numerous documents in connection with the deportations and murders.[170] At the preliminary stage, 130 files on 130 suspects were opened and forwarded for prosecution.[171] The commission also took a great many verbal and written statements, including from some 26 parliamentary deputies, who were forbidden to leave Istanbul because of the danger they would flee.[172] A questionnaire was also sent to War Ministry employees asking for information on the events surrounding the entry into war and the formation of the Special Organization. It was during this period, on 23 December 1918, that the government issued a general amnesty. A good number of politicians who had been banished by the Unionists were now able to return home. However, those suspected of war crimes and involvement in the Armenian genocide were not eligible for the amnesty.[173]

Three weeks after the Mazhar Commission began its investigations, it determined that sufficient documentation had been gathered to be able to proceed to trial. In January 1919, these documents were then submitted to the extraordinary court-martial, an unprecedented institution set up in advance, in December 1918.

The establishment of the extraordinary court-martial has a rather mixed history. It was, in practice, simply a continuation of martial law, under which the empire had been governed with brief interruption since April 1909.[174] A variety of military courts had been in session during the war as well, established in accordance with the twelfth Article of the Military Penal Code. However, all the existing courts were deemed inadequate for the task of trying the perpetrators of the wartime crimes; thus the government ultimately issued a decree allowing for an extraordinary court-martial.

The first decision taken to set up a court aimed specifically to further the investigation of crimes related to the Armenian massacres was made on 14 December 1918 by a special Sultanic decree.[175] The sultan claimed to take this step in response to increasing pressure from abroad and because justice through the regular courts of law would take too long to complete. The sultan claimed that the foreign powers " . . . were accusing us of still not having done a thing in regard to the criminals, and if—God forbid!—our independence were lost, the loss for us would be great indeed."[176]

The tribunals that were subsequently established were formed in accordance with the regulations on martial law of 20 September 1877.[177] A number of investigating commissions would also work under the military tribunal to further its objectives. According to the government's decree:

> Because propriety demands that measures be adopted and implemented for the sake of the security and peace of mind so sorely needed by the country, through the rapid inquiry and investigation into those who were either the main perpetrators or accessories in the crimes of oppression and assault, and which were carried out under the cover of deportation operations during the general mobilization, or which were planned with revolutionary intent, special committees have been formed in Istanbul and the relevant

provincial areas to undertake investigations of the perpetrators of the aforementioned crimes.[178]

The first of the extraordinary courts-martial was established in Istanbul with Mahmut Hayret Paşa as its president.[179] Three of the seven civil members of the Court Administrative Board were Christian, and one of these a judge. However, there would be frequent resignations from the board and new appointments. (Changes made later, on 8 March 1919, would put an end to any civil or Christian participation on the board.)

Other similar courts in operation during this time created a great deal of confusion. On 20 December, the newspaper *Vakit* refers to three separate military tribunals ongoing in Istanbul. In February 1919, some two months after the establishment of the first military tribunal, changes were made to bring order to the confusion. "To distinguish among . . . the military tribunals entrusted with the investigation of deportation cases and original military tribunals, it is befitting that the latter shall from now on be known as the Istanbul Military Administration Tribunal . . . "[180] or the "First Military Tribunal."

It was not simply enough to establish the military tribunals to investigate and prosecute. A law enacted in 1913 prohibited trial of civil servants without higher permission; thus an inquiry required special intervention to proceed.[181] The detention of a civil servant first needed permission from the provincial administration, then the Ministry of the Interior. This process would have made it virtually impossible for the military tribunals to investigate and question witnesses. Despite Interior Minister Fethi Bey's pledge, published in the press, that "all employees would be investigated, regardless of rank or grade, in fairness and justice," there was insufficient authority to do so.[182]

Thus on 22 December 1918, the minister of the interior stated that wartime cabinet members would be subject to prosecution by the military tribunals.[183] Then on 25 December 1918, this jurisdiction was extended to officers and civil servants.[184] On the same day an executive decision was taken to allow the prosecution of crimes related to the deportations in regular criminal courts in places where martial law was not in force.[185]

On 8 January 1919, appointments were made to the military tribunals in Izmir, Bursa, Tekirdağ, Edirne, Samsun and Antep.[186] On 21 January, the tribunals' scope of duties were reevaluated. The tribunals in İstanbul, Izmir, Van, Tekirdağ, Antep, Samsun, Bursa and Beyazit were authorized to hear cases from further afield. Information about the jurisdiction and area of responsibility of these tribunals was published in the papers, but confusion over the courts persisted, so yet another commission was formed to clarify their role.[187] In February the regional issue was clarified again and the Edirne and Bandirma tribunals were disbanded for lack of necessity.[188]

During this period, Tevfik Paşa issued an appeal to foreign governments to form an international commission to assist with the investigations, including crimes committed by Armenians against Turks. The British declined the invitation. Along with this legal initiative, Tevfik Paşa then began to arrest leading Unionists, but the sultan rejected the move as unconstitutional. Moreover, he condemned the government for not pursuing the investigations with appropriate speed. By March 1919, the military tribunals had been in place for three months, yet not a single war criminal had been punished. The sultan believed the delay would provide outside powers with an excuse to interfere.[189] This issue caused serious disagreement between the sultan and Tevfik Paşa's cabinet, and resulted in its resignation.

Damat Ferid Paşa's Liberty and Concord Party was then called upon to form a new government, which began its duties on 4 March 1919. Its foremost mission was to ensure that former Unionist leaders would be put on trial, and to this end important changes were made to the military tribunals. On 8 March 1919 Damat Ferid Paşa removed all civil members from the military courts' administrative board and replaced them with military personnel. The right to appeal tribunal rulings was taken away and the tribunals' jurisdiction was expanded to allow for investigation of any individual who pushed the country into war, organized massacres against Greeks, Armenians and Muslims, or who incited hatred between groups.[190]

Under the new regulations, investigations, trials, and arrests increased rapidly. Sixty-six members of the wartime cabinet, high-ranking military officers, parliamentary deputies and members of the CUP were arrested in one day. The measures taken by the new cabinet were not limited to the trials. On May 5, the government moved to outlaw the Renewal Party, the de facto heir to the CUP, as well as the Libertarian People's Party, also founded by former Unionists. The government extended the decree seizing CUP property to these other parties as well.[191]

Both in rhetoric and action, Damat Ferid Paşa's government exerted the greatest efforts to pursue, arrest, and try those responsible for the genocide and related crimes. One communiqué, issued to state employees and published in the government gazette, stated that:

> All officials, high or low, must know that, beginning now, oppression and injustice and persecution and killing and deportation, exile and banishment from this country are prohibited. Complete respect must now be shown for the liberty of all Ottomans, regardless of race or religion, and for their political and personal rights: weak or strong, all are equal in the eyes of the government and all the empire's subjects are entitled to the same protection everywhere.[192]

Further changes to the court-martial, instituted by Damat Ferid Paşa, included closing trials to the public. Also, death sentences required a two-thirds majority of the judges, while other rulings required only a simple majority.[193] The many changes in government during the postwar years were reflected in the shifting powers of the tribunals. In September 1920, a new law required that trials of high-ranking officials, both military and civilian, necessitated special permission from the sultan.[194] It was claimed that Damat Ferid Paşa issued this law to forestall any attempt to prosecute him in the future. As one former governor put it, "After his government humiliated and tormented a great number of honorable men and . . . sentenced some of them to death, they thought that they themselves might fall into the same trap in the not-too-distant future . . . Thus they safeguarded their own interests."[195]

The strong reaction to the death sentences imposed by Damat Fevid Paşa's government prompted Tevfik Paşa, who came back to power in 1920, to introduce a number of retroactive changes, particularly regarding the sentences delivered by the military courts. The appeal process was reinstated and all the decisions made by the court during the Damat Ferid Paşa period were reexamined. The panels of judges were changed and the four judges from the Damat Ferid Paşa period were arrested.[196]

It should be added that the Istanbul court-martial did not only hear cases connected to the Armenian deportations. In March 1920, the extraordinary courts-martial also began to try nationalists, who had initiated a series of insurgent activities against the Istanbul government, and to impose further death sentences. Mustafa Kemal was one of those sentenced to death. There were also trials of state employees accused of looting Yıldız Palace during the 1909 revolt against Abdul Hamid II. A number of sentences were imposed, including the death sentence.[197]

The first trial in Istanbul on 5 February 1919 concerned criminal actions against the Armenian population in the Yozgat area in central Anatolia. In addition to this trial, there were at least sixty-two other cases. Of the sixty-three cases, twelve were documented in *Takvîm-ı Vekâyi*, but the trials were reported in a number of different ways. In the first category, which includes the trials of cabinet members and members of the CUP Central Committee, there are complete or partial accounts of the trials, comprising indictments, minutes, and verdicts. In the second category are trials where only the verdict is recorded, as in the case of the Yozgat and Trabzon trials. The third category features only the sultan's confirmation of the court's sentence. Information about the other fifty-one cases can be gleaned only from the daily newspapers. Of the fifty-one other cases, twenty-two reached a judicial conclusion (seventeen of which ended with acquittals); eight were dismissed due to lack of sufficient evidence; and the results of the other twenty-one are unknown.[198]

While most of the trials dealt with specific regional cases, there were three principal trials for those with overall responsibility:

1) CUP Central Committee members and the committee's semi-covert auxiliary, the Special Organization
2) other members of the wartime Ottoman cabinets
3) the CUP party secretaries and delegates

The main trial against CUP leaders began on 28 April 1919 and continued in seven sessions until 17 May, when Greek troops occupied Izmir following a May 1919 decision at the Paris Peace Conference. These proceedings were halted abruptly and were never continued, as the defendants were subsequently taken to Malta and imprisoned by the British forces. The indictment of CUP Central Committee members and directors of the Special Organization is nonetheless highly significant for the original documents in its appendices.

The trials against party secretaries and delegates began on 21 June 1919 and continued through thirteen sessions, after which a decision was reached on 8 January 1920. Important material was produced during these trials in the course of discussions on how to define the limits of individual responsibility in a collective action.

The extraordinary court-martials began, of course, with arrests. The first arrests were made, on the Interior Ministry's orders, in Ankara, Çorum and Adana in early December 1918. Those detained for crimes related to the Armenian genocide were transferred to Istanbul.[199] The newspapers of 6 January 1919 reported that the Commission of Inquiry operating in the Adapazarı region had made arrests there and in the İzmit regions.[200] These arrests, carried out as a result of British pressure on the government, would soon be followed by others. The former lieutenant governor of the provincial region of Kırklareli, Hilmi Bey, was arrested in Istanbul on 5 January. Mehmet Tevfik Bey, commander of the Çorum gendarmerie, and Trabzon customs official Mehmet Ali Bey, along with two merchants, were all arrested on 6 January. The next day, it was the turn of the former district official of Boğazlıyan, Mehmet Kemal Bey. On 13 January, three civil servants and an army lieutenant were seized.

The arrest of more high-ranking officers and government officials began on 14 January, and by the twenty-first of the month, two former provincial governors of Sivas, the provincial governors of Mosul and Bursa and parliamentary deputies for Diyarbakır, Feyzi and Zülfü Bey had all been taken into custody. By the end of the month, the number of prominent and former officials incarcerated in Istanbul's Bekir Ağa Division had reached forty. It is not clear how many were arrested from the lower ranks.[201] The first escapee was Dr. Reşit Bey, former provincial governor of Diyarbakır, who broke from prison on 25 January, ultimately committing suicide on 6 February when he realized he was on the verge of being recaptured.[202]

The arrests went beyond those on the government's list. Three people who would eventually be tried in Trabzon and given prison sentences, for instance, were arrested after a report was filed by several young girls who had survived the massacres. They claimed they had seen "the murderers of their mother and father strolling freely in Istanbul."[203] British officials also prepared "black lists" of subjects for arrest.[204] According to the British, "All of the arrests made by the Turkish authorities were carried out (a) on their own request; (b) in response to our official, written request; (c) upon our verbal suggestion. . . ."[205]

The British prepared their lists in a number of ways. The lists dealing with the mistreatment of British prisoners were prepared by the Prisoners of War Sections of the British Solicitor-General's Office. Documents dealing with other crimes were gathered in the Office of the British High Commissioner in Turkey and at the British Supreme Command. A special commission attached to the High Commissioner's Office was entrusted with this matter.

Admiral Calthorpe, in a report dated 8 January 1919, provided some interesting information on the section's inner workings.

> The Armenian and Greek Section has two card indexes: a) an index containing the names of some 6,700 persons of whom there are strong suspicions of their participation in the oppressions . . . b) a list of the names of places in which the "oppressions" were carried out, along with the names of those persons involved. It is possible to access the information regarding any and every person and incident in a very short time. There is a file for each and every deportation, but because in the case of half of these incidents no incriminating "proof" can be found, there is no recommendation that the section make arrests. All of the information has been obtained from either the "Bureau d'information Armenienne" or by Armenians from the provinces who have come to the High Commissioner's Office to file a complaint. Only in very few cases does the section possess enough proof to [merit its] submission to the courts. All that we are able to do is to determine the sources for the evidence that can be gathered.[206]

On 1 February 1919, the Office of the High Commissioner submitted a list of twenty-three people suspected of having mistreated

British prisoners of war. While informing London of this situation, it stated that this was merely a "preliminary list," and that new lists would be sent to the Turkish government as soon as they were completed.[207] This was the first official list prepared with the request that the suspects be handed over to British officials, and as we saw earlier, the demand was refused by the government.

The crimes used as the basis for the preparation of the black lists were not limited to the First World War. Since the CUP was considered guilty of the 1913 military coup, this was also included in the crimes committed. By periodically submitting these lists to the Istanbul government, the occupation forces ensured that arrests were carried out. Diplomat and historian Bilal Şimşir reports that in the three-month period between 23 January and 20 April 1919, lists were prepared and submitted to Turkish officials for the arrest of a total of 223 people, "of whom 100 were arrested between January 23 and March 14; 61 between March 15 and April 7; 18 between April 8–9; and 41 between April 10–20."[208] Some lists were submitted verbally, and through unofficial channels. One list the high commissioner gave to Tevfik Paşa in January 1919, for instance, was unofficial. Of the people whose names appeared on this list—Ziya Gökalp among them—27 were arrested on 30 January 1919.

Tevfik Paşa admitted that a great many of the arrests were carried out as a result of a direct British initiative: "The foreign powers have submitted a list. . . . When no action was taken by the government for a whole week, they announced that they would carry out the arrests themselves." Tevfik Paşa believed that it was better for the suspects to be arrested by the Ottoman government because it was able to pardon them.[209] Thus, the grand vizier thought of the arrests as a preventive measure taken to shield the suspects.[210]

After being compelled to make the arrests, the government refused to hand the prisoners over to the British. Moreover, by notifying people of their imminent arrest or the search of their homes, the government made sure they would be found blameless.[211] As the Unionist journalist Hüseyin Cahit Yalçın remembers,

> One day Midhat Şükrü came to see me . . . to bring an important piece of news. . . . He struggled to convince me that . . . Tevfik Paşa had finally succumbed to the pressure [of those] who wanted the

Unionists arrested. It had been decided. They were to be carried out on Thursday.[212]

Similar accounts appear in many memoirs of the period. In the memoirs of Halil Kut Paşa, Enver Paşa's uncle, he claims that he was informed of his arrest order ahead of time. While he was sitting in the house of a Unionist colleague, a commissioner arrived and handed over a list of those wanted.[213]

This was no coincidence. Yunus Nadi, a leading Unionist and later founder of the daily *Cumhuriyet*, had this to say:

> No matter how hard they tried, they couldn't staff the Chief of Police's office with just their own people. There were always some kids there who loved us and kept us informed. They followed everything having to do with the arrest of a friend, every order given, and they would inform . . . us by telephone, three or four times a day if necessary.[214]

Additionally, the number of people arrested was consistently exaggerated when relayed to the occupational forces, although the British did not seem to be taken in. In his report of 24 January 1919, Admiral Calthorpe said that "On the previous day, the Grand Vizier informed me that between 160 and 200 persons had been arrested. I suspect that this is an exaggeration, although it is certain that some persons have indeed been detained."[215] In one case, Tevfik Paşa's government even lost the lists left by the previous regime. Damat Ferid Paşa complained to the British that the lists prepared by his government had disappeared from the archives.[216]

In general, Tevfik Paşa's government did not act with any great enthusiasm with regard to arrests, which played a role in his forced resignation. Nor was it only the occupation forces that complained. As we have seen, there was growing public pressure as well at this time. After Dr. Reşit Bey escaped on 25 January, the president of the Chamber of Notables, Ahmet Rıza Bey, called a special session of the upper house to debate "the need for an Imperial Council to end government indolence, conduct a house-cleaning in the cabinet and give the Sultan some necessary warnings."[217] In the face of mounting British complaints, the arrests continued throughout February 1919 and British General Milne reported that the political situation in Istanbul had improved considerably as a result.[218] Together with those detained at the end of January, there were some one hundred people arrested and held in the Bekir Ağa Division.[219]

Damat Ferid Paşa's succession to the grand vizierate was a turning point in the pace of the arrests and trials. He summed up the new government's program: "To show the Victorious Powers that we are opposed to the policies of the Union and Progress Party, to punish the war criminals, to eliminate some of those persons loyal to the CUP from the bureaucracy."[220] For this purpose Damat Ferid Paşa made changes to the court-martial system and paid a visit to the British high commissioner to declare his willingness to act according to their wishes. A great number of prominent Unionists were then arrested, including Said Halim Paşa. The arrests were not limited to Istanbul, but extended throughout the various provinces of Anatolia. Many British arrest lists were submitted in this period.[221]

The Yozgat Trial concluded at this time with a guilty verdict and death sentence for Kemal Bey in April 1919. The sultan, "in light of the proven actions of this man, did not hesitate to authorize the judgment."[222] On 10 April, Kemal was executed in Istanbul's Beyazıt Square. Admiral Calthorpe reported that "for the first time, someone has received the punishment they deserve for having taken part in the crime of massacre. After this," he said, it would have to be seen "whether or not the government would show the courage to act on a larger scale and with the same severity especially against those guilty parties who are of high rank."[223] But the Turks were of a completely different mind. The funeral ceremony on the following day quickly turned into an anti-occupation demonstration. Wreaths bore inscriptions such as "Kemal Bey, the Great Martyr of the Turks" and "To the innocent Muslim martyr." Anti-British, anti-occupation and nationalist speeches were made, with phrases like "They threw the British out of Odessa. Come, let's throw them out of Istanbul."[224]

The depiction of the deceased Kemal Bey as "the first martyr in a righteous cause" irritated both the British and the Ottoman governments. The death sentence was perceived—even by government supporters—as "more a forced concession to the Entente states than a just punishment carried out against the guilty." The British Foreign

Office rightly assessed that "not one Turk in a thousand can conceive that there might be a Turk who deserves to be hanged for the killing of Christians."[225] Despite authorizing the death sentence, the sultan was afraid that the matter "would later result in some sort of massacre in revenge. . . . It won't end with this," he warned, "it will drag on. Therefore, it is necessary to take measures now to prevent this." He then "demanded a religious ruling [a fatwa] to preempt" any kind of act of revenge and he asked that it be issued by the state's highest religious authority.[226] At this point, the British realized that the business of trying those involved in the genocide in Istanbul would be much more difficult. The more pressing problem was whether to continue even holding the suspects in Istanbul. Some began to express the opinion that it might be better to transport the suspects outside Turkey.[227] The fact that no decision on this had been reached by the time of the Paris Peace Conference in spring 1919 constituted a serious obstacle since no legal basis existed for handing the suspects over to the British.

At this point, another event occurred that would deeply affect the efforts to try those responsible for the genocide. On 16 May 1919 the western Anatolian port of Izmir was occupied by the Greeks. Despite the fact that this had been expected, when the occupation finally happened, it was a great shock to the Muslims of Anatolia and Istanbul. It was soon followed by Damat Ferid Paşa's short-lived resignation to protest the occupation, and fear intensified among Turks that the Izmir occupation would quickly turn into a massacre. The Ottoman government grasped how difficult it would be to continue the Unionist and war crimes trials while the occupation was going on, and on 17 May, the trials were halted. On 19 May, Damat Ferid Paşa asked the Office of the High Commissioner "whether or not the detainees would be sent to Malta."[228] The British were then making preparations for the possible consequences of the Greek occupation, and the high commissioner believed that it would not be "appropriate with the current state of affairs for those persons who have been detained for a variety of reasons to remain in Turkish prisons," and he requested that the detainees be moved to Malta.[229]

Demonstrations soon began in every part of the country, protesting the Greek occupation and the massacres that did, eventually, result. The protesters also sent cables to the Ottoman government in

Istanbul and to the Entente Powers.[230] Huge mass demonstrations were held in Istanbul on 20 and 23 May. There were also rumors circulating of a Bastille-like storming of the military prison at Bekir Ağa. Upon hearing this, in order to calm popular sentiment, Damat Ferid Paşa freed some forty-one prisoners, of whom the high commissioner had previously said that "there was every reason to believe that they had committed crimes in the most murderous of fashions in connection with the massacres."[231] Twenty-six of these individuals were released on the grounds that "no trial had opened for them" in the extraordinary court-martial. Following this, the interior minister instructed the Office of the Chief of Police not to make any more arrests for the present time.[232]

The British had anticipated this course of events. In a report to the Foreign Office, Admiral Webb stated that "the recent events have given rise to the possibility that some of these persons (the detainees held in the Bekir Ağa Division) or all of them would be released. There are prominent members of the Union and Progress among them. . . . It would appear necessary to prevent such an action."[233] But both the prisoner release and the protest demonstrations threw the British into a panic. The Ottoman government itself now appealed to have the prisoners sent to Malta, and steps in this direction were taken. On 28 May the British took sixty-seven prisoners out of Bekir Ağa, twelve of whom, mostly former government ministers, were sent to Mudros, while the rest were sent off to Malta. The ministers were also eventually transferred to Malta. The British continued to transfer prisoners to Malta, because they claimed that the trials in Istanbul were being conducted "in such a slow and lackluster fashion that they didn't go much further than merely presenting a deceptive façade."[234] The trials previously halted were now reconvened in Istanbul on 3 June, and the case files of the suspects were transferred for this purpose.[235] The cases involving both the Unionist leaders and former cabinet members concluded on 13 July with the imposition of a number of death sentences.

The Greek occupation of Izmir marked a turning point in the internal divisions within the Ottoman state. Days later, on 19 May, Mustafa Kemal, or Atatürk, the father of the Turkish Republic, moved from

Istanbul to Anatolia and took the helm of the emerging Nationalist Movement. Kemal, an army general, had been appointed Inspector General in Anatolia by Istanbul, which gave him considerable authority over troops in the whole region. The job—arranged by ex-CUP influence in Istanbul—positioned Kemal to lead the nationalist struggle from Anatolia and indeed his arrival at the Anatolian port of Samsun is considered the beginning of coordinated resistance to Allied control and the fight for independence. In July and September 1919 important nationalist congresses were held in the cities of Erzurum and Sivas and a Representative Council was formed to act on behalf of the movement. Kemal, at the head of the council, declared the Istanbul government illegitimate. The movement was immediately effective: orchestrated nationalist pressure resulted in Damat Ferid Paşa's resignation at the end of September and the installation of the more sympathetic Ali Rıza Paşa as grand vizier.[236]

The investigation process slowed considerably with Damat Ferid Paşa out of the picture. Ali Rıza's government, which came to power on 2 October 1919, made barely a mention of the legal proceedings against the war crimes and genocide suspects in Malta.[237] Nevertheless, the new government did show some initiative in contending with the problem, even though it was closely allied to the Nationalist Movement in Anatolia, almost bound to it. After coming to power, the new grand vizier sent a cable to the nationalist center in Sivas in Anatolia, claiming that it was "of the same mind and agrees to the demand for national sovereignty," and that his government was allied with the Representative Council."[238] Some cabinet ministers even asked to be accepted as representatives of the Representative Council. The news of Ali Reza Paşa's incoming government was reported and received abroad in terms of "the Young Turks [being] in power again—the real directors of the new cabinet."[239] It was this connection and the resulting accusation that the government represented a revived "Unionism" that ultimately pushed it to take several steps toward dealing with the problem of the Armenian genocide.

During a visit to the British High Commissioner' Office on 11 October 1919, the new grand vizier "gave assurances that the legal prosecution that had begun in order to punish those guilty of deportation, massacre and hoarding would bear results, and that Turkey would thereby redeem its sullied honor."[240] The first action was taken on 30 October: The government complained that the extraordinary courts-martial had yet to bear fruit,[241] and announced the formation of a commission with the aim of addressing the situation. The commission decided that cases concerning the deportations would no longer be heard in the places where the crimes had been committed and changes were considered (but not implemented) regarding the issue of compensation.[242]

But these measures were mostly for show. The government's decisions in fact undermined the legal action against those responsible for the genocide. According to a 10 November 1919 decree, for example, the government decided "to defer the legal proceedings against the [former] mayor of Giresun, Feridunzâde Topal Osman Ağa and his 169 companions, who had fled and sought refuge in the province of Sivas before being tried in connection with the 'deportation and massacre.'"[243] Along the same lines, a decision was made on 26 October that forbade Armenians seeking to return to their former homes from entering the region of western Anatolia (the Izmir region). One of the main reasons for this was the increasing hostility with which the returnees were greeted by the Muslim population of Anatolia. According to political scientist Sina Akşin, "the Office of the Lieutenant Governor of Kayseri has, in response to a request by the Muslim population, called for a prohibition on their return." Additionally, "the decision to postpone the prosecution of the crimes [committed by Armenians] prior to the deportations" was reversed on 6 November. Despite the high commissioner's complaints, the government decided to "stand firm in its decision."[244]

Even before the new cabinet came to power, the British authorities in Istanbul were aware that the situation regarding the prosecution of perpetrators was deteriorating. In a report dated 21 September, High Commissioner Admiral de Robeck wrote,

> In view of the unfavorable general conditions now prevailing in this country as compared with a few months ago, I have decided to refrain until further notice from making suggestions to the Turkish Government for the arrest of further persons implicated in the deportations and massacres. . . . [245]

The British were convinced that the new government was not interested in taking serious steps to investigate the genocide. On 17 November 1919, Admiral de Robeck noted the reason for this reluctance:

> The present Turkish Government . . . [is] so dependent on the toleration of the organizers of the National Movement that I feel it would be futile to ask for arrest of any Turk accused of offences against Christians, even though he may be living openly in Constantinople.[246]

Investigation and prosecution of suspected war criminals was thus slowed and only accelerated when Damat Ferid Paşa returned to power yet again, in April 1920.

Meanwhile, parliamentary elections were held in October 1919 as a result of the Amasya Protocol, an agreement made between Ali Rıza Paşa's government in Istanbul and the Nationalist Forces in Anatolia regarding the dissolution of parliament and new elections. The new parliament took its seats on 12 January 1920. Nearly all the incoming parliamentary deputies were Anatolian nationalist candidates. For the entire period in which parliament was in session there was not a single debate directly concerning the Armenian genocide. The main reasons for this were the increased concern over the foreign occupation of Anatolia and the strength of the nationalists in the Chamber of Deputies. The Nationalist Movement in Anatolia had blocked the election of certain groups that were sensitive to the issue, such as Damat Ferid Paşa's Liberty and Concord Party, which were the most likely to be insistent on the prosecution of those responsible for the massacres and deportations. As a result of the nationalists' interference, the Liberty and Concord Party had boycotted the election "because of the impossibility of free elections, due to the tyranny in the name of the Nationalist Movement."[247] The forces in Ankara had also made sure that Christians were not entitled to vote in the election. A circular sent to the provinces by Mustafa Kemal on 17 March 1920 stated that "non-Muslim elements shall not be allowed to participate in the elections."[248]

The Nationalist Movement established a factional group within the chamber, Peasants of the Homeland (*Felâh-ı Vatan*), and this was the only group to act as an organized unit within parliament. The issues that the new deputies discussed mainly were the onerous peace conditions and the injustices being done to Turkey, the Entente Powers' failure to implement Wilson's Fourteen Points, the occupation of Anatolia, the murder of Turks, the efforts to establish Armenian and Kurdish states and the need for a national resistance movement. At a secret session of the chamber on 28 January 1920, the "Declaration of the National Pact" was adopted. According to this declaration, a national struggle would be waged for a Turkish state based on the Ottoman borders of 30 October 1918. This declaration was approved by the entire chamber amid great applause on 17 February.

The nationalist atmosphere in the chamber was very oppressive. In debates on the new government's program, a great many speeches and proclamations were delivered, filled with nationalist bluster such as "The Turk is not afraid of death," "The Turk entered the world on the day it was created by God, and he has made history; he has changed the map . . . the nation shall live eternally." Such statements were continually interrupted by applause.[249] Not only was there no discussion of the Armenian genocide, the chamber even refused to acknowledge that the Ottoman state had lost the war. In the words of one deputy, "Gentlemen, we were not defeated. By following the call of all humanity, which has pledged justice and truth for this oppressed world, we saluted the victors with our weapons."[250]

During this period the investigations relating to the genocide were discussed three times, and then only indirectly and negatively. The parliament intended to stop the investigations. At the 12 February session, a motion was submitted for the ministers of war and justice to address the question of whether "the formation of special courts-martial for the instances of deportation and massacre was contrary to the Constitution."[251] This argument had been used by former Unionist leaders and government members in the trials heard in the extraordinary court-martial. The government responded to the motion by denying that such courts were in violation of the Constitution, but in the speeches that followed all claims that they were indeed a violation were met with cries of "bravo" and hearty applause.[252]

A second motion was submitted calling for Damat Ferid Paşa and his entire cabinet to be handed over to the High Court of Justice for "having permitted the Greek occupation of Izmir and the formation of the Extraordinary Courts-Martial and [other] special courts in violation of Constitutional precepts." The motion was adopted without being brought to a vote and then passed to the relevant parliamentary commission for review.[253] The debates on the question of prosecuting those responsible for the genocide, and the demand to put Damat Ferid Paşa on trial showed that the situation had changed greatly within the past year, and clearly revealed the nationalist position.

A discussion was also held on the subject of the prisoners in Malta. A proposal was submitted "regarding the questioning of the government as to the manner in which a number of men and children of the homeland (Ottoman subjects), who were deported to Malta, were handed over to foreigners, and whether or not the government protested this matter."[254] This issue was also taken up in the Chamber of Notables, since some of its members were also being held on Malta. There was a proposal that these imprisoned notables should be considered "excused" and thus continue to receive their salaries. As a result of lengthy debate, the matter was referred to the Constitutional Commission for study.[255]

The growing power of the Nationalist Movement made the Allied plans to partition the empire and prosecute those responsible for the genocide nearly impossible. The British believed that to implement their plans, it would be necessary to occupy Istanbul fully, with complete control, and "have the dangerous Nationalist leaders arrested."[256] The high commissioner's conviction of the need to take such steps was reinforced by a fresh outbreak of Armenian massacres in Maraş, where French forces had withdrawn abruptly, leaving the returning Armenians unprotected. Lloyd George believed that "if the information regarding the massacres is correct, an accounting must be demanded of the Turkish Government."[257] According to him, it was "not enough to warn the Turks. We have done this numerous times. . . . There is no point in the Allies insisting on the statutes of the Peace Agreement before order is restored. . . . The time has already arrived for taking effective measures and performing serious deeds."[258] Despite the objections of the British High Command, the decision was ultimately taken to occupy Istanbul.

Rauf Orbay, the former commander of the navy and current representative of the Nationalist Movement in Istanbul, was informed by the Italians that the capital was to be placed under occupation.[259] And, indeed, the occupation was carried out on 16 March 1920. One of the first tasks undertaken by the occupying forces was to arrest the prominent members of the Nationalist Movement in Istanbul, and both Rauf and Unionist Kara Vasıf were among them. The goal of the arrests was not simply to seize suspects of war crimes or involvement in the genocide but also representatives of the movement in Ankara. In all some thirty people were detained, of whom eleven were immediately deported to Malta. Besides those accused of war crimes and the genocide, the exiles now included the direct representatives of the nationalists in Ankara, who were subsequently classified "undesirable nationalists."

These arrests inevitably provoked a harsh response from Ankara. Mustafa Kemal, who had expected events to unfold in this way, had earlier decided on 22 January 1920 that "because of the possibility that the foreigners will increase their assault and begin to arrest some of the government ministers and parliamentary deputies, foreign officers in Anatolia will be arrested in response."[260] A subsequent order was sent out to the provinces controlled by the nationalists calling for "British officers found in Anatolia [to] be arrested in response."[261] After this, Britain was forced to take Ankara into account in regard to investigating the perpetrators of the Armenian genocide. For its part, the nationalists used their British captives as leverage for its own people held on Malta. Ultimately, they succeeded in securing the prisoners' release.

With the Allied occupation of Istanbul, the last Ottoman parliament went into recess. Seventy of the 186 parliament members who supported the nationalists reconvened for an official opening of a unilaterally declared parliament in Ankara on 23 April 1920. An election, largely limited to representatives from the Defense of Rights Committees, was held to fill the remaining seats. The Ankara parliament declared itself the legitimate and legal successor to the Ottoman chamber and a bill was drafted to invalidate the decrees of the cabinet in Istanbul, still functioning, although now under the restored control of Damat Ferid Paşa. On June 7, the Ankara government approved Law Number 7, which voided all laws and agreements made in Istanbul, retroactive to 16 March, the day of Britain's occupation of the capital.[262] Ankara also banned all contact with the Istanbul government and decided to strip Damat Ferid Paşa of his citizenship and put his cabinet on trial as "traitors."[263] Thus there were now two competing political bodies claiming legitimacy. Clearly, the question of responsibility for the Armenian genocide would pale beside the national struggle underway.

CHAPTER 8

THE TURKISH NATIONAL MOVEMENT'S
POSITION ON THE GENOCIDE

IT IS DIFFICULT TO SPEAK OF A SINGLE, CONSISTENT APPROACH TAKEN by the Turkish National Movement in regard to the Armenian genocide. The main reason is that the National Movement approached the issue as a secondary aspect of what it called the National Pact—that is the creation of a Turkish state within the boundaries established by the armistice agreement in 1918. One factor which influenced the National Movement's attitude was the overwhelmingly Unionist character of the movement. Another was a continuing conflict over eastern Anatolia with the new Armenian state established in the Caucasus within the former Russian boundaries in May 1918 as a consequence of the Bolshevik revolution. The new Armenian republic sought to expand its territory to include parts of eastern Anatolia.

The Turkish National Movement was frequently accused of being Unionist in character by both the Allied Powers and the political opposition. In fact, given the exigencies of foreign policy, the nationalists disavowed any connection with the Unionists on many occasions. They did not wish to be associated with the wartime atrocities and the Armenian genocide. But no matter how much they protested, it was clear that a large majority of the movement's leaders—including Mustafa Kemal himself—were either former members or closely associated with the CUP. Halil Paşa, Enver's uncle, claimed that "there were Unionists leading the movement in Erzurum and organizing people in the Aydın and Aegean regions. But we had to hide that the movement . . . was a Unionist movement."[1] Among the nationalists themselves, however, there was, of course, no reason to hide this fact. Mustafa Kemal did not hesitate to state that he had been a Unionist. Celal Bayar, the Unionist secretary in the Aegean and later president of the Republic, recounted that Kemal once said: "You know, I too am a Unionist."[2] And despite all the criticism directed at the CUP, of which he was a member, and especially at its leadership, Mustafa Kemal never left the party.

Doubtless, there were differences of opinion between Mustafa Kemal's emerging faction and the entrenched Unionist leaders, Talât and Enver, differences that gradually made themselves felt openly. Indeed, the National Movement saw itself as in some ways "settling accounts" with the CUP. Foremost among these differences was Mustafa Kemal's rejection of the idea of multinational empire, that is, Pan-Turanism and Pan-Islamism. He strove instead for a Turkish state whose borders would only encompass those areas in which the Turks were a majority.[3] Early in his military career, he had been an open advocate of Turkish nationalism. He supported detaching the various Arab provinces from the empire. In his view, "The Constitutional Regime must not be built upon the corpse of the Ottoman Empire, which has lost its coherence and is now outmoded; on the contrary, it must be based upon the part of the empire in which the Turkish majority lives. . . . A Turkish state must be established."[4]

As a strong nationalist, Mustafa Kemal opposed the efforts of the Talâts and Envers to hold together a crumbling empire and expand eastward—to where there was no Turkish majority—on the basis of a Pan-Turkish, Pan-Islamic ideology. But from the viewpoint of the numerous Unionist members, this difference was seen as nothing more than one of many such differences within the movement.

It should be mentioned that although Mustafa Kemal had long been a Unionist, he had never really distinguished himself within the movement. He had no prominent political profile in 1918–19. And so the sultan and the British authorities had seen no problem in entrusting him with the job of military inspector in Anatolia. Kemal himself later explained that he remained in the "back row" during the CUP's early revolutionary years because of his rivalry with Enver Paşa, something which could be referred to as Kemal's "Enver complex." The two were the same age, but because Enver had graduated from the Ottoman military academy two years before Kemal his rank was higher. During World War I, Mustafa Kemal openly opposed Enver's strategy and found himself in frequent conflict with the German General Staff. But it was precisely these differences that allowed his star to ascend in the period after the armistice of 1918.[5]

Despite the various clashing viewpoints, the Unionists all knew each other and considered themselves friends.[6] It is not surprising that one of the places Mustafa Kemal frequented when in Istanbul was the location where the suspects of the Armenian genocide were being held. According to journalist Ahmet Ernin Yalman, "The open terrace on top of the Police Ministry became a sort of public meeting place. Mustafa Kemal Paşa also came. He would speak at great length with the detainees he knew, and especially with Fethi Okyar Bey."[7] When the suspects were transferred to prison the visits continued. Kemal visited his friends in the Bekir Ağa Division numerous times before departing Istanbul.[8]

In his biography of Atatürk, Lord Kinross gives an account of one of these visits:

> He found his friends on the top floor, in cells facing each other along a dark narrow passage. Here were ministers, politicians, journalists, public men of importance—all treated as war criminals. As he opened the doors of the cells they gathered around him, eager to talk. . . .[9]

Another regular visitor was General Kâzım Karabekir, whose appointment as the head of the nationalist Eastern Army made him the second most powerful person in the movement.[10] This general friendship had a significant effect on the Nationalist Movement's attitude towards the Armenian genocide. Some of the Unionists directly implicated also occupied a prominent place in the movement in Anatolia. However much Mustafa Kemal may have disapproved of the wartime deportations and massacres, he knew that the National Movement was fundamentally based on Unionist foundations. In a letter to ex–finance minister Cavid, Dr. Nâzım says that beyond the CUP there was "no national resistance," that the movement was led by Unionists and that the success of "Blondie," the Unionists' nickname for Kemal, depended heavily on how well he could work with them.[11]

Modern Turkish historiography has tended to downplay the CUP's role in the National Movement. After Mustafa Kemal purged the remaining Unionist leaders in 1926, the connection between the CUP on the one hand, and the attempt to establish an independent Turkey on the other, was even more consciously severed, and great efforts were made to portray the Anatolian nationalists as entirely separate from the CUP, ex nihilo. The Unionists were cast as having an insignificant role in the independence movement, more as human resources employed by the organization and its leaders.[12] But as we know, extensive plans for a resistance in Anatolia had been devised by the Unionists in the early years of World War I. In 1918, when defeat seemed imminent, these plans were reviewed, and began to be put into effect. They were remarkably similar to later nationalist strategies.

During the war, the Special Organization had stockpiled weapons at secret depots throughout Anatolia. With the armistice, they began to make strenuous efforts toward organizing armed resistance to occupation and partition, and a number of reports appeared in the Western press of CUP members fanning out through Anatolia, establishing committees to oversee the resistance.[13] They quickly created the Defense of Rights (*Müdafaa-yı Hukuk*) associations, building on a Unionist organizational foundation. These associations, along with nationalist units, were established as a continuation of the Unionist tradition.

The idea of setting up a national defense organization went back at least as far as the Ottoman-Italian War of 1911. In that year, the National Support Committee was established. Its goals were later broadened with the empire's defeat in Balkans, and on 31 January 1913, the National Defense Committee was founded. This was an umbrella organization and it included among its members many high state functionaries, among them the sultan and the grand vizier. Its aim was ostensibly "to develop and strengthen national education, health and the general intellectual level of the nation." Additionally, the committee had a military purpose:

The committee would, in the face of war, prepare the population for war, on the one hand, and provide them with the education that would give them the strength and physical training to succeed in the field of battle, and protect the population from harm.

Another important characteristic of the committee was that it stood apart from political struggles, remaining "completely free from any political or partisan sentiment."[14] In its first statement, the committee said that it "would embrace every hand extended to save the homeland. . . . We shall rescue the homeland."[15]

The Defense of Rights associations, founded in 1918–19, were based on the tradition and legacy of these previous organizations.[16] There was considerable continuity of staff between the older and more recent organizations as well. The founders of the first Defense of Rights association in 1918 had been active members of the National Defense Committee in 1913.[17] The nationalists' military wing, the armed National Forces, also had historical antecedents. The term "national force" was first used by the Unionists after the Balkan defeat, when the Ottoman government was forced to cede western Thrace to Greece. Some members of the CUP did not accept the defeat and established a "Temporary Government of Western Thrace" in the region. Its military units were called the National Forces, and many of those who served in them were found in their later incarnation in Anatolia after the world war.[18]

After the defeat, the remaining Unionist leaders began to organize military units and associations across Anatolia based on the hope promised in the Wilsonian principles, such as "the right of a people to determine its own fate." They hoped that partition of the remaining Ottoman land might then be averted if the Great Powers were convinced that most of Anatolia was inhabited by a Turkish majority. The first Defense of Rights Committees, in fact, were established through the direct efforts of Talât Paşa and the CUP Central Committee. Some of the more important of these committees were:

1) The Ottoman Committee for the Defense of Thrace-Paşaeli, established on 7 November 1918 and centered in Edirne. Its founder, Faik Kaltakıran, was one of the movement's leaders. The committee was established through the direct initiative of Talât Paşa,[19] yet was

subsequently supported by the entire Istanbul government. Even Damat Ferid Paşa's government provided a four thousand lira grant for the organization in April and May 1919.

2) The Committee for the Defense of National Rights for the Eastern Provinces was established in Istanbul in November 1918 with the direct support of the government. Among its founders were a number of Unionist parliamentary deputies who would later be arrested by the British occupational forces. One of its founders, Süleyman Nazıf, a journalist and former governor of several provincial regions, was also an active member of the main Defense of Rights Committee. The central office was a room within the Defense of Rights Committee building.[20] The Trabzon Committee for the Defense of National Rights was also established in this region on 12 February 1919. The organization also opened a branch in Erzurum on 6 March 1919. The Erzurum and Trabzon committees later organized the nationalist Erzurum Congress (23 July–7 August 1919), in which Mustafa Kemal decided to participate. Discussions at the Paris Peace Conference about giving the Armenians control of the eastern provinces provided the impetus for the establishment of these defense organizations.

3) The Izmir Committee for the Defense of Ottoman Rights was founded on 1 December 1918. Other committees followed in Balıkesir, Alaşehir and Nazilli, called the National Movement and the Resistance to Occupation. Later, dozens of organizations bearing similar names sprang up throughout Anatolia. The founders of all these committees were essentially local Unionist members and ex-members of the Special Organization.[21] "The Defense of Rights Committees showed themselves to be largely identical to the local CUP organizations."[22] This relationship was so strong that when all these groups united under the banner of the Anatolia and Rumelia Defense of Rights Committee and became a party, former members of the Liberty and Concord Party were formally excluded.[23]

4) The Government of the National Resistance of the Southwest Caucasus: This was established on 17–18 January 1919, following a number of nationalist congresses organized after the armistice. The National Resistance of the Southwest Caucasus proclaimed an independent state when Kars and the surrounding provinces came under the postwar control of British forces and the whole region was under consideration as an Armenian homeland. Dr. Esat Paşa, a prominent

Unionist, played a major role in setting up this local government and in the resistance, as did commanders in the Ottoman army.[24]

After the main Unionist leaders had fled, those remaining took over the movement's organization. According to one member, Şeref Çavuşoğlu,

> We who remained assembled ourselves under the leadership of Esat Paşa and began to implement our plan. . . . We set to work organizing the resistance in Istanbul and Anatolia.[25]

There were four dimensions of activity undertaken by the CUP to organize resistance in Anatolia: "1) overt political activities; 2) covert activities; 3) the role of the provincial branches [of the CUP]; 4) the role of the army."[26] The most overt of the political activities was the formation of the National Congress on 11 December 1918. The congress encompassed sixty-three political, social, cultural and professional organizations[27] and was connected to the National Movement in Anatolia. Several older Unionist organizations such as the Red Crescent, the National Committee for Education and Instruction and Turkish Hearth were also involved. Esat Paşa, the Istanbul representative to the National Council government in Kars, led the organization.

The National Congress went to great lengths to disseminate the National Movement's demands in Istanbul, engaging in a variety of publishing activities to convince the West of the righteousness of the Turkish position. One of these books addressed the "Armenian question," justified the massacres, and blamed the Armenians for them.[28]

One of the most effective institutions in organizing the national resistance was the Karakol (The Provincial Guard). This secret organization was set up under the direct orders of Talât and Enver Paşa for the purpose of continuing the covert work of the CUP. "While they were in Istanbul, Talât, Enver and Cemal Paşa saw that the situation of the country was worsening and [established secret organizations] with the purpose of taking steps for a final defense against any and all possible situations."[29] The actual date that the organization was founded remains uncertain, and although 13 November 1918 has been claimed, preparations for the organization had already begun at the end of October. The establishment of the Karakol coincided with another significant event, the decision to change the Special Organization's name to the General Islamic World Revolutionary Committee.[30]

Mustafa Kemal claimed that the Karakol was "a way . . . to conceal the activities of the CUP from the victorious powers. . . . Its objective was the same as the abolished party," and it was "closely connected with Enver Paşa."[31] The central aim of the Karakol was to provide protection—hiding places and escape routes—for members being sought for their role in the Armenian genocide. It had a list of regulations and a program for action.[32] The job of forming the organization was given to Unionist strongman and wartime cabinet member Kara Kemal. He, in turn, commissioned Unionist Kara Vasıf with the task, telling him:

> Vasıf . . . according to the order I received when I visited Talât Paşa, those who will keep to the Unionist way must be linked to each other through a secret organization. . . . The British are ordering the arrests, one by one, of the Unionists involved in the deportation and massacre of the Armenians. We must protect ourselves through an organization.[33]

Among the organization's most significant activities were "covertly taking the measures necessary to prevent violent action against Turks by the minorities who were likely to collaborate with the enemy in Istanbul. . . ." Rauf Orbay, considered the second-ranking leader in the National Movement after Mustafa Kemal, recounted that he worked closely with the organization when he was in Istanbul.[34]

Karakol played a leading role in the formation of both the Defense of Rights Committees and the newly established National Forces units. In many regions, these were directly set up by Karakol members. As for its own activities, the Karakol was successful in both protecting Unionists being sought for war crimes and in recruiting a broad group of people for the national resistance in Anatolia. In a way, the organization represented a symbolic connection between the Armenian genocide, and the Turkish National Movement in Anatolia since all the leading members of Karakol—Rauf Orbay Bey and his brother Kâzım, Kâzım Karabekir Paşa, Bekir Sami Bey, and Ali Çetinkaya—had all been influential members of the CUP. Because of Rauf's role in Karakol, in fact, it was not considered necessary to send any other delegates from the organization to the Erzurum Congress.[35]

Many of the memoirs of the period identify Karakol as the organization that ultimately persuaded Mustafa Kemal to assume the leadership of the nascent Nationalist Movement in Anatolia.[36] The organization even communicated with the War Ministry to facilitate his appointment to Anatolia as a military inspector.[37] Nonetheless, Mustafa Kemal looked upon the Karakol organization with suspicion, because it was under the control of Enver Paşa. He took care to convince government circles that he was not a Unionist. The army's chief of staff Cevat Paşa was convinced, which laid the groundwork for Kemal's appointment to Anatolia.

By the time Kemal arrived in Anatolia in May 1919, he had come to a clear agreement, in principle, with Karakol. In his memoirs, Şeref Çavuşoğlu reports that Kemal had a number of conditions before he accepted the National Movement's leadership. First, that there would be sufficient funding for the organization. Then, that he would only come to Anatolia if a position was arranged that gave him authority over the army commanders in the region.[38] The organization then sent Rauf Orbay Bey the necessary funds for expenses. Rauf would later write that this money was enough to cover all of the needs of Kemal's delegation while they were in Amasya.[39] Despite all this, in a famous 1927 speech, he claimed that he only learned of the Karakol organization during the Erzurum Congress in July 1919.[40] But there are numerous sources testifying to the fact that Kemal had previously had detailed information about the Karakol. In his memoirs, his friend and colleague General Ali Fuat Cebesoy confirmed that Mustafa Kemal was on intimate terms with the Karakol during his time in Istanbul in November 1918–May 1919.[41] He even collaborated with the organization on a plan to assassinate the sultan[42] and kidnap the grand vizier.[43]

Mustafa Kemal claimed to have been unaware of the existence of the Karakol, because the organization was not under his control. He conveyed his uneasiness in a conversation with Kara Vasıf at the Sivas Congress:

Your goal is to resurrect the disbanded Union and Progress [Committee]. This means you hope to come to power again. I have noticed this and I know the name of your secret commander-in-chief: it is Enver Paşa. . . . You want to lead the country off into

another adventure. You're all still in communication with Enver·
Paşa. . . .[44]

Kara Vasıf admitted that he had taken his orders from Talât Paşa,
but that his commander-in-chief was now Mustafa Kemal.[45] Apart
from the fact that the organization still took directions from Enver
and Talât, Kemal knew that any hint of Unionism would bring more
harm than good to the nationalists in Anatolia.[46] Thus, during this
conversation, he proposed the Karakol organization be shut down
and its members absorbed into the Anatolian movement.

While he had no objection to working with Unionists, nor even
with Kara Vasıf, who had been put in charge of the Representative
Committee in Istanbul,[47] tension between the Unionist core and
Kemal persisted throughout the Turkish struggle for independence;
Kemal's intervention in the October 1919 parliamentary elections
was one example.[48]

While in Ankara, Mustafa Kemal received great support from the
Karakol, which enjoyed close relations with the Istanbul government.
Kemal would send Istanbul a list of the military officers he required,
after which the Karakol would use its contacts in the War Ministry,
still staffed with ex-Unionists, and succeed in getting these officers
appointed to Anatolia.[49]

Mustafa Kemal understood that it was politic to distance himself
from the Unionist organization. After the establishment of the Turkish Republic in 1923, the tension turned into a genuine political
struggle that ended with the gallows for some Unionists in 1926. Nevertheless the conflict was essentially a factionalist fight among the
Unionists. As discussed, the National Movement was heir to the
Unionists both in terms of membership and its modernizing and
nationalizing policies, even as the nationalists rejected the Pan-
Turanist CUP aims. With Mustafa Kemal in the lead, the Anatolian
movement defended the CUP against attack. Kemal's comments to a
British representative he met in Istanbul are one example. The man,
Frew, told Kemal that he

"first should accept the crimes of the Union and Progress," to which
Kemal replied: "I am not a representative of the Union and

> Progress! . . . But if you will allow me, let me say that the Union and Progress was a patriotic association. . . . It may have been very flawed. But its patriotism is beyond dispute.
> He also stated that he held to the CUP's general line.[50]

While calling for punishment of the Unionist leaders, Kemal nevertheless insisted on making a clear division between those responsible for the crimes and the rest of the party members. He had stressed this in his correspondence with Ali Rıza's cabinet in the fall of 1919, and had rejected any policy of general hostility toward the CUP. According to Kemal, "the unwavering hostility toward Unionism, fanned by the non-Muslim elements and the Entente governments for political purposes," was fundamentally misplaced. The perpetrators of the war crimes were "but a small party of Unionists who conned the country into the war through their misadministration and abuses." It was wrong—even dangerous—to sully the reputation of the CUP's honorable members.[51]

He also rejected claims that the National Movement was Unionist in its policies. On 9 October 1919, after the Sivas Congress, Kemal sent a telegram to the Istanbul government's minister of war, Cemal Paşa, in which he stated that accusations of Unionism were a ploy by Damat Ferid Paşa's government—now out of power—and Great Britain, the Greeks and the Armenians to discredit the nationalists.[52] To stop these accusations, delegates to the Sivas Congress had publicly "vowed not to work to resurrect the Committee of Union and Progress, and a copy of this pledge was published throughout the country."[53] On the first day of the congress, 4 September 1919, delegates swore:

> by Allah that I shall not pursue any aim, personal or otherwise, other than the happiness and tranquility of the homeland, that I shall not work to resurrect the Committee of Union and Progress, and that I shall not serve the political aspirations of any but the present political parties.[54]

But even this declaration was insufficient for the government in Istanbul, and so it was repeated in the Amasya Protocol. "The reawakening of Unionism, of the ideas of the Union and Progress Committee within the country, even the appearance of certain signs of it, is politically detrimental."[55]

This rejection of Unionist connections was not an isolated incident. Even the Renewal Party, the direct successor to the Unionists, had sworn that it had no connections with the CUP. On 1 November 1918, at the final CUP Congress, where the party dissolved itself and set up the new party in its place, the following resolution was passed: "Relations between this party and members of the Committee of Union and Progress and its General Assembly have been severed."[56] The CUP was formally dissolved on 5 November, and the new party made official six days later. The skepticism that met these vows was not unjustified. A veteran Unionist who refused to take the oath in Sivas was told by his companions that it "was ultimately just a formality."[57]

The question of the Nationalist Movement's relationship to the CUP had a prominent place in Mustafa Kemal's speeches, and he took every opportunity to distance himself and the movement from Unionism. "[This charge of] Unionism [is a] calumny. . . . We have declared to all creation both through the oath that was taken at the general congress and through the official declarations we have published, that we are not attached to any party whatsoever, and that we have no connection to Unionism."[58] According to Kemal, "Unionism had passed into history," and "since neither the central government nor the West[ern powers] wished its resurrection, the nation would not, of its own volition, resurrect it either."[59]

Mustafa Kemal's criticism of the CUP remained focused on its expansionism and imperialism. In an interview with the daily *Tasvir-i Efkâr*, Kemal stated:

Politically speaking, the Committee of Union and Progress is bankrupt. . . . While they were in power, the individuals of that party followed an expansionist policy without any regard for the needs and situation of our nation. A policy that turns the eyes of the nation to other distant points while its own land is in need of care and protection is a flawed policy. Thus it was doomed to collapse.[60]

Mustafa Kemal used all available means to criticize the CUP's Pan-Turanist and Pan-Islamist policies. In a conversation on 21 Sep-

tember 1919 with General Harbord, the head of the American delegation to the Middle East investigating the possibility of a mandate for
Armenia, Kemal said, "We believe that 'Turanism' is detrimental."[61]
Additionally, in a memo he wrote to Harbord about the Anatolia and
Rumelia Defense of Rights Committee and its objectives, Kemal
called Turanism "a dangerous concept"[62] On 4 March 1920, when
journalists of the Istanbul press asked what the press should be doing,
Kemal recommended not spreading "any Turanist or Pan-Islamic
propaganda in publications concerned with the Islamic world, and to
present the Anatolia movement as independence organizations."[63] On
24 April 1920, at a secret session of the National Assembly, Kemal
repeated that "we do not wish to expand beyond our borders with all
the human resources and advantages that exist within the borders of
our nation."[64] In a speech made on 1 December 1921, Kemal
described what he understood by Pan-Islamism: "Certainly, we desire
that all our coreligionists throughout the world should live in happi-
ness and prosperity." But that was all. "It is a fantasy to imagine this
community" of the world's Muslims "as an immense empire, an
actual material empire administered from one [location]! It goes
against knowledge, logic, and science."

But he also gave more practical reasons for rejecting Pan-Turkism
and Pan-Islamism.

> Gentlemen . . . we are not a deluded kind of people who pursue
> great illusions, who appear to go after things they cannot accom-
> plish. . . . Because of posing as if we have done great things without
> actually having done so, we have brought . . . the anger, rancor and
> hostility of the entire world upon this nation. We have not brought
> about Pan-Islamism. Perhaps "we are doing so," or "we will do so,"
> as we have said. So our enemies said, "Let's quickly kill them to stop
> them from doing so" . . . instead of adding to the enemies we have
> or to the threats against us by running after illusions that we will
> not and cannot achieve, let us return to our natural borders, our
> rightful borders. Let us know our limits.[65]

Mustafa Kemal's critique of Pan-Islamic or Pan-Turkic policies
remains a point of contention today. Some argue that his rejection was
based not on the principles involved, but on the practical realization

that they were dangerous to implement.[66] Indeed, there is some ambiguity. The debate in the Ankara National Assembly over the correct understanding of the National Pact—establishing a Turkish state within the armistice borders—is one example of this ambiguity. The fact is there was no unequivocal definition of the state's borders in the pact, which was adopted at nationalist congresses in Erzerum, Sivas and finally in the Chamber of Deputies in Istanbul on 28 January 1920. On 16 October 1921, during a debate in the Ankara Assembly, the deputies demanded a clear answer as to where the borders lay. Mustafa Kemal replied that "there is no predetermined and definite border in our National Pact. The border will be the boundary that we shall establish with our power and our strength. . . . We shall establish the borders according to the degree of our power and our strength."[67]

However, in the British archives in particular, there is ample information documenting the Anatolian movement's Pan-Islamist policy and its secret activities in other Muslim countries.[68] These documents in the British archives exist because Kemal believed that it was in Turkey's interests to have the British fear a broad Islamic movement. Hüsamettin Ertürk, who directed the activities of a new Special Organization in Ankara during this period, recalled that false reports were intentionally disseminated.[69] At the National Assembly's secret session of 24 April 1920, Kemal claimed that the movement had embarked on such overseas activities quietly to allay foreign fears. He suggested that it was reasonable for a Muslim nation to find common ground with other Muslim countries to resist their enemies. He added that "although it was not declared publicly, this point of solidarity was indeed sought without hesitation."[70]

Mustafa Kemal listed these activities. "It was first of all necessary to establish contact with our coreligionists on our borders. We entered into relations in various ways with all of these, with the Islamic nations of the Caucasus in the East, and with western Thrace in the West."[71] What is important is that these relations with the greater Islamic world were not in fact based on Pan-Islamic or Pan-Turkish ideologies. The nationalists' main objective was neither Islamic nor Turkic unity; Kemal believed that the idea of one center governing the whole Muslim world was "pure fantasy."[72]

He developed a consistent attitude to this issue and refused calls from various other resistance movements—in particular from Syria and Saudi Arabia—for an Islamic political union, emphasizing that each state's national independence was fundamental. The ties between them should be the relations of two separate nations. To a proposal along these lines from Emir Faisal, Kemal replied that "just as we (the Turks) are independent within our own borders, the Syrians must also be free and independent within their own borders, according to the principle of national sovereignty."[73]

In a sense, the Turkish National Movement was part of the ongoing conflicts between the various ethnic groups that made up the Ottoman Empire. Thus the establishment of the Turkish nation-state can be seen as the final stage of the nation-building process—and of ethnic-religious conflict—in the Balkans and Anatolia.

The main catalyst for the Turkish resistance in Anatolia was the "Armenian and Greek danger." The first organizations were essentially founded to counter and forestall the danger that the land still in possession of the Ottoman state would be given to the Greeks or the Armenians. To achieve this goal, the local organizations struggled to prove that the region that they represented belonged to a Turkish majority, historically, geographically, and demographically. They sent delegations to the Paris Peace Conference armed with "scientific" studies and reports, and they engaged in propaganda and publishing activities. The organizations included articles in their regulations mandating members to attend "the Peace Conferences for the purpose of advocating [for the Turkish cause] according to the Wilsonian Principles.[74] The Committee for the Defense of National Rights for the Eastern Provinces, established in Istanbul, was active along these lines and began to publish two newspapers, one in French, the other in Turkish.[75]

The committee fell into a panic on 26 February with the delivery of a memo from the Armenian delegation to the Paris Peace Conference which claimed rights to Cilicia and eastern Anatolia. As a result, a branch of the organization was established in Erzurum only days later, on 6 March, and its first act was to declare "that the Eastern Provinces had been the country of the Turks since time immemorial, that the Armenian population in the region nowhere exceeded 15 percent, and that therefore the Armenians had no right to these provinces." The same declaration categorically rejected claims that atrocities had been inflicted on the Armenians during the deportations.[76]

In the founding documents of the Izmir Committee for the Defense of National Rights, which was established on 6 November 1918, we see the same principles at work. The aim of the committee was to prove to the civilized word, using scientific means, that Muslims in that region comprised a majority. At its 13 March 1919 meeting, the committee decreed that Izmir and its surrounding area could not be subjected to "foreign rule . . . according to the 12th Article of Wilson's principles."[77]

After the Greek occupation of Izmir it was understood that propagandistic activities alone would no longer be enough. The decision was taken to oppose the Greek and Armenian minorities through armed struggle. The Trabzon Committee for the Defense of National Rights, for example, decreed at its second congress (22 May 1919) that "the minorities should be opposed with arms."[78] When Kâzım Karabekir arrived on 3 May in Erzurum, the headquarters of the Fifteenth Army Corps to which he had been appointed commander, his first action was to meet with the Erzurum Committee. The meeting produced a joint request that Erzurum not be conceded to the Armenians, and that the Turks would fight to the last man.[79] As the British general Milne reported, "The very phrase 'greater Armenia' is igniting the flames of the National Movement."[80]

The Greek presence in Izmir prompted the same result in western Anatolia. A British officer claimed that:

[The National forces were] established solely for the purpose of fighting the Greeks. . . . The Turks . . . are willing to remain under the control of any other state. . . . There was not even an organized resistance at the time of the Greek occupation. Yet the Greeks are persisting in their oppression, and they have continued to burn villages, kill Turks and rape and kill women and young girls and throttle to death children.[81]

These organizations basically looked upon the empire's non-Muslim communities (the Armenians and Greeks) as competitors, and were founded with the aim of struggling against them. This view was expressed at the committees' congresses and in their regulations. At the Erzurum Congress in July 1919, considered the founding event of the National Movement, the decision was made to adopt "the principle of a united defense and resistance," since any occupation or intervention would be understood as support for Greek and Armenian organizations that aimed to separate states.[82]

The same position was repeated at the Sivas Congress in September 1919 where the delegates approved

a united defense and resistance, as in the case of the national struggles on the Aydın, Manisa and Balıkesir fronts, against the invasion and occupation of any portion of the Ottoman realm, and against each movement directed at creating independent Greek and Armenian entities.[83]

When Mustafa Kemal tendered his resignation to Istanbul in July 1919, he repeated the need for action against the Armenian and Greek danger.[84]

Over the years this ethnic and religious aspect of the National Movement's founding principles has gradually been consigned to oblivion. Instead, there is the widely held belief that it was an anti-imperialist movement responding to foreign occupation. But the defense committees never intended to fight against the Allied Powers; they were designed to "convince" the Entente Powers of the Turkishness of Anatolia. In a cable Mustafa Kemal sent to the lieutenant governor of Urfa, Ali Rıza, he described how the Nationalist Movement never in any way planned attacks on the Entente Powers.[85] Direct opposition to the Allies developed only because the Allies insisted on partitioning Anatolia and punishing the Turks for the Armenian genocide.

In his famous thirty-six hour speech delivered over six days, between 15 and 20 October 1927 at the second congress of the Republican People's Party, Mustafa Kemal said that during the Turkish War of Independence, the nationalist forces took great pains not to adopt an attitude of "hostility toward the Entente States"; and "not to offend the great states like England, France and Italy."[86] The National Movement went even as far as to offer the Great Powers an overall mandate for the former Ottoman Empire rather than have the territory partitioned among various ethnic groups. The American journalist Lewis Edgar Browne, who attended the Sivas Congress, was told that the congress would agree to an American mandate if America itself would accept it.[87] Similar ideas were voiced to the head of the American delegation to Anatolia, General Harbord. The general later recounted that Mustafa Kemal himself told him "the aim of the Nationalist Movement . . . is the preservation of the territorial integrity of the Empire under a mandate of a single disinterested power, preferably America. America is the only country able to help us."[88] This mandate question was one of the primary topics of debate at the Sivas Congress in September 1919. Ultimately, the congress adopted the decision to make an official request to the United States to send a delegation to discuss the mandate question.[89]

The same ideas were repeated to Georges Picot, who came to visit Kemal in Sivas on 5–6 December 1919, while he was serving as the French high commissioner for Armenia and Syria.

In these discussions Kemal stated his willingness to accept a French economic mandate over all of Anatolia. He also . . . indicate[ed] his readiness tô consider help from Britain, but made it clear that what he sought was the assistance of a single power, preferably France.[90]

The Defense of Rights Committees founded in Anatolia had a positive attitude toward the British and French occupation forces, whose arrival was greeted with demonstrations of affection. One French officer serving in occupied Cilicia wrote:

25 June 1919: We left for Mersin (Cilicia). We are making a very good impression on the population. They greet us like royalty and form victory arches with our flags for our soldiers to pass under. . . . 29 June: We arrive in Adana. Here they greeted us even better than in Mersin. The people hand out refreshing drinks. . . . Again, we pass under victory arches. . . . They throw flowers in our path.[91]

Fearing Greek occupation, special delegations from some western regions of Anatolia appealed to the Entente Powers to occupy their cities, among them Isparta, Bayındır, Tire and Ödemiş. In Isparta, for instance, the population appealed to the Italians through a delegation and asked them to occupy their city.[92]

The only armed struggle undertaken directly against the Allied Powers during the Turkish War of Independence was against the

French forces in the Antep, Urfa and Maraş regions, which included Armenian volunteers among their ranks who demanded the return of lost property. There was no conflict during the British occupation of this same region until the end of 1919. In fact, no members of these cities under occupation felt the need to attend either the Erzurum or Sivas nationalist congresses.

The situation was not much different in eastern Anatolia where British occupation forces were also greeted warmly. The Islamic Council, founded in Kars on 5 November 1918, established warm relations with the British, who entered the city on 13 January 1919. The British officially recognized the council, saying that "the Administrative Council is getting along splendidly with the [British] military administration."[93] The reason for the eventual rift between the two, and for the Administrative Council's arrest and transfer to Malta was the council's refusal to countenance the return of Armenian exiles to Kars.[94]

The thing that ultimately mobilized the Muslim population of western Anatolia was not Izmir's occupation per se, but its occupation by Greeks, which was seen as a tremendous insult. The British high commissioner was told that "Greece's occupation came to mean humiliation and oppression."[95] The Turks would have preferred British occupying forces. The day the Greek occupation began, a retired Turkish officer told a British officer, "We want to tell you that we can remain only under the rule of this great state."[96]

Even when the decision was taken to begin armed resistance to the Greek occupation, no hostility was shown toward the Allied Powers. On the contrary, displays of good will and efforts to win friendship continued. The Nationalist Movement in the Alaşehir region sent a 23 August 1919 telegram to General Milne in Istanbul stating that its objective "was only to prevent the unjust, treacherous assault and abhorrent crimes committed by the Greeks during the occupation and offensive." There were no ill feelings toward the Allied Powers, only a demand that the Greeks withdraw and be replaced by the British forces.[97] Four days later, National Committee of Nazilli sent Milne a similar cable.[98] The British officers stationed in the area were told by the Muslims: "We will agree to a British occupation without terms or conditions."[99] The British and French supervisory officers also attended the various congresses of the National Movement, even speaking to the assemblies.[100]

Despite these overtures, the Allied Powers remained aloof from the Turks. "They didn't indulge them in the least," due to their desire for Ottoman territory and to punish Turkey for the genocide and the war. More than Turkish anti-imperialism, the Entente Powers maintained a harsh stance, keeping the Turks at arm's length.

After Greece's occupation of western Anatolia, supported by the victorious powers, and in response to the Armenian efforts to establish a state, the religious aspect of the nation-building process within the Ottoman Empire, although much denied, became ever more virulent. The process that had begun with mutual "ethnic cleansing" in the Balkans and progressed, with World War I, to the expulsion and massacre of Christians in Anatolia, entered a new period following the Ottoman defeat. After 1919, the Greek, Armenian and Turkish National Movements all either massacred or forcibly expelled the other groups under their control. For the first time, the Kurds also emerged as a significant political actor. The Kurds were torn between joining the Muslim Turkish National Movement and seeking support from the British forces for their own ends. While the British had promised the Kurds an independent state, the Turks had promised autonomy and Muslim solidarity against returning Armenians.

However, Turkish and Kurdish interests began to conflict in this period, and the Turkish National Movement, irritated by the Kurds' attempts to gain a level of independence, added them to their list of targets. The Koçgiri Uprising in 1919–21[101] is an example of a Kurdish attempt at independence followed by repression. There were massacres throughout 1920–23, the period of the Turkish War of Independence—especially of Armenians in the east and the south, and against the Greeks in the Black Sea region. Massacres of Turks were also carried out by the Greek and Armenian forces.[102]

The National Movement was fundamentally defined by religion, despite all claims to the contrary. In numerous speeches to the National Assembly, Mustafa Kemal repeatedly spoke of the National Pact as a movement common to all Muslim peoples within the borders of the newly emerging Turkish state:

Let it not be thought that there is only one Muslim nation within these borders. There are Turks, there are Circassians.

Therefore, the nation we are determined to preserve and defend naturally does not consist of one element. It is composed of various Muslim peoples . . . Kurds as well as Turks.

If there is one thing we're sure of it is that the Kurd, the Turk, the Laz, the Circassian and others, all of these Islamic peoples within the national border have equal rights. They have pledged to work together.[103]

The Muslim character of the National Movement was very clear during the elections for the National Assembly in Ankara. A circular sent to the provinces by Mustafa Kemal on 17 March 1920 stated that "non-Muslims shall not be allowed to participate in the elections."[104] In response, army commander Kâzım Karabekir said that he particularly appreciated this part of the statement: "It is very fitting that the elections be restricted to Muslims."[105]

Christians were not only excluded from the election process, they became targets for massacres. Ebubekir Hazım Tepeyran, who served as governor-general of the Sivas Province for part of 1919, said that the massacres were so horrible that he could not bear to report on them,[106] referring to atrocities against Greeks in the Black Sea region and against Kurds in Koçgiri. According to the official tally, some 11,181 Greeks were murdered in 1921 by the Central Army under the command of Nurettin Paşa, established in a joint effort by Ankara and Istanbul to pacify Anatolia. In addition, the entire population of Greek males residing in the coastal villages and towns was deported.[107]

The massacres occurred on such a scale that they came up for discussion at one of the National Assembly's closed sessions. Some parliamentary deputies demanded that Nurettin Paşa be sentenced to death.[108] The assembly, which had de facto control of the army, decided to relieve Nurettin Paşa of his command and put him on trial,[109] although the trial was later revoked through the intervention of Mustafa Kemal.[110] According to one newspaper, Nurettin Paşa had suggested not only deporting the Greek and Armenian populations remaining in Anatolia, but also killing them, a suggestion rejected by Kemal.[111]

The situation in the southwest Caucasus was complicated by frequent changes in the political landscape. From 1878 until 1915 the region had been under Russian control. After the Bolshevik revolution the Ottoman army regained some control, formalized in March 1918, under the Brest-Litovsk Treaty, signed with the Soviet state. It was agreed that the Ottomans would govern the areas that reflected their empire's boundaries in 1878. However, the Turks took more territory than the terms allowed, and forced the fledgling Georgian, Armenian, and Azerbaijani Soviet Republics, founded in May 1918, to accept the Batum Agreement of 4 June 1918, which meant more loss of territory to the Ottomans and greater Ottoman influence in the region. Then, after the collapse of the empire in October 1918, part of the region came under British control. Thus, the Armenians controlled cities such as Kars in conjunction with the British until the end of 1920. After the British withdrew, the Turkish army, with the assistance of the Bolsheviks, retook the territory. Because of the constantly chang-ing borders, populations moved back and forth, causing great tension between ethnic groups and leading eventually to massacres.

In the period under consideration, the first wave of massacres was in 1918. Shortly after the Bolshevik Revolution, the CUP hoped to realize its Pan-Turkic and Pan-Islamic dream to occupy the Caucasus and Central Asia. Vehip Paşa, the Third Army commander after 1916, assured Armenian leaders that the ideal of Pan-Turanism now burned more strongly than ever:

> Destiny draws Turkey from the West to the East. We left the Balkans, we are now leaving Africa, but we must extend toward the East. Our blood, our religion, our language is there. And this has an irresistible magnetism. Our brothers are in Baku, Daghestan, Turkestan and Azerbaijan. . . . You Armenians are standing in our way . . . you must draw aside and give us room.[112]

One way to realize this plan, German sources suggest, was "to annihilate all the remaining Armenians."[113] In March, when news of massacres by Turkish forces reached Berlin, the German government made attempts to intervene.[114] Reports from German officers serving in the region testify to the murders committed by units under the command of Enver Paşa's brother Nuri and his uncle Halil Paşa, which advanced into the Caucasus in violation of the Brest-Litovsk Treaty. The German general Lossow sent reports on 15 and 23 May 1918:

The unlimited-Turkish demands towards those regions which are purely Armenian . . . are intended to achieve a border further than the Brest Treaty, to monopolize the economic exploitation of the Caucasus and bring about the complete annihilation of the Armenians of Transcaucasia.

The aim of Turkish policy . . . is to attain the Armenian regions and to annihilate the Armenians. . . . All of the utterances of Talât and Enver to the contrary are lies. . . . There will be no place left for Armenians to live.[115]

By 20 July 1918, approximately six hundred thousand Armenians from the Caucasus had fled before advancing Turkish units.[116] The German general Kress von Kressenstein, in Tiflis (Tblisi) at the time, wrote: "The Turks' policy toward the Armenians is painfully clear. The Turks have by no means abandoned fundamentally extirpating the Armenians."[117]

In his memoirs, Halil Paşa admits that he took part in these massacres. He claims that he gave a speech to a group "who knew Halil Paşa as the person who had carried out these massacres . . . in which almost everyone had lost a relative, a father, a brother," by saying that he "had worked to eliminate the Armenian Nation to the last individual" because they had sought the complete destruction of his homeland.[118] The massacres continued through the summer and autumn of 1919. The American high commissioner for Armenia, William N. Haskell, was so shocked by the scale of the killings that he sent a warning to President Wilson on 16 August, saying that the United States should withdraw the Twelfth Article of his Peace Declaration regarding the Turks unless Turkish officials took effective measures to stop the massacre in the Caucasus.[119]

The massacres in the region resumed in 1920 to 1921 under the Turkish army. In a sense this was a continuation of the Ottoman policy, as well as the result of advances made by Turkish military units under the command of Kâzım Karabekir in the fall of 1920. The members of the new Turkish parliament in Ankara understood their Armenian policy as an attempt to complete the unfinished work of the previous government. During a debate in parliament, one deputy suggested that the Armenians left in Anatolia should be shipped abroad: "I'll make you a sound proposal. Let's finish this job properly.

Let's sift out the Armenians and send them off to Yerevan. That way they'll be comfortable and so will we. . . . (Howls of approval were then heard)."[120]

Charles P. Grant from the American Committee reported from Gümrü in May 1921 that a great proportion of those killed that year were women and children. He estimated that the number killed ranged between twelve and fifteen thousand.[121] The reason for the large number of massacres in the region can also be inferred from a coded telegram sent to Kâzım Karabekir Paşa from the Turkish foreign minister in Ankara, which states that "the most important thing is to eliminate Armenia, both politically and materially."[122]

There was also significant continuity between the organizers of the massacres between 1915–17 and 1919–21. Among those who served the army in this region during both periods were Nuri and Halil Paşa, Deli Halit Paşa and Topal Osman.[123] In addition, Ibrahim Avras, a former deputy, wrote, "valuable officers such as Yenibahçeli Şükrü, Hilmi and Nail Beys, . . . were attached to the 15th Army Corps." After naming these commanders, Arras described these commanders as "honorable conquerors" and their action as the "uproot[ing] of a 'den of treachery.' "[124]

Russian sources contain many documents relating to these killings of Armenians. The Bolsheviks, who had preferred to remain neutral observers in the region in order to maintain good relations with the Turkish nationalists, finally felt compelled to act. In an 18 January 1921 telegram sent by Soviet foreign minister Chicherin to the Caucasus, he stated that a policy of silence on the issue of the Armenians was no longer possible. It was "traitorous" to "stand by and watch the destruction of the Soviet Republic" and he recommended taking action.[125]

One day later the Armenian foreign minister protested to the Turkish Grand National Assembly in Ankara that "violence and murder had taken a general character in the form of organized plunder and real carnage."[126] The document stated that villages had been attacked, property looted, and all men between the ages eighteen and fifty taken away. After listing the areas affected, the minister reported that "armed military companies are attacking the Armenian villages, looting them, raping the women and killing the inhabitants." Over two hundred Armenians in one region had been killed in a single day (13 January 1921).[127] He had sent a similar letter of protest on 10 December 1920, in which he accused the Ankara government of pursuing "the old policy of implacable hostility toward Armenia," and as a result the Turkish army was devastating the land, committing "violence and murder" as well as "organized plunder and real carnage," which have taken "a general character."[128]

Referring to these events in late 1920 and early 1921, S. I. Aralov, Soviet ambassador to Ankara, wrote: "The Turkish forces . . . inflicted bloody pogroms, mass killings on the Armenians. More than 69,000 people were murdered."[129] A Soviet encyclopedia from 1961 gives the number of victims in the areas under Turkish occupation during the Turkish-Armenian war at close to 198,000.[130] In his memoirs, British officer Alfred Rawlinson, who was held hostage by Kâzım Karabekir Paşa in Erzurum for months as leverage against Turkish prisoners held by the British in Malta, tells of the Armenian captives that he saw during his own imprisonment, and concludes that the ultimate aim of the Turks was "to exterminate" the Armenians. In his opinion, this goal "is and has long been a deliberate policy of the Turkish Government."[131]

One of the main reasons that these massacres in the Caucasus, which V. N. Dadrian characterized as "miniature genocide,"[132] were carried out without too much opposition was the Russian revolution. In their relations with the Bolsheviks, the Turks "were able to characterize their war against the Armenians as a war against the Entente, thus allowing them the chance to mask their aggressive intentions in Transcaucasia."[133]

During the period of 1919–22, similar massacres were directed at the Muslim communities of western Anatolia by the Greeks,[134] and by the Armenians in the Caucasus. Acts of revenge in the eastern provinces were first carried out by the advancing Russian forces in 1916, assisted by Armenian volunteers. During the 1916 offensive, it is estimated that some two to three thousand Muslims were killed in Bitlis.[135] Having witnessed the systematic massacre of Armenians and suffered intermittent attacks from Kurdish irregulars, most Russian commanders came to hold abiding prejudice against Kurds and Muslims in general. Cossack units in particular visited merciless retribution upon local Muslims. One witness wrote, "The Cossacks and the Armenian *comitadchis*, like our Kurd guerrillas, killed without mercy all the enemy wounded and defenseless that fell into their hands." When Cossack troops retook Ardahan, "a massacre occurred. The Cossacks looted the bazaar, burnt the Moslem quarter, and killed on sight any Turk they saw."[136] Armenian volunteer detachments, later re-formed as rifle corps, similarly showed little compassion to Kurdish and Turkish communities.[137] In his testimony to the Mazhar Commission of Inquiry, General Vehip Paşa confirms accounts of acts of revenge that occurred around Erzurum.[138] A second wave of revenge took place after the Russian evacuation from Erzurum following the October Revolution. These massacres were witnessed not only in Erzurum itself, but also in Erzincan, Kars and many other places.[139] "The frenzied troops and bands retreating from Erzurum killed any Muslims falling into their hands and burned the Turkish villages that lay in their path."[140] Vehip Paşa gives a detailed account of these acts in his testimony and set the number of killed at 3,000 for the Erzincan and Bayburt region.[141] Another eyewitness account gives the number 3,000 for the Erzurum area.[142] In the Kars region, the number of Muslim dead in the spring of 1918 is given as 20,000.[143]

At the beginning of 1919, the Armenian forces reoccupied the territories they had left after the Bolshevik Revolution, whereupon

massacres and pillaging of the Muslim population reached tremendous proportions. A Soviet writer, Borian, himself an Armenian, states that the Armenian politicians had organized state authority not to administer the country, but to exterminate the Muslim population and loot their property.[144]

One Turkish source gives the number 6,500 for the deaths during the winter and spring of 1919 in Kars.[145] In a protest to the Armenian Republic on 22 March 1920, Kâzım Karabekir put the number at 2,000 in certain villages and regions in Kars.[146] These massacres were then used as an excuse for the Turkish offensive in the fall of 1920 that led to the Turkish occupation of the region.

British and German sources also confirm massacres against the Muslim population. In an 11 February 1918 report, K. Axenfeld, director of the Orient and Islam Commission of the German Protestant Mission, states that the Armenian government admitted that Armenian units withdrawing before the Turkish forces had committed vengeance operations.[147] The British foreign minister, Lord Curzon, mentioned in a speech in the House of Lords on 11 March 1920 that the massacres carried out by the Armenians were "barbaric, blood-thirsty assaults."[148] Other evidence of these post-1917 massacres can be culled from the German archives.[149]

Despite the fact that the newly formed Armenian government tried to put a halt to the activities of these gangs, formed explicitly to take revenge on the Muslim population, it never fully brought them under control.[150] "Guerrillas and freedom fighters in the years of struggle against Turkish oppression, [they] now robbed and looted in broad daylight, a government unto themselves . . . freedom fighters turned outlaws."[151]

The famous Armenian general Antranik and his activities is a well-known example. After rejecting the Turkish-Armenian Batum Agreement of 4 June 1918, Antranik's forces crushed one Tatar village after another. In Nakhichevan, Zangezur and Karabagh, Armenian "bands slaughtered the Muslim population." The Armenian government tried to prevent these acts and show that it was not implicated. "The hero of the Turkish Armenians was *persona non grata* and would be disarmed if he entered the bounds of the Republic."[152] Armenian Army Corps commander Nazarbekoff's reply (dated 27 June 1918) to a telegraph from Kâzım Karabekir which protested the massacres in the region of Nakhichevan confirms that Antranik was beyond the control of the Armenian government. "I urge that you make known to the Turkish Commanding forces that many of the Antranik atrocities and massacres which took place . . . [in] the area of Nakhichevan around June 5, 1918, occurred because of a failure to obey my orders."[153]

We should add that some efforts were made in the Armenian Republic to integrate Caucasian Muslims into the local state apparatus. Obviously, in the end, this did not work.

Certain considerations bear emphasizing. It is important that we do not equate these events with the Armenian genocide. It is a frequent mistake to "equate" or "balance" the massacres in the Caucasus with the genocide, an error often made in Turkish histories, which cite acts of Armenian revenge as proof that the murders of 1915 were not genocide. Previous massacres are never a justification for subsequent massacres. Or, in the Turkish case, subsequent massacres can never justify earlier genocide. The second problem is the reliability of the sources. Most of the figures cited are freely invented by the authors. For example, one study of the Vilayet of Erzurum puts the number of massacred Muslims in the spring of 1918 as 25,000.[154] After examining Turkish military publications, Dadrian claims that "the number . . . as a compilation of various statistical data embedded in the wartime records of the Ottoman Third Army, reveals that alto-gether some 5,000–5,500 victims are involved."[155] German sources also refer to these exaggerations.

Nuri Paşa (Enver's brother) claimed that more than thirty villages were destroyed in one such massacre. General Kress claimed that Nuri had greatly exaggerated the figures, as the events in question had not affected more than ten villages or so, and some of these could hardly be classified as villages, containing as they did no more than four or five inhabitants. Such reports were systematically exaggerated or out-right fabrications, delivered in order to reinforce the image of the "Armenian peril."[156]

The third issue is how to evaluate the events between 1917 and 1922, whether the terms "acts of revenge" or "continuation of the genocide" are accurate. There is no doubt that the events in Caucasus were part of a historical continuity in the region. However, while there is continuity of the actors, there are significant changes to the context in which these events took place. The decline of empires and rise of new nation-states changed the nature of the events in very important ways that negate a description of Muslim deaths during this period as simply "acts of revenge." The newly formed Armenian state was itself attempting to establish an ethnically homogenous nation. After the suppression of a Bolshevik uprising in May 1920 in Yerevan, "the government . . . turned the regular army and Western Armenian detachments against the constantly defiant Muslim-populated districts. . . ."[157] In a note to General Harbord, Mustafa Kemal writes:

> We know that the Armenians of this new state, following the orders of Armenian detachment commanders, are acting to annihilate the Muslims. We saw actual copies of these orders. The fact that Yerevan Armenians are following a policy of extermination is corroborated

by the fact that our borders are flooded by innumerable Muslims fleeing death.[158]

The years between 1918 and 1922 were a period in which nationalist politics were decisive in determining the course of events, in which massacres and countermassacres were frequent, directed toward expanding national borders and achieving homogenous populations.

During a conversation with Russian foreign minister Chicherin, Yusuf Kemal Tengirşenk, the foreign minister of the Ankara government, noted: "We must immediately stop the massacre of Muslims, which has been continuing for the past several months in Kars, Nahçivan and Şahtahtı. . . . The two sides are murdering one another. This, unfortunately, is a common practice in both countries."[159] Answering a memo from the Soviet Armenian government, Foreign Minister Bekir Sami, who preceded Yusuf Kemal, concluded, "When there are no regions left where a majority of Turks live under Armenian sovereignty, nor a majority of Armenians who live under Turkish sovereignty, there will be true peace and brotherhood between the two peoples." In other words, until what today we might call the ethnic cleansing in the two regions was complete, mutual massacres were to be expected.[160]

Although it is outside our topic, it must be added that the massacres in Anatolia were not limited to the Greek and Armenian populations. Atrocities were also carried out by the Ankara nationalists against the Turkish Muslim population to suppress various rebellions in support of the caliphate. These uprisings were primarily motivated by opposition to the Ankara regime and were stirred up by the Istanbul government. Killings became so widespread that army commanders created a militia force, separate from the regular army, which could carry out these atrocities. In this way, the officers, who were both military commanders and the heads of armed gangs, eliminated any potential legal obstacles.[161]

After March 1920, when Damat Ferid Paşa returned to power and Britain fully occupied Istanbul, the struggle between Ankara and Istanbul turned more violent.[162] To suppress resistance the National Movement in Ankara established Independence Tribunals by the "Law of Fugitives" issued on 11 September 1920.[163] Chief among the courts' tasks was the trial and punishment of those suspected of crimes against the Nationalist Movement, and assisting the suppression of revolts by trying rebels. Many executions were carried out, even without trial. The fact that the number of dead hanged by the Independence Tribunals is higher than the number of dead at the Western and Caucasus fronts during this period shows the enormity of the internal conflict among the Turks.[164]

In memoirs of the period, we read of army commanders possessing the broadest possible authority to suppress the various revolts. For instance, "The Saga of Sergeant Selahattin" noted that "the authority to hand out punishments such as imprisonment, death, razing villages and expulsion were all given to Lieutenant Colonel Osman Bey, who had been appointed to the command of the Mobile Retribution Forces for the Province of Bursa."[165] It is no coincidence that one encounters examples like the following in the correspondence between army commanders: "I request that the women be excluded from the oppressive measures that you have adopted, and that the punishments of exile and banishment not be applied to the womenfolk."[166]

Another important reason for the Muslim uprisings lay in the social character of the National Forces. They were largely composed of bandits who roamed the mountains, military deserters, criminals on the lam, released convicts and adventurers interested in plunder.[167] "They intimidated, frightened and plundered the population; they carried out actions calamitous for the local population."[168] This brutality of the National Forces was one of the causes of the Bozkır revolt that erupted in September 1919. The local villagers only ended their uprising when the government promised not to send any persons or units of the National Forces to the region.[169]

The 1920-23 struggle against British and French occupation and Greek and Armenian territorial claims—later known as the Turkish War of Independence—was, to a great extent, an attempt to establish an independent Turkish national state based on the principles of the National Pact, which called for the preservation of the six eastern provinces of Anatolia. The Armenians, in accordance with promises made by the Allied Powers, claimed these provinces as their own, and indeed the Istanbul government had been willing to negotiate over them. The nationalists' approach to the question of the genocide, therefore, was governed solely by the determination to maintain control of these areas. It is no coincidence that the first appearance of the local nationalist defense committees, which were the seeds of the National Movement, was in these eastern regions or that the first nationalist congress took place in Erzurum.

Responding to a declaration of the Istanbul government stating its willingness to cede these lands to Armenia, Mustafa Kemal said,

> although the government may have no alternative but to bow its head to this grievous obligation, the nation has declare[d] to the world, through the decisions at the Erzurum and Sivas Congresses, that it will not abandon an inch of land to Armenia, and that it claims its own lawful rights in its defense.[170]

Despite Mustafa Kemal's clear attitude toward the question of land in eastern Anatolia, the ranks of the National Movement debated the issue, at least in its early period. This question was included in the first talks with the Bolsheviks after the revolution. Halil Kut Paşa and Cemal Paşa, who spoke on behalf of the National Movement, claimed during their 1919 meeting in Moscow they had received instructions from Mustafa Kemal himself that certain areas of Van and Bitlis Provinces would be ceded to the Armenians.[171] This was the postwar position of some of the former CUP leaders, but whether this was a directive from Ankara is doubtful. The willingness of CUP leaders in Moscow to hand these areas over to the Armenian Republic caused a serious diplomatic problem. In the end, Turkish chief of staff İsmet İnönü surveyed army officers by telegram on 14 October 1919, on the issue of leaving the Van and Bitlis regions. The idea was vehemently rejected. The parliament in Ankara then rejected any compromise on the land issue.[172] With the Turkish defeat of Armenia in December 1920, the land issue resolved itself.[173]

Generally, the existence of the Armenian Republic was seen by Ankara as the greatest "threat" to its own survival. Kâzım Karabekir said that this state "in its current form and in the future remains as a disaster," and his suggestion to Ankara was an immediate occupation of Armenian territories.[174] The Ankara government defined its relationship to the Armenian Republic as "at war" according to international law. Since Turkey had concluded no peace agreements with any of the Caucasian republics at the time, it is significant that it never used this legalistic argument against Azerbaijan or Georgia. They "did not set themselves to basely exploit our (the Turks') weakness following the armistice, or to again [commence with] hostile actions." As for the attitude toward the Armenians, it was a war "which continued, in both the legal and the active sense."[175]

From Ankara's vantage point, the new Republic of Armenia was dangerous not only because it desired to include the eastern provinces, but also because of its ambition for a "Greater Armenia," which included Cilicia. The new parliament in Yerevan made a decision on 28 May 1919, known as the "Act of United Armenia," which declared the intention to "unify and liberate the ancestral lands located in Transcaucasia and the Ottoman Empire."[176] The means would be the "annexation of Turkish Armenia" and this was nothing less than a "declaration of war to the Turks.[177] The seven provinces of Van, Bitlis, Harput, Diyarbakır, Sivas, Erzurum and Trabzon "would be merged with the Armenian Republic."[178]

A "bifurcated" approach to Armenia was evident in Ankara's policies during this time, one primarily for public consumption and one only for internal discussion. In public, Ankara declared that it "positively" received the establishment of an Armenian state beyond Ottoman borders. Mustafa Kemal's speeches follow this line; for instance, he expressed the official position, saying that Ankara "looks favorably upon an Armenia established beyond the Ottoman borders."[179] Additionally, there are a number of speeches given by Kemal before secret sessions of the Turkish parliament that support this view. "We recognize the independence of those Armenians who have founded and formed the Armenian Republic. . . ."[180]

While repeating this line in November 1920, Foreign Minister Ahmet Muhtar sent his counterpart in the Armenian Republic a response to terms for a proposed peace treaty between the two countries. It read: "Turkey vows to provide all manner of facilitation within its power to secure the development of [its] neighboring nations with independence and security." However, in a secret internal correspondence, he instructed the commander of the Eastern Army, Karabekir Paşa, that "it was of the utmost necessity that Armenia be both politically and physically eliminated." But the implementation of this principle was dependent upon "our strength and the overall political situation."[181] To this second, coded message the minister added: "These instructions, which represent the true aim of the cabinet, are confidential. They are only meant for you personally."[182]

After sending these telegrams, the foreign minister, Ahmet Muhtar, gave a speech before a secret session of the Turkish parliament that justified the secret Armenian policy and clarified what the government meant by "elimination." The goal was to eliminate the threat, not the nation.[183] Clearly this statement is open to interpretation. If one believes the minister's argument, it is not terribly different from the stated policy of acceptance of an Armenian state. However, this acceptance required the Armenian state to refrain from demanding any territory that had been part of the Ottoman Empire. It is also clear that despite the minister's comments, Ankara viewed the mere existence of an Armenian state as a serious threat and formulated its policies accordingly.

For the National Movement the massacres of the Muslims on the Eastern Front were far more critical than the "ancient history" of the genocide. Thus, whenever the question of the genocide came up, it was raised in tandem with the subject of massacres perpetrated by the Armenians themselves.

In their communications, the nationalists frequently referred to the killings of Muslims. In a cable Mustafa Kemal mentioned that "elimination by massacre of the Muslims in Maraş at the hands of the French and Armenians continues and is reaching frightening dimensions."[184] Ankara went so far as to organize a propaganda campaign that mentioned Muslim massacres whenever the Armenian case was raised, especially in Europe. A campaign abroad regarding the massacres perpetrated against the Armenians by the Turks was countered with a plan "that . . . would . . . eliminate the effect through a counter-campaign." Kemal "requested that a list be made up, complete with documentation, of all of the Armenian crimes, without exception. . . . All the atrocities and offenses that the Christians . . . deemed suitable [to inflict on] the Muslims should be reported in detail."[185]

Within this context, the genocide was always considered irrelevant since it happened in the past. In a speech at a secret parliamentary session on 24 April 1920, Mustafa Kemal spoke of the massacres of Muslims being carried out "within the area [controlled by] the Government of Armenia," and mentioned the genocide as "an incident which was *in any case* perpetrated during the World War."[186] What was most significant for the Turks was that Muslims were then being killed. "The Armenians . . . are perpetrating extraordinary oppression and persecution and perpetrating massacres against the Muslim peoples."[187] In short, any discussion of the Armenian genocide was overshadowed by the ongoing war with the newly founded Republic of Armenia and by the cycle of massacres in the region; thus it was approached as an issue that had lost its immediacy and importance.

At the same time, the nationalists were influenced by the steady stream of accusations that the movement was essentially a Unionist reincarnation, and would therefore carry out more massacres against Christians. They were very aware that their actions were under observation and positive results at the Paris Peace Conference depended on foreign assessments of their intentions.

Since the European community was convinced that the nationalists were Unionists in disguise, it was no easy task to persuade them otherwise. The press was full of such opinions. "The movement of M. Kemal is Unionist in its essence. . . . He [M. Kemal] . . . has inherited the spirit of the Union and Progress. . . . "[188] A London *Times* correspondent reported that the CUP existed "almost intact."[189] This conviction repeatedly appears in the reports sent by British officers serving in Anatolia at the time. The author of one British intelligence report wrote, "Having had the opportunity of closely watching the proceedings at the Congress held at Balikessir [Balıkesir] and coming into touch with a good many of the leaders, I am today more than ever convinced that the Committee of Union and Progress is at the bottom of this Nationalist Movement, whatever may be said to the contrary. I have personally satisfied myself that about three-fourths of the leaders I have come across are old Committee of Union and Progress members."[190]

The Istanbul government and the Armenian patriarchate played significant roles in encouraging this opinion of the Ankara movement. Damat Ferid Paşa frequently accused the Anatolian movement of being "Neo-Unionist." "Mustafa Kemal," he claimed, was "an employee of the CUP."[191] The leitmotif in much of the Istanbul press's criticism of Ankara was that it was Unionist, even Pan-Turkic.[192] In some articles it was even claimed that the Istanbul governments were under Unionist control.[193]

In addition to the accusation of Unionism, the crucial assumption was that the Nationalist Movement was planning future massacres of the non-Muslim population. The congress in Erzurum was seen to be "plotting to eliminate the Armenians," and "making preparations for a general massacre."[194] It was believed there would be a second campaign of annihilation against the Armenians, and that the Erzurum Congress had been convened for this purpose.[195]

In April 1919, the British *Daily Mail* reported that "the Christians of the East are afraid that they will be massacred on a large scale when the Peace Conference decisions are announced."[196] There were also similar reports in the rest of the Western press. In February 1919, for instance, the *Journal des débats* reported that "the massacres and brutal mistreatment, all manner of oppression of the Christians continues in the villages." In mid-February 1919, *Le Temps* reported that "the Union and Progress Party is continuing its labors in Anatolia. . . . The aim is to eliminate the Christian land owners. A new massacre is in the works."[197] Almost every day, without exception, the dailies carried headlines proclaiming "Turkish Atrocities in Asia Minor," "The Killing of the Greeks by the Turks," "Brutal Treatment Meted Out to the Greeks in Thrace," "The Killing of Greek Children in Aydın," and such.

After the massacres against the Armenians of Maraş and the surrounding area in the spring of 1920 (February–May), British opposition circles began claiming that Mustafa Kemal possessed a national program that consisted of killing all of the Christians residing in Cilicia.[198] The patriarchate tried to influence attitudes toward the nationalists, saying: "The Turkish army . . . is making preparations to kill the Armenians of the Caucasus. . . . The threat is serious, you must intervene" and "[t]he Christians are confronted by a new massacre."[199]

Well aware of these persistent attitudes, Ankara used all means at its disposal to counter these accusations. In his report, General Harbord writes:

> Mustafa Kemal Paşa has assured me in no uncertain terms that this National Movement will not result in assaults and displays of violence against non-Muslims. He also said that he would publish a declaration in order to dispel the fear of this and the despair into

which the Armenian citizens have fallen, and has followed through on his promise by publishing such.[200]

Mustafa Kemal informed Kâzım Karabekir about his correspondence with Harbord.

> Upon his request we spoke in complete privacy for three or four hours. . . . In the lengthy and detailed responses that were given to the questions he asked, the following points were expounded. . . . 4) We have no untoward plans against the Armenians, just as there are none against any of the non-Muslim communities living within our country. On the contrary, we are completely respectful of all of their various civil rights. Rumors to the contrary are the result of meddling and British misrepresentations.

To Harbord's claims that "there were rumors circulating that efforts were underway to bring about the aims of Pan-Turkism," Kemal said in response that "this was utterly baseless and unfounded."[201] In accordance with their understanding, a memorandum was delivered to Harbord on 24 September 1919, which, in addition to repudiating any connection to Unionism, contained the following promise in regard to the Christians:

> We have no other opinion or sentiment regarding our non-Muslim fellow citizens (Armenians, Greeks, Jews, etc.), with whom we have dwelt together for a great length of time, than to foster the best intentions and sincere feelings and to consider them on a level of complete equality with us.[202]

Harbord reported that Mustafa Kemal gave a statement on 15 October that "we [the nationalists] guarantee no new Turkish violence against the Armenians will take place."[203] During this same period, Kemal made similar promises in interviews given to the American Radio Gazette: "We have no plans for expansion whatsoever. . . . We give a guarantee that there shall be no new atrocities against the Armenians,"[204] and to the Turkish papers as well: "The national organization harbors no ill will or ulterior motives toward the non-Muslim elements."[205]

The Representative Council constituted at the Sivas Congress adopted many resolutions stating that such charges were groundless. On 16 September 1919, for instance, "It was decided that a general circular should be composed stating that the national organization was not opposed to non-Muslims and foreigners," and eight days later, another decision was made that a written declaration should be delivered to the commissioners of the Entente Powers and to the embassies of neutral countries stating that "the National Movements were not opposed to the non-Muslim nations."[206]

Despite the Turks' attempts to appear tolerant, massacres had been carried out in the Maraş region in the first two months of 1920, which was one of the factors in the British decision to occupy Istanbul on 16 March of that year. While speaking of the necessity of occupying Istanbul at the Paris Peace Conference, Lord Curzon placed at the top of his list of reasons the need to punish the Turks for the Maraş massacres.[207] In the first general circular to be issued after the Allied Powers' occupation of Istanbul, the Ankara regime took up the matter of Maraş. It stated that "the humane treatment that we have shown toward the Christian population living within our country is of great importance," and added that those who mistreated the Christians "would be punished most severely."[208]

In a speech made in the Turkish National Assembly the following year, Mustafa Kemal mentioned this circular as an important event among the achievements of the National Movement in preventing violence against its non-Muslim citizens.

> We have viewed it as a crucial civilizing task to ensure the safety of those Armenians dwelling within our country from any sort of assault. . . . We have informed all of the offices of state of the need to safeguard the well-being of the Armenian population. . . . Not a single Armenian has been subjected to any sort of violent assault whatsoever, even though they have not enjoyed the protection of any foreign power: this is a significant point that should shame intriguing Europe. . . . [209]

However, as we have seen, the National Movement had many members who had indirectly profited from the genocide or even directly participated. Of these members, one group comprised the newly emergent class in Anatolia of people who had reaped great financial profit from the genocide. These new "notables," having grown rich on the abandoned property of the deportees, were fearful that returning Armenians might take revenge or demand their property back, encouraged by Allied plans for the region. Then there were the former members of the CUP and the Special Organization, who, with or without an official connection to Karakol, the CUP successor, had fled to Anatolia to evade arrest by the British, and once there, filled the ranks of the National Forces.[210]

Despite the relative failure of the Istanbul government's attempts to relocate and compensate Armenian deportees, the fear of Armenian volunteer units in the areas under the control of the occupational forces was sufficient to frighten the nouveau riche. In Cilicia the French forces that arrived in this region at the end of 1918 were accompanied by a special Armenian Legion composed of four hundred soldiers;[211] in fact, the first shot in the Turkish War of Independence was fired against these Armenians.[212] After the acts of revenge turned to killing on 10 January 1919, the ensuing uproar was only stilled through British intervention. The French authorities were compelled to disband the legion.[213]

In an agreement made between the French and the British on 15 September 1919, French military units and Armenian volunteers assumed control of the cities of Maraş, Urfa and Antep. Armenians throughout Anatolia who felt unsafe had also begun migrating into Cilicia. The Istanbul government decided on 26 October 1919 that this southward migration of Armenians from the rest of Anatolia should be stopped.[214] In response, on 27 November, "the High Commissioners of the Entente [countries] . . . decided that [the Ottoman Government] would not be allowed to prevent the migration."[215] According to French sources, "some 12,000 Armenians had resettled in the southern provinces by the end of 1919."[216] Those Armenians began to take back property that had been confiscated or seized, and to take the women who had been forcibly converted to Islam and reconvert them to Christianity.[217]

This specter of returning Armenians motivated the newly rich class to support the nationalists. In the words of Turkish historian Doğan Avcıoğlu: "While the common people feared that atrocities would be perpetrated against them by returning Armenians thirsting for revenge, the notables feared not only for their lives but also for their property."[218]

It is significant that during the British occupation of Cilicia there was no Turkish opposition to the foreign presence or support for the Nationalist Movement. This changed when Britain turned the region over to the French forces and the Armenians began to return in October 1919. "The British occupying forces treat the Turks well in Maraş" because the official in charge of political affairs, who was a Muslim soldier from the Indian subcontinent, would repeatedly turn away Armenians who appealed to him to get back their properties, saying, "We have come here to preserve peace and order; the place for your request is the official offices of the Ottoman Government. Go there to appeal."[219] For this reason, the region's prominent Muslim individuals sent no delegation to the Erzurum and Sivas congresses organized by the national resistance.

Many recent works identify this connection between those who benefited from plundering Armenians and the Turkish national movement. As one author writes:

> The transfer of the property of deported Armenians . . . to Turkish notables, and their status as "accomplices" of the Unionist [regime] in this crime were significant factors in frightening this class and therefore causing them to draw closer to the government in Ankara.[220]

It is therefore no coincidence that many of the newly rich were among the leadership of the Defense of Rights associations throughout Anatolia. Doğan Avcıoğlu provides the following profile for Erzurum:

> Hilmi, a member of the Unionist Central Committee, Ebulhindili Cafer . . . who had grown rich through the Armenian deportations, and Deli Halit Paşa, a member of the Special Organization . . . were all members of this organization.[221]

Those serving under Mustafa Kemal also included a number of people who had grown rich from the Armenian genocide. One of these was Topal Osman, who would later become commander of

Kemal's special "Bodyguard Regiment." Another was Ali Cenani, a former Unionist deported to Malta by the British. He later served as minister of trade and commerce in the republic.

Ali Şükrü, an opposition deputy from Trabzon, spoke in the National Assembly in Ankara on 6 December 1920, admonishing the other deputies: "Look at what happened to the property left by the deportees when the country was saved . . . it is still in the possession of those who seized it."[222] It thus becomes easy to see why measures taken by the Istanbul government between 1918 and 1919 to return this property to its rightful owners—even if these measures were only for show—were eventually abrogated (14 September 1922) by the new regime in Ankara.[223]

By examining the members of the National Forces and the Defense of Rights Committees, we can see a close connection between the guiding forces of the Turkish War of Independence and the Armenian genocide. As we have seen, a significant portion of the National forces units were founded by members of the Special Organization, who were sought in connection with their role in the deportation of Greeks and Armenians during the war.[224] In the Marmara region, the founders of the National Forces included Dayı Mesut, Kara Arslan and İpsiz Recep, all of whom had hidden to avoid arrest and then established armed gangs. Special Organization member Yenibahçeli Şükrü Oğuz began to consolidate these gangs, receiving the directive for such an effort from Karakol founder Kara Kemal: "Through this directive the first armed forces were established in Kocaeli through the efforts of . . . Yenibahçeli Şükrü, Dayı Mesut [Gürbüz], Fehmi Yavuz, Bafra Gendarmerie Commander Nail, Hulusi and Demir Beys."[225]

A similar situation existed in the Black Sea region, where Topal Osman was sought for his role in the Armenian genocide in the Trabzon area. Not only had he been a central figure in the deportations and massacres, but he had greatly enriched himself as a result—the main reason he fled to the mountains after the armistice and gathered a gang of outlaws.[226]

Apart from Topal Osman, other prominent organizers of the national resistance in the area were Lieutenant Colonel Deli Halit, who assembled the Ardahan Congress on 7 January 1919,[227] and Yahya Kaptan and Ahmet Barutçu, founders of the Trabzon Organization for the Defense of National Rights. All of these had played decisive roles in the Armenian genocide and were members of the Special Organization.[228]

Similarly in the Aegean region, those who organized the earliest resistance to the Greeks and formed National Forces units had connections to the genocide. Former Izmir chief of police Hacım Muhittin, a member of the Special Organization, led most of the congresses organized in western Anatolia. Kazım Bey, the army commander in western Anatolia, had also been a member. In addition to organizing the congresses, these men distributed the program of the Karakol movement.[229] In his memoirs, Celal Bayar, later president of the Turkish Republic, at the time a prominent Unionist leader in Izmir, recalled that

> the former gendarmerie regiment commander Colonel Avni Bey (and later parliamentary Deputy for Cebel-i Bereket, Avni Paşa) was suspected in the deportation of Armenians from Adana. He was in hiding because they were looking for him. The gendarmerie Sergeant Edip Bey (he would later take the name Sarı Efe Edip) also withdrew from the public eye because he was being followed. The government was making concerted efforts to find both of them.[230]

Bayar himself was also sought for his role in the deportations. He recalls that in March 1919 he decided, together with the gendarmerie officers, to flee to the inner provinces of the Aegean region to join the resistance to the likely Greek occupation.[231] Süleyman Sururi, a sergeant in the Special Organization, Serezli Parti Pehlivan, and district official Köprülü Hamdi Bey, are but a few who played critical roles in the Aegean resistance.[232]

The story of Halit Paşa reveals Mustafa Kemal's attitude toward some of those responsible for the genocide. In hiding to avoid arrest, Halit Paşa nonetheless continued to lead his division, as per the understanding between him and the commander of the Fifteenth Army, Kâzım Karabekir. Mustafa Kemal deemed this arrangement inappropriate, and demanded that Halit Paşa carry out this role publicly. Summoning Halit, Kemal gave him the title "Commander of the National Forces for Trabzon and its Environs."[233] He later explained this move:

It was necessary for two reasons. The first and most important was the need to raise morale by showing Istanbul that its summons would not be observed, and by showing the nation—and the army, in particular—that they had no need to fear or hide away.[234]

Essentially, Kemal wanted those involved in the deportations and genocide to stop hiding and to join the National Movement.

When he began to organize and coordinate the revolt in Anatolia, Mustafa Kemal received great assistance from former Unionists sought for their involvement in war crimes. Doğan Avcıoğlu gives one example:

Atatürk received support from Küçük Kâzım, one of the Unionist *fedaîs* who had been thoroughly involved in the Armenian massacres. . . . He also appealed to Halis Turgut, who was guilty of both crimes against the Armenians and of Unionism and was being sought [by the authorities]; he had fled to the mountains.[235]

People involved in Unionist and/or Special Organization activities and now being pursued proved an important source of manpower for the National Forces. In short, Mustafa Kemal

led the struggle for independence . . . by relying on those . . . who had been forced into resistance by Greek and Armenian vengeance, and on Unionists who were being legally prosecuted for the Greek and Armenian incidents.[236]

Flight to inner Anatolia and to the national resistance was for these members a vital necessity. The only other alternatives were surrender or eventual capture, both of which would result in severe punishment, quite possibly execution. Journalist and confidant of Mustafa Kemal, Falih Rıfkı Atay, gave a succinct depiction of the situation: "With the end of the war the British and their allies would begin to demand an accounting from the Unionists and for the Armenian murders, so whoever was the object of even the slightest hint of suspicion armed themselves and joined a gang."[237]

Thus it is quite difficult to speak of Mustafa Kemal and a single attitude toward the Armenian genocide. He generally called it a "massacre" organized by "a small committee that had seized control of the government." He often gave speeches in which he both criticized the events and minimized their importance. He did not see the question as a matter of the first order. For Kemal, the most pressing matter was the establishment of an independent Turkish state on the basis of the borders at the time of the armistice. The criminal prosecution of those who perpetrated the crimes were, in his words, "a detail." He spoke openly about this while visiting his comrades at the Bekirağa prison:

> The matter of the arrests and trials of the Bekirağa prison detainees is the simplest of things to resolve. The basic problem that has to be solved is the future existence of the state, which is presently in danger. As soon as this fundamental question is resolved . . . a very simple little detail like the Bekirağa prison odyssey will disappear by itself.[238]

For Kemal, the emerging Armenian state threatened Turkey. Immediately after landing at Samsun he warned Erzurum of the increased danger arising with British support.[239] Such a development had to be prevented at all costs.[240]

Aware of the gravity of accusations of genocide, he approached the issue with a great deal of caution and sensitivity, especially when meeting representatives of Western states. He admitted, for instance, in a conversation with General Harbord that some eight hundred thousand Armenians had been killed. Harbord later said that "he was also disapproving of the Armenian massacres."[241] What is most significant here is that Kemal confirmed the official Ottoman position on the number of Armenian deaths, given on 13 March 1919 by the Ottoman interior minister, Cemal, which had provoked an eruption of controversy. But Kemal continued to insist that "the killing and expulsion of the Armenians [was] the work of a small committee that had seized control of the government."[242]

Speaking with foreign journalists, he made rather progressive demands on the issue of punishing the guilty. Kemal "attacked the Unionist leaders. He accused them [as responsible] and said it would be right to hang them for their deeds. What were the Allied Powers waiting for before hanging these scoundrels?"[243] He continued to express this attitude. In 1926 he said, "These leftovers from the former Young Turk

Party, who should have been brought to account for the lives of millions of our Christian subjects ruthlessly driven *en masse* from their homes and massacred, have been agitating under republican rule."[244]

Kemal's attitude was slightly different when he spoke in the Turkish parliament, as in one lengthy speech he gave on 24 April 1920. While he condemned the genocide, he spoke of it as "shameful acts belonging to the past." He leveled particularly scathing criticism of British claims "that catastrophes like this were still being carried out."[245] On 6 May 1920, in a cable he sent to Kâzım Karabekir in connection with foreign policy, he repeated this opinion. He feared that Western powers would accuse the Turks of "committing massacres" in the inevitable war with Armenia. He even proposed delaying an army offensive against the Armenian republic to avoid this accusation.

> Just as the Armenian incidents were among the most important factors turning the entire Christian world against us, eliminating the Armenian government through the power of our army . . . naturally means a renewed massacre of Armenians. . . . Our army is at present being very careful to avoid any official or public attack or hostile action. . . . [246]

Yet, despite his indictment of the old CUP leadership and distancing himself from the genocide, Kemal also held the foreign powers and the Armenians themselves responsible and he tried to focus attention on Armenian massacres of Muslims. To General Harbord he argued that mass killings "are occurring in America, France, and England as well, but only Turkey is held accountable for the massacre of 800,000 of its own citizens."[247] According to Kemal, "foreign intrigues caused the calamities that occurred in Turkey."[248] In a speech to a group of prominent Ankara residents he said that "whatever happened to the non-Muslim communities living in our country, it is the result of partition politics that they themselves, swept away by foreign intrigues and abusing their privileges, pursued in a most brutal manner."[249] His words are eerily reminiscent of Talât Paşa's only a short time earlier: "The responsibility for the events belongs first and foremost to those who brought them about."[250] İsmet İnönü, chief negotiator and later second president of the republic, expressed similar sentiments, and over time, this view was adopted as the "official" Turkish version, and would be often repeated.

The clearest expression of Mustafa Kemal's views on the Armenian genocide, however, is evident in the call to punish the perpetrators in the Amasya Protocols, and in the discussions he held with the Istanbul government prior to their signing. But behind his condemnation and his insistence on punishment, in both his private correspondence and in the protocols themselves, we can see the specter of the Paris Peace Conference and the future of the Turkish state. The Amasya Protocols' demands were accepted by Ankara because it knew that "both the Entente States and non-Muslim citizens oppose [the policies of the CUP]. . . . " Any resistance to the process of justice would, Kemal realized, "inevitably bring disaster upon the homeland" and so he acted to prevent the "opposition and intervention that would be against us."[251] The important point is that there was not one single special initiative on the subject that came from the movement in Ankara. It was the Istanbul government that continually brought up the issue and discussed it. One example is the statement of purpose published by Ali Rıza Paşa's newly formed government, which was deemed inadequate by the Istanbul parliament. The deputies called for more extensive explanations, including a condemnation of the Armenian massacres.[252]

This unenthusiastic attitude is also evident in Ankara's internal political debates. The deportations and massacres of 1915–17 are never discussed in detail. On the contrary, there appears to be an almost conscientious effort not to take up the question. In Kemal's speech to prominent figures of Ankara, he mentioned the genocide as "certain situations unworthy of mention, which accrued in Turkey." Nevertheless, this situation "demands a thorough explanation and apology." Furthermore, "we are clearly suggesting that the situation was not even half the scale as things that were done without apology in the states of Europe. In short, such events may well have transpired, but there are good explanations for them." Kemal goes on in this speech to criticize the Western powers, who, by means of the Armenian massacres, have accused the nation of "incompetence . . . and cruelty." These two charges, he said, were "sheer calumny," because "ours is the only nation that has respected the religions and nationhood of other peoples." He then went on to provide examples of the special rights accorded to Ottoman Christians and how they had prospered as a result, and declared that whatever had happened to the Armenians, it had resulted from their own actions and he was therefore unable to hold Muslims responsible.[253]

In Kemal's approach to this issue, three aspects emerge as noteworthy: First, when speaking to representatives of foreign powers or the Ottoman government in Istanbul, his emphasis differed from his internal political discussions. This difference is starkly illustrated in speeches, both public and closed, in the National Assembly in Ankara. Second, Mustafa Kemal preferred to touch on the subject of the Armenian genocide as little as possible. When it was unavoidable, he would pass over it quickly with a brief condemnation of the events and move on to the Armenians' current assaults. Third, he was sharply opposed to the issue being used as a tool of political pressure. In his parliamentary speech where he mentions the genocide as "shameful acts belonging to the past," he only touches on the subject to answer British accusations regarding massacres still going on.[254] For him, the central objective was always Turkish independence in the sovereign Ottoman territory set down in the armistice agreement.

Nevertheless, his condemnation of the Armenian calamities is noteworthy. Although Mustafa Kemal was surrounded by Unionists and though the national struggle he waged relied on the organizational and personal support of the Union and Progress Party, he did not refrain from calling the 1915 genocide "a shameful act," even in a closed session of parliament. He was not required to make such declarations in closed parliamentary sessions. His longsighted conviction that the new Turkish Republic should be free of the taint, both political and moral, of this "shameful act" could serve as an important model for Turkey today.

CHAPTER 9

THE FINAL PHASE OF THE TRIALS

THE INITIAL POSITION OF THE NATIONAL MOVEMENT, CONDEMNING the massacres and favoring trials for those involved, soon gave way to a more equivocal stance, even to the extent of protecting suspects from prosecution. This was due to two major developments. The first was the Treaty of Sèvres, 10 August 1920, and its implicit understanding that Anatolia was to be partitioned among the Great Powers and then any remaining territories among the Kurds, Armenians, Greeks, and Turks. The prosecution of war crimes suspects was thus no longer justifiable as the necessary price to be paid for the promise of a new state conserved along the lines of the National Pact. The second development was that the military court in Istanbul began to pass death sentences on the leaders of the National Movement.

Prior to the full British occupation of Istanbul in March 1920, pronationalist members of the Istanbul government had succeeded in slowing the process of prosecutions. But on 5 April, Damat Ferid Paşa again became grand vizier and the arrest and imprisonment of massacre suspects resumed in earnest. Fourteen suspects were sent to

Malta in May. With the signing of the Sèvres Treaty, "the hunt for suspects in the massacre of Christians was accelerated."[1]

At the same time, the struggle between the Istanbul and Ankara governments turned violent. Istanbul begin to marshal armed units to counter Ankara's National Forces. These were led by former Special Organization member Ahmet Anzavur.[2] On 11 April, the Şeyhülislam Dürrizade Abdullah Efendi, the highest religious authority, published fatwas condemning the National Forces as infidels, sanctioning their murder.[3] The Istanbul government further established a special military group called the Forces of Order (Kuva-yı İnzibatiye), under the command of General Şefik Paşa, with the specific objective of eliminating the National Forces.[4] Meanwhile, Damat Ferid Paşa was handing the British lists of names of the various leaders of the Anatolian movement.

The polarization between Ankara and Istanbul intensified. While the Ankara center opposed the division of Anatolia, the Istanbul government, which had signed the Treaty of Sèvres, had already consented to plans for its partition and also remained committed to punishing those suspected of war crimes and massacres. Then the Istanbul courts and legal bodies originally set up for that purpose turned their attention to the leaders of the Anatolian movement. Sixteen people with links to the National Forces were sentenced to death and four were eventually executed on 12 June 1920, for attempting to assassinate Damat Ferid Paşa. According to İ. M. K. İnal,

> Dramalı Rıza Bey, ex-Naval Captain Halil İbrahim Efendi, Mehmed Ali Bey, the official for the Doğancılar neighborhood (within the Üsküdar Municipality), and Tevfik Sükuti Bey, the first commissioner of the Finance Ministry's personnel budget, were all among those accused of conspiring to murder [Damat] Ferid Paşa and Ali Kemal Bey, the ex-minister of interior, and of belonging to an extensive clandestine organization. . . . They were sentenced to death . . . hanged on the morning of [12 June 1920] in Beyazıt Square.[5]

One of the four, Tevfik Sükuti, was a member of the Karakol and it was alleged that the assassination plot had been ordered from Ankara.[6] The same court tried Mustafa Kemal in absentia along with other leading nationalists and sentenced them to death. Overall, one hundred death sentences were imposed and a list of those convicted was published in *Takvîm-i Vekâyi*.[7] These trials succeeded in blurring the line between two distinct issues, the first being national sovereignty and second punishment for the massacres, and thus led the Ankara government to act to protect war crimes suspects as well as its own members.

Meanwhile, the military courts continued hearing cases of suspects in the massacre. On 20 July 1920 the prefect of Urfa, Nusret Bey, was sentenced to death and on 22 July, Abdullah Avni, Erzincan gendarmerie officer, was executed.[8] On 5 August, Nusret Bey was hanged in Beyazıt Square.

Although the Istanbul government had blurred the crime of participation in the National Movement with the crimes of the genocide, it is incorrect to conclude that all members of the Ankara center were guilty of genocide or that most in Istanbul were innocent. Both factions included some participants in the events of 1915. Among those who joined in the 1920 rebellion against Ankara included past members of the Special Organization.[9]

The Treaty of Sèvres put an ultimate end to the Nationalist Movement's tolerance of the trials. There was no longer any reason to soften its stance to achieve more favorable conditions from Europe. Mustafa Kemal wrote that he would exploit every opportunity and do whatever was necessary to save those arrested by the British and suspected of massacres "from the dungeons of Malta."[10]

After the Allied occupation of Istanbul on 16 March 1920, and the full split between the Istanbul and Ankara governments, Ankara moved to invalidate Damat Ferid Paşa's cabinet decrees. On 7 June, the Ankara government approved Law Number 7, which declared the Istanbul government illegal as well as all agreements that it already had and might make, unless approved by Ankara, retroactive to 16 March 1920.[11]

Once the parliament in Ankara declared itself the legal and legitimate successor to the parliament in Istanbul, it also began to undo decisions pertaining to the massacre and war crimes trials. The first move in this direction had come earlier, on 29 April, when the Ankara government demanded the release of all prisoners being held by the military courts in Ankara itself, arguing that the dossiers for these prisoners had been sent to the appeals court in Istanbul, which had never responded.[12] Then an amnesty proposal was examined on 11

May by the assembly and subsequently sent to the cabinet. However, the amnesty excluded those prisoners released in April who had been convicted of massacres. In any case, the proposal was rejected. At the same session of the assembly, Mustafa Kemal announced the government's decision that "those under arrest for crimes [connected to the] massacres are to be tried without detention."[13] The government had already decreed, three days earlier, on 8 May, to try these suspects without keeping them in custody. The decree stated that many people had used the deportations to further their own interests and that those who had behaved unlawfully would be punished, but that the decision had been adopted primarily to prevent further injustice.[14] Since most of the detainees were in Istanbul or Malta and thus out of nationalist control, the decision was largely a symbolic gesture made to state Ankara's attitude toward the massacres.

Another proposal was submitted on 21 July 1920 to revoke all rulings issued by the Istanbul extraordinary court-martial; however, the proposal was rejected since the assembly had already invalidated, revoked and annulled all Istanbul's decisions and decrees.[15] The final step came on 11 August 1920 when the Ankara government decided to abolish the courts altogether.[16] Previously, action had been taken to eliminate individual, regional courts. On 13 May, a proposal had been presented to the assembly for abolishing the court-martial in Çine.[17] On 31 July, another draft proposed closing the court-martial in Samsun.[18] Following the cabinet's decision of 11 August, the assembly examined these decisions one by one and decided to shut down all of the courts-martial.

The actions of the Ankara assembly were not confined merely to ending the prosecution of war criminals. In addition, a series of decisions were passed that clearly favored the suspects. One ordered the payment of salaries for the exiles in Malta;[19] another proclaimed the executed Kemal, the prefect of Boğazlıyan, and Nusret Bey, one of the defendants in the Bayburt trials, "national martyrs." On 12 August 1920, the day of Nusret's execution, he was declared a "glorious martyr" and the assembly stopped its proceedings for five minutes as a sign of respect.[20] It also arranged for salaries for the families of those sentenced to death. On 30 November 1920 a bill was drafted awarding a salary to Kemal's family and after passing through various committees the bill was accepted on 26 August 1922.[21] A similar bill for Nusret's family was introduced in parliament, which asked for the confirmation of a government decision from 7 October 1920. It passed on 25 December 1920 amid laudatory speeches about Nusret.[22] "A neighborhood, a school and an avenue in Urfa all still bear the name Mârtyr Nusret Bey."[23] Other bills were introduced to honor others of the defendants, which all ended in 1926 with a general law to give a pension, property and land to the twelve families of all the defendants and victims of Armenian revenge killings after the war, including Talât, Enver and Cemal.[24]

With regard to prisoners outside Ankara's control, in August 1920, the National Assembly had called on the cabinet to take firmer steps to prevent further executions. The urgent reason was that some detainees from Malta had been brought to Istanbul for trial and it was feared that they too would be executed. The Ankara Interior Ministry replied that "the British and the Istanbul government have been made aware that there are many reciprocal measures that will ensue if they take any actions such as this."[25] This warning was delivered in a letter written by Mustafa Kemal to the British headquarters in Istanbul on 12 August, two days after the Treaty of Sèvres was signed.

"The Ottoman government," the letter said, "continues to hang children of the homeland for allegations of deportation and massacre that have lost all meaning." The letter's language made it clear that such executions should only be carried out when they fulfilled a purpose. Meaningless executions should be stopped immediately. The letter also took note of reports that "fifteen of the Malta exiles have been brought to Istanbul to be handed over to the Istanbul government," and claimed that there were plans to have them executed, saying, "We have not a shred of doubt that the intention of the British is to surrender these hapless people to destruction at the hands of Damat Ferid Paşa and his henchmen."

The letter continued:

> ... should any of the detainees either already brought or yet to be brought to Istanbul be executed, even at the order of the vile Istanbul government, we would seriously consider executing all British prisoners in our custody.[26]

The threat paid off. No further death sentences were imposed. British military courts were similarly cautious. From then on the exiles' lives were guaranteed by the Ankara government even if they were prosecuted—which itself was difficult enough.

Damat Ferid Paşa's seventh and last cabinet collapsed on 17 October 1920, undermined by pressure from the Allies, who now sought to negotiate with Ankara. Thus the pro-nationalist Tevfik Paşa was returned to power. This dealt a fresh blow to the ever-diminishing stature of Istanbul courts-martial. On 7 December 1920, the panel of the first court-martial was changed. Its president, Nemrut Mustafa, and three other members, had been arrested on 14 November for irregularities involving Nusret's death sentence. On 10 December 1920, the court's new president, Hurşit Paşa, began to release prisoners, one after another.

On 9 December, the Supreme Military Court had begun to examine the issue of whether membership in the National Forces was a punishable offence. The Istanbul War Ministry issued a declaration on 16 April 1921 saying, "Collaborating with the National Forces is worthy of applause. Drop all such cases."[27] In fact, the military court had already begun releasing prisoners in February 1921. On 24 April, the Supreme Military Court ruled that:

> collaborating with the National Forces is not a crime. All property placed in [the government's] custody because of such an allegation must therefore be restored to its owners. . . . Incriminating the National Forces conflicts with the honorable duty of defending the homeland.[28]

Thus ended the prosecution of the National Forces, which had begun 11 May 1920 and had resulted in about one hundred death sentences, most of which were imposed in absentia.

On 24 April 1922, the last Istanbul government was forced to declare that it had no jurisdiction to try members of the National Forces. According to a newspaper report of 11 April 1922 no cases in fact remained before the court.[29] On 11 July of that year, it was reported that the government had abolished the extraordinary courts-martial.[30] After Istanbul was taken by the National Forces on 6 November 1922, the laws passed by the National Assembly in Ankara were extended to Istanbul and declared the new law of the land. The remnants of the conflict were resolved finally with the general amnesty announced at the Lausanne Conference in 1923.

As we have seen, the Ankara-based National Movement was not especially keen to prosecute crimes connected with the Armenian deportations and massacres. This owed much to the general hostility toward the Armenians, an attitude that is apparent in the National Assembly's speeches. The deputies expressed their animosity in both open and closed sessions.

During closed discussions on the border disputes between Moscow and Ankara, some deputies' speeches took on a defensive tone regarding the massacres—even justifying them. Deputy Hasan Fehmi said:

> This deportation business, as you know, has put the whole world in an uproar, and has branded us all as murderers. We knew even before this was done that the Christian world would not stand for it, and that they would turn their fury and hatred on us because of it. But why should we call ourselves murderers? Why have we gotten involved in so vast and intractable an affair? These things that were done were to secure the future of our homeland, which we hold more sacred and dear than our very lives.[31]

In the same session, Mazhar Müfit, a Hakkari deputy, likened the Armenians to a pig that had swallowed a diamond, and claimed that he would not hesitate to strangle them to retrieve it:

> It is not possible to give even an inch, Gentlemen. I am firmly convinced that Islam's wells of courage have not yet dried up. Yes, we have been defeated. But we have not been destroyed. And is it not impossible that one day we will rise again? It has been said, "Choose the lesser of two evils." Very well. Gentlemen, . . . I accept this "lesser of two evils" notion. Here is an example: If a pig swallowed a diamond, should you spare the diamond or spare the pig? That gem, that diamond must not be sacrificed to spare the Armenian swine.[32]

Another deputy, Salih Efendi, suggested that they sift out the Armenians and send them off to Yerevan.[33] Hüseyin Avni Bey, a deputy from Erzurum known for his liberal views, said:

> Your humble servant doesn't fear armed Armenians but the unarmed ones. The armed Armenians are the Dashnaks, and whenever they use their arms against us we have the power to crush them. But I fear those Armenians who wrap themselves in the red flag and work to corrupt and damage our country from within. This is certain to happen.

The root of the problem, as he saw it, was that "the Armenians are a scheming nation and they will try to destroy us from the inside."[34] Mustafa Kemal then took the floor and said, "Gentlemen, what Hüseyin Avni Bey said about the Armenians is absolutely true. And as we discuss this issue with the Russians, we are trying to bring this reality home to them. He is absolutely right."[35] This attitude dominated the assembly and even shaped policy toward the Armenian people.

Thus all attempts to try those suspected of war crimes had failed. Meanwhile, some 200 Turks were still being detained in Malta. What was to become of them? In which court were they to be tried? And according to what law? None of these issues had been resolved by the Treaty of Sèvres, so Britain decided to take the initiative and try the suspects itself. That effort also came to naught and the whole question had to await a deal between the British and the Ankara government.

Since they had expected a solution to the problem from the Paris Peace Conference, the British had compiled no indictments against the suspects. When they finally began to prepare indictments, there was disagreement over who had the authority to do so. The British high commissioner in Istanbul, whose office had overseen the arrests and deportation to Malta, claimed no such authority.[36] In his report, High Commissioner Calthorpe classified the exiles into three categories: those exiled during the war as a precautionary measure; those exiled for their part in the massacre of Christians; and those who had been arrested and exiled for mistreatment of British prisoners of war.[37]

Admiral de Robeck, who replaced Calthorpe as high commissioner, presented a report on 21 September 1919, in which he classified the Turks to be punished into four categories, according to where the suspects were at the time. Regarding the Malta exiles he had this to say: "The choice [to deport them to Malta] was made hastily and not based on known criminal acts, but rather general principles were applied."[38] On 6 December 1919 the high commissioner classified the Malta exiles in more precise fashion, according to their alleged offenses: "those accused of acts of gross injustice (massacre), 16 persons, former members of government who turned a blind eye to acts of injustice, 17 persons, and those who cannot be said to have had any part in this unjust policy (mostly members of parliament), 21 persons." This classification was not comprehensive because it included only fifty-four of the almost 200 exiles, focusing on those accused of involvement in the Armenian genocide.

Meanwhile, the Committee for the Investigation of War Crimes set up in the Office of the British Procurer General drew up another list of 37 names of those who had mistreated prisoners of war, based on the high comissioner's report. This list included both suspects who had not yet been captured and those already in Malta. On 2 January 1920, the War Office asked the Foreign Office to have the high commissioner draw up a report specifying these individuals' degree of guilt.

The high commissioner duly sent three lists to London on 12 February 1920: those who had committed acts of violence against British prisoners of war, 18 persons; those who had committed violence against the Christians of Turkey, 130 persons; and, those who had violated the terms of the armistice, 9 persons—totalling 157 prisoners.

These prisoners were to be handed over to the Allies after the signing of the Treaty of Sèvres so that they might be tried for their offenses. On 16 May 1920, seventeen more names were added to the list of those suspected of violence against the Armenians.[39] This list had been drawn up by the high commissioner's Armenian-Greek Section. Of the people on it, only nineteen or twenty were ultimately arrested, another was sentenced to death by the court-martial in Istanbul and executed, and two others were murdered.[40]

After the signing of the Sèvres Treaty, the British Foreign Office wrote to the procurer general asking for "information on the prosecution of individuals responsible for the Armenian massacre as provided for in Article 230 in the Turkish peace treaty." The answer was pithy: "Given the present situation of the Turkish peace treaty it is impossible to answer the question."

It is easy to determine whether or not a crime has been committed; the difficult part is finding the evidence to incriminate individuals. Documents must be found, analyzed, and classified according to the law. The Allies had a mountain of documents related to the Armenian genocide, but these were mostly general and did not clearly implicate specific individuals. So the problem of finding enough evidence to take individuals to court remained unresolved.

We have already seen that a large portion of the relevant documents had been destroyed or stolen, and there was no coordination between British and Turkish authorities. The British never requested incriminating documentation. "There was probably some evidence in the archives of the courts martial in Istanbul," wrote W. S. Edmonds of the Oriental Desk of the British Foreign Office, "but it was no doubt slipped out before we began to investigate."[41] Sir Lindsey-Smith, a British judge, expressed a similar conviction: "The Turkish government collected a considerable amount of incriminating evidence, but hoping to lay our hands on it is in vain."[42]

Even at the beginning of investigations, in August 1919, High Commissioner Calthorpe had said, "It is clear that there is no chance of collecting evidence against the majority of the suspects."[43] Admiral de Robeck was similarly concerned. "It would be hard under these conditions to convict most of the exiles before an Allied court.[44] Thus, the British ultimately gave up on the idea of prosecution and decided to hold the exiles as hostages against British prisoners of war. As to why the documents collected at the Istanbul military courts were not given to the British and why the British did not press for them, we have no answer.

One possible explanation was provided by Sir Horace Rumbold, the third high commissioner, who claimed that "since the Peace Treaty has not yet come into force, no pressure has been put on the Turkish government or [its] officials. That is why no Turkish official documents have been obtained."[45] This is rather difficult to comprehend, for even prior to the full occupation, the British were powerful enough to do whatever they wanted. Admiral Webb at the High Commissioner's Office wrote on 19 January 1919 that the British authorities

> have control over appointments to governorships, the press and the railways. They released Armenians and Greeks from prisons at will,[46] and rescued Armenian women and girls from Turkish houses, and laid their hands on everything.[47]

Why the British authorities, who had interfered in the appointments of ministers, who had drawn up lists of suspects and presented them to the government and, since March 1920, officially occupied Istanbul, failed to press for the surrender of such documents is totally incomprehensible.

Harry H. Lamb, a senior official in the Office of the High Commissioner, wrote a detailed report explaining why evidence had not been found. He listed the following difficulties:

1) It is impossible to obtain from the central government or the [provincial] governors any documents containing orders or instructions on this subject.

2) The Allied governments' hesitation in taking part in the trials of massacre suspects.

3) As can be seen from their answers to questions put to them by the High Commissioner, officials in the Near East are completely indifferent when it comes to this issue.

4) A large part of the male Armenian population in the provinces and almost all their intellectuals had been murdered.

5) Lack of public security means that people who could present evidence are afraid to come forward for fear of reprisals; the Allies' intentions in this respect are not trusted.

6) News is circulating that the Malta exiles will be released in the end.[48]

On 16 March 1921 High Commissioner Rumbold sent all the materials available on the Malta exiles along with preliminary indictments to London. "No evidence was obtained from any Allied or neutral country" for the reports, he stated, adding that "the main conduit was the Armenian patriarchate." Furthermore, the commissioner went on, because freedom of movement was restricted in Anatolia, few witnesses were able to come to Istanbul in order to testify.[49] Thus Rumbold confirmed Harry H. Lamb's points. Since the documents the British had obtained were simply not sufficient to go to court, they contacted the Americans, hoping they might possess a more comprehensive archive. On 21 March 1921, Lord Curzon telegrammed Sir Auckland Geddes, Britain's ambassador to the United States, and asked for supplementary documents.[50]

The U.S. State Department found in its archives 138 reports dating from 1915 to 1921 and covering the massacre, of which 60 were dispatches from the three American consuls who served in the region during the deportation and 78 were from diplomats at the American Embassy in Istanbul. Nevertheless, the answer to Lord Curzon's request was not encouraging. Although "the Americans do have a lot of documents on the deportation and massacre of the Armenians," Geddes replied, these documents "are more about the crimes committed than the people involved. . . . Looking at these documents, I doubt that they would be useful as evidence against the Turks held in Malta."[51]

In response to Geddes's assessment, a list of the Malta detainees was sent to Washington on 16 June 1921, with the request to seek concrete, incriminating evidence against any of them. The result was negative: "There is nothing in these documents that can be used as evidence against the Turks who are being held in Malta pending trial."[52] This news from America shattered all British hope for being able to bring the detainees to trial. On 29 July 1921, the British procurer general wrote a long letter to the Foreign Office explaining that the evidence in hand would not be enough to convict any of these individuals. "What can be understood from this letter," commented W. S. Edmond, "is that our chance of convicting any of the exiles is almost zero."[53] In a letter to the high commissioner in Istanbul on 10 August, Lord Curzon grumbled about his uncooperative allies, the French and Italians, regarding the formation of a court as stipulated under Article 230 of the Treaty of Sèvres.[54] The only course of action left was to strike a deal with the nationalist government in Ankara in order to arrange a prisoner exchange. Harry H. Lamb had already warned his government that this was likely to occur if there was no cooperation among the Allies.

As long as there is no sincere cooperation or desire for action among the Allies, the trials will come to nothing and the murder, directly or indirectly, of one million Christians will remain unpunished. I wish that, instead of this, the Allies had never made any declarations on this issue.[55]

The issue of the Malta prisoners frequently arose in talks between the British and the Ankara government. The Ankara government promised to try the war and genocide criminals in its own courts. The first promise came from Bekir Sami, the Turkish foreign minister, during discussions in London in March 1921. Lord Curzon reported that Bekir Sami

contrasted the situation of the German war crimes suspects with that of the Turkish suspects. . . . He tried to reassure me that they are ready to punish those [responsible for the] crimes . . . then he said that this task must be left to his government.[56]

However, it was decided in the London Agreement drafted in March 1921 that the British would try all the suspects. A stipulation was attached requiring Turkey to release all the British prisoners it held while the British would not release anyone involved in massacres against Armenians or who acted against British soldiers. It was this point that caused the Ankara government to reject the agreement because it would not give a foreign government jurisdiction over Turkish subjects.[57] In Mustafa Kemal's words, it was "nothing but the old requirement of the Sèvres Treaty" presented again.[58]

On 28 July 1921 Ankara foreign minister Yusuf Kemal Tengirşenk informed Lord Curzon "that the Allies had accepted Germany's right to try Germans accused of war crimes. Turkey's national pride required that she be given equal treatment as a sovereign nation."[59] The Turkish foreign minister's offer was a reciprocal release of prisoners.

Ankara's second promise to try the suspects was delivered by Safâ Bey, the foreign minister of the Istanbul government, on 11 June 1921. According to a Foreign Office record, "The Turkish Cabinet in Istanbul invited the British ambassador and proposed, in the name of the Turkish nationalists, the release of all the Malta exiles. He said that, as with the German detainees in Germany, the suspects would have to be tried before an impartial court in Ankara."[60]

Ankara's final promise came from its minister of the interior, Refet Bele on 14 September 1921:

> I have here a firm promise from Refet Paşa, the Interior Minister of the [the government in] Ankara . . . that the detainees will be marched from the port straight to their respective states where they will be tried for the crimes of which they are accused.[61]

In all these promises, Germany was cited as a precedent; the Turks said they would try their suspects on the model of the Leipzig trials. The agreement for the return of the Malta exiles was signed in Istanbul on 23 October 1921, and on 31 October, the exiles arrived in Turkey. Most of them moved to Ankara and were given posts in the nationalist government.

Many of those who had been under suspicion for crimes of war rose to occupy high-ranking positions in the Ankara government. Şükrü Kaya, who became both foreign and interior minister of the new Turkish Republic, as well as secretary-general of Mustafa Kemal's Republican People's Party, had been head of the office for the Settlement of Tribes and Immigrants. His department had been in charge of the Armenian deportations, which is why he was often referred to as the "dispatcher general."

Rössler, the German consul in Aleppo, mentioned him twice in his correspondence. On one occasion, the consul was trying to secure the release of some Armenians who had worked for the Germans. Şükrü told him: "You don't seem to understand what we want. We want an Armenia without Armenians."[62] A German engineer reported to Rössler that Şükrü had said, referring to the 1915 massacres: "The final result has to be the destruction of the Armenian race. This eruption is merely an open flare-up of the continuous struggle between Muslims and Armenians. The weaker side will be eliminated."[63]

Şükrü had been sent to Malta by the British, but on 6 September 1921 he escaped along with several other Unionists, making his way to Ankara to join the nationalists.

Another example is Mustafa Abdülhalik Renda. During the deportations, he served as the provincial governor, first of Bitlis, then of Aleppo. Rössler described him "working with great energy for the destruction of Armenians."[64] General Vehip Paşa, commander of the Third Army from February 1916, mentioned Abdülhalik in his testimony to the Mazhar Commission, claiming that Abdülhalik had, among other things, burned thousands of people alive in the Muş Province—a claim corroborated by German and other sources.[65]

Abdülhalik was also among those arrested and sent to Malta, and the British included him in the core group that bore the greatest responsibility for the massacres. For this reason he was not included in a first exchange of prisoners on 16 March 1921. He was eventually released with the rest of the exiles on 31 October 1921 and went on to serve as minister of finance, of education and finally of defense. Later, he served as speaker of the assembly, even becoming president of the Turkish Republic—albeit for only one day—following the death of Mustafa Kemal.

Abdulahad Nuri had worked with Mustafa Abdülhalik in Aleppo and amassed great wealth during the course of the deportations. He was arrested in Istanbul after the war and immediately put on trial by the Ottoman authorities. There were many witnesses against him—twenty in all—including a certain İhsan, who had served as the prefect of Kilis during the deportations. İhsan gave a damning account of how Abdulahad Nuri relayed the elimination order and its source: "I contacted Talât Bey and got the elimination order from him personally. It is for the safety of the country."[66]

Abdulahad Nuri was the brother of Yusuf Kemal Tengirşenk, minister of finance and a later foreign minister. During Nuri's trial, Yusuf Kemal sent a warning to Istanbul that if his brother was executed, he would kill at least two or three thousand Armenians. Soon thereafter Nuri was released.[67]

Dr. Tevfik Rüştü Aras was married to Dr. Nâzım's sister. During the war, he served on the Supreme Hygiene Council, whose task was to destroy the bodies of Armenian victims. According to a secret document presented to the military court by the police director-general Mustafa Reşad, Rüştü was sent, with thousands of kilograms of lime, to the provinces where massacres had taken place. The bodies were dumped in wells that were then filled with lime and sealed with earth. Tevfik Rüştü was given six months to complete his task, after which he returned to Istanbul.[68] H. W. Glockner, a British prisoner of war, wrote in his memoirs that he had seen the bodies of murdered Armenians in Urfa thrown into large ditches and covered with lime, just as Dr. Rüştü had been instructed to do.[69] Rüştü became a long-serving foreign minister (1925–38) under successive republican governments.

The list goes on: Arif Fevzi Pirinççizade, a former deputy for Diyarbakır, registered as prisoner no. 2734 in Malta, was included among those "accused of acts of gross injustice." It was alleged that he, along with Dr. Reşit, the governor of Diyarbakır, had set up and directed a Special Organization Unit.[70] He became minister of public works from 21 July 1922 to 27 October 1923. Ali Cenani Bey, a former deputy from Antep, prisoner no. 2805 in Malta, enriched himself through the deportations. Turkish author Bilâl Şimşir said, "His file in the British archives is very damning."[71] Ali Cenani Bey served as minister of trade, from 22 October 1924 to 17 May 1926.[72]

Although this list could continue for pages, it is sufficient to demonstrate that prosecuting the suspects would have been an extremely complicated task for the Ankara government. Celaleddin Arif personified the complications. The lawyer who defended many of the accused in the Istanbul trials, he was elected speaker of the nationalist assembly, and later became minister of justice in the Ankara cabinet.

By the time of the Lausanne Peace Conference (1922–23)—convened to fix the boundaries of Turkey, among other outstanding problems left by the demise of the Ottoman Empire—the Armenian genocide was no longer a point of discussion. The emphasis had shifted to facilitating the return of the surviving Armenians and establishing a "national home for the Armenians" within Turkey. Various Armenian bodies tried to influence the conference, the most important among them being representatives from the Soviet Armenian Republic and the Armenian diaspora. These later combined to form the United Armenian Delegation.

The delegation petitioned the governments of Britain, France and Italy to include a list of promises that had been made to the Armenians. The first of these was made on 26 March 1922, in London, and committed to give the Armenians the territory they had been guaranteed. The second, made in Paris at a meeting of foreign ministers, pledged to "consider measures for the foundation of a national home for the Armenians with the help of the League of Nations."[73] In another memo submitted to the Lausanne Conference by the Arme- ·

nians, we learn that the General Assembly of the League of Nations had voted unanimously in 1921 to establish a national home. And again, on 22 September 1922, during discussions over a trade agreement with Turkey, the League of Nations made the decision to address the issue of an "Armenian national home."[74]

Yet despite the vigorous efforts of the Armenian delegation, they were ultimately not allowed to take part in the Lausanne Conference. They were, however, allowed to deliver a speech before a session of the Sub-Commission on the Protection of Minorities on 26 December 1922. The Turkish delegation boycotted this meeting in protest. The Armenian representative recounted the Allies' promises. One aim was to restore the borders of the Soviet Armenian Republic, which had been significantly reduced by two agreements in 1921, the first beween the Soviets and Turkey and the second between Moscow and the Caucusus republics. Among specific demands of the Armenians were access to the sea and the establishment of a small Armenian state within Turkey in the Çukurova region. But it was all in vain. As the representatives left the Lausanne Conference, they noted: "The Entente Powers have forsaken the Armenian question."[75]

The best explanation for why the Allies ultimately abandoned the Armenian question came from one British diplomat. While the United Armenian Delegation was lobbying to be allowed to participate in the Lausanne Conference, they met Vanisttart, Lord Curzon's representative responsible for running the Eastern Desk at the Foreign Ministry, and for Turkish-Armenian relations in particular, and with the undersecretary Sir Eyre Crowe. What was said gives some indication of what the Armenian question actually meant to the Allies and why the prosecution of war criminals was no longer being pursued.

"The Allies can no longer employ real and serious means to influnce Turkey," said the British representatives,

> the Turks have understood the situation well and will take things as far as they possibly can. There is no consensus on this issue among the Allies, some of whom even want to supply the Turks with money and weapons. The Armenian claims are not a vital question for the Allies, who are more concerned with the Straits issue. Allies will not sever their relations with Turkey for the sake of the Armenian question.[76]

This also explains why the Allies took no further steps toward prosecuting crimes committed against Armenians during World War I. M. Montagne, the head of the Minorities Sub-Commission in Lausanne, made his position clear: "We are no longer laboring to correct the wrong behaviors or responsibilities of the past."[77]

İsmet İnönü, Turkey's lead negotiator, delivered a speech that seemed like an official justification for why the Armenian question ought to be closed. The speech is historically significant as the first declaration of what was to became the official long-standing Turkish position on the massacres.

Since both the Turkish government and nation were forced to take punitive measures and to respond fully, but always and without exception only after their patience was exhausted, the responsibility for the disasters that befell the Armenian community within the Turkish Empire belongs entirely to the Armenian community itself. . . . For as long as the Christian elements did not abuse the generosity of the country in which they lived for centuries in comfort and plenty, the Turks never denied them their rights.

Thus, what had been done to the Armenians was a "punitive measure," the reason for which had been the Armenians' "desire for independence and statehood," as well as other states' "desire to interfere in the country's internal affairs under the pretext of protection of minorities," and on whose behalf the Armenians "carried out provocations and received rewards."[78]

In some speeches at Lausanne, the massacres were described as a "challenge to civilization" and the speakers took note of the "sorrow" and the "great tragedy" that befell the Armenians. However, the prevailing mood was "against the opening of old accounts." In his speech to the opening session, Lord Curzon proposed a broad "general amnesty" for all war crimes committed since 1 August 1914.[79] The Treaty of Lausanne did ultimately proclaim a general amnesty for all political and military crimes committed between 1 August 1914 and 20 November 1922, effectively closing the book on the past and on any chance of retribution.[80]

The only remaining issues surrounded returning and resettling the Armenians who had survived the deportations.[81] "Turkey must provide in her own territory in Asia the gathering centre that the Armenians desire," proposed Lord Curzon at the opening session. "It could be in her northern/eastern provinces or in the southeast of Cilicia and the Syrian border."[82] The Allies' treaty drafts posited an Armenian homeland near the Syrian border. But İsmet İnönü said that such a move could have no meaning other than to "partition Turkey" and that he "saw no possibility of even beginning to discuss such an arrangement."[83] At the meetings of the Minorities Sub-Commission, the Turkish delegation repeatedly said that, as a matter of principle, it would not discuss such an issue, which, they said, was nothing more than a return to the old European tricks. When the Allies pressed the matter at various points, delegate Rıza Nur declared at the 6 January 1923 session that he considered "all notices presented as not received and invalid" and walked out of the meeting.[84]

The minorities question did in fact cause the conference to break down temporarily. When it reconvened after several months, the proposal for an Armenian homeland had been dropped. What remained on the table were the general amnesty and the collective return of Armenian deportees. Yet the Turks protested even these provisions touching on the collective return. Finally, with the declaration of a general amnesty, the whole issue was consigned to oblivion.

CHAPTER 10

WHY THE POSTWAR TRIALS FAILED

AS THE EXPRESSION GOES, THE MOUNTAIN LABORED AND BROUGHT forth a mouse. It would be hard to find a more fitting phrase to describe the postwar investigations into the Ottoman crimes committed during World War I, especially the Armenian genocide.

Initially, expectations were high. The first use of the concept "crimes against humanity" was a significant contribution to international case law, as well as the fact that the Ottoman cases were investigated within the framework of national criminal law in a single country. But the failure of the three different attempts to prosecute the suspects meant that the concept of "crimes against humanity" was set aside, reemerging on the international stage only at Nuremberg after World War II.

A number of factors led to this failure. Significantly, these factors remain relevant today.

The sanctity of national sovereignty and the international necessity of punishing those who carry out crimes against humanity are not easily reconciled. This question of how to balance these two principles persists. The impasse between these two conflicting demands ultimately played a crucial role in ensuring that the legal prosecution of those guilty of the Armenian genocide would come to nothing. The nascent Turkish government in Anatolia continually blocked efforts by the Entente Powers to punish suspects by asserting its right of national sovereignty. A nation cannot be punished with the violation of its sovereignty, it argued.[1] Any attempts in this direction were perceived as an assault.

The Allied desire to partition Anatolia and their desire to punish the perpetrators in the name of humanity were so interwoven that the Turkish National Movement perceived the punishment of perpetrators as a blow to national independence. None of the various actors of the time were able to separate these two issues successfully. Thus the assumption took hold that "accusations of . . . 'the Armenian massacres' were merely fig leaves, concocted 'crimes' and 'criminals' used by the British to realize its colonialist aspirations and reduce the Turkish nation to servitude."[2]

Violations of national sovereignty inevitably occur for one of two reasons, either over universalist aims such as the defense of human rights, or for imperialist interests. In terms of postwar Turkey, it is hard to argue that the British desire to violate Ottoman sovereignty was due solely to universal principles rather than colonial interests. When universalist principles coincided with colonialist aims, both were easily implemented by the Great Powers. But when these interests clashed universal principles quickly dropped away. Thus international efforts in this context evaporated.

What might have happened had the Allies accepted the importance of the National Pact and its territorial demands, had they recognized the sovereignty of the Ottoman state while demanding the prosecution of those guilty of war crimes in exchange? If the question of punishing the Turks had not been tied to the partition of Anatolia, there might have been a very different outcome to the Istanbul trials.

Andrew Ryan, an official in the Office of the British High Commissioner, recounted that during the initial period of the armistice, the Turks were exhausted and that "most of the population would have been greatly pleased with any peace, regardless of the conditions." A similar impression is left by a speech given on 27 April 1920 by General Fevzi Paşa, who had served as minister of war in the postwar Istanbul government before joining the National Movement in Ankara. Addressing the British, he said, "You cannot achieve anything by threats. . . . If you will recognize our right to life we are prepared to do everything."[3] What drove the general to abandon Istanbul for Ankara was the British failure to recognize this national "right to life" for the Turks, in particular, the occupation of Izmir by the Greeks with Allied collusion, and the plans for partition in the Treaty of Sèvres that hardened the Turkish resistance to the peace conditions. The British chief of staff understood this. He reported that "the very great majority of the people are war weary in the full sense of the word. But the people will also be prepared to fight most determinedly in order to prevent a section of its lands from being given to either Greece or Armenia. . . . Resistance will increase with the broadening of the region under occupation."[4]

There were several approaches among the Entente states that advocated very different policies regarding the sovereign rights of the Ottoman state. On several occasions President Wilson and Prime Minister Lloyd George promised to respect the principle of the sovereignty of the Ottoman state. Wilson's Fourteen Points included the assurance that a Turkish state would be established in the areas in which the majority of the population was Turkish. This principle became a matter of U.S. policy: "Turkey shall continue its separate existence as a state under the Turkish Government. This shall perhaps be the existing government or perhaps another government."[5] Lloyd George stated on 5 January 1918: "We are not fighting in order to leave Turkey devoid of its capital, or of the rich and renowned lands which are inhabited largely by persons of the Turkish race, lands such as Asia Minor and Thrace."[6]

Ultimately, however, instead of maintaining Turkey's sovereign integrity, the Allies agreed to the Greek occupation of western Anatolia. When the Allied leaders were reminded of their past statements, they claimed to have "forgotten" them.[7] The partition dealt a heavy blow to the prosecution of those involved in the Armenian genocide. In the words of British minister of defense Winston Churchill, "Righteousness has now switched sides. Justice has now passed to the other camp."[8]

The British high commissioner, Admiral Calthorpe, had come out strongly against the Greek occupation of Izmir, and therefore official British policy.

I hope that the Monarchy of Helen will not be extended to the eastern shore of the Aegean Ocean. This hope of ours does not derive from a lack in the strength of sympathy that we have felt for the hopes of being rid of this oppression in the past, but rather from not having believed that this action would be of service to any one of the concerned parties. . . .⁹

But despite these warnings the occupation was carried out. On 23 November the new British high commissioner, Admiral de Robeck, wrote that "the Turks had to be punished, but the British . . . did not have to extract this penalty in the form of dividing up, to their own advantage, the provinces in which the Ottomans were the great majority."¹⁰

In the initial period following the armistice, there were clear indications from the Turkish camp that they were ready to swallow the pill of punishing the perpetrators of the genocide in order to secure their sovereignty. Thus began the Istanbul trials. When the Istanbul trials turned to prosecute those fighting for sovereignty, the process collapsed. The argument being made is not that Ankara was eager to try the perpetrators of the Armenian massacres, but rather it was a matter of realpolitik, a willing concession as long as it might improve the peace conditions. Ankara did not hesitate to protect the same perpetrators when there was no longer an advantage to prosecuting them.

The Turkish example shows that there is a sharp—and perhaps irreconcilable—contradiction between the right of states to national sovereignty, on the one hand, and the pursuit and prosecution of crimes against humanity, on the other. The dilemma might be circumvented through the insertion of a concept of "crimes against humanity" into the framework of national law in a manner that does not contradict a state's rights.

In this context, the importance of the Istanbul trials is clearly evident. For the first time a crime of premeditated mass murder, committed by a state, which is a crime according to international law, was prosecuted according to the principles of national law. When international bodies lack significant powers of sanction, making the concept of "crimes against humanity" an inseparable part of national legal systems can have certain advantages.

However, this is not an argument to reduce crimes such as genocide to the level of a "domestic problem" of any country, which could open the door to the danger of multiple definitions of "humanity."[11] Thus, investigations of crimes against humanity should not be conducted exclusively within the framework of national institutions, in which, as Montesquieu explained, each state would be considered as an individual.[12]

"Crimes against humanity" would thus rest on shared legal norms that are as valid for nations as for individuals, for the rulers as for the ruled, for ministers as for ordinary citizens.

As a rule, if a crime is committed by one group against another ethnic or religious collective group, it is nearly impossible for the perpetrator to punish itself. The Istanbul trials stand as a ringing example, showing quite clearly just how unreliable the internal legal and social processes of a nation are in the prosecution of its own crimes against humanity. In the Turkish case, the nation's difficulty facing up to the stain of guilt also played a large role in the collapse of the trials. The trial and punishment of people who had represented the nation was perceived as "a national humiliation" and "the punishment of an entire nation." Mithat Şükrü, the secretary-general of the Union and Progress Party, interpreted the trials as "self-condemnation by the government and the court, and a condemnation of the Turkish nation."[13]

In general, those who resort to mass murder on a collective scale always put forward the justification that they acted on behalf of the nation. This too is the case with the CUP and the Armenian genocide. The genocide was presented as a struggle over the Turkish nation's very existence, and the policy was pursued with a certain level of popular support among Muslims even though the party itself was authoritarian and ruled through dictatorship. Halil Menteşe expressed this when he stated that "the number of Turks in Anatolia who have no connection to this deportation is small indeed."[14] In crimes as extensive as this, the main problem is where to draw the line of inclusion for potential legal sanction and prosecution. Politically speaking, how should we understand the concept of "the guilt of a nation"? How can such a term be defined as a legal category? These questions remain unanswered.

Agreement among the world powers is an indispensable condition for proceeding against the perpetrators of such crimes. This element was lacking in the case of the Armenian genocide. The Allied powers had conflicting interests in the Middle East and humanitarian objectives were only achievable when they managed to reconcile their various state objectives. In the absence of any such understanding, it was naive to believe that the Great Powers would intervene for strictly humanitarian purposes.

Regarding the Armenian genocide, the Allied powers' own national and imperialist self-interests took precedence over any demands for justice. Thus Britain excluded France from the armistice negotiations with Turkey and occupied areas promised to France. Britain and France allowed the Greeks to occupy areas considered Italy's zone of influence.

As tensions with Britain grew, the French and Italians began to seek ties with the nationalists in Anatolia. The French sent their own representatives to the nationalists in Ankara to conclude their own agreement, bearing the message that they desired "the existence of an independent Turkish state." Paris subsequently placed great importance on pleasing the Turks. As High Commissioner Calthorpe wrote to Lord Curzon in May 1919:

> The French are wholeheartedly devoting themselves to creating the impression that only they among the Entente countries have insisted on defending the rights of Muslims, and they are expending great efforts to ensure that Istanbul remains in Turkish hands and that the Ottoman Empire not be partitioned.[15]

Italy also sent its own representative to Sivas for talks with the nationalist leaders.[16]

According to Turkish historian Nur Bilge Criss, "Almost everyone then . . . shared the opinion that the Italians were 'the noble occupiers,' the French were 'harmless,' apart from the Senegalese, who harassed women, and the Americans were 'of pure and sound character,' but the British were 'the enemy.'"[17]

The area of Istanbul skirting Anatolia, which was under Italian control, quickly became an important passageway for those fleeing the capital for the interior. According to reports received by Admiral

Bristol, U.S. high commissioner, "a great number of nationalists in Istanbul had found refuge on Italian warships, and they were going to be sent to Anatolia via the Italian area."[18] False documents and passports were provided to a great number of Turks by the French and Italian passport offices, allowing their passage to Anatolia. In addition to standing by while the National Movement organized in the regions under their control, the Italians also provided active support for the nationalists in the form of weapons and supplies.[19] French support for the National Movement became quite overt, even providing constant intelligence regarding movements of the Greek forces in Anatolia. The secret, Ankara-allied organization Felâh, active in Istanbul,

> was in very frequent and intimate communication with the 2nd Office of the French General Headquarters and received great amounts of assistance . . . from the French in their attempts to gather military intelligence on the condition and disposition of Greek units. The French passed all of the data they acquired from British Headquarters directly to this department.[20]

In the end, the British remained alone in their tenacious desire to punish the perpetrators of the genocide and Muslim hostility increased.[21] In a debate in the British parliament, a summary was given:

> During the two years between the armistice at Mudros and the signing of the treaty of Sèvres, . . . the Allied coalition virtually dissolved. By 1920 most of the victors no longer included among their aims the punishment of Turkish war criminals. . . . The United States had repudiated the Versailles treaty and was retreating into isolationism. . . . The French made no provision for war crimes trials in an initial draft treaty with Turkey. . . . At the same time, the Italians evaded a British request for the arrest of former Young Turk leaders. . . . The French and Italians hoped to secure concessions in Asia Minor and did not want to antagonize powerful factions in Turkey unnecessarily, particularly the rising Nationalists.[22]

After 1920, the British also ultimately abandoned their demand to punish those responsible for the Armenian massacres in the hope of reaching an understanding with the National Movement. On

30 March 1921, the Entente countries announced that their position on the Greek-Turkish fighting in Anatolia was one of neutrality. Having signed an agreement with Ankara in October 1921, the French gave the Turkish National Movement official recognition. France, Italy and Britain all ultimately desired to conclude agreements with the nationalist government—so much so, in fact, that they had no hesitation undermining what remained of the Istanbul government and forcing the Ottoman grand vizier, Damat Ferid Paşa, to resign. What is interesting is that the British took a leading role in the final days of the Ottoman state.[23] The human rights question was consigned to oblivion.

Interventions in the domestic affairs of nation-states are extremely problematic. In most cases, they produce results that are more detrimental than advantageous. Post–World War II developments in Germany appear to be the exception. There are two main reasons for the difficulty: Without the necessary resolve, those interfering will be unable to monitor and oversee the outcome of their intervention. And of course, states rarely intervene in the affairs of other states on purely humanitarian grounds. As a rule, humanitarian goals mask their imperialist policies and interests. Furthermore, in many cases, demands for intervention for humanitarian purposes are manipulated for internal political reasons. Thus in the nineteenth century, the Armenian question was manipulated in the interests of internal British policy. In 1890, a liberal British parliamentarian, William Summer, stated that "both Gladstone and myself concern ourselves with the Armenian question simply as a way of placing the Salisbury Cabinet in a difficult position."[24]

André Mandelstam, a dragoman who served for decades in the Russian Embassy in Istanbul, succinctly summed up this tension between real and alleged aims:

> The interventions of the Western powers into the Ottoman Empire
> are generally assessed from diametrically opposed positions. The
> Turks and their defenders claim that the interventions are under-
> taken with the aim of serving the selfish interests of the states who
> carry them out. In this vein, the chief Turkish negotiator at Lausanne,
> İsmet Paşa, strove in a lengthy speech to prove that the protection of

minorities had been nothing other than an excuse that the powers gladly used to interfere in the internal affairs of Turkey. As for the other, opposing interpretation, it claims that the actions of the Great Powers within Turkey are done in the name of humanity, a humanitarian intervention.[25]

Despite the numerous historical examples that could be presented for both of these positions, what is important is how Turkish society perceived "human rights" and "democracy" in this context. Because the Great Powers used these terms to legitimize the most obvious colonial moves, Turks began to view both notions as "Western hypocrisy."[26] Beyond the specific historical reasons, the fundamental problems that lay behind the failure to bring the perpetrators of the Armenian genocide to justice persist to this day. If it is not possible to draw a clear line of division between humanitarian goals, on the one hand, and a state's economic and political interests, on the other, then how are we to come to a consensus about ethical norms? And on what legal and theoretical grounds shall we justify international interventions? These questions remain unanswered.

NOTES

Abbreviations

AA   Austrian Foreign Office Archive
AMMU   Directorate of Tribes and Immigrants in the Ottoman Interior Ministry (*Aşair ve Muhaciri Müdüriyet Umumiyesi*)
BAO/DH/SFR Priministerial Archive, Office of the Cipher in the Ottoman Interior Ministry (*Başbakanlık Osmanlı Arşivi Dahiliye Nezareti Şifre Kalemi*)
FO   British Foreign Office
HHStA PA   Austrian State Archive, Political Archive
IAMM   Office of Tribal and Refugee Settlement in the Ottoman Interior Ministry (*İskan-ı Aşair ve Muhacirin Müdiriyeti*)
MAZC   Minutes of the Ottoman Chamber of Notables (*Meclis-i Ayan Zabıt Ceridesi*)
MMZC   Minutes of the Ottoman Chamber of Deputies (*Meclis-i Mebusan Zabıt Ceridesi*)
PA-AA   German Foreign Office, Political Archive (also appears as DE/PA-AA).
PO   British Public Record Office
TBMM   Grand National Assembly of Turkey (*Türkiye Büyük Millet Meclisi*)

Preface

1. *Foreign Relations of the United States, 1915: The World War,* p. 981, quoted in: J. F. Willis, *Prologue to Nuremberg, The Politics and Diplomacy of Punishing War Criminals of the First World War* (London, 1982), p. 26.
2. Seha L. Meray and Osman Olcay, *Osmanlı İmparatorluğu'nun Çöküş Belgeleri* (Ankara, 1977), pp. 113–14.
3. Information on some of these trials can be found in *Takvîm-i Vekâyı* and in Ottoman dailies from the period. This book does not provide a comprehensive list of the trials, preferring instead to concentrate on the evidence from a few proceedings. For a detailed account of the trials, see the forthcoming *The Protocols of the Istanbul Military Tribunals on the Investigation of the Armenian Genocide,* with Vahakin N. Dadrian.
4. Aram Andonian, *Documents officiels concernant les massacres Arméniens* (Paris, 1920). For the claims that the documents contained in this book are forgeries, see Şinasi Orel and Süreyya Yuca, *Ermenilerce Talât Paşa'ya Atfedilen Telgrafların Gerçek Yüzü* (The True Nature of the Telegrams attributed by the Armenians to Talât Paşa) (Ankara, 1983) and Türkkaya Ataöv, *The Andonian Documents Attributed to Talât Paşa Are Forgeries* (Ankara, 1984). A critique of the official Turkish position on the Andonian documents can be found in V. N. Dadrian, "The Naim-Andonian Documents on the World War I Destruction of Ottoman Armenians: The Anatomy of a Genocide," *International Journal of Middle East Studies* 18, no. 3 (August 1986), p. 343. I shall not enter into the debate over their authenticity here, except to stress: It is possible to prove that at least some of the published and unpublished documents in the possession of scholars share the same contents as documents published by Andonian. One authentic cable quoted here, which was read at the Istanbul trial of CUP leaders and which suggests the involvement of Ottoman army units in the massacres, as well as other documents published later, contain sentences identical with those found in the documents published by Andonian. For more information on the Andonian documents, see the forthcoming *Denial and Rewriting History,* by Taner Akçam.
5. Başbakanlık Devlet Arşivleri Genel Müdürlüğü, *Osmanlı Belgelerinde Ermeniler, 1915–1920* (Ankara, 1994), Document no. 71, pp. 68–69.
6. These incidents are also mentioned in German consular reports. "Reşit, governor-general of Diyarbakır Province, commissioned the local gendarmes with carrying out the massacres. If preventive measures are not taken, the 'lower class' would begin massacring the Christian [population]." It was the governor of the provincial district of Mardin, who was in Diyarbakır at the time, who provided the information. These reports from the consulates were passed on by the German Embassy in Istanbul directly to Talât Paşa and an explanation was demanded. Talât used the descriptions found in the reports in cables he sent. When he referred to public opinion in these messages what he most likely meant

NOTES: PREFACE | 379

was these initiatives by the foreign embassies. See for instance PA-AA/Bo. Kons./ BD 169, Mosul consul Holstein's reports dated 10–15 July 1915; the message written by the German ambassador in French to Talât Paşa, dated 12 July 1915.

7. Among the many German Embassy and consular reports one can find numerous accounts which initially approve of, or at least show understanding for, the measures adopted by the Unionists. Many of these accounts were not published by Lepsius, and we shall evaluate some of them at greater length below. See, for example, PA-AA/Bo. Kons./B. 169, two separate messages from Ambassador Wangenheim, dated 4 June 1915, to the priest of the Elazığ (Ma'mûretûl-aziz) orphanage and to the German Consulate in Erzurum; and the telegram from Erzurum consul Scheubner-Richter dated 10 June 1915. Similar content is to be found in the May reports of the Austrian Embassy in Istanbul. Only near the end of June does mention begin to appear that the events that are unfolding are not simply "ordinary" deportations but massacres. See Artem Ohandjanian, *Österreich-Armenian 1872–1936: Faksimliesammlung diplomatischer Akenstücke* (Vienna, 1995), vol. 6 (1914–15), p. 4556, for the May 1915 reports.

8. PA-AA/Bo. Kons./B. 191, Report of Consul Mordtmann, dated 30 June 1915. Dr. Mordtmann, who knew Turkish well, was appointed by Ambassador Wangenheim to follow the Armenian question. This particular was written in old-style German script and was not sent to Berlin by Wangenheim.

9. Johannes Lepsius, Albrecht Mendelssohn-Bartholdy, Friedrich Thimme, eds., *Die Grosse Politik der Europäischen Kabinette, 1871–1914.* Sammlung der diplomatischen Akten des Auswärtigen Amtes, im Auftrage des Auswärtigen Amtes, 40 vols. (Berlin: Deutsche Veragsgesellschaft für Politik und Geschichte, 1922–27).

10. It is not clear whether these distortions were made with Lepsius's knowledge. Wolfgang Gust found that most of the changes were made by the German Foreign Office before they were sent to Lepsius. There are, however, documents that were changed to some extent by Lepsius. For more information see www.armenocide.net.

11. One example of a report from which condemnatory descriptions of the Armenian organizations were excised is PA-AA/Bo. Kons./B. 168, Report by Louis Mosel, dated 26 March 1915. The report contains information about the arming of the Armenian Dashnak organization. Examples of such reports from which the interesting sections were removed include: PA-AA/R 14089: Reports from Consul Rössler (Aleppo), dated 8, 16 November 1915. From these reports the name of Graf Wolffskeel, the German officer who suppressed the revolt in Urfa, has been removed in Lepsius's reproduction (see J. Lepsius, *Deutschland und Armenien: 1914–1918: Sammlung Diplomatischer Schriftstücke* [Potsdam, 1919], Document no. 193, p. 202). It should be added that other reports, which hint that Graf Wolffskeel also played an instrumental role in the events at Zeytun (present-day Süleymaniye), are utterly absent. PA-AA/R 14087: Report by Consul Rössler (Aleppo), dated 27 July 1915, Appendix 1. Lepsius left out Appendix 1 in its entirety, because it contained accounts by certain Turkish officers, who condemn the murders and hold the

Germans directly responsible for what occurred (see Lepsius, *Deutschland und Armenien*, Document no. 120, pp. 108–12; PA-AA/R 14085: Report by Ambassador Wangenheim dated 11 August 1915). In the report sent to the embassy by Anders, the German consul in Erzurum, information regarding the names of fourteen members of a committee formed in the Erzurum area and the fact that a certain Dashnak leader had been in continual contact with the Russian Consulate was removed (Lepsius, *Deutschland und Armenian*, Document nos. 9, 193, pp. 9, 202). Additionally, Lepsius does not as a rule include reports containing eyewitness accounts of events. Some reports do appear, however, which contain some observations about how the Turks disapproved of what was being done (see Lepsius, *Deutschland und Armenian*, Document no. 123, p. 113).

12. See: Wolfgang Gust, ed., *Der Völkermord an den Armeniern 1915/16: Dokumente aus dem Politischen Archiv des deutschen Auswärtigen Amts* (2005).

13. An important selection of American documents was compiled by Ara Sarafian, ed., *America and the Armenian Genocide of 1915* (Cambridge, UK: Cambridge University Press), 2004.

14. In particular, various persons who served in the Special Organization have provided us with extremely valuable information about plans that were made from the beginning of 1914. Memoirs and other works by these people are discussed in greater detail later on, but for now it bears mentioning that no systematic review of Turkish-language memoirs has been carried out in regard to the Armenian genocide. For further information see: Vahakn N. Dadrian, "Documentation of the Armenian Genocide in Turkish Sources," in Israel W. Charny, ed., *Genocide: A Critical Bibliographic Review*, vol. 2 (New York: Facts on File), 1991.

15. *Ati*, 24 February 1920.

16. Çerkez Hasan, "Peki Yüzbinlerce Ermeni'yi Kim Öldürdü?" ("Well then, who *did* kill hundreds of thousands of Armenians?"), *Alemdar*, 5 Nisan (April) 1919.

17. This contradiction is pointed out in ibid.

18. For fuller development of these ideas, see: Taner Akçam, *From Empire to Republic: Turkish Nationalism and the Armenian Genocide* (London, 2004).

19. Kazım Öztürk, ed., *Atatürkün TBMM Açık ve Gizli Oturumlardaki Konuşmaları*, vol. 1 (Ankara: Kültür Bakanlığı, 1992), p. 59.

1. The Ottoman State and Its Non-Muslim Populations

1. Richard G. Hovannisian, "The Historical Dimensions of the Armenian Question 1878–1923," in Richard G. Hovannisian, ed., *The Armenian Genocide in Perspective* (New Brunswick and London, 1991), p. 20.

2. The question of whether or not the Ottoman state possessed a theocratic character is the subject of debate. The concept here is being used in the general sense that the basis for legitimizing political power was drawn from religion. For a detailed discussion of this issue, see *Bilgi ve Hikmet* (Summer 1995), p. 11.

3. It is a commonplace to depict the Ottoman Empire as a regime characterized by violence and terror, especially by the descendants of its Christian subjects (the Serbians, Bulgars, Rumanians, Greeks, and Armenians, among others). I am of course aware of this depiction, which is based mostly on prejudice. I am aware as well of the pointlessness of examining past empires through the filter of contemporary judgments, which have been shaped by our current moral values. My argument here is that the perception of earlier periods as "relatively peaceful" was influenced by the greater violence of later Ottoman-Christian relations during the nineteenth century.

4. İlber Ortaylı, *Türkiye İdare Tarihi* (Ankara, 1979), pp. 1, 282.

5. Halil İnalcık, "Osmanlı Hukukuna Giriş," *SBF Dergisi* 13, no. 2 (Haziran/ June 1958), p. 102.

6. Ömer Lütfi Barkan, "Türkiye'de Din ve Devlet İlişkileri," *Cumhuriyet'in 50. Yildönümü Semineri* (Ankara, 1975), p. 55.

7. Ömer Lütfi Barkan, *Kanunlar* (Istanbul, 1943), vol. 1, p. xiv.

8. In Islam, there are various law schools each with its own law collections usually written or compiled by its founders. For detailed information, see Mohammad Hashim Kamali, "Law and Society," in *Oxford History of Islam*, ed. John L. Esposito (Oxford: Oxford University Press, 1999) pp. 107–53.

9. For more detailed information concerning this subject, see Karl Binswanger, *Untersuchungen zum Statut der Nichtmuslime im Osmanischen Reich des 16. Jahrhundert* (Munich, 1977); Orhan Münir, *Minderheiten im Osmanischen Reich und in der neuen Türkei* (Cologne, 1937); Gülnihal Bozkurt, *Alman İngiliz Belgelerinin ve Siyasi Gelişmelerin Işığı Altında Gayrimüslim Osmanlı Vatandaşlarının Hukuki Durumu 1839–1914* (Ankara, 1989).

10. For a good general overview on this topic, see Benjamin Braude and Bernard Lewis, eds., *Christians and Jews in the Ottoman Empire*, vol. 1 (New York, 1982); Adel Khoury, *Toleranz im Islam* (Munich, 1980); Mustafa Fayda, "İslam Tarihinin İlk Dönemlerinde Gayrimüslimler," *Türk Tarihinde Ermeniler Sempozyumu* (Izmir, 1983); Bat Ye'or, *The Decline of Eastern Christianity under Islam: From Jihad to Dhimmitude* (Madison, NJ, 1996); Bat Ye'or, *Islam and Dhimmitude: Where Civilizations Collide* (Madison, NJ, 2002).

11. For more information on jizya', see Cizye in: *İslam Ansiklopedisi*, vol. 3 (Ankara: Milli Eğitim Bakanığı), pp. 199–201.

12. In addition to the term *"zelil ve hakir"* the phrases *"küçük düşürme"* (to humiliate) and *"boyunlarını bükme"* (to abase, submit to) are used in the Turkish translations. There are a number of works written about the meaning of the words found in this passage. For a partial list, see Bernard Lewis, *The Jews of Islam* (Princeton, 1984), p. 195, n. 9.

13. Münir, *Osmanischen Reich*, p. 29.

14. Roderic Davison, *Reform in the Ottoman Empire, 1856–1876* (Princeton, 1963), p. 13.

15. For detailed information and discussion on the establishment of the *millet* system, see Benjamin Braude, "Foundation Myths of the *Millet* System," in Braude and Lewis, *Christians and Jews*, pp. 69–88.

16. In a nineteenth-century work on the legal status of the Greek minority within the Ottoman Empire, the author claims that the church authorities could also hear criminal cases and decree punishments: "In a situation in which one Greek demanded that another Greek be punished, the *Episcopos* (Bishop) could accept the complaint and mete out punishment, just like in civil cases. The precondition for this was simply that both the plaintiff and the defendant voluntarily accept the *Episcopos*'s judgment." Dr. Gustav Gelb, *Darstellung des Rechtzustandes in Griechenland, Während der Türkischen Herrschaft und bis zur Ankunft des König Otto I* (Heidelberg, 1835). Even so, such punishments had to receive the sultan's approval.

17. Servet Armağan, *İslam Hukukunda Temel Hak ve Hürriyetler* (Ankara, 1987), p. 47. In the period of the Prophet Muhammad and the *Rashîdûn*, or (first) four Rightly-Guided Caliphs, in particular, there are examples of such practices.

18. M. Cevat Akşit, *İslam Ceza Hukuku ve İnsani Esasları* (Istanbul, 1976), p. 122.

19. These prohibitions are based on a *Hadîth* that is attributed to the Prophet himself. See Khoury, *Toleranz im Islam*, pp. 147–48.

20. Binswanger, *Osmanischen Reich*, pp. 165ff.

21. For further information see Münir, *Osmanischen Reich*, pp. 60–69.

22. J. Kirakossian Arman, *British Diplomacy and the Armenian Question, from the 1830s to 1914* (Princeton and London, 2004), p. 21.

23. Davison, *Reform*, p. 72.

24. İhsan Sungu, "Tanzimat ve Yeni Osmanlılar," *Tanzimat*, vol. 1, p. 791.

25. Edmund Hornby, *Autobiography* (London, 1928), p. 93. Quoted in Davison, *Reform*, pp. 73–74, n. 75. Although I suspect that this number is high, the fact that the Ottoman government passed the Law on Ottoman Citizenship in 1869 to put a stop to this practice shows how widespread it was.

26. Enver Ziya Karal, *Osmanlı Tarihi, Islahat Fermanı Devri (1856–1861)*, vol. 6 (Ankara, 1988), pp. 40–42; for an English translation of the Regulation for the Administration of Lebanon, 9 June 1861, see J. C. Hurewitz, *Diplomacy in the Near and Middle East, A Documentary Record: 1535–1914* (Princeton, 1956), vol. 1, pp. 165–98.

27. For details, see Taner Akçam, *Siyasi Kültürümüzde Zulüm ve İşkence* (Istanbul, 1993).

28. İber Ortaylı, "Tanzimat," *Tanzimattan Cumhuriyete Türkiye Ansiklopedisi* (Istanbul, 1985), p. 1545.

29. A good example of this is the bill written by Ali Paşa, the Ottoman grand vizier and foreign minister for much of the 1850s and 1860s, from Crete, where he had gone in order to suppress a revolt in 1867. For the complete text of this proposal, see A. D. Mordtmann, *Stambul und das moderne Türkentum* (Leipzig, 1877–78).

30. İlber Ortaylı, *Tanzimattan Cumhuriyete Yerel Yönetim Geleneği* (Istanbul, 1985), p. 20.
31. Taner Timur, *Osmanlı Kimliği* (Istanbul, 1986).
32. Davison, *Reform*, p. 45.
33. Ibid.
34. A. H. Ongunsu, "Tanzimat ve Amillerine Bir Bakış," *Tanzimat*, vol. 1, p. 11.
35. Edouard Philippe Engelhardt, *Tanzimat* (Istanbul, 1976), p. 33.
36. Bernard Lewis, *The Emergence of Modern Turkey*, 2nd ed. (Princeton, 1968), p. 107.
37. Karal, *Osmanlı Tarihi*, vol. 5, p. 250.
38. The documents concerning the edict are taken from: Engelhardt, *Tanzimat*, pp. 93–94; Karal, *Osmanlı Tarihi*, vol. 5, pp. 250–51; vol. 6, p. 15; Davison, *Reform*; and F. Eichmann, *Die Reformen des Osmanischen Reiches* (Berlin, 1858).
39. Davison, *Reform*, pp. 123ff.
40. M. A. Ubicini, *Türkiye 1850* (Istanbul, n.d.), vol. 1, p. 67.
41. Halil İnalcık, "Tanzimatın Uygulanması ve Sosyal Tepkileri," *Belleten*, no. 112 (Ekim/October 1964), p. 633.
42. For details, see Gülnihal Bozkurt, *Batı Hukukunun Türkiye'de Benimsenmesi* (Ankara, 1966).
43. Engelhardt, *Tanzimat*, pp. 232ff.
44. For the articles under discussion, see Tarhan Erdem, *Anayasalar ve Seçim Kanunları 1876–1982* (Istanbul, 1982), p. 34.
45. Ibid., p. 4.
46. Cevdet Paşa, *Tezakir* (prepared for publication by Cavid Baysun) (Ankara, 1986), p. 79.
47. Ibid., pp. 78–81.
48. Lewis, *Emergence of Modern Turkey*, p. 107.
49. Davison, *Reform*, p. 43.
50. Inalcık, "Tanzimatın," p. 624.
51. Enver Ziya Karal, "Gülhane Hattı Hümayunu'nda Batı'da Etkisi," *Belleten*, no. 112 (Ekim/October 1964), p. 582. Mustafa Reşit Paşa, the chief architect of the 1839 Tanzimat Edict, was referred to as "Gâvur Paşa," having "gained this name not only because of his personal westernisms, but because of his belief in the need to treat with equality people of all creeds within the empire." Davison, *Reform*, p. 37.
52. Cevdet Paşa, *Tezakir*, no. 10, p. 68.
53. Gülnihal Bozkurt, *Turkiye*, pp. 60–61.
54. Feroz Ahmad, *İttihatçılıktan Kemalizme* (Istanbul, 1985), p. 121.
55. Enver Ziya Karal, *Osmanlı Tarihi*, vol. 6, p. 11.
56. Ibid., p. 94.
57. Ibid., p. 63.

58. Ibid.

59. The assessment of British diplomat Sir Henry Bulwer, who served in Istanbul in the 1860s, the 1861 report of the British consulate in Izmir, and the 1873–74 report of the German Consulate in Bursa are among the relevant examples.

60. *Great Britain, Parliamentary Papers* (1861), vol. 67: *Accounts and Papers*, vol. 34; "Condition of Christians in Turkey, 1860," no. 8, as cited in Davison, *Reform*, p. 106, n. 77.

61. Ibid.

62. Bekir Sıtkı Baykal, *Şark Buhran ve Sabah Gazetesi* (Ankara, 1948), p. 148.

63. Norbert Elias, *Studien über den Deutschen* (Frankfurt am Main: Suhrkamp, 1989), p. 467.

64. Hüseyin Tuncer, *Türk Yurdu Üzerine Bir İnceleme* (Ankara, 1990), p. 47, quoting an article by Yusuf Akçura in: *Türk Yurdu*, vol. 3 (1329/1913).

65. Mümtaz Türköne, *Siyasi İdeoloji Olarak İslamcılığın Doğuşu* (Istanbul, 1991), p. 70.

66. Ibid.

67. Karal, *Osmanlı Tarihi*, vol. 6, p. 70.

68. Salahi Sonyel, "İngiliz Belgelerine Göre Adana'da Vuku Bulan Turk-Ermeni Olayları (Temmez 1908–Aralık 1909)," in *Belletin*, no. 51, 1987.

69. Lewis, *Jews of Islam*, p. 168.

70. E. Uras, *Tarihte Ermeniler ve Ermeni Meselesi*, expanded second edition (Istanbul, 1987), p. 177.

71. Yves Ternon, *Ermeni Tabusu* (Istanbul, 1993), pp. 58–59.

72. Ibid.

73. Uras, *Tarihte Ermeniler*, p. 178.

74. For the entire text of the agreement, see Hurewitz, *Diplomacy*, vol. 1, pp. 153–56.

75. H. V. Kremer-Auenrode and P. Hirsch, eds., *Das Staatarchiv, Sammlung der Offiziellen Aktenstücke* (Leipzig, 1877), no. 6360, pp. 156–57.

76. Uras, *Tarihte Ermeniler*, p. 189.

77. Regarding the Armenian officers serving in the Russian Army and their successes, see *Armenier und Armenien* (a brochure published by the Bulgarian-Armenian Committee) (Sophia, 1941), p. 60; Hamdullah Suphi, *İkdam* (17 Aralık/26 December 1912), cited in Paul Rohrbach, *Armenien* (Stuttgart, 1919), p. 45.

78. For the complete text of this report and the detailed story of other developments that followed the 1877–78 war, see Artem Ohandjianian, *Armenien, Der verschwiegene Völkermord* (Vienna, Cologne, Graz, 1989), pp. 20–37.

79. Uras, *Tarihte Ermeniler*, p. 207.

80. Kirakossian, *British Diplomacy*, p. 67.

81. Uras, *Tarihte Ermeniler*, p. 225.

82. Hurewitz, *Diplomacy*, p. 190.

83. A detailed account of the initial British initiatives and the Ottomans' delaying tactics can be found in Cevdet Küçük, *Osmanlı Diplomasisinde Ermeni Meselesinin Ortaya Çıkışı, 1878–1897* (Istanbul, 1986).

84. Akdes Nimet Kurat, *Türkiye ve Rusya* (Ankara, 1990), p. 103.

85. Uras, *Tarihte Ermeniler*, p. 274.

86. Yusuf Hikmet Bayur, *Türk İnkılabı Tarihi*, vol. 1, part 1 (Ankara, 1983), p. 21.

87. Karal, *Osmanlı Tarihi*, vol. 3, p. 133.

88. For more detailed information on the Hamidiye Regiments, see Mehmet Bayrak, *Kürtler ve Ulusal Demokratik Mücadeleleri* (Istanbul, 1993), pp. 61–73; Bayram Kodaman, *Hamidiye Hafif Süvari Alayları* (a special printing of the *İstanbul Üniversitesi Edebiyat Fakültesi Tarih Dergisi*) (March 1979); Necati Gültepe, "Hamidiye Alayları," *Hayat Tarih Mecmuası* (July 1976); Osman Aytar, *Hamidiye Alaylarının Köy Koruculuğuna* (Istanbul, 1972); Bayram Kodaman, *Şark Meselesi Işığında Sultan Abdülhamit'in Doğu Anadolu Politikası* (Istanbul, 1983).

89. Kendal, "Die Kurden unter der Osmanischen Herrschaft," in Gerard Chaliand, ed., *Kurdistan und die Kurden*, vol. 1 (Göttingen, 1988), p. 61.

90. See, for instance, Orhan Koloğlu, *Abdulhamit Gerçeği* (Istanbul, 1987), p. 337; Sonyel, "İngiliz Belgelerine Göre Adana'da," p. 1242.

91. Joan Haslip, *The Sultan: The Life of Abdul Hamid II*, first American edition (New York, 1973).

92. Mithat Sertoğlu, "Türkiye'de Ermeni Meselesi," *Belgelerle Türk Tarihi*, vol. 1 (Kasım, 1967), p. 48. For a fuller account of events at Sasun, see V. N. Dadrian, *History of the Armenian Genocide: Ethnic Conflict from the Balkans to Anatolia to the Caucasus* (Providence, RI, 1995), pp. 114ff; and Dadrian, "The 1894 Sassoun Massacre: A Juncture in the Escalation of the Turko-Armenian Conflict," in *Armenian Review* 47, nos. 1–2 (2001), pp. 5–39. For a contrasting account of the events at Sassoun, see Jeremy Salt, *Imperialism, Evangelism and the Ottoman Armenians, 1878–1896* (Oregon, 1993).

93. From the memoirs of Kâmil Paşa, who was made grand vizier shortly after this incident. Cited in Karal, *Osmanlı Tarihi*, vol. 8, p. 138.

94. Uras, *Tarihte Ermeniler*, p. 295.

95. Bayur, *Türk İnkılabı Tarihi*, p. 78.

96. Cited in Salt, *Imperialism*, p. 88.

97. Yves Ternon, *Tabu Armenien: Geschichte eines Völkermords* (Frankfurt/M-Berlin, Ullstein Sachbuch, 1988), pp. 73–74.

98. Uras, *Tarihte Ermeniler*, pp. 297–326, provides for comparison the complete texts of the proposals and notes delivered by the three powers and accepted by the Ottoman government.

99. For a more detailed account of these massacres, see Johannes Lepsius, *Armenien und Europa* (Berlin, 1897); Dadrian, *History of the Armenian Genocide;* and Ternon, *Tabu Armenien.*

100. Even the works that seek to protect Abdul Hamid II stress this strong connection between his reform edict to the regions and the massacres. See Salt, *Imperialism*, p. 141.

101. Lepsius, Bartholdy, and Timme, *Europäischen Kabinette*, vol. 10, p. 251.

102. Cited in V. N. Dadrian, "The Role of [the] Turkish Military in the Destruction of the Ottoman Armenians: A Study in Historical Continuities," *Journal of Political and Military Sociology* 20, no. 2 (Winter 1992), pp. 255–56.

103. Lepsius, *Armenien und Europa*, p. 20.

104. Ternon, *Tabu Armenien*, p. 149.

105. Some examples of this were the memorandum delivered by Great Britain on 20 October 1896, the reform package announced by Abdul Hamid II on 8 November and the memorandum delivered to the Porte by Russia on 19 December 1896. For the full text of these communications, see Uras, *Tarihte Ermeniler*, pp. 356–73.

106. This claim has been repeated in a number of works. See for instance Peter Lanne, *Armenien: der erste Völkermord des 20. Jahrhundert* (Munich, 1977), pp. 86–90; Fritjof Nansen, *Betrogenes Volk* (Leipzig, 1928), pp. 288–303; Ohandjanian, *Armenien*, pp. 26–36; Lepsius, *Armenien und Europa*, pp. 73–85.

107. For similar views on the matter of how the foreign interventions and the agreements that they produced brought attempts to solve the Armenian problem to an impasse, and how, by their negative effect, they resulted in massacre and mass slaughter, see V. N. Dadrian, "Der Genozid an den Armenien und das Völkerrecht," in Deutsch-Armenische Gesellschaft, ed., *Phönix aus der Asche* (Frankfurt, 1996), pp. 35–45, and *History of the Armenian Genocide*, pp. 61–113.

108. Ali Vehbi Bey, *Abdülhamit*, pp. 12, 31, cited in Karal, *Osmanlı Tarihi*, vol. 13 (Ankara, 1988), p. 484.

109. Tahsin Paşa, *Sultan Abdülhamid, Tahsin Paşa'nın Yıldız Hatıraları* (Istanbul, 1990), p. 182.

110. Haslip, *Sultan*, p. 211.

111. Ibid.

112. Ambassador's report, dated 16 November 1894, quoted in Lepsius, Bartholdy, Timme, *Europäischen Kabinette*, p. 9; Bayur, *Türk İnkılabı Tarihi*, pp. 77–78.

113. Quoted in Wilhelm van Kampen, *Studien zur Deutschen Türkeipolitik in der Zeit Wilhelms II* (Kiel, 1968), p. 122.

114. The politics of Pan-Islam has been examined in detail in a number of different works. See, for instance, Mümtaz Türköne, *Siyasi İdeoloji*; J. M. Landau, *The Politics of Pan-Islamism, Ideology and Organization* (Oxford, 1990); Bernard Lewis, "The Ottoman Empire in the Mid-Nineteenth Century: A Review," *Middle Eastern Studies* 1, no. 3 (April 1965); Azmi Özcan, *Panislamizm, Osmanlı Devleti Hindistan Müslümanları ve İngiltere, 1877–1914* (Istanbul, 1992); Cezmi Eraslan, *II. Abdülhamid ve İslam Birliği* (Istanbul: Otuken, 1992).

115. HHStA PA 413, A 1c, Constantinople, Report dated 11 October 1896.

116. For some examples, see Taner Akçam, *Siyasi Kültürümüzde Zulüm ve İşkence* (Istanbul: İletişim Yayınları, 1992), pp. 302–4.
117. For these reports, see Dadrian, "Role of the Turkish Military," p. 262.
118. Lepsius, Bartholdy, and Timme, *Europaeischen Kabinette*, vol. 10, p. 856.
119. The entire text of the note can be found in Bresnitz von Sydacoff, *Die Christenverfolgung in der Türkei unter dem Sultan Abdul Hamid, Aufzeichnungen nach amtlichen Quellen* (Berlin and Leipzig, 1896), pp. 57–58.
120. Cited in Dadrian, "Role of the Turkish Military," p. 263.
121. Koloğlu, *Abdülhamit*, pp. 227, 442.
122. FO 195/1930 (Folio 34/187). Quoted by V. N. Dadrian in "Genocide as a Problem of National and International Law: The World War I Armenian Case and Its Contemporary Legal Ramifications," reprinted in *Yale Journal of International Law* 14, no. 2 (1989), p. 243.
123. Lord Kinross, *The Ottoman Centuries* (New York, 1977), p. 560, cited by Dadrian, "Genocide as a Problem," p. 243.
124. For a more detailed account of the massacres in various cities in this period, see Ternon, *Tabu Armenien*; Lepsius, *Armenien und Europa*.
125. Yusuf Kemal Tengirşenk, *Vatan Hizmetinde* (Ankara, 1981), p. 120.
126. Reported in Haslip, *Sultan*, p. 222.

2. The Union and Progress Era

1. Ati, February 24, 1921. Talât Paşa's letter from 26 May 1915 to the grand vizier.
2. For more on this subject, see Akçam, *From Empire to Republic*, pp. 39–115.
3. Lewis, *Emergence of Modern Turkey*, p. 329. For an opposing view, see Charles Warren Hostler, *Türken und Sowjets* (Berlin, 1960), p. 107.
4. David Kushner, *The Rise of Turkish Nationalism, 1876–1908* (London, 1977), p. 5.
5. For more on the early Turkist movements, see Yusuf Akçura, *Yeni Türk Devletinin Öncüleri, 1928 Yazıları* (Ankara, 1981); Kushner, *Turkish Nationalism*; Ahâh Sırrı Levent, *Türk Dilinde Gelişme ve Sadeleşme Evreleri* (Ankara, 1960).
6. Akçura, *Yeni Türk*, p. 29.
7. Ibid., pp. 16–29.
8. For more detailed information, see Türköne, *Siyasi İdeoloji*, pp. 245ff.
9. M. C. Kuntay, *Namık Kemal, Devrin İnsanları ve Olayları Arasında*, vol. 1 (Ankara, 1949), p. 186.
10. Karal, *Osmanlı Tarihi*, vol. 7, p. 296.
11. Ibid., p. 293.
12. Lewis, *Emergence of Modern Turkey*, pp. 147–48.
13. Şükrü Hanioğlu, *Bir Siyasal Örgüt Olarak Osmanlı İttihad ve Terakki Cemiyeti ve Jön Türklük, 1889–1902* (Istanbul, 1985), p. 627.
14. Ernest E. Ramsaur, *The Young Turks* (Berkeley, CA, 1947), p. 92.

388 | Notes: The Union and Progress Era

15. Bayur, *Türk İnkılabı Tarihi*, vol. 2, part 4, p. 104. Similar utterances can be found in Hanioğlu, *Bir Siyasal*, pp. 630ff.
16. Sina Akşin, *Jön Türkler ve İttihat ve Terakki* (Istanbul, 1987), p. 169.
17. Hüseyin Cahit Yalçın, "Türkiye'yi Yaşatmak ve Batırmak İsteyenler, On Yılın Hatıraları 1935," *Yakın Tarihimiz*, vol. 1, p. 214.
18. Yusuf Akçura, *Üç Tarz-ı Siyaset* (Ankara, 1976), p. 37. The reply belongs to Ali Kemal.
19. Kushner, *Turkish Nationalism*, p. 39.
20. İsmail Kara, "Bir Milliyetçilik Tartışması," *Tarih ve Toplum*, 30 (June 1986), p. 57.
21. Halil Menteşe, *Osmanlı Mebusan Meclisi Reisi Halil Menteşe'nin Anıları* (Istanbul, 1986), p. 13.
22. Quoted from a letter dated 1901 by Şükrü Hanioğlu, *Bir Siyasal*, p. 629.
23. Kushner, *Turkish Nationalism*, pp. 29–30.
24. From a letter dated September 1906 by Bahaettin Şakir to the Muslims of the Caucasus. Quoted in Bayur, *Türk İnkılabı Tarihi*, vol. 1, part 1, p. 347.
25. Hanioğlu, *Bir Siyasal*, p. 631. The descriptions given by the author come from letters written in the years 1896–97.
26. Ibid., pp. 632–33.
27. Bayur, *Türk İnkılabı Tarihi*, vol. 2, part 4, p. 115.
28. Ibid.
29. Hanioğlu, *Bir Siyasal*, p. 649.
30. Quoted in François Georgeon, *Türk Milliyetçiliğinin Kökeni, Yusuf Akçura (1876–1935)* (Ankara, 1986), p. 14.
31. Ibid., p. 84.
32. It should be added here that there is no sociological or historical rule that every late-developing nationalism inevitably becomes aggressive or expansionist.
33. Hilmi Ziya Ülken, *Türkiye'de Cağdaş Düşünce Tarihi* (Istanbul, 1979), p. 81.
34. Tekin Alp, *Turkismus und Pan-Turkismus* (Weimar, 1915), p. 7.
35. Yusuf Akçura, quoted in Georgeon, *Yusuf Akçura*, p. 84.
36. Quoted in Tarık Zafer Tunaya, *Türkiye'de Siyasal Partiler*, vol. 3 (Istanbul, 1989), p. 320.
37. Ibid., p. 310.
38. Tunaya, quoted in Şerif Mardin, *Jön Türkler ve Siyasi Fikirleri* (Istanbul, 1983), p. 14.
39. Feroz Ahmad, *The Young Turks: The Committee of Union and Progress in Turkish Politics, 1908–1914* (Oxford, 1969), p. 155.
40. Celal Bayar, *Ben de Yazdım*, vol. 2 (Istanbul, 1966), p. 466.
41. A large portion of Gökalp's articles, in which he outlines the fundamental ideological directions of the Union and Progress movement, were published in the journals *Türk Yurdu* and *İslam* between the years 1913–14. These were subsequently collected and published in book form in 1918 under the title *Türkleşmek, İslamlaşmek, Muasırlaşmak (Turkification, Islamification, Modernization)*. Regarding Ziya Gökalp and his ideas, see Uriel Heyd, *The Founda-*

tions of Turkish Nationalism (London, 1950); Niyazi Berkes, Turkish Nationalism and Western Civilization, Selected Essays of Ziya Gökalp (London, 1959); and Taha Parla, The Social and Political Thought of Ziya Gökalp, 1876–1924 (Leiden, 1985).

42. İlber Ortaylı, Imparatorluğun En Uzun Yüzyılı (Istanbul, 1983).
43. Niyazi Berkes, Türkiye'de Çağdaşlaşma (Istanbul, 1978), p. 325.
44. Hanioğlu, Bir Siyasal, p. 620.
45. Ibid., p. 633.
46. Şevket Süreyya Aydemir, Makedonya'dan Orta Asya'ya Enver Paşa, vol. 2: 1908–1914 (Istanbul, 1981), p. 67.
47. Ibid., p. 552.
48. Bayar, Ben de Yazdım, vol. 2, p. 552.
49. Bayur, Türk İnkılabı Tarihi, vol. 1, part 1, p. 271.
50. Ibid., vol. 2, part 4, p. 18.
51. Mardin, Jön Türkler ve Siyasi Fikirleri, p. 118.
52. The paper Mechveret, which was the main French-language Unionist organ, published an article by one of the staff, Aristidi Bey, under the nom de plume G. Ümid, dealing with the Greco-Turkish War of 1897. In the article, themes are taken up that attempt to show that the Greek uprising on the island of Crete was justified. "The article reflected such an extreme separatist view that an Armenian journal felt it appropriate to reprint it." Mechveret subsequently became a target for severe attacks on account of the article. The publishers of the paper (among whom were Armenians and Greeks) were individually named, and Ahmet Rıza himself was accused in the sharpest of tones, asking why he would publish such vile things. After all of the slanderous accusations, Ahmet Rıza was kicked out of the organization. Hanioğlu, Bir Siyasal, pp. 233–39.
53. Ramsaur, Young Turks, p. 93.
54. Koloğlu, Abdülhamit, pp. 335–36.
55. Hüseyin Cahit Yalçın, "Türkiye'yi Yaşatmak," p. 214.
56. For a detailed discussion of this issue, see Hanioğlu, Bir Sayasal, and Mardin, Jön Türkler ve Siyasi Fikirleri.
57. Tunaya, Türkiye'de Siyasal Partiler, p. 399.
58. Akşin, Jön Türkler, pp. 61–62.
59. Tunaya, Türkiye'de Siyasal Partiler, pp. 135–36.
60. Ibid., pp. 136–37.
61. Ibid., p. 134.
62. Akşin, Jön Türkler, p. 159.
63. For more information, see Şükrü Hanioğlu, Preparation for a Revolution: The Young Turks, 1902–1908 (New York, 2000); Ahmad, İttihatçılıktan; Louise Nalbandian, The Armenian Revolutionary Movement (Berkeley, 1963); Richard Hovannisian, Armenia on the Road to Independence: 1918 (Los Angeles, 1967); Dikran Mesrob Kaligan, "The American Revolutionary Federation Under

Ottoman Constitutional Rule, 1908–1914," unpublished dissertation at Boston College, the Graduate School of Arts and Sciences, December 2003.

64. Y. A. Petrosyan, *Sovyet Gözüyle Jön Türkler* (Ankara, 1974), p. 267.

65. Bayur, *Türk İnkılabı Tarihi*, vol. 1, part 1, p. 372.

66. Ibrahim Temo, *İttihat ve Terakki Cemiyeti'nin kurucusu ve 1/1 no'lu üyesi İbrahim Temo'nun İttihat ve Terakki Anıları* (Istanbul, 1987), p. 42. For the entire text of the report, see Ahmet Bedevi Kuran, *Osmanlı İmparatorluğunda ve Türkiye Cumhuriyetinde İnkilap Hareketleri* (Istanbul, 1959), pp. 158–59.

67. Sükrü Hanioğlu, *Bir Siyasal*, p. 191.

68. Ibid., pp. 195, 433–37.

69. Ibid., p. 210. It is not known with which Armenian revolutionary committees the meetings were held. When reporting on the meetings, Ahmet Rıza himself told Mizancı Murat that he met "with everyone." Ibid., p. 211.

70. Ibid., p. 217.

71. Ibid., p. 220, n. 252.

72. Mardin, *Jön Türkler ve Siyasi Fikirleri*, p. 144.

73. See Hanioğlu, *Bir Siyasal*, p. 232, for a reflection of this in their correspondence.

74. Ibid., pp. 315, 392–93.

75. Ibid., p. 358, n. 971 and n. 972.

76. *Mechveret*, 1 October 1896, quoted in Ternon, *Tabu Armenien*, p. 153.

77. Mardin, *Jön Türkler ve Siyasi Fikirleri*, p. 150.

78. Ibid.

79. Bayur, *Türk İnkılabı Tarihi*, vol. 1, part 1, p. 374.

80. Ibid., vol. 2, part 4, p. 117.

81. For Sabahettin's views on this subject, see A. B. Kuran, *Osmanlı İmparatorluğunda*; A. B. Kuran, *İnkilap Tarihimiz ve Jön Türkler* (Istanbul, 1945); Bayur, *Türk İnkılabı Tarihi*, vol. 1, part 1, and vol. 2, part 4; Cavit Orhan Tütengil, *Prens Sabahettin* (Istanbul, 1954).

82. Tunaya, *Turkiye'de Siyasal Partiler*, p. 106.

83. Avcıoğlu, *Milli Kurtuluş Tarihi: 1838'den 1995'e*, vol. 3 (Istanbul, 1987), pp. 1089–90.

84. Quoted in Bayur, *Türk İnkılabı Tarihi*, vol. 2, part 4, p. 13.

85. Avcıoğlu, *Millı Kurtuluş Tarihi*, p. 1084. Similar reports can be found in Taner Timur, *Osmanlı Çalışmaları* (Ankara, 1989), pp. 320–32; A. Alper Gazigiray, *Osmanlılardan Günümuze Kadar Ermeni Terörünün Kaynakları* (Istanbul, 1982), pp. 137–38.

86. Koloğlu, *Abdülhamit*, p. 91.

87. Sina Akşin, *İstanbul Hükümetleri ve Milli Mücadele*, vol. 1: *Mutlakiyete Dönüş (1918–1919)* (Istanbul, 1983), p. 241.

88. Sabah Külian, *Badaskanadouneru* (Those Responsible) (Beirut, 1974), p. 208. (I thank Professor V. N. Dadrian for the translation from Armenian.)

89. Bayur, *Türk İnkılabı Tarihi*, vol. 1, part 1, pp. 372–73.

90. Ibid., p. 343.

91. Ibid.

92. Although space does not allow me to discuss the history of the CUP in any detail here, I should point out that the CUP in the form we know it now was established by Talât Paşa and his friends in Salonica under another name in 1906. And this organization merged with the Paris Committee of Union and Progress, whereupon Salonica became the center. For detailed information see Şükrü Hanioğlu, *Bir Siyasal.*

93. Bayur, *Türk İnkılabı Tarihi,* vol. 1, part 1, p. 387.

94. Ibid., p. 391.

95. Ibid., p. 388.

96. Ibid., p. 391.

97. Temo, p. 148.

98. On this point, almost all Turkish researchers are in agreement. Mardin, *Jön Türkler ve Siyasi Fikirleri,* p. 219, and Hanioğlu, *Bir Siyasal,* pp. 69–70, are but two examples of this assessment.

99. Hanioğlu, *Bir Siyasal,* p. 72.

100. Quoted in V. N. Dadrian, "Genocide as a Problem of National and International Law," pp. 251–52.

101. For further information based on British sources about the demonstrations of brotherhood and solidarity in the various regions after 1908, see Sonyel, "İngiliz Belgelerine Göre Adana'da."

102. The proclamation of the second constitutional period in 1908 has been deceptively called a "revolution," which misleads one to believe that there was a mass uprising of some kind. However, the majority of the people did not even know about the proclamation. It was announced by the sultan and published in the daily newspapers. Even Union and Progress members learned this from the newspapers. Hüseyin Cahit Yalçın wrote in his memoirs that after he had read the news in the paper he could not believe his eyes and did not believe that the news was true. (Hüseyin Cahit Yalçın, "Meşrutiyet Hatıraları 1908–1918," in *Fikir Hareketleri* 3, no. 71, 28 Şubat/February 1935).

103. Feroz Ahmad, *İttihat ve Terakki,* p. 41.

104. Tunaya, *Turkiye'de Siyasal Partiler;* p. 8; Akşin, *Jön Türkler,* p. 83.

105. Bayur, *Türk İnkılabı Tarihi,* vol. 2, part 4, pp. 204–8.

106. Petrosyan, *Sovyet Gözuyle Jön Türkler,* p. 281.

107. Mizancı Murat, quoted in ibid., p. 192.

108. Mardin, *Jön Türkler ve Siyasi Fikirleri,* p. 67.

109. Ibid., p. 67.

110. Hanioğlu, *Bir Siyasal,* p. 671.

111. For the declarations of the Hunchak and Dashnak committees in regard to the reestablishment of the Constitution, see Uras, *Tarihte Ermeniler,* p. 573.

112. Sonyel, "İngiliz Belgelerine Göre Adana'da," p. 1245.

113. Feroz Ahmad, "Unionist Relations with the Greek, Armenian, and Jewish Communities of the Ottoman Empire, 1908–1914," in Bernard Lewis, ed., *Christians*

and Jews in the Ottoman Empire: The Functioning of a Plural Society (New York, 1982).

114. For more information on the "31 March Affair," see Sina Akşin, 31 Mart (Ankara, 1970); Doğan Avcıoğlu, 31 Mart'ta Yabancı Parmağı (Ankara, 1959); Faik Reşit Unat, İkinci Meşrutiyetin İlanı ve Otuzbir Mart Hadisesi (Ankara, 1991); İsmail Hakkı Danişment, 31 Mart Vakası (Istanbul, 1986); Edward J. Ericson, Defeat in Detail: The Ottoman Army in the Balkans, 1912–1913 (Westport, CT, 1972), p. 26.

115. For the role of economic factors in the Adana massacres see Stephan H. Astourian, "The Silence of the Land: Agrarian Relations, Ethnicity, and Power," an unpublished paper presented at "Contextualizing the Armenian Experience in the Ottoman Empire: From the Balkan Wars to the New Turkish Republic," University of Michigan, Ann Arbor, 8–10 March, 2002; this is the estimate given in the report later issued by the aforementioned investigative committee, led by Ottoman deputy Agop Babikyan (Hagop Papikian). For more information on the report, see Uras, Tarihte Ermeniler, p. 559; Hovannisian, Armenia on the Road to Independence, p. 30. Hovannisian mentions that in the French and Armenian versions of the report, the number given is 21,000 (p. 268).

116. Ternon, Tabu Armenien, p. 209.

117. Frankfurter Zeitung, 20 June 1909.

118. Quoted by Dadrian, "The Role of the Turkish Military," p. 274.

119. R. Pinon, Revue des Deux Mondes (September 1919). Quoted in Zarevand, United and Independent Turania, Aims and Designs of the Turks (Leiden, 1971), p. 32. See also Ternon, Tabu Armenien, p. 210.

120. For more detailed information on the events in Adana, see V. N. Dadrian, "The Circumstances Surrounding the 1909 Adana Holocaust," Armenian Review 41, no. 4/164 (Winter 1988); Norbert Saupp, Das Deutsche Reich und die Armenische Frage 1878–1914 (Cologne, 1990); Uras, Tarihte Erminiler, pp. 551–70; Sonyel, "İngiliz Belgelerine Göre Adana'da"; Ternon, Tabu Armenien.

121. For a detailed account of the dimensions of these relations and the activities of the joint committees between 1909–1912, see Dikran Mesrob Kaligian, "The Armenian Revolutionary Federation Under the Ottoman Constitutional Rule 1908–1914," unpublished dissertation, Boston College Graduate School of Arts and Sciences, 2003, pp. 19–182; Feroz Ahmad, İttihatçılıktan, pp. 148–63; Sarkis Atamian, Armenian Community: The Historical Development of a Social and Ideological Conflict (New York, 1955), pp. 156–65; Michael A. Reynolds, "The Ottoman-Russian Struggle for Eastern Anatolia and the Caucasus, 1908–1918: Identity, Ideology and the Geopolitics of World Order," unpublished dissertation presented to the faculty of Princeton University, November 2003, pp. 170–71.

122. Quoted in Feroz Ahmad, İttihat ve Terakki, p. 148.

123. Akçura, who claimed that the "union of [Ottoman] peoples," or İttihad-ı Anasır, was an illusion, first asked these questions in 1910. For the full text, see Georgeon, Yusuf Akçura, pp. 131–32, Appendix 8.

124. Akşin, *Jön Türkler,* p. 149.
125. *Meclisi Mebusan Zabıt Ceridesi 5* (Ankara, n.d.), pp. 26–27. Regarding this law—and the aforementioned articles in particular—there were extremely heated debates within the assembly, with the non-Turkish and non-Muslim deputies coming out strongly in opposition to the article forbidding the establishment of nationally or ethnically based associations. Ultimately, the law passed on a vote of 90 to 60.
126. Lewis, *Emergence of Modern Turkey,* p. 217.
127. Tunaya, *Türkiye'de Siyasal Partiler,* p. 209.
128. İlhan Tekeli and Selim İlkin, *Osmanlı İmparatorluğu'nda Eğitim ve Bilim Üretim Sisteminin Oluşumu ve Dönüşümü* (Ankara, 1993), p. 86.
129. Osman Ergin, *Türk Maarif Tarihi,* vols. 3–4 (Istanbul, 1977), p. 1292.
130. For detailed information on failed attempts at conscription, see Erik Jan Zürcher, "The Ottoman Conscription System in Theory and Practice," in Erik J. Zürcher, ed., *Arming the State: Military Conscription in the Middle East and Central Asia, 1775–1925* (London, 1999), pp. 79–95.
131. The "Law on the Conscription of Non-Muslim Communities" was adopted on 8 Temmuz 1325 (21 July 1909): *Meclisi Mebusan Zabıt Ceridesi,* pp. 475–86. Published in the Official Gazeteer, *Takvim-i Vekâyı* on 25 Temmuz, 1325 (7 August 1909).
132. Tekeli and İlkin, *Osmanlı,* p. 89.
133. Zürcher, ed., *Arming the State,* p. 87.
134. Ergin, *Türk Maarif Tarihi,* p. 1293–95.
135. Ibid.
136. For more on the Albanian revolt, see J. Stanford Shaw and Ezel Kural Shaw, *History of the Ottoman Empire and Modern Turkey,* vol. 2 (Cambridge, 1977), pp. 287–88; Süleyman Külçe, *Osmanlı Tarihinde Arnavutluk* (Izmir, 1944), pp. 351–419.
137. Shaw and Shaw, *Ottoman Empire,* p. 289.
138. For more detailed information concerning the oppressive measures implemented by the CUP between 1908 and 1913, see Feroz Ahmad, *İttihat ve Terakki,* pp. 106–16; Tunaya, *Türkiye'de Siyasal Partiler,* vol. 3, pp. 388–94; and Akşin, *Jön Türkler,* pp. 140–49.
139. Tunaya, *Türkiye'de Siyasal Partiler,* p. 388.
140. Feroz Ahmad, *İttihat ve Terakki,* p. 266.
141. Bayur, *Türk İnkılabı Tarihi,* vol. 2, part 4, p. 476.
142. Lewis, *Emergence of Modern Turkey,* p. 218.
143. Berkes, *Türkiye'de Çağdaş,* p. 393.
144. *Tanin,* 27 Temmuz 1910, quoted in Feroz Ahmad, *Young Turks,* p. 84.
145. Gooch and Temperly, *British Documents on the Origin of the War, 1898–1914,* vol. 9 (London, 1926), part 1, no. 181, p. 208. Cited in Lewis, *Emergence of Modern Turkey,* p. 218.

146. Gooch and Temperly, *British Documents*, pp. 207–8, cited in Lewis, *Emergence of Modern Turkey*, pp. 218–19.

147. In the report sent on 14 October 1910 from the Austrian Consulate in Monastir, the information concerning Talât's speech is almost word-for-word identical with that given in the British report. AA Türkei 159, no. 2, p. 12. For more information about the French, British, and German reports, see Dadrian, *The History of the Armenian Genocide*, pp. 179–84.

148. Bayur, *Türk İnkılabı Tarihi*, vol. 2, part 4, p. 13.

149. French Foreign Ministry Archives, *Turquie*, new series, vol. 7, no. 486 (23 November 1910).

150. Bayur, *Türk İnkılabı Tarihi*, vol. 2, part 4, p. 13.

151. Tekin Alp, *Türkismus und Pantürkismus* (Weimar, 1915), p. 45.

152. From the Central Committee's report, submitted to the 1911 congress of the Committee of Union and Progress. *Tanin*, 30 Eylül 1327 (13 October 1911), no. 1118.

153. Ibid., 28 Eylül 1327 (11 October 1911), no. 1116.

154. Ibid., 30 Eylül 1327 (13 October 1911), no. 1118.

155. Ibid.

156. Tunaya, *Türkiye'de Siyasal Partiler*, p. 189.

157. AA Türkei, PA 38414. The report by Karl, the Austrian consul in Salonica, dated 13 November 1911.

158. For more details on these reports, see Jacob M. Landau, *Pan-Turkism in Turkey, A Study of Irredentism* (London, 1981), pp. 48–55.

159. Ternon, *Tabu Armenien*, p. 189; J. Lepsius, *Der Todesgang des Armenischen [V]olkes* (Potsdam, 1919), pp. 220–22. The reports given by both Ternon and Lepsius regarding the decisions made at the congress are incorrect.

160. U. Heyd, *Foundations of Turkish Nationalism: The Life and Teachings of Ziya Gökalp* (London, 1950), pp. 71–72.

161. "Seeing the language question [alone] as insufficient, I thought it necessary to raise the issue of Turkish nationalism in all of its principles and in its entirety. I wrote and published in *Genç Kalemler* the poem 'Turan,' which contained all of these ideas." Ziya Gökalp, *Türkçülüğün Esasları* (Istanbul, 1978), p. 10.

162. On Ziya Gökalp's influence on *Genç Kalemler*, see Ali Canip Yöntem's recollections in *Yakın Tarihimiz*, vol. 1, pp. 371–73.

163. Heyd, *Foundations*, p. 109.

164. Ziya Gökalp, *Türkleşmek, İslamlaşmak, Muasırlaşmak* (Istanbul, 1988), pp. 39–40.

165. Tunaya, *Türkiye'de Siyasal Partiler*, vol. 3, p. 8.

166. Bayur, *Türk Inkılabı Tarihi*, vol. 1, part 4, p. 203. Additionally, it was mentioned [to] both the Prince and certain persons who were with him that it would be best if they returned to Europe. Ali Haydar Mithat, *Hatıralarım* (Istanbul, 1946), p. 201.

167. Akşin, *Jön Türkler*, p. 107.

168. Lewis, *Emergence of Modern Turkey*, p. 214.

169. Mardin, *Jön Türkler ve Siyasi Fikirleri*, p. 144.

170. Ömer Kürkçüoğlu, *Türk-İngiliz İlişkileri (1919–1926)* (Ankara, 1978), p. 30.
171. Quoted in Avcıoğlu, *31 Mart'ta*, pp. 35–36.
172. Bayur, *Türk İnkılabı Tarihi*, vol. 2, part 3, p. 94.
173. Regarding the German plans for Anatolia and the Balkans, see Wilhelm van Kampen, "Studien zur Deutschen Türkeipolitik in der Zeit Wilhelms II," unpublished dissertation, Christian-Albrechts University (Kiel, 1968).
174. Quoted in Mardin, *Jön Türkler ve Siyasi Fikirleri*, p. 117.
175. The article was written on 4 August 1911, shortly after the Italian invasion of Tripoli. It has been transliterated and reprinted in *Tarih ve Toplum* 70 (October 1989), pp. 43–50.

3. Turkish Nationalism

1. The rise of Turkish nationalism in the Ottoman Empire has been studied in detail in several works: Yusuf Akçura, *Yeni Türk Devletinin Öncüleri, 1928 Yılı Yazıları;* (Ankara, 1981); İsmail Habib, *Edebi Yeniliğimiz* (Istanbul, 1931); Sadık Tural, *Osmanlı İmparatorluğu'nun Son Yıllarında (1908–1920) Edebiyatımızda Türkçülük Akımı* (Ankara, 1978); Ağâh Sırrı Levent, Türk Dilinde Gelişme, Yusuf Sarınay, *Türk Milliyetçiliğinin Tarihi Gelişimi ve Türk Ocakları 1912–1931* (Istanbul, 1994); Lewis, *Emergence of Modern Turkey;* Heyd, *Foundations;* Kushner, *Turkish Nationalism;* Landau, *Pan-Turkism;* Suavi Aydın, *Modernleşme ve Milliyetçilik* (Ankara, 1993).
2. For more in-depth discussion of these sources, see Lewis, *Emergence of Modern Turkey,* pp. 341–58; Gökalp, *Türkçülüğün,* pp. 32–34. For a different list of sources for Turkish nationalism, see Ersanlı Behar, *İktidar ve Tarih: Türkiye'de 'Resmi Tarih' Tezinin Oluşumu (1929–1937)* (Istanbul, 1992), pp. 60–78.
3. Lewis, *Emergence of Modern Turkey,* p. 348.
4. For more on the pattern of development of eastern nationalisms, see Miroslav Hroch, *Die Vorkämpfer der nationalen Bewegung bei den kleinen Völkern Europas* (Prague, 1968).
5. The debates on these topics during this period have been analyzed in different Turkish studies, among which Tarık Zafer Tunaya's work holds a special place. His articles were recently compiled in various volumes by Bilgi University. See especially *Türkiye'de Siyasal Gelişmeler 1876–1938: Kanun-ı Esasi ve Meşrutiyet dönemi,* vol. 1 (Istanbul Bilgi Üniversitesi, 2001); *Türkiye'nin Siyasi Hayatında Batılılaşma Hareketleri* (Istanbul Bilgi Üniversitesi, 2004); and *İslamcılık Cereyanı* (Istanbul Bilgi Üniversitesi, 2003); see also Bayur, *Türk İnkılabı Tarihi,* vol. 2, part 4; and Hilmi Ziya Ülken, *Türkiye'de Çağdaş Düşünce Tarihi* (Istanbul: Ülken, 1979).
6. Bayur, *Türk İnkılabı Tarihi*, vol. 2, part 4, p. 399.
7. Berkes, *Türkiye'de Çağdaş*, p. 394.
8. Landau, *Pan-Turkism*, p. 45.
9. Ibid., pp. 45–46.

10. Harry Luke, *The Making of Turkey from Byzantium to Angora* (London, 1936), p. 157; quoted in ibid, p. 46.

11. Georgeon, *Yusuf Akçura*, p. 38. David Kushner has advanced a different theory on this issue. He claims that the Union and Progress leaders had read the works of the original "Turkist" movement, but had not been particularly impressed.

12. Gökalp, *Türkleşmek*, pp. 12, 14, 44.

13. A good example of this is that of Yusuf Akçura. Concerning his relations with the committee and its ideologue Ziya Gökalp and the problems between them, see Georgeon, *Yusuf Akçura*, pp. 54–55, 62ff, 221.

14. Bayur, *Türk İnkılabı Tarihi*, vol. 2, part 4, p. 314.

15. Ergin, *Türk Maarif Tarihi*, pp. 1296–301.

16. For more on the debates between the Unionists and the traditional Islamists, see İsmail Kara, *Türkiye'de İslamcılık Düşüncesi*, vol. 1 (Istanbul, 1986), pp. i–xiv; Hüseyin Kâzim Kadri (İsmail Kara, ed.), *Ziya Gökalp'ın Tenkidi* (Istanbul, 1989), pp. 50–71. In addition, for more on the intellectual currents, one may also consult the aforementioned works by T. Z. Tunaya.

17. Bayur, *Türk İnkılabı Tarihi*, vol. 2, part 4, pp. 409–13.

18. The words are of the well-known Islamist thinker of the period, Mehmet Akif Ersoy, quoted in Tunaya, *Türkiye'de Siyasal Partiler*, vol. 3, p. 464.

19. Ibid., p. 310.

20. The real reason for this coup was that the Unionists had learned that the government was preparing to ban the party. On this date, the Union and Progress organization had already been closed down and its members were being investigated. As of early November, there were some fifty-five Unionists in custody in Istanbul alone. Akşin, p. 220.

21. Bayar, *Ben de Yazdım*, vol. 3, p. 814.

22. Ibid., p. 808.

23. Ibid., pp. 813–14.

24. Bayur, *Türk İnkılabı Tarihi*, vol. 2, part 4, p. 423.

25. Ibid., p. 245.

26. Shaw and Shaw, "Osmanlı İmparatorluğu'nda Azınlıklar Sorunu," in *Tanzimattan Cumhuriyete Türkiye Ansiklopedisi*, vol. 4, p. 1004.

27. Ibid., p. 1005.

28. Davison, *Reform*, p. 173, n. 32.

29. Aydemir, *Enver Paşa*, vol. 2, p. 296.

30. Quoted in *Tarih ve Toplum* (March 1991), p. 87.

31. Arnold J. Toynbee, *The Western Question in Greece and Turkey* (New York, 1970), p. 139.

32. Ohandjanian, *Armenien, Die Veschweigerten Völkermord*, p. 36. For more information about the migration from the Balkans, see Bilal N. Şimşir, *Rumeli'den Türk Göçleri: Belgeler*, vol. 2 (Ankara, 1989), pp. ix–clxxxii.

33. Bayur, *Türk İnkılabı Tarihi*, vol. 2, part 2, p. 410.

34. Tunaya, *Türkiye'de Siyasal Partiler*, p. 235.
35. It was claimed that Gökalp's selection to the CUP Central Committee was based on the fact that he could create a theoretical model to fit the practical needs of the party. Mehmet Emin Erişirgil, *Bir Fikir Adamının Romanı* (Istanbul, 1984), p. 67. Likewise, see Yalçın Küçük, *Aydın Üzerine Tezler*, vol. 2 (Istanbul, 1985), p. 566.
36. Kazım [Nami] Duru, *Ziya Gökalp* (Istanbul, 1949), pp. 61–62.
37. Ibid.
38. Quoted in Ülken, *Türkiye'de Çağdaş*, p. 310.
39. Gökalp, *Türkleşmek*, pp. 71–76.
40. Ibid., pp. 73, 80.
41. For a more detailed treatment of the economic aspects of Turkish nationalism, see Zafer Toprak, *Türkiye'de 'Milli İktisat' 1908–1918* (Ankara, 1982), pp. 173–76.
42. Ibid., pp. 21, 32.
43. Heyd, *Foundations*, p. 57.
44. For more information on the preparation of the Union and Progress Party's ethnicity and resettlement policy, see Fuat Dündar, "Türk Milliyetçiliğinin Dinamikleri, İttihat ve Terakki'nin Etnisite Araştırmaları," *Toplumsal Tarih* 16, no. 91 (July 2001), pp. 43–51.
45. Enver Behnan Şapolyo, *Ziya Gökalp ve İttihad [ve] Terakki ve Meşrutiyet Tarihi* (Istanbul, 1974), p. 149.
46. The society's regulatory charter was published on 12 Kanunuevvel 1324 (25 December 1908), according to which, its aim was to establish a "Turkish society of a non-political, cultural nature." Akçura, *Yeni Türk*, pp. 188–89.
47. Erol Şadi Erdinç, "Meşrutiyet Sonrasi Parti ve Cemiyetler Hakkında Bir Kalem Denemesi (1906–1920)" (unpublished manuscript) 1983, p. 21.
48. This institution described its goal as "to assist the Turks in acquiring the means and the initiative to raise themselves to a higher level of intellect and knowledge." Akçura, *Yeni Türk*, pp. 191–92.
49. The initial attempts at establishing the Turkish Hearth actually began with the efforts of 190 military medical school students in May 1911. An account of these efforts can be found in ibid., pp. 195ff.
50. Erdinç, "Meşrutiyet," p. 77/a, b.
51. According to François Georgeon, the financial support (to the organization)— and from Enver Paşa in particular—was not public, being instead of a secret nature. It was only after the 1913 Balkan defeat that it began to be given openly. Georgeon, *Yusuf Akçura*, p. 59.
52. Quoted from the responsible delegate for the Türk Gücü Cemiyeti, Kuzcuoğlu Tahsin Bey, in Zafer Toprak, "II. Meşrutiyet Döneminde Paramiliter Gençlik Örgütleri," in *Tanzimattan Cumhuriyete Türkiye Ansiklopedesi*, vol. 2, p. 532.
53. Ibid. German influence was pervasive in all of these associations (p. 535).
54. Ibid., pp. 531, 533.

55. This society was deemed as "beneficial to the public" by the Council of Ministers in 1914 and subsequently performed important services during the First World War.

56. Tunaya, *Türkiye'de Siyasal Partiler*, vol. 3, p. 336.

57. A detailed report on the matter of companies being founded by the Unionist party leadership was submitted to the 1914 annual Union and Progress party congress. For the full text of the report, see Toprak, *Türkiye'de 'Milli İktisat,'* p. 393.

58. Ibid., pp. 79–83.

59. Quoted in Zeki Sarıhan, *Kurtuluş Savaşı Günlüğü*, vol. 1 (Ankara, 1984), p. 68.

60. This committee was established by the government with the aim of preventing wartime profiteering and speculation. For more detailed information, see Toprak, *Türkiye'de 'Milli İktisat,'* pp. 294–302.

61. Ibid., p. 57.

62. Minutes of the main trial of the former Unionist leaders, fifth session, 12 May 1919. *Takvîm-i Vekâyı*, no. 3554. The printed date of "14 May" is incorrect.

63. *Takvîm-i Vekâyı*, no. 3547.

64. Henry Morgenthau, *Ambassador Morgenthau's Story* (London, 1918), p. 51.

65. Ibid.

66. Halil Menteşe, *Osmanli Mebusan Meclisi Reisi Halil Menteşe'nin Anıları* (Istanbul, 1986), p. 165.

67. Eşref Kuşçubaşı was one of the central figures in the notorious Special Organization, which carried out the operations aimed at cleansing Anatolia of its non-Turkish elements. His utterances are quoted in Bayar, *Ben de Yazdım*, vol. 5, p. 1578.

68. Gökalp, *Türkleşmek*, p. 401.

69. In a 1911 issue of *Genç Kalemler*, Gökalp had written that "For the Turks, the homeland is neither Turkey nor Turkistan / the homeland is a great and eternal country: Turan." Ibid., p. 63.

70. Ibid.

71. Gökalp, quoted in Tunaya, *Türkiye'de Siyasal Partiler*, vol. 3, pp. 319–20.

72. Regarding Turkish nationalism and Pan-Turanism, see also Gotthard Jäschke, "Der Turanismus der Jüngtürken," in *Die Welt des Islams* 23 (1941); Ahmed Muhiddin, *Die Kulturbewegung im Modern Türkentum* (Leipzig, 1921); Günter Schöld, "Zur Entstehung des Türkischen Nationalismus," in *Österreichische Osthefte* Jahrgang 27 (Vienna, 1985); Ernst Werner, "Wesen und Formen des Türkischen Nationalismus," *Zeitschrift für Geschichtswissenschaft* Jahrgang 16, 10. Heft 10 (Berlin, 1968); Zehra Önder, "Pantürkismus in Geschichte und Gegenwart," in *Österreichische Osthefte* Jahrgang 19, vol. 2 (May 1977); Richard Hartmann, "Ziya Gökalp's Grundlagen des Türkischen Nationalismus," in *Orientalische Literaturzeitung*, no. 9/10 (1925). Even though some scholars try to define the differences between Pan-Turanism, Turkism, Turanism, and Turkism, the terms were seldom used in the nationalistic literature to indicate distinct meanings. In most cases, Turkish authors used the terms interchangeably. For a discussion of these terms, see Jacob M. Landau, *Pan-Turkism, From Irredentism*

to *Cooperation* (Bloomington and Indianapolis: Indiana University Press, 1995), pp. 7–74.

73. A. Mil, "Umumi Harpte Teşkilat-ı Mahsusa," *Vakit,* Installment no. 1 (2 İkinciteşrin/2 November 1933). A. Mil is the alias of Arif Cemil, one of the CUP's so-called responsible secretaries, who served within the Special Organization in eastern Anatolia during World War I.

74. Ibid.

75. Yuluğ Tekin Kurat, *Osmanlı İmparatorluğu'nun Paylaşılması* (Ankara, 1986), p. 24.

76. Philip H. Stoddard, *Teşkilat-ı Mahsusa, Osmanlı Hükümeti ve Arapları 1911–1918: Teşkilat-i Mahsusa Üzerine Bir Ön Çalışma* (Istanbul, 1993), p. 48.

77. The works cited in the previous two paragraphs are, in order, Tevfik Bıyıkoğlu, *Trakya'da Milli Mücadele,* vol. 1 (Ankara, 1987), pp. 88–89; Bilge Criss, *İşgal Altında İstanbul, 1918–1923* (Istanbul, 1993), p. 145. Criss claims that he reached this conclusion as a result of a conversation he had with Special Organization member Fahri Özdilek; Fuat Balkan's recollections are found in *Yakın Tarihimiz,* vol. 2, p. 37; Cemal Paşa, *Hatıralar ve Vesikalar* (Istanbul, n.d.), p. 89.

78. Cemal Kutay, *Birinci Dünya Harbi'nde Teşkilât-i Mahsusa ve Heyber'de Türk Cengi* (Istanbul, 1962), pp. 39–40. Kutay made a similar claim in another work, *Talât Paşa'nın Gurbet Hatıraları,* vol. 2 (Istanbul, 1983), p. 905.

79. The minutes of the questioning sessions were kept by Necmettin Sahir (Sılan) Bey and later published in book form: *Said Halim ve Mehmet Talât Paşalar kabinelerinin Divan-ı Âli'ye sevkleri hakkında divaniye mebusu Fuat Bey merhum tarafından verilen takrir üzerine berayı tahkikat kura isabet eden Beşinci Şube tarfından icra olunan tahkikat ve zabt edilen İfadati muhtevidir* (*Meclis-i Mebusan,* no. 521, *Devre-yi İntihabiye:* 3, *İçtima:* 5) (Istanbul, 1334/1918), p. 42. Due to its lengthy title, further references to the book shall be made as simply 5. *Şube Tutanakları.* The page references are according to the transcription made by Erol Şadi Erdinç. (The pagination begins anew for each suspect who was brought before the commission for questioning.)

80. See the minutes of the fifth session of the trial (12 May 1919), the depositions of Cevat Bey, Mithat Şükrü and Ziya Gökalp, *Takvîm-i Vekâyı,* no. 3554 (14 Mayıs 1335/14 May 1919).

81. From the questioning of Cevat and Atıf Bey at the trial's second session (4 May 1919). *Takvîm-i Vekâyı,* no. 3543 (4 Mayıs, 1335/4 May 1919). The same testimony was repeated by all of the defendants at the fifth session.

82. Tunaya, *Türkiye'de Siyasal Partiler,* vol. 3, p. 276; minutes from the first session of the main trial—Principal Indictment. *Takvîm-i Vekâyı,* no. 3540 (27 Nisan 1335/27 April 1919).

83. During the Balkan War, some Special Organization members with representatives of the Ottoman military established a provisional government in western Thrace in summer 1913. Thrace was given back to the Greeks a few months later.

For more information, see Abdürrahim Dede, *Balkanlar'da Türk İstiklal Hareketleri* (Istanbul, 1978), pp. 33–55.

84. Bayar, *Ben de Yazdım*, vol. 5, p. 1570. The quotation is from Kuşçubaşı Eşref, who sent Bayar a file regarding the Special Organization. The government of western Thrace was, in accordance with the Ottoman-Bulgar agreement, obliged to surrender the region to the Bulgarians no later than 25 October 1913. In fact, the Bulgarian occupation was completed on 30 October. (Bıyıkoğlu, *Trakya'da Milli Mücadele*, pp. 85–88.) According to this chronology, the Special Organization appeared at the same time that Enver Paşa was the minister of war (January 1914).

85. Galip Vardar, *İttihat ve Terakki İçinde Dönenler* (Istanbul, 1960), pp. 274–77.

86. See the reports of the third and fourth sessions of the main trial of Unionist government defendants. *Takvîm-i Vekâyı*, nos. 3547 and 3549 (6 and 8 Mayıs 1335/6 and 8 May 1919, respectively).

87. The minutes from the main trial of the Unionist leaders, second session (4 May 1919), in *Takvîm-i Vekâyı*, no. 3543 (4 Mayıs 1335/4 May 1919).

88. *Takvîm-i Vekâyı*, no. 3543 (4 Mayis 1335/4 May 1919); he reiterated the same claim at the third session, *Takvîm-i Vekâyı*, no. 3547 (6 Mayis 1335/6 May 1919).

89. Minutes from the main trial, first session. *Takvîm-i Vekâyı*, no. 3540 (27 Nisan 1335/27 April 1919).

90. Minutes from the main trial, second session *Takvîm-i Vekâyı*, no. 3543 (4 Mayıs 1335/4 May 1919).

91. Fifth session, *Takvîm-i Vekâyı*, no. 3554 (14 Mayis 1335/14 May 1919). There is a typographical error. The correct date should be 12 Mayis 1335.

92. See the daily newspapers *Alemdar* and *Yeni Gazete*, 3 August 1919.

93. *Ati*, October 28, 1919. Trial against the party secretaries, fifth session, 27 October, 1919.

94. Hüsamettin Ertürk, *İki Devrin Perde Arkası* (Istanbul, 1964), pp. 109–10.

95. Vardar, *İttihat ve Terakki*, p. 274.

96. Kutay, *Birinci*, p. 36.

97. Ibid., p. 18.

98. Aram Andonyan, *Balkan Savaşı* (Istanbul, 1999), p. 227.

99. Bayur, *Türk İnkılabı Tarihi*, vol. 2, part 1, p. 50.

100. For the situation in eastern Anatolia before the Balkan Wars see: Dikran Mesrob Kaligian, "The Armenian Revolutionary Federation," pp. 217–33.

101. Bayur, *Türk İnkılabı Tarihi*, vol. 2, part 3, p. 81.

102. Ibid., p. 68.

103. Ibid., p. 70.

104. The Russian Armenians arranged a large assembly in Tbilisi on 7 October 1912, with the aim of submitting an appeal to the czar. Ibid., p. 22.

105. Davison, "The Armenian Crisis, 1912–1914," in R. H. Davison, *Essays in Ottoman and Turkish History, 1774–1923: The Impact of the West* (Austin, TX, 1990), p. 184.

106. For a general overview of Russian-Armenian relations during this time, see

Ronald G. Suny, *Looking Toward Ararat: Armenia in Modern History* (Bloomington, IN, 1993), pp. 31–79.

107. Ibid., p. 185.

108. Regarding the Kurdish uprising, about which we cannot go into detail here, there are a large number of German consular reports. See, for instance, PA-AA/R 14083, R 14084, R 14085, Reports by Consul Anders (Bitlis), dated 16 February, 21 June, 25 July; Bo. Kons./B. 168, dated 20 April 1914.

109. Bayur, *Türk İnkılabı Tarihi*, vol. 2, part 3, p. 26.

110. Ibid., vol. 2, part 4, p. 304. The question of whether or not this temporary law was actually within the authority of local administrators is highly debatable. Those historians who are best known for their detailed works on local administration have claimed that the aforementioned law brought no significant changes, and that "the measures in force since 1864 were, with some minor changes, largely preserved." Musa Çadırcı, "Tanzimat'tan Cumhuriyet'e Ülke Yöntemi," *Tanzimattan Cumhuriyete Türkiye Ansiklopedisi*, vol. 1, p. 227. Nevertheless, according to İlber Ortaylı, "the 1913 Temporary Law on the Provinces was the beginning of an application [of legal measures] that would over a long period open all of the doors of autonomy for local democracy and administration." İlber Ortaylı, "Tanzimat ve Meşrutiyet Dönemlerinde Yerel Yönetimler," *Tanzimattan Cumhuriyete Türkiye Ansiklopedisi*, vol. 1, p. 244.

111. Bayur, *Türk İnkılabı Tarihi*, vol. 2, part 4, p. 304.

112. Kurat, *Osmanlı*, p. 207.

113. In his memoirs, Halil Menteşe claimed that he initiated these reforms after his discussions in Paris with the Socialist leader Jean Jaurès on the subject of reforms, and reported him as having said the following: "A greater danger is emerging for you. The propaganda for reform has begun in Armenia. I fear lest the Russians should take this up in order to deal the final blow. Commence yourselves with the fundamental reforms there, and perhaps you will in this way be able to avert the danger." Menteşe, *Halil Menteşe'nin Anıları*, p. 167.

114. This was the reform issue described by Marling, the British chargé d'affaires in Istanbul, in a report of the meetings that he sent to London. See Bayur, *Türk İnkılabı Tarihi*, vol. 2, part 3, p. 131.

115. Ibid., vol. 2, part 3, p. 140.

116. Ibid., p. 117.

117. André Mandelstam, *Das Armenische Problem im Lichte des Völker und Menschenrechts* (Berlin, 1931), p. 31.

118. Vienna, HHStA PA XII, 463 Yeniköy, 11 July 1913, Nr. 38 / B.

119. Lewis, *Emergence of Modern Turkey*, p. 356.

120. Tunaya, *Türkiye'de Siyasal Partiler*, vol. 3, p. 374.

121. Bayur, *Türk İnkılabı Tarihi*, vol. 2, part 3, p. 86; quoting a report dated 21 May 1913 by the German ambassador Wangenheim.

122. Ibid., p. 87.

123. Hüseyin Cahit Yalçın, "Ölüm Yıldönümünde Talât Paşa," *Yakın Tarihimiz*, vol. 1, p. 89. See also Falih Rıfkı Atay, *Çankaya, Atatürk'ün Doğumundan Ölümüne Kadar* (Istanbul, 1980), p. 450.

124. Halil Menteşe's memoirs, serialized in *Cumhuriyet* (section 24, 9 Kasım/November 1946), quoted in Bayur, *Türk İnkılabı Tarihi*, vol. 2, part 4, pp. 654–55.

125. The CUP leaders were aware of the conspiracy [in advance]. In his memoirs, Cemal Paşa, who at the time was the police chief for Istanbul, says that he had been told of a conspiracy being planned. (Cemal Paşa, *Hatıralar*, p. 59.) Talât Paşa also claimed, in a 1914 debate on the subject in the Chamber of Deputies, that "the government had been aware" of a conspiracy being planned. Tunaya, *Türkiye'de Siyasal Partiler*, vol. 3, p. 139. Thus, it has been argued that the Unionists, who had detailed information as to a plan being hatched, willfully closed their eyes to it, and were thereby hoping to rid themselves of both Mahmut Şevket Paşa and the opposition.

126. Bayur, *Türk İnkılabı Tarihi*, vol. 2, part 4, p. 314.

127. Kutay, *Birinci*, p. 10.

128. Cemal Kutay, "Türkiye Nereye Gidiyor?" *Sohbetler* 10 (Eylül/September 1969), p. 69.

129. Kutay, *Birinci*, p. 18.

130. Kuşçubaşı Eşref's memoirs, quoted in Bayar, *Ben de Yazdım*, vol. 5, p. 1573.

131. Ibid.

132. Ibid. Regarding the meetings and the fact that the plans that had been prepared were kept secret even from government members.

133. Nurdoğan Taçalan, *Ege'de Kurtuluş Savaşı Başlarken* (Istanbul, 1970), p. 65.

134. Bayar, *Ben de Yazdım*, vol. 5, p. 1574.

135. Ibid., p. 1576.

136. Menteşe, *Halil Menteşe'nin Anıları*, p. 166.

137. Kutay, *Birinci*, p. 62.

138. Taçalan, *Ege'de Kurtuluş*, pp. 71–73.

139. Bayur, *Türk İnkılabı Tarihi*, vol. 2, part 3, p. 255.

140. Arnold Toynbee, *The Western Question in Greece and Turkey* (London, 1992), p. 140.

141. Ibid.

142. Ibid., p. 143.

143. Hıfzı Erim, *Ayvalık Tarihi* (Ankara, 1948), pp. 60–62 (chapters 1 and 2 are translated from a book by Yorgi Sakkarin of the same name).

144. MMZC, Period 3, Assembly Period 5, vol. 1, 23 Teşrinisani 1334 (23 November 1918) 17. İnikad, p. 186.

145. Morgenthau, *Ambassador Morgenthau's Story*, pp. 324–25. Morgenthau adds that, unlike the Armenians, the Greeks were not subjected to a general massacre.

146. Ibid., p. 325.

147. Avcıoğlu, *Milli Kurtuluş*, vol. 3, p. 1138.

148. Bayar, *Ben de Yazdım,* vol. 5, p. 1568.

149. Menteşe, *Halil Menteşe'nin Anıları,* p. 166.

150. Kutay, *Birinci,* p. 6. Celal Bayar, who draws extensively from Kuşçubaşı's memoirs, gives some separate figures for specific cities. The total number of these is the same as the figure above. Bayar, *Ben de Yazdım,* vol. 5, p. 1576.

151. FO/AMG, 7 N 1653, no. AC3602, Confidential.

152. MMZC, Period 3, Assembly Period 5, vol. 1, pp. 285, 287.

153. Ibid., 4 Teşrinisani 1334 (4 November 1918), 11, İnikad, p. 109.

154. Ibid., 11 Kânunuevvel 1334 (11 November 1918), Çarşamba, 24, İnikad, pp. 284–87.

155. Ibid., p. 285.

156. Ibid., p. 289.

157. Ibid., p. 287.

158. Ibid., p. 288.

159. Ibid.

160. Ibid., 12 Kânunuevvel 1334 (12 December 1918), Perşembe, 25, İnikad, pp. 316–17.

161. Ibid., pp. 313–15.

162. Ibid., 11 Kânunuevvel 1334 (11 December 1918) Çarşamba, 24, İnikad, pp. 288, 290–94.

163. For example, some sections of the reports by France's ambassador in Istanbul, Bompard, can be found in Bayur, *Türk İnkılabı Tarihi,* vol. 2, part 3, pp. 256–60.

164. Toynbee, *Western Question,* p. 138.

165. For the numbers of Muslims expelled during the Balkan War, see Ahmet Halaçoğlu, *Balkan Harbi Sırasında Rumeli'den Türk Göçleri (1912–1913)* (Ankara, 1994), p. 63.

4. What Led to the Decision for Genocide?

1. Morgenthau, *Ambassador Morgenthau's Story,* p. 323.

2. Bayur, *Türk İnkılabı Tarihi,* vol. 2, part 3, p. 254. As we saw in the previous chapter, these Greeks were forced to sign documents attesting to their choice to emigrate. MMZC, Period 3, Assembly Period 5, vol. 2, p. 288.

3. Ahmet Refik, *İki Komite, İki Kıtal* (Istanbul, 1919). Transliteration/simplification by Hamide Koyukan (Ankara, 1994), p. 27.

4. I have evaluated the question of Ottoman entry into the war particularly connected with the Armenian genocide. For more detailed accounts, see the following: Kurt Ziemke, *Die Neue Türkei* (Stuttgart, 1930); Ulrich Trumpener, *Germany and the Ottoman Empire* (New Jersey, 1968); Frank G. Weber, *Eagles on the Crescent: Germany, Austria and the Diplomacy of the Turkish Alliance, 1914–1918* (London, 1970). Additionally, the archival materials for this period of all the countries involved (apart from the Ottoman Empire) have been published.

Unfortunately, in Turkey serious research on the subject of the Ottoman entry into the war and the reasons therefore is paltry.

5. It must be emphasized that the desire to free themselves from the Capitulations in particular played an important role in determining the Ottoman leaders' preference for entering the war.

6. From Said Halim Paşa's deposition, 5. *Şube Tutanakları*, p. 3.

7. Bayur, *Türk İnkılabı Tarihi*, vol. 3, part 1, p. 65.

8. Landau, *Pan-Turkism*, p. 51. Other references and examples of this thinking can be found on pp. 48–55.

9. Bayur, *Türk İnkılabı Tarihi*, vol. 3, part 1, p. 317.

10. Alp, *Türkismus*, p. 50. Quoted in Luke, *Making of Turkey*, p. 161.

11. Liman von Sanders, *Fünf Jahre Türkei* (Berlin, 1919), p. 51.

12. Subsequently, General Ali Fuat Erden's memoirs, quoted in Bayur, *Türk İnkılabı Tarihi*, vol. 3, part 1, p. 198.

13. Landau, *Pan-Turkism*, pp. 52–53.

14. Ibid., p. 55.

15. MMZC, p. 361.

16. The *Times*, 19 February 1920.

17. Kâzım Karabekir, *İstiklal Harbımız* (Istanbul, 1960), p. 901.

18. M. Cemil Bilsel, *Lozan*, vol. 1(Istanbul, 1933), pp. 125–26.

19. Translated and prepared for publication by M. Şükrü Hanioğlu, *Kendi Mektuplarında Enver Paşa* (Istanbul, 1989), Letter no. 166, p. 242.

20. Tunaya, *Türkiye'de Siyasal Partiler*, vol. 3, p. 465.

21. Ertürk, *İki Devrin*, p. 121.

22. Author's personal archive.

23. Bayar, *Ben de Yazdım*, vol. 5, p. 1082.

24. Bilsel, *Lozan*, p. 126.

25. Ahmet Hamdi Tanpınar, *Sahnenin Dışındakiler* (Istanbul, 1973), p. 54.

26. Bilsel, *Lozan*, p. 127.

27. Bayur, *Türk İnkılabı Tarihi*, vol. 3, part 1, p. 427.

28. A. Mil, "Umumi Harpte," Installment nos. 9 and 10, İkinciteşrin (November) 1933.

29. Quoted in Jäschke, *Der Turanismus*, p. 7.

30. *Tanin* (14 Kasım 1914), quoted in Ş. S. Aydemir, *Makedonya'dan Ortaasya'ya Enver Paşa*, vol. 3, p. 20.

31. Bayar, *Ben de Yazdım*, vol. 4, p. 1082.

32. The verses are from a poem written about Enver Paşa by Ziya Gökalp. Quoted in Tunaya, *Türkiye'de Siyasal Partiler*, vol. 3, p. 321.

33. Galip Kemal Söylemezoğlu, *Başımıza Gelenler, Yakın bir Mazinin Hatıraları, Mondros'tan Mudanya'ya 1918–1922* (Istanbul, 1939), p. 128.

34. Cemal Paşa, *Hatıralar*, p. 502.

35. Wolfgang Gust, *Der Völkermord an den Armeniern: die Tragödie des ältesten Christenvolkes der Welt* (Munich: Carl Hanser, 1993), p. 153.

36. The letter, dated 31 July 1919, was sent from Mondros, where Halil was being held by the British. Quoted in Şimşjr, *Malta Sürgünleri*, p. 276.
37. Ibid., p. 281.
38. Kurt Ziemke, *Die neue Türkei: politische Entwicklung, 1914–1929* (Stuttgart: Deutsche Verlangsanstalt, 1930), p. 271.
39. Institut für Armenische Fragen, *Tagebücher von Westenek* (Munich, 1986), pp. 69–74.
40. PA-AA/R 14085, Report from Wangenheim, dated 2 February 1915.
41. Bayur, *Türk İnkılabı Tarihi*, vol. 3, part 3, p. 12.
42. Menteşe, *Halil Menteşe'nin Anıları*, p. 175.
43. Lepsius, *Der Todesgang*, pp. 195–96.
44. FO 371/515/E. 2476 Malta, Polverista, 16.3.1920, quoted in Şimşir, *Malta Sürgünleri*, pp. 279–80. Some of the English documents cited by Şimşir and Jäschke are translations from the Turkish. Some have been replaced with English originals if they were available in Dadrian, *"Genocide as a Problem."*
45. Joseph Pomiankowski, *Der Zusammenbruch des Osmanischen Reiches, Erinnerungen an die Türkei aus Zeit des Weltkrieges* (Zürich, Leipzig, Vienna, 1928), p. 162.
46. Henry Morgenthau, "The Greatest Horror in History," *The Red Cross Magazine* (March 1918). Quoted in Dadrian, *History of the Armenian Genocide*, p. 207.
47. FO 371/3658/75852, Dossier 441. 2 (19 May 1919).
48. PA-AA/Bo. Kons./B. 169, Report by Vice-Consul Scheubner-Richter, dated 28 July 1915.
49. PA-AA/R 14087, Report, dated 27 July 1915.
50. PA-AA/Bo. Kons./B. 169, Telegram from Ambassador Wangenheim, dated 17 June 1915.
51. Trumpener, *Germany and the Ottoman Empire*, p. 127.
52. Vienna, HHStA PA XII 463 Konstantinopel, 7 Kasım 1915, Nr. 93/P. B. Artem Ohandjanian, ed., *Österreich-Armenien 1872–1936*, vol. 7, p. 4818. For a similar statement, see Ziemke, *Neue Turkei*, p. 271.
53. AA Türkei 158/14, 18, 17 October 1915.
54. Bayur, *Türk İnkılabı Tarihi*, vol. 3, part 3, p. 22.
55. Halil Menteşe, *Cumhuriyet* (9 November 1946) (Installment no. 24). Quoted in Bayur, *Türk İnkılabı Tarihi*, vol. 2, part 4, pp. 654–55.
56. *5. Şube Tutanakları*, testimony from Cavit Bey, p. 14.
57. From a German General Staff document dated 4 August 1914, quoted by Wolf Dieter Bihl, *Die Kaukasus-Politik der Mittelmächte, Teil I: Ihre Basis in der Orient-Politik und ihre Aktionen 1914–1917* (Vienna, Cologne, Graz, 1974), p. 41.
58. HHStA PA 1522, Yeniköy, 20 July, 1914, Report no. 338, in Ohandjanian, *Armenien*, p. 4388.
59. From reports by Ambassador Wangenheim and State Minister Zimmermann. Quoted in Bihl, *Kaukasus-Politik*, Tiel I, p. 59.
60. *5. Şube Tutanakları*, testimony from Çürüksulu Mahmud, p. 4.

61. Ibid., p. 19. In his testimony, Cavid Bey claimed that the Russian ambassador also told him of such actions during a visit in August. The ambassador said that the Russians were conscious of such provocations, but had decided to turn a blind eye toward them; ibid., Cavid Bey, p. 29.

62. Sixth session, *Takvîm-i Vekâyı*, no. 3557 (14 May 1335).

63. *Renaissance* (15 April 1919).

64. Bayur, *Türk İnkılabı Tarihi*, vol. 3, part 1, p. 226.

65. Bihl, *Kaukasus-Politik*, Tiel I, p. 59.

66. Mil, "Umumi Harpte," Installment no. 23 (25 November 1933).

67. Ibid., Installment no. 46 (18 October 1933). For another memoir discussing this issue, see Ömer Türkoğlu, *Binbası Süleyman Bey'in Manzum Anıları* (Ankara, 1997).

68. 5. *Şube Tutanakları*, testimony from Cavid Bey, p. 40.

69. Avcıoğlu, *Milli Kurtuluş*, vol. 3, p. 1138.

70. Karal, *Osmanlı Tarihi*, vol. 5, p. 73.

71. Elias, *Deutschen*, p. 13.

72. Lewis, *The Emergence of Modern Turkey*, p. 127.

73. Tunaya, *Türkiye'de Siyasal Partiler*, vol. 3, p. 511.

74. Ibid., pp. 512–13.

75. Elias, *Deutschen*, p. 476.

76. Refik, *İki Komite, İki Kıtal*, p. 44.

77. Colonel Seyfi was also counted, in a secret document obtained by the English during the armistice period, as one of the top five persons who had planned the genocide (FO 371/4172/1307).

78. For details, see V. N. Dadrian, "The Secret Young Turk Ittihadist Conference and the Decision for the World War I Genocide of the Armenians," *Holocaust and Genocide* 7, no. 2 (Spring 1998).

79. Fifth session, *Takvîm-i Vekâyı*, no. 3554 (14 Mayıs, 1335/1919).

80. Tunaya, *Türkiye'de Siyasal Partiler*, vol. 3, p. 514.

81. Aydemir, *Makedonya'dan Ortaasya'ya Enver Paşa*, vol. 3, p. 228.

82. Bayur, *Türk İnkılabı Tarihi*, vol. 3 part 3, pp. 83–87.

83. Ibid.

84. Elias, *Deutschen*, p. 465.

85. HHStA PA III 171, Yeniköy, 26 August 1914. Telegram no. 494, in Ohandjanian, *Armenien*, vol. 6, p. 4402.

86. Şeref Çavuşoğlu, "İttihat ve Terakki'nin Gizli Planı," *Yakın Tarihimiz*, vol. 1, p. 263.

87. Selahattin Tansel, *Mondros'tan Mudanya'ya Kadar*, vol. 1 (Ankara, 1973), p. 142.

88. Taçalan, *Ege'de Kurtuluş*, p. 166.

89. Çavuşoğlu, *İttihat ve Terakki*, p. 263.

90. Bayur, *Türk İnkılabı Tarihi*, vol. 3, part 2, p. 714.

91. Pomiankowski, *Der Zusammenbruch des Osmanischen Reiches*, p. 117.

92. Sixth session, *Takvîm-i Vekâyı*, no. 3557 (14 May 1335).

93. Yahya Kemal Beyatlı, *Siyasi ve Edebi Porteler* (Istanbul, 1976), p. 323.
94. Ahmet Emin Yalman, *Turkey in the World War* (New Haven, 1930), p. 220.
95. Ahmet Emin Yalman, *Yakın Tarihte Gördüklerim ve Geçirdiklerim*, vol. 1 (Istanbul, 1970), p. 332.
96. Aram Andonian, *The Memoirs of Naim Bey: Turkish Official Documents Relating to Deportation and Massacre of Armenians* (Newton Square, PA, 1964), pp. 49–52.
97. Hasan Fehmi Bey, from a speech given at a secret session of the TBMM on 17 Teşrinievvel 1336 (October 1920). TBMM *Gizli Celse Zabıtları*, vol. 1 (Ankara, 1985), p. 177.
98. Lepsius, *Der Todesgang*, p. 189.
99. Uras, *Tarihte Ermeniler*, p. 612. The declaration was made in response to a note delivered to the Porte by the Entente governments after reports of the Armenian genocide had begun to reach European capitals.
100. According to Lepsius's reports, in the Erzurum region these arrests had even begun to be made at the end of March, so that "by April 12 the great majority of Dashnaks were behind bars" (Lepsius, *Der Todesgang*, p. 42).
101. Ibid., p. 21.
102. Pailadzo Captanian, *1915 Der Völkermord an den Armenien, eine Zeugin berichtet* (Berlin, 1993), p. 18. The author claims that her father died of torture after having been arrested in Samsun in the month of April.
103. Mil, "Umumi Harpte," Installment no. 11 (2 İkinciteşrin/2 November 1933).
104. In addition to the above information about the reconstitution of the Special Organization, see also the testimonies of Talât and Atıf, second session, *Takvîm-i Vekâyı*, no. 3543 (4 May 1919).
105. Mil, "Umumi Harpte," Installment no. 11 (2 İkinciteşrin/2 November 1933).
106. Cited in Bihl, *Kaukasus-Politik*, Tiel I, p. 40.
107. Mil, "Umumi Harpte," Installment no. 13 (15 İkinciteşrin/November 1933).
108. Second session, *Takvîm-i Vekâyı*, no. 3543 (4 May 1919).
109. Fifth session, *Takvîm-i Vekâyı*, no. 3554 (12 May 1919). The printed date of "14 Mayıs" is incorrect.
110. These documents were read into the record at the fifth and sixth sessions of the main trial of Unionist leaders after the war, upon the defendants' rejection of any connection between the Unionist party and the Special Organization. For other examples, see *Takvîm-i Vekâyı*, no. 3554 (12 Mayıs 1335/12 May 1919) and no. 3557 (14 Mayıs 1335/14 May 1919).
111. Mil, "Umumi Harpte," Installment no. 2 (3 Teşrinievvel/3 November 1933).
112. Ibid. Mil mentions many persons by name here.
113. Second session, *Takvîm-i Vekâyı*, no. 3543 (4 Mayıs 1335/4 May 1919).
114. Bihl, *Kaukasus-Politik*, Tiel I, p. 230. From a report of Undersecretary of State Zimmermann to State Secretary Jagow.

115. HHStA PA XII 941, ZI 54/P, Trabzon, 2 September 1914. In Ohandjanian, *Armenien*, vol. 6, p. 4403.

116. Fifth session, *Takvîm-i Vekâyı*, no. 3554 (12 Mayıs 1335/12 May 1919). (Incorrectly dated 14 Mayıs.)

117. Ali İhsan Sabis, *Harp Hatıralarım, Birinci Dünya Harbi*, vol. 2 (Istanbul, 1990), p. 197.

118. Mil, "Umumi Harpte," Installment no. 3 (4 İkinciteşrin/4 November 1933).

119. Later on, he would flee abroad a full two months before Talât, Enver and Cemal, but after Talât's assassination he would also be assassinated, along with Bahaettin Şakir, in Berlin by an Armenian vengeance organization.

120. Ertürk, *Iki Devrin*, p. 111.

121. Ali İhsan Sabis, *Harp Hatıralarım*, vol. 2, p. 175. Hafız Hakkı Paşa was the previous commander. When he died of typhus at the Caucasus front on 2 February 1915, his position was filled by Mahmut Kamil Paşa.

122. Ibid., pp. 192, 197–98. See also Arif Bayın, *İlk Dünya Harbinde Kafkas Cephesi* (Istanbul, 1946), pp. 49–51.

123. Mil, "Umumi Harpte," Installment no. 6 (7 İkinciteşrin/7 November 1933).

124. First session, *Takvîm-i Vekâyı*, no. 3540 (27 Nisan 1335/27 April 1919).

125. Mil, "Umumi Harpte," Installment no. 13 (15 İkinciteşrin/15 November 1933).

126. Askeri Tarih Belgeleri, *Ermeni Belgeleri Özel Sayısız*, Installment no. 32 (Mart [March] 1983), p. 83, Document no. 1894.

127. Ibid., Installment no. 94 (6 Şubat/6 February 1933).

128. Second session, *Takvîm-i Vekâyı*, no. 3543 (4 May 1919).

129. Ibid.

130. This letter was signed by Hilmi and is dated 23 Ağustos 1330 (4 September 1914) (from the author's personal collection).

131. Mil, "Umumi Harpte," Installment no. 4 (5 İkinciteşrin/5 November 1933).

132. Ibid.

133. Ibid., Installment no. 27 (29 İkinciteşrin/29 November 1933).

134. Ibid., Installment no. 19 (21 İkinciteşrin/21 November 1933).

135. From the interrogations in the Fifth Department of the Ottoman parliament (İbrahim Bey's testimony, p. 41).

136. Sixth session, *Takvîm-i Vekâyı*, no. 3557 (14 Mayıs 1335/14 May 1919).

137. Tunaya, *Türkiye'de Siyasi Partiler*, vol. 3, pp. 285–86.

138. Sixth session, Takvîm-i Vekâyi, no. 3557 (14 Mayıs 1335/14 May 1919).

139. Ibid.

140. Fifth session, *Takvîm-i Vekâyı*, no. 3554 (12 Mayıs 1335/12 May 1919).

141. Falih Rıfkı Atay, *Zeytindağı*, (Istanbul, 1985), pp. 35–36.

142. Fifth session, *Takvîm-i Vekâyı*, no. 3554 (12 Mayıs 1335/12 May 1919).

143. HHStA PA 1942, ZI 79/P, Trabzon, 8 November 1914. Ohandjanian, *Armenien*, vol. 6, pp. 4462–63.

144. Fifth session, *Takvîm-i Vekâyı*, no. 3554 (12 Mayıs 1335/12 May 1919).

145. Refik, İki Komite, İki Kıtal, p. 27.
146. Mil, "Umumi Harpte," Installment no. 39 (11 Birincikanun/11 December 1933).
147. HHStA PA I 942, ZI 79/P, Trabzon, 8 November 1914. Ohandjanian, Armenien, vol. 6, pp. 4462–63.
148. Stoddard, Teşkilât-ı Mahsusa, p. 52.
149. Hovannisian, Armenia on the Road, pp. 41–43.
150. Uras, Tarihte Ermeniler, pp. 596–600. The author also quotes a correspondence by the Armenian deputy from Erzurum, Karakin Pastirmacıyan, who would later serve in the Russian army in a voluntary Armenian unit in the Caucasus during the war.
151. Ibid., p. 600. For more details on the subject, see Kamurun Gürün, The Armenian File (New York, 1985), pp. 187ff; Ermeni Komitelerinin A'mal ve Harekât-ı İhtilâliyyesi (Ankara, 1983) (a reprint of a 1916 official Ottoman government publication); Alper Gazigiray, Osmanlılardan Günümüze Kadar Vesikalarla Ermeni Terörünün Kaynakları (Istanbul, 1982), pp. 223–38; Talat Paşa'nın Anıları (Istanbul, 1986), pp. 67–79; İhsan Sakarya, Belgelerle Ermeni Sorunu (Ankara, 1984), pp. 156–61.
152. Mil, "Umumi Harpte," Installment no. 13 (14 İkinciteşrin/14 November 1933).
153. Ibid., Installment no. 15 (17 İkinciteşrin/17 November 1933).
154. Fifth session, Takvîm-i Vekâyı, no. 3554 (12 Mayıs 1335/12 May 1919).
155. Lepsius, Der Todesgang, p. 35.
156. Quoted in Mil, "Umumi Harpte," Installment no. 15 (17 İkinciteşrin/17 November 1933).
157. Mütekaid Kaymakam Şerif Köprülü, Sarıkamış İhata Manevrası ve Meydan Muharebesi (Istanbul, 1338/1922), p. 119 (the page number given is actually from a transcribed copy in our possession).
158. PA-AA/R 14085, Report by Consul Paul Schwarz (Erzurum), dated 5 December 1914.
159. Aziz Samih, "Umumi Harpte Kafkas Cephesi Hatıraları," Kurun, Installment no. 19 (19 April 1935).
160. AA (Bonn) Weltkrieg, 11 d secr., B. 4, A 9305, from the report by Louis Mosel, dated 3 March 1915.
161. Ibid., A 37451, from the report by German officer Schulenburg, Erzurum, dated 28 November 1915.
162. Quoted in Bihl, Kaukasus-Politik, Tiel I, pp. 67–68.
163. Refik, İki Komite, İkı Kital, p. 41. Artvin was occupied on 24 November 1914, Ardahan on the twenty-ninth.
164. Lepsius, Der Todesgang, pp. 78–79.
165. Henry Barby, Au pays de l'épouvante (Paris, 1917), pp. 230–40. The massacres carried out in this region are recounted here in detail on the basis of the reports supplied to Barby by the Italian consular agent in Van. Cited in V. N. Dadrian, "The Role of the Special Organization in the Armenian genocide during the First World War," in Panikos Panayi, ed., Minorities in Wartime (Berg: Oxford, 1993), pp. 63–64.

166. Wolfgang Gust, "Der Völkermord an den Armenien," in *Der Tragödie des Erste-sen Christianvolkes der Welt* (Munich, 1993), p. 175. For German and Austrian reports, see V. N. Dadrian, "The Armenian Question and the Wartime Fate of the Armenians as Documented by Officials of the Ottoman Empire's World War I Allies: Germany and Austria-Hungary," *International Journal of Middle East Studies* 34 (February 2002), pp. 68, 69, 82 (n. 59–66).

167. AA (Bonn) Weltkrieg, 11 d secr., B. 4, A 9305, from the report by Louis Mosel, dated 3 March 1915.

168. Dadrian, "Role of the Special Organization," pp. 52–53.

169. İbrahim Arvas, "Tarihi Hakikatlar, Eski Van Mebusu İ. Arvas'm Hatıraları," *Yeni İstiklal* (7 Nisan[April] 1965), p. 234. For other information about the develop-ments in this region, see Stefanos Yerasimos, *Milliyetler ve Sınırlar* (Istanbul, 1994), pp. 271–391.

170. Mil, "Umumi Harpte," Installment no. 62–63 (3–4 İkincikanun/3–4 January 1934).

171. Lepsius, *Der Todesgang*, p. 53.

172. Viscount Bryce and A. J. Toynbee, eds., *The Treatment of the Armenians in the Ottoman Empire: Documents Presented to Viscount Grey of Fallodon* (London, 1916), Document no. 23, p. 88. In Lepsius, *Der Todesgang*, it is reported that the situation was almost identical in every city.

173. Archive of the Armenian patriarchate in Jerusalem, Carton 21, Dossier M, Docu-ment no. 479. This telegram was also published in the Armenian newspaper *Nor Giank* (a fact made known to me by Professor V. N. Dadrian). Telegram no. 169, dated 27 June 1915, from the acting commander of the Kayseri Detachment, Sahabettin, to the acting commander of the Ankara Army Corps, Halil Reca'i.

174. Archive of the Armenian patriarchate in Jerusalem, Carton 17, Dossier H, Docu-ment no. 606. This report was also published in the Armenian newspaper *Nor Giank* (again, a fact made known to me by Professor V. N. Dadrian). From a telegram from Sahabettin, the acting commander in Kayseri, dated 28 July 1915.

175. Aziz Samih, "Umumi Harpte Kafkas Cephesi Hatıraları," *Kurun*, Installment no. 19 (19 Nisan/19 April 1935).

176. Lepsius, *Der Todesgang*, p. 183.

177. Mil, "Umumi Harpte," Installment no. 15 (17 İkinciteşrin/17 November 1933).

178. Lepsius, *Der Todesgang*, p. 28.

179. Archive of the director-general of security of the Interior Ministry, Dossier 44, 844/51. Cited in Gürün, *The Armenian File*, p. 205.

180. Askeri Tarih Belgeleri Dergisi, *Ermeni Belgeler Özel Sayısı 2* 32, no. 83 (Mart [March] 1983), Document no. 1894.

181. Archives du Ministère des affaires étrangères (A. M. A. E.) *Guerre 1914–1917*, vol. 887, pp. 184–87. See also V. N. Dadrian, "The Armenian Genocide: An Interpretation," in Jay Winter, ed., *America and the Armenian Genocide of 1915* (New York, 2003), pp. 62–63.

182. Dinkel, "German Officers and the Armenian Genocide," *Armenian Review* 44, 1

(Spring 1991), p. 38; V. N. Dadrian, *German Responsibility in the Armenian Genocide: A Review of the Historical Evidence of German Complicity* (Watertown, MA: Blue Crane Books, 1996), p. 146; see also Ernst Jäckh, *The Rising Crescent* (New York: Farrar & Rinehart, 1944), p. 19.

183. Rafael de Nogales, *Vier Jahre unter dem Halbmond: Erinnerungen aus dem Weltkriege* (Berlin, 1925), p. 35.

184. PA-AA/R 14085, Report from Wangenheim, dated 29 December 1914. When citing Wangenheim's report in his work, Johannes Lepsius excised the parts about the Armenian patriarchate blaming the Germans. Lepsius, *Der Todesgang*, p. 23, Document 13.

185. Pomiankowski, *Der Zusammenbruch des Osmanischen Reiches*, p. 93.

186. Morgenthau, *Ambassador Morgenthau's Story*, p. 302.

187. Bryce and Toynbee, *Treatment of the Armenians*, Document 23, p. 88.

188. Lepsius, *Der Todesgang*, p. 55.

189. Ibid., pp. 112–13.

190. H. C. Yalçın, *Siyasi Anılar* (Istanbul,1976), p. 233.

191. Lepsius, *Der Todesgang*, pp. 161–62.

192. PA-AA/Bo. Kons./B. 168, Report dated February 1915 This report concerns the conditions of the Ottoman Armenians.

193. Askeri Tarih Belgeleri Dergisi (Documents of Military History), *Ermeni Belgeleri Özel Sayısı 3* 34, no. 85 (Ekim [October] 1985), Document no. 1999.

194. From German consular reports, it can be seen that the disarming of Armenian soldiers had been carried out on a broad scale. See, for instance, PA-AA/Bo. Kons./B. 168, Report by Consul Scheubner-Richter (Erzurum), dated 3 March 1915; R 14085, Report by Ambassador Wangenheim, dated 23 March 1915.

195. Jakob Künzler, *Dreizig Jahre Dienst am Orient* (Basel, 1933), p. 54.

196. Morgenthau, *Ambassador Morgenthau's Story*, pp. 302–3.

197. For reports from the Muş, Sivas and Bitlis regions, see Bryce and Toynbee, *Treatment of the Armenians*, Document no. 23, p. 88; Lepsius, *Der Todesgang*, pp. 55, 112–13; Arnold Toynbee, *Armenian Atrocities: The Murder of a Nation* (London and New York, 1915), pp. 81–82; Samuel Zurlinden, *Der Weltkrieg, Vorläufige Orientierung von einem Schweizerischen Standpunkt aus Band 2* (Zurich, 1917–18), pp. 63–69.

198. HHStA PA XXXVIII 368, Trabzon, 4 September 1915, Z. 54/P.A., in Ohandjanian, *Armenien*, p. 4724.

199. Jakob Künzler, *Im Lande des Blutes und der Tränen, Erlebnisse in Mesopotamien Während des Weltkrieges* (Potsdam, 1921), pp. 17ff.

200. AA Türkei, 183/44, A 24663, Dossier no. 1. Cited in Dadrian, *History of the Armenian Genocide*, p. 258. Additionally, one section of this document is reproduced in: *Germany, Turkey and Armenia: A Selection of Documentary Evidence Relating to the Armenian Atrocities from German and Other Sources* (London, 1917), pp. 80–85.

201. AA Türkei, 183/38, A 28109, K. No. 90/B. No. 1950, Dossier no. 1.

202. Written testimony of Vehip Paşa submitted to the chairman of the Commission of Criminal Inquiry in the Office of Public Security. The copy used by this author was found in the archives of the Armenian patriarchate in Jerusalem. Carton 7, Dossier H, Document nos. 171–82.

203. Morgenthau, Ambassador Morgenthau's Story, pp. 303–4.

204. Sakarya, Belgellerle Ermeni Sorunu, p. 181. A telegram from the Office of the Governor-General of Adana to the Interior Ministry, dated 26 February 1915. For the approval of the Interior Ministry, see T. C. Başbakanlık, Devlet Arşivleri Genel Müdürlüğü, Osmanlı Belgelerinde Ermeniler (1915–1920) (Ankara, 1994), p. 20.

205. Lepsius, Der Todesgang, p. 11. According to some Armenian sources, an estimated 800 Armenian men were initially sent from Dörtyol, and within a month or so all the town's young people. The full deportation of families began afterward, and ended by August 1915. See: Aram Arkun, "The Fall of the Eagles' Nest: The Fate of the Armenians of Hajin, Zeitun, Sis, and Marash, 1914–1921" (unfinished dissertation). The numbers of deportees who were sent from Zeytun to the Konya region (within Anatolia) were about 5,000 of approximately 26,500. See: Bryce and Toynbee, eds., The Treatment, Document no. 120.

206. Plenty of information regarding the events at Zeytun and subsequent deportation can be found in the standard works on the period. Among the Turkish sources, see Gürün, Ermeni Dosyası (Ankara, 1988), pp. 260–62; Sakarya, Belgellerle Ermeni Sorunu, pp. 172–73; 185–87. For European language sources, see Lepsius, Der Todesgang, p. 411; Ternon, Tabu Armenien, pp. 138–39; Stanley Elphinstone Kerr, The Lions of Marash: Personal Experiences with American Near East Relief, 1919–1922 (Albany: State University of New York Press, 1973), pp. 18ff.

207. "Halep Valisi Celal'ın Anıları," Vakit, 12 Aralık (December) 1918.

208. See in particular the following two reports: PA-AA/R 14085, Report by Wangenheim, dated 29 March 1915; PA-AA/R 14085, Report by Consul Rössler (Aleppo), dated 12 April 1915.

209. The Armenian Catholicos of Adana, for instance, wrote a detailed report of the events on 21 April 1915. Its contents are nearly identical to the accounts of Celal and Rössler. PA-AA/Bo. Kons./B. 168. Report by the Adana Consulate, dated 26 April 1915. For a comparison of the Turkish versions with information contained in the consular reports and accounts of eyewitnesses, see Gust, "Der Völkermord an den Armenien," pp. 167–72.

210. Ample information on the first deportations from Çukurova can be found in Lepsius, Der Todesgang, pp. 4–20.

211. İsmet Parmaksızoğlu, ed., Ermeni Komitelerinin İhtilal Hareketleri ve Besledikleri Emeller (Ankara, 1981), pp. 79–80.

212. PA-AA/Bo. Kons./B. 168, Report from Consul Büge (Adana), dated 13 March 1915.

213. For a number of these reports, see Lepsius, Deutschland und Armenien, Document nos. 19–25, 27, pp. 32–45, 49–50.

214. PA-AA/Bo. Kons./B. 168, Supplement to the report by Büge (Adana), dated 13 March 1915. Also, see PA-AA/R 14085, Report by Ambassador Wangenheim, dated 15 April 1915.

215. Telegram from Sir H. Bax Ironside (Sofia), FO /371/2484, No. 25167 (4 March 1915). Quoted in Muammer Demirel, *Ermeniler Hakkında İngiliz Belgeleri, 1896–1918* (Ankara, 2002), Document no. 417, pp. 667–68. From the other documents published in this book, we understand that the offer came from the Armenian Committee in the Balkans and the same offer was made to the French and Russian forces as well.

216. FO/371/2428, No. 0152/4717, quoted in ibid., Document no. 420, p. 669.

217. Gürün, *The Armenian File*, p. 206.

218. PA-AA/Bo. Kons./B. 168, Report from Zimmermann, dated 26 March 1915.

219. PA-AA/R 14085, Report by Consul Rössler (Aleppo), dated 12 April 1915; PA-AA/Bo. Kons./B. 168, Report by Vice-Consul Scheubner-Richter (Erzurum), dated 15 May 1915. Compare with Lepsius, *Deutschland und Armenien,* Documents 25 and 51, pp. 51ff, 68. These lines were omitted in Lepsius's publication of the German documents.

220. FO 424/220, Report from the British Consulate in Mersin on the massacres in Adana, p. 70.

221. This information was taken from the memoirs of one of the Armenian leaders of the period. Cited in V. N. Dadrian, "The Circumstances Surrounding the 1909 Adana Holocaust," *Armenian Review* 41 (1988), p. 2.

222. Lepsius, *Der Todesgang*, p. 37.

223. Ibid., pp. 23–24, 37–39, 55–56. The author provides detailed accounts of the terror tactics and torture used in various provinces in the name of gathering weapons. Similar reports of arrests and torture for this purpose can be found in Morgenthau, *Ambassador Morgenthau's Story*, pp. 304–5.

224. HHStA PA 1942, Trabzon, 8 November 1914, ZI. 80/P. in Ohandjanian, *Armenien,* vol. 6, p. 4464.

225. PA-AA/R 14085, Report from Consul Rössler (Aleppo), dated 12 April 1915.

5. The Decision and Its Aftermath

1. *Azatamard* (an Armenian-language Dashnak newspaper), quoted by Lepsius, *Der Todesgang*, pp. 186–88.

2. PA-AA/R 14085, Report by Consul Paul Schwarz (Erzurum), dated 5 December 1914, and PA-AA/Bo. Kons. /B. 168, Report by Consul Paul Schwarz (Erzurum), dated 26 April 1915.

3. PA-AA/Bo. Kons./B. 168, Report of the German-Armenian Society dated 20 April 1915, and Report by Chief Consul Mordtmann (Istanbul), dated 26 April 1916 containing information sent by General Posseldt.

4. Künzler, *Dreizig Jahre Dienst am Orient*, p. 456.
5. Lepsius, *Der Todesgang*, p. 36.
6. Bryce and Toynbee, eds., *Treatment of the Armenians*, Document no. 23, p. 127.
7. Ibid., Document no. 64, p. 258.
8. PA-AA/Bo. Kons./B. 170, Report by Consul Scheubner-Richter (Erzurum), dated 28 July 1915.
9. V. N. Dadrian, "The Secret Young-Turk Ittihadist Conference and the Decision for the World War I Genocide of the Armenians," *Holocaust and Genocide Studies* 7, no. 2 (Fall 1993), p. 180. .
10. Mil, "Umumi Harpte," Installment no. 15 (17 Teşrinisani/November 1933).
11. Ibid., Installment no. 13 (13 Teşrinisani/November 1933). A letter from Hilmi to Bahaettin Şakir on 3 September 1914.
12. Bihl, *Kaukasus-Politik*, Tiel I, p. 74.
13. The sources containing documents on the campaign in the Caucasus also mention the gangs pillaging and looting Muslim villages. Refik, *İki Komite, İki Kıtal*, p. 41; AA (Bonn) Weltkrieg, 11 d secr., vol. 4, A 9305, Report by Louis Mosel, dated 3 March 1915; Mil, "Umumi Harpte," Installment nos. 74 and 101 (15 İkinci Teşrin/January and 13 Şubat/February 1934).
14. Mustafa Ragıp Esatlı, *İttihat ve Terakki Tarihinde Esrar Perdesi* (Istanbul, 1975), pp. 400–402, 405. In this section are listed all the crimes of Yakup Cemil at Çorum and Hasankale, Erzurum, that irritated the army.
15. Mil, "Umumi Harpte," Installment no. 96 (8 Şubat/February 1934).
16. Ibid., Installment no. 107 (19 Şubat/February 1934).
17. At the time when Bahaettin Şakir was in Istanbul and this correspondence took place, Artvin had not yet fallen. "But before long," Artvin was evacuated, on 23 March. So Şakir must have been in Istanbul by the beginning of March at the latest; ibid., Installment no. 96 (18 Şubat/February 1934). Basing his analysis on the memoirs of Ali İhsan Sabis, V. N. Dadrian concludes that Şakir probably set off for Istanbul on 13 March. V. N. Dadrian, "Role of Special Organization," p. 18.
18. Mil, "Umumi Harpte," Installment no. 98 (10 Şubat/February 1934).
19. "Dr Bahaettin Şakir Bey brought them (the documents he had acquired) to the attention of the CUP Central Committee in Istanbul and busied himself with measures designed to rescue the army from a grave threat. " Ibid., Installment no. 100 (12 Şubat/February 1934).
20. Ibid., Installment no. 98 (10 Şubat/February 1934); Installment no. 100 (12 Şubat/February 1934).
21. BAO/DH/SFR, 51–215, 1333CA 20. I thank Fuat Dündar for bringing the document to my attention.
22. Menteşe, *Halil Menteşe'nin Anıları*, pp. 213–16. After relating news of Talât, Menteşe claims that "there was no answer for a long time," but he does not mention when the answer did come. The period of time he spent in Berlin was "close

to two months," he says. If we assume that he went to Berlin on 18 March, then he must have returned around the beginning of May.

23. "Maliye Nazırı Cavit Bey'in Notları, Türkiye'nin I. Dünya Savaşına Girmesi," *Tanin*, 22, 24, 27, 28 Birincikanun (December) 1944.

24. PA-AA/R 1409, Report by Paul Rohrbach, dated 13 May 1916.

25. First session, Main Indictment, *Takvîm-i Vekâyı*, no. 3540 (27 Nisan 1335/27 April 1919).

26. "Halep Valisi Celal'in Anıları," *Vakit*, 12 Kânunuevvel (December), 1918.

27. First session, main indictment, *Takvîm-i Vekâyı*, no. 3540 (27 Nisan 1335/27 April 1919).

28. Testimony of Vehip Paşa; Vehip Paşa's testimony, supplied to the Inquiry Commission on 5 December 1918, played an important part in the Harput and Trabzon trials, as well as in the main trial. In the 29 March 1919 session of the Trabzon trial, it was read out in full, and was actually included in the verdict of the Harput trial.

29. Ibid.

30. *Tercümanı Hakikat*, 5 Ağustos (August) 1920.

31. PA-AA/Bo. Kons./B. 170, Report by Stange, dated 23 August 1915.

32. The extensive summary is published in Muammer Demirel, *Birinci Dünya Harbinde Erzurum ve Çerçevesinde Ermeni Hareketleri 1914–1918* (Ankara: Genelkurmay Basımevi, 1996), p. 53. For the sources which mention the document see: Kamuran Gürün, *Ermeni Dosyası* (Ankara: Bilgi Yayınevi, 1988), pp. 277–78; Azmi Süslü, *Ermeniler ve 1915 Tehcir Olayı* (Van: Yüzüncü Yıl Üniversitesi Rektörlüğü Yayını, Yayın No: 5, 1990), p. 110.

33. *Ati*, 24 February 1920.

34. Demirel, *Birinci Dünya Harbide*, p. 53.

35. *Ati*, 24 February 1920, "Devlet-i Aliyye'nin Fihrist-i Mesail-i Hayatiyyesi arasında mühim bir fasıl iştigâl olan bu gailenin esâslı bir suretde hal ve faslı ile külliyen izâlesi esbâbının tehiyye ve ihzârı tasavvur ve mülâhaza edilmekde iken. . . ."

36. Henry Morgenthau, *United States Diplomacy on the Bosphorus: The Diaries of Ambassador Morgenthau, 1913–1916*, compiled with an introduction by Ara Sarafian (London: Taderon Press with Gomidas Institute, 2004), p. 273.

37. Morgenthau, *Ambassador Morgenthau's Story*, p. 333. Although the book gives the date 3 August for this conversation, Morgenthau's diary records no such conversation on that date. There is a long discussion on the Armenian question with Talât recorded on 8 August.

38. PA-AA/R 14094, Report by Vice-Consul Scheubner-Richter (Erzurum), dated 4 December 1916. In his reprinting of this report, Lepsius omitted the parts containing information on the allegation, widely held in Turkey and used against Scheubner-Richter, that the massacre was the Germans' idea and was carried out with their practical support.

39. PA-AA/Bo. Kons. /B. 170, Report by Stange, referring to Scheuber-Richter, dated 23 August 1915.
40. PA-AA/Bo. Kons./B. 191, Report of Consul Mordtmann, dated 30 June 1915.
41. 5. Şube Soruşturması, from the testimony of Said Halim Paşa, pp. 30–33.
42. Ibid., testimony of İbrahim Bey, p. 32.
43. Cemal Kutay, Birinci Dünya Harbinde, p. 18.
44. Bayur, Türk İnkılabı Tarihi, vol. 3, part 1, p. 484.
45. 5. Şube Soruşturması, testimony of Çürüksulu Mahmut Paşa, p. 19.
46. Ibid., testimony of Ahmet Şükrü, p. 4.
47. Kutay, Talât Paşa'nın Gurbet Hatıraları, vol. 2, pp. 906–7.
48. The issue of temporary laws remained extremely controversial for a long period of time. See Tunaya, Türkiye'de Siyasi Partiler, vol. 3, pp. 385–88.
49. Second session, Takvîm-i Vekâyı, no. 3543 (4 Mayıs 1335/4 May 1919).
50. Fifth session, Takvîm-i Vekîyı, no. 3554 (12 Mayıs 1335/12 May 1919).
51. Ibid.
52. Refik, İki Komite, İki Kıtal, pp. 38–39.
53. PA-AA/Bo. Kons./B. 169, Report by Consul Bergfeld (Trabzon), dated 2 July 1915; Report by Carl Schlimme, dated 5 August 1915.
54. DE/PA-AA/Bo. Kons./B. 169, Telegram by Scheubner-Richter, dated 18 June 1915. The numbers are given by Lepsius, Deutschland und Armenien, p. xxiv.
55. PA-AA/Bo. Kons./B. 169, Report by Consul Rössler (Aleppo), containing information regarding Mikusch's report.
56. PA-AA/Bo. Kons./B. 170, Report dated 28 July 1915, containing the observations of Wedel-Jarlsberg.
57. For other examples of reports containing information on the involvement of Special Organization units in the massacres, see PA-AA/Bo. Kons./B. 169, and R 14088, Reports by Consul Scheubner-Richter (Erzurum), dated 18 June and 5 August 1915; Bo. Kons./B. 169 and R 14086, Reports by Ambassador Wangenheim, dated 25 June and 9 July 1915; R 14087, Report by Consul Rössler (Aleppo), dated 27 July 1915.
58. Takvîm-i Vekâyı, no. 3616 (6 Ağustos/August 1919), from the verdict of the Trabzon trial for the deportation and massacre; similar information is in the verdict of the Yozgat trial, Takvîm-i Vekâyı, no. 3617 (7 Ağustos/August 1919).
59. Such testimony is to be found in almost all sessions of the Yozgat trial. Eyewitness accounts of these events are available in many works. For example, see Gabriele Yonan, Ein vergessener Holocaust (Giessen, 1989), pp. 218–50.
60. The 5 May session is a model of such testimonies. See Alemdar, 6 May 1919.
61. V. N. Dadrian, "Armenian Genocide: An Interpretation," in Jay Winter, ed., America and the Armenian Genocide (Cambridge, 2003), pp. 98–99.
62. For the seventh sitting: Ati, 13 November 1919; for the eighth sitting: Alemdar, İkdam, Ati, 23 November 1919.
63. Aurora Mardiganian, The Auction of Souls: The Story of Aurora Mardiganian, the

Christian Girl Who Survived the Great Massacre (London, 1968); Levon Mesrob, *Verabroğner Der Zor* (Paris, 1955).

64. BAO/DH/SFR, 50-141-1333R/15, 17 Nisan 1331 (2 March 1915). Telegram from the Interior Minister Talât to the Adana region.

65. BAO/DH/SFR, 52-93-1333-C9, 11 Nisan 1331 (26 April 1915). Telegram from the Ministry of the Interior to Cemal Paşa. For the actual document see: Başbakanlık Devlet Arşivleri Genel Müdürlğü (General Directory of the State Presidential Archives), in *Osmanlı Belgelerinde Ermeniler*, pp. 23–24; BAO/DH/SFR, 52-112-1333-C11, 13 Nisan 1331 (26 April 1915). Telegram from the Ministry of the Interior to the governor's office in Maraş, Adana, and Halep regions; BAO/DH/ SFR, 52-253-1333-C. 21, 23 Nisan 1331 (6 May 1915), Telegram from the Ministry of the Interior to the governor's office in Maraş.

66. BAO/DH/SFR, 52-94-1333-C. 9, 11 Nisan 1331 (24 April 1915). Telegram from the Ministry of the Interior, EUM, to the regional office of Ankara; BAO/DH/SFR, 52-100, 11 Nisan 1331 (24 April, 1915). Telegram from the Ministry of Interior, EUM, to the regional office of Ankara.

67. BAO/DH/SFR, 52-253, 23 Nisan 1331 (6 May 1915). Telegram from the Ministry of Interior, EUM, to the governor's office of Maraş; BAO/DH/SFR, 52-338, 29 Nisan 1331 (12 May 1915). Telegram from the Ministry of the Interior to Adana.

68. Başbakanlık Devlet Arşivleri Genel Müdürlğü, *Osmanlı Belgelerinde Ermeniler, 1915–1920* (Ankara, 1994), pp. 28–29, 32–33; Lepsius, *Der Todesgang*, p. 43.

69. Başkâtipzade Ragıp Bey, *Tarih-i Hayatım* (Ankara, 1996), pp. 59–60.

70. PA-AA/R 14085, Report by Ambassador Wangenheim, dated 6 May 1915; PA-AA/R 14086, Report by Consul Rössler (Aleppo), dated 10 May 1915; PA-AA/Bo. Kons./B. 168, Report by Consul Scheubner-Richter (Erzurum), dated 15 May 1915.

71. MAZC, Period 3, Assembly Period 5, vol. 1, p. 123.

72. *İkdam*, 5 Kânunuevvel (December) 1918.

73. From the testimony of Vehip Paşa.

74. Cemal Kutay, *Celal Bayar'ın Yazmadığı ve Yazamayacağı Üç Devirden Hakikatler* (İstanbul, 1982), p. 12; Tunaya, *Türkiye'de Siyasal Partiler*, vol. 3, p. 210.

75. *Takvîm-i Vekâyı*, no. 3586 (21 Haziran 1335/21 June 1919).

76. Fifth session, ibid., no. 3554 (12 Mayıs 1335/12 May 1919).

77. Verdict in responsible secretaries trial, ibid., no. 3772 (8 Ocak 1336/8 January 1920).

78. See, for example, the sixth session, ibid., no. 3557 (14 Mayıs 1335/14 May 1919). Reşit Paşa (Kastamonu) was sacked by Responsible Secretary Hasan Fehmi Efendi; the lieutenant governor of Yozgat by Necati; and Ali Hilmi, the acting lieutenant governor of Bolu, was sacked by Dr. Mithat. All these officials were replaced by people who would be directly involved in the massacres.

79. Archive of the Armenian Patriarchate of Jerusalem, Box 21, Dossier M, no. 492.

80. This information is mentioned in the verdict of the trial of the CUP responsible secretaries, dated 8 January 1920, *Takvîm-i Vekâyı*, no. 3772 (10 Şubat/February 1920).

81. The British were skeptical about Ahmet Esat and his documents. For discussions of the authenticity of these documents and their content, see Dadrian, "Secret Young Turk–Itthadist Conference," pp. 173–201.

82. FO371/3172/31307, Report dated 10 February 1919, p. 396.

83. See, for example, the trial's fourth session, *Takvîm-i Vekâyı*, no. 3549 (8 Mayıs 1335/8 May 1919).

84. *Renaissance*, 6 and 7 March 1919. The eleventh session of the Yozgat trial (5 March 1919).

85. Archive of the Armenian Patriarchate of Jerusalem, Box 21, Dossier M, no. 494.

86. *Alemdar*, 28 Mart (March) 1919.

87. *Tercüman-ı Hakikat*, 5 Agustos (August) 1920; *Vakit*, 6 Ağustos (August) 1920.

88. De Nogales, *Vier Jahre unter dem Halbmond*, pp. 104–5.

89. *Takvım-i Vekâyi*, no. 3771, 9 February 1920, the verdict of the Mamüretülaziz trial, p. 236.

90. Yalçın, *Siyasi Anılar*, p. 236. Yalçın claims that during these tours Bahaettin Şakir "seems to have exceeded the limits of his authority and presented his own ideas as if they were the requests of the Central Committee and the Committee [of Union and Progress]." Yet the documents we have presented indicate that what transpired was not merely Şakir's idea.

91. *Alemdar*, 3 Ağustos (August) 1919.

92. First session (indictment). *Takvîm-i Vekâyı*, no. 3540 (27 Nisan 1335/27 April 1919).

93. Verdict in the Mamüretülaziz trial, *Takvîm-i Vekâyı*, no. 3771 (9 Şubat 1336/9 February 1920).

94. For example see: PA-AA/Bo. Kons./B. 169, Report by Consul Scheubner-Richter (Erzurum), dated 9 July 1915.

95. First session (main indictment), *Takvîm-i Vekâyı*, no. 3540 (27 Nisan 1335/27 April 1919).

96. *Renaissance*, 11, 12 Şubat (February) 1919; *İkdam*, 11 Şubat (February) 1919.

97. *Alemdar*, 25 Mart (March) 1919.

98. Lepsius, *Der Todesgang*, p. 76.

99. After the armistice, Dr. Reşit was captured as a war criminal. He managed to escape from prison, but committed suicide when he understood that he would be captured again.

100. Abidin Nesimi, *Yılların İçinden* (Istanbul, 1977) pp. 39–40.

101. PA-AA/Bo. Kons./B. 169, Telegram from Consul Holstein (Mosul), dated 16 July 1915.

102. *Alemdar*, 11 Mayıs (May) 1919.

103. *Zhamank*, 12 Aralık (December) 1919.

104. Archive of the Armenian Patriarchate of Jerusalem, Box 21, Dossier M, Document nos. 519–20.

105. PA-AA/Bo. Kons./B. 169, 170, R 14088, Report by Consul Scheubner-Richter (Erzurum), dated 20 May 1915.

106. PA-AA/Bo. Kons./B. 169, 170, R 14088, Reports by Consul Scheubner-Richter (Erzurum), dated 26 June, 28 July, and 5 August 1915.

107. For example, see PA-AA/Bo. Kons./B. 169, Report dated 21 June 1915.

108. In various sources, I have the names of approximately fifteen other governors-general and lieutenant governors who were sacked because they refused to carry out the order.

109. "Tehcirin imha maksadina müstenit bulunduğu," first session (indictment), *Takvîm-i Vekâyi*, no. 3540 (27 Nisan 1335/27 April 1919).

110. Archive of the Armenian Patriarchate of Jerusalem, Box 17, Dossier H, Document no. 616. Telegram from Mustafa, Commander of the Boğazlıyan regiment to Halil Recai, dated 5 August 1915.

111. Archive of the Armenian Patriarchate of Jerusalem, Box 21, Dossier M, Document no. 511.

112. Ibid. For information on the ninth session see the 23 February 1919 issues of *Renaissance, Yeni Gün* and *İkdam*.

113. Archive of the Armenian Patriarchate of Jerusalem, Box 21, Dossier M, Document no. 506; *Renaissance*, 21 February 1919 and 7 March 1919.

114. Verdict (dated 8 Ocak 1336/8 January 1920) in the responsible secretaries trial, *Takvîm-i Vekâyi*, no. 3772 (10 Şubat/February 1920).

115. PA-AA/R 14089, Report by Ambassador Wolff-Metternich, dated 7 November 1915.

116. First session (main indictment), *Takvîm-i Vekâyi*, no. 3540 (27 Nisan 1335/27 April 1919).

117. AA Bonn, Bo. Kons./B. 170, Telegram from Schmitt, dated 9 September 1915. As previously mentioned, Cemal Paşa said similar words in March 1916 to Loytved, the German consul to Damascus.

118. PA-AA/R 14088, Report by Ambassador Hohenlohe-Langenburg, dated 25 September 1915. For Talât Paşa's telegrams and related responses from the various foreign consulates, see also Lepsius, *Deutschland und Armenien*, pp. xxvi-xxxiii.

119. AA Türkei 159, no. 3, vol. 4, A 24679, Report by Ambassador Wolff-Metternich, dated 16 September 1916.

120. Haus und Hof Archiv, PA 12, Box 209, nos. 72 and 73, Reports by Ambassador Pallavicini, dated 3 and 8 September 1915.

121. PA-AA/Bo. Kons./B. 170, Telegram from Consul Büge (Adana), dated 10 September 1915.

122. Hüseyin Cahid Yalçın, *Siyasi Anılar*, p. 148.

123. Atay, *Zeytindağı*, pp. 24–25.

124. Menteşe, *Halil Menteşe'nin Anıları*, p. 216.

125. Morgenthau, *Ambassador Morgenthau's Story*, p. 145. The full account of the visit is found on pages 140–45.

126. Reported by V. N. Dadrian, "Documentation of the Armenian Genocide in

German and Austrian Sources," in Israel W. Charney, ed., *Genocide: A Critical Bibliographic Review*, vol. 2 (London and New York, 1991), pp. 109–10.

127. İlhan Selçuk, *Yüzbaşı Selahettin'in Romanı*, vol. 1, p. 292.

128. FO 371/7869/E7840, File 262, p. 2 (1 August 1922).

129. *Alemdar*, 27 March 1919.

130. FO371/4172/31307, p. 390, Report, dated 10 February 1919.

131. *Renaissance*, 6 May 1919; *Hadisat*, 7 May 1919.

132. Andonian, *Documents Officiels*, pp. 16 and 57: Talât Paşa's cables, dated 3 Mart (March) 1915 and 20 Şubat (February) 1916.

133. Bryce and Toynbee, *Treatment of the Armenians*, p. 652.

134. For a summary of this phenomenon, see ibid., pp. 635–50.

135. First session, trial of Unionist leaders (indictment), *Takvîm-i Vekâyı*, no. 3540 (27 Nisan 1335/27 April 1919).

136. *Vakit* and *İkdam*, 4 Nisan (April) 1919.

137. *Renaissance* and *Journal d'Orient*, 6 April 1919, and *Renaissance*, 1 May 1919.

138. *Renaissance*, 20 May 1919.

139. PA-AA/Bo. Kons./B. 170, Report by Stange, dated 23 August 1915.

140. Fuat Balkan, "İlk Türk Komitacısı Fuat Balkan'ın Hatıraları," in *Yakin Tarihimiz*, vol. 2, p. 297. In May 1919, Colonel Seyfi said to Colonel İsmet (İnönü), who was serving as advisor to the Ministry of War at the time: "You cannot possibly have problems with money. I have transferred all the Special Organization's secret funds to you as it is." V. N. Dadrian emphasizes Seyfi's role in "The Secret Young Turk–Ittihadist Conference," pp. 173–98.

141. *Ariamard*, an Armenian newspaper, reported this information on 13 December 1918, citing *Sabah*. A news story in *Akşam* of 12 December 1918 said that some of the documents taken by Dr. Nâzim, and which contain important information on the massacre, were given to Bahaettin Şakir. The police later found the documents in the house of one of Şakir's relatives, an attorney named Ramiz.

142. FO 371/4173, File 345, Report dated 20 May 1919.

143. For more information on the army units' role in the planning and implementation of the massacre, see Dadrian, "Role of Special Organizations in the Armenian Genocide," and by the same author, "Role of the Turkish Military in the Destruction of Ottoman Armenians," pp. 257–88.

144. Zurlinden, *Der Weltkrieg*, part 2, p. 640.

145. Bryce and Toynbee, *Treatment of the Armenians*, p. 103.

146. Halil Paşa, *İttihat ve Terakki'den Cumhuriyet'e Bitmeyen Savaş*, ed. M. Taylan Sorgun (Istanbul, 1972), p. 241. In these memoirs Halil said: "Three hundred thousand Armenians . . . maybe more, maybe less; I did not count them. Wherever they rebelled against my country I used my reserve forces to move them and punish them. Wherever they were likely to rebel I ordered state authorities to deport them and I had them deported" (p. 274).

147. PA-AA/1409, Report by Consul Scheubner-Richter (Erzurum), dated 4 December 1916, written in Munich.
148. PA-AA Türkei (Bonn), 183/54, A44066, Report by Count Lüttichau, dated 18 October 1918.
149. Many consular dispatches exist that report eyewitness accounts. For example, PA-AA/R 14087, Report by Consul Rössler (Aleppo), dated 27 July 1916. Also see Lepsius, Deutschland und Armenien, Document no. 120, pp. 108–12, and the subsequent documents for the months of July and August.
150. Leslie A. Davis, The Slaughterhouse Province: An American Diplomat's Report on the Armenian Genocide, 1915–1917 (New York, 1989), p. 62.
151. PA-AA/R 14086, Appendix to Report by Ambassador Wangenheim, dated 16 July 1915; R 14090, Appendix 2 to Report by Consul Rössler (Aleppo), dated 3 January 1916. An Armenian woman who was deported from Samsun stated in her memoirs that after the announcement of the deportation, a Muslim religious scholar visited their house two or three times a week to press them to convert to Islam. (Captanian, 1915 Der Völkermord, p. 20).
152. PA-AA/Bo. Kons./B. 168, Report by Consul Scheubner-Richter (Erzurum), dated 2 June 1915; PA-AA/R 14086, Report by Ambassador Wangenheim, dated 7 July 1915 (quoting the report by the Trabzon consul of 26 June); PA-AA/Bo. Kons./B. 170, Report by Chief Consul Mordtmann (Istanbul), dated 21 December 1915. Many German consular reports state that those who converted were not deported; for example, see PA-AA/Bo. Kons./B. 172, Telegrams by Werth, the vice-consul in Sivas, dated 27 June and 27 July 1915.
153. PA-AA/R 14089, Appendix to Report by Zimmermann, undersecretary to the Foreign Ministry, dated 12 December 1915.
154. Osmanlı Belgelerinde Ermeniler 1915–1920, Documents 58 and 72, pp. 58, 69. The English translation is from Kamuran Gürün, Ermeni Dosyası, p. 212.
155. PA-AA/Bo. Kons./B. 170, Report by Wedel-Jarlsberg, in which she recounts her observations, dated 28 July, 1915.
156. PA-AA/R 14090, Report by Consul Rössler (Aleppo), dated 31 January 1916; PA-AA/Bo. Kons./B. 173, Report by Consul Julius Loytved-Hardegg (Damascus), dated 30 June 1916; and PA-AA/Bo. Kons./R 14092, Report by Consul [Dr.] Brode (Jerusalem), dated 26 June 1916.
157. HHStA PA XL 274, Istanbul, 6 January 1916. In Ohandjanian, Armenien, vol. 7, p. 5007.
158. Many such reports exist. For examples, see PA-AA/R 14086, Report by Consul Kuckhoff (Samsun), dated 4 June 1915; and Report by Ambassador Wangenheim, dated 7 July 1915. PA-AA/Bo. Kons./B. 169, Report by Ehmann, dated 26 June 1915; and Report by Consul Holstein (Mosul), dated 15 July 1915.
159. PA-AA/Bo. Kons./B. 169, Note by Mordtmann, dated 21 July 1915. Also see Lepsius, Deutschland und Armenien, p. xxix.

160. *Osmanlı Belgelerinde Ermeniler 1915–1920,* Documents 76 and 83, pp. 72, 77–78. In a coded cable sent in August 1915, the same order is repeated for both Catholics and Protestants (ibid., Document 99, p. 87).

161. For example, see PA-AA/Bo. Kons./B. 170, Report on İzmit, dated 19 August 1915. Reports by Consul Rössler (Aleppo), dated 9 and 12 September 1915, and Report by Ambassador Hohenlohe, dated 11 September 1915.

162. PA-AA/R 14087, Report by Consul Rössler (Aleppo), dated 13 August 1915.

163. United States National Archives, RG 59, 867.4016/148, Report by J. B. Jackson, dated 19 August 1915.

164. PA-AA/Bo. Kons./B. 170, Report by Consul Mordtmann (Istanbul), dated 21 August 1915.

165. PA-AA/Bo. Kons./B. 170, Report by Göppert, dated 31 August 1915.

166. PA-AA/Bo. Kons./R 14087, Report by Ambassador Hohenlohe, dated 4 September 1915. The German translations of the aforementioned telegrams are attached to the report. The same report includes other news from the provinces.

167. PA-AA/Bo. Kons./B. 170, Reports and Telegrams by Consul Büge (Adana), dated 10 September 1915, and by Ambassador Hohenlohe, dated 11 September 1915, and by Consul Rössler (Aleppo), dated 12 September 1915.

168. For examples of such telegrams see: BAO/DH/SFR, 54-A/27ł, 1333-N.23, Telegram sent by Talât to Adana Province on 4 August 1915; BAO/DH/SFR, 54-A/384, 1333-N.30, Telegram sent by Talât to the Adana and Haleppo provinces on 11 August 1915.

169. *Osmanlı Belgelerinde Ermeniler 1915–1920,* Document nos. 109, 111–13, pp. 94–97.

170. PA-AA/Bo. Kons./B. 170, Report by Ambassador Hohenlohe, dated 16 September 1915.

171. For some examples, see PA-AA/R 14091, R 14092, Reports by Ambassador Wolff-Metternich, dated 11 May 1916 and 10 July 1916; and by Consul [Dr.] Brode (Jerusalem), dated 26 June 1916.

172. PA-AA/R 14090, Report by Erzberger, dated 3 March 1916. Erzberger was a member of the German Reichstag who had just returned from Istanbul.

173. PA-AA/R 14093, Report by Ambassador Wolff-Metternich, dated 18 September 1916.

174. On the congregations in Ankara, see PA-AA/R 14096, Report by Zimmermann, dated 25 June 1916.

175. PA-AA/R 14097, Report, dated 14 July 1916.

176. PA-AA/R 14098, Report by Ambassador Bernstorff, dated 16 December 1917.

177. BAO/DH/SFR, 63-188-1334-B.1 (4 May 1916). A ciphered telegram sent from the Interior Ministry Department of AMMU to the provinces and districts of Ankara, Konya, Kayseri, Niğde, etc.

178. BAO/DH/SFR, 56/290/1333.ZA.26. For the regulations regarding different Muslim groups see: Fuat Dündar, *İttihat ve Terakki'nin Müslümanları İskan*

Politikası (1913–1918) (Istanbul, 2001), pp. 262–73. In this work the resettlement of Muslim population is well documented.

179. This explains why some Armenian neighborhoods were not deported. BAO/DH/SFR, 55/59/1333.L.6.

180. BAO/DH/SFR, 54/308/1333.Ş22.

181. BAO/DH/SFR, 54/413/Ş.29.

182. This is a topic requiring much further research, including local studies of various regions, before any conclusions should be drawn.

183. *Alemdar,* 5 April 1919.

184. PA-AA/Bo. Kons./B. 170, Report by Consul Scheubner-Richter (Erzurum), dated 28 July 1915. In his reproduction of this report, Lepsius omitted certain passages. See Lepsius, *Deutschland und Armenien,* Document no. 123, p. 113.

185. PA-AA/R 14086, Report dated 9 June 1915. Lepsius, who published this report as Document no. 109, omitted these sentences. Lepsius, *Deutschland und Armenien,* pp. 99–101.

186. PA-AA/R 14088, Report by Vice-Consul Scheubner-Richter (Erzurum), dated 5 August 1915. In his presentation of this document, Lepsius omitted this and other sentences in which Turks condemn the massacres, as well as the parts where Turks express the view—widely held at the time—that the Germans were the main culprits. Lepsius, *Deutschland und Armenien,* Document no. 129, pp. 116–21.

187. PA-AA Türkei (Bonn), 183/54, A 44066, Report by Count Lüttichau, dated 18 October 1918.

188. First session of Unionist leaders trial (indictment), *Takvîm-i Vekâyı,* no. 3540 (27 Nisan 1335/27 April 1919).

189. This statement was read at many sessions. See *İleri,* 19 Şubat (February) 1919; *Alemdar,* 25–30 Mart (March) 1919.

190. HHStA PA XXXVIII 368, Nr. 68/P, Report dated 6 October 1915. Found in Ohandjanian, *Armenien,* vol. 6, p. 4756.

191. Captanian, *1915 Der Völkermord,* p. 60. He tells the story of one man who saved thirty Armenians, saying, "We are Kurds, not Turks." In the Dersim region, however, the convoys were set upon by Kurdish tribesmen.

192. Davis, *Slaughterhouse Province,* pp. 66, 98; Garo Sasunu, *Kürt Ulusal Hareketleri ve 15. Yüzyıldan Günümüze Ermeni Kürt İlişkileri* (Istanbul, 1992), pp. 162–65.

193. Henry H. Riggs, *Days of Tragedy in Armenia: Personal Experiences in Harpoot, 1915–17* (Ann Arbor, MI, 1997), pp. 108–17. Report of Leslie A. Davis, American consul in Harpoot, 9 February 1918 (U.S. State Department Record Group 59, 867.4016/392) in Ara Sarfyan, ed., *United States Official Documents on the Armenian Genocide,* vol. 1: *The Lower Euphrates* (Watertown, MA, 1994), pp. 110–15.

194. *Alemdar,* 3 August 1919; Captanian, *1915 Der Völkermord,* recounts one of these attacks (pp. 62–70).

195. *İleri,* 30 Temmuz (July) 1919.

196. PA-AA/Bo. Kons./B. 169, Report by Consul Scheubner-Richter (Erzurum), dated 18 June 1915, speaks about Kurdish villagers' attacks against Armenian convoys on the way from Erzincan to Harput; Report by the consul in Mosul, dated 15 July 1915, speaks about the attacks and massacres in Christian villages near Diyarbakır.

197. For an example, see HHStA PA XXXVIII 366, Aleppo, 27 August 1915, Z. 12/P. Found in Ohandjanian, *Armenien*, vol. 6, p. 4704.

198. PA-AA/R 14087, Report by Consul Rössler (Aleppo), dated 27 July 1915, Appendix 1. This report is also found in Lepsius, *Deutschland und Armenien*, Document no. 120, pp. 108–12, but omitted the whole of Appendix 1 because it contains statements by Turkish officers blaming the Germans for the events in question.

199. For a news story on how a convoy from Erzurum was attacked by gangs on the road and defended by the gendarmes, some of whom were killed, see *Tasvir-i Efkâr*, 3 Tesrinisani (November) 1919; and De Nogales, *Vier Jahr unter dem Halbmond*, pp. 78–98. The author himself witnessed some incidents in which the gendarmes protected the convoys from attacks by the locals. Captanian claims that the gendarmes pretended to be protecting the convoys but in fact did not interfere. He says that the looting by Muslim Turks was done by "permission" of the gendarmes. Captanian, *1915 Der Völkermord*, pp. 40–42.

200. PA-AA/R 14088, Report by Consul Scheubner-Richter (Aleppo), dated 5 August 1915, quoting an Armenian who survived the attacks. The gendarmes who clashed with the Kurds to protect the convoy were the same people who later massacred them.

201. PA-AA/Bo. Kons./B. 169, Report by Consul Rössler (Aleppo), dated 8 July 1915.

202. Gabriele Yonan, *Ein vergessener Holocaust*, p. 296, Document no. 38; Davis, *Slaughterhouse Province*, p. 82.

203. For example, see PA-AA/R 1408, 14093, Reports by Consul Rössler (Aleppo), dated 13 August 1915 and 5 September 1916.

204. *Alemdar*, 25 Mart (March) 1919.

205. *İkdam*, 5 Kânunısani (January) 1919. Armenians were deported from Izmir in November 1916. The deportations were stopped upon Liman von Sanders's intercession. PA-AA/R 14094, Reports by Radowitz, of the consular staff, dated 13 November 1916, and by Field Marshall Liman von Sanders, dated 17 November 1916.

206. *Alemdar*, 4 Nisan (April) 1919; similar statements were given at the seventh session of the trial (8 April): *Alemdar*, 9 Nisan (April) 1919.

207. *Alemdar*, 16 Nisan (April) 1919.

208. MMZC, Period 3, Assembly Period 5, Sitting 24, 11 December 1334 (1918), p. 300.

209. PA-AA/Bo. Kons./B. 170, Report by Wedel-Jarlsberg, containing her observations, dated 28 July 1915.

210. For examples of such reports, see PA-AA/R 14093 and 14098, Appendices to Reports by Consul Rössler (Aleppo), dated 29 July and 16 November 1915. Lepsius omitted some of the eyewitness reports.

211. PA-AA/Bo. Kons./B. 168, Report by Dr. Liparit, dated 2 April 1915, regarding the condition of Armenians.

212. PA-AA/Bo. Kons./B. 168, Report by Consul Rössler (Aleppo), dated 3 May 1915.

213. PA-AA/Bo. Kons./B. 168, Cable by Consul Scheubner-Richter (Erzurum), dated 22 May 1915.

214. PA-AA/Bo. Kons./B. 169, Report by Consul Scheubner-Richter (Erzurum), dated 22 May 1915.

215. BAO/DH/SFR, 53/21/1333.B.3.

216. *Osmanlı Belgelerinde Ermeniler 1915–1920*, Document nos. 51 and 68, pp. 53–54, 65–66.

217. Controversy over numbers is a feature of almost all sources. For a careful consideration of this issue, see Sarkis J. Karajian, "An Inquiry into the Statistics of the Turkish Genocide of the Armenians, 1915–1918," *Armenian Review* 25 (Winter 1972); also Gürün, *Ermeni Dosyası*, pp. 120–47, 290–98.

218. The interior minister's statement was published in the 16 March 1919 editions of *Vakit, Alemdar* and *İkdam*.

219. *Alemdar,* 18 Mart (March) 1919.

220. Bayur, *Türk İnkılabı Tarihi*, vol. 3, part 4, p. 787.

221. Ibid., vol. 3, part 3, pp. 43–44.

222. Çerkez Hasan, "Peki Yüzbinlerce Ermeniyi Kim Öldürdü?," *Alemdar,* 5 Nisan (April) 1919.

223. PA-AA/Bo. Kons./B. 169 and R 14088, Reports by Consul Scheubner-Richter (Erzurum), dated 22 June and 5 August 1915.

224. Archive of the Armenian Patriarchate of Jerusalem, Box 21, Dossier M, Document nos. 519–20.

225. PA-AA/R 14086, Report by Ambassador Wangenheim, dated 17 June 1915.

226. PA-AA/R 14089, Report by Ambassador Wolff-Metternich, dated 27 December 1915.

227. PA-AA/R 14091, Report by Ambassador Wolff-Metternich, dated 28 April 1916.

228. PA-AA/R 14093, Report dated 14 August 1916.

229. "Halep Valisi Celal'in Anıları," *Vakit,* 12 Kânunuevvel (December) 1918.

230. Ibid.

231. PA-AA/R 14090, Report by Consul Loytved (Damascus), passed on by Ambassador Wolff-Metternich on 29 March 1916.

232. Cemal Paşa issued many directives specifically ordering that the massacring of convoys on the roads be stopped. For information regarding Cemal's efforts, see PA-AA/Bo. Kons./B. 170, Reports by Consul Rössler (Aleppo), dated 12 August, and by Ambassador Hohenlohe, dated 4 August 1915; B. 172, Reports by Consul

Rössler (Aleppo), dated 10 January 1916, 8 and 17 June 1916; R. 1409, dated 12 April 1916; and R. 1409, Report by Ambassador Wolff-Metternich, dated 28 April 1916.

233. PA-AA/R 14092, Report by Ambassador Wolff-Metternich, dated 19 June 1916, to which is attached Consul Loytved Hardegg's report of May 30 1916. Lepsius omitted the sentence that talks about Hüseyin Kâzım's acceptance of secret help from the document he published in *Deutschland und Armenien*, Document no. 275, p. 73.

234. Hüseyin Kâzım Kadri, *Türkiye'nin Çöküşü* (Istanbul, 1992), p. 205. In his memoirs, Hüseyin Kâzim claims that he remained in Syria for six years *(Hatıralarım* [Istanbul,1991], p. 255). German consular reports mention a Hüseyin Kâzım Bey who was in Damascus in 1917 and was in charge of settling migrants. This individual tried to save those Armenians who reached Syria alive; and according to him about thirty thousand did. I did not investigate whether this is the same person as Hüseyin Kâzım Kadri Bey. (PA-AA/R 14096, Report from Consul Loytved [Damascus], dated 23 March 1917.)

235. "Tehcirin İçyüzü, Çerkez Hasan Bey'in Hatıraları," *Alemdar*, 26 Haziran (June) 1919.

236. Ibid., 27 Haziran (June) 1919. Although the day's installment finishes with the promise "continued tomorrow," it was not, as the Unionists' threats were effective in preventing its publication.

237. Başbakanlik, "Devlet Arşivleri Genel Müdürlüğü," Document no. 71, pp. 68–69, cable from the Ministry of Interior to Diyarbakır on 12 July 1915.

238. The Turkish summary of the telegram translates "halin işarı" of the original Ottoman text as "investigate." This is incorrect. The correct translation is "inform."

239. For the entire text of the decision, see Süslü, *Ermeniler ve 1915*, pp. 111–13.

240. For the entire text of the manual, see ibid., pp. 114–16.

241. For the entire text of Manual for the Administrative State of Affairs of the Personal and Real Property of Armenians, Forcibly Deported from Their Homes Due to Conditions of War and Exceptional Political Necessity, see *Askeri Tarih Belgeleri Dergisi (Journal of Historical Military Documents)* 31, no. 81 (December 1982), pp. 149–62; Süslü, *Ermeniler ve 1915*, pp. 117–21.

242. For the instructions given by the Interior Ministry to the regions on 3 and 15 August, see Yusuf Halaçoğlu, *The Armenian Deportation and Reality (1914–1918)* (1984), pp. 68–69; Bayur, *Türk İnkılabı Tarihi*, vol. 3, part 3, pp. 45–46.

243. Ibid., p. 46.

244. Hilmar Kaiser, "Armenian Property, Ottoman Law and Nationality Policies During the Armenian genocide, 1915–1916," unpublished paper presented at a conference in Leiden, 2000.

245. MAZC, Period 3, Assembly Period 2, pp. 133–35, in the minutes of the council for 7 December 1915, when Ahmet Rıza's proposal was discussed in the Cham-

ber of Notables, it says that while the proposal "has appeared worthy of consideration, because it has been understood through examination that the temporary law whose amendment is being requested was submitted to the Chamber of Deputies, it is requested of the general assembly that this proposed amendment would have to be suggested during the course of discussions when the aforementioned temporary law reaches the Chamber of Notables." Although the time between the date on which Ahmet Rıza submitted his proposal and the date of the council's decision was some two and a half months, the issue was not discussed in the Chamber of Deputies. In the minutes of the discussions in our possession, there is no evidence whatsoever that this topic was ever taken up.

246. Başbakanlık Devlet Arşivleri Genel Müdürlüğü, *Osmanlı Belgelerinde Ermeniler, 1915–1920*, pp. 176–77, 180–81; Fuat Dündar, *İttihat ve Terakki'nin Müslümanları İskan Politikası*, p. 88.
247. BAO/DH/SFR, 54-346-1333.Ş24. The IAMM was established in 1914 within the Ministry of the Interior. A law of 14 March 1916 expanded its authority, and it grew in power and influence under its new title of Ministry of the Interior's Directorate of Tribes and Immigrants (Aşair ve Muhacirin Müdüriyet Umumiyesi [AMMU]).
248. BAO/DH/SFR, 59-239-1334.Ş.29.
249. BAO/DH/SFR, 60-129-1334.RA.20.
250. BAO/DH/SFR, 60-277-1334.R.3.
251. BAO/DH/SFR, 64-39-1334.B.13.
252. BAO/DH/SFR, 65-37-1334.Ş.17.
253. BAO/DH/SFR, 61-247-1334.R.28.
254. BAO/DH/SFR, 63-261-1334.B.7.
255. BAO/DH/SFR, 54-382-Ş.27.
256. BAO/DH/SFR, 55-A-143-1333.L.28.
257. BAO/DH/SFR, 67-106-1334.L.27. For the transition from IAMM to AMMU see note 247 in this chapter.
258. As mentioned earlier, these telegrams have been cited by Yusuf Halaçoğlu. The documents show quite openly that the state used the income to cover its expenses for "deportation and maintenance."
259. BAO/DH/SFR, 57-342-1333.Z.30.
260. BAO/DH/SFR, 57-348-1333.Z.30.
261. BAO/DH/SFR, 57-349-1333.Z.30.
262. BAO/DH/SFR, 52-292-1333.C.24, Telegram sent by Talaat Pasha to the Konya regional office on 26 Nissan 1331 (9 May 1915).
263. BAO/DH/SFR, 64-18-1334.B.11.
264. BAO/DH/SFR, 54-A-218-1333-N.20 (1 August 1915).
265. Kaiser, "Armenian Property," p. 12.
266. MAZC, vol. 1, session 3, Assembly Year 2, p. 134.
267. Çerkez Hasan, "Peki Yüzbinlerce Ermeni'yi Kim Öldürdü?," *Alemdar*, 5 Nisan (April) 1919.

268. First session (indictment), *Takvîm-i Vekâyı*, no. 3540 (27 Nisan 1335/27 April 1919).
269. Second session, *Takvîm-i Vekâyı*, no. 3543 (4 Mayıs 1335/4 May 1919).
270. *Takvîm-i Vekâyı*, no. 3573 (3 June, 1919).
271. For evidence of the destruction and removal of documents, see Dadrian, "Documentation of the Armenian Genocide," pp. 104–7.
272. Aydemir, vol. 3, p. 468.
273. FO 371/4172/31307, Report by Heathcote Smith, dated 4 February 1919. V. N. Dadrian reprinted it in "The Secret Young Turk–Ittihadist Conference," pp. 174–75. It was Ahmet Esat who provided the information.
274. 1926 Ankara'daki İstiklal Mahkemesi, *İzmir Suikasti İddianame ve Savunmalar* (draft text), p. 36.
275. Hüsamettin Ertürk, "Milli Mücadele Senelerinde Teşkilat-i Mahsusa" (typed text) (Ankara Stratejik Araştırmalar ve Askerlik Tarihi Estitüsü: no date), p. 14. Reported by Bilge Criss, *İşgal Altında İstanbul*, p. 147.
276. For the full text of the Council of Ministers' Deportation Decree, see *Osmanlı Belgelerinde Ermeniler*, pp. 30–32.
277. For a list of these official documents, see Yusuf Halaçoğlu, *Ermeni Tehciri ve Gerçekler (1914–1918)* (Ankara, 2001), pp. 47–53; Süslü, *Ermeniler ve 1915*, pp. 106–21.
278. Gürün, *Ermeni Dosyası*, p. 206.
279. *5. Şube Soruşturmaları*, testimony of İbrahim Bey, p. 25.
280. T. C. Başbakanlık, Devlet Arşivleri Genel Müdürlüğü, *Osmanlı Belgelerinde*, pp. 23–36.
281. Willis, *Prologue to Nuremberg*, p. 26.
282. Bayur, *Türk İnkılabı Tarihi*, p. 39.
283. Bryce and Toynbee, *Treatment of the Armenians*, p. 648.
284. Lepsius, *Deutschland und Armenien*, document no. 157, p. 146.
285. The role of the "activities of Armenian organizations as provocation" thesis is discussed in Robert Melson, "Provocation or Nationalism: A Critical Inquiry into the Armenian Genocide of 1915," in Richard G. Hovannisian, ed., *The Armenian Genocide in Perspective* (New Brunswick, NJ, 1987), pp. 61–84, and Robert Melson, *Revolution and Genocide: On the Origins of the Armenian Genocide and the Holocaust* (Chicago, 1992), pp. 49–53, 151–59.
286. For information on Ottoman intelligence's reporting of the congress's decisions, see Mim Kemal Öke, *Ermeni Sorunu 1914–1923* (Ankara, 1991), pp. 101ff. Also see Uras, *Tarihte Ermeniler*, pp. 581–95.
287. Arakel Babakhanian Leo, *Türkiye'deki Ermeni Devrimi'nin İdeolojisi*, vol. 2 (Paris, 1935), p. 117. Uras adorned his book with extensive quotes from the works of Leo, an Armenian historian. But Uras does not say that *Horizon*, the newspaper that declared war on the Turks, belonged to Caucasian Armenians. He makes it appear as though the declaration of war came from Ottoman Dashnaks.
288. For detailed information, see Hovannisian, *Armenia on the Road*, pp. 42–45.
289. Leo, *Türkiye'deki*, vol. 2, p. 120.

290. PA-AA/Bo. Kons./B. 168, Note by Ambassador Wangenheim, dated 15 February 1915.

291. Leo, *Türkiye'deki,* vol. 2, p. 119.

292. AA (Bonn) Weltkrieg, 11 d secr., B IV, A 9305, Report by Louis Mosel, dated 3 March 1915.

293. Mil, "Umumi Harpte," Installment no. 82 (25 Ocak/January 1934).

294. Ibid., Installment no. 66 (7 Ocak/January 1934).

295. İbrahim Arvas, *Tarihi Hakikatler* (Ankara, 1964), pp. 21–22; Arvas does not name Antranik, but Stefanos Yerasimos, quoting Arvas, mentions Antranik's name; see Stefanos Yerasimos, *Milliyetler ve Sınırlar* (Istanbul, 1994), p. 284.

296. Süslü, *Ermeniler ve 1915* (Van, 1990), p. 77.

297. For a detailed account of the Van uprising in the records of the Turkish army command, see Ergünöz Akçora, *Van ve Çevresinde Ermeni İsyanları (1896–1916)* (Istanbul, 1994), pp. 163–70.

298. PA-AA/R 14088, Report by Von Tyszka, a German journalist, on the region, dated 1 October 1915. Lepsius omitted all this information (29 September 1915, Appendix 2) in his version of the report. J. Lepsius, *Deutschland und Armenien,* pp. 156–61, Document no. 176.

299. Yerasimos, *Milliyetler ve Sınırlar,* p. 286, quoting G. Korganoff's *La Participation des Armeniens à la Guerre mondiale sur le front du Caucase.* Also Azmi Süslü, "Van Zeve'deki Türk Katliamları," in *Yakın Tarihimizde Van Uluslararası Sempozyumu* (Ankara, 1990), pp. 27–35.

300. Aziz Samih, "Umumi Harpte Kafkas Cephesi Hatıraları," *Kurun,* Installment no. 10, 10 Nisan (April) 1935.

301. PA-AA/R 14085, Report by Ambassador Wangenheim, dated 15 April 1915. Lepsius reproduces this report as "Dokument 26," but he omits the part in it which says that the information contained therein has been corroborated by accounts of German officers who took part in the war. Lepsius, *Deutschland und Armenien,* Document no. 26, pp. 45–49.

302. Samih, "Umumi Harpte," Installment no. 11, 11 Nisan (April) 1935.

303. PA-AA/R 14085, Report by Consul Rössler (Aleppo), dated 16 October 1915. Lepsius's version of this report (Document 11) omits the part that discusses the negative attitude toward the Germans then prevalent in the region. (Lepsius, *Deutschland und Armenien,* Document no. 11, p. 21.)

304. PA-AA/Bo. Kons./B. 168, Report by Consul Büge (Adana), dated 13 March. 1915. Lepsius published this report but omitted this sentence. (Lepsius, *Deutschland und Armenien,* Document no. 19, pp. 32–34.)

305. For detailed information, see Hovannisian, *Armenia on the Road,* pp. 40ff; Gürün, *Ermeni Dosyası,* pp. 253ff.

306. Kamuran Gürün has reproduced some documents of the Turkish Army Command and some accounts of foreign observers in *Ermeni Dosyası,* pp. 257–75.

307. Nuri Dersimi, *Hatıralarım* (Stockholm, 1986), pp. 44–47.

308. For example, Abraham Hartunian, *Neither to Laugh Nor to Weep: A Memoir of the Armenian Genocide* (Boston, 1968), p. 58. This book is an important source on the massacre. The author claims that these gangs killed some sixty Turks in one village.

309. Samih, "Umumi Harpte," Installment no. 34, 7 Mayıs (May) 1935.

310. PA-AA/Bo. Kons./B. 168, Report by Consul Büge (Adana), dated 18 March 1915.

311. Samih, "Umumi Harpte," Installment no. 2, 2 Nisan (April) 1935.

312. Ibid., Installment no. 11, 11 Nisan (April) 1935.

313. Ibid., Installment no. 38, 12 Mayıs (May) 1935.

314. This subject was talked about in some novels as well. See Ömer Polat, *Saragöl* (Istanbul, 1974).

315. For example, see consular reports from Erzurum and Adana. AA Türkei 183/45 A33457, Report dated 4 December 1916; and AA Bo. Kons./B. 168 (no. 2540), Report dated 26 April 1916.

316. De Nogales, *Vier Jahre unter dem Halbmond*, p. 100.

317. Davis, *Slaughterhouse Province*, p. 157.

318. PA-AA/Bo. Kons./B. 168, Note by Chief Consul Mordtmann (Constantinople), dated 29 May, 1915; Cable by Ambassador Wangenheim, dated 30 May 1915.

319. PA-AA/Bo. Kons./B. 168, Cable by Consul Scheubner-Richter (Erzurum), dated 2 June 1915.

320. Archives of the Armenian Patriarchate of Jerusalem, Box 21, Dossier M, Document no. 479 (numbered 169 and dated 14/27 July 1915).

321. *Renaissance* and *Orient*, 21 February 1919.

322. Archives of the Armenian Patriarchate of Jerusalem, Box 17, Dossier H, Document no. 458. Also, *Renaissance*, 22 February 1919.

323. *Renaissance*, 6 March 1919.

324. For Şebinkarahisar, see Lepsius, *Der Todesgang*, pp. 63ff.

325. German reports offer detailed information on the events in Urfa. Count Wolff-skeel, a German officer, was on duty at the time that the uprising was suppressed. PA-AA/R 14089, Reports by Consul Rössler (Aleppo), dated 8 and 16 November 1915. Lepsius's reproduction of these reports omits the parts in which the name of the German officer is mentioned. (Lepsius, *Deutschland und Armenien*, Document nos. 193 and 202.) Also PA-AA/R 14090, Report by Consul Rössler (Aleppo), dated 3 January 1916, Appendix 1. In this latter report, Rössler includes the observations of the Swiss-German missionary Jakob Künzler. For detailed information, see Künzler, pp. 64ff.

326. PA-AA/R 14089, Report by Consul Rössler (Aleppo), dated 16 November 1915.

327. Mil, "Umumi Harpte," Installment no. 22 (22 İkinciteşrin/November 1933). The report was published in late August 1914.

328. De Nogales, *Vier Jahre unter dem Halbmond*, pp. 60–61.

329. Lepsius, *Deutschland und Armenien*, p. 471.

330. Onnig Mikhitarian, "The Defence of Van, (Part III)," *Armenian Review* 1, no. 3 (Summer 1948), p. 133. There is a vast body of sources concerning the events in

Van, primarily from missionaries serving in the area. Through these sources it is possible to follow the developments on a day-by-day basis. For a few examples, see Kæthe Ehrhold, *Flucht in die Heimat* (Dresden, Leipzig, 1937); de Nogales, *Vier Jahre unter dem Halbmond.*

331. Archives of the Armenian Patriarchate of Jerusalem, Box 21, Dossier M, Document nos. 519–20. This is from a 24 May 1915 telegram to the minister of the interior, Talât. Tahsin served in Van as the governor, before he was moved to Erzurum.

332. PA-AA/R 14085, Reports by Consul Rössler (Aleppo), dated 12 April 1915.

333. "Tarihi Hakikatler, İ. Arvas'ın Hatıratı," p. 6.

334. PA-AA/Bo. Kons./B. 168, Report, dated 2 April 1915.

335. Pomiankowski, p. 160.

336. Gust, *Der Völkermord an den Armeniern*, pp. 177–78.

337. Reported by ibid., p. 178.

338. PA-AA/R 14085. Report by Ambassador Wangenheim, dated 30 April 1915.

339. PA-AA/R 14085, Report by Ambassador Wangenheim, dated 8 May 1915. Also see Bo. Kons./B. 168, Report by Consul Scheubner-Richter (Erzurum), dated 15 May 1915.

340. See Gust, *Der Völkermord an den Armeniern*, pp. 172–85.

341. For example, Leo, *Türkiye'deki*, pp. 145–54.

342. For example, see PA-AA/R 14086, Report by Ambassador Wangenheim, dated 7 June 1915.

343. PA-AA/Bo. Kons./B. 169/R 14088, Report by Consul Scheubner-Richter (Erzurum), Appendix 1, dated 5 August 1915. In reproducing this report, Lepsius omitted the appendix. Lepsius, *Deutschland und Armenien*, Document no. 130, pp. 121–22.

344. Davis, *Slaughterhouse Province*, p. 157.

345. For some examples, see PA-AA/Bo. Kons./B. 168, Report by Consul Büge (Adana), dated 13 March 1915 and PA-AA/R 14085, Report by Ambassador Wangenheim, dated 15 April 1915.

346. Cengiz Kürşat's introduction to Esat Uras's *Tarihte Ermeniler*, p. clxiii.

347. For more information on the psychological aspects of Turkish denial and justification strategies, see Akçam, *From Empire to Republic*, pp. 208–43.

348. Uras, *Tarihte Ermeniler*, p. 631.

349. One of the most interesting of these incidents was the hanging on 15 June 1915 of twenty-one members of the Hunchak Armenian socialist party. An Armenian expelled from the Hunchak organization long before the war had sent four Armenians connected to Şerif Paşa, an Ottoman dissident in Paris, to Istanbul to carry out assassinations. There, they were arrested in 1914 and detained for a year. Later, they were accused, along with seventeen other Armenians, of plotting a conspiracy and hanged. For information on this incident, see *Osmanischer Lloyd* (in German), in Istanbul, issue nos. 126–37 (9–22 May 1915).

350. That is how Marling, the British chargé d'affaires in Istanbul, described the

reform plan in a report to London concerning the talks. Bayur, *Türk İnkılabı Tarihi*, vol. 2, part 3, pp. 141–42.

351. Wien, HHStA PA XII 463 Yeniköy, dated 11 July 1913.

352. *Osmanlı Belgelerinde Ermeniler 1915–1920*, Document no. 99, p. 87.

6. The Question of Punishing the "Turks"

1. Genelkurmay Başkanlığı, *Türk İstiklal Harbi Mondros Mütarekesi ve Tatbikatı* (Ankara, 1992), pp. 47–49.

2. Tansel, *Mondros'tan Mudanya'ya Kadar*, vol. 1, p. 32.

3. Genelkurmay Başkanlığı, *Türk İstiklal Harbi Mondros*, pp. 179–81.

4. Gotthard Jäschke, "Mustafa Kemal und England in neuer Sicht," *Die Welt des Islams* 26 (1975), p. 225.

5. Bayur, *Türk İnkılabı Tarihi*, vol. 2, part 3, pp. 144, 477, 475.

6. For more information on these various treaties: Paul C. Helmreich, *From Paris to Sèvres: The Partition of the Ottoman Empire at the Peace Conference of 1919–1920* (Columbus, OH, 1974), pp. 5–10, 341–47.

7. Jäschke, "Beiträge zur Geschichte des Kampfes der Türkei um ihre Unabhangigkeit," *Die Welt des Islams* 5 (1958), p. 2.

8. Jäschke, *Kurtuluş Savaşı ile İlgili İngiliz Belgeleri* (Ankara, 1971), p. 36.

9. Bayur, *Türk İnkılabı Tarihi*, vol. 3, part 4, p. 627.

10. Kurat, *Türkiye ve Rusya*, p. 32.

11. Jäschke, "Beiträge," p. 2.

12. Both statements of Lloyd George were quoted in David Walder, *The Chanak Affair* (London, 1969), pp. 87, 240.

13. Jäschke, *Kurtuluş Savaşı*, p. 54.

14. Jäschke, "President Wilson als Schiedsrichter zwischen der Türkei und Armenien," *Mitteilungen des Seminars für orientalische Sprachen zu Berlin (M.S.O.S.)*, vol. 38 (1935), p. 77.

15. The full text of the speech was published in *Takvîm-i Vekâyı*, 17–21 July 1920.

16. Helmreich, *From Paris to Sèvres*, p. 110.

17. Jäschke, "Beiträge," p. 2.

18. Arnold J. Toynbee, *Acquaintances* (London, 1967), pp. 149–50.

19. Willis, *Prologue to Nuremberg*, p. 191, n. 14.

20. Ulrich Trumpener, *Germany and the Ottoman Empire, 1914–1918* (Princeton, NJ: Princeton University Press, 1968), p. 210.

21. Ibid.

22. H. W. V. Temperly, *History of the Peace Conference in Paris*, vol. 6 (London, New York, Toronto, 1969), p. 23.

23. Reported by David Lloyd George, *Memoirs*, vol. 2 (Boston, 1934), p. 64.

24. Speech made at the Lausanne Conference on 12 December 1922, Tuesday session; reported by Seha Meray, *Lozan Barış Konferansı, Tutanaklar-Belgeler* (Istanbul, 1993), vol. 1, p. 181.

25. Ali Fuat Türkgeldi, *Görüp İşittiklerim* (Ankara, 1987), p. 187. Tevfik Paşa was saying that he was expected to execute those accused of involvement in the Armenian massacre, just as Fuat Paşa had executed the perpetrators of an earlier massacre against Christians. In 1858, some Muslims in Lebanon and Syria rebelled in protest of the Reform Decree of 1856, which proclaimed equality between Muslims and Christians in the Ottoman Empire, and in some cities, Christians were massacred. The incident caused uproar in Europe and prompted France, the protector of Lebanese Christians, to send troops to Beirut. In response to the strong reaction in the West, the Ottoman government sent Fuat Paşa to investigate. He dealt harshly with the rebellion, hanging so many people that he earned himself the soubriquet *ipçi*, or the rope man.

26. FO 371/4174/118337, file 253.

27. Ibid.

28. These utterances came from two British officials, Admirals Webb and Calthorpe. Quoted by Jäschke, *Kurtuluş Savaşı*, p. 38.

29. In the first forty days alone, the sultan tried three times to establish contacts. Akşin, *İstanbul Hükümetleri ve Milli Mücadele*, vol. 1, p. 146.

30. Ibid., p. 24.

31. Bilâl Şimşir, *Malta Sürgünleri* (Ankara, 1985), p. 15. Milne made this statement on 12 January 1919.

32. Tunaya, *Türkiye'de Siyasi Partiler*, vol. 2, p. 27.

33. Statement of Lord Curzon, 4 July 1919, W. Woodsward and R. Butler, *Documents on British Foreign Policy 1919–1936*, 1st series (London, 1952), vol. 4, p. 661.

34. Yahya Akyüz, quoting from the journals *Le Temps* and *Journal des Débats* (2 November 1918). Y. Akyüz, *Türk Kurtuluş Savaşı ve Fransız Kamuoyu, 1919–1921* (Ankara, 1988), p. 70.

35. Richard G. Hovannisian, "The Allies and Armenia, 1915–18," *Journal of Contemporary History 3*, no. 1 (1968), p. 148.

36. FO 371/4173/53351, Dossier no. 192/93.

37. *MAZC*, Period 3, Assembly Period 5, vol. 1, p. 122.

38. Helmreich, *From Paris to Sèvres*, p. 109.

39. Ibid., p. 109.

40. Ibid., p. 110.

41. Ziemke, *Neue Türkei*, p. 83.

42. Helmreich, *From Paris to Sèvres*, p. 110.

43. Twelve governments took office in postwar Istanbul between 11 November 1918 and 4 November 1922. Five of them—three between 4 March and 30 September 1919 and two between 5 April and 17 October 1920—were set up by Damat Ferid Paşa. For a complete list of governments that took office during this period, known as the armistice period, see Tunaya, *Türkiye'de Siyasal Partiler*, vol. 2, p. 37. For more on the Telegram War, see Sina Akşin, *İstanbul Hükümetleri*, vol. 1, pp. 534–89.

44. Mustafa Kemal, *Nutuk*, vol. 1 (Istanbul, 1934), p. 161.
45. Ibid., vol. 3, Document no. 142, pp. 164–66.
46. Ibid., p. 165.
47. Ibid., Document no. 159, pp. 193–94.
48. Akşin, *İstanbul Hükümetleri ve Milli Mücadele*, vol. 2, p. 316.
49. Mustafa Kemal, *Nutuk*, vol. 3, Document no. 142, pp. 166–67.
50. Ibid., Document no. 159, pp. 193–94.
51. The document presented as the third protocol in Mustafa Kemal's *Nutuk* (Document no. 160) is in fact a proposed reformulation by Mustafa Kemal of the sixth article of the first protocol presented and accepted by the Istanbul government. (Akşin, *İstanbul Hükumetleri ve Milli Mücadele*, vol. 2, p. 445.)
52. Mustafa Kemal, *Nutuk*, vol. 3, Document no. 160, p. 194.
53. Ibid., vol. 1, p. 174.
54. Ibid., p. 177.
55. Ibid., vol. 3, Document no. 159, pp. 193–94.
56. Excerpted from a letter sent by Mustafa Kemal to Sultan Vahdettin on 2 October 1920, ibid., vol. 3, Document no. 97, p. 94.
57. In a speech of Mustafa Kemal's when he entered Ankara in December 1919, ibid., Document no. 220, p. 260.
58. For detailed information on the evolution of the concept of crimes against humanity in international law, see Gerd Hankel and Gerhard Stuby, eds., *Strafgerichte gegen Menschheitsverbrechen* (Hamburg, 1995).
59. M. Charif Bassiouni, "Das 'Vermächtnis von Nürnberg,'" in *Strafgerichte gegen*, p. 16.
60. Reported by Alain Finkielkraut, "Der Barbie-Prozess und die Nürenburg Urteile," *Mittelweg* 36, no. 1 (1993), p. 78.
61. Rudolf Laun, *Die Haager Landkriegsordnung* (Hanover, 1950), pp. 14–23.
62. J. Litawski, "Outline of the Developments of the Laws of War prior to the First World War," in The United Nations War Crimes Commission, *History of the United Nations War Crimes Commission and the Development of the Laws of War* (London, 1948), pp. 25ff.
63. Ibid., p. 28.
64. Christopher Simpson, "Die seinerzeitige Diskussion über die in Nürnberg zu verhandelnden Delikte," in Hankel and Stuby, *Strafgerichte gegen*, p. 42.
65. Anette Höss, "Die Türkischen Kriegsrichtverhandlungen 1915–21" (unpublished Ph.D. thesis, University of Vienna, 1991), p. 43.
66. Lewis, *Emergence of Modern Turkey*, p. 356.
67. For the cancellation decision, see Kraelitz Greifenhorst, "Die Ungültigkeitserklärung des Pariser und Berliner Vertrages durch die Osmanische Regierung," *Österreichische Monatsschrift für den Orient*, no. 43, pp. 56–60.
68. Helmreich, *From Paris to Sèvres*, pp. 12–13.
69. Ibid., p. 21.

70. For a detailed history of the relationship between the Inquiry Commission and Wilson's principles, see Lawrence E. Gelfand, *The Inquiry: American Preparations for Peace, 1917–1919* (New Haven and London, 1963), pp. 134–454.
71. Jäschke, "President Wilson als Schiedsrichter," p. 75.
72. Ibid., p. 76.
73. Ibid., p. 77. However, Wilson was to protest vigorously when in 1920 the Paris Peace Conference decided to allow the Turks to stay in Istanbul.
74. Fritz Dickmann, *Die Kriegsschuldfrage auf der Friedenskonferenz von Paris 1919* (Munich, 1964), pp. 20–21.
75. For all the documents cited, see ibid., pp. 19ff.
76. The commission's report was published many times. The information here was taken from the relevant report. See "Commission on the Responsibility of the Authors of the War and on Enforcement of Penalties: Report," *American Journal of International Law* 14 (New York, 1920), pp. 95–155. Henceforth, it will be referred to as *Report*.
77. Ibid., p. 115.
78. Ibid., p. 117.
79. Dickmann, *Die Kriegsschuldfrage*, p. 40.
80. Simpson, "Die Seinerzeitige Diskussion," p. 45.
81. Meray and Olcay, *Osmanlı, İmparatorluğu'nun*, pp. 113–14.
82. Jäschke, *Kurtuluş Savaşı*, p. 221.
83. David Lloyd George, *Memoirs of the Peace Conference* (London, 1939), p. 811. Quoted in Dadrian, "Genocide as a Problem of National and International Law," p. 247.
84. Ibid.
85. For details, see Akaby Nassibian, *Britain and the Armenian Question, 1915–1923* (London, New York, 1984), pp. 33–67.
86. Hovannisian, "The Allies and Armenia, 1915–1918," p. 147.
87. Jäschke, *Kurtuluş Savaşı*, p. 21.
88. Ibid., p. 21.
89. FO 371/4173/45590, from the Ministry of War to the consulates in Istanbul, Cairo and Baghdad. Quoted in Şimşir, *Malta Sürgünleri*, p. 289.
90. FO 371/4172/170560, Letter from Calthorpe, dated 2 January 1919. Quoted in Şimşir, *Malta Sürgünleri*, pp. 27–28.
91. Ibid., p. 28.
92. FO 371/4172/12905, no. 34/1335, Coded Telegram from Calthorpe, dated 7 January 1919. Quoted in Şimşir, *Malta Sürgünleri*, p. 27.
93. FO 371/4174/118377, Dossier no. 334.
94. Report from Calthorpe, dated 10 January 1919. Quoted in Şimşir, *Malta Sürgünleri*, 36.
95. FO 371/4172, Coded Telegram from the Foreign Office to Calthorpe (London), dated 5 February 1919, no. 233. Quoted in Şimşir, *Malta Sürgünleri*, pp. 37–38.

96. Jäschke, *Kurtuluş Savaşı*, p. 175; Şimşir, *Malta Sürgünleri*, p. 38. The crime categories laid out in the 5 February letter of instructions are as follows: 1. The insufficient application of the conditions of the armistice. 2. The obstructing of the fulfillment of these conditions. 3. The insulting of British commanders and officers. 4. The mistreating of prisoners. 5. The seizing of any subjects of the Armenian or other races whether in Turkey or in Azerbaijan. 6. The taking part in looting or destruction of property. 7. The violating of the laws and customs of war.

97. Ibid.

98. Ibid.

99. FO 371/4172/26088, Coded Cable from the Ministry of War to the consulates in Istanbul, Cairo and Baghdad. Quoted in Şimşir, *Malta Sürgünleri*, p. 204.

100. Ibid., pp. 30–31.

101. FO 371/4173/42787, Franchet d'Espèrey'den Calthrop'a, Istanbul, 11 February 1919. Quoted in Şimşir, *Malta Sürgünleri*, pp. 40–41.

102. Jäschke, *Kurtuluş Savaşı*, p. 176.

103. Ibid., pp. 175–76; Şimşir, *Malta Sürgünleri*, p. 41.

104. Şimsir, *Malta Sürgünleri*, p. 74.

105. FO 602/244/3749, Dossier no. 315, letter from Admiral Webb, dated 19 February 1919. The full text of the Ottoman reply, in French, is in FO 602/247/4222, Dossier no. 177. "Bearing in mind that international law gives each country the right to try before its own courts crimes committed by its own citizens on its own soil, your demand directly conflicts with this country's sovereignty rights. . . . [Moreover,] by signing an armistice agreement with the Ottoman Empire, His Britannic Majesty's government has recognized, both *de facto* and *de iure*, the Ottoman Empire as a sovereign state. That the empire's government is fully entitled to the free practice of all the rights of sovereignty is beyond dispute."

106. FO 371/4172/2972, Dossier no. 364. Quoted in Şimşir, *Malta Sürgünleri*, p. 56.

107. Ibid., pp. 56–75.

108. Jäschke, *Kurtuluş Savaşı*, p. 177.

109. Tarık Mümtaz Göztepe, *Sultan Vahdettin Mütareke Gayyasında* (Istanbul, 1969), pp. 103–5. This decision was published under the heading "Note to the governments of Sweden, Holland, Spain and Denmark on the participation of neutral judges," in *Osmanlı Belgelerinde Ermeniler, 1915–1920*, p. 195, Document no. 223, BOA. HR. MÜ, 43/17, but the text of the document does not appear here.

110. Şimşir, *Malta Sürgünleri*, p. 60.

111. FO 371/4173/47590, Letter from the Foreign Office to Balfour, dated 4 April 1919. Quoted in Şimşir, *Malta Sürgünleri*, p. 210.

112. FO 608/244/3700, Dossier no. 3112.

113. Dadrian, "Genocide as a Problem of National and International Law," p. 66.

114. FO 371/4174/102553, Note from Admiral Webb to the Ottoman Foreign Minister (Istanbul), dated 26 June 1919, no. R/1956. Quoted in Şimşir, *Malta Sürgünleri*, p. 206.
115. FO 371/4174/129560, Dossier no. 43031. The Foreign Office's inquiry was launched by the deputy foreign secretary, J. A. C. Tilley.
116. FO 371/4174/129560, Dossier no. 4303. Quoted in Şimsir, *Malta Sürgünleri*, p. 212.
117. Ibid.
118. Ibid.
119. Ibid., p. 207.
120. Jäschke, *Kurtuluş Savaşı*, p. 182.

7. Ottoman Government Initiatives

1. Menteşe, *Halil Menteşe'nin Anıları*, p. 232.
2. "Ankara İstiklal Mahkemesi (İzmir Suikasti, İddianame ve Savunmalar)" (unpublished, 1926), pp. 18, 57.
3. M. Şükrü Bleda, *İmparatorluğun Çöküşü* (Istanbul, 1979), pp. 123–25.
4. For the developments surrounding the attempts to form a new cabinet, see Tansel, *Mondros'tan Mudanya'ya Kadar*, vol. 1, pp. 22–23.
5. Ahmet İzzet Paşa, *Feryadım*, vol. 2 (Istanbul, 1933), p. 14.
6. MMZC, Period 3, Assembly Period 5, vol. 1, 19 Teşrinievvel 1334 (19 October 1918), 4, İnikad, pp. 28–29.
7. Ibid., p. 29.
8. İzzet Paşa refers to the Unionist triumvirate of Talât, Enver and Cemal as "flawed patriots." Tansel, *Mondros'tan Mudanya'ya Kadar*, p. 31.
9. Ahmet İzzet Paşa, *Feryadım*, p. 31.
10. Hüsamettin Ertürk, "Milli Mücadele Senelerinde Teşkilat-ı Mahsusa" (unpublished transcription), p. 14, cited in Bilge Criss, *İşgal Altında Istanbul*, p. 147.
11. Cemal Kutay, *Osmanlı'dan Cumhuriyet'e, Yüzyılımızda Bir İnsanımız*, vol. 4 (Istanbul, 1992), pp. 257–58.
12. Ibid., p. 261.
13. Yenibahçeli Şükrü "Hatıralar" (copy of unpublished memoirs), p. 7.
14. AA Türkei 183/54, No. 1839, Cable from Ambassador Bernstoff, dated 27 October 1918.
15. Refik Halit, "Efendiler Nereye?," *Zaman*, 6 November 1918.
16. A complete list of the members of the Tevfik Paşa cabinet can be found in Tunaya, *Türkiye'de Siyasal Partiler*, vol. 2, Document no. 3, p. 40.
17. The Turkish expression, "not leaving one stone on top of the other, one head on its shoulders," was frequently used by the press of the period in regard to the desired fate of the CUP. Ali Fuat Türkgeldi, p. 166.
18. Zeki Sarıhan, *Kurtuluş Savaşı Günlüğü*, vol. 1 (Ankara, 1986), p. 21.

19. Asaf Muamber, *Söz* (15 Kasım/November 1918), quoted in Sarıhan, *Kurtuluş*, p. 41.

20. İbnülemin Mahmud Kemal İnal, *Son Sadrazamlar*, vol. 4 (Istanbul, 1953), pp. 1943–44.

21. Ahmet İzzet Paşa, *Feryadım*, p. 288, Appendix 12. In their explanatory letters, Enver Paşa was the only triumvir who did not mention the issue of giving an account for his actions and of possible trials. In his letter, he states that he is "traveling to the Caucasus, where I hope to finish the task in an auspicious manner." His goal, he claims, "[is] to be of assistance in the bringing about of an Islamic revolution in the Caucasus," and he promises to continue to struggle "to return with the same objective . . . when the possibilities of being of service would be produced in the furture." Ibid., pp. 287–88, Appendix 11.

22. *Minber* (9 Kasım/November 1918).

23. *İkdam* (8 Kânunısani/January 1919).

24. *Alembar* (21 Kânunuevvel/December 1918).

25. *Alemdar* (12 Mart/March, 4 Nisan/April 1919).

26. For a complete account of the party's activities during the armistice period, see Tunaya, *Türkiye'de Siyasal Partiler*, vol. 2, pp. 654ff.

27. Akşin, *İstanbul Hükümetleri*, vol. 1, p. 182.

28. Ibid., p. 151.

29. MMZC, 14 Teşrinievvel 1334 (14 October 1918), 4, İnikad, p. 32.

30. Ibid., 19 Teşrinievvel 1334 (19 October 1918), 4, İnikad, p. 32.

31. Ibid.

32. Ibid.

33. Ibid., pp. 32–33.

34. Ibid.

35. Ibid., Period 3, Assembly Period 5, 24 Teşrinievvel 1334 (24 October 1918), 6, İnikad, p. 47.

36. Ibid., 4 Teşrinisani 1334 (4 November 1918), 11, İnikad, p. 95.

37. Ibid.

38. Ibid., p. 106.

39. Ibid., p. 109.

40. Ibid.

41. Ibid., p. 110.

42. Ibid., p. 111.

43. Ibid. The Turkish deputies who responded were Mehmet Emin Bey, a deputy for Trabzon, deputy for Muş İlyas Sami Bey and Kastamonu deputy Rüştü Bey. İlyas Sami would later be arrested for having taken part in the genocide.

44. Ibid., p. 112.

45. Ibid.

46. Ibid.

47. Ibid., p. 114.

48. Ibid., p. 115.
49. Gotthard Jäschke and Erich Pritsch, *Die Turkei seit dem Weltkriege, Geschichts-kalender 1918–1922* (Berlin, 1929), p. 65.
50. MMZC, 4 Teşrinisai 1334 (4 November 1918), 11, İnikad, p. 101.
51. Ibid., 7 Teşrinisani 1334 (7 November 1918), 12, İnikad, pp. 122–38.
52. Ibid., 18 Teşrinisani 1334 (18 November 1918), 14, İnikad, p. 136.
53. Ibid., pp. 140–43.
54. Ibid., p. 144.
55. Ibid., pp. 157–58.
56. Şimşir, *Malta Sürgünleri,* pp. 351–54.
57. MMZC, 18 Teşrinisani 1334 (18 November 1918), 14, İnikad, p. 160.
58. Ibid., 23 Teşrinisani 1334 (23 November 1918), 17, İnikad, pp. 186–87.
59. Ibid., 9 Kânunuevvel 1334 (9 December 1918), 23, İnikad, p. 257.
60. Ibid., 11 Kânunuevvel 1334 (11 December 1918), 24, İnikad, pp. 289–93.
61. Ibid., p. 294.
62. Ibid., p. 296.
63. Ibid.
64. Ibid., pp. 300–301.
65. Ibid., 12 Kânunuevvel 1334 (12 December 1918), 25, İnikad, pp. 313–15.
66. Ibid., pp. 315–16.
67. Ibid., pp. 316–17.
68. Ibid., p. 317.
69. Ibid., p. 318–19.
70. Ibid., p. 328.
71. Ibid., 24 Kânunuevvel 1334 (24 December 1918), 29, İnikad, p. 362.
72. Ibid., 4 Teşrinisani 1334 (4 November 1918), 11, İnikad, p. 103.
73. Tarhan Erdem, *Anayasalar ve Seçim Kanunları 1876–1982* (Istanbul, 1982), p. 5.
74. Ibid., p. 11.
75. The Ottoman lower house, or Chamber of Deputies, was divided into various departments and branches according to the places represented by the deputies. Some of the deputies who would be investigated by the Fifth Department, which was randomly selected to conduct the investigations, were actually members of this department.
76. *5. Şube Soruşturmaları,* from the deposition of Çürüksulu Mahmud Paşa, p. 3.
77. One example is the information provided by Hans Humann, the military attaché in Istanbul and a close friend of Enver Paşa. Sterling Library, Yale University, Jäckh papers, Hans Humann's letter of 23 October 1914 (*Besprechungen mit Enver Pasha*), Box 1, Folder 15.
78. *5. Şube Soruşturmaları,* from the deposition of Said Halim Paşa, pp. 38–40; ibid., p. 32.
79. *İleri,* 20 Aralık (December) 1918.
80. *5. Şube Soruşturmaları,* from the deposition of Said Halim Paşa, p. 42.

81. Ibid., from the deposition of İbrahim Paşa, p. 29.

82. Ibid., p. 25.

83. Ibid., p. 32.

84. According to the twenty-fourth article of the decree dated 19 Ağustos 1326 (1 September 1910), which ordered the establishment of courts-martial, "Rulings handed down by the courts-martial shall be carried out upon the order of the local commander to whom the martial law is subject, and death sentences shall only be carried out by permission of and the issuing of an Imperial decree [to this effect]," Osmanlı Belgelerinde Ermeniler (1915–1920), Document no. 220, p. 190.

85. Ibid., p. 41.

86. For the complete text of the order, see Tunaya, Türkiye'de Siyasal Partiler, vol. 3, p. 627.

87. MAZC, Period 3, Assembly Period 5, vol. 1, 19 Teşrinievvel 1338 (19 October 1918), 2, İnikad, pp. 8–9.

88. Ibid., 21 Teşrinievvel 1334 (21 October 1918), 3, İnikad, p. 28.

89. Ibid., p. 29.

90. Ibid., p. 32.

91. Ibid., p. 34.

92. Ibid., 4 Teşrinisani 1334 (4 November 1918), 7, İnikad, pp. 64–68.

93. Ibid., 14 Teşrinisani 1334 (14 November 1918), 9, İnikad, p. 90.

94. Ibid., 21 Teşrinisani 1334 (21 November 1918), 11, İnikad, p. 117.

95. Ibid.

96. Ibid., p. 118.

97. Ibid., pp. 118–22.

98. Ibid., p. 123.

99. Ibid., 2 Kânunuevvel 1334 (2 December 1918), 13, İnikad, pp. 146–47.

100. Ibid., p. 148.

101. MMZC, 4 Teşrinisani 1334 (4 November 1918), 11, İnikad, pp. 97–98.

102. Türkgeldi, Görüp İşittiklerim, p. 166.

103. Tansel, Mondros'tan Mudanya'ya Kadar, vol. 1, p. 76.

104. Türkgeldi, Görüp İşittiklerim, p. 169.

105. Ibid., p. 182.

106. "Ahval-i harbiye ilcaatı ile memleket dahilinde bir mahalden diğer mahalle nakil ve tehcir," MAZC, 19 Teşrinievvel 1334 (19 October 1918), 4, İnikad, p. 29.

107. Ibid.

108. Ibid., p. 24.

109. As an example of how the population participated in the expropriation process, one may refer to the eyewitness reports of the American consul in Harput, Leslie A. Davis, in his recollections of the period, Davis, The Slaughterhouse Province, pp. 53–55.

110. U.S. National Archives, Record Group 59, Dossier no. 867. 4016/210, Report by Oscar S. Heizer, dated 13 August 1915. For similar eyewitness accounts, see the report by German ambassador Count von Wolff-Metternich, dated 30 June 1915, found in Lepsius, *Deutschland und Armenien*, Document no. 282, p. 277.

111. HHStA PA XII 209, Nr. 62/P, Report dated 23 August 1915, inserted with Nr. 71/PB, in Report by Ambassador Pallavicini, dated 31 August 1915. Found in Ohandjanian, *Armenien*, vol. 6, p. 386.

112. HHStA PA XL 275, Confidential Report, no. 47, Constantinople 27/2/1917. Found in Ohandjanian, *Armenien*, vol. 7, p. 5275.

113. Halide Edib, *Memoir of Halide Edib* (London, 1926), p. 386.

114. HHStA PA XII 209, Nr. 72/P-H, Jeniköj (Yeniköy), Report dated 3 September 1915. Found in Ohandjanian, *Armenien*, vol. 6, p. 4721.

115. Doğan Avcıoğlu, *Türkiye'nin Düzeni*, vol. 1 (Istanbul, 1987), p. 293.

116. *Osmanlı Belgelerinde Ermeniler 1915–1920*, correspondence dated 21 Teşrinisani 1334 (21 November 1918), no. 214, p. 182.

117. Ibid., pp. 182–83.

118. Ibid., Document no. 209, pp. 175–76.

119. Ibid., Document no. 210, pp. 176–77.

120. Ibid., Document no. 212, pp. 179–80.

121. Ibid., Document no. 214, 215, 224, 227, pp. 182–84, 195, 203.

122. MMZC, Period 3, Assembly Period 5, vol. 1, 29 İnikad (21 Kânunuevvel, 1334/21 December 1918), p. 362.

123. Tayyib Gökbilgin, *Milli Mücadele Başlarken*, vol. 1 (Ankara, 1959), p. 16.

124. *Osmanlı Belgelerinde Ermeniler 1915–1920*, Document nos. 221, 232, 234, pp. 191–92, 207–10.

125. FO 371/5088/E9664, no. 1070/M/3190, Report by de Robeck to the Foreign Office.

126. Sir Robert Graves, *Storm Centres of the Near East: Personal Memories 1879–1929* (London, 1933), p. 324.

127. Akşin, *İstanbul Hükümetleri ve Milli Mücadele*, vol. 1, p. 32.

128. Tercüman-ı Hakikat, 27 March 1919.

129. Jäschke, *Kurtuluş Savaşı*, p. 37; Selahattin Tansel, *Mondros'tan Mudanya'ya Kadar*, vol. 1, pp. 73–74.

130. Ali İhsan Sabis, *Harp Hatıralarım, Birinci Dünya Harbi 4* (Istanbul, Nehir, 1991), pp. 331–32.

131. Jäschke, *Kurtuluş Savaşı*, p. 38.

132. For an example from the second Tevfik Paşa government, see *Osmanlı Belgelerinde Ermeniler (1915–1920)*, Document no. 249, pp. 222–23.

133. *Osmanlı Belgelerinde Ermeniler (1915–1920)*, Document no. 254, p. 230.

134. *Memleket*, 12 March 1919.

135. Akşin, *İstanbul Hükümetleri ve Milli Mücadele*, vol. 2, p. 221. The decree in question was published in *Takvîm-i Vekâyi*, no. 3445 (12 Kânunısani 1336/12 January 1920).

136. PA-AA/R 14089, Report by Ambassador Wolff-Metternich, dated 27 December 1915.

137. For some of these published official documents, see *Osmanlı Belgelerinde Ermeniler (1915–1920)*, Document nos. 45, 47, 79, 82, 119, 179, pp. 50–51, 74–77, 100–101, and 141, respectively.

138. BAO/DH/SFR, 63/142/1334.C.26 for a similar telegram, see BAO/DH/SFR, 59/150/1334. S.21.

139. The document in which this is stated comes from the Archives of the Armenian Patriarchate in Jerusalem; it is numbered 343, but I am unable to make out the complete archival information for it from the photocopy in my possession.

140. BAO/DH/SFR, 63/60/1334.C.16.

141. For one example of these protests, see PA-AA/Bo. Kons. 172, Report by Ambassador Wolff-Metternich, dated 20 December 1915.

142. *Osmanlı Belgelerinde Ermeniler (1915–1920)*, Document nos. 92, 93, p. 83.

143. Both Webb and Calthorpe's reports are quoted by Jäschke, *Kurtuluş Savaşı*, p. 40.

144. Ibid.

145. Celal Bayar, *Ben de Yazdım*, vol. 5, p. 1503. Other examples of this phenomenon are mentioned in Kemalettin Şükrü, *Mütareke Acıları* (Istanbul, 1930), pp. 64–68; Halide Edip (Adıvar), *The Turkish Ordeal* (London, 1928), pp. 16–19.

146. *Osmanlı Belgelerinde Ermeniler (1915–1920)*, Document no. 250, pp. 224–25.

147. MMZC, Period 4, Assembly Period 1, vol. 1, p. 103.

148. Seha L. Meray, *Lozan Barış Konferansı*, set 1, vol. 1, book 2, p. 224.

149. Jäschke, *Kurtulus Savaşı*, p. 39.

150. Quoted in Avcıoğlu, *Milli Kurtuluş Tarihi*, vol. 3, p. 1292.

151. Ibid., p. 1293.

152. Ibid., p. 1292.

153. Publication no. 6 of the Directorate of the Office of Refugees in the Interior Ministry (Istanbul, 1922), p. 14. Quoted in Gürün, *Ermeni Dosyası*, p. 313.

154. For example, in the Maraş region during the first days of occupation (22 February 1919), the British and the Armenians returning with them made numerous attempts to take back the confiscated and looted properties of the Armenians, and to collect Christian women and children from Muslim houses. But for a variety of reasons, these efforts quickly met with failure. For more detailed information, see Yaşar Akbıyık, *Milli Mücadele Güney Cephesi (Maraş)* (Ankara, 1990), pp. 191–93.

155. The article in question was the third article of the draft concerning the protection of minorities. Meray, *Lozan Barış Konferansı*, vol. 2, p. 161.

156. For more details, see ibid., pp. 157, 161, 183–84.

157. Ibid., vol. 8, p. 93. and vol. 2, p. 254. (There are two different dates, 20 and 30 October, in the protocols; generally it must be accepted as the beginning of British occupation in Istanbul.)

158. Jäschke and E. Pritsch, *Die Türkei*, p. 65.
159. Gökbilgin, *Milli Mücadele Başlarken*, p. 15.
160. Ibid., pp. 8–9, 11.
161. The decision was published with the signatures of the minister of war and Grand Vizier Tevfik Paşa, in *Takvîm-ı Vekâyi*, no. 3407 (30 Teşrinisani 1334/30 November 1918), which is when it went into effect.
162. The court's ruling to this effect was published in *Takvim-i Vekâyi*, no. 3416 (12 Aralik 1334/12 December 1918).
163. Tunaya, *Türkiye'de Siyasal Partiler*, vol. 3, p. 557.
164. *Vakit*, 24 November 1918.
165. *Sabah*, 25 November 1918.
166. *Osmanlı Belgelerinde Ermeniler (1915–1920)*, Record nos. 219 and 220, pp. 188–89.
167. *İkdam*, 8 and 9 December 1918.
168. Ibid., 12 December 1918.
169. *Ati*, 15 December 1918.
170. For information about the activities of the commissions see V. Dadrian, "The Documentation of World War I: Armenian Massacres in the Proceedings of the Turkish Military Tribunal," *International Journal of Middle East Studies* 23 (November 1991), pp. 552–53.
171. United States National Archives, Record Group 256, 867.00/59 at 3 (U.S. Commissioner at Istanbul Lewis Heck's report of 20 January 1919 to State Department), transcribed by Dadrian, "Genocide as a Problem of National and International Law," p. 295.
172. Our knowledge of this prohibition derives from a report on the subject informing the occupation powers. See British Foreign Office Archives, Public Records Office, Kew, FO 371/4141/49194. *The Committee of Union and Progress*, chap. 2, s. 4. G.H.Q. Intelligence Report (3 August 1919).
173. The government's decision to set up the court was published in *Takvîm-i Vekâyi*, no. 3427 (24 December 1918).
174. For the suspension of Martial Law, see *Takvîm-i Vekâyi*, no. 1186, 24 July 1912. On the reestablishment of Martial Law, see ibid., no. 1249, 7 October 1912. For further information, see Tunaya, *Türkiye'de Siyasal Partiler*, vol. 3, p. 268.
175. *Ati* and *Hadisat*, 16 December 1918.
176. Turkgeldi, *Görüp İşittiklerim*, p. 173.
177. *Osmanlı Belgelrinde Ermeniler (1915–1920)*, Record no. 220, p. 190.
178. Ibid., pp. 189–90.
179. The 16 December decision of the government was published in *Takvîm-i Vekâyi*, no. 3424, 21 December 1918.
180. *Tercüman-ı Hakikat*, 14 February 1919; *Yeni Gazete*, 15 February 1919.
181. This law, which was enacted on 4 February 1913, was published in *Takvîm-i Vekâyi*, no. 1751, 24 February 1913.
182. *Hadisat*, 22 October 1918.

183. *İstiklal*, 21 December 1918.

184. *Takvîm-i Vekâyi*, 28 December 1918; *Ati*, 26 December 1918.

185. The decision was published in *Takvîm-i Vekâyi*, no. 3430, 28 December 1918. There is information about this decision in the daily newspapers of the time. *Yeni Gazete*, 1 January 1919.

186. This decision, dated 8 January 1919, was published in *Takvîm-i Vekâyi*, no. 3445, on 14 January 1919.

187. *Tercüman-ı Hakikat*, January 25, 1919; *Yeni Gazete*, 1 January 1919.

188. *Takvîm-i Vekâyi*, no. 3452 (21 Kânunısani 1335/21 January 1919).

189. Tansel, *Mondros'tan Mudanya'ya Kadar*, vol. 1, pp. 79–80.

190. Transcribed from *Alemdar*, 9 March 1919, quoted in Nejdet Bilgi, *Ermeni Tehciri ve Boğazlayan Kaymakamı Mehmed Kemal Bey'in Yargılanması* (Ankara: Köksav serisi 16, 1999) p. 59.

191. Tunaya, *Türkiye'de Siyasal Partiler*, vol. 2, Document no. 9a, p. 134.

192. The communiqué, dated 8 Mart/March 1919, was published in *Takvîm-i Vekâyı*, no. 3491, on the following day.

193. *Takvîm-i Vekâyı*, no. 3837 (26 Nisan 1336/26 April 1920). The decree also appears in Ebubekir Hazim Tepeyram, *Zalimane Bir İdam Hükmü* (Istanbul, 1946), pp. 121–23.

194. *Takvîm-i Vekâyı*, no. 3496 (4 Eylul 1336/4 September 1920). See also Teperyan, *Zalimane*, pp. 221–22.

195. Tepeyran, *Zalimane*, p. 219.

196. The new regulations were published in the official gazette, *Takvîm-i Vekâyı*, no. 3996 (1 Teşrinisani 1336/1 November 1920). For more discussion of these changes in the press, see *Vakit*, 13 October and 1 November 1920. For information about the arrests, see *Vakit*, 16 and 17 November 1920.

197. The death sentence imposed on Mustafa Kemal was published in *Takvîm-ı Vekâyı*, no. 3864 (27 Mayis 1336/27 May 1920). For other decisions, see *Takvîm-ı Vekâyı*, no. 3866 (30 Mayıs 1336/13 May 1920) and no. 3883 (21 Haziran 1336/21 June 1920). For a full list of death sentences see Tunaya, *Türkiye'de Siyasal Partiler*, vol. 3, pp. 559–60. The decision in the Yıldız looting case was published in *Takvîm-i Vekâyı*, no. 3969 (30 Eylül 1336/30 September 1920).

198. For a detailed list of the 63 trials and their outcomes see Dadrian and Akçam, *The Protocols of the Istanbul Military Tribunals*, introduction.

199. *İkdam*, 2 Kânunuevvel 1334 (2 December 1918).

200. *Alemdar*, 6 Kânunısani 1335 (6 January 1919).

201. Figures taken from Şimşir, *Malta Sürgünleri*, pp. 43–47.

202. "Dr. Reşid'in İntiharı," *Yakın Tarihimiz*, vol. 2, pp. 339–41.

203. *İkdam*, 8 Kânunısani 1335 (8 January 1919).

204. Şimşir, *Malta Sürgünleri*, p. 50.

205. FO 371/4174/118377, Dossier no. 251262, Report from Calthorpe to the Foreign Office, dated 8 January 1919.

206. FO 371/4174/118377, Folios 251–62, Message from Calthorpe, dated 1 August 1919.

207. FO 371/4172/22373, Dossier no. 248, Message from Calthorpe, dated 2 May 1919.

208. For the relevant lists, in chronological order, see FO 370/4173/50501, 62442, 63315, and 68109. Quoted in Şimşir, *Malta Sürgünleri*, pp. 68–69.

209. Türkgeldi, *Görüp İşittiklerim*, p. 187; and Kemal, *Son Sadrazamlar*, vol. 9, p. 1724.

210. Information found in British documents would seem to contradict Tevfik Paşa's statements. In a report by Admiral Calthorpe dated 1 August 1919, it is mentioned that the first arrests made in the month of January (especially the twenty-seven arrested on 30 January) were entirely the result of the Turkish goverment's initiative.

211. In his memoirs, Ali Münif Yeğena, who had served in the wartime cabinet of Talât Paşa, recounts that he was informed that his house would be searched, upon which he got rid of all the documents in his possession. "Eski Nafia Nazırı Ali Münif Yeğena'nın Hatıraları: İstibdattan Cuhuriyet'e," *Akşam*, Installment no. 47, 1956. Also found in *Ali Münif Bey'in Hâtıraları* (prepared for publication by Taha Toros) (Istanbul, 1996), p. 96.

212. Yalçın, *Siyasal Anılar*, p. 258.

213. Halil Paşa, *İttihat ve Terakki'den Cumhuriyet'e Bitmeyen Savaş* (prepared for publication by M. Taylan Sorgun), p. 262.

214. Yunus Nadi, *Kurtuluş Savaşı Anıları* (Istanbul, 1978), p. 19.

215. Report by Calthorpe, dated 24 January 1919, quoted in Şimşir, *Malta Sürgünleri*, p. 35.

216. Ibid., p. 64.

217. Akşin, *İstanbul Hükümetleri ve Milli Mücadele*, vol. 1, p. 187.

218. FO 371/4172, no. 14674, Cable from Milne to the War Office, dated 2 February 1919. Quoted in Şimşir, *Malta Sürgünleri*, p. 57.

219. Ibid., p. 58.

220. Mehmet Tevfik [Biren], *"Bir Devlet Adamının" Mehmet Tevfik Bey'in (Biren) II. Abdühamid, Meşrutiyet ve Mütareke Devri Hatılraları*, vol. 2 (Istanbul, 1993), p. 137.

221. It has been perceived that the British were very impressed by the rapidity of the new government's activity. A communication by Webb, the assistant to the high commissioner, dated 11 March 1919, indicates that it was the speed with which the new cabinet acted that did much to influence the British in their decision to forego their demand that the criminals be handed over to them. Jäschke, *Kurtuluş Savaşı*, pp. 177–78.

222. Türkgeldi, *Görüp İşittiklerim*, p. 203.

223. FO 371/4173/61185, no. 789, Coded Cable from Calthorpe (Istanbul) to the Foreign Office, dated 17 April 1919. Quoted in Şimşir, *Malta Sürgünleri*, p. 76.

224. FO 371/4173/72536, no. 59, Report, dated 12 April 1919.

225. Jäschke, *Kurtuluş Savaşı*, p. 178.

226. Türkgeldi, *Görüp İşittiklerim*, pp. 203–4.
227. FO 371/4173/61185, Note from the Foreign Office, dated 22 April 1919. Quoted in Şimşir, *Malta Sürgünleri*, p. 79.
228. Jäschke, *Kurtuluş Savaşı*, p. 179.
229. FO 371/4174/102588, no. 1315, Note by Webb, dated 15 May 1919.
230. This was the period in which Mustafa Kemal had landed at Samsun and entered Anatolia. Having been sent as an inspector for Anatolia, he sent letters saying that protest cables be sent to all of the provincial governorships and army commanders as well as to the government in Istanbul and the Allied Powers. Kemal, *Nutuk*, vol. 1, p. 167.
231. FO 371/4174/88761, Dossier 9, Note from General Calthorpe to London, dated 30 May 1919.
232. *Spectateur d'orient*, 21 May 1919.
233. FO 371/4174/76582, no. 1082, Cable from Webb to the Foreign Office, dated 19 May 1919.
234. FO 371/4174/88761, no. 887/R.1315.D, Report from Calthorpe (Istanbul) to Curzon and Balfour, dated 30 May 1919. Quoted in Şimşir, *Malta Sürgünleri*, p. 104.
235. This decision was published as an insert to *Takvim-i Vekâyi*, no. 3571 (3 Haziran 1335/3 June 1919).
236. Damad Ferid Paşa sent Governor-General Ali Galip to Sivas while the nationalist Sivas Congress was convening with the purpose of arresting Mustafa Kemal and shutting the conference down. The action ultimately failed, but in response Mustafa Kemal called for a massive "telegraph campaign" to boycott all correspondence to Istanbul. Most of Anatolia obeyed Mustafa Kemal's call and Damad Ferid Paşa was ultimately forced to step down.
237. The government read its program to the 9 February 1920 session of the Chamber of Deputies, which had been reformed after new elections held in the winter months. MMZC, Period 4, Assembly Period 1, vol. 1, pp. 73ff.
238. Mustafa Kemal, *Nutuk*, vol. 1, p. 154.
239. *The Times*, 13 October 1919. Quoted in Akşin, *İstanbul Hükumetleri ve Milli Mücadele*, vol. 2, p. 34.
240. Akşin, *İstanbul Hükumetleri ve Milli Mücadele*, vol. 2, p. 181.
241. Ibid.
242. Ibid.
243. Ibid., p. 182.
244. Ibid.
245. FO 371/4174/136069, Folios 466–73.
246. FO 371/4174/156721, Folios 523–52. Quoted in Dadrian, *Genocide as a Problem of National and International Law*, p. 286.
247. From the daily *Alemdar*, quoted in Tunaya, "Osmanlı İmparatorluğu'ndan Türkiye Büyük Millet Meclisi Hükümeti Rejimine Geçiş," in *Ordinarius Prof. Muammer Raşit Seviğ'e Armağan* (Istanbul, 1956), p. 375 (separate offprint).

248. Kâzım Karabekır, *İstiklal Harbimiz*, p. 544.
249. MMZC, Devre 4, İçtima Senesi 1, vol. 1, pp. 80–82.
250. Ibid., p. 79.
251. Ibid., p. 98. The proposal was submitted by Sırrı Bey, a deputy for İzmit.
252. Ibid., pp. 214–18.
253. Ibid., p. 105.
254. Ibid., p. 229.
255. MAZC, Period 4, Assembly Period 1, vol. 1, p. 4, İnikad (26 Kânunısani 1336/26 January 1920), pp. 22–26; 6, İnikad (3 Şubat 1336/3 February 1920), pp. 43–48; İnikad (1 Mart 1336/1 March 1920), pp. 164–72.
256. FO 406/43, p. 190191, no. 96, Telegram from the Office of the High Commissioner to Lord Curzon, dated 5 March 1920. Quoted in Bilal Şimşir, *İngiliz Belgelerinde Atatürk*, vol. 1 (Ankara, 1973), no. 144, p. 428.
257. Helmreich, *From Paris to Sèvres*, p. 278.
258. Ibid.
259. Rauf Orbay, *Cehennem Değirmeni: Siyasi Hatıralarım*, vol. 2 (Istanbul, 1993), p. 27.
260. Mustafa Kemal, *Nutuk*, vol. 1, p. 267.
261. Ibid., Document no. 226.
262. TBMM *Zabit Ceridesi*, Period 1, Assembly Period 1, vol. 2, pp. 126–32.
263. Zeki Sarıhan, *Kurtuluş Savaşi Günlüğü*, vol. 3, p. 33; TBMM *Zabit Ceridesi*, Period 1, Assembly Period 7, p. x. İçtima, vol. 1, pp. 342–43.

8. The Turkish National Movement's Position on the Genocide

1. Halil Paşa, *İttihat ve Terakki'den*, p. 259.
2. Ibid., p. 261. Bayar stated that M. Kemal said this to him during the 1923 elections, at which time he did not want to campaign in the Izmir region because he feared that he would get a hostile reception for having been a former Unionist. To this, M. Kemal told him that there was no need to hesitate, and said that "he should go without care."
3. Fuat Cebesoy, *Sınıf Arkadaşım Atatürk* (Istanbul, 1981), p. 116.
4. Ibid., p. 114.
5. For the personal and political conflicts between Mustafa Kemal and Enver, see Erik Jan Zürcher, *The Unionist Factor: The Role of the Committee of Union and Progress in the Turkish National Movement 1905–1926* (Leiden, 1984), chap. 2, pp. 45–67; Cemal Kutay, *Atatürk Enver Paşa, Yakın Tarihin Meçhul Sahifeleri* (Istanbul, 1956); Şevket Süreyya Aydemir, *Tek Adam, Mustafa Kemal*, vol. 1 (Istanbul, 1976); Kâzım Karabekir, *İstiklal Harbimizde Enver Paşa ve İttihat Terakki Erkânı* (Istanbul, 1990).
6. Alongside these bonds of friendship, a large number of these persons were also related through blood or nuptial ties. For a partial listing of such relations, see Zürcher, *Unionist Factor*, pp. 47–48.

7. Ahmet Emin Yalman, *Yakin Tarihte Gördüklerim ve Geçirdiklerim*, vol. 1 (Istanbul, n.d.), p. 340.

8. Jäschke, "Beiträge zur Geschichte des Kampfes der Türkei um ihre Unabhangigkeit," *Die Welt des Islams* 5 (1958), p. 2.

9. Lord Kinross, *Atatürk: The Rebirth of a Nation* (London, 1964), pp. 168–69.

10. Akşin, *Istanbul Hükumetleri ve Milli Mücadele*, vol. 1, p. 278.

11. Dr. Nâzım's letter, dated 11 May 1921, to Cavit, in Hüseyin Cahit Yalçın, *İttihatçı Liderlerin Gizli Mektupları*, ed. Osman Selim Kocahanoğlu (Istanbul, 2002), p. 124.

12. For histories taking this line, see Dankwart A. Rustow, "The Army and the Founding of the Turkish Republic," *World Politics* 11 (1959), pp. 513–52; A. A. Cruickshank, "The Young Turk Challenge in Post-War Turkey," *Middle East Journal* 22 (1968), 17–28; Lord Kinross, *Atatürk*. Zürcher, *Unionist Factor*, represents the main exception to this trend. With only a few exceptions, works by Turkish scholars tend to give insufficient consideration of this subject.

13. For some of these reports, see Zürcher, *Unionist Factor*, p. 149.

14. Tunaya, *Türkiye'de Siyasal Partiler*, vol. 3, p. 293.

15. Tevfik Bıyıklıoğlu, *Trakya'da Milli Mücadele*, vol. 1 (Ankara, 1987), p. 66.

16. Ibid.

17. For more detailed information on both the Defense of Rights Committees and the National Movement, in general, see Nazım H. Polat, *Müdafaa-yı Milliye Cemiyeti* (Ankara, 1991).

18. Bıyıklıoğlu, *Trakya'da Milli Mücadele*, p. 80; Fuat Balkan, "İlk Türk Komitacısı Fuat Balkan'ın Hatıraları," *Yakın Tarihimiz*, vol. 2, pp. 135–36, 164–66, 196–98.

19. Talât Paşa called Faik Bey and instructed him as follows: "Take the train to Edirne tonight, speak with the friends (i.e., other CUP members) and make sure that such a committee is established." Bıyıklıoğlu, *Trakya'da Milli Mücadale*, vol. 1, pp. 127–28.

20. Fuat Balkan, *İlk Komitacı*, p. 297.

21. For more on the role of former members of the Special Organization in the Defense Organization in western Anatolia, see Emel Akal, *Milli Mücadelenin Başlangıcında: Mustafa Kemal Ittihat Terakki ve Bolşevizm* (Istanbul, 2002), pp. 222–26.

22. Mete Tunçay, *Türkiye Cumhuriyetinde Tek Parti Yönetiminin Kurulması (1923–1931)* (Ankara, 1981), p. 36.

23. Ibid., p. 34.

24. S. Esin Dayı, *Elviye—i Selase'de Kars, Ardahan, Batum—Milli Teşkilatlanma* (Erzurum, 1997), pp. 72–112.

25. Şeref Çavuşoğlu, *İttihat ve Terakkinin Gizli Planı*, p. 263.

26. Zürcher, *Unionist Factor*, p. 72.

27. Tunaya, *Türkiye'de Siyasal Partiler*, vol. 1, pp. 417–20, and vol. 2, p. 153.

28. For more detailed information on the Congress's activities, see ibid., pp. 150–62. One of its important publications in the English language was related to the

Armenian genocide. Congress tried to justify the genocide with certain critiques of Unionist leaders. National Congress of Turkey, *The Turco-Armenian Question: The Turkish Point of View* (Istanbul, 1919).

29. Fethi Tevetoğlu, *Milli Mücadele Yıllarindaki Kuruluşlar* (Ankara, 1988), p. 22.
30. Mesut Aydın, *Milli Mücadele Dönemi'nde TBMM Hükumeti Tarafindan İstanbul'da Kurulan Gizli Gruplar ve Faaliyetleri* (Istanbul, 1992), p. 23.
31. Hüsamettin Ertürk, *İki Devrin Perde Arkası*, pp. 344–45.
32. For the first paragraph of these regulations and its five-point program, see Tunaya, *Türkiye'de Siyasal Partiler*, pp. 521–23.
33. Ertürk, *İki Devrin Perde Arkası*, p. 217.
34. Tevetoğlu, *Milli Mücadele*, p. 223.
35. Ibid., pp. 13–15. The author also provides the names of other members of this organization.
36. There are several accounts about who offered Mustafa Kemal the leadership of the National Movement. Yenibahçeli Şükrü claims Refik İsmail was the one who made the offer. Şükrü, *Hatıralar*, p. 33. Şeref Çâvuşoğlu recounts that the proposal to lead the movement was delivered to Mustafa Kemal by Istanbul deputy Rıza Bey. Çavuşoğlu, *İttihat ve Terakkinin Gizli Planı*, p. 264.
37. Şükrü, *Hatıralar*.
38. Çavuşoğlu, *İttihat ve Terakkinin Gizli Planı*, p. 264.
39. Tevetoğlu, *Milli Mücadele*, p. 23.
40. Mustafa Kemal, *Nutuk*, vol. 1, pp. 52ff.
41. General Ali Fuat Cebesoy, *Milli Mücadele Hatıraları* (Istanbul, 1953), p. 75.
42. Falih Rifki Atay, *Çankaya*, pp. 108–9.
43. Rauf Orbay, *Cehennem Değirmeni*, vol. 2, p. 232.
44. Ertürk, *İki Devrin Perde Arkası*, pp. 244–345.
45. Ibid., p. 344.
46. Ali Fuat Cebesoy published a telegram from Mustafa Kemal, in which Kemal criticized Kara Vasıf and Unionist attitude towards the National Movement, Cebesoy, *Milli Mücadele*, pp. 138–40.
47. Moreover, Kemal himself had invited many well-known Unionists to Anatolia, such as Enver's uncle, Halil Paşa. But because he feared being smeared with the Unionist brush, Kemal not only kept secret the fact that he had met with Halil Paşa and former CUP Central Committe member Küçük Talât at Sivas, but even kept their presence in Anatolia a secret. Both Halil and Küçük Talât were later appointed to a variety of positions within the movement.
48. Mustafa Kemal wrote an open letter, which was published in the Istanbul papers on 10 November 1919. Quoted in Zeki Sarıhan, *Kurtulus Savaşi Günlüğü*, vol. 2, pp. 201–2.
49. Ali Fuat Cebesoy prepared the list of officers with Kemal and sent it to Kara Vasıf to be sure those officers would be appointed to Anatolia through his channels in the war ministry. *Milli Mücadele*, p. 75.

50. Falih Rıfkı Atay, *Atatürk'ün Bana Anlattıkları* (İştanbul, 1955), p. 99.

51. Mustafa Kemal, *Nutuk*, vol. 3, p. 165.

52. Ibid., Document no. 142, pp. 164–65.

53. Ibid., p. 165.

54. Mazhar Müfit Kansu, *Erzurum'dan Ölümüne Kadar Atatürk'le Beraber*, vol. 1, p. 219.

55. Mustafa Kemal, *Nutuk*, vol. 3, Document no. 159, p. 193.

56. Tunaya, *Türkiye'de Siyasal Partiler*, p. 412.

57. Kansu, *Erzurum'dan Ölümüne Kadar Atatürk'le Beraber*, vol. 1, p. 219.

58. From a speech given in Sivas on 11 October 1919, printed in *Yedigün* newspaper. Quoted in *Atatürk'ün Söylev ve Demeçleri*, vol. 3 (Ankara, 1989), p. 3.

59. From a series of written reponses given on 13 October 1919 to questions from the newspaper *Tasvir-i Efkâr*. Quoted in *Atatürk' ün Söylev ve Demeçleri*, vol. 3, p. 8.

60. From an interview with *Tasvir-i Efkâr* on 24–25 October 1919. Ibid., pp. 12–13.

61. Seçil Akgün, *General Harbord'un Anadolu Gezisi ve Ermeni Meselesine Dair Raporu* (Istanbul, 1918), p. 112, n. 210.

62. Kaynak Yayınları, *Atatürkün Bütün Eserleri*, vol. 4 (1919) (Istanbul, 2000), pp. 111–12.

63. Seyfettin Turhan, *Atatürk'te Konular Ansiklopedisi* (Istanbul, 1995), p. 436.

64. Kazım Öztürk, *Atatürk'ün TBMM Açık ve Gizli Oturumlarındaki Konuşmaları*, vol. 1 (Ankara, 1992), pp. 79, 81.

65. Ibid., pp. 66–69. After the establishment of the Republic in 1927, he continued to criticize Pan-Islamism and Pan-Turkism as dangerous policies that should be avoided. Mustafa Kemal, *Nutuk*, vol. 2, p. 2.

66. The ultranationalists in Turkey in fact preferred just such a reading. Dr. Hikmet Tanyu, in his work entitled "Atatürk and Turkish Nationalism," gave a very similar interpretation to a similar statement by Mustafa Kemal from 1930: "this depiction . . . does not demand that the description of the policies of Turanism and Turkish unity be openly examined as the policy of the state and at the rank of state minister, and on the basis of political reasons or conditions. But it presents it as state policy, as national policy." (Hikmet Tanyu, *Atatürk ve Türk Milliyetçiliği* [Ankara, 1981], p. 72). For other, similar analyses, see Yalçın Toker, *Türk Milliyetçiliğinin Yasal Kaynakları* (Istanbul, 1979); Arun Engin, *Yükseliş Savaşımızda Jüpiter* (Istanbul, 1971).

67. TBMM *Gizli Celse Zabıtları*, vol. 2, p. 355.

68. Akşin, *İstanbul Hükümetleri ve Milli Mücadele*, vol. 2, pp. 275–82. The author gives a general summary of the reports sent by the British agents in these places regarding the Pan-Islamic activities under way there.

69. Hüsamettin Ertürk, "Milli Mücadele Senelerinde Teşkilât-ı Mahsusa," Report, quoted in Akşin, *İstanbul Hükümetleri ve Milli Mücadele*, vol. 2, p. 281.

70. Kazim Öztürk, *Atatürk'ün*, vol. 1, pp. 79–80.

71. Ibid., p. 80.
72. *Atatürk'ün Söylev ve Demeçleri*, vol. 1, p. 215.
73. Kazim Öztürk, *Atatürk'ün*, vol. 1, p. 81.
74. From the internal regulations of the Trabzon Committee for the Defense of National Rights, established on 19 February 1919. Mahmut Goloğlu, *Erzurum Kongresi, Milli Mücadele Tarihi*, vol. 1 (Ankara, 1968), p. 143.
75. Mustafa Kemal, *Nutuk*, vol. 3, Document 7, p. 5.
76. Goloğlu, *Erzurum Kongresi*, vol. 1, p. 21.
77. Ibid., p. 150.
78. Selek, *Anadolu İhtilali*, p. 100.
79. Karabekir, *İstiklâl Harbimiz*, p. 23.
80. Jäschke, *Kurtuluş Savaşı*, p. 445.
81. A report sent from Akhisar (a small town in western Anatolia) on 3 September, 1919. Quoted in Celal Bayar, *Ben de Yazdim*, vol. 7, pp. 2364–65.
82. Goloğlu, *Erzurum Kongresi*, p. 201.
83. Goloğlu, *Sivas Kongresi, Milli Mücadele Tarihi*, vol. 2 (Ankara, 1969), p. 232. It is worth noting the subtle difference between this decision and the one taken at the Erzurum Congress. While at Erzurum the problem was taken up solely in regard to the Greek-Armenian axis; at Sivas, this point again formed the basis of discussion, but it was added that even occupations of regions devoid of Armenians and Greeks would also be resisted.
84. *Yakin Tarih Ansiklopedisi*, vol. 12 (Istanbul, 1990), p. 27.
85. Mustafa Kemal, *Nutuk*, vol. 3, Document no. 108, p. 112.
86. Ibid., vol. 1, p. 8.
87. Akgün, *Genral Harbord'un Anadolu Gesısi*, p. 105.
88. General Harbord, "Report of the American Military Mission to Armenia," *International Conciliation*, no. 157 (June 1920), pp. 294–95.
89. The debates surrounding this question that took place at the Sivas Congress can be found in a variety of sources. See, for instance, Vehbi Cem Aşkun, *Sivas Kongresi* (Sivas, 1945); Mustafa Kemal, *Nutuk*, vol. 1, pp. 62–82; Kadir Kasalak, "Sivas Kongresi Öncesinde 'Manda ve Himayenin' Türk Basınında Tartışılması ve Komutanlar Arasında Yazışmalar, *Atatürk Yolu 3*, no. 10 (November 1982), pp. 186–211.
90. Helmreich, *From Paris to Sèvres*, p. 183.
91. Yahya Akyüz, *Türk Kurtuluş Savaşı ve Fransız Kamuoyu, 1919–1921* (Ankara, 1988).
92. Mehmet Nadir, the deputy for Isparta in the First National Assembly in Ankara, was the one directing this movement. In a parliamentary commission that was later established, he was described as guilty of betrayal of the homeland, and the whole incident was covered up. See Damat Arıkoğlu, *Hatıratım* (Istanbul, 1961), pp. 178–79. Arıkoğlu had been one of the members of the parliamentary commission of inquiry in question.

93. Avcıoğlu, *Milli Kurtuluş Tarihi*, vol. 3, p. 10.
94. For more detailed information regarding the council, see Ahmet Ender Gökdemir, *Cenubi Garbi Kafkas Hükümeti* (Ankara, 1989), pp. 63–171.
95. Utterance of the governor-general of Aydın, İzzet. Quoted in Jäschke, *Kurtuluş Savaşı*, p. 78.
96. Ibid., p. 79.
97. İlhan Tekeli and Selim İlkin, *Ege'deki Sivil Direnişten Kurtuluş Savaşı'na Geçerken Uşak Heyeti Merkeziyesi ve İbrahim (Tahtakılıç) Bey* (Ankara, 1989), p. 205.
98. Celal Bayar, *Ben de Yazdim*, vol. 7, Document no. 136, p. 2391.
99. Ibid., p. 2249.
100. Ibid., p. 150.
101. David McDowell, *A Modern History of the Kurds* (London, 1997), pp. 87–112.
102. The various uprisings and cycle of massacres that took place during the 1919–1923 period has not been examined here separately because it is an area of study in its own right. We will instead content ourselves with simply noting that they were a continuation of the process that had begun at the outset of the century.
103. From Mustafa Kemal's speeches of 24 April, 31 May, and 27 July 1919. Quoted in Kazim Öztürk, *Atatürk'ün*, vol. 1, pp. 127, 130, 196.
104. Karabekir, *İstiklal Harbimiz*, p. 544.
105. Ibid., pp. 545–46.
106. Ebubekir Hazım Tepeyran, *Belgelerle Kurtuluş Savaşı Anıları* (Istanbul, 1982), p. 81.
107. Genelkurmay Harb Tarihi Dairesi, *Türk İstiklal Harbi*, vol. 6: *İstiklal Harbinde Ayakanmalar (1919–1921)* (Ankara, 1974), p. 294.
108. For the debates on the subject, see TBMM *Gizli Celse Zabıtları*, vol. 2, pp. 204ff., 252–87, 626–50.
109. For more detailed information on Nurettin Paşa and the Central Army, see Mustafa Balcıoğlu, *İki İsyan Koçgiri, Pontus, Bir Paşa, Nurettin Paşa* (Ankara, 2000).
110. Kazim Öztürk, *Atatürk'ün*, vol. 1, p. 84.
111. *Akşam*, 1 May 1965. Quoted in Zeki Saruhan, vol. 4, p. 804. It is possible that the newspaper date is incorrect.
112. Hovannisian, *Armenia on the Road*, p. 195.
113. Ibid., p. 178.
114. For some examples of this attempt at intervention, see PA-AA/R 14099, 14100, Reports by State Minister v. d. Bussche, dated 22, 24 March, 15 April 1918.
115. PA-AA/R 14100, Reports by General Lossow, dated 15, 23 May 1918. For similar reports, see PA-AA/R 14100, Report by Consul Rössler (Aleppo), dated 15 May 1918; R 14103, Eyewitness report by Sergeant Walker of a massacre perpetrated by a Tatar unit in the environs of Tbilisi, dated 14 June 1918; R 14102, Report by Consul Schulenburg (Tbilisi), dated 19 June 1918.

116. PA-AA/R 14103, Report, dated 2 August 1918. The report also gives the figures regarding the number of Armenians killed in a number of areas of settlement.

117. PA-AA/R 14104, Report by General von Kressenstein, dated 5 August 1918.

118. Halil Paşa, *Ittihat ve Terakki'den,* pp. 240–41.

119. Quoted in Gotthard Jäschke, "Ein Amerikanishes Mandat für die Türkei," *Die Welt des Islams* 8 (new series) (1962–63), p. 222.

120. Speech of Erzurum deputy Salih Efendi on the peace discussions with Armenia, 9 November 1920. *TBMM Zabıtlarında Doğu ve Güneydoğu Meselesi* (compiled by Nurettin Gülmez) (Istanbul 1992), p. 36.

121. FO 371/7878, Folio 180, May 1921.

122. Quoted in Karabekir, *İstiklal Harbimiz,* p. 901.

123. İhsan Ilgar, "Bir Asır Boyunca Ermeni Meselesi," *Hayat ve Tarih Mecmuası,* vol. 2, no. 10 (October 1975), p. 10. The activities of the aforementioned individuals concerning the periods 1915–17 and 1919–21 are discussed in numerous Turkish sources. For some examples dealing with the actions of Deli Halit and Topal Osman, see İhsan Birinci, "Sarıkamış Kahramanları," *Hayat ve Tarih Mecmuası* 1, no. 1 (February 1967), pp. 88–91; 2, no. 7 (August 1967); Sabis, *Harb Hatıraları,* vol. 2, p. 192; Mil, "Umumi Harpte"; General Fahri Belen, *Birinci Dünya Savaşında Türk Harbi, 1916 Yılı Hareketleri,* vol. 3 (Ankara, 1965), p. 34; Tevfik Bıyıklıoğlu, *Atatürk Anadolu'da 1919–1921* (Ankara, 1959), p. 37; Cemal Şener, *Topal Osman Olayı* (Istanbul, 1992), pp. 55, 61, 76, 80.

124. Avras, *Tarihi Hakikatler,* p. 24.

125. Document dated 18 January 1921, translated by Stefanos Yerasimos, "Turkish-Soviet Relations from the October Revolution to the National Struggle," Document no. 75 (Istanbul, 1979) p. 292.

126. Andrew L. Zapantis, *Greek-Soviet Relations, 1917–1941* (New York, 1982), p. 73.

127. Yerasimos, "Turkish-Soviet Relations," Document no. 76 (19 January 1921), pp. 293–95.

128. Zapantis, *Greek-Soviet Relations,* p. 72.

129. Ibid., p. 79. In a cable sent to Soviet foreign minister Chicherin in 1921, Alexander Miassignian, the president of the Council of Peoples' Commissars for Soviet Armenia, estimated the number of persons killed in 1921 alone at around sixty thousand. Quoted in E. K. Sarkisian and R. G. Sahakian, eds., *Vital Issues in Modern Armenian History* (Watertown, MA, 1965), p. 56.

130. Sarkisian and Sahakian, *Vital Issues,* p. 66.

131. Alfred Rawlinson, *Adventures in the Near East, 1918–1922* (London, 1923), pp. 307, 335. Quoted in Dadrian, *History of Armenian Genocide,* pp. 360–61.

132. Dadrian, *History of Armenian Genocide,* p. 360.

133. A. B. Kadishchev, *Intervention and Civil War in Transcaucasia.* Quoted in Sarkisian and Sahakian, *Vital Issues,* p. 57.

134. For atrocities in western Anatolia, see Permanent Bureau of Turkish Congress

at Lausanne, *Greek Atrocities in the Vilayet of Smyrna (May to July 1919)* (Lausanne, 1919); Zekeriya Türkmen, *Belgelerle Yunan Mezallimi* (Ankara, 2000).

135. PA-AA/R 14090, Report by Ambassador Wolff-Metternich, dated 7 March 1916.

136. AVPRI, f. 151, op. 482 (Politarkhiv), d. 3504, ll. 29-29ob. This letter's recipient, V. Sharbin, forwarded the letter to the Russian Foreign Ministry, which highlighted this passage. For a similar account by a Cossack officer who found Armenians gruesomely slaughtered and violated on the retreat from Van in summer 1915, see F. I. Eliseev, *Kazaki na Kavkazskom fronte* (2001), p. 130. This and following information taken from Peter Holquist, "Forms of Violence during the Russian Occupation of Ottoman Territory and in Northern Persia (Urumiah and Astrabad), October 1914–December 1917" (unpublished paper, 2004), pp. 24–25. See also: Michael A. Reynolds, "The Ottoman-Russian Struggle for Eastern Anatolia and the Caucasus, 1908–1918: Identity, Ideology, and the Geopolitics of World Order" (Ph. D. dissertation, Princeton University, 2003), p. 260.

137. Philips Price, *War and Revolution in Asiatic Russia*, p. 208, quoted in Holquist, "Forms of Violence," pp. 24–25.

138. Written testimony of Vehip Paşa, pp. 7–8; for detailed information about early acts of revenge, see Muammer Demirel, *Birinci Dünya Harbinde Erzurum ve Çevresinde Ermeni Hareketleri (1914–1918)* (Ankara, 1996), pp. 71–74.

139. Much information regarding these massacres directed at Muslims can be found in Turkish works on this period, for instance, Başbakanlık Devlet Arşivleri Genel Müdürlüğü, *Arşiv Belgelerine Göre Kafkaslar'da ve Anadolu'da Ermeni Mezalimi, 1919*, vol. 2 (Ankara, 1995); Halil Kemal Türközü, *Osmanlı ve Sovyet Belgeleriyle Ermeni Mezalimi* (Ankara, 1995); M. Fahrettin Kırzıoğlu, *Kars ve Çevresinde Ermeni Mezalimi (1918–1920)* (Ankara, 1970).

140. Hovannisian, *Armenia on the Road*, p. 135.

141. Written testimony of Vehip Paşa submitted to the chairman of the Commission of Criminal Inquiry in the Office of Public Security (*Emniyet-i Umumiye Dairesi'nde Tahkik-i Seyyi'at Komisyonu Riyaseti*). The copy cited here is from the archives of the Armenian Patriarchate in Jeruslam. Carton 7, Dossier H, Document nos. 171–82, p. 10.

142. Aydemir, *Makedonya'dan Ortaasya'ya Enver Paşa*, vol. 3, p. 464.

143. Gökdemir, *Cenubi Garbi Kafkas*, p. 18.

144. Firuz Kazemzadeh, *The Struggle for the Transcaucasia* (New York, 1951), p. 214.

145. Gökdemir, *Cenubi Garbi Kafkas*, pp. 18, 145–46. Kars and the surrounding areas changed hands several times during the period of 1918–21. The region was first under Russian control. During the winter and spring of 1918, the region fell under Turkish control, which lasted almost one year; with the defeat of the Ottomans, the region came under British, Georgian and Armenian control, between spring 1919 and December 1920. Turks took control at the end of 1920.

146. Karabekir, *İstiklal Harbimiz*, pp. 555–56.

147. PA-AA/R 14098, Report by Karl Axenfeld, dated 11 February 1918.

148. Ömer Kürkçüoğlu, *Türk-İngiliz İlişkileri (1919–1926)* (Ankara, 1978), p. 67.

149. For but a few of the many examples, see PA-AA/R 14098, Report by the chairman of the Orient and Islam Commission, Karl Axenfeld, dated 11 February 1918; PA-AA/R 14099, Evaluation of affairs, Berlin, dated 19 March 1918. When reproducing the 11 February report, Johannes Lepsius omitted several negative assessments regarding the Armenians. In regard to the 19 March document, he also omitted the negative judgments of the Armenians as well as the sections concerning the barbaric actions by the Armenian militias and armed gangs. Lepsius, *Deutschland und Armenien,* Document nos. 370 (pp. 368–71) and 377 (pp. 375–76), respectively.

150. PA-AA/R 14104, Reports by General von Kressenstein, dated 5, 22 August 1918. The general also reported on 3 September that similar difficulties were being experienced on the Turkish side.

151. Richard G. Hovannisian, "The Republic of Armenia," in *The Armenian People From Ancient to Modern Times,* vol. 2 (New York, 1997), p. 310.

152. Hovannisian, *Armenia on the Road,* pp. 194, 214.

153. *Journal of Historical Military Documents* 81 (31 December 1982), Document no. 1983, p. 472 (Ankara, 1982).

154. Demirel, *Birinci Dünya Harbinde,* p. 8.

155. V. N. Dadrian's revision to "The History of Armenian Genocide" (unpublished manuscript), p. 1.

156. PA-AA/R 14104, Report by General von Kressenstein, dated 3 September 1918.

157. Hovannisian, "The Republic of Armenia," p. 338.

158. Mustafa Kemal, "24 Eylül 1919 General Harbord'a Verilen Muhtıra, Kaynak Yayınları," *Atatürkün Bütün Eserleri,* vol. 4, p. 111.

159. Tengirşenk, *Vatan Hizmetinde,* p. 160.

160. A letter of Bekir Sami dated 5 February 1921, in Yerasimos, *Turkish-Soviet Relations,* Document no. 78, pp. 299–300. For more on the relationship of demography to ethnic cleansing and nation states in the Caucasus, see Eddie Arnavoudian's review of *Antranig and His Times,* vol. 2, by Hratchig Simonian (Yerevan: Gaysa Publishers, 1996), in GROONG (Armenian News Network), 12 July 2006.

161. For more information regarding officers who carried out such massacres, see Mete Tuncay, "Ankara İstiklâl Mahkemesinde Bir Heyeti Fesadiye Davası ve Kuva-yı Milliye," *Bilineceği Bilmek* (Istanbul, 1983), pp. 107–31.

162. For a general overview of the "Muslim" uprisings against the Nationalist Movement, see Sabahattin Selek, *Milli Mücadele,* vol. 1, *Anadolu İhtilali* (Istanbul, 1966), pp. 348–60; Genelkurmay Harb Tarihi Dairesi, *Türk İstiklal Harbi,* vol. 6: *İstiklal Harbinde Ayaklanmalar (1919–1921)* (Ankara, 1974); Fahri Belen, *Türk Kurtuluş Savaşı* (Ankara, 1973), pp. 194–214, 223–27.

163. For more information about these tribunals, see Ergün Aybars, *İstiklal Mahkemeleri, 1920–1927,* vols. 1–2 (Izmir, 1988), pp. 26–29.

164. Tevfik Çavdar, "... Vaziyet ve Manzara-i Umumiye," in *Milli Mücadele Başlarken Sayılarla* (Istanbul 1971), pp. 195–96.

165. *Yüzbaşı Selahattin'in Romanı* (Istanbul, 1975) (prepared for publication by İlhan Selçuk), pp. 209–10.

166. Ibid., pp. 252–53.

167. Selek, *Anadolu İhtilali*, vol. 1, pp. 120–29.

168. Ibid., p. 127.

169. Tansel, *Mondros'tan Mudanya'ya Kadar*, vol. 2, p. 155.

170. Mustafa Kemal, *Nutuk*, vol. 3, Document no. 196, p. 231.

171. Karabekir, *İstiklal Harbimiz*, p. 737; Kâzım Karabekir, *İstiklal Harbimizde Enver Paşa ve İttihat Terakki Erkânı*, pp. 4–5, 13–17.

172. Yerasimos, *Turkish-Soviet Relations*, p. 190.

173. For other sources on this topic, see Tengirşenk, *Vatan Hizmetinde*, pp. 161–62; Feridun Kandemir, *Atatürk'ün Kurduğu Türkiye Komünist Partisi ve Sonrası* (Istanbul, n. d.); Ahmet İzzet Paşa, *Feryadım*, vol. 1, p. 283.

174. Kâzım Karabekir, *İstiklal Harbimiz*, pp. 670–73.

175. From a speech given before the TBMM on 11 November 1920 by the acting foreign minister Muhtar Bey, in regard to the peace talks then under way with the Armenian Republic. TBMM *Zabıtlarından Doğu ve Güneydoğu Meselesi* (prepared for print by Nurettin Gülmez) (Istanbul, 1992), pp. 44–45.

176. Hovannisian, "The Republic of Armenia," p. 323.

177. Kazemzadeh, *The Struggle*, p. 286.

178. Tansel, *Mondros'tan Mudanya'ya Kadar*, vol. 2, p. 229.

179. *Atatürk'ün Söylev ve Demeçleri*, vol. 3, p. 17.

180. Kazim Öztürk, *Atatürk'ün*, vol. 1, p. 196.

181. Karabekir, *İstiklal Harbimiz*, pp. 900–901.

182. Ibid., p. 901.

183. TBMM *Gizli Celse Zabıtları*, vol. 1, p. 244.

184. A cable sent to Sivas, 25 January 1919. Turhan, *Atatürk'te Konular*, p. 213. The Turkish word for genocide, *soykırım*, only came into use after 1945. The word originally used here by Kemal, *katliam*, or "massacre," is translated by the author into modern Turkish as *soykırım*, which is incorrect. The fact that the words are not interchangeable in Turkish, and that the author repeatedly uses *soykırım* for *katliam* seems to be an intentional attempt on his part to create a "parity" between these actions and the Armenian genocide.

185. A communication sent to the provincial governor of Erzurum on 25 June 1919, ibid., p. 214. See similar references to killings of Muslims in *Atatürk'ün Söylev ve Demeçleri*, vol. 1, p. 6, and Kaynak Yayınları, *Atatürkün Bütün*, p. 111.

186. Kazim Öztürk, *Atatürk'ün*, vol. 1, p. 85.

187. Ibid., p. 182. From the secret parliamentary session of 7 June 1920.

188. Jäschke, *Mustafa Kemal und England*, pp. 222–24.

189. Helmreich, *From Paris to Sèvres*, p. 107. For another example, see from Calthorpe to Curzon on 30 July 1919; FO 371/4158/118411. Reproduced in Şimşir, *British Documents on Atatürk*, vol. 1, Document no. 22, p. 56.

190. FO 406/41, p. 409411, no. 185/1. Reproduced in Bilâl Şimşir, *British Documents on Atatürk*, vol. 1, Document no. 86, p. 239.

191. Jäschke, *Mustafa Kemal und England*, p. 223.

192. For selected passages from some of the articles accusing Ankara of Unionist or Pan-Turkish tendencies, see Tunaya, *Türkiye'de Siyasal Partiler*, vol. 3, pp. 288–92.

193. Ali Kemal, *Sabah*, 19 Kânunısani 1335 (19 January 1919).

194. Paul Dumont, *Mustafa Kemal* (Ankara, 1993), p. 356.

195. *Le Temps*, 11 July 1919. Quoted in ibid., p. 35.

196. From *Le Temps* and *Journal des débats* (2 November 1918). Quoted in Yahya Akyüz, *Türk Kurtuluş Savaşı ve Fransız Kamuoyu, 1919–1921* (Ankara, 1988), p. 75.

197. Ibid., p. 76.

198. İzzet Öztoprak, *Türk ve Batı Kamuoyununda Milli Mücadele* (Ankara, 1989), p. 89.

199. Yahya Akyüz, *Türk Kurtuluş*, p. 82.

200. "Rauf Orbay'ın Hatıraları," *Yakın Tarihimiz*, vol. 3, p. 179.

201. Karabekir, *İstiklal Harbimiz*, p. 225.

202. Kaynak Yayınları, *Atatürkün Bütün Eserleri*, vol. 4, p. 108.

203. General Harbord, "Report of the American Military Mission," p. 295.

204. Şimşir, *British Documents on Atatürk*, vol. 1, p. 171.

205. *Atatürk'ün Söylev ve Demeçleri*, p. 4.

206. Bekir Sami Baykal, *Heyeti Temsiliye Kararları* (Ankara, 1974), pp. 5, 10, 24, 28. The adoption of similar resolutions on 29 September and 11 October 1919 shows the level of seriousness with which the Representative Council approached the issue, and their grave concern as to its outcome.

207. Helmreich, *From Paris to Sèvres*, p. 278.

208. Mustafa Kemal, *Nutuk*, vol. 1, p. 296.

209. Kazim Öztürk, *Atatürk'ün*, vol. 1, p. 67.

210. The point here is not that the War of Independence was solely led by those who had participated in the genocide or had grown rich as a result of it. Rather, it is only to emphasize one of the characteristics of circles who supported the movement.

211. Kasım Ener, *Çukurova Kurtuluş Savaşında Adana Cephesi* (Ankara, 1996), p. 3.

212. Avcıoğlu, *Milli Kurtuluş Tarihi*, vol. 1, pp. 5–7.

213. Jäschke, *Kurtuluş Savaşı*, p. 46. The clashes that began when the Armenian regiment turned to acts of vengeance were appeased only after the British forces intervened and mediated. The Armenian force was later disbanded by the French.

214. Tansel, *Mondros'tan Mudanya'ya Kadar*, vol. 2, p. 208. Of the Armenians in the areas of Tokat, Amasya, Kayseri, Yozgat, Ankara, Konya, Afyonkarahisar and

Izmir who migrated to Cilicia, one portion concluded that their lives were in danger from the growing National Movement in Anatolia and another simply acted in accordance with the desire of both the Entente Powers and the acting Armenian patriarch. In a newspaper interview he gave at the time, the Armenian patriarch Zaven Efendi claimed that the migrations began out of fear of the National Movement.

215. Akşin, *Istanbul Hükümetleri ve Milli Mücadele*, vol. 2, p. 229.

216. Yaşar Akbıyık, *Milli Mücadele'de Güney Cephesi (Maraş)* (Ankara, 1990), p. 16.

217. Ibid., p. 210.

218. Avcıoğlu, *Türkiye'nin Düzeni*, vol. 1, p. 293.

219. Akbıyık, *Güney Cephesi*, p. 19.

220. Baskin Oran, *Atatürk Milliyetçiliği* (Ankara, 1990), p. 74.

221. Doğan Avcıoğlu, *Milli Kurtuluş Tarihi*, vol. 3, p. 1183.

222. "Ali Şükrü Bey'in Meclis Konuşmalarindan," in *Yakin Tarihimiz*, vol. 4, p. 77.

223. Gotthard Jäschke, *Türk İnkilap Tarihi Kronolojisi 1918–1923*, trans. N. R. Aksul (Istanbul, 1939), p. 136.

224. Zürcher, *The Unionist Factor*, p. 88.

225. Dr. Fahri Can, "İzmir Suikast Teşebbüsü ve Kara Kemal Bey," and "İlk Milli Kuvvet Nasıl Kuruldu?," *Yakın Tarihimiz*, vol. 1, pp. 169, 334 (respectively).

226. Cemal Şener, *Topal Osman Olayı*, pp. 118–19.

227. Abdüllah M. Çay and Yaşar Kalafat, *Doğu ve Güneydoğu Anadolu'da Kuva-yı Milliye Hareketleri* (Ankara, 1990), p. 33.

228. The names were taken from Avcıoğlu, *Milli Kurtuluş Tarihi*, vol. 3, pp. 1167–201.

229. Çarıklı Hacim Muhittin, *Balıkesir ve Alaşehir Kongreleri ve Hacim Muhittin'in Kuvayı Milliye Hatıraları* (Ankara, 1967), pp. 14–20.

230. Celal Bayar, *Ben de Yazdim*, vol. 5, p. 1648.

231. Ibid.

232. The names are taken from Avcıoğlu, *Milli Kurtuluş Tarihi*, vol. 3, pp. 1176–81.

233. Mazhar Müfit Kansu, vol. 1, p. 301.

234. Mustafa Kemal, *Nutuk*, vol. 1, p. 334.

235. Doğan Avcıoğlu, *Milli Kurtuluş Tarihi*, p. 1181.

236. Ibid., p. 1233.

237. Falih Rıfkı Atay, *Çankaya, Atatürk'ün Doğumdan Ölümüne Kadar* (Istanbul, 1980), p. 236.

238. Yunus Nadi, *Kurtuluş Savaşı Anıları*, p. 81.

239. In letters to Erzurum to the command of the Fifteenth Army Corps (i.e., to Kâzim Karabekir Paşa) on 29–30 May 1919. Tansel, *Mondros'tan Mudanya'ya Kadar*, vol. 1, p. 244.

240. *Le Temps*, 11 July 1919. Quoted in Dumont, *Mustafa Kemal*, p. 35.

241. "Rauf Orbay'ın Hatıraları," p. 179.

242. Ibid.

243. An interview with a French journalist in March 1920. Maurice Prax, Constantinople, *Lectures pour tous* (March 1920), p. 829. Prax was a reporter for the French daily *Petit Parisien*. Part of this interview was translated and reproduced in the May 1920 issue of *Current History*, no. 12, pp. 334–36. Information taken from Dadrian, "Documentation of the World War I Armenian Massacres," p. 552, n. 20.

244. Emile Hildebrand, "Kemal Promises More Hangings of Political Antagonists in Turkey," *Los Angeles Examiner*, 1 August 1926 (Sunday edition, section 6). Some Turkish authors challenge the authenticity of this interview.

245. *Atatürk'ün TBMM Açık ve Gizli Oturumlardaki Konuşmaları*, p. 59.

246. Karabekir, *İstiklal Harbimiz*, p. 707.

247. "Rauf Orbay'ın Hatıraları," p. 179.

248. Ibid.

249. Mustafa Kemal, *Nutuk*, vol. 3, Document 220, p. 257.

250. These words were uttered by Talât at the last CUP Party Congress, in November 1918. Quoted in Bayur, *Türk İnkılap Tarihi*, vol. 3, part 3, p. 44.

251. Mustafa Kemal, *Nutuk*, vol. 3, Document nos. 159, 160, pp. 193–94.

252. Ibid., Document no. 137, p. 161.

253. Ibid., vol. 3, Document no. 220, pp. 256–57.

254. *Atatürk'ün TBMM Açık ve Gizli Oturumlarındaki Konuşmaları*, p. 58.

9. The Final Phase of the Trials

1. Şimşir, *Malta Sürgünleri*, p. 195.

2. Anzavur had been a member of the Special Organization. He was "enrolled in our Special Organization by order of His Excellency the Minister, upon the recommendation of Messrs. . . . He was sent to the Eastern Front, where his auspicious service was demonstrated." (Ertürk, p. 377.) Whether his "auspicious service" in the East included his taking part in the massacre is a question worth investigating.

3. For the full text of these fatwas, see: İbnülemin Mahmut Kemal İnal, *Son Sadrazamlar*, pp. 2054–57.

4. The decree was published in *Takvîm-i Vekâyi*, no. 3835 (24 Nisan 1336/24 April 1920).

5. İbnülemin Mahmut Kemal İnal, *Son Sadrazamlar*, vol. 4, p. 2058.

6. Zeki Sarıhan, *Kurtuluş Savaşi Günlüğü*, vol. 3, p. 71.

7. The death sentence against Mustafa Kemal was published in *Takvîm-i Vekâyi*, no. 3864 (27 Mayıs 1336/27 May 1920). For the other decisions, see *Takvîm-i Vekâyi*, no. 3866 (30 Mayıs 1336/30 May 1920); and no. 3883 (21 Haziran 1336/ 21 June 1920).

8. *Takvîm-i Vekâyi*, no. 3917 (31 Temmuz 1336/31 July 1920). Turkish sources offer little information on this execution. Ebubekir Hazım, who had been minister of

the interior in Salih Paşa's government, mentioned it in his remembrances of the period. Tepeyran, *Zalimane Bir İdam Hükmü* (Istanbul, 1946), pp. 147–50. Falih Rıfkı Atay (*Çankaya,* pp. 225–26) talked of Avni's last days; and Altan Deliorman gives some information on the execution in his *Ermeni Komiteciler* (Istanbul, 1973), pp. 249–50. However, the accounts provided by these authors are contradictory in regard to the information on Avni's character.

9. For specific names, see Ertürk, *iki Devrin Perde Arkası,* pp. 375–81.

10. Mustafa Kemal, *Nutuk,* vol. 1, p. 272.

11. TBMM *Zabıt Ceridesi,* Devre 1, İçtima Senesi 1, Sayı 145, vol. 2 (Ankara: TBMM, 1940), pp. 126–32.

12. TBMM *Zabıt Ceridesi,* vol. 1, p. 148.

13. Ibid., p. 272.

14. *Düstur,* 1928 (Istanbul), 3. Seri, vol. 1, p. 8.

15. The proposal, dated 21 July, can be found in the TBMM *Zabıt Ceridesi,* vol. 2, p. 341. The assembly's rejection of the proposal is in ibid., vol. 3, p. 52.

16. Sarıhan, *Kurtuluş Savaşi Günlüğü,* vol. 3, p. 167.

17. TBMM *Zabıt Ceridesi,* vol. 1, p. 281.

18. Ibid., vol. 3, pp. 268–69.

19. TBMM *Zabıt Ceridesi,* Devre 1, İçtima Senesi 1, vol. 3, p. 15 (31 July 1920). The discussion began in the 41st session with a proposal that, by the 120th session (23 Aralik 1920), had taken the form of a draft law (ibid., vol. 6, pp. 516–23).

20. TBMM *Zabıt Ceridesi,* vol. 3, p. 170.

21. For the draft bill see, TBMM *Zabıt Ceridesi,* vol. 6, pp. 141, 271; for the decision see vol. 22, pp. 317–18, 322.

22. TBMM *Zabıt Ceridesi,* vol. 7, pp. 6–10.

23. İsmail Özçelik, *Milli Mücadele'de Güney Cephesi, Urfa (30 Ekim 1918–11 Temmuz 1920)*(Ankara, 1992), p. 58.

24. The related law, no. 822, was passed in parliament on 30 May 1926 and published in the government gazette on 27 June, no. 405.

25. TBMM *Zabıt Ceridesi,* vol. 3, pp. 170–71.

26. The letter was sent to Ahmet İzzet Paşa, the first prime minister after the armistice, with the intention of its being delivered to the British high commissioner. Şimşir, *Malta Sürgünleri,* p. 334.

27. Sarıhan, *Kurtuluş Savaşi Günlüğü,* vol. 3, p. 313.

28. Ibid., pp. 399, 449, 493.

29. Peyam-ı Sabah, 11 April 1922.

30. *Tercüman-ı Hakikat,* reported in Sarıhan, vol. 4, p. 521.

31. Hasan Fehmi Bey's speech to the closed session of the TBMM on 17 Teşrinievvel 1336 (17 October 1920). TBMM *Gizli Celse Zabıtları,* vol. 1, p. 177.

32. From the speech of Mazhar Müfit Bey, a deputy from Hakkâri, to the closed session of the National Assembly on 17 Teşrinievvel 1336 (17 October 1920). Ibid., p. 179.

33. Speech of Erzurum deputy Salih Efendi on the peace discussions with Armenia, 9 November 1920. TBMM *Zabitlarında Doğu ve Güneydoğu Meselesi* (compiled by Nurettin Gülmez) (Istanbul, 1992), p. 36.
34. Hüseyin Avni Bey's speech to the TBMM on 1 January 1921. Ibid., pp. 96–97, 99.
35. Ibid., p. 99.
36. FO 371/4174/118377, Letter from Calthorpe to the Foreign Office, dated 1 August 1919, no. 1364/5056/14, quoted in Şimşir, *Malta Sürgünleri*, p. 215.
37. Şimşir, *Malta Sürgünleri*, p. 216.
38. FO 371/4174/136069, Report from Admiral de Robeck to Curzon, cited in ibid., p. 217.
39. All of these figures from ibid., pp. 216–25.
40. FO 371/5089/E. 1346, Note from the Foreign Office, cited in ibid., p. 224. FO 371 6509 E. 11651, Letter from the Foreign Office to the Office of the Procurer General, dated 29 September 1920, and E. 12773, Letter from the Office of the Procurer General to the Foreign Office, dated 15 October 1920; cited in ibid., p. 227.
41. FO 371/6509/E. 8745, Folios 232–34.
42. FO 371/6509/E. 10023, Folios 100–101, 24 August 1921.
43. FO 371/4174/118377, Letter from Calthorpe to the Foreign Office, dated 1 August 1919, no. 1364/5056/14. Cited in Şimşir, *Malta Sürgünleri*, p. 215.
44. FO 371/4174/136069, Letter from High Commissioner de Robeck to Curzon, cited in ibid., p. 217.
45. FO 371/6500/E. 3557, Letter from High Commissioner Rumbold to Curzon (Istanbul), dated 16 March 1921, no. 277/1984/24, cited in ibid., p. 239.
46. The majority of the prisoners released were not political prisoners. According to Halide Edib, "There were no 'politicals' among the prisoners here. Mostly they were brought here because of murder and other crimes. That day the colonel ordered the release of all prisoners from minority groups." Edib, *Turkish Ordeal*, p. 16.
47. FO 371/4164, 19127; cited in Akşin, *İstanbul Hükümetleri ve Milli Mücadele*, vol. 1, p. 162, n. 42.
48. FO 371/6500/W. 2178, Appendix A (Folios 385–118, 386–119), 11 August 1920; cited in Dadrian, "Genocide as a Problem," p. 287, n. 238.
49. FO 371/66500/E. 3557, Letter from Rumbold to Curzon; (Istanbul), dated 16 March 1921, no. 277/1984/24, cited in Şimşir, *Malta Sürgünleri*, p. 242.
50. FO 371/6500/E. 3552, Cable from Curzon to Geddes (London), dated 31 March 1921, no. 176, cited in ibid., p. 242.
51. FO 371/6503/E. 6311, Cable from Geddes to Curzon (Washington), dated 2 June 1921, no. 374, cited in ibid., p. 243.
52. FO 371/6504/E. 8519, Cable from Craigie to Curzon (Washington), dated 13 July 1921, no. 722, cited in ibid., p. 244.
53. FO 371/6504/E. 8745, cited in ibid., p. 245.
54. FO 371/6504/E. 8745, Letter from Curzon to the high commissioner in Istanbul, dated 10 August, 1921, cited in ibid., p. 246.

55. FO 371/6500 (Folio 118), Letter from Lamb to the High Commissioner's Office, dated 11 August 1920. Cited in Anette Höss, "Die Türkischen Kriegsgerichtsverhandlungen 1919–1921," Ph.D. diss., University of Vienna, 1991, p. 55.

56. FO 371/6499/E. 3110 (Folio 190), Report by Lord Curzon on his meeting with Bekir Sami.

57. Mustafa Kemal, Nutuk, vol. 2, p. 110.

58. Ibid., p. 239.

59. Willis, Prologue to Nuremberg, p. 161.

60. FO 371/6504/E. 9112 (Folio 47).

61. FO 371/6504/E. 10411 (Folio 130), Cable from General Harrington to the Ministry of War, dated 14 September 1921.

62. The conversation was in French. Rössler wrote down the French text along with the German translation. (AA Türkei 183, vol. 40, A468, 20 December 1915.)

63. The German engineer said the conversation took place on 18 December 1915. Rössler's report is dated 3 January 1916. (AA Türkei 158, vol. 24, SA1373.)

64. AA Türkei 183, vol. 41, A4215, 9 February 1916.

65. For the German report on these incidents: AA Türkei 158, vol. 48, A34435, October 1917); additionally, extracts from memoirs of the period can be found in Dadrian, "Naim-Andonian Documents," p. 354, n. 96.

66. Takvim-i Vekâyı, no. 3540 (27 Nisan 1335/27 April 1919).

67. Since Damat Ferid's last government fell on 17 October 1920, the threat must have been delivered sometime over the summer. V. N. Dadrian cited this information from Krieger, "Aram Andonianee Huradargadz Tourk Bashdonagan Vaverkarerou Vaverganoutiunu," 1915–1965 Houshamadian Medz Yeghernee ("The authenticity of the official Turkish documents Aram Andonian did not publish," Commemorative Compendium on the Great Holocaust, 1915–1965).

68. Archive of the Armenian Patriarchate of Jerusalem, Box 21, File M, Document no. 249.

69. H. W. Glockner, Interned in Turkey 1914–1918 (Beirut, 1969), p. 47.

70. FO 371/6500 (Folio 7780).

71. Şimşir, Malta Sürgünleri, p. 317.

72. Nuran Dağlı and Belma Aktürk, eds., Hükümetler ve Programları, vol. 1: 1920–1960, TBMM yayını no. 12 (Ankara, 1988), pp. 8–9, 26, 33.

73. Cited in Uras, Tarihte Ermeniler, p. 716.

74. From the notice given by the Armenian Delegation to the Lausanne Conference in November 1922, quoted in ibid., p. 719.

75. Announcement by the Armenian Delegation on 2 February 1923, quoted in ibid., p. 741.

76. Uras, Tarihte Ermeniler, p. 714. The author transcribed the names of the British officials from the Armenian alphabet, so he wrote them as Vankirat and Akporn.

77. Meray, Lozan Barış Konferansı, vol. 2, p. 275.

78. Uras, *Tarihte Ermeniler,* p. 717. For the full text of İsmet Paşa's speech, see Meray, vol. 1, pp. 188–200.
79. Meray, *Lozan Barış Konferansı,* vol. 1, p. 185.
80. Ibid., vol. 8, p. 923.
81. Since the issues of confiscated property and children have been dealt with above, I will limit my discussion here to the question of an Armenian homeland.
82. Meray, *Lozan Barış Konferansı,* vol. 1, p. 184.
83. Ibid., pp. 212, 298.
84. Ibid., vol. 2, pp. 156, 280.

10. Why the Postwar Trials Failed

1. See this argument in the nationalist organ, the daily *Hakimiyet-i Milliye* (20 January 1920) as a reply to a speech by British prime minister Lloyd George that appeared in the Istanbul papers sixteen days earlier. Quoted in İsmet Öztoparak, *Türk ve Batı Kamuoyunda Milli Mücadele* (Ankara, 1989), p. 63.
2. Şimşir, *Malta Sürgünleri,* p. 198.
3. Jäschke, *Kurtuluş Şavaşı,* p. 152.
4. Jäschke, *Mustafa Kemal und England,* p. 210.
5. Jäschke, "President Wilson als Schiedsrichter," p. 75.
6. Jäschke, "Beiträge zur Geschichte des Kampfes," p. 2.
7. Jäschke, "Ein amerikanisches Mandat," p. 222.
8. Jäschke, "Beiträge zur Geschichte des Kampfes," p. 6.
9. Jäschke, *Kurtuluş Savaşı,* p. 61.
10. Akşin, *İstanbul Hükümetleri ve Milli Mücadele,* vol. 2, pp. 246–47.
11. Alain Finkelkraut, *Der Barbie Prozess und die Nürnberger Urteile,* p. 78.
12. Quoted in ibid., p. 72.
13. Şükrü, *İmparatorluğun Çöküşü,* p. 62.
14. "Bu tehcir işiyle alâkadar olmıyan Türk, Anadolu'da pez azdır," "Halil Menteşe'nin Hatıraları, No. 4: Malta'ya Sürgün," *Yakın Tarih,* vol. 9, no. 8 (Eylül, 1973), p. 22.
15. FO 406/41, Letter from Calthorpe to Curzon, dated 6 May 1919. Quoted in Criss, *İşgal Altında İstanbul,* p. 101.
16. Akşin, *İstanbul Hükümetleri ve Milli Mücadele,* vol. 2, pp. 235–36.
17. Criss, *İşgal Altında İstanbul,* p. 96.
18. Ibid., p. 104.
19. Numerous reports to this effect were sent by British officers serving throughout Anatolia. See the one from Admiral Webb to the Earl of (Lord) Curzon, dated 22 January 1920, D.B.F.P., 1st series, vol. 4, pp. 1076–80, n. 674. Quoted in Şimşir, *British Documents on Atatürk,* vol. 1, Document no. 117, pp. 341–46.
20. FO/371/6533/E. 11670, quoted in Şimşir, *British Documents on Atatürk,* vol. 4, Document no. 12, p. 41.

21. For some of these practices, see Criss, *İşgal Altında İstanbul*, p. 104.
22. Willis, *Prologue to Nuremberg*, p. 158.
23. For the British reports explaining these developments, see Şimşir, *British Documents on Atatürk*, vol. 2, Document nos. 122–25, 128, 137, 147, 148.
24. Lepsius et al., *Die Grosse Politik der Europäischen Kabinette 1871–1914*, vol. 9 (Berlin, 1923), Document no. 2178, p. 194.
25. Mandelstam, *Das Armenische Problem*, p. 89.
26. Akçam, *From Empire to Republic*, pp. 96–107.

ACKNOWLEDGMENTS

The origins of this book go back to my Ph.D. thesis at the University of Hanover in Germany in 1995. I would like to give special thanks to my mentors, Professor Vahakn Dadrian and Professor Peter Gleichmann. Professor Dadrian has put at my disposal much material on the subject, which he has collected for close to thirty years. He also translated some Armenian sources for me. For his part, Professor Gleichmann has labored, through his meticulous critique and persistence, to teach me to balance the engagement and distance that Norbert Elias called on social scientists to display, and to show me how this balance is concretely achieved in academic work.

This English edition is a substantially revised version of my book *İnsan Hakları ve Ermeni Sorunu,* published in Ankara in 1999, which was itself a substantially revised and expanded version of my thesis. This English edition would not exist were it not for the Zoryan Institute, which assisted greatly in the translation and revision. I wish to thank Paul Bessemer for his translation and Julie Gilmour and George Shirinian of the Zoryan Institute for their assistance revising the English text. I would also like to thank Margaret Lavinia Anderson, whose careful reading and helpful comments proved invaluable. I owe special thanks to all the staff at Metropolitan Books, and in particular to my editor, Riva Hocherman, who winnowed the text as if it were a field of wheat and gave it new shape.

INDEX

Vehip Paşa, 4, 145, 154, 162–63, 324, 328, 363
Veli Bey, 249
Venizelos, Eleutherios, 106, 107
Versailles, Treaty of (1919), 221, 232, 374
Vienna, Congress of (1814–15), 27
Volkan (newspaper), 68

Wangenheim, Hans von, 100–101, 118, 121, 123, 126–27, 138, 142, 153, 196–97, 214
war crimes. *See* Armenian massacres of 1915–17; extraordinary courts-martial
War Ministry, 94–96, 102–4, 125, 131, 136, 157–58, 171, 191, 194, 244, 263–64, 276, 283
"war of aggression," 229
Webb, Admiral, 216–17, 277–80, 295, 359
Wedel-Jarlsberg, nurse, 158, 181
Wilhelm II, kaiser of Germany, 42, 113, 228–29, 232
Wilson, Woodrow, 210–12, 214, 218, 226–30, 232, 244, 299, 307, 317–18, 325, 370
Wolff-Metternich, Count, 121, 177, 185
World War I, 97, 101, 102, 105–6, 111–48, 151, 156, 183, 207, 218–19, 225, 322

World War II, 125, 375
World Zionist Organizaton, 210

Yalman, Ahmet Emin, 128–29, 305
Yavuz, Fehmi, 342
Yeni Hayat (journal), 88
Yeniköy Accord (1914), 101, 119, 204, 224–25
Young Ottomans, 34, 48–49
Young Turks, 48–50, 57, 62, 64, 67–68, 79–80, 83, 120–21, 138, 154–55, 296, 345
Yozgat region, 140, 158, 162, 164–65, 168, 171, 179–81, 199–200, 288, 293
Yugoslavia, 222
Yuvanidis Efendi, Yorgi, 258

Zekeriya Bey, 107
Zeki Bey, 74
Zeytun region, 42, 145–47, 159–61, 182, 192, 197–98, 202
Zhamank (Armenian newspaper), 167
Ziemke, Kurt, 118–19
Ziya Paşa, 34
Zohrab Efendi (Zöhravi), 250, 265
Zoryan Institute, 13
Zülfü Bey, 289

ABOUT THE AUTHOR

TANER AKÇAM, sociologist and historian, was born in Ardahan Province, Turkey, in 1953. He was granted political asylum in Germany after receiving a nine-year prison sentence in Turkey for his involvement in producing a student journal, which resulted in his adoption in 1976 by Amnesty International as a prisoner of conscience. He is the author of ten scholarly works of history and sociology, as well as numerous articles in Turkish, German, and English. He currently teaches at the Center for Holocaust and Genocide Studies at the University of Minnesota.